THE PRACTICE OF MARKET RESEARCH

Visit *The Practice of Market Research, 3rd edition* Companion
Website at **www.pearsoned.co.uk/mcgivern** to find valuable
student learning material including:

- Links to useful websites.
- A student guide to writing a brief and proposal for an
  assignment.
- A student guide to learning from case studies.

We work with leading authors to develop the strongest
educational materials in business and marketing,
bringing cutting-edge thinking and best learning practice
to a global market.

Under a range of well-known imprints, including
Financial Times Prentice Hall, we craft high quality
print and electronic publications which help readers
to understand and apply their content, whether
studying or at work.

To find out more about the complete range of our
publishing, please visit us on the World Wide Web at:
www.pearsoned.co.uk

Third Edition

THE PRACTICE OF
MARKET RESEARCH

An Introduction

Yvonne McGivern

Prentice Hall

FINANCIAL TIMES

An imprint of **Pearson Education**

Harlow, England • London • New York • Boston • San Francisco • Toronto • Sydney • Singapore • Hong Kong
Tokyo • Seoul • Taipei • New Delhi • Cape Town • Madrid • Mexico City • Amsterdam • Munich • Paris • Milan

Pearson Education Limited
Edinburgh Gate
Harlow
Essex CM20 2JE
England

and Associated Companies throughout the world

Visit us on the World Wide Web at:
www.pearsoned.co.uk

First published 2003
Second edition published 2006
Third edition published 2009

© Yvonne McGivern 2003, 2009

ISBN: 978-0-273-71707-2

British Library Cataloguing-in-Publication Data
A catalogue record for this book is available from the British Library

Library of Congress Cataloging-in-Publication Data
McGivern, Yvonne.
   The practice of market research : an introduction / Yvonne McGivern. — 3rd ed.
      p. cm.
   Includes bibliographical references and index.
   ISBN 978-0-273-71707-2 (pbk. : alk. paper)   1. Marketing research—Methodology.   2. Social
sciences—Research—Methodology.   I. Title.
   HF5415.2.M3827   2009
   001.4—dc22

                                                                    2008034380

10   9   8   7   6   5   4   3   2
12   11   10

Typeset in 10/12pt Minion by 35
Printed and bound by Ashford Colour Press Ltd., Gosport

BRIEF CONTENTS

CONTENTS

Supporting resources

Visit **www.pearsoned.co.uk/mcgivern** to find valuable online resources

Companion Website for students

- Links to useful websites.
- A student guide to writing a brief and proposal for an assignment.
- A student guide to learning from case studies.

For instructors

- Chapter-by-chapter teaching notes, links to useful websites and updated end of chapter question solutions.
- A Lecturers guide to using ARK as a teaching and learning resource. (ARK is a source of questionnaires, survey and teaching datasets and qualitative research archives such as downloadable interviews etc.)
- Useful tables and boxes from the text reproduced in downloadable PDF format for use in class.
- A PowerPoint lecture for each chapter and slides of all the useful figures and tables from the book.

For more information please contact your local Pearson Education sales representative or visit **www.pearsoned.co.uk/mcgivern**.

FOREWORD

In recent years the research sector has enjoyed a period of buoyancy and considerable change – driven not least by a booming global economy and growth in new sectors and markets. Research has been able to grasp new opportunities, powered by significant client investment and interest in the ever-evolving field of customer insight. Over the past few decades methods of data collection have developed at a rapid pace. From online questionnaires to surveys using mobile phone text messaging, researchers use technology to provide businesses with a wide range of in-depth information. On one hand, this has lowered costs and increased efficiency. On the other, it has reinforced the need to ensure that researchers understand the fundamentals of research so that they are able to provide high quality information and insight.

At the heart of successful research remains a series of important basic principles which enable it to provide insights into problems and information on which sound decisions can be based. It is vital that anyone undertaking research understands these principles and the ethics that underpin them. The MRS Advanced Certificate in Market and Social Research Practice supports this process as it provides a benchmark of the knowledge, skills and understanding which researchers need in the early part of their careers. Since its launch in 2002, the MRS Advanced Certificate has grown to become an essential tool in developing new research practitioners. As Managing Director of Operations at Ipsos MORI, a research organisation with strong roots in both market and social research, I believe that the Advanced Certificate is ideally suited for all our researchers. In the UK, seven out of the ten largest research suppliers incorporate the qualification into their professional development programmes and currently 25 per cent of all candidates who sit the qualification are from client-side organisations. More and more global suppliers are rolling out the Advanced Certificate to researchers around the world, and having a textbook such as *The Practice of Market Research: An Introduction*, which matches the syllabus of the qualification, is important in assisting this process.

This third edition of *The Practice of Market Research: An Introduction* has been comprehensively revised to reflect the changes in the MRS Advanced Certificate Syllabus and expanded in areas such as project management and quantitative data analysis to provide a clear pathway for candidates wishing to progress to the MRS Diploma in Market and Social Research Practice. Both qualifications are one way of ensuring that practitioners of the future understand the fundamentals of good research while equipping them to be able to respond to rapidly changing technological and global research needs.

Rowland Lloyd
MRS Chairman and Managing Director of Operations, Ipsos MORI

- With members in more than 70 countries, MRS is the world's largest association serving all those with professional equity in provision or use of market, social and opinion research, and in business intelligence, market analysis, customer insight and consultancy.

- MRS has a diverse membership of *individuals* at all levels of experience and seniority within agencies, consultancies, support services, client-side organisations, the public sector and the academic community.

- It also serves MRS Company Partners agencies, suppliers of support services, buyers and end-users – of all types and scale who are committed throughout their *organisations* to supporting the core MRS values of professionalism, research excellence and business effectiveness.

- In consultation with its individual members and Company Partners, MRS supports best practice by setting and enforcing industry standards. The commitment to uphold the MRS *Code of Conduct* is supported by the Codeline service and a wide range of specialist guidelines.

- MRS contributes significantly to the enhancement of skills and knowledge by offering various qualifications and membership grades, as well as training and professional development resources.

- MRS enables its members and Company Partners to be very well-informed through the provision of a wide range of publications, information services and conferences.

- MRS offers many opportunities for meeting, communicating and networking across sectors and disciplines, as well as within specialisms.

- As 'the voice of market research', MRS defends and promotes research in its advocacy and representational efforts.

- Through its media relations and public affairs activities, MRS aims to create the widest possible understanding of the process and value of market, social and opinion research, and to achieve the most favourable climate of opinion and legislative environment for research.

April 2008

PREFACE

The aim of this book

This book provides a comprehensive, straightforward account of the practice of market research – the techniques and the day-to-day tasks of the researcher – that is both easy to read and easy to understand.

Who should use this book?

This book provides a thorough introduction to the practice of market research. It is suitable for undergraduates on research methods or research skills courses, and is suitable for undergraduates and postgraduates on courses where there is a requirement to complete a research project or dissertation. In addition, research practitioners will find it useful as a reference text and source of information and ideas on both method and practice.

The book was also designed with the MRS Advanced Certificate in Market and Social Research Practice in mind. This is a degree-level qualification that follows the research process from problem definition to reporting the findings. It aims to help candidates to develop a wide range of research skills. The book covers the syllabus for this qualification and there is a section setting out where candidates can find the information they need as they work through each element of the syllabus.

New to this edition

In preparing this new edition of the book some changes have been made to the basic structure in response to customer feedback and to changes in the syllabus of the MRS Advanced Certificate in Market and Social Research Practice. In brief, Chapter 9 – which covered designing questions to measure attitudes – has been merged with the chapter on designing questionnaires to give a new, comprehensive Chapter 9; and the chapter on analysing quantitative data has been expanded into two chapters, Chapters 12 and 13. Material in all chapters has been revised and where necessary updated. Below is a list of the major changes made for this edition.

Revised Chapter 1 on the practice of market research

Since technology is now embedded in how research is done, with online methods of data collection now widely used and accepted as standard research practice, the section on technology and the practice of research was no longer relevant and has been removed. It has made way for some additional material on ethics and the practice of research. A new case study on the McDonald's brand has been added.

Revised Chapter 5 on secondary research

The focus of this chapter is now on doing secondary research or desk research, as it is often called, with updated information on secondary sources and new sections on writing a literature review and citing sources.

Revised Chapter 6 on planning and conducting qualitative research

This chapter has been reorganised with clearer headings and some expanded content. It offers material on methods of data collection in qualitative research (including online methods), interviewing and moderating skills and how to design an interview or discussion guide.

Expanded Chapter 8 on sampling

There is a slightly expanded section in this chapter on sampling in qualitative research.

Expanded Chapter 9 on designing questions

There was some overlap between the chapters devoted to researching attitudes and designing questions. Since designing questions on attitudes poses many of the same problems as designing questions on other things it was decided for this edition to bring them together in an expanded Chapter 9: Designing questionnaires. This change also reflects changes in the MRS Advanced Certificate syllabus.

Expanded Chapter 10 on managing a research project

This chapter contains new material on project management including sections on the role of the project manager, project management tools, communication, leadership and managing resources as well as a revised section giving an overview of the analysis process.

Revised and expanded Chapters 12 and 13 on analysing quantitative data

In the previous edition Chapter 13 covered the basics of quantitative data analysis including univariate and bivariate analysis and the use of inferential statistics. This material has been developed and expanded to look at the whole process of analysis in a slightly different way across two chapters. Chapter 12 focuses on understanding data and how they are transferred from questionnaire to analysis package through to univariate descriptive analysis. Chapter 13 takes the reader through bivariate descriptive analysis and data reduction, and on to explanatory and inferential analysis, setting out some of the more commonly used techniques.

Expanded Chapter 14 on communicating the findings

This chapter contains a new section on what is meant by added value in the research process.

Ethical and professional practice: the MRS Code of Conduct

In each chapter, where relevant, new material has been added that highlights key aspects of ethical and professional practice, drawing attention to the rules and guidance set out in the MRS Code of Conduct.

Case studies drawn from real life research projects

As in the previous edition, most chapters contain several case studies drawn from real-life research projects. For this new edition the range of topics covered by the case studies has been expanded. To make the case studies more accessible – and to increase the value of them as teaching and learning tools – each one has been revised and given a new introduction, new headings, an edited key word list and a new section detailing why that case study is worth reading. The aim of the case studies is to show research in action, to illustrate and/or provide examples of the techniques and practices covered in the chapter. They aim to demonstrate why research was done and how it was done. In addition, they illustrate the usefulness and value of research, how research relates to and addresses the decision maker's problem. They also show how researchers overcome difficulties in setting up and running projects, and finally, they highlight innovative approaches to research practice – from design through to dissemination.

Distinctive features

METHODS AND PRACTICE

The book is unusual in that it covers research methods *and* the practical tasks involved in running a research project. Few other textbooks do this. For this reason the book is particularly valuable to practitioners as well as students. There is comprehensive coverage of the following:

- research design;
- sampling;
- secondary research;
- qualitative data collection techniques including ethnography, semiotics and online methods;
- quantitative data collection including online methods;
- questionnaire design; and
- qualitative and quantitative data analysis.

An entire chapter is devoted to the analysis of qualitative data, a topic which few other market research texts cover in any detail.

In terms of the practical tasks involved in setting up and running a project and bringing it to completion, there is comprehensive coverage (with examples) of the following:

- how to prepare a brief;
- how to write a proposal;
- how to manage a project – including how to brief interviewers, how to prepare a coding frame, how to write a data processing specification;
- how to prepare and write a report;
- how to design and give an oral presentation;
- how to evaluate research findings; and
- professional practice and the MRS Code of Conduct.

REAL-LIFE CASE STUDIES AND EXAMPLES

As noted above, throughout the book there are examples of research in action, some new to this edition. They cover a wide variety of sectors and topics in market and social research. On the market research side there are examples of research on well-known brands from the arts, media, telecommunications, financial services, retailing and fast moving consumer goods (FMCG) sectors including Barclays Bank, the BBC, BT, Levi Strauss, McDonald's, Shell International, Spider-Man/Columbia Tri-Star Pictures, *The Mirror* newspaper, Unilever Bestfoods Europe and Van den Berghs. On the social research side there are examples of research for government and charities on complex social issues including anti-social behaviour, AIDS awareness, exclusion from school, teenage pregnancy, and child abuse and neglect.

In addition to the case studies, there are examples of the key documents and outputs of research. These include examples of a brief; a proposal; terms and conditions of business; project timetables and costing grids; a sampling summary; discussion and interview guides; questions and sections of questionnaires; interviewer briefing notes; findings from pilot studies; a coding frame and list of extractions; an analysis specification; an audit list for analysis of qualitative data; charts and diagrams; a checklist for preparing a report; and examples of key bits of a report – an abstract and summary, conclusions and recommendations.

CLEAR STRUCTURE

The book is divided into three parts: Part I, Introducing market and social research; Part II, Getting started; and Part III, Getting on and finishing up. Part I provides an introduction to market and social research; Part II deals with getting a project up and running, from thinking about the decision maker's problem and on to the research problem through to designing the questionnaire or discussion guide; and Part III deals with getting on and finishing up, getting the project into the field, analysing, communicating and reviewing the findings.

SUPERB PEDAGOGY TO AID LEARNING

Each chapter opens with an **Introduction** which summarises the aim of the chapter. A list of **Topics covered** is then presented. Next, there is **Relationship to MRS Advanced Certificate Syllabus**, a useful tool that shows how the material in the chapter relates to the MRS Advanced Certificate Syllabus. Next, **Learning outcomes** show exactly what you should be able to do after reading each chapter. **Key words** pulled from the case study texts are presented after a short summary of the focus of the **Case study** to show at a glance what the case study illustrates. In addition, under the heading **Why this Case study is worth reading** there is a **list of reasons** that highlights the value of the case study in terms of what it shows about research practice and the research process.

At the end of the chapter you will find **Chapter summaries**. These help to reinforce the main points made in the chapter, and are useful as a revision tool. **Questions and exercises** at the end of each chapter are designed to test the reader's knowledge and understanding and the ability to apply that knowledge and understanding to research scenarios. These can be used by the reader for self-study and/or in-class discussions. Each chapter ends with **References** and **Recommended reading** which provide more detail on the topics or issues covered in that chapter. Finally, at the end of the book, is the **Bibliography**.

WEBSITE

A range of support materials, including suggested solutions to the questions and exercises in this book, is available to lecturers and students on the website for this book. To access, visit **www.pearsoned.co.uk/mcgivern**. To obtain a password, contact your local Pearson Education sales representative.

GUIDE TO THE MAIN FOCUS OF CASE STUDIES

	Case study title	What it is about	Research techniques and issues covered	Quantitative research	Qualitative research	Market research	Social research
1.1	McDonald's listens	How research helped to re-establish the brand's credibility and regain customers' trust.	• Market research in action; • importance of staying in touch with customers; • importance of understanding changing environment; • end result of research – actions taken, impact on organisation and brand.	✔	✔	✔	
1.2	Levi Strauss: research compels the business to act	How the company overhauled its approach to market research and the effect this had on business.	• Where the research function sits in large organisations; • links between internal research team and external research supplier; • examples of types of research used by an organisation; • role of research in achieving business goals; application of research findings.			✔	
1.3	The government reaches an understanding	How the government uses research to develop policies and strategies.	• Application of research in policy development and implementation.		✔		✔
1.4	Improving performance	How the right sort of research at the right time can improve business performance.	• What happens when a charity/public sector organisation acts without doing the right research; • what happens when the right research is done at the right time.	✔		✔	
2.1	Use of a panel	Reasons for using a panel survey, how it works and what the findings have been used for.	• Example of a panel in action; • design and set up of a panel; • link between information needs and design; • application of the findings.	✔			✔
2.2	Investigating SPIDER-MAN	Why research was needed and what the findings revealed.	• Reasons for research; • links between organisation's marketing and business goals and the research; • exploratory research enquiry; • international research; • the output from the research.		✔	✔	
2.3	'I know what you did last summer'	How valuable information on customer behaviour and market characteristics was retrieved by secondary analysis of box office data.	• Example of secondary data analysis; • use of a database; • descriptive research enquiry; • how valuable insight can be extracted from existing data; • end uses of 'insight'.	✔		✔	
2.4	The Scottish Executive: dealing with anti-social behaviour	How research was conducted on a complex topic, anti-social behaviour.	• Why research was needed; • research objectives; • use of primary and secondary research; • structure of a research project and key elements of it.	✔	✔		✔

Case study title		What it is about	Research techniques and issues covered	Quantitative research	Qualitative research	Market research	Social research
3.1	Looking at *The Mirror*: identifying the business issues	The challenges faced by a national daily newspaper at a time of great change.	• Issues in unpacking business problem and defining research problem and information needs; • issues in 'selling' research findings to internal audience.			✔	
3.2	Should I talk to you?	How the initial phases of a research project for a charity were handled.	• Need for research; • research objectives; • need to be precise in defining target audience for research.	✔			✔
3.3	Banner advertising on the net: the effect on the brand	How an online tracking study using a repeated cross-sectional design helped work out the impact of banner advertising on the advertiser's brand and product.	• Example of repeated cross-sectional design; • online research; • identifies need for research.	✔		✔	
3.4	Seeing the big picture	Why an FMCG company would use a panel rather than an ad hoc, cross-sectional approach to understand consumer behaviour and what drives it.	• Decision-making criteria in choosing one research design over another; • links between design and client's information needs; • advantages of a panel design and disadvantages of a cross-sectional design; • identifies need for and end uses of the data.	✔		✔	
3.5	What happens when you win the lottery?	The sort of design used to examine organisations' use of funding over time.	• Research objectives; • link between research aim and research design; • benefits of the approach taken; • how client used the data.		✔		✔
3.6	Experimenting with incentives	How an experimental design was used to examine the effects of incentives on the response rate to a postal survey.	• Example of an experimental design; • research objective; • how research was done; • findings.	✔		✔	
4.1	Why do we need research?	Why a complex social research project was commissioned.	• How a complex social research project was commissioned.				✔
5.1	Insight from secondary data	How data recorded at point of sale proved useful in understanding customer behaviour.	• Example of secondary data analysis/secondary research; • issues in using database data; • insight from data records; • how findings not what expected; • some end uses of the research.	✔	✔	✔	

	Case study title	What it is about	Research techniques and issues covered	Quantitative research	Qualitative research	Market research	Social research
5.2	Which site? Geodemographics has the answer	How geodemographics can be used in deciding where to site retail stores.	• Example of use of secondary data; • how geodemographic data used to reduce risk in decision making; • how the data were used; • variables used in decision-making process.	✔		✔	
5.3	Leveraging the Census for research and marketing	How UK Census data can be used to help researchers and marketers.	• Example of use of secondary data; • value of the Census as a source of information.	✔		✔	
6.1	Applications of ethnography	How ethnography can be used in market research to understand consumer behaviour and choice.	• What an ethnographic approach can offer the client.		✔	✔	
6.2	Understanding binge drinking	How ethnographic and traditional qualitative research techniques were used to understand social phenomenon of binge drinking.	• Structure of a project using traditional and non traditional techniques; • benefits of using 'ethnographic films'.		✔	✔	✔
6.3	Talking to teenagers about sex: part 1	How and why paired in-depth interviews were used to gather data on a sensitive subject. (Case study 1.2 describes the background to the research and why it was commissioned; and Case studies 6.9 and 6.10 describe other aspects of the project.)	• Links between topic, research objectives and method of data collection; • rationale for use of in-depth interviews; • how recruitment/sampling was done.		✔		✔
6.4	Researching SPIDER-MAN 2	The content of the first stage of a research project designed to get feedback on a movie sequel. See also Case study 2.2.	• Use of group discussions – focus groups; • example of a project plan – scope, sample, number of groups, geographic coverage; • research aims; • what covered in groups.		✔	✔	
6.5	Researching the media habits of minority ethnic groups	How a range of qualitative research methods including workshops were used to explore media use and attitudes to advertising among minority ethnic communities in Britain.	• Link between objectives, sample and methods used; • range of qualitative methods of data collection used; • sample and how it was recruited.		✔		✔

	Case study title	What it is about	Research techniques and issues covered	Quantitative research	Qualitative research	Market research	Social research
6.6	Keeping the consumer in sight: Levi's Youth Panel	Describes how a qualitative consumer panel was used to investigate product design and development issues, among other things. See also Case study 1.2.	• Rationale for use of a panel; • details of panel make-up, recruitment and data collection; • shows link between sample and research objectives; • highlights contribution that information from the panel makes to the business.		✔	✔	
6.7	New ways for new products: Unilever NPD research online	How asynchronous online discussion forums were used with great success in new product development research for an FMCG company.	• Online group discussions; • link between method of data collection and information needs or research objectives; • benefits of the approach; • how the method can be used with other data collection tools.		✔	✔	
6.8	Talking to teenagers about sex – part 2	Approach taken to interviewing teenagers about sex, contraception and pregnancy.	• Link between topic, sample and method; • approach to interviews and rationale for approach; • how interviews were structured; • use of pre-task journals.		✔		✔
6.9	Understanding the lives of teenagers	How journals were used in a study among marginalised teenagers to help the government devise a strategy in relation to teenage pregnancy.	• Why a particular approach was chosen; • how task was set up; • how journals generated rich, insightful data; • end benefits to client.		✔		✔
6.10	Developing a brand proposition for *The Mirror*	The approach taken to gather evidence with which to address the business challenges faced by a national daily newspaper. See also Case study 3.1.	• Link between business problem, information needs and research approach; • overview of a research project; • research approaches and rationale for their use; • development and use of stimulus material; • semiotic analysis in action.		✔	✔	
6.11	What's wrong with taking the bus?	How a semiotic analysis was used to find out what it is that puts people off taking the bus.	• Link between business problem, information needs and research approach; • detailed guide to how a semiotic analysis was done.			✔	
7.1	Interviewing in gay bars	How and why fieldwork for a 1986 study of attitudes and behaviour in relation to AIDS was conducted in a non-typical venue.	• Link between sample and fieldwork location; • issues in interviewing in a non-typical venue; • how fieldwork was managed in unusual conditions.				✔

Case study title		What it is about	Research techniques and issues covered	Quantitative research	Qualitative research	Market research	Social research
7.2	Asking about child abuse and neglect: face to face or not?	The rationale for the choice of method of data collection in a study into child abuse and neglect for a charity.	• The thinking behind decisions about methods of data collection; • how the data collection process was structured.	✔		✔	✔
7.3	What do you do all day? The BBC wants to know	The methods used to gather data about daily life in the UK in order to understand how people use their time and use the media.	• Details of project plan including sample; • links between research objectives and choice of method of data collection; • use of a diary and a questionnaire; • rationale for using electronic over paper data collection; • issues in design of script for electronic diary; • response rate; • findings and their end use.	✔		✔	
7.4	BT: Measuring customer satisfaction by post	The approach taken by a telecommunications company, to find out – among other things – what its residential customers and some of its non-customers thought about it at a time of rapid change in the telecoms market.	• Explains need for research; • research objectives; • rationale for use of postal over telephone data collection; • decisions taken about format of questionnaire; • content of questionnaire; • survey set up and management; • respondent follow up survey; • reasons for non-response; • response bias.	✔		✔	
7.5	Unilever Bestfoods: a panel full of insight	How data from a panel provided insight into who consumers are, what they do and why they do it.	• Business objectives, research objectives and research design; • advantages of using a panel design; • application of panel data; • sample and response rate; • what was measured; • end use of the data.	✔		✔	
8.1	The sampling decision in a consumer telephone survey	How a research agency reached a sampling decision for a consumer telephone survey.	• Decision-making process for sampling; • link between aim of research, sampling approach and method of data collection; • sampling approach; issue of 'representativeness'.	✔		✔	
8.2	The sampling decision in a survey of 16 year olds	How a review of a survey of young people led to a decision to switch from a sample of 12–17 year olds derived from a household sample to an independent sample of 16 year olds.	• Decision-making process in choosing a sampling approach; • process of getting access to a suitable sampling frame; • sampling approach in detail; • response rate.	✔			✔

Case study title		What it is about	Research techniques and issues covered	Quantitative research	Qualitative research	Market research	Social research
8.3	Sampling the general public and gay men	The sample design for an investigation into knowledge, attitudes and behaviour in relation to AIDS for a government programme of public education and publicity.	• Description of two sampling operations; • rationale for choice of approaches; • sample design for a repeated cross-sectional study; • random location sampling; • purposive sampling to get at a hard to find population.	✔			✔
8.4	Finding teenagers at the 'margins'	How the research team gained access to teenagers 'at the margins'.	• Issues in sampling hard to reach groups; • network sampling; • ethical issues related to topic and target population.		✔		✔
9.1	Barclays Bank: monitoring brand health	Why a questionnaire underwent a major redesign and what happened as result.	• Importance of designing with research objectives and respondent and interviewer experience in mind; • benefits of CAPI; • benefits of pilot studies.	✔		✔	
9.2	What do you mean, anti-social behaviour?	How to define the intangible concept of anti-social behaviour for use in a questionnaire.	• Importance of a working definition of 'thing' the client wants to find out; • process of arriving at a definition; • link between concept and concrete examples or indicators of it.	✔			✔
9.3	How do you ask that?	The questionnaire design issues that arose in researching AIDS and how they were resolved. See also Case study 7.1.	• Questionnaire design in action – what was done and why; • some key techniques and rationale for their use; • impact of questionnaire design and interviewing on data quality and on interviewer and respondent experience of taking part in research.	✔			✔
9.4	Just checking: an informal pilot test	The pilot study for a school meals self-completion survey.	• The value of pilot testing on the target audience.	✔		✔	
9.5	How do we do it? Finding out about child abuse	Issues involved in designing, pilot testing and administering a questionnaire on a sensitive topic – child abuse. Interesting comparison re mode of administration between this and Case study 9.3.	• Process of questionnaire design; • issues in designing a survey on a sensitive and complex topic; • structure of questionnaire and interview; • pilot testing; • use of two forms of data collection within one interview (interviewer-administered and self-completion); • respondents' view of interview.	✔			✔

Case study title		What it is about	Research techniques and issues covered	Quantitative research	Qualitative research	Market research	Social research
9.6	It has to change: findings from a pilot study	Some of the changes suggested after a face-to-face briefing with mock interviews and 60 face-to-face pilot interviews.	• Changes suggested by a pilot study – question wording, additions to pre-coded lists, changes to the order of question modules.	✔			✔
10.1	Shell International: central versus local	An approach to international research.	• Example of how a multinational corporation approaches international research; • two main approaches described – buying centrally and buying locally with benefits and disadvantages of each; • responsibilities of co-ordinator and suppliers in research process; • links between elements of research process; • importance of understanding client's needs and research task.			✔	
10.2	Finding gay men	How researchers got access to a hard to find sample.	• Example of a strategy used to find a hard to reach population and the issues involved.	✔			✔
10.3	What's the incentive?	Choosing an incentive for a postal survey on customer satisfaction among customers, non-customers and new customers.	• Description of the thinking underlying the decision and the client's and agency's ideas; rationale for the choice of incentive; description of the effect of the incentive.	✔		✔	
11.1	Marrying theory and data to get a clearer view	How theory helps at the analysis stage.	• Firsthand account of how someone tackled analysis; • the issues faced in data analysis; • an example of how ideas and theory from elsewhere helped develop thinking.		✔		✔
13.1	Anti-social behaviour: who experiences it?	Hypotheses tested in a study to understand experiences of anti-social behaviour on buses or at bus stops.	• Ideas tested out in the data; • use of bivariate descriptive analysis; • difference between researchers' perceptions and what data showed.	✔			✔
13.2	Weighting for household size	How weighting is used to compensate for disproportionate household size in a random sample survey.	• Why weighting is needed; • how weighting is done.	✔			✔

	Case study title	What it is about	Research techniques and issues covered	Quantitative research	Qualitative research	Market research	Social research
13.3	Vons Superstores: targeting local needs	An example of the application of cluster analysis in designing grocery stores to meet the needs of local shoppers.	• Cluster analysis in action; • the process – what goes on before cluster analysis and what happens to findings; • usefulness of the demographic profile and sales data; • how 'targeting' works.			✔	
14.1	Seeing is believing: consumer videos	How those who commission research can get as much benefit from it as possible by taking an innovative approach to disseminating the findings.	• Limitations of traditional approach to a debrief; • advantages of a more innovative one; • rationale for use of approach.			✔	

ACKNOWLEDGEMENTS

Author's acknowledgements

A lot of people have been enormously helpful to me while I was writing this book and when I was preparing the new edition. I would like to thank Paula Devine and Katrina Lloyd at Queen's University, Belfast and Lizanne Dowds, not only for the pieces they contributed and for the use of the Life and Times Survey material, but also for their help and encouragement along the way.

I am very grateful indeed to a number of people at MRS: David Barr and Debrah Harding for permission to use extracts from the *International Journal of Market Research* and MRS *Conference Proceedings*; and to past and present members of the fantastic Professional Development team – Karen Adams, Samantha Driscoll, Margaret Quirke and Hayley Dack – for their support and good humour, and for their help with information on the syllabus for the MRS Advanced Certificate in Market and Social Research Practice.

I am very grateful to Raehaneh Ghazni, Managing Director of Acuity Computing Enterprise Technology, for her feedback and encouragement throughout. I would also like to thank Kate Dann, Managing Director of kd consulting, for taking the time to talk to me about the research job market. I would like to thank Petra van der Heijden, Director, Network Research and Marketing Ltd, for her many useful suggestions and for allowing me to use the extract on the sampling decision in a telephone survey. Thanks are due also to Alison Park, Director, National Centre for Social Research, for permission to reproduce questions from British Social Attitudes surveys.

I would also like to thank the reviewers for this third edition – Ruth McNeil, Response Consulting Ltd. London; Dr Ann Hartl, CEUSS School of Business, Denmark; Fiona Daview, Cardiff Business School; Paul Kiff, University of Westminster; Wybe Popma, Brighton Business School; and Michael De Domenici, Greenwich University. Their suggestions were invaluable and much appreciated. Thanks are also due to the team at Pearson, Managing Editor Amanda McPartlin and Desk Editor Joy Cash, for their patience and their help.

I would also like to thank Peter Carter, Managing Director of Consumer InSight, and Jeremy Green, Chief Executive, Hall & Partners, USA, for their patience, guidance and humour during my formative years as a researcher at Millward Brown.

Finally, and not least, I would like to thank my friends and family for putting up with me (and my excuses) during the writing and editing process. I am hugely grateful for the support and encouragement of all of them, especially my husband Barry.

Yvonne McGivern
Autumn 2008

Publisher's acknowledgements

We are grateful to the following for permission to reproduce copyright material:

Extracts from the MRS Code of Conduct on Chapter 1, page 5, Chapter 1, pages 52–53, Box 3.4, Box 4.4, Box 6.1, Box 7.2, Box 7.8, Box 7.9, Box 8.11, Box 8.12, Box 9.1, Chapter 9, pages 11–12, Chapter 9, pages 17–18, Box 10.3, Box 10.5, Box 11.10, Box 11.14 and Box 14.14, with permission from MRS; Case Study 1.1 from How research saves scapegoat brands © retaining brand and business perspective in troubled times, Proceedings of the MRS Conference 2008 (Davidson, G. & Payne, C. 2008), with permission from MRS; Case Study 1.2, Case Study 6.6 and Box 14.4, part 2 adapted from Inspiring the organisation to act: a business in denial, Proceedings of the MRS Conference 2002 (Flemming, Thygesen & McGowan 2002), with permission from MRS; Case Study 1.3, Case Study 6.3, Case Study 6.9, Case Study 6.10 and Case Study 8.4 adapted from Teenage sex at the margins, Proceedings of the MRS Conference 2005 (Cohen, J. 2005), with permission from MRS; Box 1.2 from Do we listen to journalists or clients? The real implications of change for the market research industry, Proceedings of the MRS Conference 2005 (Chadwick, S. 2005), with permission from MRS; Box 1.3 from How research drove the metamorphosis of a public sector organization, Proceedings of the MRS Conference 2005 (Butcher, J. Strutt, S. & Bird, C. 2005), with permission from MRS; Box 1.5 from www.esomar.org/uploads/pdf/professional-standards/ICCESOMAR_Code_English.pdf, published by ESOMAR, © Copyright 2007 by ESOMAR® – The World Association of Research Professionals, reproduced with permission; Case Study 2.1 by Dr. Katrina Lloyd, Queen's University, Belfast, reproduced with permission; Case Study 2.2 and Case Study 6.4 adapted from KERPOW!!KERCHING!! Understanding and positioning the Spider-man brand, Proceedings of the MRS Conference 2005 (Palmer, S. & Kaminow, D. 2005), with permission from MRS; Case Study 2.3 and Case Study 5.1 adapted from I know what you did last summer: arts audiences in London 1998–2002, Proceedings of the MRS Conference 2004 (Brook, O. 2004), with permission from MRS; Case Study 2.4, Case Study 9.2 and Case Study 13.1 adapted from Perception, prevention, policing and the challenges of researching anti-social behaviour, Proceedings of the MRS Conference 2005 (Granville, S., Campbell-Jack, D. & Lamplugh, T. 2005), with permission from MRS; Case Study 3.1 and Case Study 6.11 adapted from Capturing the emerging zeitgeist, Proceedings of the MRS Conference 2003 (Clough, S. & McGregor, L. 2003), with permission from MRS; Case Study 3.2 adapted from Never work with children and graduates?, Proceedings of the MRS Conference 2002 (Capron, M., Jeeawody, F. & Parnell, A. 2002), with permission from MRS; Box 3.7 adapted from Qualitative data analysis for applied policy research in *Analyzing Qualitative Data*, edited by R. Bryman and A. Burgess, Routledge (Ritchie, J. & Spencer, L. 1994), reproduced with permission from Taylor & Francis Books (UK); Case Study 3.3 adapted from How advertising frequency can work to build online advertising effectiveness, *International Journal of Market Research*, 42, 4, pp. 439–57, WARC (Broussard, G. 2000), with permission from WARC; Case Study 3.4 and Case Study 7.5 adapted from Bridging the gap between dreams and reality, Proceedings of the MRS Conference 2004 (Gibson, S., Teanby, D. & Donaldson, S. 2004), with permission from MRS; Case Study 3.5 adapted from Quality time: cohort and observation combined – a charity case, Proceedings of the MRS Conference 2001 (Halls, K. & Browning, S. 2001), with permission from MRS; Case Study 3.6 adapted from The effects of monetary incentives on the response rate and cost-effectiveness of a mail survey, *International Journal of Market Research*, 33, 3, pp. 229–41, WARC (Brennan, M., Hoek, J. & Astridge, C. 1991), with permission from WARC; Box 4.1 adapted from It's all in the brief, Proceedings of the MRS Conference 2000 (Pyke, A. 2000), with permission from MRS; Case Study 4.1, Case

Study 7.2, Case Study 9.5 and Box 10.7 adapted from The prevalence of child abuse and neglect: a survey of young people, Proceedings of the MRS Conference 2001 (Brooker, S., Cawson, P., Kelly, G. & Wattam, C. 2001), with permission from MRS; Case Study 5.2 and Case Study 13.3 from The application of geodemographics to retailing: meeting the needs of the catchment, *International Journal of Market Research*, 39, 1, pp. 201–24, WARC (Johnson, M. 1997), with permission from WARC; Case Study 5.3 adapted from Opportunities to leverage the Census for research and marketing, Proceedings of the MRS Conference 2003 (Leventhal, B. & Moy, C. 2003), with permission from MRS; Box 5.5, Case Study 8.2 and Case Study 13.2 by Paula Devine, ARK, Queen's University, Belfast; reproduced with permission; Box 5.6, Case Study 7.4 and Case Study 10.3 adapted from Breaking through boundaries – MR techniques to understand what individual customers really want, and acting on it, Proceedings of MRS Conference 2003 (Macfarlane, P. 2003), with permission from MRS; Case Study 6.1 adapted from The power of ethnography, *International Journal of Market Research*, 41, 1, pp. 75–87, WARC (Mariampolski, H. 1999), with permission from WARC; Case Study 6.2 from The qual remix, Proceedings of the MRS Conference 2004 (Griffiths, J., Salari, S., Rowland, G. and Beasley-Murray, J. 2004), with permission from MRS; Case Study 6.5 from Dreaming the global future, Proceedings of the MRS Conference 2004 (Desai, P., Roberts, K. and Roberts, C. 2004), with permission from MRS; Box 6.3 from 21st century qualitative research, Proceedings of the MRS Conference 2005 (Langmaid, R. 2005), with permission from MRS; Box 6.4 adapted from People power in politics, *International Journal of Market Research*, 41, 1, pp. 87–95, WARC (Mattinson, D. 1999), with permission from WARC; Case Study 6.7 adapted from Asynchronous online discussion forums: a reincarnation of online qualitative, Proceedings of the MRS Conference 2003 (Balabanovic, J., Oxley, M. & Gerritsen, N. 2003), with permission from MRS; Box 6.11 adapted from I shouldn't be here: the experiences of working adults living at home, Unpublished qualitative research project for M.Sc. in Applied Social Research by P. Fleming, S. Ni Ruaidhe & Kathryn McGarry, with permission from Kathryn McGarry; Case Study 6.12 adapted from De-mystifying semiotics: some key questions answered, Proceedings of the MRS Conference 2002 (Lawes, D. 2002), with permission from MRS; Case Study 7.1, Case Study 8.3, Case Study 9.3, Box 9.25 and Case Study 10.2 from What we have learned from researching AIDS, *International Journal of Market Research*, 39, 1, pp. 175–200, WARC (Orton, S. & Samuels, J. 1997), with permission from WARC; Case Study 7.3 adapted from The way we live now: Daily life in the 21st century, Proceedings of the MRS Conference 2004 (Holden, J. and Griffiths, G. 2004), with permission from MRS; Box 7.5 and Box 7.6 adapted from Innovation in online research – who needs online panels?, Proceedings of the MRS Conference 2003 (Comley, P. 2003), with permission from MRS; Box 7.10 adapted from Mystery customer research: cognitive processes affecting accuracy, *International Journal of Market Research*, 39, 2, pp. 349–61, WARC (Morrison, L., Colman, A. & Preston, C. 1997), with permission from WARC; Case Study 8.1 from The viability of random digit dialling in the UK, *International Journal of Market Research*, 33, 3, pp. 219–227, WARC (Foreman, J. & Collins, M. 1991), with permission from WARC; Box 8.4 adapted from Paula Devine, Technical notes, www.ark.ac.uk/nilt, reproduced with permission; Case Study 9.1 adapted from Improving the research interview experience, Proceedings of the MRS Conference 2000 (Miles, K., Bright, D. & Kemp, J. 2000), with permission from MRS; Box 9.7 adapted from Research in new fields, *International Journal of Market Research*, 38, 1, pp. 19–31, WARC (Mytton, G. 1996), with permission from WARC; Box 9.8 and Box 10.11 from the Life and Times Survey 2000, used with permission; Box 9.11 from the Life and Times Survey and the National Centre for Social Research, used with permission; Box 9.12 and Box 9.21 from the Life and Times Survey 2003, used with permission; Chapter 9, p. 40, 'Showcard' from The Life and Times Survey 2006, used with permission; Box 9.14 and Box 9.18 from the British Social Attitudes Survey,

© National Centre for Social Research, used with permission; Box 9.20 from the Life and Times Survey 1999, used with permission; Box 9.24 adapted from Solpadol – A successful case of brand positioning, *International Journal of Market Research*, 39, 3, pp. 463–80, WARC (Hurrell, G., Collins, M., Sykes, W. & Williams, V. 1997), with permission from WARC; Box 9.26 from ARK Young Life and Times Survey 2007, www.ark.ac.uk/ylt/2007/YLT07quest.pdf, used with permission; Case Study 10.1 adapted from Buying international research, *International Journal of Market Research*, 38, 1, WARC (Childs, R. 1996), with permission from WARC; Box 10.4 adapted from Getting it done properly, *International Journal of Market Research*, 38, 1, WARC (Wilsdon, M. 1996), with permission from WARC; Box 11.1 adapted from Analysis and interpretation of qualitative findings, Report of the Market Research Society Qualitative Interest Group, *International Journal of Market Research*, 35, 1, pp. 223–25, WARC (Robson, S. & Hedges, A. 1993), with permission from WARC; Case Study 11.1 By Diarmaid O'Sullivan, reproduced with permission; Box 12.4 from ARK & the Northern Ireland Life and Times Survey Team, University of Ulster and Queen's University Belfast, reproduced with permission; Box 14.1 adapted from Connecting with clients: Re-thinking the debrief, Proceedings of the MRS Conference 2006 (Niven, A. & Imms, M. 2006), with permission from MRS; Case Study 14.1 adapted from Seeing is believing, Proceedings of the MRS Conference 2001 (Walter, P. & Donaldson, S. 2001), with permission from MRS; Box 14.3 adapted from PowerPoint is not written in stone: Business communication and the lost art of storytelling, Proceedings of the MRS Conference 2004 (Parsons, J. 2004), with permission from MRS; Box 14.4 adapted from Nothing about us without us: Meeting the challenges of a national survey amongst people with learning difficulties, Proceedings of the MRS Conference 2003 (Emerson, E., Malam, S., Joyce, L. & Muir, J. 2003), with permission from MRS; Box 14.4, part 3 adapted from Insight as a strategic asset – the opportunity and the stark reality, *International Journal of Market Research*, 46, 4, pp. 393–410, WARC (Wills, S. & Williams, P. 2004), with permission from WARC; Box 14.7 adapted from Do interviewers follow telephone survey instructions?, *International Journal of Market Research*, 38, 2, p. 161, WARC (Kiecker, P. & Nelson, J. 1996), with permission from WARC; Box 14.8 from Healthy Ageing in Ireland: Policy, Practice and Evaluation in *The 2003 Healthy Ageing Conference* edited by Y. McGivern, © National Council on Ageing and Older People (O'Shea, E. & Connelly, S. 2003), reproduced with permission; Box 14.9 from Housing, social interaction and participation among older Irish people in *Towards a Society for All Ages* edited by Y. McGivern, © National Council on Ageing and Older People (Fahey, T. 2001), reproduced with permission; Figure 6.1 adapted from Inside the consumer mind: consumer attitudes to the arts, *International Journal of Market Research*, 34, 4, pp. 299–311, WARC (Cooper, P. & Tower, R. 1992), with permission from WARC; Figure 11.1 adapted from I'm in Politics Because There's Things I'd Like to See Happening, Unpublished project report, M.Sc. in Applied Social Research by Derek Beattie, J. Carrigan, J. O'Brien & S. O'Hare, 2005, with permission from Derek Beattie; Figure 11.2 from On and Off the Treadmill: A Typology of Work-Life Integration for Single Workers Aged 35–44, Unpublished project report, M.Sc. in Applied Social Research by G. Breslin, F. Comerford, Fiona Lane & F. O'Gabhan, 2006, with permission from Ms Fiona Lane, B.S.S. (CQSW), M.Sc..

In some instances we have been unable to trace the owners of copyright material, and we would appreciate any information that would enable us to do so.

Part I   INTRODUCING MARKET AND SOCIAL RESEARCH

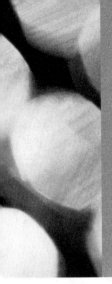

Chapter 1

THE PRACTICE OF MARKET RESEARCH

Introduction

The aim of this chapter is to provide an overview of what research is, why it is done and how it operates. We look at the role of research in business and society, its uses and its limitations. We look at the roles of the in-house and the agency researcher. We look at ethics and data protection and what they mean for the practice of research.

Topics covered

- What is research?
- The use and value of market and social research
- Research roles
- Ethics and the practice of research
- Data protection and the practice of research

Relationship to MRS Advanced Certificate Syllabus

The material covered in this chapter is relevant to Element 1 – Introduction to Market and Social Research. In particular, it covers the following Element 1 topics: the role of research in effective decision making within business and public sector organisations; the structure of the research profession and the roles within it; and the key ethical and legal underpinnings of research.

Learning outcomes

At the end of this chapter you should be able to:

- understand the nature of research;
- recognise the value and contribution of research;
- understand the limitations of research;
- understand the roles of the research supplier and the person commissioning research;
- understand the ethical and legal framework within which research operates and the implications of that framework for the practice of research.

What is research?

Research is about enquiry; it is about systematic observation or investigation to find things out. It is the process by which we produce evidence or knowledge about the world. It is founded on scientific methods, which are in turn supported by philosophical principles about the nature of knowledge and how we construct that knowledge.

Box 1.1 Definitions of research on the web

- Research involves collecting information about a subject from a variety of sources including books, journals and the Internet or by carrying out experiments or talking to people and analysis of this information.
  www.abdn.ac.uk/aim4uni/terms.shtml
- A formal, systematic application of the scientific approach to the study of a problem to discover new information or expand and verify existing knowledge.
  www.ag.ohio-state.edu/~aged885/Glossary/GLOSSARY.htm
- The process of collecting information and data about a topic being studied.
  education.jlab.org/beamsactivity/6thgrade/vocabulary/index.html
- Inquiry into a topic to discover or revise facts or add to knowledge about the topic.
  www.usg.edu/galileo/skills/ollc_glossary.html
- The systematic investigation into, and study of materials, sources etc in order to establish facts and reach new conclusions.
  library.wit.ie/library/olas/glossary.htm
- Research in the most general sense is simply a search for knowledge or truth. The search process itself may be as simple as informally consulting a friend or as complex as designing and implementing a formal billion dollar scientific study.
  library.dts.edu/Pages/RM/Helps/glossary.shtml

What is sometimes called 'pure research' is research undertaken to gain knowledge or understanding of something without having in mind a specific application of that knowledge or understanding. 'Applied research' is the term given to research undertaken to gain the knowledge or understanding needed to address a specific need. Applied research is conducted in many fields. In this book we focus on the practice of applied market and social research.

ICC/ESOMAR (www.esomar.org) in its International Code on Market and Social Research (2007) defines research (market, social and opinion research) as:

> the systematic gathering and interpretation of information about individuals or organisations using the statistical and analytical methods and techniques of the applied social sciences to gain insight or support decision making. The identity of respondents will not be revealed to the user of the information without explicit consent and no sales approach will be made to them as a direct result of their having provided information.

MRS (www.mrs.org.uk) in its Code of Conduct (2005) defines research as:

> the collection and analysis of data from a sample or census of individuals or organisations relating to their characteristics, behaviour, attitudes, opinions or possessions. It includes

all forms of market, opinion and social research such as consumer and industrial surveys, psychological investigations, qualitative interviews and group discussions, observational, ethnographic, and panel studies.

MARKET AND SOCIAL RESEARCH

The distinction between market and social research is based largely on the subject matter which the research addresses – the nature of the problem to be researched and the context of the problem – and not because there are differences in method or approach. Both market and social research require the same clear thinking to define the problem. Both require an understanding of the research process. Both involve the systematic collection and analysis of data. Both require skill to draw out the findings and knowledge to interpret and apply the findings in the wider context or setting of the problem or area under investigation. However, while market and social researchers may use the same research skills set, each is likely to be a specialist in the field in which they apply their findings and to have detailed knowledge of the substantive area in which they work. For market researchers, this body of knowledge is typically business in general (including economics, business strategy and business process) and marketing in particular (including product development, pricing, advertising and promotion, competitive strategy, segmentation, consumer behaviour). The body of knowledge which social researchers draw on is the social sciences including the disciplines of sociology, anthropology, criminology and psychology.

The use and value of market and social research

Research is now a widespread activity. Indeed you only have to look through the Research Buyers' Guide (www.rbg.org.uk) to see the current scope of market and social research applications. Organisations are listed that specialise in research on transport and distribution, training and education, sports, leisure and the arts, property and construction, policing, the environment, agriculture and farming, local and central government, politics, housing, employment, and information communication technologies. It is also a worldwide activity.

Organisations, not just those in the private sector but those in the public and not-for-profit sectors, rely on research to inform and improve their planning and decision making. In all organisations resources are scarce. For an organisation to survive and prosper it must use its limited resources wisely. To do this effectively it must understand the needs and opinions of both its customers and other stakeholders (employees and shareholders, for example, in the case of private sector organisations, and citizens – taxpayers and voters – in the case of public sector organisations). This is where the value of research lies: in its ability to provide high-quality information for planning and decision making in often very complex decision-making environments in which all sorts of other information sources – whose quality and value are often harder to assess – vie for attention. Decisions based on robust and credible research evidence should lead to better quality decision making, better use of resources, better products and services, better policies and better relationships with customers and other stakeholders, increased customer and stakeholder satisfaction and ultimately greater longevity for the organisation than if research were not conducted. Thus research influences what is provided and the way in which it is provided. It connects people with organisations whose products or services they use, or whose policies affect their lives, and so gives them a voice, a role, a degree of influence.

There is evidence that organisations which spend more on research are more successful in the long run. Research is therefore perhaps best viewed as an investment and not as a cost.

However, because of the difficulty in communicating the outcome of research in terms of bottom line value or profitability (see, for example, Wills and Webb, 2006), it is easy to understand why organisations see research as a cost. As Tanner (2005) points out, to see research as an investment, researchers need to show decision makers the link between the research objectives and the business or corporate objectives; they need to set the research findings into the wider business or social context – which may mean combining the research data with other data such as financial data and sales data; and they must communicate the findings in the language of the business or policy context and not in the language of research. This last point is worth bearing in mind when you come to read Chapters 11 to 13 on data analysis and Chapter 14 on communicating research findings.

THE USE OF MARKET RESEARCH

For what kind of planning and decision making does market research provide data? One example is set out in Case study 1.1 below. If you are unfamiliar with the marketing process, however, you might find the following paragraphs useful in understanding the sort of planning and decision making that are often involved.

Marketing process

The Chartered Institute of Marketing (www.cim.co.uk) defines the marketing process as 'the management process responsible for identifying, anticipating and satisfying customer requirements profitably'. Although this management process may not be formalised, or even recognised, as marketing in some organisations, the task of identifying, anticipating and satisfying the needs of the customer exists nevertheless. A marketer's job is to seek out (business) opportunities – opportunities that will serve the interests of the organisation. When an opportunity is discovered, the marketer's role is to develop a *marketing plan* to apply the organisation's resources to achieving measurable *marketing objectives*, and so contribute to the organisation's goals. Marketing objectives are statements of what is to be achieved. For example, a marketing objective might be to launch a new savings account into the online banking market and to achieve a five per cent market share within a year, or to launch a new cancer screening service and achieve an uptake of 80 per cent of the target market.

In order to develop a marketing plan and set marketing objectives, marketers need a clear understanding of the environment in which they operate. They need to understand the wider external environment that is made up of or influenced by social (and cultural), legal, economic, political and technological factors (you may have come across these factors under the acronyms SLEPT or PEST), and the internal environment and resources of the organisation. They need a clear picture of both the opportunities and threats posed by the external environment and also of their organisation's strengths and weaknesses. The process of examining the external environment and the resources of the organisation is referred to as a *marketing audit*. The analysis of strengths and weaknesses, opportunities and threats is called a *SWOT analysis*.

Once a marketing audit and a SWOT analysis have been completed and a business opportunity established and evaluated, a marketing plan can be developed and marketing objectives set. To achieve the marketing objectives a *marketing strategy* is developed – a plan for achieving the objectives. This plan will involve defining the *marketing mix*, which consists of the four Ps: the *product* (or service) – its design, its features, its packaging; its *price*; how it will be *promoted* – advertising, direct mail, public relations and so on; and *place* – the distribution and sales channels, and the level of customer service. The marketer's task is to implement the marketing plan and monitor and evaluate its success in achieving the marketing objectives.

Not only are individual products and services marketed to customers but the organisation itself is marketed to its customers and to a wider audience of stakeholders, including employees and shareholders, in the case of private sector organisations (see Case study 1.1), and taxpayers and voters, among others, in the case of public sector organisations.

CASE STUDY 1.1

MCDONALD'S LISTENS

In this case study we see how a well-known brand, McDonald's, went from being popular with consumers to being unpopular, and how research helped to re-establish the brand.

Why this case study is worth reading

This case study is worth reading for several reasons: it is an example of market research in action; it highlights some of the issues that a large organisation faces in staying in touch with its customers and in understanding the changing environment in which it operates; it describes the end result of the research – the actions taken – and their impact on the organisation and its brand.

The key words are: consumer reaction, consumer habits, reluctance, denial, fight back, research, consumers' perceptions, listening campaign, champion, open-mindedness, understanding, action, trust rebuilt, sales up.

Introduction

The first McDonald's restaurant opened in the UK in 1974. It brought a new style of eating: relaxed, fun, quick and cheap. Consumer reaction was overwhelmingly positive. The brand thrived. By 1983 – nine years later – there were one hundred restaurants; three years after that, another one hundred. By 2000 there were over 1,200.

In 1988 concerns were expressed about the chlorofluorocarbons or CFCs used in McDonald's packaging; in fact, by 1988 CFCs had been removed. In 1989 there was a rumour that beef cattle to supply McDonald's were being grazed on land cleared from South American rainforests. A not-dissimilar story – soya from growers' deforestation of the Amazon – emerged in 2006. In 1993 MP Glenda Jackson led a campaign against opening a McDonald's in the London suburb of Hampstead; the designer, Valentino, did the same in Rome. Things had changed but McDonald's had stayed the same. Why should they change? The formula worked, did it not?

What had happened?

Lifestyles had changed; consumer habits had changed; eating behaviour had changed. More people were buying ready meals and fast food. Obesity became an issue. Government and media looked for someone to blame. McDonald's became a target. People began actively to dislike McDonald's.

The reaction – what not to do

At first there was a reluctance on McDonald's part to recognise what was happening. This is the *first practical point* to note – 'lack of good intelligence and understandably, in part as a result, denial'. The company then tried to fight back: among other actions it tried to sidestep the health issue with the launch of salads. This is the ▶

second practical point – 'Sidestepping can be a dodging, alarm-based reaction'. The launch risked being seen as 'atonement', 'proving', consumers would say, 'we were right all along'.

Then came the development of a lexicon of McDonald's words – in particular, McJob and McLibel. In the so-called McLibel case two people, Morris and Steel, accused McDonald's of exploitation and ecological abuses. McDonald's won in court but lost on public opinion. This is the *third practical point* – 'Attack may not be the best form of defense'; it can look like bullying if you are bigger. McDonald's was now the high street pariah. Sales suffered. Franchisee cash flow declined. The business model became harder and harder to sustain. Pressure grew internally to do something.

Research to the rescue

Research led the thinking. This is the *fourth practical point* – 'The need for a strong perspective so that you understand what is going on.' First, it was important to understand consumers' perceptions in more detail. Everyone needed to realise the extent of distrust of the brand. In 2004 McDonald's ran a Listening Campaign that included 40 qualitative group discussions across the UK with consumers, franchisees, store managers and crew. The new CEO, Peter Beresford, attended every session – the research had a champion.

The *fifth practical point* is 'open-mindedness'. This was evident in the extent to which new techniques were tried and in the depth in which the data were collected and mined. McDonald's began to understand 'who was leaving the brand and why' through segmenting standard tracking studies (that is, looking at the data and seeing if there were specific groups of people who thought or acted in similar ways and working out what demographic groups they belonged to, e.g. mothers with young children, young adults and so on). Critical was an understanding of the current consumer reaction to food and the need to be clearer about ingredients, nutritional content, provenance and processing.

Using techniques designed by American political polling experts Penn Schoen Berland, McDonald's began to see whom they needed to influence. The technique used a presentation of consumer issues and concerns together with potential solutions. The analysis focused on which solutions had most impact among 'swing voters'. It became clear this was the first target audience to focus on. Other audiences were identified to whom specific issues were addressed. This highlights the open-minded not 'one-size fits all approach' in thinking. The final and *sixth practical point* was 'open mindedness in building a relationship with audiences in actions and communication'.

The research led to action: trans fatty acids were removed from the food; genetically modified ingredients were removed from the food chain; beef was bought from British and Irish farmers only; organic milk and free-range eggs were served; fruit bags were introduced. The website 'Make Up Your Own Mind' allowed consumers to ask anything about McDonald's, allowed them to co-create the advertising, and in 2007 McDonald's worked with Greenpeace, as noted on the Greenpeace website: 'An unlikely union [. . . which] successfully pressured multinational commodities brokers into signing a two-year moratorium on buying soya from newly deforested land in the Amazon' (http://www.greenpeace.org.uk/blog/forests/the-odd-couple, accessed 1 April 2008).

Redemption

The results have been positive. Trust in the brand has been rebuilt; people are coming back to the restaurants and are happy to do so; sales are up; franchisees have positive cash flow. A lot has been done but there is a lot more to do. You Gov's Brand Index (which monitors attitudes to 1,200 brands) shows McDonald's as a low scorer: respondents say they hear more negative things about McDonald's than positive – but the trend is upward. The brand has changed; consumer perceptions are changing, slowly.

Source: Adapted from Davidson, G. and Payne, C. (2008) 'How research saves scapegoat brands©: retaining brand and business perspective in troubled times', MRS Conference, www.mrs.org.uk.

Think of all the information needs – the research needs – that this marketing process involves if it is to be done effectively, if the goal of marketing – to 'identify, anticipate and satisfy customer requirements profitably' – is to be met. Market research can be used to achieve the following:

- understand the wider environment and how it affects the organisation;
- identify opportunities and threats;
- identify markets, competitors and customers;
- help with priority setting and direct the use of resources;
- build knowledge for longer-term benefit;
- understand customers and market dynamics;
- monitor customer and stakeholder satisfaction;
- understand how to build and enhance customer relationships;
- monitor and evaluate competitors/competitive activity;
- identify or monitor market changes and trends;
- develop marketing strategies;
- test different marketing strategies;
- monitor and control marketing programmes;
- understand how to influence customer attitudes and behaviour;
- understand how best to communicate with customers and stakeholders;
- develop advertising and communication strategies;
- develop and test advertising executions; and
- develop or select a product or service, a brand name, a pack design, a price point, a distribution channel.

THE USE OF SOCIAL RESEARCH

Social research is commissioned for much the same reason as market research – to obtain information, to understand what is going on in the wider environment, to understand people's attitudes, opinions and behaviour – in order to provide data for effective planning and decision making in relation to policy development and implementation. In social research, the wider external environment is society, the attitudes of interest are 'social' attitudes, attitudes to 'social issues', and the behaviour of interest is how we live and behave in the 'social' world. Social research might be commissioned, for example, to describe the living standards of older people in the community, or to understand decisions taken during a crisis pregnancy, or to

LEVI STRAUSS: RESEARCH COMPELS THE BUSINESS TO ACT

This case study describes how Levi Strauss, maker of Levi's® 501 jeans, overhauled both its approach to market research and to how the research findings were communicated and used within the organisation, with positive effects on its business.

Why this case study is worth reading

This case study is worth reading for a variety of reasons: it shows where the research function sits within a large consumer organisation; it shows how the internal research team linked up with external research suppliers, and it shows how that relationship can work; it gives examples of the types of research that such an organisation uses; it illustrates the job that research must do for an organisation in achieving its business goals; and it shows how an organisation shifted its focus from the detail of the research process to the business application of the research findings.

The key words are: growth, sales, consumer insight, role of research, passive information provision, research process, application, usage, equity tracking, interview, barrier, understanding, core market, opinion leading market, inertia, responsibility, message, company culture, credibility, engage, partnership, internal team, external agencies, business objectives, greater depth.

Introduction

As a company, Levi Strauss settled into a work style where double digit growth on an annual basis became accepted as a natural state of affairs. Beating the sales plan was normal. 'Consumer insight' was the exclusive domain of a handful of designers, and product innovation was essentially expressed through new ways of communicating 501 jeans which represented in excess of 60 per cent of all sales in bottoms. Increasingly, we allowed our focus to wander away from consumers and the market place to internal supply chain issues and how to better reward ourselves for the great work we were achieving. Because Levi Strauss had grown to expect success, the role of research became that of principal cheer leader: market share only went up, equity only improved, and in focus groups consumers always spoke in glowing terms about the brand. Inadvertently, we created a platform from which it became increasingly difficult to be critical of anything that the Levi's® brand did. Likewise, it reduced the role of the (small) research organisation to passive information provision which focused on the actual research process rather than on the application and usage of the consumer insights which resided in the information but which went largely unexplored.

The research tools in place at the time were largely focused on advertising. We had no research around either product or retail, two areas that would prove to be massive areas of weakness once the bottom fell out of the 501 jeans trend. Our main equity tracking tools were set up to only interview consumers who had bought jeans in the last six months. A 'great' idea in a stable market but a major barrier to understanding what is happening to your brand when the category goes into double digit decline and the competition comes from outside of jeans!

Essentially, research became 'due diligence'; we did it because we 'had to' not because we were committed to working with consumer insights. By early 1997, there were clear indications that all was not well but we chose to ignore them: the jeans market amongst young men (our core market) declined by 6 per cent, equity in Scandinavia (which was talked about as an opinion leading market) was in decline, a qualitative 501 jeans study showed that young consumers were beginning to sign out of 501 jeans.

On the verge of a crisis

By the end of 1997 we started to pull the various strands of information together to create a complete analysis of the consumer, market and brand situation across Europe. The picture wasn't pretty.

The jeans market was in free fall, consumers were drifting to stores such as Zara, Mango, H&M, Gap etc and they were finding other garments than jeans to wear: combat pants, casual trousers, outdoor wear, high tech fibres etc. By the end of 1997, consumption of Levi's® jeans amongst young men and women had declined by 6 per cent compared to the previous year. A number which was to get much worse as we'd go on to lose over 50 per cent of our consumption amongst young consumers between 1997 and 2000! The way consumers talked about the Levi's® brand was increasingly distant. Just another fat American corporation: 'Levi's® is in a panic. They are losing share and are desperate to stay cool.' Product ubiquity and lack of innovation: '501 jeans fit every ass fabulously, unfortunately every ass wears one.'

Equity numbers, when we started to expand the scope of our study just a little to include designer jeans, declined dramatically. It was the first clear sign that we had been too narrow in our 'internal' view of the market we were in and that as competition was toughening and moving forward, we were falling backwards fast by standing still.

The internal challenge

The biggest internal challenge was how to overcome the business inertia and mentality that research only brings good news. The initial response to the situation analysis was one of 'what do you mean equity is down, you do know that the sales forecast is up, right?'

The fundamental choice from a research point of view was how far does your responsibility extend? Is it to inform the business of the situation it is in and allow it to make a choice on how to act or is it to compel it to act? In choosing the second route, we put our necks on the line. We continuously sought out a senior audience to pound home the message that, though we as a company expected more success from our current formula, the signs from consumers and the market place were that more of the same was a route that would quickly take us nowhere but backwards.

Taking a well thought through and firm position, which went against company culture, ultimately gave us an infinite amount of credibility when reality caught up with us and the sales forecast suddenly did go down. It created a platform that allowed a total overhaul (and growth) of the research tools in our kit. More importantly it allowed a fundamental change in the way in which we engaged with the broader company, establishing us as partner with a stake in the actions taken.

Engagement with outside partners

To get into this position, and to respond when given the opening, placed specific requirements on the internal research team and it required a shift in focus away from the research process itself to the take-out from that process to the actual usage. It meant thoroughly understanding the brand and business needs, often better than the ▶

people employed to make the decisions. It meant being both willing and able to engage in a debate about what actions to take, and inspire colleagues to follow the path which we believed in, based on the consumer insight generated.

To allow us to shift our focus from the detail of the research process to the business application, it was essential to ensure partnership with our external agencies. To achieve this we invest our time to present our business plans and results to them. We share internal meetings, we have regular contact regardless of whether or not there is a project ongoing, and we have established a non competitive environment across the research companies we use which allows us to cross reference information between them (which means that we forfeit the practice of shopping around for a 'bargain'). The result is that our external partner can truly support us to develop useful research programs and generate insights which can propel the business forward. Because we have a common vested interest in the success of the business, we achieve much greater depth of insights.

Source: Adapted from Flemming from Thygesen and McGowan, P. (2002) 'Inspiring the organisation to act: a business in denial', MRS Conference, www.mrs.org.uk.

explore drug use in prisons, or to establish the healthcare needs of homeless people. This information will be valuable to policy makers, service providers and resource managers, for example. Case study 1.3 offers an example of governnment-commissioned social research and Case study 1.4 is an example of research in the public/charity sector.

CASE STUDY 1.3

THE GOVERNMENT REACHES AN UNDERSTANDING

This case study describes a government's need for information to help it develop appropriate policies and strategies for addressing an important social issue – marginalised teenagers' attitudes to sex, condoms and teenage pregnancy.

Why this case study is worth reading

This case study is worth reading for two reasons: it is an example of social research; and it shows the sort of information that a government needs from research in order to develop suitable policies and strategies.

The key words are: evidence, policies, strategies, goals, clinical and support services, strategic research objectives, programme of research, aim of the study.

Introduction

From 1998 to 2000 the UK Government reviewed evidence and developed policies and change strategies in the area of teenage pregnancy. In the 1970s the UK had similar teenage pregnancy rates to other European countries, but while they achieved dramatic falls in the '80s and '90s, the rates in the UK remained the same. While there is no single explanation for this, two factors stand out:

Ignorance

UK teens lack accurate knowledge about sex and what to expect in relationships. While the need for better sex education has been recognised, delivery is still patchy. Unsurprisingly, it is easy for teens to get confused between playground rumours and fact.

Mixed messages

The UK has a simultaneously puritanical and prurient culture: teenagers are bombarded with sexually explicit messages and an implicit message that sexual activity is the norm, while 'family' campaigners hope that if sex isn't talked about, it won't happen.

The recommendation

After reviewing the evidence, the Social Exclusion Unit, [then] part of the Office of the Deputy Prime Minister, recommended that the specific issue of teenage pregnancy required a specific remedy. It highlighted two main goals:

- Reduce the rate of teenage conceptions, with the specific aim of halving the rate of conceptions among the under 18s by 2010
- Move more teenage parents into education, training or employment, to reduce their risk of long-term social exclusion.

Strategic research objectives

As a matter of priority, the Department of Health wished to find out about teenage attitudes towards sex and contraception, and the best way of communicating to this audience. An extensive programme of research to 'get under their skin' was commissioned by the Central Office of Information (COI), the UK Government's marketing communications arm, to provide the Department of Health with real depth and useable insights for future marketing and communications. The principal aim of the study was to develop key learnings about teenage sex, pregnancy, contraception and sexually transmitted diseases (STDs) that could be transferred and used in a successful communications campaign.

Source: Adapted from Cohen, J. (2005) 'Teenage sex at the margins', MRS Conference, www.mrs.org.uk.

Clearly the need for high-quality information is no less important in the social arena than it is in the business or marketing arenas. Plans and decisions have to made about how our society operates, about how we deal with 'social issues', about how we allocate scarce resources, about what services should be provided, how they should be designed, to whom they should be targeted and how they should be implemented. Plans and decisions about policy and public service provision are nowadays subject to scrutiny and often require justification. They should therefore be based on robust, defensible evidence; the best way of providing that evidence is via objective research.

Social research is commissioned by government departments, public bodies, public services, local government, non-governmental organisations, charities, policy studies groups, the media, think-tanks, academia and research institutes. The topic areas are many and varied, and include health and social care, crime, transport, leisure and the arts, work and family life, housing, labour force participation, and training and skills needs. A social research project might be commissioned for many of the same reasons that a market research project is commissioned – for example to achieve one or more of the following:

- to help with priority setting and to direct the use of resources;
- to understand the wider environment;
- to identify or monitor changes and trends;
- to build knowledge for longer-term benefit;
- to develop policies and programmes;
- to monitor or evaluate programme delivery;
- to identify relevant stakeholders;
- to understand the beliefs and values and attitudes of stakeholders;
- to understand how to influence stakeholder attitudes and behaviour;
- to understand how to build and enhance stakeholder relationships;
- to monitor stakeholder satisfaction; and
- to understand how best to communicate with stakeholders.

CASE STUDY 1.4

IMPROVING PERFORMANCE

This case study shows how research was used to improve the performance of an environmental campaigning agency called ENCAMS, which is part funded by the UK Government (and better known as Keep Britain Tidy).

Why this case study is worth reading

This case study is worth reading for several reasons: it describes the transformation in an organisation's thinking about the research it conducts; it describes what happens when an organisation acts without conducting suitable research; and it describes what happens when appropriate research is conducted at an appropriate time.

The key words are: research, public and charity sector, evaluations, quantitative, research after the event, stakeholders, satisfaction study, cost, benefit, targeting.

Introduction

Market Research is a term that often doesn't exist in the public and charity sector. That doesn't mean that research isn't carried out; a variety of projects are often undertaken but in a multitude of departments and often under the heading of research and development, or evaluations. Research is seen in parts of this sector as something to do after something has happened, to prove the level of success. When research is carried out to understand an issue before work is developed it is in the majority of cases through a large scale quantitative study with huge amounts of data analysis and modelling, answering the 'what's' and the 'when's', but not the 'how's' and the 'why's'. This was the position that ENCAMS was in in 2001. Since then it has revolutionised the way it works and market research was central to this change.

Where ENCAMS was

ENCAMS' work is about the improvement in quality of the local environment, covering issues such as litter, dog fouling, graffiti and vandalism. Although campaigns have been running for years it is only since 2000 that market research has influenced these in any way. Prior to this, they were based on a 'one size fits all' approach. The thinking behind this was to ensure that the messages were not excluding any sectors of the population. The messages for these campaigns were developed based on the desired outcome, therefore if the aim was to reduce the amount of littering by encouraging people to bin their rubbish then the campaign slogan or message would be something to that effect. Channel selection was fairly simple: use widely-targeted media within the constraints of the budget. Most of the research done at this time was research conducted after the event to measure success and determine percentage awareness and recall.

Changes afoot

It became apparent that this approach was not working. The campaigns were only effective or appealing for the minority – effectively preaching to the converted. ENCAMS realised that the focus needed to move away from the converted to the real culprits. To do this it was necessary to understand why people were littering in the first place, and to understand the triggers and barriers that help people to stop littering.

The success of the research

Research was commissioned – qualitative and quantitative – and the findings not only informed a subsequent advertising campaign, they drove the message, the imagery, the channel, the timings and the tone of the execution. Research is also the driving force behind many new products developed by ENCAMS such as the awards for beaches, Blue Flag and Seaside Awards, and the environmental award for schools, Eco-schools. And, since ENCAMS works in partnership with everyone from MPs to Local Authority employees, an annual stakeholder satisfaction study is now in place to monitor these relationships. ENCAMS has been ruthless about stopping work in areas where research suggests that no need exists.

Market research does cost money but if carried out in the right way the benefits far exceed the costs. Money invested in research enables the communication budget to be spent more effectively, targeting the right people with the right product or message.

Source: Adapted from Butcher, J., Strutt, S. and Bird, C. (2005) 'How research drove the metamorphosis of a public sector organisation', MRS Conference, www.mrs.org.uk.

THE LIMITATIONS OF RESEARCH

The value of research depends on its providing actionable, insightful, high-quality information that can be used in the decision-making process. What limits its value? Research is only of value if it fulfils its purpose – if it provides information and knowledge that contribute to the planning and decision-making process. Research is a means to an end, not an end in itself. It will be of use only if it is based on a clear understanding of what problem or issue it is to address, if it has clear aims and objectives, if there is a clear understanding of what kind of information is needed for effective decision making. In fact, there are many factors that limit the value of a piece of research, including the following:

■ poor definition of the problem;
■ lack of understanding of the problem (or the brief);

- poor or inappropriate research design;
- the limitations of the methods used;
- poor execution of the research itself;
- the interpretation of the results;
- the status of knowledge;
- the time that elapses between commissioning the research and delivering and applying the findings;
- the use or misuse or non-use of research evidence by the decision makers.

Poor definition of the problem

This is a key stage in the research process. A clear and accurate statement or definition of the problem is essential if the research is to provide useful information for the decision-making process (Bijapurkar, 1995). Good quality research is relatively easy to carry out but it all means nothing if it does not address the problem or issue under investigation. It will not be able to address the problem if it is not clear what the problem is. A key skill for a researcher is to be able to define or help the client define the problem to be researched. To do this effectively the researcher must understand the wider context of the problem and the decision to be made on the basis of the research evidence, including the factors that may affect the implementation or action to be taken as a result of the research findings. It is important therefore that the researcher checks that all those in the client's decision-making unit (DMU) have been consulted about what it is the research is to investigate so that (at the other end of the research process) they are clear about what can be done – what decisions made, what actions taken – with the evidence collected by the research.

Lack of understanding of the problem (or the brief)

If the researcher fails to understand what the research must deliver, or misinterprets what is needed, he or she may design research that is inappropriate and so of little or no value. The person commissioning the research has a responsibility to ensure that the research brief is clear and unambiguous. This does not mean that the brief or the statement of the research problem should go unchallenged. The researcher has a duty to ensure that he or she understands the research problem and the brief (Pyke, 2000), and understands what evidence is needed from the research.

Poor or inappropriate research design

The value of any research will be limited by the research design – by its suitability in providing the kind of evidence needed to address the problem. If the research design (and this includes the sample design) is poor, the research will be of little value. Good research design is dependent on a clear and accurate definition of the problem and a clear understanding of the research brief. For example, if the client needs to know how effective its advertising campaign is in delivering messages about its brand to its target audience, conducting a one-off study after the first burst of advertising spend may not provide appropriate evidence. A more effective design, one that might provide more robust evidence, may be to track attitudes to the brand over a longer period of time.

The limitations of the methods used

The data collected will only be as good as the methods used to collect them. If, for example, you need a detailed, in-depth understanding of women's facial cleansing routines, the data collected via a telephone interview may be limited; it may be more appropriate to use qualitative methods – interviews and observation – to get at the sort of understanding needed. A random sample survey that achieves a 55 per cent response rate may not provide data that is representative of the target population.

Poor execution of the research itself

Research can be badly executed. Errors can arise in questionnaire design, in sampling, in field-work, in data processing and in data analysis. For example, a badly worded question, a failure to brief interviewers in the handling of probes and prompts to survey questions, a failure to brief coders in how to code respondents' answers may all lead to poor quality data.

The interpretation of the results

Research data and research findings can be misinterpreted, and any misinterpretation limits the value of the research. The researcher must guard against any possible misinterpretation by making sure that he or she clearly understands how to analyse and read the data (quantitative or qualitative) in an objective and systematic way, in a way that is free of bias.

The status of knowledge

Research does not produce 'right answers' – the findings from any research are always partial and contingent, and dependent on context (Shipman, 1997). Knowledge is not 'value free' – it is influenced by the social and cultural context in which it was collected, and by the view of the respondent and by the researcher designing the study and collecting and interpreting the data. Although we strive to conduct objective research we can never be completely objective – our ways of knowing and finding out about things are always filtered through our own way of thinking and our way of seeing and knowing the world. Throughout the research process – in designing and conducting research as well as interpreting and using it – we need to be aware of these possible sources of bias, and their influence.

Time

The time that elapses between commissioning the research and delivering and applying the findings can limit the value of the research. Data become out of date – the passage of time erodes the value of research simply because the data are time dependent. As Sorrell (2002), quoted in Chadwick (2005), remarked, 'How often do I hear a CEO say "By the time we send out a questionnaire, have consumer responses and analyse the data dump, the problem has changed."'

The use, misuse or non-use of research evidence by the decision makers

The value of research also lies in whether the findings are used, and if they are used, how they are used. They may be used well or badly, or they may be ignored. They may be ignored for a number of reasons – the decision makers may simply not believe them, or may not believe that they are valid or reliable; they may find them hard to understand, or unconvincing, or irrelevant; or they may fail to see how they could be used or they may have problems integrat-ing them into the decision-making process. Research findings are not always clear-cut – they can be inconclusive, which may limit their use, or lead to the wrong decision being taken. An organisation's culture and/or any internal political issues may affect the use, misuse or non-use of the research findings; or its structure, systems or level of skills and resources may get in the way of integration or use of the findings (Wills and Williams, 2004). In ensuring that the value of any research is maximised, it is important to clarify with the decision makers at the outset what they want from the research; what they think it will deliver; how they would like you (the researcher) to handle or present the findings; and what they plan to do with the findings – how they envisage using them and what decisions are to be made on the basis of the research. As a researcher you have a role in managing the expectations of the research buyer in terms of what the research can and cannot provide.

RESEARCH BUYERS' VIEWS OF THE RESEARCH PRODUCT

What do research buyers and users think are the limitations or the weaknesses of the service provided by researchers?

In discussions with research managers and research users, and from a review of the literature, Bairfelt and Spurgeon (1998) found that research often did not meet expectations. They found that research buyers perceived that it was not well managed, that findings were poorly presented, and that it failed to deliver value for money. Interviews with research users in Spurgeon's organisation, Shell, revealed a perception that too few researchers are 'commercially oriented' and most have little knowledge of or interest in the way the client's business works; they would rather focus on data than insights and implications. In addition, it was felt that the data produced are 'nice to know but not directly actionable' and tend to be historical, not future focused. Research is perceived to be a discipline of 'black box techniques' and the research process 'shrouded in mystery'. It is viewed as lacking creativity in design and delivery – the output (and the way it is presented) seen as 'too often dull and uninspiring'.

Simmons and Lovejoy (2003) believe that research sometimes fails to deliver the understanding that CEOs need because researchers do not worry enough 'about what the research actually means'. In Tanner's (2005) study of what CEOs want from research, one CEO said, 'We want results that demonstrate the hard reality of whatever's being researched will lead to profitable results.' Another respondent in the same study remarked that 'It's almost as though they're talking a different language. You brief them [the researchers] . . . but the responses are often in terms of intangibles. It's frustrating. I'm often left thinking that I've paid them to do this and I don't have anything I can easily grasp . . . I have to ask "Have I wasted my money? Would I do this again?" '. Tanner notes that because most researchers do not speak the same language as the decision maker, important findings 'are lost at senior management levels where they are necessary for strategic business decision making'. Bijapurkar (1995) believes that in order to contribute better to strategic decision making researchers should improve their problem-definition skills and their understanding of the business context of the decision, and learn to look to the future rather than describe the present.

Kreinczes (1990) believes that the market research industry holds 'a production rather than a marketing orientation, . . . concentrated on selling what it makes, rather than on what its customers want to buy'. He believes that researchers 'need a greater degree of insight, creativity, innovation and individual responsibility: a greater degree of pride of ownership in the results; a genuine, burning desire to champion the findings'. Chadwick (2005) notes that clients 'expect more proactivity in the delivery of insight, more integration of information . . . , more consulting and more senior involvement'. Edgar and McErlane (2002) argue that researchers should position themselves as the client's 'integrated business partner', that clients will 'go back to researchers who can provide them with business solutions and knowledge not just research data'. Furthermore, they note that clients will pay these researchers more, and give them the most interesting jobs.

Box 1.2 What do clients want?

Simon Chadwick reports the key findings from two studies investigating what clients want from researchers.

Key words are: primary data collection, knowledge management, business decision support, value added, integration of information, insight generation, multiple data sources, analysis, reporting, project management, data processing, quality control, strategic, fabric of decision making, extracting value, partnership.

A taxonomy of need

In 2002, the research agency NOP World conducted 35 in-depth interviews with research directors and marketers in Fortune 500 companies in both the US and Europe. Key findings suggested that there existed a taxonomy of needs among clients, which ranged from the very basic (mere primary data collection) to the ultra-sophisticated (knowledge management and business decision support). Overall, clients tended to fall into five distinct categories (or Value Added Levels) where their needs and demands of their research suppliers were concerned:

Level 5 Knowledge Management and Business Decision Support
Level 4 Integration of information and insight generation across multiple data sources
Level 3b Design, analysis, reporting and generation of insights across multiple studies [that is, the cumulative experience with the client]
Level 3a Design, analysis, reporting and generation of insights from the current study alone
Level 2 Project management, data processing and quality control
Level 1 Primary data collection

What research directors want

The majority of research directors (two-thirds) demanded service ranging between Levels 1 and 3a from their research companies. Indeed, they felt uncomfortable if anything beyond that was offered, viewing this as competition to the role that they felt that they should play within the organisation. A third, however, were expecting at least Level 3b and even Level 4 from their suppliers, as they themselves reengineered their own departments to be more consultative and influential within their own companies' management structures and business decision-making fabrics.

What marketers want

The majority of marketers in the study (primarily marketing directors and above) wanted Levels 4 and 5 service from research companies. Their concept was of research companies as experts from whom they could derive insight and advice born of experience in the market, the category or the discipline.

From research to knowledge

In a qualitative study conducted by Cambiar in 2004 with research directors from ten multinational companies (five in the US and five in the UK) matched by size and ▶

sector, the themes uncovered in 2002 were reiterated. Respondents talked of 'becoming involved in the fabric of decision making' and of the critical importance of 'managing relationships with other parts of the business'. The directors involved saw their role in a much more strategic light. As one UK technology company research head put it: 'It's about integrating information from all around the business. It's no longer about delivering the project. We need fewer projects, more time and more use for the research.' As another put it, 'Less research, more knowledge.' Respondents referred to themselves and their departments as 'thought leaders' and 'integrators'. Their job is to generate insight, which can impact on strategy, and they do it, as one respondent put it, by 'extracting value from the research and from the knowledge of the team.'

Many recognised that they would need fewer 'pure' researchers and project managers and more 'insight-type' people who were possessed of consulting and communications skills. But will research companies be relegated to the role of data collectors and project managers? According to the clients themselves, the answer is a very definitive 'no'. What they wish to see is their research partners leveraging the knowledge and experience that they already possess and bringing integrated insights to them as part of the partnership.

Source: Adapted from Chadwick, S. (2005) 'Do we listen to journalists or clients? The real implications of change for the market research industry', MRS Conference, www.mrs.org.uk.

In conclusion

So what is to be learnt from all this research on researchers? It is clear that the value and the perception of research can be enhanced by turning data into information and knowledge. This means paying attention to drawing out the implications of the research findings, and interpreting the findings in the context of the client's business environment, rather than just presenting data. As Chadwick (2005) points out, researchers need to sharpen their skills, 'emphasising consulting, business savvy and the ability to integrate data across studies and data sets'. Not only do you need to know what Smith (2005) calls 'the "content" of market research' but you also need to be able to communicate what it means to those who are going to use it, typically senior management. You must be what Smith calls a 'trusted information advisor'. This involves the following, according to Smith:

- being able to work in partnership with clients;
- being able to get to grips with and make sense of the data;
- being able to interpret what the data mean by applying 'contextual understanding';
- being able to develop robust arguments that help clients make informed judgements;
- being able to present the research evidence in an active, engaged way and not in a passive, detached way;
- being able to engage in the decision-making process.

Being able to operate as 'a trusted information advisor' depends on several things, including your skills set, your confidence in your skills and abilities, and your credibility with the client (Smith, 2005). It also depends on the client's willingness to engage in this way, which – as Chadwick (2005) above and others (Pyke, 2000) have found – is not always the case.

Box 1.3 What clients want: advice from a public sector client

Here Jo Butcher of ENCAMS, an environmental campaigning agency, and Simon Strutt and Carolyn Bird of The Marketing Works offer advice to researchers based on their experience of research in the public sector.

Key words are: unuseable information, credibility, conclusions, presentation, engage, senior staff, quality thinking, aims of organisation, early stages, strategic thinking, feedback.

1 Be consultants and not just research providers

If the client asks for something that isn't going to help, advise them to stop them wasting their budgets: having unuseable information stacked up on their shelves only undermines the credibility of market research advice. Data must not only be correct, it must also be in a form that clients can understand and buy into – not just the research specialists, but throughout the organisation. This requires simple conclusions, visual presentation of findings that energise and inspire rather than confuse and befuddle the non-specialists. If research is not used to make decisions then the industry has failed.

2 Aim high

Engage senior staff, make them interested in the information, give them some personal and intellectual reward from presentations, make the market research section of their meetings fun and inspirational, and provide quality thinking that includes a full appreciation of the aims of the organisation and of the senior staff.

3 Get in early

Research can help most at the early stages of strategic thinking. The research industry has a duty to maintain a constant stream of accurate feedback to the government machine, not only exploring what the people will stand for, but also how they will react to changes in policy and advice. This gives the research industry a crucial role in delivering democratic government that doesn't waste money trying to do the impossible for a population who do not want it.

Source: Adapted from Butcher, J., Strutt, S. and Bird, C. (2005) 'How research drove the metamorphosis of a public sector organisation', MRS Conference, www.mrs.org.uk.

Research roles

Now that we have had an overview of what research has to offer, it is time to look in more detail at the roles and day-to-day tasks in the research process.

There are effectively three main roles in the research process – research supplier, research buyer and research user. The research supplier, as the name suggests, is the person who supplies the research. The supplier is typically responsible for the research design, for overseeing its execution and for reporting the findings to the research buyer and/or the research user. The research buyer, again as the name suggests, buys or commissions research data or research expertise from a source either inside the organisation – for example from a knowledge centre or from a department or team called marketing planning, marketing services, consumer insight, market research or merely research – or from outside the organisation – for example from a research agency or a consultant. In some organisations the research buyer is also the research user. For example, as you will have seen from the discussion above, research may be commissioned by a brand manager or a marketing director, by a planner in an advertising agency, or by a policy maker in the public sector. In other organisations the research user might commission research via an intermediary, an internal or in-house researcher, for example, a research manager, a marketing planner or a consumer insight executive – someone from within the organisation who either conducts the research or briefs an external organisation to conduct it (see Case study 1.2, for example). Below we look at the role of the client or in-house researcher, the different types of research supplier, the roles within a research agency and, in particular, the role of a research executive.

CLIENTSIDE ROLES

The clientside research role will depend on the type of organisation, the nature of its business and the way it views research. Some organisations no longer have a market research department. There may be several reasons for this – for example it may be as a result of changing business practices that have led to outsourcing research services; or it may be the result of the integration of the research function into a broader function involving, for example, information or knowledge management, marketing services, business or strategic planning, or policy making. While in some organisations client researchers find themselves in a fairly traditional research department, others now belong in this broader function and job titles (and roles) reflect this. A scan of the job advertisements in the trade press demonstrates the variety of clientside roles. There are advertisements for market research managers, marketing planning managers, market analysts, brand planners, information managers, customer, consumer or market insight managers and insight analysts. Many organisations have reorganised to ensure that the customer is the focus of their business, with the result that research and market planning functions have been renamed and, to some extent, reconfigured, as customer or consumer insight. In some cases this may be a change in name only, in order to refocus or redefine the research role. In others it reflects a change in the traditional market research role, in recognition of the need to manage and use data from a variety of sources, including scanner data and other data contained in databases as well, geodemographic data, for example, and not just traditional market research data generated mostly via primary research. In some organisations researchers are now involved in the earlier stages of the business or marketing or policy-making process, at the development of ideas and initiatives, rather than at a later stage when formal research is being commissioned.

THE DAY-TO-DAY JOB OF AN IN-HOUSE RESEARCHER

The in-house researcher may be responsible for research into a particular market or product or service or area. The job is likely to involve liaising with or working alongside decision makers, for example in strategy, marketing, sales, production or policy formulation. It may involve an internal consultancy role, advising on the use of research and ensuring that research insights are integrated into the planning process – in effect ensuring that research and other data are converted to information and knowledge and applied effectively to move the business or the issue forward. Case study 1.2 offers a good example of this sort of role in action. The role may involve providing guidance and advice to internal data analysts; it may involve managing and developing databases and decision support systems. The role is also likely to involve providing and/or commissioning research, managing the research process, and managing the relationship with the research supplier.

TYPES OF RESEARCH SUPPLIER

Research suppliers can be divided into three broad groups: full service agencies, specialist suppliers and limited service suppliers. Full service agencies offer a full research service in qualitative research or quantitative research or both, supplying everything from research design, fieldwork and data processing to analysis and reporting of the findings and their implications. Specialist suppliers are those that specialise in a particular data collection method, for example telephone research; or those that specialise in a particular market sector, for example pharmaceuticals, media or business-to-business research; or those that specialise in a particular technique, for example consumer panels, mystery shopping or product testing. There is some overlap between categories – for example, qualitative research agencies may be considered to be specialist suppliers; those specialising in particular quantitative methods or in particular sectors or techniques may also be full service agencies. There are various kinds of limited service suppliers, suppliers that specialise in a particular part of the research process, usually fieldwork only (including recruitment for qualitative research) or data processing only or both – known as field and tab – or in statistical analysis. There are those – usually independent consultants – who provide research advice and consultancy, research design, project management, qualitative fieldwork, data interpretation and reporting services.

ROLES WITHIN A RESEARCH AGENCY

Most full service research agencies and most specialist agencies will have a client service department, a field department and a data processing department. Each of these services can be provided as a stand-alone service and, as we saw above, limited service agencies are those that specialise in one or more of these. Within each of these departments or service functions there will be executives at different levels of seniority. These executives will have different titles depending on custom and practice within the organisation. The most common, in order of increasing seniority, are research executive or field or data processing executive; senior executive; research or field or data processing manager; associate director; perhaps even senior associate director; and director. Within an organisation's fieldforce there are interviewers, supervisors and area managers or area controllers. In the data processing department there may be data entry and coding staff as well as script writers or programmers (for setting up the programmes needed for computer-aided data collection and analysis) and specification (spec) writers or data analysts who prepare and execute the analysis.

THE CLIENT SERVICE ROLE

The job of the client service department and so the job of a research executive involves managing and being a part of the client's research business. Obviously, responsibility for various aspects of the business and the level of involvement will vary with seniority, and will depend on the size of the research team and the nature of the project. Basically, however, the job involves everything from the research briefing stage (and sometimes before it) through to the delivery of the research findings and their implications (and sometimes beyond). In

Box 1.4 The role of the agency research executive

The main duties of a research executive are to carry out the following:

- liaise with the client;
- help define the problem or issue to be researched;
- design the research;
- cost the research;
- write the proposal;
- discuss the proposal with the client and with colleagues;
- design the discussion guide or questionnaire;
- set up the research and manage it;
- conduct a pilot study;
- refine the research plan/questionnaire or discussion guide in the light of the findings from the pilot study;
- brief the fieldwork team or the recruiters;
- brief the data processing team including coders;
- prepare stimulus material (e.g. for qualitative research);
- liaise with field staff on progress of the work;
- attend (or conduct, in the case of qualitative research) fieldwork;
- prepare an analysis plan;
- write the analysis specification for data processing;
- check the data tabulations for accuracy;
- analyse and interpret the data;
- prepare a report of the findings and/or a presentation;
- give the presentation, drawing out the implications for the client;
- take part in follow-up discussions with the client;
- organise archiving and storage of project documents.

addition to this role, which is typically a mixture of project management and client-facing consultancy, the research executive may be involved in preparing new business sales pitches and perhaps even undertaking internal development work. Also, some of their time may be devoted to keeping up to date with developments in research practice on the one hand – the content of the job – and developments in their clients' business areas on the other – the context of the job.

ROLES WITHIN THE DATA PROCESSING SERVICE

The data processing (DP) department or DP service provider typically consists of a team of data processing executives or data analysts including programmers (scriptwriters who write the questionnaires for computer-aided interviewing; specification writers who write the programs for running tables and analysis), coding staff and, if paper questionnaires are processed, data entry staff – all managed by a data processing manager, who in turn may report to a DP or data services director. In addition, there may be executives with specialist statistical expertise and those with specialist IT knowledge.

The coding section of a DP department is responsible for the development of code lists or coding frames from the open-ended questions on a questionnaire. Most quantitative studies will include some open-ended questions, such as 'Please explain why . . .'. The responses given to these questions must be coded – individual elements of a response to a particular question extracted from all questionnaires, listed under a heading and assigned a numeric code in order to be entered into the analysis package and appear in tabulations. We look in more detail at how to prepare a coding frame in Chapter 10. The research executive provides the coder with a brief on how responses are to be treated – guidance on how to construct the coding frame. The coder liaises with the research executive and the DP executive or manager about a study's coding needs in order to plan how the coding is to be organised and completed accurately and on time for the data processing schedule.

If you are working with paper questionnaires then the next stage in data processing will involve data entry and data verification. If data capture has involved computer-aided methods the data entry stage is not needed. During the data collection process the interviewer or the respondent enters responses directly into the computer. The data are therefore already held in electronic form and can be downloaded into an analysis package. If, however, paper-based methods are used to collect the data – data are recorded on a paper questionnaire – then the data must be transferred from the questionnaire to the computer analysis package. This data entry process is conducted either by computer operators experienced in touch-typing alphanumeric data or by electronically scanning the questionnaires. (To use scanning techno-logy, however, requires that the questionnaire be designed in a way that the scanner can read.) Once the data have been entered verification takes place – to ensure that codes from the questionnaire have not been incorrectly entered.

Data processing executives write, test and implement the programs necessary for data capture, data entry, verification, and those for producing data tabulations and statistical cal-culations. The research executive prepares an analysis specification (sometimes called a tab spec or a DP spec) that sets out for the DP executive how the data are to be coded, tabulated and analysed and what statistical tests or special analyses are to be conducted. We look in detail at how to prepare a DP specification in Chapter 10. On the basis of this specification the DP executive writes the program that will produce the tables and the necessary analysis. In addition, in some larger agencies or in specialist DP or IT consultancies, DP executives may be involved in software development, including database design.

The role of the DP manager is to manage the workload of the DP department and liaise with clients and researchers about their needs. DP managers may be involved in preparing costings for data processing tasks. They may be responsible for quality control and are likely to be involved in recruiting, training and supervising staff. They may have responsibility for managing a DP budget. The DP director is responsible for the success of the DP operation, for overall quality control, business development, keeping up to date with developments in technology and for implementing systems that will deliver to the needs of the clients and researchers.

ROLES WITHIN THE FIELDWORK SERVICE

The field executive's role involves preparing fieldwork costings, liaising with research executives on questionnaire design and on sample design and selection of sampling points, and setting up and managing fieldwork. Fieldwork management involves allocating work, setting quotas for the number of interviews to be completed per interviewer day, preparing briefing notes for interviewers, running briefing and training sessions, and checking on the progress of fieldwork. It may also include attending fieldwork or supervising fieldwork, administering interviewer pay, training and recruiting interviewers, and generally managing the fieldforce.

Depending on the size of the organisation, the size of the fieldforce and the volume of field-work conducted, the field executive's role may be more differentiated, to the extent that some of these tasks are conducted by specialists. For example, there may be a dedicated interviewer trainer; a dedicated fieldwork allocator; there may be an administrator who deals mostly with interviewer pay claims and fieldwork expenses.

If international, multi-country research is involved an international fieldwork co-ordinator may be part of the field or client service team, or part of a separate international co-ordination unit. The role of a co-ordinator is to ensure that the fieldwork in each country is conducted to the same standards. This will involve liaising with in-market fieldwork suppliers, ensuring that those conducting the fieldwork are fully briefed about the project requirements and per-haps even training local in-market fieldworkers. It will involve checking that questionnaires and discussion guides are adapted to suit the market and that they, together with all related material, are translated accurately. Back-translation, that is, retranslating into the original language, is often carried out to ensure that any meaning is not lost or distorted as a result of translation. The co-ordinator will also check that questionnaires and discussion guides in different languages are measuring the same thing. The role may also involve briefing research executives to ensure that they are aware of the environmental factors – cultural, social, eco-nomic, technological, legal and political – that will affect how the research is conducted or the data obtained, including for example use of recruitment and sampling techniques, methods of data collection, wording of questions and use of stimulus material. The co-ordinator may also be involved in overseeing the handling of the data at the end of fieldwork, and the processing of the data, including retranslation of responses to open-ended questions and translations of transcripts of focus groups and depth interviews.

Now that we have looked at the role of research and the roles of those within it, we turn our attention to the 'rules of the game', the wider framework within which research operates.

Ethics and the practice of research

First of all, we look at the ethical principles that underpin research, moving on in the next section to the more formal framing of those principles in the codes of conduct of professional bodies, including the MRS Code of Conduct. In the final section in this chapter we look at data protection legislation and its implications for research practice.

WHAT ARE ETHICS?

Ethics are moral principles that are used to guide behaviour. The study of ethics is the study of standards of conduct, of the rights and wrongs of the behaviour of a particular person or group. Ethical principles are used to set standards of conduct for groups or professions in how they deal with people. The research profession is no exception. Ethical standards are important in a research context in order that those involved in research – researchers, research participants, clients and other users of research and the wider community – know what is and what is not acceptable behaviour in the conduct of research. A researcher's ethical code extends to the treatment of clients, in relation to, for example, recommending research that is unnecessary, or misreporting findings, or to the disclosure of confidential client data, and to the treatment of other researchers and their work. The primary focus of most ethical codes, however, is the setting of standards of behaviour in relation to the treatment of research participants, on whom research depends.

GETTING CO-OPERATION

Why do people agree to take part in research? We ask a lot of research participants and we give them little in return. We intrude into their lives – we observe, measure and question their behaviour, their attitudes and their opinions, and we analyse, interpret and report what they tell us. We often ask them to divulge personal, sometimes sensitive, information – and to someone who is a stranger to them. There is little tangible or intangible reward for taking part – it is rare that research directly serves the interest of the individual respondent. Given these circumstances it is unlikely that people would willingly co-operate in research if they felt that they could not trust the researcher. One way of creating trust is to ensure, and demonstrate, that research is conducted in an acceptable and ethical way. This is done to a large extent by publishing and promoting a formal code of conduct by which research practitioners agree to abide. Various research industry bodies (ESOMAR – www.esomar.org; the Social Research Association – www.the-sra.org.uk; the MRS – www.mrs.org.uk) have set out codes of practice and/or sets of ethical guidelines with a view to enhancing the public's confidence in research by outlining the rights and safeguards to which they are entitled, and by making it clear to researchers the need to behave responsibly when conducting research, particularly research among vulnerable groups of people. In relevant places throughout the book we note what one such code, the MRS Code of Conduct, says about research practice. Here we look in more detail at the ethical principles that underlie codes of practice.

ETHICAL PRINCIPLES IN THE TREATMENT OF RESEARCH PARTICIPANTS

The ethical principles that are the basis of most standards of conduct in relation to research participants are as follows:

- voluntary participation;
- no harm to the participants;
- informed consent;
- anonymity, confidentiality (privacy);
- transparency;
- not deceiving subjects.

Voluntary participation

Voluntary participation is the cornerstone of an ethical code: it requires that no one should be forced or deceived into taking part in research. The researcher should obtain an individual's or an organisation's consent and this consent should be based on a clear understanding of what the research will involve and how the data collected will be used. The participant should be told that they have the right to withdraw from the research at any time and are under no obligation to answer any of the questions asked.

No harm to the participants

At all times during the conduct of research participants should be treated with respect and sensitivity. The onus is on the researcher to ensure respondents' emotional as well as physical well-being and to take steps 'to ensure that respondents are not harmed or adversely affected as a result of participating in a research project' (MRS Code of Conduct, 2005). It should be relatively easy to recognise what might cause physical harm to respondents, and to avoid it. For example, if the research involves a respondent testing a product, the client and the researcher should take steps to ensure the safe use of the product, for instance by providing clear instructions about its use. It is more difficult to recognise what might cause people emotional harm, however. There are many possible causes – the very fact of being researched can cause anxiety and stress (Gordon and Robson, 1980). Intruding on respondents at unsuitable or inconvenient times can cause annoyance and distress. Asking questions about sensitive topics can embarrass and distress respondents. Reporting or publishing the findings of research in which individuals or research settings are identifiable can cause embarrassment or distress, and may damage participants' self-image or public reputation (Lee, 1992).

Informed consent

The principles of voluntary participation and no harm to participants form the basis of informed consent. Research should not proceed without the informed consent of the participants. Respondents should be clearly and unambiguously informed about what is involved and how the data they provide will be used. It is the researcher's responsibility to ensure that the nature of the research is not misrepresented in any way. We revisit the principle of informed consent in the discussion about data protection legislation below.

Anonymity and confidentiality

Ensuring the anonymity and confidentiality of participants and the data they provide are two ways in which the well-being and interests of respondents can be protected. Anonymity and confidentiality are often confused, and sometimes taken to mean the same thing. They are different, and it is important to remember this when such assurances are given to a participant. If you promise confidentiality it means that, while you can identify a particular response with a particular respondent, you agree not to do so publicly. If, however, you promise anonymity it means that you cannot identify a response with a particular respondent. Promises of anonymity are not always possible in research. In most projects personal data are collected for quality control and verification purposes and they remain attached to the data record at least until quality checks have been made. Respondents are therefore not anonymous. Data records can be anonymised – by removing all identifying information – and it is good practice to do this as soon as possible after quality checks on the data have been made. If it is necessary to recontact a respondent, any personal data should be stored separately from the data record (and only those involved in the research should have access to that information). If respondents are promised anonymity – in some projects it may be necessary to do this in order to secure co-operation (for example studies of sexual behaviour, illegal drug taking or criminal activity) – no personal data should be recorded on the data record that could identify them with their responses. This will mean that quality or verification checks cannot be made. If you assure a respondent of confidentiality or anonymity you would be acting unethically if you were to breach that assurance. For example, say you give the respondent's data to the client to add to or enhance their customer database, or you write up your findings for publication and the description makes a respondent identifiable, you would be in breach of your agreement with the respondent, and so you would be acting unethically. If it is not your intention to keep data confidential you should not promise confidentiality, or describe the research as confidential. You must tell potential respondents what the purpose of data collection really is. If you assure the respondent that the employee satisfaction survey in which he or she is taking part will be anonymous, and you print the respondent's staff number, for example, on the questionnaire, then the data record is not anonymous. You have breached your assurance to the respondent. If you do not inform respondents honestly about the nature and purpose of the research you may not have complied with the principle of informed consent and you may be guilty of deceiving them.

Transparency

Research can be conducted without the promise of either anonymity or confidentiality. For example, data can be collected on an attributable basis. This, however, can be done only with the consent of the participant and the data can only be used for the purpose described to the participant at the time of collection. The person or organisation collecting the data must be transparent about the purpose of the research, the end use of the data and the fact that anonymity or confidentiality is or is not promised.

Not deceiving subjects

Deceiving subjects in order to get them to take part in research is unethical. For example, it would be unethical to tell a respondent that the interview will take 15 minutes if you know that it will take 45 minutes. Deceiving subjects into thinking that they are taking part in research when they are not is unethical. The reputation of research has been harmed, and co-operation rates have declined, as a result of the practice of 'sugging' or selling under the guise of research (and 'frugging', fund raising under the guise of research). Subjects should not be misled or deceived in any way; it should be made clear to them (transparency again) that they are taking part in bona fide research and they should be informed honestly about what that research involves.

ETHICAL CONSIDERATIONS TO CLIENTS AND THE RESEARCH COMMUNITY

Researchers' ethical responsibilities do not rest only with respondents; they also have ethical responsibilities to the clients or the funders of the research (Lovett, 2001), to fellow researchers and to the wider community. As a result, researchers have an ethical responsibility to behave in a way that does not cause the public or the business community to lose confidence in research or the research profession. They should not recommend or undertake unnecessary research. They should not make claims about their qualifications or experience that are untrue, for example. In conducting a research project researchers are entrusted with confidential and commercially sensitive information – they have an ethical responsibility not to disclose this information. When proposing or conducting research or reporting on the findings of research, researchers have an ethical responsibility to be open and honest about the way in which research will be or was conducted, and its limitations or shortcomings. If difficulties are encountered, or mistakes made, these should be pointed out – in order to allow others to learn from them, and for the wider research community to benefit, and to allow others to judge the validity and reliability of the research. Researchers also have an ethical responsibility to ensure that research results – whether positive or negative – are reported accurately and honestly and that they are not used to mislead in any way. They have a responsibility to ensure that they do not use or take advantage of the work of another researcher without that researcher's permission. These issues are captured in the codes of conduct we examine below.

AMBIGUITIES IN THE INTERPRETATION AND APPLICATION OF ETHICAL PRINCIPLES

The principles outlined above are widely accepted – most researchers would agree that informed consent should be obtained, that respondents should not be deceived or coerced

Box 1.5 ICC/ESOMAR Code of Practice (2007): Articles 1 and 2

Article 1 Basic principles

(a) Market research shall be legal, honest, truthful and objective and be carried out in accordance with appropriate scientific principles.

(b) Researchers shall not act in any way that could bring discredit on the market research profession or lead to a loss of public confidence in it.

(c) Market research shall be conducted with professional responsibility and conform to the principles of fair competition, as generally accepted in business.

(d) Market research shall be clearly distinguished and separated from non-research activities including any commercial activity directed at individual respondents (e.g. advertising, sales promotion, direct marketing, direct selling etc).

Article 2 Honesty

(a) Market research shall not abuse the trust of respondents or exploit their lack of experience or knowledge.

(b) Researchers shall not make false statements about their skills, experience or activities, or about those of their organisation.

Source: © Copyright [2007] by ESOMAR® – The World Association of Research Professionals. This paper first appeared in www.esomar.org/uploads/pdf/professional-standards/ICCESOMARCodeEnglish.pdf published by ESOMAR.

into taking part in research, or deceived about the use of the data they provide, and that data should be treated in confidence unless agreed otherwise. It all seems fairly straightforward at first glance. There are complications, however. Here are some things to think about.

- How far do you go in encouraging the unwilling to take part? If you try to persuade a subject to take part have you violated the principle of voluntary participation? Does it depend on what you say or do in order to persuade? If only those who are willing actually take part what implications does this have in terms of representativeness of the sample (and so the external validity of the research)?

- If you do not get the subject's consent at the start of the data collection process is participation really voluntary, or are you deceiving the subject into participating? Does it depend on the type of research situation? In observation exercises, such as mystery shopping, where the validity of the research relies on the subject not knowing that he or she is being observed, is it justifiable not to get the subject's permission before data collection begins?

- How much should you tell subjects about the research in order to comply with the principle of informed consent (Robson, 1991)? Should you tell them everything about it? What is everything anyway? Is it justifiable to withhold some of the details about the research where you believe that they might bias the respondent's answers, or is this deception, and/or a compromise of the principle of informed consent? For example, what do you do if you are conducting a customer satisfaction study in which the services of several organisations are being compared and you feel that telling the respondent the name of the client might bias the responses?

- You promise participants in a video-recorded group discussion that the data they provide and the recording of the group will be treated in confidence and used for research purposes only. Is it justifiable to use the video recording in a research training session? Does this use of the material count as research? Have you broken your promise of confidentiality? Have you deceived participants about the use of their data?

- You are researching the experiences of employees in a relatively small organisation and the client (the employer) wants to know if experiences vary by department and grade. Will individuals be identifiable in the data if their names are not used but either their department or grade is? You interview the employees at convenient breaks in their working day. Will colleagues, or those involved in commissioning the research, be able to determine who was interviewed? In these circumstances can you promise respondents confidentiality or anonymity? Are there implications for the quality of the data if respondents feel that confidentiality might be compromised? Will the openness and honesty of their answers be limited by their perception of the confidentiality of the project? Can you be sure that no harm will come to respondents as a result of their participation in the research?

- A further question for consideration is that of who owns the data collected and whether research participants have rights to their data. If participants have rights to their data do they have the right to give or withdraw consent for how the data are used? What implications does this have for confidentiality and anonymity? Do they have rights to their data record once it has been anonymised?

As these questions and dilemmas show, ethical issues are rarely clear-cut. Questions about how to apply ethical principles will always arise. It is to address such questions, and to ensure a professional and consistent standard of practice, that professional bodies representing researchers, such as ESOMAR and MRS, among others, have developed formal codes of conduct.

Professional codes of conduct

As we have seen, many issues and circumstances that arise in the practice of research are ambiguous and open to interpretation from an ethical point of view – what one person judges to be ethical behaviour in a particular situation another may not. In order to define clearly what is and what is not ethical or acceptable in the conduct of research, professional bodies that represent researchers have developed formal codes of conduct. The purpose of these codes is to establish good practice among their members and to set minimum standards of ethical behaviour. The codes aim to do this by ensuring that important ethical issues are identified and addressed and by trying to clear up any ambiguity in the interpretation of ethical principles. Most codes cover three areas: the researcher's responsibilities to research participants, to those who fund the research, and to other researchers. Members of ESOMAR, the professional body representing researchers worldwide (www.esomar.org), are bound by the International Chambers of Commerce (ICC)/ESOMAR International Code of Marketing and Social Research Practice. Members of MRS are bound by its Code of Conduct, which incorporates the ICC/ESOMAR Code. The Social Research Association (www.the-sra.org.uk) publishes Ethical Guidelines.

The codes and guidelines are self-regulatory and, although they may incorporate principles that are covered by legislation, they do not replace or take precedence over legislation. They are, as ESOMAR notes, 'to be applied against the background of applicable law and of any stricter standards or rules that may be required in any specific market.'

MRS CODE OF CONDUCT

The MRS Code was first published in 1954 and has been revised and updated regularly to take account of changes in research practice and in legislation. As MRS points out, it is the responsibility of members to keep themselves updated on changes to any part of the Code. A full version of the Code, which contains notes about its interpretation, is available at the MRS website (www.mrs.org.uk). To give researchers a more detailed framework for the

Box 1.6 The MRS Code of Conduct

The purpose of the Code

The Code of Conduct is designed to support all those engaged in market, social or opinion research in maintaining professional standards. The Code is also intended to reassure the general public and other interested parties that research is carried out in a professional and ethical manner.

The principles of the Code

These are the core principles and are based on the ESOMAR principles (www.esomar.org):

1. Market researchers will conform to all relevant national and international laws.
2. Market researchers will behave ethically and will not do anything which might damage the reputation of market research.
3. Market researchers will take special care when carrying out research among children and other vulnerable groups of the population.
4. Respondents' co-operation is voluntary and must be based on adequate, not misleading, information about the general purpose and nature of the project when their agreement to participate is being obtained and all such statements must be honoured.
5. The rights of respondents as private individuals will be respected by market researchers and they will not be harmed or disadvantaged as the result of co-operating in a market research project.
6. Market researchers will never allow personal data they collect in a market research project to be used for any purpose other than market research.
7. Market researchers will ensure that projects and activities are designed, carried out, reported and documented accurately, transparently, objectively and to appropriate quality.
8. Market researchers will conform to the accepted principles of fair competition.

The structure of the Code

Section A of the Code sets out the general rules of professional conduct. Section B sets out the more specific rules as they apply in different aspects of research. The appendix sets out the ICC/ESOMAR International Code of Marketing and Social Research Practice for reference only.

Source: http://www.mrs.org.uk/standards/downloads/code2005.doc

interpretation of the principles of its Code of Conduct, MRS also publishes a series of Guide-lines (also available at its website). These Guidelines interpret the Code for the practice of different types of research. In addition, MRS operates an advice service called Codeline, which is staffed by research experts who will provide practical advice to respondents, researchers, clients and other interested parties about the application of the Code of Conduct and the Guide-lines series. You can submit a query to the Codeline experts by email at codeline@mrs.org.uk. Throughout the rest of the book, where relevant, we highlight key rules from the MRS Code of Conduct.

Research and data protection legislation

In 1995 the European Union adopted the Data Protection Directive. One of its aims, stated in Article One, was to 'protect the fundamental rights and freedoms of natural persons, and in particular their right to privacy with respect to the processing of personal data'. Individual EU member states introduced legislation to comply with this Directive. In the United Kingdom the legislation is the 1998 Data Protection Act. The ethical principles discussed earlier are incorporated in this data protection legislation – in particular the principle of informed consent and the principle of confidentiality.

THE SCOPE OF THE 1998 DATA PROTECTION ACT: PERSONAL DATA ONLY

The aim of the Act is to ensure confidentiality in the collection and use of *personal data*. In the context of the Act, personal data are data that can be used to identify a living natural person (children and adults). An identifiable person is someone who can be identified by 'an identification number or by physical, physiological, mental, economic, cultural or social characteristics, either directly or indirectly'.

Rights of access to personal data

When personal data are attached to a data record such as a questionnaire, the data subject – the respondent to the questionnaire – has, under the Act, the right to request access to these personal data. This right, however, does not apply once the data have been depersonalised – once personal identifiers have been removed from the data record. It is worth considering, therefore, how soon in the data handling process data can be depersonalised. In many research projects personal data are collected and held for quality control purposes – to verify that the research has been conducted. Once quality control checks have been made personal data can be deleted from the data record.

Storing personal data

Compliance with the Act does not mean that data should be depersonalised in order for it to be stored. In fact the Act states that personal data can be kept indefinitely as long as this does not conflict with the Fifth Principle of the Act, which says that personal data must not be kept beyond fulfilling the purpose for which they are collected. This is particularly relevant for attributable research where the issue of depersonalising the data does not arise. The issue for researchers therefore is not the need to depersonalise the data (although this is certainly advisable from an administrative point of view) but to ensure that the data are held securely and that unauthorised access is prevented.

> ## Box 1.7 Respondents' rights of access to personal data: researcher's responsibilities
>
> Under data protection legislation respondents have rights of access to their personal data. This means that if a respondent asks to see the data held on them the researcher should give them contact details of the data owner, and/or the researcher must notify the data owner within 40 days of the respondent's request. If the respondent asks to be removed from the database, or requests that incorrect data are corrected or removed from the data record, or asks the data owner to contact them, the researcher should give the respondent contact details of the data owner, and/or notify the data owner within 40 days of the respondent's request. The researcher should inform the respondent of any action taken on the respondent's behalf.

THE TREATMENT OF PERSONAL DATA

There are eight principles that govern the treatment of personal data under the 1998 Data Protection Act:

- *First principle*: personal data must be processed fairly and lawfully.
- *Second principle*: personal data must only be used for the specified, lawful purposes for which it was collected.
- *Third principle*: personal data shall be adequate, relevant and not excessive.
- *Fourth principle*: personal data shall be accurate and kept up to date.
- *Fifth principle*: personal data must not be kept beyond fulfilling the purpose for which it was collected.
- *Sixth principle*: personal data shall be processed in accordance with the rights of the data subjects.
- *Seventh principle*: personal data must be kept secure.
- *Eighth principle*: personal data shall not be transferred from the European Economic Area unless adequate protections are in place.

Processing personal data

In the context of the 1998 Act the term 'processing' means obtaining, recording or holding data; it refers to any operation conducted on the data, such as organising, adapting or altering them. It also covers the processes involved with retrieving and consulting the data or using the data. It covers the processes involved in disclosing data by transmitting or disseminating them and any process involved in destroying the data.

Treatment of personal data for research purposes

The 1998 UK Act treats the processing of personal data for research purposes in a special way. It allows for personal data to be reprocessed if the purpose of this further processing is in line with the original purpose as described to the research participant. It allows personal data to be kept indefinitely, as long as this does not conflict with the Fifth Principle of the Act (that personal data must not be kept beyond fulfilling the purpose for which they were collected).

As we saw earlier, while data subjects have the right to request a copy of their data record if it contains information that could identify them, they do not have the right to request access once any personal identifiers have been removed. To be eligible to be treated this way, however, three conditions must be met:

- Data must be used for research purposes *only*.
- Data should not be used in a way that would cause substantial damage or distress to the data subject.
- Data should not be used to support actions or decisions in relation to particular individuals.

In recent years there has been huge growth in the use of databases, particularly customer databases, and an attendant rise in research using these databases for sampling. This raises issues in relation to data protection legislation. If researchers use databases for sampling purposes, can they pass on information from the individual to the data owner? Can they pass on information about the individual to the database owner? For what purposes can the data owner use that information? In other words, what feedback is allowed under the Act?

THE TREATMENT OR CLASSIFICATION OF MARKET RESEARCH

In order to clarify the type and extent of feedback or data disclosure allowed from research projects under the 1998 Act, MRS, the professional body representing researchers, agreed a classification of research projects with the Information Commissioner's Office (ICO), an independent body appointed by the Crown to oversee the Act and to protect personal information (www.ico.gov.uk). The classification divides projects into six categories. Five of the categories are described as 'classic' research; the sixth category contains projects that do not meet the requirements of classic research. One way of distinguishing classic and non-classic research projects is to think about the purpose for which the data are collected, or the end use of the data. Data gathered in classic research projects – those in Categories One to Five – are used to understand and predict attitudes and behaviour; data gathered in Category Six projects are used to take action – direct marketing, for example, aimed at the individuals identified. The categories are not mutually exclusive – a project could be classified as belonging to more than one category, depending, for example, on the source of the sample and the end use of the data.

Implications for research practice in general

What implications does this have for the practice of research? MRS members must ensure that there is no ambiguity when respondents consent to take part in research (the principles of informed consent and transparency). The researcher must make it clear to the respondent how the data that he or she supplies will be used. It is important therefore that confidential research is clearly distinguished from research that will make use of personal data for purposes other than research. Confidential or classic research – projects in Categories One to Five – meets the strict terms of the MRS Code of Conduct. In conducting classic research, the MRS Code of Conduct requires the following:

- respondents give informed consent to their personal data being used for specified other purposes;
- they have the opportunity to opt out of any follow-up activities;
- if sensitive data are being collected, consent is based on a detailed explanation of how the data will be used.

Box 1.8 MRS classification of research projects

- *Category One* covers classic confidential research in which there is no feedback of any personal data except to those involved in the project who are bound by the MRS Code of Conduct and agree to use the data for research purposes only.
- *Category Two* covers projects that use samples drawn from client customer databases or other third party owned lists. To comply with the Fourth Principle of the 1998 Data Protection Act – that personal data shall be kept accurate and up to date – those using the database or list (the researcher) can notify its owner where an individual is either 'no longer at this address' (but not of any new address) or has died.
- *Category Three* also covers projects that use client or third party owned customer databases or lists for sampling. To prevent the over-researching of individuals on a database or list, the researcher can give the database owner names or identification numbers of those contacted, including those who declined to be interviewed on that occasion, solely for the purpose of setting up a 'do not select for research' marker.
- *Category Four* covers projects that involve feedback about specific complaints. A respondent or the client can request that interviewers give details of specific complaints to the client for investigation. The respondent must give his or her consent to the principle of this feedback happening and to the content of the complaint (to ensure accuracy). The only details given to the client are the respondent's contact details plus a description of the complaint. The client can use the information to deal only with the issue raised and for no other purpose.
- In *Category Five* projects the client gets the results of the research at an individual respondent level (for example, a videotape of a group discussion) with the condition that the data at this personal level are used for research purposes only. This must be part of the project contract between researcher and client. These sorts of projects are described in the MRS guidelines as collecting data for 'attributable' purposes.
- *Category Six* includes projects in which the data are to be used in attributable form, for example by the client, for purposes in addition to or other than confidential research.

In conducting Category Six projects – in which data are collected for purposes other than, or in addition to, research – MRS members must ensure the following:

- that the purpose(s) for which personal data will be used have been clearly described to the respondent;
- that such purpose(s) are legal;
- that the respondent has given consent to the data being used for each of the purposes described;
- that the respondent has been given the chance to stop personal data being used for any purpose(s) to which they object (so called 'opt out');
- that the data are not subsequently used for any further purpose without getting permission from the respondent.

When carrying out non-market research exercises or exercises which are for mixed purposes including market research, MRS advises members to do the following:

■ adhere to an established code of conduct or practice relevant to the activity, for example Direct Marketing Association Code of Practice (http://www.dma.org.uk/content/Pro-Code.asp);
■ screen against any relevant 'opt out' lists which are legal requirements, for example the Telephone Preference Service (www.tpsonline.org.uk/tps/), when conducting direct marketing related activities.

Chapter summary

■ Research plays a vital role in providing robust and credible evidence for the planning and decision-making processes in organisations in the public, private and not-for-profit sectors.

■ The value of research can be limited by many things, including the following:
  ■ poor problem definition;
  ■ lack of understanding of the brief;
  ■ poor or inappropriate research design;
  ■ the limitations of the methods used;
  ■ poor execution of the research itself;
  ■ the interpretation of the results;
  ■ the status of knowledge;
  ■ the use or misuse of research evidence by the decision makers;
  ■ the time that elapses between collecting the data and applying the findings.

■ The research industry is made up of research suppliers and those who buy and/or use research. There are several kinds of research supplier, including the full service agency, the specialist agency and the independent consultant.

■ The role of the in-house client researcher varies from organisation to organisation. It can involve an internal consultancy role, advising decision makers on the use of research, and ensuring that research and other data are converted to information and knowledge and applied effectively. The role may also involve providing and/or commissioning and managing external research.

■ The role of the agency researcher is to manage a research project from the initial client briefing, through research design and set-up, fieldwork and data processing to analysis, interpretation and presentation of the findings and their implications to the client.

■ Various professional bodies, including MRS and ESOMAR, represent researchers and the research industry to the wider world and aim to ensure that research is conducted in a professional and ethical manner.

■ Ethics are moral principles that are used to guide behaviour. Ethical principles are used to set standards of conduct for groups or professions in how they deal with people. They are important in a research context in order that those involved in research – researchers, research participants, clients and other users of research and the wider community – know what is and what is not acceptable in the conduct of research. ▶

- The ethical principles that are the basis of most standards of conduct in relation to research participants are the following:
  - voluntary participation;
  - no harm to the participants;
  - informed consent;
  - anonymity, confidentiality (privacy);
  - transparency;
  - not deceiving subjects.

- Ethical issues are rarely clear-cut. Questions about how to apply ethical principles will always arise. It is to address such questions, and to ensure a professional and consistent standard of practice, that professional bodies such as ESOMAR and MRS have developed formal, self-regulatory codes of conduct. These codes help to create trust between the research profession and those who take part in research by demonstrating that research is conducted in an acceptable and ethical way.

- While these codes and guidelines may incorporate principles that are covered by legislation, they do not replace or take precedence over legislation.

- The MRS Code is revised and updated regularly to take account of changes in both research practice and legislation. Compliance with the Code should ensure that research is conducted in compliance with the UK's Data Protection Act 1998.

- There are eight principles that govern the treatment of personal data under the 1998 Data Protection Act:
  - *First principle*: personal data must be processed fairly and lawfully.
  - *Second principle*: personal data must only be used for the specified, lawful purposes for which it was collected.
  - *Third principle*: personal data shall be adequate, relevant and not excessive.
  - *Fourth principle*: personal data shall be accurate and kept up to date.
  - *Fifth principle*: personal data must not be kept beyond fulfilling the purpose for which it was collected.
  - *Sixth principle*: personal data shall be processed in accordance with the rights of the data subjects.
  - *Seventh principle*: personal data must be kept secure.
  - *Eighth principle*: personal data shall not be transferred from the European Economic Area (EEA) unless adequate protections are in place.

Questions and exercises

1 Your client has recently recruited a new internal research executive and a new marketing executive. The client has asked you, an agency researcher, to prepare a training session for them. For this session, prepare a guide on the following topics: (a) what research can and cannot offer; and (b) what an external supplier of research can offer a client organisation.

2 A retailer of mobile phones would like to conduct a series of group discussions with each of the following groups of its customers: 12–14 year olds; 15–17 year olds; and 18–21 year olds. In his brief, the marketing manager has stated that he would like the groups to be recorded on video and, in addition to using the findings to help him understand his customers better, he plans to use the recordings in training sessions with sales staff. Imagine you are writing the proposal for this research. Identify the ethical, legal and code of conduct issues that the client's brief raises and describe how you would handle these.

References

Bairfelt, S. and Spurgeon, F. (1998) *Plenty of data, but are we doing enough to fill the information gap?* Proceedings of the ESOMAR Congress, Amsterdam: ESOMAR.

Bijapurkar, R. (1995) *Does market research really contribute to decision making?* Proceedings of the ESOMAR Congress, Amsterdam: ESOMAR.

Butcher, J., Strutt, S. and Bird, C. (2005) 'How research drove the metamorphosis of a public sector organisation', *Proceedings of the Market Research Society Conference*, London: MRS.

Cambiar, L.L.C. (2004) *Study on Changes in Client Demands from Research Agencies*.

Chadwick, S. (2005) 'Do we listen to journalists or clients? The real implications of change for the market research industry', *Proceedings of the Market Research Society Conference*, London: MRS.

Codeline queries (www.research-live.com).

Cohen, J. (2005) 'Teenage sex at the margins', *Proceedings of the Market Research Society Conference*, London: MRS.

Davidson, G. and Payne, C. (2008) 'How research saves scapegoat brands©: retaining brand and business perspective in troubled times', *Proceedings of the Market Research Society Conference*, London: MRS.

Edgar, L. and McErlane, C. (2002) 'Professional development: the future's in diamonds', *Proceedings of the Market Research Society Conference*, London: MRS.

Flemming from Thygesen and McGowan, P. (2002) 'Inspiring the organisation to act: a business in denial', *Proceedings of the Market Research Society Conference*, London: MRS.

Gordon, W. and Robson, S. (1980) 'Respondent through the looking glass: towards a better understanding of the qualitative interviewing process', *Proceedings of the Market Research Society Conference*, London: MRS.

ICC/ESOMAR (2007) *International Code on Market and Social Research Practice*, Amsterdam: ESOMAR.

Kreinczes, G. (1990) 'Why research is undervalued', *Admap*, March.

Lee, R. (1992) *Doing Research on Sensitive Topics*, London: Sage.

Lovett, P. (2001) 'Ethics shmethics! As long as you get the next job. A moral dilemma', *Proceedings of the Market Research Society Conference*, London: MRS.

MRS Code of Conduct (2005) and MRS Guidelines series, London: MRS (www.mrs.org.uk).

Pyke, A. (2000) 'It's all in the brief', *Proceedings of the Market Research Society Conference*, London: MRS.

Robson, S. (1991) 'Ethics: informed consent or misinformed compliance?', *Journal of the Market Research Society*, 33, 1, pp. 19–28.

Shipman, M. (1997) *The Limitations of Social Research*, London: Longman.

Simmons, S. and Lovejoy, A. (2003) 'Oh no, the consultants are coming!', *Proceedings of the Market Research Society Conference*, London: MRS.

Smith, D. (2005) 'It's not how good you are, it's how good you want to be! Are market researchers really up for "reconstruction"?', *Proceedings of the Market Research Society Conference*, London: MRS.

The Social Research Association Ethical Guidelines (www.the-sra.org.uk).

Sorrell, M. (2002) Keynote speech to ARF Annual Conference.

Tanner, V. (2005) 'Using investment-based techniques to prove the "Bottom Line" value of research and give CEOs what they want', *Proceedings of the Market Research Society Conference*, London: MRS.

Wills, S. and Williams, P. (2004) 'Insight as a strategic asset – the opportunity and the stark reality', *International Journal of Market Research*, 46, 4, pp. 393–410.

Wills, S. and Webb, S. (2006) 'Measuring the value of insight – it can and must be done', *Proceedings of the Market Research Society Conference*, London: MRS.

Recommended reading

Bulmer, M. (ed.) (1982) *Social Research Ethics*, London: Macmillan.

Cowan, D. (1995) 'The importance of good consumer information: information – generals can't do without it. Why do CEOs think they can?', *Admap*, July.

Ereaut, G., Imms, M. and Callingham, M. (eds) (2002) *Qualitative Market Research: Principle and Practice*, London: Sage.

Gosschalk, B. (1999) 'Opinion formers' views on market research', *Admap*, April.

Holmes, D. (1998) *Market research: a backroom support function or vanguard of knowledge management*, Proceedings of the ESOMAR Congress, Amsterdam: ESOMAR.

Marks, L. (ed.) (2000) *Qualitative Research in Context*, Henley-on-Thames: Admap.

The *MRS Guide to the Data Protection Act 1998* and *The Data Protection Act 1998* and *Market Research: Guidance for Market Research Society Members* (www.mrs.org.uk). Give details about the Act and its implications for research.

The *Research Works* series: papers from the AMSO (now BMRA) Research Effectiveness Awards, Henley-on-Thames: NTC.

Spackman, N. (1993) 'Judging the value of research', *Admap*, January.

Chapter 2

INTRODUCING TYPES OF RESEARCH

Introduction

Research can be described or classified in a number of ways. For example, you might hear a piece of research described as exploratory, as quantitative research or as continuous research, or in some combination, such as exploratory qualitative research or syndicated continuous research. The purpose of this chapter is to introduce you to this terminology and what lies behind it, and to describe the main uses to which the different types of research are put. A number of case studies illustrate these different types of research in context.

Topics covered

- Types of research
- The nature of the research enquiry: exploratory, descriptive and causal research
- Mode of data collection: continuous and ad hoc research
- The type of data: quantitative and qualitative
- The source of the data: primary and secondary research
- The method of data collection: observation and interview
- The way data are bought: syndicated and customised research
- The setting of the research: consumer, business-to-business and social research

Relationship to MRS Advanced Certificate Syllabus

This chapter offers further material relevant to Element 1 – Introduction to Market and Social Research, in particular the role of commercial market and social research in effective decision making within business and public sector organisations. It also provides material useful for Element 2 – Designing a Research Project, in that it describes various types of research and their uses, and so should be useful in helping you understand what sort of research might suit a given research problem. We look in more detail at the process of research design and the nature of specific research designs in Chapter 3 and at how to prepare a brief and a proposal in Chapter 4.

Learning outcomes

At the end of this chapter you should be able to:

- understand the terminology used to describe different types of research;
- understand the basics of each type;
- be aware of the main uses of each.

Types of research

Research can be described or classified according to the following:

- the nature of the research enquiry – exploratory, descriptive and explanatory or causal research;
- the mode of data collection – continuous and ad hoc research;
- the type of data – qualitative and quantitative research;
- the status or source of the data – primary and secondary research;
- the method of data collection – observation or interview; face-to-face, telephone, postal and Internet research;
- the way in which the research is bought or sold – syndicated or customised research; and
- the setting of the research or nature of the market or population under investigation – consumer, business-to-business or social research.

A single piece of research may fall into several of these categories. For example, the research outlined below in Case study 2.2 could be described as exploratory research; ad hoc research; qualitative research; primary research; and/or consumer research. A research project may include several types of research. For example, it may have a qualitative stage or element and a quantitative stage; it may consist of secondary research – a literature review or an analysis of existing data – and primary research – a specially designed survey; it may begin with an observation exercise and have a follow-up interviewing stage.

The nature of the research enquiry

Research can be classified, according to the nature of the research enquiry and the type of evidence it aims to produce, into three categories – exploratory, descriptive and causal or explanatory. (This is a useful way of classifying research – not only can it can help you to clarify your thinking when it comes to stating your research objectives, but it will also be helpful at the other end of the research process when you are planning and executing your analysis.) Descriptive and explanatory research enquiries are sometimes referred to as conclusive research. Each of these types of research enquiry can involve primary or secondary, qualitative or quantitative research. Below is a summary of the nature and uses of each of these types of enquiry; we look at each type in greater detail in the context of research design in Chapter 3.

EXPLORATORY RESEARCH

Exploratory research is, as its name suggests, research undertaken to explore an issue or a topic. It is particularly useful in helping to identify a problem, clarify the nature of a problem or define the issues involved. It can be used to develop propositions and hypotheses for further research, to look for new insights or to reach a greater understanding of an issue. For example, you might conduct exploratory research in order to understand how consumers react to new product concepts or ideas for advertising, or to find out what business executives mean when they talk about 'entrepreneurship', or to help define what is meant by the term 'elder abuse'.

DESCRIPTIVE RESEARCH

A lot of market and social research is about description as well as exploration – finding the answers to the questions Who? What? Where? When? How? and How many? While exploratory research can provide description, the purpose of descriptive research is to answer more clearly defined research questions. Descriptive research aims to build a picture – of a market, a set of customers, a social phenomenon, a set of experiences, for example. It aims to identify, describe and in some cases count things. It can be used to examine some of the key issues facing marketers and policy makers.

Box 2.1 Examples of questions addressed in descriptive research

Market research
- How big is the market?
- Who are the main suppliers of product X?
- Which brands compete in which segment?
- What volume of sales did brand A achieve in Year 2 compared to Year 1?
- Who is buying brand B?
- What do customers think of the new advertising?
- How satisfied are customers with the new product formulation or service offer?
- How many organisations are using the technology and what are they using it for?

Social research
- How many people were the victims of a crime in the last year?
- What is the profile of those who stay in hostels for the homeless?
- What is the decision-making process of a woman with a 'crisis' pregnancy?
- What is the pattern of drug use among prisoners (who uses drugs, which drugs, when, where, how often)?
- How satisfied with the service are the users of a government employment service?

CAUSAL OR EXPLANATORY RESEARCH

Causal or explanatory research addresses the 'why' questions: Why do people choose brand A and not brand B? Why are some customers and not others satisfied with our service? Why do some prisoners and not others use drugs? What might explain this? We design explanatory or causal research to answer these types of questions, to allow us to rule out rival explanations and come to a conclusion, to help us develop causal explanations.

Mode of data collection

Continuous research, as its name suggests, is research done on a continuous basis or at regular intervals in order to monitor changes over time, for example in a particular market or among a particular population. Ad hoc (Latin for 'for this special purpose') research is research that is conducted on a 'one-off' basis, to provide a snapshot at a particular point in time.

CONTINUOUS RESEARCH

The most common way of conducting continuous research is to use a panel of respondents chosen to represent the target population; data are collected from panel members at regular intervals. The panel can be made up of individuals or households, often called a consumer panel, or it can be made up of businesses or other organisations; for example, retail panels are made up of a sample of retail outlets.

Continuous data can also be derived from independent samples of the same population, samples that are recruited anew for each round of fieldwork. For example, omnibus studies and advertising tracking studies, or product tests where the same methodology is used on similar or identical samples, can provide continuous data. Examples of this type of continuous or regular research include the General Household Survey and the National Food Survey, both conducted on behalf of the UK government.

CASE STUDY 2.1

USE OF A PANEL

Here we learn about the Northern Ireland Household Panel Survey – why it was set up, why a panel design was chosen, how it works and what the findings have been used for.

Why this case study is worth reading

This case study is worth reading for several reasons: it describes a real life panel survey; it describes why a panel design was chosen; it makes clear the link between the information requirements, the design of the study and the output from the research; it shows what the findings were used for.

The key words are: panel survey, representative sample, purpose, track, years, income, health, labour market behaviour, housing, consumption, social and political values, education, training, household members, survey design, sample, stratified, random sample, original sample members, temporary sample members, response rate, proxy interviews, attrition, incentives, policy issues, dynamics of poverty, ill-health and deprivation.

Introduction

The Northern Ireland Household Panel Survey (NIHPS) began in 2001, and is an extension of the British Household Panel Survey (BHPS) which has been running since 1991. The NIHPS follows the same representative sample of individuals – the panel – every year. The main purpose of the NIHPS is to track the movement within Northern Ireland of individuals and families across the years. While cross-sectional surveys provide valuable 'snapshots' of the state of the population on any given topic they are limited in what they can say about, for example, factors precipitating the movement of individuals into and out of poverty, employment and ill-health. This can only be achieved using panel data. The main areas of interest of the NIHPS are income, health, labour market behaviour, housing, consumption, social and political values, and education and training. The NIHPS is managed by the Institute for Social and Economic Research, based at the University of Essex, and data collection is carried out by the Northern Ireland Statistics and Research Agency.

Survey design

The survey is carried out annually between the months of September and December. The NIHPS seeks to interview (face to face) all adult members of each household (persons aged 16 years and over). From Wave 4 onwards, data were also collected from all household members aged 11 to 15 years.

Sample

The initial sample for the first round of data collection – Wave 1 – consisted of 3,170 addresses drawn from the Valuation and Lands Agency list of addresses. This complete list of private (residential) addresses was stratified into three regions – Belfast (Northern Ireland's largest city), East Northern Ireland and West Northern Ireland, and a random sample was drawn from each stratum. Approximately 2,000 households took part in Wave 1 and each member of the household (regardless of their age) was included in the panel as an Original Sample Member (OSM) – a total of approximately 5,200 people. All OSMs remain part of the sample for the lifetime of the survey and are followed at all subsequent waves, even if they split from their original household. If they form new households with people who were not OSMs, these people will become part of the sample, as Temporary Sample Members (TSMs), for as long as they live with the OSM. However, TSMs leave the panel if they cease to live with an OSM.

At the household level, the response rate in Wave 1 was 69 per cent (at least one household member participated). Within the responding households, 84 per cent of all eligible adults took part in the survey and proxy interviews were carried out on behalf of 5 per cent of adults who were not currently at home (e.g. in hospital) at the time the survey was conducted.

Attrition is an inevitable consequence of panel surveys and occurs when a panel member dies, emigrates or refuses to take part in future waves of the survey. The NIHPS uses a number of incentives to ensure that refusals are kept to a minimum, including vouchers for each participating member of a household and a report sent to all responding households outlining key findings from the previous wave. Approximately 88 per cent of the original sample members participated in the second wave.

End use of the data

Information from the NIHPS has been used to inform a number of important policy issues in Northern Ireland, and has been included in government reports, academic journals and the Director of Public Health Annual Report 2002. Data from the first two waves have enabled researchers to examine the dynamics of poverty, ill-health and deprivation within Northern Ireland, and subsequent waves of the NIHPS will offer further elucidation of these issues over time.

Source: Dr Katrina Lloyd, Queen's University Belfast, written for this book.

AD HOC RESEARCH

Ad hoc research is usually designed to address a specific problem or to help understand a particular issue at a certain point in time. For example, you might commission ad hoc research among employees to determine satisfaction with their new office accommodation, or to understand the issues faced by overseas students in their first few months at university, or to gauge whether your latest television advertisement is communicating key product messages to the target market. The types of studies that come under the heading ad hoc research include advertising pre-tests and communication testing, usage and attitudes studies, hall tests, store tests, market mix tests and brand/price trade-off research.

The type of data

One of the major distinctions in research is between quantitative and qualitative research. The differences between the two are summarised in Table 2.1.

QUANTITATIVE RESEARCH

Quantitative research involves collecting data from relatively large samples; the data collected are usually presented as numbers, often in tables, on graphs and on charts. Quantitative research is used to address the objectives of conclusive (descriptive and explanatory) research enquiries; it can also be used for exploratory purposes. It provides nomothetic description – sparse description of a relatively large number of cases. Qualitative research, on the other hand,

Table 2.1 Differences between quantitative and qualitative research

Topic	Quantitative research	Qualitative research
Research enquiry	Exploratory, descriptive and explanatory	Exploratory, descriptive and explanatory
Nature of questions and responses	Who, what, when, where, why, how many Relatively superficial and rational responses Measurement, testing and validation	What, when, where, why Below the surface and emotional responses Exploration, understanding, and idea generation
Sampling approach	Probability and non-probability methods	Non-probability methods (purposive)
Sample size	Relatively large	Relatively small
Data collection	Not very flexible Interviews and observation Standardised Structured More closed questions	Flexible Interviews and observation Less standardised Less structured More open-ended and non-directive questions
Data	Numbers, percentages, means Less detail or depth Nomothetic description Context poor High reliability, low validity Statistical inference possible	Words, pictures, diagrams Detailed and in-depth Idiographic description Context rich High validity, low reliability Statistical inference not possible
Cost	Relatively low cost per respondent Relatively high project cost	Relatively high cost per respondent Relatively low project cost

provides idiographic description, that is, description that is rich in detail but limited to relatively few cases.

Quantitative data are collected via census, sample surveys or panels. Quantitative interviews are structured and standardised – the questions are worded in exactly the same way and asked in the same order in each interview. Qualitative interviews, on the other hand, are more like conversations, on a continuum from semi-structured and semi-standardised to unstructured and non-standardised. Quantitative interviews can be conducted face to face (in the street, in a central venue, often called a 'hall test' or central location test, or at the respondent's home or place of work), over the telephone, by post, or via the Internet (email or the web). We look in detail at quantitative methods of data collection in Chapter 7.

Quantitative research is useful for describing the characteristics of a population or market – for example household spending patterns, market and brand share, use of technology, voting behaviour or intention, levels of economic activity. It is useful for measuring, quantifying, validating and testing hypotheses or theories. It has some limitations. It is not as flexible as qualitative research – data collection is structured and standardised (although this offers reliability in return). The structure and standardisation can produce superficial rather than detailed description and understanding. The use of closed questions does not allow us to collect responses in the respondent's own words, and so we may lose out on 'real' responses, and on detail and context; the standardisation means that we may miss the subtleties, the slight differences in response between respondents. Both can contribute to low validity.

QUALITATIVE RESEARCH

Qualitative research typically involves relatively small sample sizes. The techniques used include interviewing, via group discussions (also known as focus groups) and in-depth interviews, observation (including ethnography) and accompanied visits (for example to a doctor, a supermarket or bar and involving interviewing and observation). The findings are expressed as words (or pictures), rarely (but sometimes) as numbers.

Qualitative research is concerned with rich and detailed description, understanding and insight rather than measurement. It aims to get below the surface, beyond the spontaneous or rational response to the deeper and more emotional response. It is often used to gain insight into and understanding of the 'what' and particularly the 'why': what people do, what they think, what they feel, what they want; and why they do and think and feel and want. It seeks to discover what accounts for certain kinds of behaviour, for example drug use in prison, or what makes customers loyal to a particular brand. It is good at uncovering a range of responses, and the subtleties and nuances in responses and meanings. It is both less artificial and less superficial than quantitative research and can provide highly valid data. It is suitable in exploratory and descriptive research enquiries. It is more flexible than quantitative research – the researcher has the scope during fieldwork to modify or adapt the interview guide or the sample to suit the way in which the research is developing. The less structured and less standardised approach can, however, mean that it is relatively low in reliability. This is something that qualitative researchers acknowledge and take steps to address (via training, addressing one's own feelings, opinions and biases before undertaking fieldwork, discussing approach and findings with other researchers or team members, for example). It is possible using qualitative research to tackle complex issues, for example understanding the decision-making process in a crisis pregnancy. Qualitative research is sometimes criticised on the grounds that the findings from the research sample cannot be said to be representative in the statistical sense of the wider population from which the sample was drawn. This is a misguided criticism: the findings from a qualitative research study are not meant to be statistically representative. The logic that underpins the choice of a qualitative research sampling strategy is very different from the logic (and objectives) that underpin the choice of sampling strategy in a quantitative research study. We look at this in more detail in Chapter 8. Suffice to say that in designing a qualitative study the qualitative researcher will have chosen a sampling strategy that is suited to the project objectives and one in which there is a clear and meaningful relationship between the sample and the wider population from it is drawn. The process of selecting the sample for qualitative research should be just as rigorous and systematic as that used in quantitative research.

Qualitative research is used in a wide variety of settings. It is used to generate, explore and develop ideas for products, services and advertising, for example, and for understanding social issues. It is used to provide information to help guide and develop policy and strategy – for business, for marketing, advertising and communications, and for development of social policy. It is used to evaluate policies and strategies, and their implementation. It can be used in conjunction with quantitative research to great effect. At the beginning of a study it can be used to generate and develop ideas or hypotheses; to define the issues under investigation; and to find out how people think and feel and behave, how they talk about an issue or a product. This type of information is particularly useful in helping to structure quantitative research and design the questionnaire. Qualitative research is also useful at the other end of a study – in exploring the findings of a quantitative study in greater depth, providing a wider context in which to understand and interpret them.

While the cost per respondent is greater in a qualitative study than in a quantitative one, the relatively small overall sample size often means that the total project cost can be smaller. We look at qualitative methods of data collection in Chapter 6.

CASE STUDY 2.2

INVESTIGATING SPIDER-MAN

In this case study we discover the rationale for research into the SPIDER-MAN movie brand and we see the findings that the qualitative research (using focus groups) revealed. We look in more detail at the make-up of the groups in Case study 6.4.

Why this case study is worth reading

This case study is worth reading for lots of reasons: it sets out why research was needed, and shows how this links to the organisation's marketing and business goals; it is an example of an exploratory research enquiry; it offers an example of what qualitative research can achieve.

The key words are: knowledge, understanding, competitive environment, research, stage one, focus groups, commissioned, global health check, key strengths, brand, exploration, understand, evaluate, marketing campaign.

Introduction

The Columbia TriStar Marketing Group was keen to equip itself with the knowledge and understanding necessary to optimise SPIDER-MAN 2's (the movie sequel to SPIDER-MAN) chance of success in an industry and competitive environment where years of hard work and millions of dollars of investment can be so easily lost in a film's opening weekend.

Research stage one – focus groups

Prior to the creation of SPIDER-MAN 2's marketing campaign, First Movies was commissioned to undertake a 'global health check' for the SPIDER-MAN brand via a series of focus groups in the United Kingdom; Germany; France; Spain; Italy; Japan and Australia. In each territory, nine groups were conducted among children and adults.

The focus groups gathered together an extensive and comprehensive mix of cinemagoers who had seen the first film, allowing us to explore the key strengths of the brand and of the first movie, coupled with an exploration of any barriers facing the second instalment and potential traps facing the long-term health of the franchise. Through 'off-targets' we would understand why the first film had not been bought into and evaluate whether any mistakes could be avoided, potential viewers salvaged or, at least, to know who would be beyond the reach of even the most sophisticated marketing campaign and why.

Findings

Common to focus groups in all markets researched was the sense that the first film's strengths came from the special effects; the action; its successful transition from comic book to silver screen; and the credibility and believability of the lead actor (the, at the time, relatively unknown Tobey Maguire). All this built on the core strength and essence of the franchise: the character of SPIDER-MAN himself. Respondents also identified traps into which comic book movies often fell, and of which the first SPIDER-MAN movie was seen to be guilty of falling prey to – namely, predictability and an innate appeal to 'just children'. Additionally, this kind of movie was also seen as spawning disappointing sequels (and therefore as falling short of expectations) and as containing shallow and weak storylines.

Conclusion

Clearly, all these obstacles needed to be combated by the marketing, prior to the release of SPIDER-MAN 2, with the need to convince the public that the film was bigger and better than its predecessor; that there was a strong story on offer (with unexpected plot twists, more complexity and character progression); that there were more special effects and that there was more action.

Source: Adapted from Palmer, S. and Kaminow, D. (2005) 'KERPOW!! KERCHING!! Understanding and positioning the SPIDER-MAN brand', MRS Conference, www.mrs.org.uk.

The source of the data

Primary research is designed to generate or collect data for a specific problem; the data collected – primary data – do not exist prior to data collection. Secondary data, on the other hand, are data that were originally collected for a purpose other than the current research objectives – in revisiting them you are putting the data to a second use. Searching for, analysing and using secondary data is called secondary research.

PRIMARY RESEARCH

The role of primary research is to generate data to address the information needs in relation to a specific problem or issue. For example, imagine you are interested in understanding how customers have reacted to changes to the service you provide. There are no pre-existing data available – you need to conduct primary research. Primary research may be exploratory, descriptive and/or causal; qualitative or quantitative; syndicated or customised. Primary data can be collected face to face, by telephone, by post, via the Internet or via observation; on a one-off or on a continuous basis; and in almost any market or on any issue.

CASE STUDY 2.3

'I KNOW WHAT YOU DID LAST SUMMER'

This case study shows how valuable information on customer behaviour and market characteristics was retrieved from the secondary analysis of (audience) box office data.

Why this case study is worth reading

This case study is worth reading for several reasons: it is an example of secondary data analysis; it is an example of a descriptive research enquiry; it shows how valuable insight can be extracted from existing data; it identifies the end uses of this 'insight'.

The key words are: millions of records, patron data, valuable information, customer behaviour, market characteristics, wide-ranging uses, tactical, strategic marketing planning, audience profiling.

What?

A ground-breaking project analysing millions of records of patron data collected through the box offices of many of London's performing arts venues produced valuable information on customer behaviour and market characteristics. It was the first time that London organisations had pooled data on such a scale, and the first time that the subsidised and commercial sectors had collaborated on such a project.

Why?

The results have wide-ranging uses, from tactical and strategic marketing planning to PR, political lobbying, product development, and provision planning on the part of Arts Council England (who funded the project) and local government.

How?

A user-friendly software package for producing sophisticated audience profiling (such as ticket yield, product crossover, audience churn, Mosaic Group and Type, Income and Lifestage [a geodemographic segmentation], and trend information) quickly and easily from any box office software package, was used by three of the regional audience development agencies in the UK. It takes data from venues and provides a benchmark of audience information, looking at markets for each artform, their size, characteristics (demographic profile, geographic spread) and behaviour (frequency, value, drive distance, advance purchase, churn, ticket yield, programme choice etc.).

Source: Adapted from Brook, O. (2004), 'I know what you did last summer: arts audiences in London 1998–2002', MRS Conference, www.mrs.org.uk.

SECONDARY RESEARCH

You will see secondary research referred to as desk research – the sort of research or data collection you can do without leaving your desk. In contrast, primary research is sometimes referred to as field research – you have to go into the field, do fieldwork. The process of secondary research involves identifying suitable sources – often referred to as secondary sources; finding those sources and getting access to them; reviewing them and assessing their suitability for your research objectives, and evaluating their quality; learning from them; and using them or assimilating them into your own research and/or your thinking about your own research.

There are many sources available to you for secondary research. Secondary sources include books, journal articles and research reports of all kinds as well as existing data or datasets. Secondary data may be data from outside the organisation – external data, for example government-produced statistics; or, as we saw above, data generated by the organisation – internal data, sales data or data from previous research projects, available from the organisation's database or data archive, its in-house management information system or decision support system.

The role of secondary research is very often exploratory and/or descriptive and it can be used in explanatory or causal studies. For example, secondary research might be used to explore the background to a problem or issue, to describe its wider context, to help define the problem or issue, or to generate or test hypotheses or ideas. To illustrate: searching the published literature on a topic to reach a greater understanding of the issues involved, or to help develop interview questions or a framework for analysis, is secondary research; consulting the report and/or the data from a previous study conducted by another researcher to help you understand or set in context issues related to current changes is a form of secondary research; analysing sales data to determine the impact of the changes in pricing or analysing a database to determine patterns of spend are forms of secondary research, secondary data analysis. In all these cases the research was conducted and/or the data gathered for another purpose; you are revisiting the source with your research objectives in mind.

We look at secondary research and the evaluation of secondary sources in more detail in Chapter 5.

The method of data collection

Data can be collected by observation and via interviews. Observational techniques are used in quantitative and qualitative research. Interviewing can be used to collect qualitative and quantitative data. It can also be classified into personal interviewing – face to face and by telephone – and self-completion, delivered typically by post, email or via the Internet. We look in detail at qualitative methods of data collection in Chapter 6 and quantitative methods in Chapter 7. Here we look at the main features of observation and interviewing, and at the main distinctions between their use in quantitative and qualitative research.

OBSERVATION

Observational techniques, based on ethnographic methods used in anthropology and sociology, are well established in social research and are increasingly used in market research. The main advantage of observation over interviewing is that in an interview the respondent is recalling and recounting his or her behaviour to the researcher whereas in observation the researcher sees it at first hand – without the filter of memory or selection. Observation is also useful in the following situations:

- when you do not know or are unsure about what questions to ask;
- when you are starting a project in a setting with which you are not familiar;
- when you want to examine an activity or process in a new way;
- when you want to observe an individual act in detail;
- when you want to see things happen in context;
- when you want to gather data from another perspective;
- when you want greater detail or greater understanding of a process or behaviour;
- when you want to observe unconscious or habitual behaviour;
- when the target audience cannot communicate verbally;
- when you have concerns about the validity or reliability of interview data;
- when you want to observe the behaviour of people en masse.

Observation can be used to generate both qualitative and quantitative data. Observation methods to collect quantitative data tend to be mechanical or electronic. These surveillance methods also tend to be unobtrusive – that is, those being observed are largely unaware of it. Also they tend to collect data on the activity rather than on the person and the activity. Examples of mechanical or electronic observation devices include traffic counters, devices that record the number of cars or pedestrians passing a particular point; electronic scanners, including those devices that read and log the bar code or the Unique Product Code on goods, recording customer purchases for storage on a database; closed circuit television systems that record people flow; web counters that count and log visits to a website; and 'cookies', messages given to a web browser by a web server that enable it to identify users entering a website. The main advantage of these methods of collecting data is their thoroughness in counting and/or recording activity. The main disadvantage is that they can generate high volumes of data that may be difficult to handle, process and/or analyse.

Observation to collect qualitative data tends to be done in person by a researcher, sometimes with the help of a mechanical or electronic recording device – a camera, tape recorder or video recorder. This sort of observation tends to be more intrusive – the observed are aware that they are being watched, the aim being to collect data on the individual and the activity – and requires the consent of those involved. We look in more detail at the issues observation raises – the effect that awareness of being observed has on the data collected and the ethical considerations around observation – as well as at other practical aspects of observation in the chapters on qualitative and quantitative data collection, Chapters 6 and 7.

INTERVIEWING

Interviewing is a form of primary research. You can collect qualitative or quantitative data via interviews.

Quantitative interviews

To collect quantitative data researchers use standardised structured or semi-structured 'forms' – interview schedules or questionnaires and diaries. There are two ways of getting a sample to complete these 'forms'. You get the respondent to do it themselves – this is called 'self-completion'; or you get an interviewer to ask the questions of the respondent, either in person face to face or via the telephone, and record his or her answers on the 'form' – this is called 'interviewer administered'. The option you choose will depend on a number of things. You will need to determine how suitable the method is for the following:

- the study and its objectives;
- the topic or issues under investigation;

- reaching the right sample;
- achieving the right numbers;
- the time and budget available.

For example, if you have a subject of a very sensitive nature the telephone may be the best option as it offers the respondent a degree of anonymity and distance that a face-to-face interview does not. If you have a sample that is hard to reach in person – a sample of business executives, for example – the telephone or a postal or email survey may be the only way of contacting them. If you need to show respondents stimulus material, for example an advertisement, or get them to try a product, a face-to-face approach may be the only feasible one. If you need to achieve a particular sample size you may decide against a postal survey or an email survey unless you are fairly sure that the return or completion rate (which can sometimes be hard to predict) will give you the numbers (and the sample) you need. If you are working to a tight budget you might consider a postal survey – with no interviewer costs it can be cheaper than a telephone or face-to-face survey. If you are working to a tight deadline a postal survey may not be appropriate – turnaround times are often relatively long – therefore a telephone or email survey might be considered. We look in more detail at these methods of data collection in Chapter 7.

Qualitative interviews

What distinguishes qualitative interviews from quantitative interviews is the style of the interview. Whereas quantitative interviews are standardised and most of the questions are structured, closed questions, qualitative interviews are more like 'guided conversations' (Rubin and Rubin, 1995) or 'conversations with a purpose' (Burgess, 1984) – less structured and less standardised, making use of open-ended, non-directive questions.

Qualitative interviews are more flexible (Sampson, 1967 and 1996) than quantitative interviews. The interviewer has the freedom to react to what the respondent is saying and adapt the interview accordingly. They can alter the way the questions are asked, the order in which they are asked, and can insert follow-up questions if the respondent mentions something that the researcher would like to clarify or explore in greater detail.

We look in more detail at qualitative interviewing in Chapter 6.

The choice of interview rather than observation, while driven to some extent by the nature and objectives of the research, often comes down to the practicalities of time and cost – interviewing tends to be more cost effective. Interviewing is also more suitable when the objectives of the research are clearly defined, and when it is necessary to gather data from a greater range and number of people or settings.

The way the data are bought

Syndicated or multi-client research refers to research that has been put together by an organisation (usually a specialist research organisation) and sold to a number of different clients, to whom it may be equally relevant. For example, a financial services organisation with a small research budget may buy into a syndicated advertising tracking study along with several other financial services organisations as a cost-effective way of finding out how its advertising is being received by its target market. Omnibus surveys are a form of syndicated research, with clients buying space for their questions (for which it may not be feasible to conduct an ad hoc survey) alongside questions placed by other clients. Continuous research can be expensive and is often syndicated in order to spread the cost. Customised research is research that is commissioned by a single organisation, usually to meet their research objectives alone. Most ad hoc projects are customised.

The setting of the research

Research can be classified according to the nature of the topic under investigation (we saw this in Chapter 1 with the distinction between market and social research). It can also be classified according to the type of respondents involved in the research.

CONSUMER RESEARCH

Consumer research, as its name suggests, is conducted among consumers – individuals and households. The purpose of consumer research is usually to understand consumer behaviour and consumer attitudes and opinions in relation to products and services and the marketing activity that surrounds them. Most of the case studies in this book could be classed as consumer research projects.

SOCIAL RESEARCH

As we noted in Chapter 1, social research involves researching aspects of society, the social world, social life and social issues. Topics that fall under the social research heading tend to be those associated with health, education, law and order, religion, politics, policy and culture. Case study 2.4 is an example of a social research project; there are many others throughout the book.

CASE STUDY 2.4

THE SCOTTISH EXECUTIVE: DEALING WITH ANTI-SOCIAL BEHAVIOUR

This case study describes how research was conducted on a complex topic, anti-social behaviour. We look at other aspects of this project in Case study 9.2 (questionnaire design).

Why this case study is worth reading

This case study is worth reading for a variety of reasons: it is an example of social research; it is an example of a descriptive enquiry; it sets out why research was needed and states the research objectives; it is an example of a project in which primary and secondary research and qualitative and quantitative research were conducted; it describes how the research project was structured and identifies the key elements of it.

The key words are: crime, anti-social behaviour, commission research, objectives, competitive tendering process, steering group, methodology, desk research, paired/triad depth interviews, depth interviews, quantitative (in-home) surveys.

Background

Dealing with crime and the effects of crime is one of the most important issues in Great Britain today. There is an awareness that there may be a gap between the way the public perceives crime, in terms of numbers and effect, and the actual experience of crime. There are many different constituent elements or actions that form crime and these need to be examined separately and sensitively if an accurate picture is to be formed. Anti-social behaviour is one of these elements. Anti-social behaviour on public transport was identified in a consultation exercise as an area that 'consultees felt it was important that the Scottish Executive take steps to deal with' (Scottish Executive, 2003).

There are a number of reasons for examining anti-social behaviour on public buses:

- the overall prevalence of travel by bus;
- the financial impact of anti-social behaviour on public bus companies; and
- anti-social behaviour on buses is likely to have wider social costs.

The Scottish Executive decided to commission research as part of its annual Transport Research Programme to investigate the extent and impact of anti-social behaviour on buses, and to propose ways to tackle the problem. Specifically, the objectives of this research were to identify:

- the extent of anti-social behaviour on Scottish buses and the perceived extent of anti-social behaviour on buses by members of the public;
- the types of anti-social behaviour that are most likely to occur on buses;
- the times at which, and places where, anti-social behaviour is most likely to occur;
- the effects of anti-social behaviour on drivers and driver recruitment;
- the types of people who are most likely to behave in an anti-social manner and those who are most likely to be affected by anti-social behaviour;
- the effect of anti-social behaviour on other passengers;
- the wider societal impact of anti-social behaviour on buses;
- measures currently in place to tackle anti-social behaviour on buses and their relative impact;
- successful ways of reducing anti-social behaviour on buses.

The research agency was appointed following a competitive tendering process.

How the survey was carried out

A steering group was set up for this project, including representatives from the research agency team and the Scottish Executive, a local council representative with experience of related issues and a representative from the Confederation of Passenger Transport UK (CPT). This group provided a firm knowledge-base from which to establish a flexible and accurate methodology. In consultation with the steering group, the following structure was drawn up:

- desk research,
- paired/triad depth interviews with bus drivers,
- depth interviews with bus company management staff,
- quantitative in-home surveys of residents,
- quantitative survey of bus drivers,
- quantitative survey of bus company management staff,
- depth interviews with key stakeholders.

Why this research is important

The research has proved useful in highlighting the extent of anti-social behaviour on Scottish buses and its impact. The research highlighted the need for close inter-agency working to implement a range of different initiatives encompassing physical, preventative and diversionary approaches.

References

Scottish Executive (2003) Scotland's People: Results from the 2003 Scottish Household Survey.

Source: Adapted from Granville, S., Campbell-Jack, D. and Lamplugh, T. (2005) 'Perception, prevention, policing and the challenges of researching anti-social behaviour', MRS Conference, www.mrs.org.uk.

Chapter summary

- Research can be described or classified according to the following:
  - the nature of the research enquiry – exploratory, descriptive and explanatory or causal research;
  - the mode of data collection – continuous and ad hoc research;
  - the type of data – qualitative and quantitative research;
  - the status or source of the data – primary and secondary research;
  - the method of data collection – observation and interviewing; face to face, telephone, postal and Internet methods;
  - the way in which the research is bought or sold – syndicated or customised research; and
  - the nature of the setting, market or population under investigation – for example consumer or social research.
- A single piece of research may fall into several of these categories. For example, the research outlined in Case study 2.2 could be described as exploratory; ad hoc; qualitative; primary; customised; and/or consumer research.
- A research project may include several types of research. For example, it may have a qualitative and a quantitative stage; it may consist of secondary research and primary research; it may begin with observation and have a follow-up interviewing stage.
- One of the most important distinctions is between qualitative and quantitative research. Quantitative research involves collecting data from relatively large samples; description of this large number of cases tends to be sparse. Qualitative research involves relatively small samples; description of these relatively few cases is rich and detailed. Quantitative research tends to be used in conclusive (descriptive and explanatory) research enquiries; qualitative research in exploratory and descriptive enquiries.

Questions and exercises

1 Review Case studies 2.1 to 2.4. For each one, list the type or types of research involved and give the reasons why you think the use of that type of research was justified.

References

Brook, O. (2004) 'I know what you did last summer: arts audiences in London 1998–2002', *Proceedings of the Market Research Society Conference*, London: MRS.

Burgess, R. (1984) *In the Field: An Introduction to Field Research*, London: Allen & Unwin.

Granville, S., Campbell-Jack, D. and Lamplugh, T. (2005) 'Perception, prevention, policing and the challenges of researching anti-social behaviour', *Proceedings of the Market Research Society Conference*, London: MRS.

Palmer, S. and Kaminow, D. (2005) 'KERPOW!! KERCHING!! Understanding and positioning the SPIDER-MAN brand', *Proceedings of the Market Research Society Conference*, London: MRS.

Rubin, H. and Rubin, I. (1995) *Qualitative Interviewing: The Art of Hearing Data*, London: Sage.

Sampson, P. (1967 and 1996) 'Commonsense in qualitative research', *Journal of the Market Research Society*, 9, 1, pp. 30–8 and 38, 4, pp. 331–9.

Scottish Executive (2003) Scotland's People: Results from the 2003 Scottish Household Survey.

Recommended reading

Besides reading all of the papers from which the case studies are drawn, the following are recommended:

Chisnall, P. (2004) *Marketing Research*, Maidenhead: McGraw-Hill.

Collins, L. (1991) 'Everything is true but in a different sense: a new perspective on qualitative research', *Journal of the Market Research Society*, 33, 1, pp. 31–8.

Marks, L. (ed.) (2000) *Qualitative Research in Context*, Henley-on-Thames: Admap.

The Research and Development Sub-committee on Qualitative Research (1979) 'Qualitative research – a summary of the concepts involved', *Journal of the Market Research Society*, 21, 2, pp. 107–24.

The *Research Works* series: papers from the AMSO (now BMRA) Research Effectiveness Awards, Henley-on-Thames: NTC.

Shields, G. (2001) 'Meeting the need for actionable consumer insight – the Scottish Courage perspective', *Proceedings of the Market Research Society Conference*, London: MRS.

Warren, M. (1991) 'Another day, another debrief: the use and assessment of qualitative research', *Journal of the Market Research Society*, 33, 1, pp. 13–18.

Part II **GETTING STARTED**

Chapter 3

PLANNING AND DESIGNING RESEARCH

Introduction

In this chapter we look at what is involved in planning and designing research. We start with defining the problem to be researched – the first stage in the planning and design process and arguably the most important. Everything else flows from this. If the problem is not clearly defined, the information needs not clearly identified, the use of the information not clearly established, any research that follows is likely to be a waste of time and money. Next we look again at the three main types of research enquiry – exploratory, descriptive and explanatory. Understanding the nature of the research enquiry is a useful step in the research design process. We then look at the 'who' or the 'what' of research enquiry – from whom or what do we need to gather data. Finally we look at four types of research design – cross-sectional, longitudinal, experimental and case study.

In the next chapter, Chapter 4, we look at how to prepare two key documents in the research process: the research brief, in which you set out the problem to be researched; and the research proposal, in which you set out your research design.

Topics covered

- What is research design?
- Defining the problem
- The nature of the research enquiry
- Units of analysis
- The time dimension
- Research designs

Relationship to MRS Advanced Certificate Syllabus

This chapter is relevant to Element 2 – Designing a Research Project. The aim of Element 2 is to enable you to begin to develop effective research proposals. This chapter covers material that should help you understand what research design is so that you can choose an appropriate research design for a given research problem. In Chapter 4 we look in detail at how to use this knowledge to prepare a brief and a proposal.

Learning outcomes

At the end of this chapter you should be able to:

- understand how to define the problem to be researched;
- understand what is meant by research design and why it is important;
- understand the concept of validity and its importance in research design;
- understand the nature of research enquiry (exploratory, descriptive or explanatory/causal) and how this relates to research design;
- understand what is meant by units of analysis;
- understand the main types of research design (cross-sectional, longitudinal, experimental and case study), their features and their strengths and weaknesses.

What is research design?

Some people confuse research design with choice of research method, seeing it as a decision to use qualitative or quantitative methods, for example, or to use face-to-face interviews rather than telephone, or an omnibus survey rather than a tailor-made one. All these decisions are part of the research design process but they are not the whole of it. It is easiest to think of research design as having two levels. At the first level, research design is about the logic of the research, its framework or structure. It is at this level, given what we know about the problem to be researched and the sort of research enquiry (exploratory, descriptive or explanatory) which that demands, that we make decisions about the structure of the research. The structure may comprise a cross-sectional, a longitudinal or an experimental design or a case study. We will also need to make decisions about the units of analysis – the 'who' or 'what' to question or observe. At the second level research design is about the 'mechanics' of the research – what type of data (primary or secondary, qualitative or quantitative or a combination), what method of data collection, what sampling strategy, and so on. The first level is about designing the overall structure of the research so that it can deliver the sort of evidence you need to answer the research problem; the second level concerns decisions about how to collect that evidence. The steps in the research design process are set out in Box 3.1.

Box 3.1 The research design process

First level design issues
- Defining the research problem
- Thinking about the end use of the data
- Deciding on the sort of evidence you need
- Deciding on the unit or units of analysis
- Deciding on the logic and structure of the research
- Choosing the research design or structure that will deliver the evidence you need

Second level design issues

Deciding on the type of data and the method of data collection:
- Primary or secondary or both
- Quantitative or qualitative or both

Designing a sampling strategy:
- Identifying the target population
- Identifying the sampling units and the sample elements
- Choosing a sampling approach
- Choosing a sample size

Deciding on the method of data collection:
- Face to face, telephone, Internet/online; groups, in-depth interviews and so on

Designing the data collection instrument:
- Defining the concepts, choosing indicators, operationalising the concepts
- Designing the questionnaire or discussion guide

WHY IS RESEARCH DESIGN IMPORTANT?

The purpose of research design is to structure the research so that it delivers the evidence necessary to answer the research problem as accurately, clearly and unequivocally as possible. A sound research design is the framework on which good quality research is built. If you get the research design wrong you will not be able to provide credible or even useful evidence

Box 3.2 Validity and research design

Validity is a key concept in assessing the quality of research. It refers to how well a research design (and the research method and the measures or questions used) delivers accurate, clear and unambiguous evidence with which to answer the research problem. Put another way, validity is an indicator of whether the research measures what it claims to measure. There are two types of validity: internal and external validity.

Internal validity
Internal validity in the context of research design refers to the ability of the research to deliver credible evidence to address the research problem. It is the job of the research design to ensure that the research has internal validity. In causal or explanatory research, for example, it is about the ability of the research design to allow us to make links or associations between variables, to rule out alternative explanations or rival hypotheses and to make inferences about causality. Internal validity must also be considered when designing the data collection instrument and constructing questions. In this context, internal validity refers to the ability of the questions to measure what it is we think they are measuring.

External validity
When a piece of research has external validity it means that we can generalise from the research conducted among the sample (or in the specific setting) to the wider population (or setting). The ability to generalise from the research findings is a key aim in almost all research enquiries and must be considered at the research design stage as well as at the sample design stage.

to address the research problem, you will not be able to make credible claims about what you 'know' based on the research, and so the time and money spent doing the research will largely be wasted. The key is of course understanding the problem to be researched – without a clear idea of what you need to know you will not be able to plan the best way of finding out.

Defining the problem

Regardless of the nature or context of the problem, the steps in the research design process are largely the same:

- Identify and define the problem clearly and accurately.
- Identify the nature of the research enquiry.
- Identify the information needs – the objectives of the research.
- Establish the end use to which this information will be put.
- Choose the design that will give you the sort of information you need.

Defining the problem is the first step. The importance of defining the problem clearly and accurately cannot be overstated. Everything follows from this. It does not matter how good the research is (how suitable the design, how robust the sample, how well designed the questionnaire or discussion guide), if the problem has not been clearly and accurately defined you will not be generating the information or gathering the evidence that you need to address the problem and it is likely that the research will be a waste of time and money. You may end up wrongly advising your client, which may lead to a wrong and costly decision being taken.

There are really two problems to be unravelled if you are to design (or commission) good quality actionable research: first, the business or the decision maker's problem; and, second, the research problem. The decision maker needs information on which to base a decision – he or she wants to take action but what action to take? If it is clear what action to take – if the decision maker has a full understanding of the issues around the problem, if there are no information gaps or questions in his or her mind – research will not be needed. If, however, questions do exist, if there is a lack of understanding, a gap in information then research is needed to get that information. The information you need – this is the research problem; the end use of the information – decision maker's problem – the context of the research, the action to be taken.

Box 3.3 What kind of problems are we talking about?

Selling cars

A large car dealership has found that although the number of inquiries it is handling and the number of visitors to the showroom have remained the same compared to the previous year, sales have fallen dramatically (as has market share). It realises that external market forces – largely economic factors – may be affecting this. It is particularly concerned about the rise in the number of purchases of imported cars. It wants to understand what is happening among the car-buying public in order that it can take some action to at least halt the sales decline.

Good enough to eat?

A private sector organisation manages a railway station with local, national and international services and is responsible for leasing out retail units. The leases of several catering outlets are soon to come up for renewal. The management team sees this as an opportunity to review current provision. It has available to it key data about the sales and financial performance of each of the catering outlets. The team, however, wants to understand two other things: current trends in food retailing; and how station users view what is currently on offer. Armed with this information the management team believes that it will be better placed to make effective decisions about future provision.

Launching a new service

An airline has launched a new service to the United States. The launch was accompanied by an advertising campaign that had been used successfully in several other markets. It was used in this new market with very little modification. The client has several questions: How is the advertising working among the airline's target market? Is it communicating the message intended? Is it creating the right image for the airline? Should it be run unchanged during the next phase of the campaign or should new advertising be developed especially for this new market?

Making use of technology

A government department with responsibility for economic development set out an action plan to help businesses speed up their adoption of information technology. The action plan set objectives that were to be achieved by a certain date. In order to develop policy for the coming year, and to set new objectives, the department wants to review the current situation. It would like to know how successful organisations have been in meeting the original objectives. It also wants to gauge what effect the use of technology has had on their business in particular and on their industry and their markets in general. Is it increasing competition? Is it reducing the cost of market entry? Is it making new markets or industries more accessible?

Understanding effective opposition

A private waste management organisation applied for planning permission to site a waste incinerator on a piece of derelict ground between two long-established housing developments. The two communities set up and ran a campaign that resulted in planning permission being refused. An environmental agency wants to understand what made this campaign successful when most community-led campaigns on similar issues fail.

Getting directions

A small pharmaceutical company has just begun developing a new product for the care and treatment of wounds. The company has a limited budget for new product development. To make an effective decision about the level of investment that it should make, if any, the decision makers would like a detailed picture of the current market for wound care products, and current and likely future developments in this area.

FROM BUSINESS PROBLEM TO RESEARCH PROBLEM

Look again at the car dealership example in Box 3.3. The issue here is a decline in sales over time. The manager needs to take action to stop the decline in sales. But what action should be taken? This is the management or decision maker's problem. The researcher and the decision maker must be clear about what action might be taken because the aim of the research is to deliver the information that will allow the decision maker to take the most effective course of action.

Looking at the wider context

In the car dealership case, the answer to the question 'What action should we take to stop the decline in sales?' depends on understanding or explaining why sales are declining. To understand why sales are declining we need to examine the wider context or setting of the problem. What is going on in the external environment that might be affecting the sales of cars? What is going on in the car dealership itself that might be affecting sales? This is where background or exploratory research can be very useful in getting to grips with and defining the 'problem'.

What you learn from informal exploratory research

Imagine that you discover via some informal exploratory research (interviews with the sales staff and key account customers; a review of recently published reports on the car industry) that external factors, particularly the cost savings to be had in buying an imported car, and internal factors, such as customer service, are having an impact on sales. You now have an idea about what might be going on. You can make some tentative suggestions – that the cost savings to be had in buying an imported car are affecting the sales of the dealership's non-imported cars; that the perceptions of the service that the dealership offers is affecting sales. These suggestions or ideas or statements about connections between things are called hypotheses. While in the early stages of problem definition, when you are trying to get to grips with what exactly the problem is, these hypotheses are likely to be fairly vague statements – for example that there is a link between perception of customer service and sales. As you work to uncover the problem these hypotheses are likely to emerge more clearly. The aim of the research is to gather evidence that will allow you to 'test' these hypotheses, to give you information about whether your ideas are 'correct' or not. Even further into the process, when you have collected data, you may develop and test more specific hypotheses – for example that existing customers with a higher score on a customer service rating scale, indicating a positive view of customer service, are more likely to buy from the dealer than those with a lower score.

Refining the definition of the problem

With the information now available from the exploratory research the manager identifies some possible courses of action to halt the sales decline: a move to selling imported vehicles; a price promotion on selected marques and models currently stocked; a training programme to improve customer service; an advertising campaign focusing on quality of customer service. Gaps in knowledge remain, however – the manager knows very little about how the dealership is perceived by its target market in general and its customers in particular, and how it compares to its competitors. The manager is also unsure, given the changes in the market (the popularity of importing a car), about who the competitors really are. After further discussion, client and researcher agree on the research problem: research is needed to identify what factors are influencing consumers in the car-buying process, and to determine the perceived strengths and weaknesses of the dealership compared to its competitors. The information provided by the research will be used to decide the best course of action to take to halt the decline in sales.

Setting the specific research objectives

Now that you have a clear definition of the research problem you need to pin down the specifics. You need to move from the fairly broad research objective, your general research question, 'Identify what factors are influencing consumers in the car-buying process, and determine what the dealership's strengths and weaknesses are compared to its competitors', to the specific research objectives – in other words, what you need the research to tell you. This is a crucial stage – it will give you a framework on which to build the research design. It will clarify the sort of information you need (in this case descriptive and explanatory).

Research objectives should be as specific and precise as possible. In the car dealership example we need the research to tell us:

- What factors are involved in an individual's buying decision?
- Who is involved in the decision-making process?
- What range of marques and models is considered?
- What influences the range of marques and models considered?
- What sales options are considered, e.g. new or used; dealership or private buy; import or domestic?
- What criteria are used in selecting which sales option to take?
- What likes and dislikes do buyers have about the buying situation?
- How do they rate the chosen option in terms of customer service?
- What is the profile of those who buy:
  - from approved dealers;
  - new cars;
  - dealer-approved used cars;
  - imported cars?

Summary of the process

In this example, a number of steps were needed to achieve a clear definition of the problem to be researched:

- The first step was the client identifying a business problem – how to address a decline in sales.
- This raised the question of why sales are declining – a lack of information meant that this was something that research could help with.
- Information that would help throw light on this was available from within the organisation and from external sources. This could be called an exploratory research stage, designed to bring the problem into sharper focus.
- Collecting this information helped clarify the business problem – it helped to identify some courses of action to address the decline in sales.
- This information also helped clarify the research problem – it helped identify what the client needs to know in order to make a decision about what action to take.
- In clarifying these information needs – and listing the research objectives – it became apparent what sort of research enquiry was needed: descriptive and explanatory.

> **Box 3.4** Professional practice and the MRS Code of Conduct: designing research
>
> Here are the rules set down in the MRS Code of Conduct that members must take into account at this stage of the process:
>
> B1 Members must not knowingly take advantage, without permission, of the unpublished work of another research practitioner which is the property of that other research practitioner.
> *Comment: This means, where applicable, that Members must not knowingly carry out or commission work based on proposals prepared by a research practitioner in another organisation unless permission has been obtained.*
> B2 All written or oral assurances made by any Member involved in commissioning or conducting projects must be factually correct and honoured by the Member.
> B3 Members must take reasonable steps to design research to the specification agreed with the Client.
> B4 Members must take reasonable steps to design research which meets the quality standards agreed with the Client.
>
> *Source*: MRS Code of Conduct 2005. Used with permission.

Another example

In the airline example in Box 3.3, the client's business problem is more clearly defined to begin with – a decision needs to be made about whether to stick with the existing advertising in this new market, modify it or develop new advertising. This raises the question of how the advertising has been received in this new market. This is the research problem. Understanding how the advertising has been received will allow the client to decide what course of action to take.

Case study 3.1 is another real life example. It is about the issues faced by a leading British newspaper, *The Mirror*, in a changing economic, social and political environment. It shows how complex some problems can be, and how much work is needed at the front end – and how important that work is – to enable client and researcher to make the right decisions about the sort of research needed to address the issues.

Identifying the problem and the decision that the client needs to take is the first step in designing research. Once you know what the client needs to do you can clarify the information needed to help them make that decision. You will know not only what information is needed but how and in what context that information is to be used. You have defined the problem and in so doing have uncovered what sort of evidence you need to address it. This is essential information to have in designing good quality, actionable research.

PRIORITISING INFORMATION NEEDS

It is important during this 'project scoping' phase – deciding what research is necessary to address the business problem – to make sure that the focus of the research is neither too broad nor too narrow. The research should tackle what we *need to know* – providing information that is relevant to the problem and that will be used to address the problem – and should not be

LOOKING AT *THE MIRROR*: IDENTIFYING THE BUSINESS ISSUES

This case study describes the challenges faced by *The Mirror* newspaper at a time of great change in its operating environment. Later, in Case study 6.10, we look at some of the methods of data collection used in the subsequent research.

Why this case study is worth reading

This case study is worth reading for several reasons: it shows how hard it can be to tease out the business issues and work towards a definition of the research problem; it identifies a range of information needs; it recognises the potential difficulties in 'selling' the research findings to its internal audience.

The key words are: opportunity, brand, competitors, future, sales decline, strategic plan, shifts in society, fundamental questions, challenge, proposition, core audience, category insight, brand insight, consumer insight, existing research, multi-dimensional product, organisation, brand strategy, brief.

Introduction

The Mirror is a big brand. With over 65 billion copies sold since the end of the Second World War, it is the biggest English language newspaper in the world. It is also a brand with a long history and rich heritage.

In September 2001, following changes in the organisation, there was an opportunity to take stock and to develop a strategic plan to maximise the future value of the brand. For too many years, *The Mirror* had lived in the shadow of its competitors. It needed sharpening up. At the same time, events conspired to give the paper's editor a glimpse of what the future might look like for the brand. The momentous events of September 11th 2001 had a profound effect on *The Mirror*'s editorial philosophy. The paper abandoned its trivia-led approach, went big on the story and stayed big, devoting more pages, more analysis and more reporters abroad filing in than anyone expected. Long after *The Sun* (its main competitor) had reverted to its standard fare, the editor was continuing to produce a radical, campaigning, questioning newspaper that provided serious comment and analysis on the new, uncertain situation that its readers now found themselves in. Sales responded with uplifts throughout September and October, far in excess of expectations. This led the editor to the insight that his readers weren't quite who he thought they were.

The events of September 11th also threw some of the initial insights emerging from the strategic work on the brand into sharp relief. *The Mirror* had always been the paper of the working classes. Huge changes have taken place in British society over the past 25 years, changes that have had their most profound impact on working class consumers. These include huge shifts in the political landscape, religion, community, employment, education and opportunity, the family and the welfare state to name but a few. The media landscape has also undergone momentous changes with new media brands and channels competing for a share of consumers' attention. The more we learnt about these shifts in society, the more it felt as though newspapers were standing by watching as the world changed rapidly around them.

As we entered a new and uncertain age there were two fundamental questions we needed to answer in order to build on recent achievements and create a vision for the long-term future of *The Mirror* brand: what was the emerging *Zeitgeist* or spirit of the ▶

times for our readers; and how could *The Mirror* best capture this in order to secure a central role in the lives of its audience in the future?

Rising to the challenge

The challenge was a huge one: how to cast off the shackles of the past and build on the progress that the brand had made? Clearly we needed to develop a new proposition for the brand – a proposition that took into account the colossal changes that had taken place in the lives of its core audience since *The Mirror*'s glory days.

Central to the development of any successful brand proposition are three sources of insight – category insight, brand insight and consumer insight. Existing research and analysis had armed us with plenty of the first two. What was missing was deep consumer insight: an understanding of the needs, values and passions of our readers. Only by gaining this insight could we reconnect *The Mirror* with its readers and establish a role for the brand in their lives by developing a truly motivating brand proposition. As a brand that had built its reputation as the champion of the working classes we needed to understand our readers' lives as we entered the 21st century. Was the label working class even relevant to people these days? What were the shared values central to their lives? How did media fit in? And most importantly what role should *The Mirror* play in their lives in the future? We needed to tap into the emerging future needs of our audience, rather than simply playing back the established norms of today or those of the past. Gaining this kind of insight was absolutely critical for success.

Beyond the difficulties faced in generating future focused consumer insight, there were also numerous challenges posed by the sheer complexity of national newspapers as products and organisations. National newspapers are fluid, almost living, breathing products that change many times each day. Different elements are important to different people – one reader might be passionate about national news or a certain columnist; another might only be interested in the crossword or special offers. How were we to design a single proposition that could unite such a complex and multi-dimensional product?

Finally, there were a whole set of challenges around aligning the organisation behind a new vision for the future of *The Mirror* brand. For almost a century *The Mirror* had been the newspaper of the working classes and it was filled with people who were passionate about what their paper stood for and who had spent years fighting tooth and nail against the old enemy, *The Sun*. Moreover, journalists are the sworn enemies of spin. Branding, propositions and consumer insight are prime examples of spin. How could we get beyond this cynicism and unite the organisation behind a vision for the future?

It was at this point that we called in the research agency to help us determine how best to capture the emerging *Zeitgeist* and to help bring all elements of the brand strategy together – quite a brief!

Source: Adapted from Clough, S. and McGregor, L. (2003) 'Capturing the emerging Zeitgeist: aligning *The Mirror* to the future', MRS Conference, www.mrs.org.uk.

expanded to include what would be *nice to know*. In preparing a research brief, which we look at in detail in Chapter 4, you may want to set out the information needs in order of priority so that if there are time and budgetary constraints the research can focus on delivering the information most relevant to the problem. In narrowing the focus, however, you need to be careful not to define the problem or the information needs too narrowly, and so run the risk of failing to collect the data needed to understand or interpret the findings or take action.

BEING CLEAR ABOUT THE FOCUS OF THE RESEARCH

Case study 3.2 below shows that part of the work at the problem definition stage of the research process involves defining who exactly the research is to be conducted among – that is, the population of interest. We look at this in more detail in Chapter 8 Sampling, in relation to choosing a sample. Suffice to say at this stage of the research process – the design stage – it is important to be clear about the population of interest so that you can decide what sort of research enquiry is needed.

CASE STUDY 3.2

SHOULD I TALK TO YOU?

This case study describes research conducted for the charity, The Prince's Trust, by research trainees on BMRB International's graduate development scheme.

Why this case study is worth reading

This case study is worth reading for several reasons: it is an example of social research; it identifies the need for research; it states the research objectives; and it illustrates the need to be precise in defining the target audience for research.

The key words are: understanding, tailor, objectives, ascertain, attitudes, aim, opinions, examine, definition, narrow, purpose.

Researching young people excluded from school

The client, The Prince's Trust, is an organisation concerned with creating opportunities for disadvantaged young people. They believed that these young people were at risk from social isolation as a result of their exclusion from school. A greater understanding of school excludees, their experiences, and the reasons behind exclusion was needed to enable the Trust to tailor its schemes to help excludees.

Our client was concerned with giving school excludees a voice. Thus, the objectives of our research were to explore the attitudes and aspirations of young people who had been excluded from school to ascertain the problems they faced and to find out what they believed they needed to succeed. Within this broader aim, the research aimed to investigate attitudes and opinions of excludees towards school and exclusion, and to examine how these attitudes differed from those of non-excludees.

But which type of excludees? There are three official main types of exclusion: fixed term (suspension), which can be an exclusion of up to 45 days consecutively; indefinite, an exclusion for an unspecified number of days; and permanent (expulsion) whereby the pupil is prohibited from returning to that particular school. It was decided to interview only permanently excluded pupils as it was felt these young people were most at risk and were more likely to experience difficulties in being reintegrated into mainstream education.

Research revealed that in addition to official exclusions there are also many 'unofficial' exclusions per annum, where a pupil is asked to leave voluntarily and may not return to that school. Hence, a definition restricted to official excludees would have missed all 'unofficial' excludees and been too narrow. Therefore, for the purpose of this study, permanent exclusion was defined as 'those pupils who have been excluded from school either officially or unofficially, and are prohibited from returning to that particular school'.

Source: Adapted from Capron, M., Jeeawody, F. and Parnell, A. (2002) 'Never work with children and graduates? BMRB's class of 2001 demonstrate insight to action', MRS Conference, www.mrs.org.uk.

WHO GETS INVOLVED?

Defining the decision maker's problem and the research problem, getting to the specific research objectives and defining the population of interest, can involve several rounds of discussion with the owner of the problem, the decision maker, or the organisation's internal researcher (if there is one). Most of this discussion may take place between the decision maker and the internal client researcher before an external researcher is involved; on the other hand, the external researcher may be involved (and may be able to provide valuable insights) at this early stage. Some of the discussion may be revisited if, upon receipt of the brief, the external researcher finds that some elements of it are not clear.

INVESTING IN RESEARCH: THE PRACTICALITIES

There are two important issues to be considered in deciding how to proceed: how much time is available in which to complete the research and what resources (people and money) are available with which to undertake it. Both will have a bearing on the type and scope of research that can be conducted. For example, if a decision must be made within a week of identifying the problem, it may be that primary research is not feasible; the budget may not stretch to a tailor-made survey but it might accommodate including questions on an omnibus survey or a review or reanalysis of secondary data. A decision must be made as to the importance of the research in the decision-making process and enough time and resources should be set aside to reflect this. In deciding on the budget (and to some extent the time available for the research) the client should consider the value of the information that the research will provide to the organisation and to the decision to be taken. The value of the information (the benefit) should be greater than the money spent to get it (the cost).

One way of doing this is to assess the risk (and the cost) involved in making a decision without the help of the information generated by the research: is the risk (and the cost) of making the wrong decision greater than the cost of the research? If, for example, you are planning to spend €3 million on the launch of a new service, the decision to spend €50,000 researching the effectiveness of the launch campaign may be a relatively straightforward one. The risk is that you spend the €50,000 to find out that the launch campaign is highly effective. If you do not spend the €50,000 on research you take a bigger risk – the risk of spending €3 million on an ineffective launch. In the car dealership case, if the business is losing sales equivalent to €4 million annually, the decision to spend €30,000 on research to determine the most effective action may be relatively easy.

Determining the value of the information is, however, not always so straightforward. In some cases, depending on the nature of the decision, the type of organisation or the size of the potential investment, more formal risk assessment or cost–benefit analyses, for example using decision tree theory or Bayesian statistical theory, might be made. It is also important to note the wider and longer-term value of the information to the client organisation. The insights derived from research have strategic, long-term value (Wills and Williams, 2004) as well as tactical, short-term value. In other words, the value of a piece of research may go well beyond what it contributes to a particular decision; it may contribute to the greater understanding of, for example, a particular area, or a particular customer group, product or market.

The nature of the research enquiry

As we saw in Chapter 2, research is often categorised according to its purpose into three types of enquiry: *exploratory*, *descriptive* and *explanatory or causal*. (Sometimes descriptive and explanatory research appear under the heading of *conclusive* research.) In some texts all three types – exploratory, descriptive and explanatory or causal – are referred to as research designs; it is perhaps easier to think of them as types of research enquiry that tell you something about the nature of the evidence you need (and the sort of analysis you will need to do). As you will have seen above, you may need your research to deliver all three types of evidence. It is worth having a closer look at each of these types.

EXPLORATORY RESEARCH

As we saw in Chapter 2, an exploratory research enquiry, as its name suggests, aims to explore, to allow you to become familiar with a topic or the issues around a problem. It is particularly useful in helping to 'unpack' issues or topics, identify a problem, clarify the nature of the problem and define its scope – in other words, to reach a greater understanding. It is useful in looking for insights, determining the feasibility of conducting further research, and developing propositions and hypotheses for further research. The main disadvantage of exploratory research is that it may not deliver a definitive or conclusive answer to the research problem – this is not its nature or purpose. (The main reason it cannot do this is to do with sampling and representativeness: in exploring something it is likely that you will not have the sort of information about it to be able to determine accurately the population of interest, and so it is unlikely that you would be able to deliver a representative sample.)

Box 3.5 Examples of exploratory research studies

Use of mobile phones
Brief: to explore attitudes to and usage of mobile phones among 16–19 year olds.
End use of data: to help understand attitudes and usage habits, to identify the language used, to help design a further detailed study.
Research design: cross-sectional.
Data collection methods: secondary research; observation; in-depth interviews; group discussions.

Political engagement and voter behaviour
Brief: to understand why some young people do not vote and why others are politically active.
End use of data: to help understand what is involved, to clarify the nature of the issue, to define more precisely the problem to be researched and the most suitable research approach.
Research design: cross-sectional.
Data collection methods: review of the relevant literature (including previous research) on the topic; qualitative in-depth interviews with young people who do not vote and those who are politically active.

Eating habits
Brief: to get a picture of the use of food outlets in a railway station including level of awareness of outlets, profile of users of each outlet, users' opinions of provision in general as well as opinion of outlet used.　▶

End use of data: to help define the nature and scope of the problem to be researched; to help design a full-scale study.
Research design: cross-sectional.
Data collection methods: analysis of sales data from outlets; observation; small scale qualitative study with short, mini-depth interviews.

Recycling habits
Brief: to get a picture of household recycling habits over a period of time.
End use of data: to understand why some households are keen recyclers and others are not; to help develop a campaign to encourage recycling.
Research design: longitudinal.
Data collection methods: analysis of available quantitative panel data to determine the characteristics of households that recycle and those that do not; a series of group discussions with a panel of householders at intervals over a three-month period from the introduction of a recycling scheme.

Drug use
Brief: to understand the issues involved in methadone maintenance programmes; to identify the issues around methadone use; to explore users' perspectives; to identify the terminology involved.
End use of data: to clarify the issues involved in preparation for a major study; to help develop methods for the study.
Research design: case study of a methadone maintenance clinic.
Data collection methods: review of the relevant literature; qualitative in-depth interviews with users and clinicians; and observation.

DESCRIPTIVE RESEARCH

As we saw in Chapter 2, much market and social research is about description: describing people, places, things, events, situations, experiences – finding the answers to the Who? What? Where? When? How? and How many? questions. The difference between exploratory research and descriptive research is that, while exploratory research can provide description, in descriptive research we usually have a clearer idea of what is needed and are looking for answers to more clearly defined questions. Examples of quantitative descriptive research include the Census of Population; the Northern Ireland (and the British) Household Panel Survey (see Case study 2.1); the European Social Values Survey; and the Life and Times Survey (www.ark.ac.uk/nilt). The aim of many qualitative research studies is to provide description.

EXPLANATORY OR CAUSAL RESEARCH

Descriptive research will give you a picture – of a market, a set of customers, the users of a product or service, a set of experiences, for example. But very often you will want to know more – you will want to know why the patterns you see in the data exist. In other words, you want an explanation. Your descriptive study may have told you that some customers prefer brand A and some prefer brand B. You will need explanatory research to tell you

Box 3.6 Examples of descriptive research studies

IT products

Brief: to find out about market size and structure for product A in country X.

Research questions to include the following:

- How big is the market for this product (in value and volume terms)?
- What is the nature of the supply chain?
- Who are the main competitors?
- What are their strengths and weaknesses?
- What are their brands?
- What are the values of each of the brands?
- What are the most popular products?
- What is the annual sales turnover per product?
- What is the level of advertising/promotional spend per brand per year?
- What form of marketing communications do buyers prefer?
- What is their customer profile by brand and by product?
- Who is involved in the buying decision?
- Who makes the buying decision?

End use of data: to decide whether or not it is feasible to enter this market with product A.
Research design: cross-sectional.
Research approach: secondary research to gather market size, structure and competitor intelligence data; qualitative in-depth interviews with specifiers of the product and those involved in the buying decision (including IT consultants, internal IT specialists, chief technology officers); quantitative, semi-structured telephone interviews with end users of the product.

why some prefer A and some prefer B. Research that provides explanations that help identify causes or even help predict behaviour is known as explanatory or causal research. Explanatory or causal research allows you to rule out rival explanations and come to a conclusion – in other words, it helps you develop causal explanations. But what exactly are 'causal explanations'?

Causal explanations

A causal explanation might be that sales of brand A are affected by advertising spend (or that income is related to level of educational attainment). In other words a causal explanation says that one thing, call it variable Y (sales of brand A, say, or income), is affected by another thing, call it variable X (advertising spend on brand A or educational attainment).

Covariance and correlation

It is relatively easy to see if there is a relationship or an association between two variables (by examining cross-tabulations of one variable against the other or by plotting graphs of one variable against the other or by using the statistical techniques of covariance and correlation, which we look at in Chapter 13). Sales of brand A might indeed increase if advertising spend is increased, for example, or income may be greater among those with higher levels of educational attainment. In a relationship between two variables there may be a direct causal relationship – the change in Y (sales of product A) is caused directly by X (ad spend on brand A). On the other hand, there may be an indirect causal relationship – in the link between X and Y there may be an *intervening* variable or variables that produce the change in Y. For example, occupation may be the intervening variable through which educational attainment and income are related. If you want to be able to rule out the possibility that there is another variable involved, the research design must allow you to do this. If there is an intervening variable at work, the research design must enable you to examine its effect.

It is, however, important to remember that just because there is a relationship or an association between two variables, does not mean that that relationship is a *causal* relationship. The two things – the variables – might *co-vary*, that is, one might follow the other; a change in X is accompanied by a change in Y – ad spend increases, sales increase. It might be that X and Y – ad spend and sales – are strongly correlated. But it is possible to observe covariation and correlation *without* there being any causal relationship between X and Y at all. For example, the correlation between advertising spend and sales may be *spurious* (that is, not causally related at all); it may be that the correlation you see is the result of another variable, an *extraneous* (or confounding) variable (competitor activity, for instance). The research must be designed – structured – in such a way that you can determine what sort of a relationship there is, and what variables are involved in it.

Inferring causation

So you can see covariance, association and correlation but you cannot see causation – you have to infer it. In order to make sound inferences about cause you must make sure that the research design allows you to do the following:

- look for the presence of association, covariance or correlation;
- look for an appropriate time sequence;
- rule out other variables as the cause;
- come to plausible or common-sense conclusions.

Presence of association, covariance or correlation

If there is a causal relationship between X and Y then you should expect to see an association between them – a change in X associated with a change in Y. In assessing the evidence for cause you should take into account the degree of association between X and Y. You might make one inference on the basis of a strong association and another on the basis of a weak one. But remember, even if there is an association, no matter how strong, *it does not necessarily mean that there is a causal relationship.*

Appropriate time sequence

The effect must follow the cause. If you think that X causes Y (increased ad spend causes increased sales) and you find that Y in fact precedes X (that sales increased before spend increased) then you have no evidence for causation. If, however, you observe that Y does indeed follow X then we have some evidence for causation. But in real-life research situations, where you are dealing with complex environments with lots of things going on, it can be very difficult to establish a time sequence.

Ability to rule out other variables as the cause

Although you see an association between X and Y it might be the case that a third variable is responsible for both, and that the relationship you observe exists because of the effect of this third variable. For example, occupation may be 'the cause' of income levels rather than educational attainment, and occupation may be 'caused' – in part at least – by educational attainment. In fact there may be a whole causal chain of other variables linking X and Y. The ability to rule out other variables rests to some extent with your ability to identify what other variables might be involved. But even if you identify the key variables – we live in a complex world so it is unlikely that we would ever be able to identify all the variables in the marketing or social environment of the research – how do we rule them out? For example, it is unlikely that sales of brand A are determined by ad spend alone – other elements of the marketing mix as well as competitor activity are likely to have had some effect. Thus a more realistic, 'real-world', causal explanation is that variable Y is affected, directly or indirectly, by a number of variables besides X.

Plausible or common-sense conclusions

You also need to ask: Is it possible that one thing might have caused the other? How likely is the explanation? Does it pass the common-sense test? What does other evidence tell us?

Knowing that this is the type of evidence you need to make inferences about cause, you need to make sure that the research you design delivers it. This means understanding the research problem clearly and in detail; thinking about what relationships might exist between variables, and what the obvious explanations and the alternative explanations for these relationships might be; and thinking about what interpretations you might place on the data. This front-end thinking is crucial. If all of these things are clearly thought out – possible relationships, explanations and interpretations – it is much easier to design research that will deliver the evidence needed to make sound causal inferences. At the same time, you need to recognise that you will never be able to collect 'perfect information' and that your inferences will be only that, inferences and not fact. Research will always be constrained by the complexities of the social and marketing environment and those of human behaviour and attitudes.

While we have made clear distinctions between these three types of research, as we noted above and as you will know from your own experience, research projects do not usually fall into only one of these categories. It is more often the case that the purpose of a research project is two- or three-fold: to explore and describe; to explore, describe and explain; or to describe and explain. You will notice this when you come to define the problem and plan the research – you may find yourself wording the research objectives in just this way. Have a look back at the car dealership example. You will see that the list of research objectives includes both descriptive and explanatory ones.

Here is another example: imagine that you have been asked to evaluate a healthy ageing programme run in gyms across the country. You might start by *exploring* the nature of the programme, what it involved, who it was targeted at, what the outcomes of it were. You might want to *describe* or profile those who completed the programme and those who enrolled but did not complete it. You might want to *explain* why some people completed it and some did not. Take another example: imagine that you have been asked to evaluate an advertising campaign for a soft drink. You might want first of all to *explore* with the advertising's target audience – say 16 to 34 year olds – their consumption of soft drinks. This might include an exploration of their brand preferences, their usage occasions, their likes and dislikes about advertising in the soft drinks market and so on – building up a picture of opinions, attitudes, use, the context of use. You might want to find out about other aspects of the target audience's

Box 3.7 What sort of objectives?

The type of research objectives you have will depend on the nature of the problem and the questions to be addressed. Your research may need to address more than one sort of objective. Here are some examples of 'types' of research objectives (adapted from Ritchie and Spencer, 1994) – besides exploratory, descriptive and explanatory, Ritchie and Spencer also include evaluative and strategic objectives:

Exploratory: discovering or clarifying the form and nature of something
Examples: What is the nature of the market or subject area?
            What products or services are on offer?
            Who buys or uses a product or service?
            How do people talk about a service or product?

Contextual or descriptive: describing the form and nature of something
Examples: What is the nature of someone's experience?
            What processes are at work?
            What wants or needs does the population have?
            What perceptions do people hold of a product or service?

Diagnostic or explanatory: examining the causes or reasons for something
Examples: What factors are involved in a decision?
            Why is a particular pathway or action or decision taken?
            What factors might explain perceptions or attitudes?
            Why is a product or service popular or unpopular?

Evaulative: assessing the value or effectiveness of something
Examples: How did a product or service perform during its trial period?
            How were the marketing objectives achieved?
            What factors affected the performance of a product or service?
            How does a product or service fit the brand or corporate identity?

Strategic: identifying new plans, actions, services, products
Examples: What type of product or service will fill the gap in the market?
            What actions must be taken to make a product or service successful?
            What must be done to improve a process or product or service?
            What marketing strategy is needed for success in a new market?

lives and behaviour in order to be able to *describe* or characterise them in some way. You might want to be able to *explain* to your client why one group within the target audience liked the advertising, felt that it engaged them in some way while another group did not like it.

So at this stage of the process you have answers to the following questions:

- What is the business or the decision maker's problem?
- What is the research problem?
- How will the research findings be used?
- What is the nature of the research enquiry?
- What kinds of answers are we looking for?

- What sort of evidence do we need?
- What are the research objectives?

There are two other questions that it is worth considering at this stage. The first is who or what can provide the evidence you need? In other words, what units of analysis should you be using? The second question is whether or not there is a time dimension to the research problem: can you gather the information you need at one point in time only or do you need to gather it over a prolonged period? We look at both these issues below before moving on to look at research designs.

Units of analysis

In most market and social research projects the source of the data is typically an individual, a person. We observe or interview individuals. People are of course not the only data source available – archives, documents, texts, maps, visual images are just a few examples of the data sources that might be useful and relevant. Individuals are, however, the main data source in most primary research. We gather data from them about the things that are relevant to the research study – such as the characteristics that we think will be useful in grouping them together for analysis: age, gender, social class, ethnic origin, area of residence, attitude, behaviour and so on. While we collect data from individuals it is very unusual to report the findings from each individual, especially in quantitative research. Typically, we bring them together – or aggregate them – into groups and we describe the characteristics of those groups and we report the findings for those aggregated groups of individuals.

Think back to the healthy ageing programme evaluation outlined above: imagine that you have collected data on the age and gender of those individuals who completed the programme. You now aggregate the data from these individuals and you describe the group who completed the programme as follows: 93 per cent were women; 7 per cent were men; the average or mean age of the completers was 68. You have aggregated data from individuals in order to describe the group you are studying.

Aggregation is also useful in explanatory studies. Think back to the soft drinks example above: the client believes that the advertising appeals more to the younger end of the target market. You separate out those aged 16–24 and those aged 25–34 and you examine the reactions of each group to the advertising. Here you are comparing the reactions of younger respondents to the reactions of older respondents – you have aggregated data from individuals aged 16–24 and separately aggregated data from individuals aged 25–34. While you now have two groups and you are comparing the findings from these two groups, the basic 'unit of analysis' is still the individual. You have drawn these individuals from a population of interest. You have taken them and grouped them together according to some set of shared characteristics that is useful to the purpose of your research, useful in describing or explaining the issue at hand.

It may be that you are not interested in individuals as your unit of analysis; it may be that a group – for example a household, a family, a social group (e.g. friendship pairs), or an organisation (e.g. a school) – is a more appropriate unit of analysis for the purposes of your research. For instance, imagine that you need to understand how people plan their finances. Your exploratory research tells you that while single people might make financial decisions as individuals, couples tend to undertake this activity together. You therefore need to design your research to ensure that where couples are the decision makers, they are the unit of analysis. Similarly, when investigating other issues or activities related to households or families or friendship groups you may need to give close consideration to whether it is the individual or the household or family or friendship group that should be the unit of analysis. If it is, remember that you will be collecting data from the individuals that make up the 'unit' but you will be analysing and reporting the data based on the 'unit'. It is important to be clear about this because it can lead to problems at the design stage and later at the reporting and interpretation stage.

If, for example, your aim was to find out what end users think of a product or service, for example what IT managers think of a new data warehousing service that their organisation has recently signed up to, your unit of analysis would be individual IT managers. The service is aimed at them, they need to be satisfied with how it works and what it delivers. You might report the findings in terms of what IT managers with different characteristics – for example, background, training, level of experience – think of the service. If, however, you wanted to find out what different types of organisations think of the service – you need to know if you are targeting the service to the right sorts of organisation – you might identify IT managers as best placed to provide the information you need on behalf of the organisation. However, while you collect the data you need from the individual IT managers, your unit of analysis is the organisation. You aggregate the findings across all the organisations and you report or describe the differences you found in terms of the relevant characteristics of the organisation – e.g. size, sector to which the organisation belongs, main area of business. Say, for example, in analysing the data from this research you notice that the organisations that rate the service highest are those with a relatively large proportion of IT managers with experience in using outsourced data storage; those with a relatively large proportion of IT managers with little or no experience of using outsourced data storage give the service much lower ratings. You believe that the conclusion is clear: IT managers experienced in using outsourced data storage are more likely to rate the service highly compared to those managers with little or no experience. In other words, the level of experience of the IT manager affects service rating. In drawing this conclusion, however, you are falling prey to what is called the ecological fallacy. You are drawing conclusions about IT managers when your unit of analysis is the organisation. It may be that it is the less experienced managers who are giving the higher ratings in the 'more experienced' organisations and the more experienced managers who are giving the lower ratings in the 'less experienced' organisations.

Here is another example of the ecological fallacy in action: the murder rate in cities with large numbers of university students is greater than the murder rate in cities with small numbers of university students. But you cannot claim that the murders were more likely to have been committed by students. Your unit of analysis is the city – you do not know by whom the murders were committed. If your unit of analyis is at the group level, you cannot make claims about individuals that make up that group.

It is important in designing your research to be clear about what your unit of analysis is. It will affect how you draw your sample and how you collect the data, as well as how you analyse and interpret it. Think of the problem that the research must address; be clear about what you need the research to tell you, what it is you need it to explain. Once you are clear about this, it should become clear what or whom is your data source and what unit of analysis you need – for example, whether you need to study individuals or households; business executives or business organisations; individual club members or clubs; school children or schools; and so on.

CHARACTERISTICS OF UNITS OF ANALYSIS

We mentioned above different sorts of characteristics that you might use to group together your units of analysis. For example, for individuals we often use age, gender and other demographic characteristics; for households, it is often household size, composition, housing type, even geodemographic profile; for organisations it is often size in terms of turnover or number of employees, or industry sector, or markets served, among other things. This is something that you need to think about at the planning and design stage of the research – it is after all closely related to the problem to be researched and so to how you plan to analyse and interpret the findings. It may be important if you plan to fuse or integrate your data with data from another source. It is therefore something that is worth thinking widely about. What ways of grouping together your unit of analysis will be useful to you in addressing the problem, in exploring, describing or explaining; in analysing and interpreting the results; in making extensive use of your data? Besides the basic demographic characteristics we mentioned above, it is not uncommon to group units of analysis together on the basis of attitudes or beliefs, or behaviour or actions. You might want to select or group them according to whether or not they have had a particular experience or attended or witnessed an event, regardless of other characteristics that they may have. To be able to group your units of analysis in whatever way is relevant to the aims of the research, you either need to know this information and select on the basis of it or you need to find it out in the course of the selection or data gathering process. We will come back to this idea of sampling and selection criteria in Chapter 8.

The time dimension

In thinking about the sort of evidence that you need to address the research problem you need to consider whether time has a role to play. Will taking a cross-sectional view of the issue – a snapshot of it at one point in time – give you the evidence you need? Or do you need to monitor the issue over a period of time (see Case study 3.5)? Answering this question will help you decide between two major types of research design: cross-sectional and longitudinal. We look at this in detail in the next section.

Research designs

As we noted above, there are four main types of research design:

■ the cross-sectional study;
■ the longitudinal study;
■ the experiment;
■ the case study.

In this section we look at what each of them involves, and what sort of evidence each one can deliver.

CROSS-SECTIONAL RESEARCH DESIGN

A cross-sectional research design is probably the most common type of design in market and social research. With a cross-sectional design you collect data from a cross-section of a population of interest *at one point in time*. The Census of Population is an example of a cross-sectional study – it describes the make-up of the population at one particular point in time. Most ad hoc research – research designed to gather information to address a specific problem – is cross-sectional. Usage and attitude surveys, for example, use a cross-sectional design, as does an advertising pre-test. A *single cross-sectional design* involves only one wave or round of data collection – data are collected from a sample on one occasion only. A *repeated cross-sectional design* involves conducting more than one wave of (more or less) the same research with an *independent* or fresh sample at each wave. The use of an independent sample at each round of data collection is what distinguishes repeated cross-sectional design from longitudinal research. In longitudinal or panel research, data are collected from the *same sample* on more than one occasion.

Uses

A cross-sectional design can be used to provide data for an exploratory or descriptive research enquiry. It can also be used for explanatory enquiry, up to a certain point – it can be used to look for and examine relationships between variables; to test out ideas and hypotheses; to help

---

Box 3.8 Examples of the use of cross-sectional design

Single cross-sectional design: buying a car
Aim: to describe and understand the decision-making process involved in buying a car.
Research method: qualitative – mini group discussions, paired (family) and individual in-depth interviews.
Analysis: comparisons made between those who took a test drive and bought a car and those who took a test drive and did not buy.

Single cross-sectional design: assessing needs
Aim: to determine the health and social services needs of older people.
Research method: quantitative survey – face to face, in-home interviews.
Analysis: comparisons made (*inter alia*) between sexes; between those living alone and those living with family members; and between those on state pension only and those on state pension plus private pension or other income.

Repeated cross-sectional design: pre- and post-advertising test
Aim: to determine the effect of an advertising campaign on attitudes to brand A.
Research method: quantitative pre- and post-advertising surveys with independent samples using face-to-face interviews.
Analysis: comparisons made (*inter alia*) between regular buyers of brand A, occasional buyers and rejectors of brand A, pre- and post-advertising.

Repeated cross-sectional design: social attitudes
Aim: to determine the prevalence of a range of social attitudes to help in planning and policy making.
Research method: quantitative survey using CAPI in-home interviews, repeated annually among a 'fresh' nationally representative sample.
Analysis: trends in social attitudes over time; comparisons made (*inter alia*) between men and women, those with children and those without, older and younger people.

Examples of social surveys using a repeated cross-sectional design include the European Social Values Survey; in the United Kingdom, the General Household Survey, the Family Expenditure Survey; in the United States, the General Social Survey.

decide which explanation or theory best fits with the data; and to help *establish causal direction* but not to *prove cause*. With a repeated cross-sectional design – a snapshot at one point in time, followed by another snapshot at a suitable interval – you can examine trends over time. Comparison of Census data from different years is one example; pre- and post-advertising 'dipsticks' are another. Most tracking studies tend to use a repeated cross-sectional design. A repeated cross-sectional design allows you to compare, for example, data from 16–24 year olds at one point in time with data from 16–24 year olds at another point in time.

With a cross-sectional design, and this is something that distinguishes it from experimental research design, we rely on there being differences within the sample in order to be able to make comparisons between different groups. In experimental research design, we create the differences within the test sample by manipulating one of the variables – the independent or explanatory variable – in order to see if it causes a change in another variable – the dependent variable. In a cross-sectional design, having specified the relevant sample and asked the relevant questions, we examine the data to see what relationships or differences exist within the sample.

CASE STUDY 3.3

BANNER ADVERTISING ON THE NET: THE EFFECT ON THE BRAND

This case study describes how an online tracking study – using a repeated cross-sectional design – was used to determine the branding impact of banner advertising on an advertiser and its product.

Why this case study is worth reading

This case study is worth reading for several reasons: it is an example of repeated cross-sectional research; it is an example of online research; it identifies the need for research.

The key words are: Internet, branding, impact, banner advertising, repeat ad exposure, methodology, online tracking study, pop-up, incentive, target audience, media schedule, brand awareness, purchase intent, product attributes, benchmark, pre-wave, post-wave.

Introduction

Advertiser B markets a technical product (Product B), and uses a variety of media and channels for customer acquisition and retention. At the time of the study, the Internet was used primarily as a branding medium. Campaign banners contained simple, attractive messages that associated Advertiser B's product with new ways of doing business. When consumers clicked on banners, they were sent to a corporate site that provided more specific information about the product and company contact information, but here there was no direct sales offer or e-commerce capability.

Analysis framework and set-up

The goal was to determine the branding impact of banner advertising on Advertiser B and Product B, keying in on the effect of repeat ad exposures.

Methodology

- An online brand tracking study was used. Site visitors were recruited via a pop-up inviting them to participate in a ten-minute survey focussing on brand-oriented metrics. The incentive to participate was a contest drawing for cash prizes. ▶

- Two sites that attract a high concentration of Advertiser B's target audience were selected for the media schedule. They agreed to host the surveys and work with the research supplier to implement the study.

Primary metrics

For both Advertiser B and Product B the following were tracked in the study:

- Brand awareness (Product B only);
- Purchase intent;
- Product attributes.

Analysis period/survey dates

There was a six-week campaign with three waves of research:

- Benchmark pre-wave – one week before the campaign start;
- Post-wave 1 – two weeks after campaign start;
- Post-wave 2 – five weeks after campaign start.

Source: Adapted from Broussard, G. (2000) 'How advertising frequency can work to build online advertising effectiveness', *International Journal of Market Research*, 42, 4, pp. 439–57, www.ijmr.com.

LONGITUDINAL RESEARCH DESIGN

Longitudinal research is common in market and social research, where it is often referred to as panel design. The main reason for using such a design is to monitor things – attitudes, behaviour, experiences, perspectives – over a period of time. With a longitudinal or panel design you collect data from the *same sample* (of individuals or organisations, for example) on *more than one occasion*. Whereas the cross-sectional design provides a 'snapshot' of a situation, the longitudinal design provides a series of snapshots (of the same people) over a period of time that can be joined together to give a moving image. The number and frequency of the snapshots or data collection points depend largely on the research objectives (and the available budget). For example, if the purpose of the research is to look at the immediate, short-term impact of an advertising campaign, a relatively small number of data collection points, fairly closely spaced in time, may suffice; to examine the longer-term impact of advertising on a brand may require a relatively large number of data collection points over many years.

What distinguishes longitudinal designs from repeated cross-sectional designs is that in longitudinal designs data are collected from the *same sample* on more than one occasion, rather than from *independent* or fresh samples each time. There is some overlap in the definitions of longitudinal and repeated cross-sectional designs, best illustrated by the way in which tracking studies or trend studies are classified. In some texts, tracking studies are classified as a longitudinal design, the argument being that the sample at each wave is effectively the same (albeit composed of different individuals). In others, and in this one, tracking studies are classed as a cross-sectional design because although the samples are matched at each wave they are nevertheless independent samples.

Secondary analysis of panel data – in which you re-analyse the data for another purpose other than the original one – is also commonplace. Although panel designs are associated with quantitative research, they can be and are used in qualitative research, as the examples in Box 3.9 and in Case study 3.5 show.

SEEING THE BIG PICTURE

Why would fast-moving consumer goods company, Unilever Bestfoods Europe, choose to use a panel rather than an ad hoc, cross-sectional approach for a project designed to understand consumer behaviour and what drives it? This case study presents the reasons behind the decision.

Why this case study is worth reading

This case study is worth reading for several reasons: it sets out clearly the decision-making criteria in choosing one research design over another – a panel, in order to address the client's information needs; it highlights the advantages of a panel design and the disadvantages of a cross-sectional design; and it identifies the need for and the end uses of the research data.

The key words are: depth, breadth, panel data, multiple layers, ad hoc studies, complexity, cost, applicability, measurability, purchased, recalling, accountability, continuous, cost effectiveness, understanding.

1 Depth and breadth

Panel data contain multiple layers of information including information on brand, product category, size, variant, promotion, where purchased, price, time of purchase, and so on. Over 500 different product categories are measured at any one time. This level of data is often unachievable in ad hoc (one-off) Usage and Attitude (U&A) studies due to the complexity and costs of data collection. In U&As, the scope of the data needs to be decided up front, and this limits the applicability of the findings at a later stage. The sample size for this study using the panel was over 5,700 – ten times the base sizes used in previous U&As. More detailed analysis could be completed. There were sufficient and statistically reliable base sizes on the detailed sub-samples.

2 Measurability

The panel data contained data on actual products purchased. These are tracked automatically and verified. Most U&As rely on the consumer recalling what they did. Even for daily diaries, it is often difficult to remember accurately exactly what was done. Most business measurements cannot be reliably and accurately done from ad hoc standalone studies.

3 Accountability

The nature of panel data is that it is continuous over time. Thus, things can be accurately measured over different periods of time on the same consumers. Ad hoc standalone studies are static – the data is collected at one point in time. Panel data is collected continuously for the same people (with three years available for analysis). Specific marketing and sales activities can be measured against the targets for which they were defined. Product launches can be tracked to compare actual buyers versus proposed, the impact of promotions can be measured. To do this using ad hoc studies would be expensive, time consuming, and lack the depth and breadth of information needed.

▶

4 Cost effectiveness

The client, Unilever Bestfoods, needed to invest in one study only and was able to use the results for many different brands and product categories. This revolutionised the efficiency of market research spend.

5 Understanding purchase with consumption data

The full understanding of the consumer was developed from all the data collected from the panel. Data from a separate piece of data collection using a diary and carried out with a sub-set of panel members enabled detailed analysis of the relationships between purchase and consumption. Broader, more useful explanations of behaviour were developed.

Understanding drivers of behaviour

Each part of the panel study was analysed and interpreted together. Psychographic attributes (values collected via a questionnaire) were interpreted and understood in respect of who people were (demographics), actual purchase (panel purchase data), and consumption (diary data). Each helped to explain the other. Each would have been less effective on its own. The level of insight we achieved into consumer behaviour and its drivers from this one data source allowed us to predict future behaviour not just understand what had happened in the past.

Source: Adapted from Gibson, S., Teanby, D. and Donaldson, S. (2004) 'Bridging the gap between dreams and reality . . . building holistic insights from an integrated consumer understanding', MRS Conference, www.mrs.org.uk.

Uses

The main application of longitudinal design is to monitor changes in the marketing or social environment, changes that occur in the normal course of things and events that are planned, for example changes as a result of an advertising campaign, a new product launch or an election. Longitudinal design can be used to provide data for descriptive research enquiry. Although it cannot be used to prove cause, it can be used to achieve the following:

- explore and examine relationships between variables;
- establish the time order of events or changes, and age or historical effects;
- help decide which explanation or theory best fits with the data;
- help establish causal direction (rather than prove cause).

Drop-out and replacement in panels

As time passes the universe or population from which the panel is recruited changes – this is especially so in fast-moving markets and in new markets as penetration and use increases (or declines). Also, the panel members themselves change – for one thing, they get older. The longer a panel lasts the greater the chance that panel members will drop out. A key question in panel design and management is whether or not to replace them. If you do not, you may end up with a very small sample and one that is likely to be unrepresentative (and so poor in terms of external validity) – those who drop out being in all likelihood different from those who stay. If you decide to replace the drop-outs, how do you go about it?

Box 3.9 Further examples of the use of longitudinal or panel research

Voters' attitudes and intentions
Aim: to determine reactions to events; to understand the decision-making processes in relation to voting intentions in the run-up to an election; to observe the impact of events on attitudes and intentions; to gain reaction to the content and wording of campaign messages.
Design: three rounds of fieldwork with the same sample of voters over a three-month period, each round timed to follow key political events and decisions.
Method: qualitative mini-depth interviews.

Attitudes to developments in technology
Aim: to determine attitudes to developments in new technology and the implications these developments might have in daily life.
Design and method: a series of nine qualitative online discussions over a one-year period with the same sample.

Behaviour in the convenience meals market
Aim: to understand buying behaviour – frequency, brands, type of meal and usage data.
Design and method: quantitative computer-aided self-completion questionnaire/diary recording meal type, time of day, meal accompaniments and so on; continuous with weekly downloading of data.

CASE STUDY 3.5

WHAT HAPPENS WHEN YOU WIN THE LOTTERY?

This case study highlights the benefits of applying a longitudinal approach in understanding how organisations made use of funding over time.

Why this case study is worth reading
This case study is worth reading for several reasons: it is an example of qualitative research; it sets out the research objectives; it links the overall research aim with the research design; it highlights the benefits of the approach taken; and it identifies how the client used the data.

The key words are: longitudinal research, quantitative methods, qualitative methods, data collection, three-year period, effective, experiences, perspectives, rich findings, impact over time, objectives.

Aims and objectives of the research
The overall aim of the research was to understand the impact over time on small voluntary organisations that receive Charities Board funding from the National Lottery. The study sample comprised organisations that had received funding over a three-year period. The core objectives of the study were to:

▶

- establish a clear picture of the goals and achievements of each participant charity;
- evaluate the impact of the Charities Board funding over time;
- examine perceptions of the Charities Board throughout;
- compare and contrast the Charities Board with other sources of charitable funding;
- establish useful advice for other small charities contemplating approaching the Charities Board for funding; and
- identify aspects of the Charities Board practices and procedures that could be improved to the mutual advantage of the charities and the funder.

Research design

A longitudinal approach using qualitative data collection methods was needed to allow analysis of the long-term outcomes. All participants were interviewed four times over the course of three years (1997–2000), coinciding with the period covered by their Charities Board grant.

The benefits of the approach

This approach proved a most effective means of tapping into the experiences and perspectives of small charities which were awarded a National Lottery grant to fund a specific project. It allowed participants to reflect, learn, and discuss, and to allow their views to mature as the research study progressed. It provided rich findings. It delivered evidence that showed how grant recipients coped with the responsibility of running a project throughout its life, how they developed and adapted to circumstances, and how they viewed and responded to the Charities Board – the overseer of the grant and the client – throughout the term of the grant.

The research helped the Charities Board focus its thinking and change procedures to address some of the practical issues that the study raised.

Source: Adapted from Hall, K. and Browning, S. (2001) 'Quality time: cohort and observation combined – a charity case', MRS Conference, www.mrs.org.uk.

There are two approaches to replacement. The first is to find out the characteristics or profile of the drop-outs and recruit replacements with exactly the same profile. It is of course important to be aware that you can never know all the characteristics of an individual (there may be characteristics that you do not use in recruiting respondents but which nevertheless have a bearing on other characteristics). The second approach is the use of a rolling panel design, a technique used in most market research panels, indeed in any long-term panel which puts a fairly heavy burden on respondents and so results in respondent fatigue and high drop-out or attrition rates. In this approach you constantly or at regular intervals refresh the panel membership by replacing 'old' or existing members with new ones, making sure that the overall panel profile remains the same throughout. The advantage of the rolling panel method is that it smoothes out drop-out. It also smoothes out conditioning (the phenomenon of responding to questions in a way that is 'conditioned' by having responded to the same or similar questions in previous rounds of data collection), which affects the quality of the data.

Data quality is also an issue with new recruits to the panel: joiners will not have provided data in the same time period as those already on the panel (which has implications for looking at data at the individual rather than the aggregate level); they are likely to be more enthusiastic (less conditioned) than established panel members and so the data they provide will be different and not comparable with that of established members. The solution here is to ignore data from new panel members for the first one or even two data collection periods of their membership.

EXPERIMENTAL RESEARCH DESIGN

You can get evidence for 'why' questions from cross-sectional and longitudinal designs. Depending on the questions you ask or the observations you make, you may be able to work out the relationship between one variable and another, or one variable and two or three other variables. However, the complexity of the environment may be such that this may prove difficult, if not impossible – you are unlikely to able to prove cause.

The purpose of an experimental research design is to allow you to examine *in isolation* the effect of one variable (the *independent* or *explanatory variable*) on another (the *dependent variable*). The idea is that the effects of all other variables will be removed or *controlled* in order to see clearly the effect of this one variable. The main application of experimental research designs is to determine if a causal relationship exists and the nature of the relationship, to rule out the effects of other variables and to establish the time order or sequence of events (which is the cause and which the effect). It is the most effective research design in determining causal connections. It is used widely in medical and pharmaceutical research, in psychological research studies and in marketing experiments, for example, to make decisions about elements of the marketing mix, to evaluate effectiveness of advertisement A or B, the weight of advertising spend or the combination of media to be used in a campaign.

Experimental design works like this. Two identical samples or groups are recruited: one is known as the *test* group, the other is the *control* group. The test and control groups are matched on key criteria – in other words the two are the same on all key characteristics. The independent variable – the one that is thought to cause or explain the change – is manipulated to see the effect that this change has on the dependent variable. This is referred to as the *treatment*. The treatment is applied to the test group but not to the control group. The purpose of the test group is to observe the effect of the treatment; the purpose of the control group is to act as a comparison. Since the treatment is not applied to the control group any changes that take place will not be due to the independent variable but to some other factor(s). The design of the experiment should be such that the effect of other factors is limited or controlled. Comparison of the test and control group allows us to determine the extent of the change that is due to the independent variable only. This type of experimental design is called the 'after with a control group'. There are variations to this design: when the independent variable and the dependent variable are measured in both groups *before* the treatment takes place the design is called a 'before and after'; if a control group is used it is called, not surprisingly, a 'before and after with a control'.

The purpose of the before measurement is to ensure that both the test and control groups are similar on the key measures. These before measurements, however, do not need to be taken if we are satisfied that the test and control group samples are the same on all measures (if, for example, each was chosen using random sampling). The post-treatment differences between the test and control groups should be sufficient to determine the change due to the action of the independent variable. We can take several post-treatment measurements, depending on the objectives of the research – for example, some effects may take longer to manifest or we may want to observe the longer-term impact of the independent variable.

The experimental designs described above deal only with the effect of one variable. This can be impractical (and expensive) if we want to look at several variables and inappropriate if we need to determine how sets of variables might interact or work together. To look at the effect of more than one variable at a time *factorial design* is required. This type of design allows us to examine the main effects of two or more independent variables and to look at the interaction between the variables (for example gender and age on quality of life; or price and pack size on sales).

The clinical terminology used in experimental design reflects its origin in the laboratory-based sciences. Experiments can, however, be carried out in the field – such as sensory testing, test marketing (including simulated test markets) and advertising tests, as well as tests about research practice, as the example in Case study 3.6 shows.

CASE STUDY 3.6

EXPERIMENTING WITH INCENTIVES

This case study describes the use of an experimental design to examine the effects of incentives on the response rate to a postal survey.

Why this case study is worth reading

This case study is worth reading for several reasons: it is an example of an experimental design; it sets out the research objective; it describes how the research was done; it sets out the findings.

The key words are: objectives, experiment, equal numbers, control group, treatment groups, statistically significant result.

One of the objectives of this experiment was to examine the relative effectiveness of prepaid cash incentives, a prize draw for cash and a prize draw for an equivalent value non-cash prize, as methods of increasing mail survey response rates.

The sample was made up of 900 New Zealand residents randomly selected from the 57 electoral rolls representing the main urban centres. Approximately equal numbers of respondents from each socio-economic level were assigned to each of nine groups – one control group and eight treatment groups; each group contained 100 respondents:

1. control – no incentive;
2. 20 cent coin in first mailout only;
3. 50 cent coin in first mailout only;
4. $1 note in first mailout only;
5. 20 cent coin in second mailout only;
6. 50 cent coin in second mailout only;
7. $1 note in second mailout only;
8. prize draw for $200 cash offered in each mailout;
9. prize draw for $200 gift voucher offered in each mailout.

All respondents were sent the same questionnaire, a covering letter and a reply-paid return envelope. The letters to the different test groups varied only in the wording of a single sentence that drew attention to the incentive.

The response rates were monitored. The results provide qualified support for the claim that monetary incentives are an effective means of increasing response rates in mail surveys; 50 cents sent with the first mailout was very effective in this regard. However, after three mailouts, this was the only incentive that produced a statistically significant result when compared to the control group, indicating that some monetary incentives are not necessarily any more effective than two reminder mailouts.

Source: Adapted from Brennan, M., Hoek, J. and Astridge, C. (1991) 'The effects of monetary incentives on the response rate and cost-effectiveness of a mail survey', *International Journal of Market Research*, 33, 3, pp. 229–41, www.ijmr.com.

Experimental designs are difficult (and expensive) to use in full in the real world – it is not always possible to isolate or account for the complexity of variables. Care must be taken in interpreting the results, especially if the experiment has been applied to real-world market-ing and social issues. It is always possible that other uncontrolled external factors may be exerting an influence. For example, imagine you need to determine the effect of advertising on sales of brand A. You could set up an experiment: choose three areas of the country that are matched in terms of key (demographic) characteristics – non-overlapping television regions if you want to test the effects of television advertising, or separate distribution channels if you want to test the effect of press or magazine advertising. In each area you could advertise with a different weight of spend. You are manipulating the advertising variable – the causal or independent variable – and you want to see if sales of the advertised brand (the dependent variable) are affected: does a difference in the weight of advertising spend affect sales? You are controlling the effect of some other variables by matching the samples in each of the three test areas – but what about other uncontrollable or unknown variables such as competitor activity? Can you rule out the effect of these variables?

It is useful to be sceptical about the extent to which a causal relationship is proven. Even with a control group external factors (known and unknown) may influence one group disproportionately. It is also important to think about the external validity of the results. The very fact of being studied makes people act differently (a phenomenon known as the Hawthorne Effect, after Elton Mayo's research into behaviour at work at the Hawthorne Plant of the Western Electric Company, Cicero, Illinois, USA between 1927 and 1932). Think about how artificial the experiment was, and whether you can generalise from the findings to the wider population.

As with panel design, in a before and after experimental design you need to go back to the same people for an 'after' measure. You might find that some drop out. It is important to bear in mind the effect this change in the sample will have on pre- and post- and test and control comparisons. Some problems may be overcome using statistical manipulation of the data. Conditioning is also an issue in experimental design – respondents can become sensitised to the research topic, and they may remember the answers they gave in the pre-stage and offer their post-answers accordingly. Timing of the post-stage measure is critical so that you do not miss the effects of the test variables (by collecting the data too early or too late); it is possible to under- or overestimate the length of the effect. Also, you have to bear in mind that the longer the time lag between the tests the more likely it is that respondents will drop out.

CASE STUDY RESEARCH DESIGN

A case study is an in-depth investigation of a 'case' for exploratory, descriptive or explanatory research purposes, or a combination. A 'case' might be, for example, a household, an organ-isation, a situation, an event, or an individual's experience. Case study research may involve examining all aspects of a case – the case as a whole and its constituent parts. For example, a case study of a particular household may involve data collection from individual members; in an organisation the elements of the case might be departments and individuals within departments. A case study design might be made up of several case studies, not just one. In designing a case study you need to think through (and present) the following: a framework for the case study that includes all the aspects that you need to examine (and how they relate to one another); the research objectives that you need to address – the client's information needs, the 'big' research questions; your sampling strategy; and your methods of data collection. A variety of methods of data collection can be used in a case study, including analysis of documents, observation and qualitative interviewing (and ethnography) and quantitative interviewing.

Box 3.10 Examples of the use of case study designs

Drug treatment centre

Aim: To understand the reason for the level of success of a particular drug treatment centre and whether lessons in relation to policy and practice could be transferred to other centres.

The case study included a review of the brochures and other documentation drawn up by the centre; a review of policies, procedures and guidelines; and qualitative in-depth interviews with management, staff, volunteers, and clients and their families.

A university programme

Aim: To evaluate the effectiveness of a pre-admission university programme.

The case study included a review of the documents related to the programme; a review of the recruitment practice of the programme; qualitative in-depth interviews with experts involved in the policy-making decisions, programme staff, students on the programme; and a self-completion survey among students on the programme.

Uses

The main application of a case study design is to get the full picture, to achieve an in-depth understanding and to get detailed (idiographic) description. It is also useful in understanding the context of attitudes and behaviour in order to reach a greater understanding of their meaning. It can be used to establish a sequence of events; to examine relationships between variables; and to understand which explanation best fits a hypothesis or theory. Case studies are common in educational and organisational research and in evaluation research.

Table 3.1 Summary of key features of research designs

Feature	Single cross-sectional	Longitudinal	Experiment	Case study
Suitable for exploratory research	+	+	−	+
Suitable for descriptive research	+	+	−	+
Suitable for causal research	+	+	+	+
Exploring relationships between variables	+	+	+	+
Establishing time sequence	−	+	+	+
Establishing association, covariance and correlation	+	+	+	−
Ruling out other variables/explanations	−	−	+	−
Understanding why one thing causes or affects another	+	+	−	+
Ability to deal with complexity	−	+	−	+
Making comparisons between groups	+	+	−	+
Ability to detect change	−	+	+	−
Representativeness	+	−	−	−
Ability to look at data at the level of the individual	−	+	−	+
Relative cost	+	−	−	−
Ease of set-up	+	−	−	+
Ease of management	+	−	−	+
Burden on respondents	+	−	−	−

+ indicates a relative strength; − indicates a relative weakness.

If the findings from a particular case study are to be used to make generalisations about the wider group or population to which the case belongs, some care must be taken in ensuring that the particular case is representative of the wider population of cases. In some instances generalisation may not be the aim of the research – the aim may be to understand fully the particular case.

Chapter summary

- Research design is about deciding on the structure the research will take in order to deliver the evidence needed to address the research problem clearly and unequivocally.

- There are two levels of research design. The first level involves getting to grips with the research problem, defining it and clarifying the nature of the evidence needed to address it; it also involves deciding on the structure of the research that will deliver the evidence. The second level involves decisions about how to collect the evidence.

- Defining the problem to be researched is crucially important – all of the other research design decisions are built around this.

- Validity is an important concept in judging the quality of research. Two types of validity are important in the context of research design: internal validity and external validity. Internal validity refers to the ability of the research design to deliver the evidence needed to address the research problem clearly and unambiguously; external validity refers to the representativeness of the research findings, the ability to generalise from the research gathered from the sample or setting to the wider population.

- There are three types of research enquiry: exploratory, descriptive and explanatory or causal. Descriptive and causal research are also known as conclusive research. Clarifying the nature of the research enquiry will help you clarify your research objectives, which in turn will help you make decisions about research design.

- Causal research is about seeking causal explanations. We can see (and measure) association, covariance and correlation; we have to infer cause. To make sound inferences about cause the research design must enable us to look for the presence of association, covariance or correlation, and an appropriate time sequence, to rule out other variables as the cause and to come to plausible or common-sense conclusions.

- It is important at this stage of the research process to think about what units of analysis you need and what characteristics of your population and sample might be useful in addressing the research objectives.

- Determining whether the time dimension is a factor in the problem to be researched will help you decide on the most appropriate research design.

- There are four main types of research design: cross-sectional, longitudinal, experimental and case study.

- Cross-sectional research design is probably the most common type of design in market and social research. In a *single cross-sectional design* data are collected once only from a cross-section of a population at *one point in time*; a *repeated cross-sectional design* involves conducting more than one wave of (more or less) the same research with an *independent* or *fresh sample* each time.

▶

- The use of an independent sample at each round of data collection is what distinguishes repeated cross-sectional design from longitudinal research. In longitudinal research, data are collected from the *same sample* on more than one occasion.

- The purpose of an experimental design is to examine *in isolation* the effect of one variable (the *independent or explanatory variable*) on another (the *dependent variable*). The effects of all other variables are removed or *controlled* in order to see clearly the effect of this one variable. The main application of experimental research design is to determine if a causal relationship exists.

- A case study is an in-depth investigation of a case (or cases) – for example a household or an organisation – for exploratory, descriptive or explanatory research purposes, or a combination of these.

- A research design can use any method of data collection.

Questions and exercises

1 Review Case studies 3.1 to 3.6. For each one, determine the following: (a) the business or decision maker's problem; and (b) the research objectives.

2 Your client operates a bus service from a commuter town to a busy city centre. The transport alternatives for this commute are limited (there is no train service). The client wants to make sure that he is offering the best service possible to his customers. He wants to understand better their views on the service and their experience of it. He has come to you for advice. Prepare a proposal for him outlining the strengths and limitations of (a) a cross-sectional study; and (b) a longitudinal or panel study.

3 You have been asked to present a paper on the following topic: 'Accurate problem definition leads to actionable research'. Explain how accurate problem definition leads to actionable research and outline the steps involved in reaching an accurate definition of the problem.

References

Brennan, M., Hoek, J. and Astridge, C. (1991) 'The effects of monetary incentives on the response rate and cost-effectiveness of a mail survey', *Journal of the Market Research Society*, 33, 3, pp. 229–41.

Broussard, G. (2000) 'How advertising frequency can work to build online advertising effectiveness', *International Journal of Market Research*, 42, 4, pp. 439–57.

Capron, M., Jeeawody, F. and Pamell, A. (2002) 'Never work with children and graduates? BMRB's class of 2001 demonstrate insight to action', *Proceedings of the Market Research Society Conference*, London: MRS.

Clough, S. and McGregor, L. (2003) 'Capturing the emerging Zeitgeist: aligning *The Mirror* to the future', *Proceedings of the Market Research Society Conference*, London: MRS.

Hall, K. and Browning, S. (2001) 'Quality time – cohort and observation combined: a charity case', *Proceedings of the Market Research Society Conference*, London: MRS, pp. 65–73.

Ritchie, J. and Spencer, L. (1994) 'Qualitative data analysis for applied policy research', in Bryman, R. and Burgess, A. (eds) *Analyzing Qualitative Data*, London: Routledge.

Wills, S. and Williams, P. (2004) 'Insight as a strategic asset – the opportunity and the stark reality', *International Journal of Market Research*, 46, 4, pp. 393–410.

Recommended reading

Babbie, E. (1998) *The Practice of Social Research*, London: Wadsworth.

De Vaus, D. (2001) *Research Design in Social Research*, London: Sage.

Mason, J. (2004) *Qualitative Researching*, London: Sage.

Chapter 4

WRITING THE BRIEF AND THE PROPOSAL

Introduction

The aim of this chapter is to offer you some guidelines for preparing a research brief and choosing a research supplier, and for responding to a brief with a research proposal. In the previous chapter, Chapter 3, we looked at the process of problem definition and research design. Here we look at communicating all of this to the relevant parties – communicating the problem to be researched via the research brief to the researcher; and communicating the research design via the proposal to the client.

The brief and the proposal are two very important documents in the research process. We look at the preparation of each document from the point of view of the person responsible for it: in the case of the brief, the client or decision maker; in the case of the proposal, the research supplier. This assumes to some extent that the preparation of these two documents are separate, distinct activities. Sometimes this is the case – each is done in isolation with little, if any, communication between the two parties – particularly when client and researcher are unfamiliar with each other. Working in isolation on the brief or on the proposal, while sometimes unavoidable, does not always produce the best outcome. Good quality, actionable research is typically the result of a collaborative, partnership approach between client and researcher – and generally speaking the earlier this process starts, the better. Here – as in all other stages of the research process – there should be dialogue and collaboration, and not just for unusual or complex projects. It is important to bear this in mind when reading the chapter. While it is the client who is responsible for the brief, it is useful to involve the researcher; and while it is the researcher who is responsible for the proposal, it is useful to involve the client.

Topics covered

- Roles in the briefing and research design process
- Preparing a research brief
- Choosing a research supplier
- Questioning a brief
- Preparing a research proposal
- Evaluating a proposal

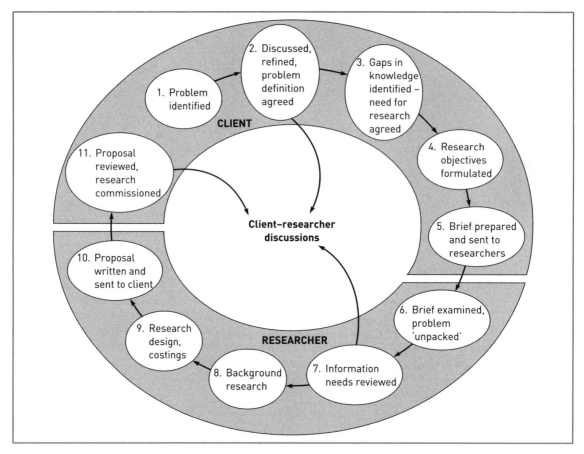

Figure 4.1 Overview of the research commissioning process

- Responding to a proposal
- The client–researcher relationship

Relationship to MRS Advanced Certificate Syllabus

The material in this chapter covers Element 2 – Designing a Research Project. This chapter should help you develop effective research briefs and effective research proposals.

Learning outcomes

At the end of this chapter you should be able to:

- develop and write a research brief;
- understand the connections between a brief and proposal in the context of the research process;
- understand what should be covered in a research proposal;
- evaluate a research proposal.

Roles in the briefing and research design process

The role of the research supplier (the researcher) is to design effective research that will deliver the information needed by the person commissioning the research (the client) and present this clearly in the research proposal. (In some situations – applying for research funding, preparing your dissertation or assignment – you may be responsible for writing both the brief and the proposal, in other words, thinking up the problem to be researched and setting out how you plan to research it.) To prepare a sound research proposal the researcher must have a clear understanding of the problem and its wider context, the type of information needed to address the problem, and how this information will be used. The role of the client, typically, is to define the problem clearly and precisely, to identify what information is needed to address it, to set out how this information will be used, to communicate all of this clearly in the research brief. Depending on the client's background and experience, the way in which the client organisation works, or the nature of the relationship between client and researcher, the client may involve the researcher in either the problem definition or information needs assessment stage. This is one way in which the researcher can 'add value' to the process – using experience and knowledge of research and the area to be researched to help the client define or refine the problem, reach a clear understanding of their information needs, and show how research might address these. Besides the problem-related material that you set out in the brief, it is also worth setting out how you as the client expect the researcher to act – what role you would like them to adopt – throughout the project (see Box 4.1 below, and Box 1.2).

Box 4.1 'It's all in the brief'

In Chapter 1 we looked at what it is that clients want from researchers (see in particular Boxes 1.2 and 1.3). Sometimes, but not always, the client will set out exactly what they want – and what sort of researcher s/he wants – in the brief or during the briefing process; similarly, the agency researcher will make it clear what sort of service s/he is offering. Here Andrew Pyke highlights the importance of doing this.

Giving attention to the brief
What should agencies expect from clients? There are three key issues for the research world: (a) the client dilemma – am I a researcher or a planner; (b) the agency dilemma – are we data providers or consultants; and (c) how do (a) and (b) impact where it matters – the marketing decision making.

The reality
My hunch is that fundamental questions in the ideal briefing process – (a) why is this project happening at all; (b) what's gone before; and (c) what will happen as a consequence of this project – are lost in the commissioning process, e.g. haggles over fees, mad diary scrambles and so on. I suspect that the momentum created by the confirmation of the project – right you've won the contract so let's get the project up and running in the next five minutes – leaves these fundamental questions (e.g. why is this project happening) uninterrogated or assumed. ▶

Why the brief should be at the hub

This is a worry for all of us. Research projects that search for and successfully apply consumer understanding to business are our lifeblood. These projects rely on unity of purpose at the outset, from the brief. Yet, this does not happen most of the time. Often, we are involved in projects where best practice happens to an extent but the ideal does not happen frequently enough.

Typologies

I contend that most of the problems lie with the roles (and resultant interaction of the roles) that both clients and agencies wish for themselves. The client modes are classic researcher mode and planner mode. The agency modes are data supplier mode and business partner mode.

Client modes

The classic client mode is that the client researcher needs the data; straight answers to straight questions. In classic mode, the client researcher will just pass the debrief (if there is one) on to the end-user. Alternatively, in the planner client mode the client needs the agency to use the project as a springboard to move thinking forward in his/her organisation.

Agency modes

In data supplier mode, the agency is very keen to prove their adeptness at supplying data across the marketing mix, all jobs considered. In business partner mode, the agency is more interested in developing the contact with the client, supplying more than just the data.

We all appear to strive to the planners/business partners modes, at least that's what everyone says is a good thing; add more value, do more than just research.

How this impacts on the brief

If the client is in planning mode, using the research project to drive change in the business, they need to be clear about this. They need personal skills beyond research competency, e.g. influencing skills, team facilitation, and entrepreneurial zeal. They need the agency to be in on the plan – otherwise the planner's initiative will have limited chance of success. The brief needs to make this clear. The context section of the brief (definition and background to the problem, why the research is needed, use of results) must state the intent. Otherwise, the research will happen, change will not and all involved will feel frustrated.

If the client is in classic mode, the research project will make a valuable contribution to the business. However, if the marketing/board end-user is using the classic data in planning mode, the client researcher/agency will suffer/be blamed as the process unfurls, often at the debrief. The context section needs to be interrogated for evidence of the mix of modes. It is remarkable how often it occurs.

To contribute meaningfully to the decision-making process, the role of the project needs to have been established at the outset. Moreover, the agency needs to know the context from the client researcher. If the client researcher is not a reliable source, the agency needs to have interrogated the client organisation to have elicited the context. Leaving it (literally) to the last minute is not a good idea. The discussion should take place at the beginning of the project – at the brief, in the context section.

How this impacts on the marketing decision-making process

When client and agency modes are matched, we are a powerful force:

- client classic and agency data supplier – delivering exactly what was required, building a deserved reputation for efficiency and reliability. Demonstrates a clear ownership of consumer insight.
- client planner and agency business partner – powerful agents of consumer-based process change. Helps to create a genuine consumer based marketing culture.

When modes are mis-matched for both agency and client researchers, the dangers are either (a) failing to meet expectations or (b) not getting the credit where it's due.

Moving forwards

Let's demand that henceforth, in each brief, the clients proactively say what mode they are in, and why. Also, clients, add in time for interrogation, saying that the job won't be confirmed until interrogation has occurred. Let's make the context section a mandatory.

Source: Adapted from Pyke, A. (2000) 'It's all in the brief', MRS Conference, www.mrs.org.uk.

Box 4.2 Recap: key things to think about in preparing a brief

- What is the issue or problem that you need to address?
- What decision is to be made and/or what action is to be taken?
- What information is needed to help make an effective decision or take the appropriate action?
- Will research help?
- What are your information needs? What specific objectives must the research address?
- How much time and money is available for the research?

Preparing a research brief

If you are commissioning research it is your responsibility to ensure that the potential research supplier understands the decision maker's problem, the context of the problem, the information needed to address it, and the nature of the constraints (time and money) within which the research must be designed. The research brief is the document in which these things are set out. It is circulated to potential research suppliers with a view to eliciting a research proposal. Verbal research briefings – either by telephone or face to face – are common but are usually accompanied by a written brief. Preparing a written brief is good practice – having to commit ideas to paper usually enhances the quality and clarity of the thinking behind them. A written brief is a valuable aid to communication and acts as a record for consultation and discussion. A draft version can be circulated to all involved in the project for comment.

Several versions may be prepared before agreement is reached on the definition of the problem and the way in which it is to be addressed. For much of its early existence the brief may be circulated internally only. However, once the final version is agreed it is sent to potential research suppliers. It provides all those involved – client, decision maker, research supplier – with a record of what is required, and can reduce the chance of a dispute arising about what is delivered. It can be used at the end of the research project to review or evaluate the process and determine, for example, if the research objectives were met and if the research provided useful information for the decision maker.

Box 4.3 Improving the quality of thinking

Usually the earlier ideas are committed to paper the better. Brainstorming with the project team and mapping ideas out, for example, can help you get at what you know and what you do not know about the problem or issue that you are thinking of researching. Mapping is also useful in helping to sort ideas and structure them into a logical order. Once ideas have been put forward, discussed and debated, mapped out and finally ordered in some way, writing can begin. It should be apparent at this drafting stage whether you have understood and defined the problem clearly or not – it is difficult to write about something that you do not fully understand or about which you are unclear. The drafting process might uncover further questions about the problem. This first draft of the brief can be a useful stimulus to further thinking and can be used as a focus for further discussion with the project team.

The brief is usually accompanied by a letter that sets out the deadline for response to the brief with client contact details, should the research supplier want to discuss the brief further. It is good practice to set up a face-to-face briefing meeting. It gives the researcher a chance to ask further questions about the brief, and perhaps test the reaction of the client to some early ideas about the shape of the research. It gives the client a chance to determine whether the researcher understands the issues involved. Thus all parties have the opportunity to assess if a working relationship is possible or desirable.

CONTENTS OF A RESEARCH BRIEF

Below is a guide to preparing a detailed brief using the following headings:

- Title
- Definition of the problem
- Background to the problem
- Why research is necessary
- Statement of research objectives
- Use of information
- Target population
- Suggested approach
- Analysis required
- Outputs
- Liaison arrangements
- Timings

- Budget
- Form of proposal
- Selection criteria

Not all briefs contain or need to contain all of this information. In cases where the research is a repeat of a similar job, or where there is an established relationship between client and researcher, some of the information may not be included. A more comprehensive brief is, however, recommended in cases where either party is fairly new to research, where the relationship between client and researcher is new, or where the project is unusual or complex.

Title

A title is important – it informs the reader immediately of the main focus of the project and draws attention to the key issue. A title may be obvious immediately or it may not be obvious until you have thought through exactly what it is you want – so it may be the last thing you decide upon.

Definition of the problem

Get to the heart of the issue immediately with a clear, accurate and precise definition of the problem. This may be harder to write than you imagine. If you do have trouble writing it down it may be that you are not clear about it yourself, and if you are not clear about it it is unlikely that the researcher will be. Use clear, jargon-free language. Avoid ambiguous words and phrases. Be as specific and precise as possible. Look back at the car dealership example. The dealership is experiencing a decline in sales; the management wishes to take action to address the decline but is unclear what action to take. It suspects – but it has no robust evidence – that the availability of cheaper, imported cars, which it does not sell, is a factor; it also suspects that perceptions of its customer service may be an issue. To make a decision on the most effective action to take to address the sales decline, the management needs accurate and robust information about these issues and their impact on sales. It therefore wishes to commission research to: 'Identify what factors are influencing consumers in the car-buying process, and determine what the dealership's strengths and weaknesses are compared to its competitors'.

Background to the problem

Give some background information about the product, service or issue to which the problem relates, and its wider setting within the organisation or within the market or subject area. It might also be useful to provide some information on the external conditions within which the organisation operates. In addition, especially if it is the first time that the researcher has been asked to prepare a proposal, you might include some background information about the organisation – its role, its aims, its responsibilities, its mission statement or business strategy – something to give a flavour of the organisation's work. This will not only help the researcher formulate the most effective research design but will be useful for interpreting the research findings and understanding the implications for the organisation.

Why research is necessary

State why you think research is necessary and, briefly, how you came to this conclusion. For example: 'Although existing data tell us that there has been a sharp decline in sales, we have no evidence as to why . . .'.

Statement of research objectives

State the research objectives – what it is you want the research to tell you. Be as specific and unambiguous as possible. Avoid vague statements such as: 'To research the market for imported cars' or even 'To conduct a study of the image of the car dealership among its target audience'. Have a look again at the main objectives of the car dealership project: to 'Identify what factors are influencing consumers in the car-buying process, and to determine what the dealership's strengths and weaknesses are compared to its competitors'. This is further specified in a series of more precise objectives, for example: 'What factors are involved in an individual's buying decision?' and 'Who is involved in the decision-making process?'

Use of the information

To ensure that the research is focused and to help the researcher determine the type and scope of information or evidence needed, and the robustness of it, state what the information will be used for, who will use it and how it will be used. For each research objective ask yourself, 'How will the information I get here be used in the decision-making process?' This is a good exercise to ensure that you are asking for the information that you really need.

Target population

Give as much detail as you can about the target audience or the target population. Specify what it is you want the unit of analysis to be. This information will help the researcher decide not only on the sampling approach but on the type of research and the method of data collection. It will also help to cost the project more accurately. Be as specific and as precise as possible. For example, if you have information on the incidence of the target market in the wider population, include it. If you have specific requirements, if there are specific groups within the population that you want to compare in the analysis – for example if you want to compare 25–34-year-old users and 35–44-year-old users; or those in employment and those not; or frequent users, occasional users and non-users; or those with children and those without, state this in the brief. This information will guide the researcher in designing the sample, in determining the number of focus groups or the number of interviews necessary for these

CASE STUDY 4.1

WHY DO WE NEED RESEARCH?

Here we learn why a piece of complex social research was commissioned. Later in Case study 9.5 and Box 10.7 we see the challenges the researchers overcame in setting up the research.

Why this case study is worth reading

This case study is worth reading for several reasons: it is an example of social research; it describes in detail the need for research on a difficult and sensitive topic; it states the research objectives; it sets out the end use of the research; it shows the links between some of the key elements of the research process.

The key words are: prevalence, general population, unrepresentative groups, establish benchmarks, monitor future changes and trends, public attitudes, research objectives, definitions, indicators, questions, operationalised, measurable, reliable.

Why research was needed

In March 1999 the National Society for the Prevention of Cruelty to Children (NSPCC) launched its Full Stop campaign, aiming to end cruelty to children within a generation. This ambitious objective requires a long-term strategy encompassing raising of awareness, public education, provision of services, and influence on the law, social policy and professional practice. In planning these initiatives the NSPCC recognised the fact that research would be needed to provide baseline information and measure progress.

Though the subject of child maltreatment appears frequently in the media, little is known about the extent of such behaviour in the general population. There is a significant body of academic research on the subject, but this focuses on special populations. In particular it focuses on the relatively tiny numbers of children whose cases have been drawn to the attention of the authorities. Furthermore, studies looking at the prevalence of maltreatment in the general population often present an incomplete picture, being based on unrepresentative groups (e.g. students), restricting the questions to certain types of abuse, or using definitions of abuse which are inflexible, thus limiting comparison of results across different studies.

We know that crimes against children are under-reported. Evidence in cases of child abuse is often difficult to obtain. Children and their families may be reluctant to talk, physical injuries can be hidden and there are rarely other witnesses. It is still difficult to know how many children die as a result of abuse or neglect because of the way in which the cause of death of an infant or child is diagnosed, recorded and assessed. Official homicide statistics suggest that currently around 70–80 children are killed in the UK each year. This is likely to be an underestimate as it only reflects cases where there is absolute certainty of the cause of death. Contrary to the image often portrayed in the media, only between five and ten of these homicides are carried out by strangers, the remainder are by those known to the child, usually a parent or carer. The number of child murders by strangers has remained fairly constant for decades.

Against this background the NSPCC realised the need for a new study, aiming to redress the deficiencies in existing data as far as possible by providing credible and reliable prevalence measures which will be robust in the context of social and cultural differences due to social class, ethnicity and region. To achieve these objectives the research had to be:

- based on definitions of abuse and neglect which have credibility and social consensus as indicators of acceptable and unacceptable behaviour towards children, and can be operationalised in measurable and reliable form;
- informed by what is currently known about the levels and nature of child maltreatment, especially in relation to age and gender of victims and identity of abusers;
- designed to allow for the possibility of abuse both inside and outside the family;
- designed to tackle the borderline areas where there is known to be uncertainty and public debate about what is acceptable care of children, and what is generally recognised as abuse or neglect.

The results will establish benchmarks which will enable the future monitoring of change in the way we treat children, and enable greater understanding of the relationship between different forms of abuse and neglect than has previously been possible.

Source: Adapted from Brooker, S., Cawson, P., Kelly, G. and Wattam, C. (2001) 'The prevalence of child abuse and neglect: a survey of young people', MRS Conference, www.mrs.org.uk.

comparisons to be made. In addition, it is important to clarify what you mean by terms such as 'frequent', or 'in employment'. Does employment mean paid employment only, for example, or would you include those in voluntary work or on home duties? Does it include those working part time as well as those working full time? Does it include those on paternity or maternity leave? Be as specific and unambiguous as possible.

Suggested approach

The amount of detail you give here may depend on your knowledge of research, or on whether you prefer the research supplier to put forward ideas that are not influenced by your own. Tell the researcher if the decision makers have a preference for a particular type of research or research evidence, for example qualitative or quantitative. If the research needs to be comparable with a previous piece of research mention this and give details. If you want the researcher to suggest a range of possible options and the pros and cons of each, say so.

Analysis required

Set out clearly what type of analysis you need and an idea of the complexity of the analysis required. In a quantitative study you are likely to want a set of cross-tabulations (data tables). Think about what headings or variables you want to include in these cross-tabulations. Also, think about what sort of statistics you will need – descriptive statistics (e.g. means, standard deviations, standard error) and/or inferential statistics (significance tests). Will you want to run other more complex analyses such as factor analysis, cluster analysis or conjoint analysis? The researcher needs this sort of information in order to make decisions about research design, design of the sample, sample size, type and level of resources to be assigned to the project, time needed to complete it and so on.

Outputs

Data tables, summary reports, full reports and presentations of findings are often referred to as 'deliverables' or outputs – the products of the research. Specify exactly what deliverables you expect during and on completion of the research. Typically they will consist of a presentation of the findings and either a written summary report or a full report, handed over at the end of the project. For some projects – especially large-scale ones – you may want interim reports of the findings. You may want to comment on a draft report before the final report is produced. In a qualitative project you may want copies of the videos or audiotapes of the interviews or group discussions and copies of the transcripts, or a summary of the findings from each group. Whatever your requirements, mention them in the research brief so that the researcher can cost them and include them in the work plan.

Liaison arrangements

Set out clearly the contact or liaison arrangements you want. For example, if you have a project team or advisory group with which the researcher must meet to discuss progress give details in the brief – frequency of meeting, type and detail of reporting needed – so that the researcher can build this into the work plan and the costing.

Timings

Give the date by which you need the research to be completed and highlight any interim deadlines (for completion of fieldwork, say, before an advertising campaign breaks or a product or service is launched). This information will not only allow the researcher to plan the work but it will also affect what sort of research can be done. For example, the time frame may put constraints on the number of interviews, or the method of data collection. Make sure the time frame is reasonable and make sure you can meet any obligations you might have – such as to approve the questionnaire, attend the fieldwork, provide samples of product or stimulus material. There is a movement promoting what is called 'Slow Research' or, more accurately, research at the right speed (Poynter and Ashby, 2005) – research 'which has been properly planned, which is fully analysed, and whose benefits will continue to be felt for a relatively long time period of time after it is completed'. It may be worth bearing this in mind when setting out your timings (and later when reviewing the proposals you receive).

Budget

If the research design and the research method are specified in detail in the brief then it may not be necessary to provide details of the budget – the researcher should have everything needed to cost the work. Even in cases where the client does not specify design and method (the more common situation) the budget may not be stated. The reason often given is that the researcher will design the research to use up this budget, whether the problem calls for it or not. This of course would not be ethical on the part of the researcher. If you have asked for more than one proposal the absence of a budget can make it more difficult for you to compare them. Different researchers will interpret a brief in different ways, making different assumptions that will impact on the cost. It is therefore worthwhile to give at least some idea of the budget so that the researcher can avoid proposing research that does not meet it and is better placed to design research that will maximise value for money.

Form of proposal

Specify clearly the way in which you want the supplier to present the proposal. For example, you might specify the headings under which the proposal should be written, the order of the headings, the nature and detail required, even the appearance of the document, method of delivery (on paper and/or electronically) and the number of copies to be submitted. Here is an alternative set of headings to those given above:

- Understanding of the problem and the client's requirements
- Details of the approach
- Any difficulties that might be anticipated and how these might be overcome
- Timetable
- Separate costing for all options proposed
- Pricing schedule outlining staff inputs and daily rates
- Details of relevant experience of organisation and proposed project staff.

Selection criteria

It is common in the tendering process for government contracts for the researcher to be told on what basis the research contract will be awarded – in other words, on what basis the proposals will be evaluated. The selection criteria might include the following:

- suitability of proposed methodology;
- relevant experience in this area;
- cost;
- demonstration of understanding of the brief.

Each proposal is rated on the extent to which it meets these selection criteria. A weighting or score may be given to each of them – for example, demonstration of understanding of the brief may be judged to be the most important, and cost the next most important.

Choosing a research supplier

Once you decide that research is necessary you must decide who is to carry it out. It may be that you can handle it internally. If you do not have the resources or the particular expertise to do so you must select an external supplier. To choose a supplier think first of all about the type of project it is and the type of supplier you might need. You may have several options, ranging from a full service agency, to a supplier of fieldwork and tabulation, to a consultant to write up the findings from data you have collected. You can obtain information on agencies and consultants from the directories of organisations representing the research industry, such as MRS (www.mrs.org.uk) and ESOMAR (www.esomar.org). The directory of the Association for Qualitative Research (www.aqr.org.uk) is a useful source of information on qualitative research organisations and independent qualitative research practitioners. The Social Research Association (www.the-sra.org.uk) can provide details of those who specialise in social research. MrWeb is a web-based service that lists suppliers including independent research consultants (www.mrweb.com) and fieldwork suppliers via the Fieldwork Exchange (www.mrweb.com/field/).

From the suppliers you have identified you may want to draw up a shortlist. The shortlist can be selected against a number of criteria including the following:

- experience in the general subject area – for example consumer, social or business-to-business issues;
- experience in the particular area – for example pharmaceutical products, older people's issues, office equipment; or advertising research, new product development, employee research;
- services available – for example full service or limited service; computer-aided interviewing or paper-based methods;
- expertise in particular research methods or techniques – for example qualitative, quantitative; omnibus, continuous research, mystery shopping.

You can determine whether researchers meet your criteria by examining their entries in directories or their advertising, by talking to those who have used their services and by talking to them directly. You can invite prospective candidates to make a 'credentials' pitch to you – a presentation outlining their experience and expertise. Once you have established your shortlist you can send out the brief.

It is preferable not to ask more than four research suppliers to tender for a project. Proposals take time and money to prepare but are provided free of charge to clients requesting them, on the understanding that the researcher has a reasonable chance of winning the job. It is judged unfair by the professional body, MRS, to ask suppliers to tender for projects for which they have less than a one in four chance of success. This guideline was developed in order to protect research suppliers from being used by clients as a source of free research advice. The cost of preparing proposals is of course built into the researcher's overheads and so ultimately affects the cost of research. The more proposals requested, the more research costs will rise in general. If more than four suppliers are involved in a pitch individual suppliers may decline to tender, or may ask the client to pay for the proposal.

Questioning a brief

We now switch to the research supplier side. When you receive a brief make sure to read it through several times and, as you start to formulate your ideas about how to structure the research, ask yourself the following:

- Is the problem clearly defined? What assumptions, if any, have been made?
- Why is the research needed?
- Is it clear what the information needs are?
- Will research help?
- Do I have all the information I need to design effective research?
  - Are there any gaps in my knowledge about the problem?
  - Are there any gaps in my knowledge about what the research is required to provide?
- If a research approach is suggested, is it feasible? Will it deliver what is needed?
- Are the research objectives clear and unambiguous?
- Are the research objectives relevant to the problem?
- Is it clear what the client expects from the research?
- Is it clear how the research will be used?
- Is the budget adequate?
- Is the time frame feasible?
- Are there any gaps in my knowledge about what the proposal should contain?

In effect, what you are doing here is conducting a critical evaluation of the brief. Even in a well-prepared brief the client may have made some assumptions about what is known or not known, or may not have fully explained some points – as a result of being too close to the problem, for example – and so some gaps or ambiguities might remain. It is therefore important to review it with a critical eye. If there is anything that is not clear, do not be afraid to go back to the client for clarification. This is as much in the client's interest as it is in yours: the better you understand the client's problem, the better you will be able to design effective research that will produce actionable insights.

Preparing a research proposal

You should now have all the information you need to write the proposal, having received the brief and clarified any issues with the client. The research proposal is the document that sets out what type of research is to be conducted, why this is suitable, how it is to be conducted, the time frame in which it will be completed and the cost that it will incur. It should demonstrate that you have a clear understanding of the problem, its context and the need for research. In writing the proposal do not assume that those reading it will be research experts or particularly research literate. Explain things clearly and simply and avoid trying to impress the reader with unnecessary jargon or technical language. Remember your aim is to show that you:

- understand the problem and the issues involved;
- understand the implications of the problem in research terms and in the wider business context;
- have the expertise to design, set up, manage and deliver good quality research that will help in the decision-making process.

TYPES OF RESEARCH PROPOSALS

Not all projects start with the sort of formal, detailed research proposal described below. The work being commissioned may be similar to, or a repeat of, a previous study and may not warrant a full proposal; or the researcher and client may have an established relationship and so the client may not require the detail of a full proposal. Time may be a factor, limiting what can be produced. About one week to two weeks' notice is needed to prepare a proposal – giving the researcher time to fit it into the work plan, arrange for costings to be prepared and so on. About one or two days will be spent thinking and writing, depending on the complexity of the project. It is good practice to prepare some sort of a written proposal – it will avoid confusion and misunderstanding. Sometimes a one or two pager – a short, less formal proposal covering the basics of introduction, a statement of the problem, the need for research, research objectives, recommended approach, reporting, timings, costs and relevant experience – is all that is needed.

THE CONTENTS OF A RESEARCH PROPOSAL

Here is a guide to what should be covered in a full proposal.

Background to the problem

Show the client that you understand the nature and setting of the problem. Do some background research – do not just reproduce the background information that the client gives you in the brief. Add in information that shows you understand the issues and the client's business problem. This can add value to the proposal, and shows the client that you are interested and willing to do that little bit extra.

Research objectives

The research objectives should state what the research will do and so should be relevant to the research problem. They may not be fully or clearly stated in the brief, so you may need to do some work to draw them out. It is crucial that your understanding of these objectives and the client's understanding of them are one and the same; and you both should agree that they will deliver the necessary information. From the research objectives, and from other information provided in the brief, you may be able to set out what general questions will be addressed in the research.

Approach to the research

Set out the research design and why this approach is the most suitable for collecting the evidence needed. Whatever you suggest, explain your reasoning and set out the limitations that the approach may have.

Sampling

State clearly the target population for the research. For example, it might be all those aged 18–64 living within a 15 km radius of the car dealership who have bought a car in the last six months or who plan to buy a car in the next six months; all those aged 55 and over living in the community; or all users of a particular Internet Service Provider (ISP). Note your assumptions about the incidence of the target population in the wider population and the basis of the assumption. Explain how you intend to draw a sample from this population, for example using quota sampling or random sampling. (We look at sampling in detail in Chapter 8.) State the intended sample size, or the number of group discussions or depth interviews, and the size of any sub-samples that are relevant to the research objectives (for example those who bought their current car from the car dealership). Explain the reasons for these choices, and the implications they have. Point out if you envisage any problems in either contacting the sample or achieving the interviews and explain how you propose to overcome these.

Method of data collection

Specify the way in which you plan to collect the data, for example whether you plan to use accompanied visits (to the car showroom or on test drives), group discussions, individual or paired depth interviews; face-to-face or telephone interviews; pen and paper methods or computer-aided methods. Mention the reason why you are recommending a particular method. Specify the expected interview length, its content or coverage and its style. You do not need to include a fully worked-up discussion guide or questionnaire but you may want to show the client that you understand what topics or question areas need to be covered in order to address the research objectives. You may even want to give examples of the type of question to be used. In a qualitative project mention whether you plan to use stimulus material or projective techniques. To provide an accurate costing you will need to use the information you have been given in the brief to estimate questionnaire or interview length. You should make this, and the assumptions on which it is based (for example an estimate of the number of open questions and the number of closed questions), clear in the proposal so that the client can see how you reached the cost. Set out the implications of using the method suggested: what are the advantages and disadvantages? For example, if you have suggested telephone interviews it is worth pointing out that this will limit the interview length to about 20 minutes. Include information on how fieldwork is to be organised. You could explain that respondents for the group discussions will be recruited by specially trained qualitative recruiters; that the fieldforce for the quantitative survey meets the standards set by the Interview Quality Control Scheme; that work is conducted in accordance with the MRS Code of Conduct or the ESOMAR Code of Practice.

Data processing and analysis

Set out how the data will be handled. For qualitative research, note whether the group discussions and individual interviews will be recorded on audio or videotape; whether tapes will be sent to the client; whether full transcripts of all interviews will be made; whether these will be sent to the client. Mention how the analysis will be tackled: will the data be analysed using specialist analysis software? If full transcripts are not made will analysis be based on the moderator's notes and the tapes? For quantitative research you may want to provide details about data processing – the extent and nature of the editing process, the verification procedure after data entry, the cleaning of the dataset, the procedure for coding responses to open-ended questions. Confirm the analysis package that will be used and the format in which the data will be made available, for example as cross-tabulations or as a datafile; hard copy or electronic, or both. Give details of any weighting that might be applied to the data. Set out the type of analysis that will be provided – cross-tabulations, significance tests, specialised statistical techniques, for example.

Outputs

Make it clear what outputs you will provide, the format, the number of copies, the dates on which they will be provided. Set out the cost of additional deliverables, for example interim summary reports, so that the client can take account of the cost implications if these are required.

Ethical issues

In any proposal you must identify any ethical issues in relation to the research that you propose, and you must set out for the client how these issues will affect how the research is conducted and how the findings are presented and used. You must set out what steps you as the researcher will take to address the ethical issues, and you must set out what the client's own responsibilities are. The sort of ethical issues that may arise may cover all or any aspect of the proper and professional conduct of research from, for example, the protection of client confidentiality to the protection of anonymity of the respondent or the confidentiality of information provided by the respondent.

Many organisations, including universities and those funding research from the public or voluntary sector, require researchers to submit details of their research plans to research ethical approval committees. These committees scrutinise the research plans to ensure that the researchers have identified and are taking steps to address any ethical issues. Typically, they ask about the sample composition and whether it contains people who might be vulnerable; they ask about how informed consent will be achieved; they ask whether research participants run a realistic risk of being harmed by taking part in the research; and they ask about data protection issues and how data will be stored. For an example of a research ethical approval committee submission form, see www.cf.ac.uk/socsi/research/researchethics/approval-form-research-and-mphil-phd.doc.

As we saw in Chapter 1, there are a number of codes of conduct or codes of practice that set out how researchers (and clients) should behave. Researchers who are members of MRS must adhere to its Code of Conduct when planning and conducting research. For those researchers who are not members of MRS, the Code of Conduct nevertheless provides a useful guide to professional standards and practice. An extract from Sections A and B of the MRS Code of Conduct (www.mrs.org.uk) in Box 4.4 shows some of the points relevant to the research commission and proposal writing stage.

Box 4.4 Professional practice and the MRS Code of Conduct: project set up and design

Section A: General Rules of Professional Conduct
A1   Research must conform to the national and international legislation relevant to a given project including in particular the Data Protection Act 1998 or other comparable legislation applicable outside the UK.
A2   Members must take reasonable steps to avoid conflicts of interest with Clients or employers and must make prior voluntary and full disclosure to all parties concerned of all matters that might give rise to such conflict.
A3   Members must act honestly in dealings with Respondents, Clients (actual or potential), employers, employees, sub-contractors and the general public.

A4   The use of letters after an individual's name to indicate membership of MRS is permitted only in the case of Fellows (FMRS), Full Members (MMRS) and Associate Members (AMRS). These letters must not be used by any individual not admitted in any of these MRS categories of membership.

A6   Members must not make false claims about their skills and experience or those of their organisation.

A7   Members must take reasonable steps to ensure that others do not breach or cause a breach of this Code.
Comment: This includes:
Members taking reasonable steps to ensure that the people with whom they work (including other Members, non-member research practitioners, colleagues, Clients, consultants, sub-contractors) are sufficiently familiar with this Code that they are unlikely to breach or cause it to be breached unknowingly or unintentionally; and Members with responsibility for implementing processes, procedures and contracts, taking reasonable steps to ensure that they are such that this Code is unlikely to be breached or caused to be breached by others unknowingly or unintentionally.

A8   Members must not act in a way which might bring discredit on the profession, MRS or its Members.

A9   Members must not disparage or unjustifiably criticise other Members or other non-member researchers.

A10 Members must take all reasonable precautions to ensure that Respondents are not harmed or adversely affected as a result of participating in a research project.

Section B: Rules of Professional Conduct Applicable to Research

Designing and Setting up a Research Project

B1   Members must not knowingly take advantage, without permission, of the unpublished work of another research practitioner which is the property of that other research practitioner.
Comment: This means, where applicable, that Members must not knowingly carry out or commission work based on proposals prepared by a research practitioner in another organisation unless permission has been obtained.

B2   All written or oral assurances made by any Member involved in commissioning or conducting projects must be factually correct and honoured by the Member.

B3   Members must take reasonable steps to design research to the specification of the Client.

B4   Members must take reasonable steps to design research which meets the quality standards agreed with the Client.

B5   Members must take reasonable steps to ensure that the rights and responsibilities of themselves and Clients are governed by a written contract and/or internal commissioning contract.

B6   Members must not disclose the identity of Clients or any confidential information about Clients without the Client's permission unless there is a legal obligation to do so.

Source: MRS Code of Conduct 2005. Used with permission.

Week	Tasks
1	Project start meeting Discuss project management issues Agree key 'milestone' dates – approval re discussion guide, questionnaire and so on Agree target population/sample for qualitative work Agree date of next meeting
2	Choose sample for in-depth interviews Design discussion guide for in-depth interviews Get client approval for discussion guide Brief recruiters Recruit for in-depth interviews
3	Conduct in-depth interviews Transcribe interviews Analyse interviews Informal telephone debrief with client on findings to date
4	In-depth interviews completed Transcribe interviews Analyse interviews Prepare and send summary report of findings to client
5	Progress meeting Discuss findings from in-depth interviews Discuss development of survey questionnaire Prepare draft survey questionnaire and send to client
6	Meet with client to discuss draft questionnaire Amend draft questionnaire and send to client for comment and approval Conduct pilot interviews with approved draft questionnaire Feedback findings from pilot interviews to internal project team and to client Agree amendments to questionnaire
7	Finalise questionnaire Fieldwork planning and set up Run survey questionnaire briefing session
8	Fieldwork set up completed Fieldwork start Fieldwork visit with client
9, 10, 11	Draw up specification for analysis of data and send to client Agree analysis spec Fieldwork ongoing Answer field queries re editing and coding Data processing set up Liaise with client Agree code frames with client and field
12	Data processing ends Standard tables produced Check tables Prepare topline summary report for client
13	Finalise tables and send to client with datafile Meet to discuss findings and plan presentation/workshops
14	Write report and design presentation Send draft summary report and draft presentation of key findings to client Do presentation to client Design workshops on findings
15	Answer client follow-up queries Deliver two workshops to internal client team

Figure 4.2 Example 1 of a draft project timetable

Timetable

Include a draft timetable or work schedule, highlighting key dates, especially those that are dependent on input from the client. Two different formats are shown below. Figure 4.2 is set out as a table showing the dates associated with key tasks or 'milestones' (you could add a third column to show the outputs associated with the tasks). Figure 4.3, a Gantt chart, shows the individual activities or tasks as bars with week numbers or days, so that it is clear when

Box 4.5 Working out project timings

Working out precise project times can be difficult – there are so many elements involved that impact on timings, for example:

the nature of the research – whether qualitative or quantitative or a combination;
the size, scope and complexity of the project;
the method of data collection and data capture;
the nature of the population under study – ease of accessing the population or sample, the strike rate or speed and ease of recruitment;
the length of the interview;
the number of interviews;
the geographic scope of the research;
the time of year (the impact of holidays);
data processing and analysis needs;
reporting requirements;
thinking time – time needed for interpretation, comparison with other data;
the extent of liaison required with the client during the project.

Table 4.1 below gives a rough idea of the time involved from briefing to reporting for a range of different projects.

Table 4.1 Guideline to approximate turnaround times for domestic research

Method	Sample	Sample size	Turnaround time
Group discussions (face to face)	Consumer	6 groups	4 weeks
In-depth interviews	Business	12	3 to 4 weeks
Street survey (pen and paper interviewing)	Consumer	300	4 to 6 weeks
Face to face/in-home (computer-aided personal interviewing) using random sample	Consumer	600	4 to 6 weeks (depending on response rate)
C-aided self-interviewing (15-min interview)	Business	400	3 to 4 weeks
CAPI hall test (20-min interview)	Consumer	400	2 weeks
Postal survey	Business	300	2 to 3 months (depending on response rate)
Email or web survey	Business	300	3 to 4 weeks (depending on response rate)

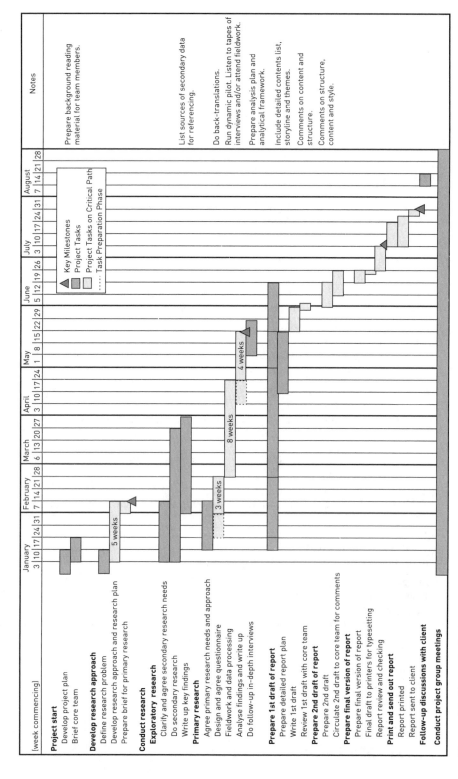

Figure 4.3 Example 2 of a draft project timetable

different phases begin and end and where they overlap. At this stage you may not be able to include exact dates – this will depend on the client giving the go-ahead – but you can put in week numbers and add in the dates when the details have been confirmed. In drawing up the timetable think of the practicalities. If possible, and it is not always possible, build in some contingency time; if the timetable is tight, mention this to the client and explain why.

Costs

Include details of the cost of conducting the research proposed and the assumptions on which these costs are based. The detail in which you present the costs may vary depending on custom and practice within your organisation, or on the level of detail requested by the client, and by the nature of the project. Some clients want to see an overall cost plus an estimate of expenses; others want to see the number of hours each staff member will spend on the project and his or her daily or hourly charge-out rate. A quantitative costing might be presented on a task-by-task basis, or as a client service cost plus a 'field and tab' cost. An example of a project costing grid for client service time for three staff grades is given in Table 4.2. The daily rates included are for illustrative purposes only.

A qualitative costing might be presented in terms of the cost per group or depth interview, or as one total cost, or it may be broken down into recruitment costs, fieldwork costs (venue hire, refreshments, transport, incentives), moderator's fee and report writing fee. Box 4.7 is an example of how a cost for a qualitative project might be presented in a proposal. Again, the costs presented are for illustrative purposes only.

Be clear about the length of time for which the costs you quote are valid. The time that elapses between submitting the proposal and being commissioned to do the work may be considerable and costs may rise (or fall) in the interim. Be clear also about the costs for which the client will be liable if they cancel. See the paragraph on terms and conditions of business below. Make sure you state whether the cost you have quoted includes or excludes any relevant sales tax. Costing international projects can be difficult, especially with fluctuating exchange

Table 4.2 Example of a costing grid for client service time

Staff/rate per hour	Director €1000	Manager €750	Senior Exec €500	Research Exec €250
Task	Estimated time			
Project team briefing	1	1	1	1
Questionnaire design	1	1	5	5
Fieldwork briefing		1	1	1
Fieldwork visit			5	5
Design of analysis spec		1	2	1
Data checking			1	4
Preparation of topline findings		1	2	7
Discussion of findings with team	2	2	2	2
Discussion of findings with client	1	1	1	1
Report preparation	1	2	4	21
Presentation preparation	2	2	2	7
Delivery of presentation	4		4	
Project administration				7
Total time per team member	12	12	30	62
Total cost per team member	€12,000	€9,000	€15,000	€15,500
Total client service cost				**€51,500**

rates. In costing an international project make it clear in which currency you are billing the client and, if exchange rates apply, what range of fluctuations in the rates (typically ±10 per cent) will be acceptable before it is necessary to recalculate the cost.

It can be difficult to price the service you offer clients: on the one hand, you do not want to under-value what it is you offer; on the other, you do not want to over-price it. You will get some feedback from clients about whether or not your costs are competitive, especially if you are involved in a competitive tendering process, and you may get some information informally from other practitioners. You may find it worthwhile consulting the ESOMAR *Global Prices Study*, which is carried out periodically, the most recent in 2007. It provides information on costs for a range of research projects and types of research (consumer and business to business; qualitative and quantitative; various methods of data collection) across more than 60 countries; it also gives information on charge-out rates for junior and senior researchers.

Box 4.6 Working out costs

The cost of a project is closely related to the expenditure of time. In particular, it will depend on the degree of difficulty obtaining respondents, the length of interview, and so number of interviews possible per shift, the total number of interviews, the location of the interview, the type of interview, the analysis requirements, and the project management and reporting requirements. Costing procedures vary. For example, the data processing and client service costs for a quantitative project may be worked out by those departments in an agency, or by the supplier, on the basis of an hourly rate for the grades of staff involved and the number of hours it is likely to entail. Hourly (and daily) charge-out rates are calculated on the basis of employee costs and overheads – the cost of office space, the cost of equipment and so on – and include a profit margin. The field department or fieldwork supplier may work out fieldwork costs. The strike rate or number of interviews achievable in an interviewer shift, the cost of that interviewer shift and its associated expenses (equipment and venue hire, travel and subsistence costs and so on) plus the cost of managing the project – the cost of supervisor time and administrative time – will all be used in reaching a total cost.

Box 4.7 Example of a qualitative research costing

The cost for completing six group discussions, from recruitment to reporting, would be £25,200 plus respondent incentives (at £65 per person and assuming eight per group) of £3,120, giving a total cost of £28,320. The cost for the four- and five-group options, as requested, is given in Table 4.3.

Table 4.3 Group costs

Option	Cost (£)	Cost per group (£)	Incentives (£)	Total cost (£)
Six groups	25,200	4,200	3,120	28,320
Five groups	23,000	4,600	2,600	25,600
Four groups	19,800	4,950	2,080	21,880

The costs include the following:

- briefing of recruiters;
- recruiters' fees (for recruitment and hosting of groups);
- recruitment costs (preparation of sampling frame, printing of recruitment questionnaires, etc.);
- venue hire;
- respondents' refreshments;
- consultant fees for project management, moderating, analysis and reporting;
- presentation;
- three copies of presentation charts and management summary report.

The costs quoted here are exclusive of VAT and do not include moderator's travel and subsistence expenses, which would be agreed when the location of the groups is decided. The cost does not include respondents' travel costs. We would recommend a contingency of £20 per respondent (£160 per group) should we need to arrange transport for respondents.

Box 4.8 Headings for a research proposal

- Introduction
- Background to the problem
- Research objectives
- Approach to the research
- Outputs
- Ethical issues
- Timetable
- Costs
- Relevant previous experience
- Project team CVs
- Terms and conditions of business

Relevant previous experience

This is your chance to sell, to show your credentials, to tell the client why *you* should conduct the research. Rather than presenting a standard credentials pitch, tailor it to the particular research brief. Think about what you bring to this subject matter, to this type of research, to this project. The client may request details of project team members. Whether this is the case or not, it is useful to include a set of short CVs or résumés of key staff designed to show experience and expertise in the area.

Terms and conditions of business

The proposal is an important contractual document as well as a selling tool. It is important to include information on your terms and condition of business, including notice of your adherence to the MRS Code of Conduct or ICC/ESOMAR Code of Practice; how you plan to bill the client; the exchange rate to be used in converting foreign currencies; an assertion of the right to amend the project cost if the client changes the specification; what payment is due if the client cancels the project after commissioning it. Two examples follow.

Statement of Terms and Conditions of Business 1

As members of the professional body, MRS, we adhere to the Society's Code of Conduct. The Code incorporates the key principles of the Data Protection Act 1998. Details of this can be found on the MRS website – www.mrs.org.uk

We invoice 50 per cent of the total cost upon commission of the project with the final 50 per cent due on delivery of the presentation and report. All invoices are payable within 30 days. We place a 5 per cent per month surcharge on unpaid invoices.

Statement of Terms and Conditions of Business 2

Payment
50% of total project cost due on commission of work
25% of total cost due at start of quantitative (Stage 2) fieldwork
25% of total cost due at delivery of final report
Payment is due within 14 days of date of invoice
A late payment charge of 1.5% per month is levied on payments outstanding after that date
Costs are valid for six weeks from today.
Fieldwork costs are calculated on a Euro/GBP exchange rate of €1.00 = £0.80
Should this rate vary by ±10% during the valid period we reserve the right to re-calculate the costs

Cancellation charges
Should you agree to undertake the research and then cancel it the following charges apply:

Cancellation up to six weeks' in advance of start	no charge
Cancellation between four and six weeks of start	20% of total cost
Cancellation between two and four weeks of start	35% of total cost
Cancellation between one and two weeks of start	50% of total cost
Cancellation within one week of start	100% of total cost

It is also worth including something asserting your intellectual property rights. Although the vast majority of clients and research agencies operate in an ethical way, some are unaware of such guidelines and others ignore them. You may want to include a short piece along the following lines:

Please note that a specification or proposal for a project drawn up by one research agency is the property of that agency and may not be passed on to another agency without the permission of the originating research agency.

Meeting the proposal submission deadline

The research proposal should be submitted on time. It creates a poor impression if the research proposal arrives late. In government tendering a deadline is set – for example 15.00 hours on 17 October – and no proposal will be accepted after that time, even one minute after it. Other clients are less precise – close of business on Thursday or Tuesday morning may be the instruction. A deadline is a deadline and you should use it as an opportunity to show that you can complete a piece of work on time.

Box 4.9 Example of key elements of a research proposal

As was noted above, the form of a research proposal will vary depending on a whole range of factors including organisation or personal style; relationship with the client; similarity of the project to previous projects. The proposal below is an 'outline' style proposal for a two-stage (qualitative followed by quantitative) multi-country research project in the business-to-business area.

Background and introduction

The John Doe Graduate Business School at Wonderland University provides postgraduate and professional business education. The aim of its one year programme, Master of Science in Marketing, is to give students – or as it refers to them, marketing advisors – practical experience in marketing and help them develop management and professional skills. More specifically, the programme aims to help its marketing advisors develop a business and marketing knowledge base and build skills in team work and team building, communication, negotiation, goal-setting and leadership. It aims to help them with their personal as well as professional development. The learning culture is one of learning by doing. By working on assignments of commercial significance to the School's partner organisations, advisors learn 'hard skills' that benefit their employers immediately they start work. The 'soft skills' they acquire via the course can help them progress quickly to senior management level.

As a result of this skills profile, the School has found that marketing advisors find jobs quickly, and in well-known, high profile organisations. Many take up positions such as assistant brand manager, marketing executive and business development executive. A number of graduates of the programme now hold senior management roles in leading national and international organisations.

The programme directors are constantly seeking ways of improving the course and the employability of its graduates. To help do this effectively they want to understand in more detail how effective marketing education really is in preparing people for senior positions in major European and international organisations. The research findings will be used to review and, if need be, improve the marketing education programme. It is likely that the findings will be published in the relevant marketing education journal.

▶

Aims and objectives: what it is you want to achieve with this research

From your brief we understand that you want to ensure that the MSc in Marketing is a first-rate qualification, one that allows its graduates to obtain jobs in major organisations and to progress rapidly to senior management posts within those organisations. To do this you need to know what it is that allows this to happen – what makes those with a postgraduate marketing degree attractive to these organisations and what makes them move quickly through the ranks to senior positions. What knowledge base do they need? What hard skills? What soft skills? What sort of experience?

The assumption in your brief is that marketers do not get senior positions within top companies – or rather they are less likely than those in other disciplines or departments (for example, finance and accounting, or law, or engineering) to secure these 'c-level' jobs. This is something that we feel is worth exploring via secondary research, which we have not costed for here but which we would be happy to discuss further with you.

This leads us to your three main objectives:

1. To understand why marketers don't get senior positions within top companies. In other words, to address the question, Why are marketers less likely than others to become C-level or board level executives, CEOs or COOs?
2. To determine where the fault lies. Is it within marketing education? If so, what are the problems with marketing training? What is missing? How could it be improved? In other words, to understand the role of postgraduate marketing education in helping marketers achieve senior positions.
3. To get guidance on the course of action for marketing education.

In other words, to address the question, What exactly do you need to do to improve graduates' employability and 'promotability'?

The sample: who to talk to?

Who has the answers to these key questions? In your brief you have identified CEOs. We would also recommend that you include senior recruitment consultants, those who recruit people to senior posts within major organisations. We believe that it may also be worth including senior human resource directors, those who are involved in recruitment and promotion. We feel that all three groups will be able to offer insight and understanding.

Suggested approach

We propose a two-stage approach: a qualitative study followed by a quantitative phase.

Location coverage

Since many of your former and current marketing advisors (and future ones) work in international organisations, and since the findings of this research may have wider significance, you have decided that the scope of the research should extend outside the UK. Specifically, you wish to talk to those in Ireland, France and Scandinavia. We would suggest two additions to the list: Germany and the Netherlands. As the biggest economy in Europe and home to many major brand owning organisations we feel it would be important to include respondents from German organisations.

We recommend the Netherlands on the same basis – it is home to many well-known brands and English is widely spoken among its business community, making it a possible place of employment for English-speaking graduates.

In addition, from our own experience researching the views of business leaders across Europe for other clients, we have found responses to be influenced by culture. Interviewing in the UK, Ireland, France, Germany, Netherlands and Scandinavia will give you a perspective on that.

At the qualitative stage of the research we would recommend conducting at least two interviews in each of five countries in order to get as wide a view as possible, cultural differences and all, to inform the quantitative. At the quantitative stage we would recommend interviewing in up to seven countries.

To help elucidate the research problem more fully, and to understand the key issues in more depth, we would suggest a programme of exploratory qualitative research. It is important, we feel, to understand what is going on from the point of view of business leaders and those recruiting future leaders.

Ideally these type of interviews should be conducted face to face. However, both the groups we have identified are 'elite' groups – they are difficult to get access to for research; they are important people with busy schedules. We would therefore recommend interviewing them by telephone at pre-arranged times. We would recommend that you conduct a minimum of ten interviews (see below). Each interview will last for about 20–30 minutes. From experience, this is the maximum length of time many of the target groups will be prepared to spend. It will be conducted by experienced researchers with expertise in this kind of interview with this type of respondent. The interview will be designed to cover key topics and issues but will be open-ended enough to allow the researcher to explore relevant issues with the respondent. To encourage respondents to take part we would advise offering them an incentive – either a thank you payment to themselves or to a charity of their choice. It can also help secure an interview by promising to send a copy of the published report to participants.

This exploratory stage should provide insight into and understanding of the key issues, useful in their own right. It will also help further define and refine the objectives for the second stage of the research, and it will provide key information for questionnaire design. A summary of the key elements of this stage are given below.

Summary of Stage 1: Qualitative telephone interviews (20 to 30 minutes)

Sample
- CEOs and C-level HR executives of major brand owning organisations
- Recruitment consultants (those recruiting senior/c-level executives to major brand owning organisations)

Location
- UK
- Ireland
- France
- Germany
- Netherlands or Sweden

▶

Number of interviews
10 in total:

- one CEO or C-level HR executive per country (at least two CEOs overall)
- one recruitment consultant per country

Recording/transcription
- Interviews will be recorded
- Recorded interviews will be translated (where necessary) and transcribed verbatim

Analysis
- Transcripts will be analysed and key issues and themes drawn out
- Findings presented in a summary report and used as basis for survey questionnaire

Stage 2: Quantitative telephone interviews (15 to 20 minutes)
The aim of the quantitative phase is to quantify the issues uncovered at the qualitative stage – to help understand how widespread they are, whether they differ by industry sector or by country.

The level of detail you want from the analysis, and the statistical precision and accuracy you require, are determined largely by sampling method and sample size. This is something we would want to talk to you about in more detail. Both have an impact on costs. For the purposes of costing this proposal we have assumed a sample size of 200. A sample of this size should deliver results that give you clear guidance on your key issues. It will, however, restrict the level of detailed analysis you can do – for example, it would be difficult to report meaningfully on the findings from CEOs of French organisations in the travel and transport sector.

We would recommend telephone interviewing as the most cost-effective and feasible method of data collection among this group. To cover the issues in some detail we believe will take 15 to 20 minutes.

A summary of the key elements of this stage is given below.

Stage 2: Quantitative telephone interviews – Summary

Number of interviews
- 200

Sample
Respondents (NB final split may depend on level of insight of each group as shown in indepth interviews):

- CEOs
- C-level HR directors
- Recruitment consultants

Location and suggested sample size by country
- Ireland and UK (50 interviews)
- Sweden, Finland and/or Norway (60)
- France (30)
- Germany (30)
- Netherlands (30)

Top brand owning companies in the following sectors (spread per country)
- Financial services
- Telecoms/electronics
- Consumer goods
- Retail
- Pharmaceuticals
- Travel and transport

Length of interview
- 15–20 minutes maximum
- Mostly closed questions bar one final open ended

Literature review
As we noted earlier, although we have not costed for it here we would strongly recommend a comprehensive review of the literature in this area. This would be certainly be helpful prior to the start of the primary research – before the qualitative work begins – but it would be advisable before writing up the findings for any academic or business journal. It would help locate the issue in its wider context.

Evaluating a proposal

How do you know if a research proposal you have received will produce effective research? Read the research proposal thoroughly, several times. Meet with the research suppliers (at your office or at theirs – meeting at their place may give you more insight into their working practices). Asking the suppliers to present or discuss the proposal is a useful way of gauging their ability to undertake the work and will help you to determine whether you can develop a working relationship with them. Box 4.10 is a guide to the sort of questions you might ask as you read the proposal or as you discuss it with the supplier.

Box 4.10 Useful questions in evaluating a proposal

The problem and the research objectives
- Has the researcher demonstrated a clear understanding of the problem?
- Has the researcher shown a clear understanding of the context of the problem and the decisions to be made on the basis of the research?
- Has the researcher clearly identified the key research objectives and the research questions?
- Has the researcher made any incorrect assumptions?

The research design
- Will the research design or approach suggested deliver the right kind of evidence?
- Has the researcher made a solid and credible case for the approach suggested? ▶

- Has the researcher identified any limitations of this approach?
- Will the data produced be credible?
- Has the researcher clearly and precisely identified the target population?
- Has the researcher made a plausible case for the proposed sampling strategy?
- Is the sampling strategy appropriate to the aims of the research?
- Is the method of data collection suitable?
- Has the researcher identified any limitations of this method?
- Has the researcher addressed quality control issues?
- To what standard is fieldwork conducted?
- Is it clear how the data are to be analysed and presented? Is this approach suitable?
- Can the researcher provide normative data for comparison?
- Has the researcher suggested a framework for interpretation of the findings?

Ethical issues
- Have any ethical or legal issues been identified and dealt with appropriately?

Timing and costs
- Is the timetable suggested in line with your own and is it manageable?
- Is the cost justified and is it clear where the costs arise? Is it value for money?
- Have all contingencies been allowed for?

Experience
- Has the researcher the right level and kind of experience to deliver the research specified?
- Is the staffing suggested appropriate? Do the personnel have the right amount and type of experience?
- Has the researcher added any value, provided useful insights, done more than you expected?
- Is the proposal clearly set out, well written and easy to follow?

Responding to a proposal

Once you have chosen the proposal that best meets your needs the next step is to inform the supplier in writing and agree to meet to discuss it in detail. This meeting is sometimes called a Project Start meeting. It gives all parties the chance to bring up any outstanding issues, to talk through how the research will happen and to clarify what each expects of the other. Any amendments to the original brief or the proposal or subsequent research plan should be agreed and put in writing. For example, it may be that the research proposed is outside your budget. You may want to discuss with the supplier what changes could be made to meet the budget (one less group discussion, a smaller sample size) without of course sacrificing or compromising the objectives.

It is good practice to inform those who have not been successful with their proposal, and to tell them why they were not successful. This allows the supplier to learn from the experience, address any weaknesses they may have and so improve the service they offer.

The client–researcher relationship

To be able to deliver, and to commission, good research it is important that client and supplier establish a good working relationship. A good working relationship is characterised by a rapport between the parties – a sense of being on the same wavelength, and each understanding the role of the other (Pyke, 2000). The client has certain expectations of the researcher: the researcher should be competent in the design and management of a research project. Yet the client does not want someone who is merely good at the mechanics of research but rather someone who can see the 'big picture' and who can put the research findings into this picture. Failure to do this is a common criticism of researchers: clients often report that researchers are too focused on the research process and the data and not focused enough on what the data say about the problem (Bairfelt and Spurgeon, 1998). The client expects the researcher to have a sound understanding of and an interest in the business and the issues they face, to think about the context of the problem, the wider issues involved and how the research can help address these. The researcher should not ignore the question of what is to be done with the information provided by the research.

It is here that we come full circle: as a researcher you must always keep in mind why the research was commissioned in the first place; you will not be able to deliver effective research if you have not paid attention to the front end of the research process. If you have not fully understood the nature of the problem, the context of it, or what the client needs from the research, you will have problems at the delivery stage. Always think of the end result at the beginning. This can be difficult – it may not be possible to get access to the decision maker or the information end user, or information about them, particularly the sort of information that might help you understand the decision-making process and the culture and politics of the organisation. You therefore rely on your relationship with the client. From the researcher's point of view, for the relationship with the client to work best there should be no hidden agendas; the client should help establish an atmosphere in which the researcher feels able to explore or question the brief and reach a full understanding of the issues. In order to improve service delivery, the researcher should ask for (and the client should provide) open and honest feedback about the service.

Chapter summary

- The start of a research project typically involves the following:
  - identifying and defining the problem clearly and accurately;
  - identifying the information needs;
  - establishing the end use to which this information will be put;
  - communicating this information to a researcher via a brief;
  - describing the approach to the research via a proposal.

- The importance of spending time identifying, defining and clarifying the problem to be researched cannot be overstated. It is essential if good quality, actionable research is to be produced.

- A detailed research brief should contain the following information:
  - definition of and background to the problem;
  - why research is necessary;   ▶

- use of information;
- research objectives;
- target population;
- suggested approach;
- analysis required;
- deliverables, timings and budget.

- It is important that the researcher understands the brief fully. Anything that is not clear should be clarified with the client.

- In preparing a proposal the aim is to show that you understand the problem and its implications in the wider business context and that you have the expertise to deliver good quality research that will provide the information to address the problem.

- A research proposal should include:
  - an introduction and background to the problem;
  - statement of the research objectives;
  - approach to the research;
  - ethical issues and how they will be handled;
  - deliverables, timetable and costs;
  - relevant previous experience and project team CVs;
  - terms and conditions of business.

- The proposal should be evaluated to ensure that the research approach described will deliver the information required.

- Once a supplier has been chosen the client and supplier should meet to discuss in detail how the research is to be conducted. It is good practice to inform those who have not been successful with a proposal why they were not successful.

- To deliver, and to commission, good quality research client and supplier should establish a good working relationship.

- The client expects the researcher to be competent in designing and managing the research and to be able to understand the implications of the findings in the wider business context.

- The researcher and the client should be aware of and adhere to their ethical and professional responsibilties when commissioning and tendering for research.

Questions and exercises

1 Here are the key elements of a research brief sent out by a client, the general manager of a not-for-profit education and training centre. Having read the brief, you decide that you would like to meet the client face to face to discuss his requirements in more detail so that you might make useful suggestions about a way forward. List the questions that you want to ask at this meeting together with your rationale for asking them.

The brief: We are a not-for-profit education and training provider specialising in the delivery of IT programmes and courses to those aged 50 and over. We are based on the outskirts of a city with a population of around 100,000. Demand for our provision has remained steady over the last five years but we expect it to increase over the next five to ten years as the population of those aged 50 and over grows. Our building is now more than 100 years old and although it is in good condition we are finding it difficult and costly to adapt it to suit our needs and to meet health and safety and other regulations. We would like to build a new state-of-the-art training suite on our current site – we have outline planning permission to do so. We understand that government funding may be available to cover the capital cost of building the new facility. To make a sound case for this funding we would like to gather evidence via a programme of research. We should like you to provide us with costs for the following: a series of focus groups with existing users of our facilities; a survey of older people within our area; and an audit of the employment opportunities available to older people who have completed our training programmes. We have a budget for this research of around €10,000. The funding application must be submitted in two months' time. We should therefore like you to provide a detailed workplan that fits this time frame.

2 Imagine you are the client and you have just received the proposal outlined in Box 4.9.

   (a) Review this proposal using the guidelines given in the section on 'Preparing a proposal', listing the information, if any, that is missing.

   (b) List the questions that you would like to raise at a meeting with the researcher.

References

Bairfelt, S. and Spurgeon, F. (1998) *Plenty of data, but are we doing enough to fill the information gap?*, Proceedings of the ESOMAR Congress, Amsterdam: ESOMAR.

Brooker, S., Cawson, P., Kelly, G. and Wattam, C. (2001) 'The prevalence of child abuse and neglect: a survey of young people', *Proceedings of the Market Research Society Conference*, London: MRS.

ESOMAR (2007) *Global Prices Study,* Amsterdam: ESOMAR.

MRS Code of Conduct (2005), London: MRS (www.mrs.org.uk).

Poynter, R. and Ashby, Q. (2005) 'Quick, quick, slow! The case for slow research', *Proceedings of the Market Research Society Conference*, London: MRS.

Pyke, A. (2000) 'It's all in the brief', *Proceedings of the Market Research Society Conference*, London: MRS.

Recommended reading

Bijapurkar, R. (1995) *Does market research really contribute to decision making?*, Proceedings of the ESOMAR Congress, Amsterdam: ESOMAR.

Hedges, A. (2002) *Commissioning Social Research: A good practice guide*, London: Social Research Association. Also available at http://www.the-sra.org.uk/commissioning_sr.htm.

Moser, C. and Kalton, G. (1971) *Survey Methods in Social Investigation*, Aldershot: Dartmouth.

Punch, K. (2000) *Developing Effective Research Proposals*, London: Sage.

Smith, D. and Fletcher, J. (2001) *Inside Information: Making sense of marketing data*, London: Wiley.

Chapter 5

DOING SECONDARY RESEARCH

As we saw briefly in Chapter 2, secondary research, is sometimes referred to as desk research (the alternative name for primary research is field research) because you can do it without leaving your desk, making use of published sources – books, journals, magazines, newspapers, CDs; research reports; and research data available from a range of sources including internal and online databases and the Internet. It can take the form of a review of the published top-line statistics about a market or a group of people; a review or re-analysis of a dataset (quantitative or qualitative) – in whole or in part; or a review of the published reports of other researchers, including reviews of the scholarly literature on a theory or on previous research studies.

In this chapter we look at what is involved in doing secondary research. We give examples of some useful secondary sources. We also look at how data is stored and retrieved for secondary use and we look at data fusion and data mining.

Topics covered

- Why bother with secondary research?
- What is secondary research?
- Secondary sources
- Assessing quality and suitability
- Data storage and retrieval systems
- Analysing secondary data – data fusion and data mining

Relationship to MRS Advanced Certificate Syllabus

This chapter includes material relevant to Element 2 – Designing a Research Project in that it examines the place and the process of secondary research, which, as noted below, is a useful tool at the problem definition and research design stage (as well as at the end stages of a project).

Learning outcomes

At the end of this chapter you should be able to:

- understand the nature of secondary research;
- understand what is meant by secondary research and secondary data analysis;
- demonstrate knowledge of secondary sources;
- develop a strategy for conducting secondary research including use of online searches;
- evaluate the quality and suitability of secondary sources;
- understand the concepts of data storage and retrieval systems;
- understand what is involved in data fusion and why it is done;
- understand what is involved in data mining and why it is useful.

Why bother with secondary research?

Almost all research projects depend on or, at the very least, benefit from a secondary research stage. It is especially useful in the early stages of a project, helping you to clarify your thinking about the issues, helping with problem definition and with research design and planning. It is also very useful later in the life of a project when it can provide a context or framework for the analysis and interpretation of the findings (Case study 11.1 is an example).

It is important to keep in mind that the value or usefulness of any piece of research or set of data is rarely exhausted on its initial or primary application. The data or the findings may be useful in the same context at a later date, or they may be useful in a different context. One set of data may be combined with others – from very different sources – making the combined set more valuable and of greater use than the individual elements. Using existing data or findings as we noted above can be much cheaper than carrying out primary research; they are also relatively quick and easy to get hold of – unlike primary data they are already available and relatively easy to gain entry to, using the World Wide Web to access material on the Internet, for example, or via online internal and external databases.

Box 5.1 Uses and benefits of secondary research

- Answers the research problem without the need for primary research.
- Leads to a better understanding of the issues and the wider context of the problem.
- Helps define the problem.
- Helps in the development and formulation of hypotheses.
- Helps determine the nature of the evidence required to address the problem.
- Helps formulate an effective research design.
- Helps in the design of effective questions.
- Enriches the analysis and the interpretation of primary data.
- Sets the findings from primary research into a wider context.

Increasingly, commerical market researchers, following established practice among academic and social researchers, are conducting a form of secondary research – a formal or informal review of the existing literature on a topic (known as a literature review) – alongside primary research. This practice is particularly valuable as it can be used to increase knowledge and understanding of the topic under investigation; it allows you to benefit from the work and the thinking of others, for example those who have tried a particular research approach or those who have done research on the same or a similar topic, and so it enhances the quality of your own thinking.

Box 5.2 The literature review

In most academic and in some social research projects a formal literature review is conducted and often written up as a chapter in the final research report. But what is a literature review? A literature review is, or should be, a synopsis of and critical assessment of the relevant literature – the stuff that you found that relates directly to your research topic, the stuff that informed how you designed and conducted your research, and how you analysed and interpreted the data.

In writing a literature review there are two main pitfalls which must be avoided: using it to show that you know 'the area'; and presenting it without any critical thinking about the content.

Here is a guide to what a literature review should aim to show (Silverman, 2005, adapted from Murcott, 1997):

- What is already known about the topic
- What you have to say about what is known
- If anyone else has conducted the same research
- If anyone has done research that is related to your topic
- Where your research fits in with what has gone before
- Why your research is worth doing in the light of what has been done already.

Secondary research is of course a type of research in its own right: it is possible that an entire set of research objectives can be addressed by doing secondary research alone – with no need at all for more expensive primary research (Case study 5.1 below is an example).

What is secondary research?

Secondary research is a process that involves the following steps:

- identifying existing relevant sources of data or information;
- gaining access to them;
- assessing their suitability for your purposes;
- reviewing them and assessing their quality;
- learning from them and using this knowledge in your research.

Secondary sources

Secondary sources in a marketing context are often classified according to whether they are internal or external. Internal sources are those produced within the organisation, for example reports and/or data from previous research; financial data; and, crucial to the marketing function, sales data. External sources are those produced by others, outside the organisation, for example market reports by commercial organisations such as Mintel; and journals such as the *International Journal of Market Research*.

INTERNAL SOURCES

Technological developments in the last 15 to 20 years have meant that it is possible to capture, store and analyse huge volumes of the sort of data that marketers find useful. For example, data can be captured at the point of interaction with the customer, whether it is in person via EPOS (electronic point of sale) scanners or remotely via telephone, wireless and Internet technology. The data collected can be stored in and retrieved from databases and data warehouses designed to function as management information systems (MIS) or marketing information systems (MkIS). Such systems are often referred to as decision support systems (DSS) or executive information systems (EIS) or sometimes even enterprise intelligence systems, and are structured in a way that allows users to search for and retrieve the data they need for planning and control, and for strategy development, for example. We look in more detail later in the chapter at how these systems are built.

It is now relatively easy and inexpensive to record and store customer transactions and – through the use of 'loyalty' cards, sometimes called 'reward' or 'club' cards – log each transaction to the record of an individual customer. It works like this: you apply for the card to benefit from the organisation's promotion schemes; when you apply you give the organisation – a retailer or an airline, for example – your personal details; each time you make a transaction and offer your 'loyalty' card, your personal details from the card are collected and logged against that transaction. The organisation now has a record of your actual buying behaviour (that is, not your claimed buying behaviour – which is the sort of data that is recorded in a survey) in your personal record in its database.

These databases are thus a rich source for secondary research, providing detailed current and historic information about *actual* rather than *reported* buyer behaviour, giving the decision maker a different view of the market from that provided by primary research. Case study 5.1 below shows how the analysis of customer information recorded at the box offices of arts venues provided greater insight into customer behaviour than did customer surveys at the venues. It shows, too, how data can be shared and used for decision making by the several parties.

CASE STUDY 5.1

INSIGHT FROM SECONDARY DATA

Here we see how data originally recorded during sales transactions at the box offices of arts venues proved useful in understanding customer behaviour.

Why this case study is worth reading

This case study is worth reading for several reasons: it is an example of secondary research; it is an example of descriptive research; it is an example of the use of database data and the issues that it raises; it shows how insight can be generated from data records; it describes how the findings were not what the researchers expected; it describes some of the end uses of the research.

The key words are: box office software, enormous databases, complex, high-quality information, customers, basic reporting, extensive analysis, benchmark data, confidentiality agreement, obstacle, data-pooling, coding, categorisations, coverage, rate of data capture, drawbacks, trend information, crossover, geographic distribution, marketing planning, demographics.

Background

Since the development of box office software, performing arts venues in London have been accumulating enormous databases of complex and increasingly high-quality data on their customers. Basic reporting is offered but arts organisations tend to lack the resources to carry out more extensive analysis of this potentially rich data. Organisations rely on audience questionnaires (which tend to represent the most loyal and older audience members) and data from the Target Group Index Survey (TGI), which, it seems, is answered rather aspirationally regarding the arts. Also, due to a number of factors – including competitive environment, lack of resources, fears about Data Protection, lack of a culture of audience-focussed planning at senior level, and a nervousness about what the figures might reveal – there has been little sharing of data or of basic audience statistics between venues.

Unlocking the data

Then there became available a user-friendly software package called data:crunch. This software allowed users to produce sophisticated audience profiles (such as ticket yield, product crossover, audience churn, Mosaic Group and Type, Income and Lifestage [see Box 5.3 below on geodemographic classification systems], and trend information quickly and easily from any box office software package. It has now been used successfully by three regional audience development agencies to take data from their members and provide a regional benchmark of audience information, looking at markets for each artform, their size, characteristics (demographic profile, geographic spread) and behaviour (frequency, value, drive distance, advance purchase, churn, ticket yield, programme choice etc). We used it in a project called Snapshot London to provide a picture of audiences and their behaviour at a number of arts organisations.

The project plan

This is what we aimed to do:

- To include up to 20 organisations from Central London, where a reasonably representative sample could be covered.
- To concentrate on those with the best and largest databases in order to make best use of the resources we had available.
- To examine five years' worth of box office data from participating organisations.
- To give each participating organisation benchmark data for London as well as its own data within the data:crunch software, enabling each to carry out its own analysis. ▶

A confidentiality agreement guaranteed that the research organisation would only present publicly results regarding the overall benchmark and not any figures which pointed directly or indirectly at individual organisations. Any reference to a venue by name is made with that venue's permission.

Coding issues

An issue that had been an obstacle to data-pooling in the past was that of artform coding: those working within venues needed to work with subtle categorisations of their product whereas, for an umbrella study, higher-level categorisations were required. This was solved by allowing each organisation to use whatever product categorisation they liked for analysing their own data, but the benchmark database was coded at a higher level of categorisation which roughly matched the categories used in the TGI Survey, in research carried out by the Society of London Theatres and Theatrical Management Association and in data-pooling exercises elsewhere in the country. The product coding took place at two levels – Artform and Style.

Data capture issues

For some artforms we had a good or excellent representation or coverage of venues – and we found that their rate of data capture was good. For other artforms (e.g. Cinema or Visual Arts) coverage of venues was poor and we found that these venues had very little data capture. This is important in making any interpretation of the results; we have tended to issue figures for which we have at least good coverage, giving careful qualification elsewhere.

There are drawbacks in working with box office data:

- Not all ticket sales are sold with name and address capture. The venues taking part here all had very high rates, often exceeding 90 per cent and in many cases 95 per cent. Many sales without capture are those taken just before a performance.
- Only the buyer's details are captured for an average of just over two tickets sold per transaction. We have allowed for this as far as possible in that the benchmark data has been analysed in most cases at household level. However, it has to be accepted that not all attenders are captured and customer records will tend to under-represent their frequency of attendance.
- Not all venues were open for the entire five year period (1998–2002) and they were removed from any analysis of trend information over the entire period. (However, this enabled us to find out what happens to a venue's audience when it closes.)

Initial key findings

We thought that we would find a very small pool of arts audiences who attended very widely and frequently. In fact, the reverse proved to be the case. The pool of arts attenders upon which venues draw is very large – we found that over the five year period, some two million households had attended one of the participating venues, seven per cent of all households in Britain. Within London, 30 per cent of households had attended. And the geographic reach was broad – the few postal sectors that had no customers were in the Highlands of Scotland. This shows that there is a significant opportunity to improve retention and increase attendances. But it also shows that the arts serve a large cross-section of the population, which is good news for public funding and its administering bodies.

Venue crossover

Audiences in London are not skipping between venues with the fleetness of foot sometimes assumed. Most households (73 per cent) attend only one venue; 13 per cent attend two; and 13 per cent attend three or more. Comparing London's two main classical music venues, the Barbican and the Royal Festival Hall, we find that of their combined audience for orchestral concerts, only 11 per cent attended both venues. Looking at the combined opera audiences for the English National Opera and the Royal Opera House, only 12 per cent of this audience had attended both venues. It seems that the more venues and performances that exist, the more audiences are drawn.

Artform crossover

The percentage of households attending only one artform over five years is 69 per cent, slightly lower than the equivalent figure for venues. In other words, people are more likely to attend another artform at the same venue than they are to attend another venue. Nevertheless, the specificity of audiences' tastes has been a surprise, challenging long-held assumptions that the general public share the eclectic cultural habits of the arts professional and the keen attenders who respond to questionnaires.

Demographic and geographic distribution

There is a general perception of arts audiences as ageing and wealthy. We found that the proportion of younger arts attenders matches the population very closely. In terms of household income, arts audiences are wealthier than the population. From a marketing planning perspective, it is useful to analyse the relationship between the price people pay for their tickets and the distance they travel, which established that the further people travel, the more they pay, the larger their party-size is, and the more likely they are to return. So, for example, not bothering to mail previous attenders who live far away from your venue is a false economy.

Opera

We were asked by the Arts Council [an arts funding body] to conduct further analysis of audiences for opera in London. This served to show just how powerful this dataset is when mined to answer specific questions.

There were two drivers for the research: 1998–2002 was a period of instability for the two opera houses, the Royal Opera House and English National Opera. For almost the first two years the Royal Opera House was closed for refurbishment, reopening late in 1999. English National Opera closed for redevelopment in 2002.

We found that when each opera house closed, their audience simply stopped attending – they did not attend the other opera house during the closure. This is despite the fact that the venues are close to one another and that their audiences appear to be demographically similar. This provides enormous strength to the justification for the Arts Council's continuing support for two opera houses in London.

Source: Adapted from Brook, O. (2004) ' "I know what you did last summer" – arts audiences In London 1998–2002', MRS Conference, www.mrs.org.uk.

'Shopping basket analysis' can show what sets of products or brands are bought together among the different segments, for instance, and which ones rarely occur together. By examining trends in behaviour over time the researcher can build models to predict behaviour, sales volumes and revenue. This information can be used to understand, for example, how profitable different groups of customers or different types of outlet are, and what type of promotion works best for which group.

Loyalty card data, however, can be limited. While they give information about customer behaviour in the store, they do not give information on behaviour outside it (for which data from traditional consumer panels may be useful); the demographic information provided may not in all cases be accurate; and people may hold more than one card for the same store (Passingham, 1998). Also, the customer may not use the card for every transaction in the store. In addition, loyalty card data cannot be used to build a full picture of a store's or a vendor's customer base as some customers may refuse the offer of a card.

As Case study 5.1 shows, databases can be analysed to identify customer behaviour and sales patterns by different outlet types and by different regions and patterns of buying behaviour among customers. Analysis can also reveal the characteristics, demographic or geodemographic for example, that are associated with different behaviour patterns. These patterns and characteristics can be used to build profiles of customers and outlets, and to identify market segments and gaps in the market.

This type of research – analysing information in databases – is a form of *Category One* research (see Box 1.8 in Chapter 1). This is *classic confidential research* in which there is no feedback of any personal data except to those involved in the project who are bound by the MRS Code of Conduct and agree to use the data for research purposes only. Should, however, the database owner use the database to generate a sample to contact people to participate in primary research, then data protection issues arise. In this circumstance the client (in the UK) must ensure that it is registered with (has notified) the Information Commissioner (www.ico.gov.uk) concerning the use of the data. If the client's 'notification' includes market research, then it is possible to use the database for this purpose. For further information have a look at *The Data Protection Act 1998 and Market Research: Guidance for MRS Members* (www.mrs.org.uk/standards/dp.htm#guide).

EXTERNAL SOURCES

External sources, which can also be integrated into an organisation's DSS (decision support system), are data generated by those outside the organisation. In the world of marketing and market research, external sources tend to be put into one of two categories: those produced by government departments, its agencies and related bodies and sometimes referred to as *official statistics*; and those produced by trade bodies, commercial research organisations and business publishers, and sometimes called *unofficial statistics*. Of course the world of available knowledge, information and data is much wider than that, including everything that one might expect to find in a library – books, reference works, scholarly journals, magazines, periodicals and newspapers as well as bibliographic databases, statistical publications and the full range of electronic resources.

Material tends to come in either print (hard copy format) or electronic format (offline CD-ROM or online).

We saw in Chapter 1 that one of the main uses of research is to reduce risk, thus helping decision makers arrive at cost-effective solutions to their organisation's problems. Case study 5.3 below shows how geodemographic data – readily available, easy to access and straightforward to use – can be used in this regard; in this case, to provide information that will help in the decision about where to site a retail store.

Box 5.3 Geodemographic information systems

Geodemographic data (sometimes called 'geodems') are a form of secondary data often used in market research. They are used to build geodemographic classification/information systems, which are then used primarily to identify and target different types of consumers.

The basis of most geodemographic information systems is more or less the same: they relate the demographic characteristics of the residential population, derived from the Census at the smallest geographical unit within the Census for which data are available, to geographic information about that area (see Case study 5.2 below). The sources of information used to construct the system and build categories and profiles may also include the electoral register, postal address files, car registration information, credit rating data, data from surveys on media use or attitudes, and data from customer databases. The end product is a classification of neigbourhoods or areas within which people with certain characteristics live. The classification or segmentation of the neighbourhoods is based on a cluster analysis. Each 'cluster' or type of neighbourhood will be different from every other cluster or neighbourhood – because the type of people – the type of consumers – living in that neighbourhood will be different. A neighbourhood in one town may be classified as belonging to the same cluster or type of neighbourhood in another town, because the characteristics of people in that neighbourhood are the same or similar.

Since they are rooted in a geographic location, knowing a person's postcode or postal address is enough to allow you to assign them to a particular geodemographic group. As a result each record held on a customer database can be assigned to a geodemographic cluster; if you know the area from which a sample, sub-sample or respondent was drawn, individual cases from a survey can be assigned to a geodemographic cluster. This means that data from different sources – from a customer database or from any type of survey – can be analysed in terms of its geodemographic profile. Thus data from a survey on buying behaviour, survey data on attitudes and values, and data from a customer database can be linked – the geodemographic classification of each unit or case being the common variable for fusing the data. The database created by this fusion allows us to examine relationships between different types of consumers, their attitudes and their behaviour.

Using geodemographic information can help organisations to gain a more in-depth understanding of their customers' habits, preferences, attitudes and opinions. This information can be used to develop strategy and to target products, services and marketing communication more effectively. Applying geodemographic codes to, say, existing sales data on customers derived from loyalty cards will help give you information on their demographic and lifestyle characteristics. If you know the geodemographic profile of your customers you can use a GIS to find where other people with similar profiles are located. This information can be useful in planning store location, store type and size, product mix within the store and so on (as Case study 13.3 shows); and in targeting marketing and advertising campaigns.

'Off the shelf' geodemographic information systems are available for most European countries as well as for the United States, Canada and Australia, New Zealand, Hong Kong and major cities in China. Several commercial organisations ▶

specialise in providing them, including CACI, which produces a product called ACORN – A Classification of Residential Neighbourhoods; Experian, which produces MOSAIC and EuroMOSAIC; and Claritas, which produces Super Profiles.

CACI's ACORN system divides the population of the UK into 56 types, which are grouped together into 17 groups spread across five categories:

A Wealthy Achievers
B Urban Prosperity
C Comfortably Off
D Moderate Means
E Hard Pressed

Within the Urban Prosperity category, for example, are three groups which cover 11 types: Prosperous Professionals; Educated Urbanites; and Aspiring Singles. In addition to a classification system on a country-by-country basis, there are also classifications for regions.

Experian's MOSAIC offers a classification system based on data from around 22 countries. This 'Mosaic Global' system divides consumers into ten groups:

A Sophisticated Singles
B Bourgeois Prosperity
C Career and Family
D Comfortable Retirement
E Routine Service Workers
F Hardworking Blue Collar
G Metropolitan Strugglers
H Low Income Elders
I Post Industrial Survivors
J Rural Inheritance.

There are other systems and products available that classify people at the individual level, according to income, buying behaviour and life stage, and which can be tied into a GIS. There are also segmentation systems that classify online customers according to their behaviour on the Internet.

CASE STUDY 5.2

WHICH SITE? GEODEMOGRAPHICS HAS THE ANSWER

This case study shows how geodemographics can be used in deciding where to site retail stores.

Why this case study is worth reading

This case study is worth reading for several reasons: it shows how geodemographic data – data readily available – can be used to reduce risk in decision making; it illustrates how the process works; it lists the variables that are used in the decision-making process.

The key words are: geodemographics, targeting local differences, site location, catchment area, catchment profile, site potential.

Introduction

Geodemographics were first used by retailers as a means of taking some of the risk out of major investment decisions involved in new store locations. Historically, location decisions were based on practical experience. Nowadays, where expansion is likely to involve the consideration of sites with risky market, cost, competition or planning characteristics, that experience needs to be supplemented by more rigorous assessments.

In the more mature retail sectors such as grocery, clothing, CTNs (Confectioners, Tobacconists and Newsagents), petrol retailing and so on, sectors where there is a requirement to target to consumer demand, ACORN and Pinpoint [geodemographic classification and analysis systems] can provide retailers with expenditure estimates for a merchandise sector or site, thereby placing a monetary value on local markets.

Typically, a site location and a definition of its catchment area are provided by the retailer in terms of either postcode sectors or radius of x kilometres from the site location. The output generated by services such as ACORN and Pinpoint compares the population and/or household profile of the area with some or all of:

- the national (GB) average
- the retailer's national profile
- the retailer's 'target' profile if this has previously been identified.

In addition it can provide for the location:

- population/household numbers
- £ value of the defined market spend available from the catchment.

When referenced against existing stores or the chain profile this provides an indicator of the site potential.

Source: Adapted from Johnson, M. (1997) 'The application of geodemographics to retailing: meeting the needs of the catchment', *International Journal of Market Research*, 39, 1, pp. 201–24, www.ijmr.com.

Government published data

Governments and related bodies collect a wide range of social, economic and business data, from the Census of Population and the demographic characteristics of the population (see Case study 5.3 below), through their spending habits, lifestyle and attitudes, to information about different market sectors, from agriculture to tourism, and information on domestic and international trade and key economic indicators.

In the United Kingdom, the Government Statistical Service (GSS) – an organisation spread among 30 or so government departments and bodies – is responsible for providing 'Parliament, government and the wider community with the statistical information, analysis and advice needed to improve decision making, stimulate research and inform debate'. Within the GSS it is the role of the Office for National Statistics (ONS), a body independent of any other government department, to collate research and statistical publications produced by government departments and related bodies in compendia publications and databases. These publications can be bought, accessed in hard copy form via libraries or accessed online via the ONS website (www.statistics.gov.uk).

Government statistical services exist in most countries. You can find a comprehensive list at the University of Michigan Website www.lib.umich.edu/govdocs/stforeig.html. In Ireland the body responsible is the Central Statistics Office (www.cso.ie); in Australia it is the Australian Bureau of Statistics (www.abs.gov.au); in the United States it is the US Census Bureau (www.census.gov); in the European Union it is Eurostat (http://epp.eurostat.ec.europa.eu). Government departments for trade and foreign affairs and the embassies of foreign governments are useful sources of data on international business environments, providing information on political, legal, economic and cultural aspects of doing business or research.

The quality and usefulness of government produced data should be assessed in the same way and with the same rigour as data from other sources.

CASE STUDY 5.3

LEVERAGING THE CENSUS FOR RESEARCH AND MARKETING

This case study describes some of the ways in which UK Census data can be used to help researchers and marketers.

Why this case study is worth reading

This case study is worth reading for several reasons: it is an example of the use of Census data; it shows how Census data can be used as a source of demographic information for area and customer profile and as a source of geographic information for building classification systems.

The key words are: valuable source, profile of the population, geographic detail, demographic resource, survey research, applications, customer analysis, locational, area profiling, customer profiling, geodemographic classifications, raw variables, 'off-the-shelf' geodems, customised discriminators, modelling, drill down.

Introduction

The UK Census represents a valuable source of data to all researchers. It provides a unique profile of the population at a level of geographic detail far beyond anything available from commercial or other government surveys. As such, it is the single most important demographic resource for informing survey research in this country.

Applications to customer analysis

Applications of Census data to customer analysis fall into two categories of use, which may be deployed either separately or in combination:

- Demographic – essentially using the Census as a source of demographic information
- Locational – using the Census as a tool for geographical location

The relevance of the Census to any specific company with domestic customers will depend on the extent to which the customer base is segmented – either demographically, through the nature of the company's products or services, or geographically, due to the company's trading area or catchment areas of its branches or outlets. If either or both forms of segmentation apply, then Census analysis should prove to be relevant and useful.

Demographic applications

The Census may be applied to gain a better understanding of the customer base through demographic profiling. Profiling is typically undertaken in two steps:

(a) Area profiling

The first step is to determine the trading area in which the majority of customers reside and obtain the Census profile of the trading area population. This gives a picture of the base population from which the company's customers have been drawn. For products available nationally, this base will therefore be the UK (or possibly Great Britain) population. For a business with a limited trading area, such as a restaurant, the base might be the population living within X miles, or Y minutes drive time, of the restaurant location.

(b) Customer profiling

Determining the corresponding Census profile for a sample of customers who reside in that trading area. The customer profile is interpreted by comparison with the base population profile from step (a) in order to identify 'what makes a customer'. Equivalent profiles may also be usefully produced for subsets of customers, such as 'high value' vs 'low value' or purchasers of different products. Confidentiality requirements prevent customers from being matched to the Census, as if it were a lifestyle database, and then profiled on their actual characteristics. Therefore, step (b) works by assigning each customer to their Output Area (OA), based upon their home postcode, and attaching the OA profile as a set of proportions for the various demographic categories. A Census customer profile can then be produced by summing those proportions – so while it will not be the actual demographic profile for those customers, it will represent the profile of their Output Areas. Experience has shown that if the customers were significantly over or under represented in certain demographic groups, this would be evident from their Census profile.

Locational analysis

Each Output Area has a known geographical location and therefore the Census may be used to find the areas that contain certain types of people. For example, if a restaurant undertakes the demographic analysis described in the last section and finds that its customers tend to be, say, 'middle aged, Social Grade AB, without children', then it could apply these criteria to search for potential site locations in areas with highest concentrations of these characteristics.

Use of geodemographic classifications

In the past, users have tended to employ geodemographic classifications ('geodems'), such as ACORN and MOSAIC, for customer analysis rather than 'raw' Census variables. The advantages of geodems were partly based on 'user friendliness' – they are easy to use and have been thoroughly built, researched and tested – and partly on cost grounds – as raw Census data historically incurred high royalty charges. For 2001, the free access to Census data should remove any cost barriers in profiling with raw variables. However, there will still be a place for 'off-the-shelf' geodems. We can expect a much larger number of these to become available, given the free data, but this also opens up the possibility for users to build their own customised discriminators. ▶

Customised discriminators

To obtain improvements over 'off-the-shelf' products one must include more discriminatory variables and/or shift from area-level to individual-level classifications. Using Output Areas as ready-made 'building bricks', customised discriminators could take a number of forms, for example:

■ 'Geodem-type' classifications built using customer data alongside Census data
■ Statistical models using Census data to predict some customer outcome, e.g. response to a campaign
■ Estimates of consumer demand based upon demographic modelling of market research sources

Subject to agreement with the Census Offices and resolution of any confidentiality issues, it may be possible to drill down within Output Areas and build an individual-level classification for people or households.

Source: Adapted from Leventhal, B. and Moy, C. (2003) 'Opportunities to leverage the Census for research and marketing', MRS Conference, www.mrs.org.uk.

Non-government published data

Sources of non-government information and data abound. They include newspapers, journals, magazines, newsletters, pamphlets, books, directories, guides, catalogues and databases. Material is produced by trade associations and professional bodies, chambers of commerce, regulatory bodies and pressure groups, academic and research institutions; as well as by commercial organisations, including market research companies and business information publishers. Much of this material can be tracked down via the source organisation's website, via specialist information host sites that list catalogues, directories, guides and databases, and via portals and information gateway sites.

There are several commercial organisations that supply market research data (standard packages as well as tailored ones) on a range of topics. They include Mintel (www.mintel.co.uk), Data Monitor (www.datamonitor.com) and Kompass (www.kompass.com); Forrester Research (www.forrester.com), ClickZStats (www.clickz.com/stats/) and eMarketer (www.eMarketer.com) among others are useful sources of new media research data. Through the Financial Times website (http://ft.com) and business directory websites such as www.business.com, www.hoovers.com/free and www.ibd-business.de you can access a wide range of information on organisations, markets, industry sectors and countries.

Other useful sources of international data include the United Nations (www.un.org), which has a wide range of links to online catalogues, bibliographic databases and directories relating to social, economic and market data; the World Bank (www.worldbank.org), the OECD (Organisation for Economic Co-operation and Development (http://www.oecd.org) and the World Economic Forum (www.worldeconomicforum.org).

For more academic-related material, there is the gateway site, Intute (www.intute.ac.uk). It provides an extensive list of links to online databases worldwide – bibliographic, numeric and full text databases – covering most education and research subjects. COPAC is a free access service to the unified online catalogues of some of the largest university libraries in the United Kingdom and Ireland and includes access to documents in around 300 languages (http://copac.ac.uk/). Voice of the Shuttle (http://vos.ucsb.edu/) is a gateway site for research

Box 5.4 Searching the web

Introduction

There are two main approaches when it comes to conducting any sort of search: 1) start with a vague idea and narrow it down as you go; and 2) start with a precise topic or issue. The approach you choose is likely to be related to the nature of your enquiry: if it is exploratory in nature then you may want to go with approach number one; if it is a descriptive enquiry with relatively clear-cut objectives then you may want to take approach number two.

Whichever it is, it is worth bearing in mind that in a research project time is usually short, there is likely to be more information available than you will be able to handle (there are billions of pages on the web) and so it will be easy to get overwhelmed by the volume of it. It is therefore worth thinking about what it is you are after before you start the search. Depending on the nature of your enquiry you may even be able to set some search criteria or parameters. These will certainly help you focus your search and/or re-focus your mind if you do get swamped. Examples include the following:

- the precise subject or topic (or as precise as you can make it);
- the sort of information you want (e.g. text or data; qualitative or quantitative);
- the source of the information (scholarly, government, commercial and so on);
- the names of any authors that you know have worked in or published on that topic;
- the titles of any works that you think might be relevant;
- the relevant dates.

During the search try not to be distracted by material that looks interesting but does not meet your search criteria.

Where or what to search

It might be that the information you need can be obtained from a particular organisation. The first step in this case is to go directly to that organisation's website. If you do not know its web address, make a guess. Leave out the http:// part and go straight to the www bit of the address. Use the full name, short name or acronym of the organisation next (e.g. mrs or cim or esomar). Then add the appropriate domain – .com for international private sector organisations; or the relevant country code (see http://www.iana.org/root-whois/index.html for a list of country codes); or .org for non-private sector organisations; or .gov for government departments and bodies; or .edu for academic bodies in the US and .ac for those in the UK. If this approach does not get you to the organisation you want, use a portal, directory or search engine and type in the name of the organisation.

Portals, directories and search engines are not only useful for searching for organisations, they are also useful in subject searches. There may be a specialist portal or directory that gets you directly into the subject area you need. Portals offer search, directory and other services, including news, access to discussion forums and basic information on popular topics. Useful commercial portals include Yahoo!, AOL, MSN and Lycos. Useful specialist ones include Intute for education and ▶

research – http://www.intute.ac.uk/; Northern Light for business (including market research – http://www.northernlight.com/portal.html); REESWeb for Russian and Eastern European studies – http://www.ucis.pitt.edu/reesweb/; Directgov for UK public service information – http://www.direct.gov.uk. A subject directory contains selected websites and classifies them into subject categories. Most portals have subject directories (see for example www.business.com). There are also specialist, stand-alone directories (for example www.lii.org, Librarians' Index to the Internet). Most search engines also have directories. Search engines work by allowing you to search the database of indexed words from web and Internet pages. Examples of large search engines are Google, Alta Vista and AlltheWeb.

It is important to remember than none of the portals, directories or search engines offer comprehensive coverage of what is available on the web or via the Internet. It is also worth remembering that there is not always overlap in content between search engines – for this reason it is useful to use more than one search engine in your search. You will find that some have more powerful search capabilities than others and this may also influence your choice of which to use.

Multiple search engines are also available. Examples include Dogpile and Mamma. These work by searching in parallel the databases of several individual search engines. The problem with using these multiple search engines is that they do not offer as comprehensive a search as you might achieve with a search of the individual search engines. They are, for example, subject to time outs when processing takes too long; some only retrieve the top ten to 50 hits from each search engine; the advanced search facilities of the individual search engines (including phrase and Boolean searches) may not be available.

How to search

You are unlikely to get what you want in only one click. This is another reason why working out in advance a search strategy with search criteria or parameters is useful. It should mean that you won't get distracted as you do your search. Your strategy should allow you to narrow the focus of your search – starting with the general or broad topic and working toward the more specific. It is, however, a good idea to be as precise as you can be at the start of the search. Rather than searching for a key word, try a Boolean search (that is, making your search more precise by using the operators *and, or, not*) or a 'phrase search' or a title field search to narrow the list of results. Almost all the portals and search engines allow you make these. A phrase search can often be particularly productive. It is a search for the words entered adjacent to each other and exactly in the order you give them. Most use double quotation marks to identify a phrase, for example: "geodemographic classification systems". To get a better match – to narrow the search further – you can add more words. The Advanced Search facility that most portals and search engines offer also allows you to exclude words. If you're not sure exactly what it is you want, start with your key word or topic, search for that then scan the results to see the sort of material it has produced. This will give you information that may help you narrow your search by adding more words or building a phrase. You can also use the Advanced Search facilities to limit your search to a title or a specific domain or a file type or a date, for example. Some Advanced Search facilities allow you to limit your search to particular sources, such as scholarly papers.

Remember, no search engine can search the entire web or the Internet, only its own database of indexed words from those pages listed with it. You will miss, with any search engine search, the content in sites that need a log-in, including material on Intranets, and, in many cases, very current information (for which the best place to search are the sites of newspapers, magazines, trade press and television and radio stations).

Keeping track of what you've done

It is important in doing your search that you keep a log of it. This is important for several reasons: you may need to show what you have done in a report or to a client or to other people working on the project; you need to attribute or cite any material you used from your search; and you or someone else may need to go back to some of the sources you found at a later date for further information or for verification purposes. You should therefore bookmark the sites you visit or add them to your 'Favorites' list; and you should also record the Internet address or URL in a log or bibliography along with the date on which you accessed it (this is good practice since the content of the site may change over time). If you need to cite the URL in a report you can either give the precise URL for the document, e.g. ESOMAR, December 2007. http://www.esomar.org/uploads/pdf/professional-standards/ICCESOMAR_Code_English.pdf. [Accessed 5 August 2008]; or you can give the details of the document and the URL of the search page from which you accessed it, e.g. ESOMAR, December 2007. ICC/ESOMAR International Code on Market and Social Research. Available from http://www.esomar.org/index.php/codes-guidelines.html [Accessed 5 August 2008].

Where possible, you should aim to keep a record of the following information for any source you consult:

■ The name of the author
■ The title of the document
■ The name of the editor (if appropriate)
■ The name of the site
■ The name of the body associated with the site
■ The date of publication or last update
■ The URL address
■ The date that you accessed the site.

on the humanities. Also look out for peer-reviewed sites and 'peer-reviewed, limited-area search engines' (Gibaldi, 2003).

Citing your sources

There are several ways in which you can cite material you use. In the Harvard System, for example, you give the author's surname and the year of publication within your text, e.g. (Hakim, 2008) or using the example above where no author is given you give the name of the organisation, e.g. (ESOMAR, 2007) and you list in your bibliography or references, the author's surname, first name, year of publication, title of the work, place of publication and name of publisher. For a book, this would be as follows: Hakim, C. (1982) *Secondary Analysis in Social Research*, London: Allen & Unwin; for a website or online journal article: Orton-Johnson, K.

(2007) 'The online student: lurking, chatting, flaming and joking' in *Sociological Research Online*, Volume 12, Issue 6, <http://www.socresonline.org.uk/12/6/3.html>. [Accessed 21 March 2008]. For further information and detail, see the brief guide produced by Bournemouth University Academic Services (2007) *Citing References – A Brief Guide*, available at http://www.bournemouth.ac.uk/library/citing_references/citing_refs_main.html.

Remember – if you use a source you must acknowledge it. If you do not, it is plagiarism – stealing someone else's ideas and presenting them as your own. It is a serious offence. When you are copying or downloading material, you must also ensure that you comply with copyright rules. If you include material from other sources in your report it is your responsibility to get the appropriate copyright permission to use them.

Assessing quality and suitability

Once you have found a secondary source you need to do two things: judge whether it is of sufficient quality to be worth using (not everything that appears in print or that is on the Internet will be sound); and judge whether it is useful to your purposes. In other words, you need to evaluate the source. Quality and suitability go hand in hand: you do not want to use work that is of poor quality, even if it is suitable; and you do not want to use work that is not suitable, even if it is of good quality.

The first questions you need to ask in your evaluation are:

- Who commissioned the work?
- Who did the work?
- Why was it commissioned?
- Where did you find the work?

The answers to these questions will help you establish whether the work has authority (Gibaldi, 2003) and credibility. For example, might the person who commissioned the work or the person who undertook it have had a particular agenda or approached the topic with a particular perspective that may mean the work is biased in some way? Is the source of the work an organisation or a person with a sound and/or long-standing reputation in this area of work? Don't forget to make use of your own knowledge and that of your colleagues in coming to a conclusion.

Next you need to establish the currency of the work – how up to date it is. The questions here are:

- When was the work done? How long ago?
- Does it make use of or rely on outdated ideas, facts, figures and so on?
- Has it been overtaken by recent discoveries/changes?

Remember, there may be a time lapse between when work was done and when it was published or uploaded to a site, so make sure to check.

Next you need to check the validity, reliability and accuracy of the research element of your secondary source. The questions that are useful here are as follows:

- What was the research design? Was it appropriate for producing valid and reliable evidence in answer to the research question?
- What sampling procedure was used? Was it appropriate to the aims of the research?
- What was the sample size and the size of any sub-samples reported? Are they robust enough for any claims made?
- What method(s) of data collection were used? Was it appropriate?

- What was the response rate? Is it large enough to ensure a representative sample?
- How good was the design of the questionnaire or discussion guide?
- How accurate are the data?
- What quality standards were employed in the research process?

You may only want to use the information you uncover via secondary research in the form in which you find it, for example to give you an overview of a topic or a market or to quote figures about product usage and so on. On the other hand, you may want to conduct further or secondary analysis. Hakim's (1982) definition of secondary data analysis is:

> any further analysis of an existing dataset which presents interpretations, conclusions or knowledge additional to, or different from, those presented in the first report on the inquiry and its main results.

The aim of secondary data analysis therefore – as with all secondary research – is to extract new findings and insights from existing data. Secondary data analysis became an important part of social research in the United Kingdom and elsewhere in the 1970s when the type of data collected by government changed from statistics derived from administrative records to data collected via sample surveys. At the same time there was an increase in access to computers for data analysis and archives were created to store and preserve computer-readable data, thus making the process of retrieval and analysis much easier than it had been.

The factors affecting the quality and usefulness of a dataset for secondary data analysis are the same as those for the use of other secondary research materials. If you are planning to conduct secondary analysis on a dataset it is important to know the source of the data and to have at least a copy of the original survey questionnaire or discussion guide and a description of the sampling techniques used. You may also find it useful to have a copy of the instructions that were given to the interviewers or moderators who conducted the fieldwork. It is also important to know the definitions and clarifications they may have given respondents. From a data processing point of view you should have a detailed description of how the data were coded and analysed. You may want to know how the dataset is structured, what technical tools were used in processing and analysis and what weighting, if any, was applied. In addition, a list of the variables and values and the coding and classification schemes used, including non-response codes, as well as any derived variables that were constructed, can be invaluable. A list of the publications produced from the data will give a better insight into the study; it will highlight the ground already covered and point to interesting questions still waiting to be answered.

Data storage and retrieval systems

There are two main types of data stores: data archives and data warehouses. Although they have much in common – they are databases of one sort or another – there are some differences.

DATA ARCHIVES

A data archive is a store or repository for data. Commercial organisations have their own data archives in the form of internal databases and data warehouses that form the basis of DSS and MIS. External organisations also maintain data archives that can be accessed by anyone interested in using the data stored there.

A vast amount of data relating to social and economic life in the United Kingdom is held at the UK Data Archive, which is administered by the Economic and Social Research

Council (ESRC) and the University of Essex. The Archive contains data collected by the ONS on behalf of the UK government from regular, repeated surveys such as the Labour Force Survey, the General Household Survey and the Family Expenditure Survey. Besides government produced data, the Archive holds academic research data – data produced with funding from the ESRC itself as well as material from other (international) archives and data from market research, independent research institutes and public bodies. The Archive website (www.data-archive.ac.uk) contains full descriptions and documentation of datasets (including qualitative data) and supports several methods of searching for information. The Archive's main online retrieval system, known as BIRON, can be used for subject and topic searches as well as searches by name of person or organisation associated with a study, or the dates and geographical location of data collection. BIRON is in effect a catalogue consisting of descriptive information (the metadata) about studies held in the Archive.

Another useful archive is the Central Archive for Empirical Social Research at the University of Cologne (www.gesis.org/en/za/index.htm). It houses German survey data as well as data from international studies and is the official archive for the International Social Survey Programme (ISSP), of which the European Social Values Survey is a part. The ISSP collects data on key social and social science issues in over 30 countries worldwide. The Central Archive provides access to the data collected from each individual country and to the file containing data from all participating countries for each year of the survey.

The archive at the Inter-University Consortium for Political and Social Research (ICPSR) at the University of Michigan (www.icpsr.umich.edu/) provides access to social science data from over 400 member colleges and universities worldwide. It also has a series of archives relating to particular topics, for example the Health and Medical Care Archive, the International Archive of Education Data and the National Archive of Criminal Justice Data.

Box 5.5 Accessing data from archives

With technological developments, especially developments in web technology, it is now relatively easy to get access to an archive in order to download data sets and individual tables to your PC. NESSTAR server software, for example, offers facilities for searching and browsing information about the data stored in the UK Data Archive, for doing simple data analysis and visualisation over the web, and for downloading data. NESSTAR makes use of developments from the Data Documentation Initiative (DDI), an initiative that aims to establish international standards and methodology for the content, presentation, transport and preservation of metadata, the data that describe the datasets. As a result of the DDI, metadata can now be created with a uniform structure that is easily and precisely searched, and which means that multiple datasets can be searched.

Source: Paula Devine, Queen's University Belfast, written for this book.

DATA WAREHOUSES

A data warehouse is a repository for data, in effect it is a very large database that contains data from one but usually more than one source. It is a central storage facility that takes the concept of a data archive one step further, in that different datasets within the warehouse are integrated and elements in one set can be related to elements in another set (known as a relational database). Data stored in the warehouse are data that are useful for supporting management decision making, for example for marketing and sales management or customer relationship management. Indeed this is the purpose of a data warehouse – to support the managament decision-making process (Inmon, 1996).

Data warehouses (and the tools used to extract information from them) are often referred to as decision support systems (DSS) or executive information systems or enterprise intelligence systems. The data warehouse is designed or structured, and data in it given context, in order to enhance this decision support role and to make access to the data in the warehouse fast and efficient. There are two main designs or structures: the relational database structure, based around a star design with a central fact table, for sales, for example, and several linked or related tables, for product group, sales region, sales period and so on, as the arms of the star; and the multidimensional database structure based around a multidimensional cube design. The database or data warehouse with a traditional relational database structure has two main advantages over the multidimensional structure: it allows you to integrate relatively easily other relational databases and is a more efficient way of storing data than the multi-dimensional approach, and so is easier to manage and easier to update. The main advantage of the multidimensional architecture is that it allows you to get a direct multidimensional view of the data. As with a data archive, data can be retrieved remotely from the warehouse via a networked workstation and interrogated and analysed using software tools designed to deal with very large volumes of data.

Building a data warehouse

Data are sent to the warehouse from what is called the *operational field* – from scanner data of transactions at the point of sale, from a geodemographic information system or from the data tables of a survey. Once in the warehouse they are referred to as being in the *informational field*. Data sent to the warehouse should be good quality: they are the raw material that will be used to support key management decisions and any inaccuracies or inconsistencies will impact on the quality of the decision making. It is good practice to clean the data before sending them to ensure that they are accurate and complete, that definitions of terms and variables, and the coding procedures used for these, are consistent so that data can be fully integrated or fused with other data in the warehouse. In addition, only data relevant to the needs of the DSS should be sent to the warehouse. Irrelevant or unnecessary data will only clog up the system and slow down access and processing time.

Organising the data in the warehouse

The end use of the warehouse should dictate how it is structured and how the data in it are organised. The data should be stored and organised in a way that allows the analyst to look at the data from relevant perspectives, for example by customer type, by brand and by market. Current data and historic data may be stored in a way that facilitates faster access to the more frequently used current data but allows older data to be called up for comparison, for examining trends or making predictions. In effect, the data warehouse is a multidimensional structure containing lots of shelves or rooms. Different datasets can be stored on different shelves or in different rooms within the warehouse.

The warehouse contains information telling users about its structure and how to find their way around the shelves and the rooms. This information is called *metadata*. Besides being a map of the warehouse, it also acts as a contents list, providing the user with details of the databases or datasets in the warehouse, the elements contained in them, and how these elements relate to elements in other datasets in the warehouse. Data in the warehouse may have been transformed in some way (changes to coding or to format) and they exist in the warehouse at different levels of detail – from what is called 'detail' through 'lightly summarised' to 'highly summarised'. The metadata also give users this information – telling them how the data were transformed, what changes were made to make them consistent, and on what basis the data are summarised.

The key characteristics of a well-designed data warehouse are as follows:

- It can store ever-increasing volumes of data without affecting processing performance.
- It is user friendly.
- Everyone has access to it regardless of location.
- Lots of users can use it at once with little effect on processing speeds.
- It facilitates analysis of data from a variety of perspectives.
- The speed of analysis and query answering is so fast that the search does not get in the way of thinking about the problem.

Analysing secondary data – data fusion and data mining

With an increase in the use of databases two techniques for analysing and making use of data in them have become popular: data fusion and data mining.

DATA FUSION

Technological developments have meant that it is possible to build an even more detailed picture of the market and the consumer by merging the data held in databases with data derived from other sources, including surveys and consumer panel data, and by merging the findings from separate surveys. The aim of data fusion is to obtain insights that could not be obtained from the sources individually (Leventhal, 1997; Macfarlane, 2003). The process of merging or integrating data from separate sources is known as data fusion. The process of fusion depends on being able to match individual records in one dataset, usually according to demographic or geodemographic details, with comparable records in another dataset. The idea is that data collected from person X1 about attitudes or buying behaviour, say, can be combined with data collected from person X2 on media usage, who is similar in his or her demographic or geodemographic characteristics to person X1. The fused data record (X1 plus X2) contains details of attitudes or behaviour and media usage for what is assumed to be the same person.

Merging datasets from different sources, however, can be problematic. Besides issues of format and software platform, which can be overcome with technology, there are also issues with the content of the datasets. If two sets of data are to be fused it is essential that there are variables common to each set. Common variables, say on demographics or product purchase, should be defined in the same way, so that they are measuring the same thing, and coded in the same way, so that the analysis program takes them to mean the same thing. This has implications at the research design stage, in particular for the design of the data collection instrument. If you know that two sets of data may be merged it is important to identify and define common variables before data collection starts. If this is not possible variables can sometimes be manipulated and redefined at the processing or analysis stage.

Box 5.6 Fusing survey data with geodemographic data

In 2002 BT carried out a census of its residential customer base. Data from this postal survey were integrated (within regulatory guidelines) with data from the BT Customer Database and data from the Claritas Life Style database, a geodemographic segmentation system. Below Phyllis Macfarlane outlines the process and the outcome.

Introduction

The questionnaire presented to customers was kept short to maximise response rates, and the focus of the questions was products and services. No demographic, life stage or life style questions were asked. Integration of the Claritas Life Style data added this dimension.

Fusing the data

Over 60 per cent of matches were achieved between the data sources, and since the postal survey sample size was so large it was feasible to work with the subset of data with complete matches – this gave a rich data source for profiling and segmentation purposes. It has enabled customer profiling in unprecedented detail, and is being used to develop and tailor products for specific customer groups.

The learning

What we learned was how feasible it is do something like this. For a relatively modest expenditure per customer, BT has built a customer database of unprecedented breadth and depth. One that can be developed over time into the sort of customer system that everyone talks about but very few companies actually achieve. We believe that this relatively straightforward, but significant start will point the way for future CRM [customer relationship management] systems.

Source: Adapted from Macfarlane, P. (2003) 'Breaking through the boundaries – MR techniques to understand what individual customers really want, and acting on it', MRS Conference, www.mrs.org.uk.

DATA MINING

The databases and data warehouses created to house data can be enormous – hundreds of thousands, even millions of rows, and thousands of variables. Until relatively recently, however, while the potential value of the information contained in them was widely recognised, there were problems extracting it. The lack of suitable tools to explore and analyse such vast datasets meant that little use was made of them: standard computer techniques could not process or analyse the volume of data fast enough or comprehensively enough for it to be of use. This is where the techniques of data mining came in.

Data mining, also known as knowledge discovery in databases (KDD), is the process by which information and knowledge useful to decision makers are mined or extracted from very large databases using automated techniques and parallel computing technology. Some of the techniques used in data mining are similar to those used in standard and multivariate data analysis. A data mining program can manipulate the data, combining variables, for example, and allowing the user to select elements or sections of the database for analysis; it can provide basic descriptive statistics, look for associations and relationships between variables, and perform cluster analysis. Where data mining differs from other data analysis techniques is in the volume of data it can process and analyse, and in its ability to discover patterns and relationships that cannot be detected with standard analysis techniques. And it does this at high speed, producing answers to queries or searches almost immediately, by using parallel computing technology. The data mining system divides the workload between a set of parallel processors, enabling streams of data to be processed simultaneously, in parallel. Speed of processing can be further enhanced if the database is structured in a particular way, for example if it is divided up or 'partitioned' into smaller units or packets; the data mining program works on each partition in parallel.

Approaches to data mining

There are two approaches to data mining: verification and discovery. In the verification approach you already have an idea about patterns of behaviour or relationships between variables – you have formulated a hypothesis, and you want to test the hypothesis in the data. You take the discovery approach, on the other hand, if you have no clear idea about patterns and you want to find out what hidden treasures exist among the mass of data. You get the computer to search and explore the database in order to find patterns and relationships. The computer program searches the database for these patterns and relationships by getting to know the data, and by learning the rules that apply within the database, identifying how all the elements relate to each other, what networks exist within the data. The mining metaphor is a good one – it is often necessary in data mining to sift through large volumes of dross before finding the high value material. It is possible to use data mining techniques on very large and complex databases containing data from several sources that would defy conventional analysis techniques. The database can be analysed at the individual level – the level of each transaction or individual customer – and at the aggregated level. And because the database is dynamic – data from the operational field are being added to it on a regular basis – information is always timely.

Box 5.7 Techniques used in data mining

- Summarising
- Learning classification rules
- Cluster analysis and segmentation
- Analysing changes
- Searching for anomalies
- Searching for dependency or neural networks.

Data mining techniques

A data mining system can examine the data and automatically formulate 'if x, then y' classification rules from its experience working with the data. For example, if the customer has a certain set of characteristics, say living in a single-person household in a large town or city with annual income greater than €60,000, then the classification rules show that he or she will be interested in range X food products. The system can build the classification rules into a model, displaying them in a hierarchical structure, such as a decision tree (similar to the output of the multivariate technique, AID analysis). For example, in searching the database of a bank it might find those customers who took out a personal loan in the last three years and those who did not. Among those who took out a personal loan it might split out those who repaid the loan early and those who did not.

The system can also look for associations between elements or variables in the data and can formulate rules about associations. For example, it might discover that on 84 per cent of occasions a customer who buys brands S and R also buys brand M. It has sequence/temporal functions that can search the data for patterns that occur frequently over a period of time. For example, it might discover what group of products is bought before buying a personal digital organiser, or what type of purchases follow the purchase of a desktop PC.

Data mining systems also run cluster analysis, working in more or less the same way as the cluster analysis or segmentation techniques used in standard analysis. The computer searches the database for cases that are similar on a characteristic or range of characteristics and it groups or clusters similar cases together. Cluster analysis can be used to identify different types of buying behaviour, for example. Besides being useful for their own sake, clusters are often used as the basis for further exploration.

Data mining can use neural networks to interrogate databases. A neural network is a mathematical structure of interconnected elements, analogous to the neural pathways in the brain, a sort of non-linear, non-sequential computer program. It is a sort of complex 'black box' technique that works by looking for all the interdependencies between a set of variables or elements in a database. It can be used to uncover patterns and trends in a very large database that standard sequential computing techniques cannot see because they are so complex. The neural network can learn from the database – in fact it can be 'trained' to be an expert in the data it has to analyse. Once trained it can be asked to make predictions by investigating 'what if' scenarios.

Criticisms of neural networks centre on the 'black box' approach, which means that there is little or no explanation of the method by which the findings are obtained. It can also take time to train the neural network in the database. The network learns by experience, by tracking back and forth between elements in the database, and so with very large databases this can be time consuming.

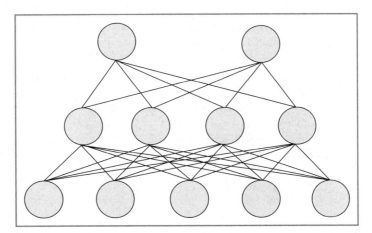

Figure 5.1 Diagram of a neural network

Data visualisation is often used with data mining techniques to help understand the data. It can help at the initial exploratory stage, by making relationships and patterns in the data easier to understand, and at a later stage for presenting or illustrating the findings.

OLAP

On-Line Analytical Processing or OLAP (Codd et al., 1993) is a category of software tools for retrieving, manipulating and analysing data in very large databases or data warehouses – those that contain elements that are interrelated and multidimensional. Multidimensional means that the database is structured in a hierarchical way (typically in the form of a multi-dimensional cube), so that the data and the relationships between data are structured and stored in a logical way. OLAP enables you to get access to and perform both simple and complex analysis of the data at speed. It understands the interrelated and multidimensional way in which the data in the database or data warehouse are organised. It has functions that allow you to perform analysis at the basic level – request descriptive statistics, for example – and at a more complex level – for example trend and time series analysis, factor analysis, pattern searching and modelling. The database might contain aggregated data on sales, say; it will also contain a multidimensional cell with data on sales classified or categorised according to different dimensions relevant to the needs of the organisation, dimensions such as brand, sales outlet type, market and so on. A single cell will contain data at the most granular level – for example, sales of brand X in Week 32 in bars in Ireland. Data can be aggregated or consolidated into larger sets (referred to as 'roll-up') – for example weekly sales into monthly sales, monthly sales to quarterly, quarterly to annual; sales via the website can be aggregated with sales via traditional retail outlets to produce total sales, or sales in each EU country can be aggregated into an EU total. Aggregated data can be disaggregated or broken down into smaller units, even down to the individual level, in a process known as 'drill down'. Data can be examined across a range of perspectives, such as by volume, by volume within market, or by volume within outlet type by market, in an operation known as 'slicing and dicing'.

Box 5.8 Examples of OLAP queries

- How many units of brands W and R did we sell in Ireland, the United Kingdom, France and Germany in the last financial year?
- How were these sales split between direct sales and agency business?
- What is the gross profit on direct sales and agency sales based on these sales figures?
- On the direct sales side, how were sales split between wholesalers and retailers?
- Among the retailers in the United Kingdom and Ireland, what was the split between on-sales and off-sales accounts?
- Were there seasonal variations in sales between these two types of outlet?
- How do sales per quarter in the last financial year compare with sales per quarter in the last two years?

Chapter summary

■ Secondary research, also known as desk research, involves looking for and analysing data that already exist – data that have not been created specifically for the purpose at hand but were originally collected for another purpose.

■ Consulting existing sources – doing secondary research – should be the first step in answering any query or researching any topic. You may discover that there is no need for expensive primary research, that the secondary sources answer the research or business problem.

■ Secondary sources may provide useful information, especially in the early stages of a project, helping with problem definition and research design and planning, and at the later stages, providing a context for the interpretation of primary data.

■ Secondary sources can be found inside the organisation (internal) or outside the organisation (external).

■ The two main external sources are those produced by government departments and related bodies (*official statistics*); and those produced by trade bodies, commercial research organisations and business publishers (*unofficial statistics*). Most are available in hard copy format, from the publisher or source, from a library, or via online and offline (CD-ROM) databases.

■ Demographic data from the census are merged with geographic data to produce geodemographic data. Geodemographic classifications can provide a better understanding of consumer behaviour than demographic data alone, and are often used as the basis of market segmentation systems.

■ It is important to evaluate the quality and suitability of secondary sources before using them.

■ Data archives and data warehouses are very large databases that contain data from one or more than one source. Management information systems or decision support systems are databases or data warehouses in which internal and external data are stored. They are useful sources of secondary data and are designed with the information needs of end users in mind.

■ Data fusion is the process of merging or fusing data from different datasets or databases and can be used to build a detailed picture or profile of the consumer. If two sets of data are to be fused it is essential that there are variables common to each set.

■ Data mining, also known as knowledge discovery in databases, is the process by which information and knowledge are extracted from very large databases using automated techniques and parallel computing technology. Its advantages over standard techniques are in the volume of data it can handle, its ability to discover patterns and relationships otherwise undetectable, and the speed at which it works.

Questions and exercises

1 You have received a report based largely on data collected from secondary sources. Describe the steps you would take to review the quality of the secondary data and explain why each is important.

2 You work for a well-known premier league soccer club. The club has a very popular website and a successful online store selling mostly clothes and club memorabilia. The marketing manager is keen to broaden the range of products sold in the online store. He is particularly interested in starting a range of mobile phone products including a club news text service, match and ticket alerts, downloadable ringtones and screen backgrounds (wallpaper). He would, however, like to have some background information about this market and these products to help him put together a business case for the finance director. He has asked you to help. Outline a programme of secondary research that will help both the marketing manager and the finance director decide whether or not to go ahead with the new range. Give reasons for the approach you plan to take and for the suggestions you make.

3 Your client, a mail order company selling plants and small trees, has a very large database that contains the records of all its transactions with its customers over a three-year period. This includes customer addresses (including postcode where relevant) and for each transaction details of product(s) bought; money spent/value of purchases; and method of payment. The client has plans to expand the business and would like you to undertake an analysis of this database in order to gain greater insight into the customers and the product portfolio. Prepare a proposal outlining your approach to the analysis, listing the sort of information you plan to provide the client. Note also what, if any, problems might be associated with use of the data.

References

Bournemouth University Academic Services (2007) *Citing References – A Brief Guide.* Available at http://www.bournemouth.ac.uk/library/citing_references/citing_refs_main.html. [Accessed 21 March 2008]

Brook, O. (2004) '"I know what you did last summer" – arts audiences in London 1998–2002', *Proceedings of the Market Research Society Conference*, London: MRS.

Codd, E.F., Codd, S.B. and Sally, C.T. (1993) *Providing OLAP (On-line Analytical Processing) to User-Analysts: An IT Mandate*, Toronto, Canada: E.F. Codd and Associates.

Gibaldi, J. (2003) *MLA Handbook for Writers of Research Papers*, New York: The Modern Language Association of America.

Hakim, C. (1982) *Secondary Analysis in Social Research*, London: Allen & Unwin.

Inmon, W.H. (1996) *Building the Data Warehouse*, 2nd edition. New York: John Wiley & Sons, Inc.

Johnson, M. (1997) 'The application of geodemographics to retailing: meeting the needs of the catchment', *Journal of the Market Research Society*, 39, 1, pp. 201–24.

Leventhal, B. (1997) 'An approach to fusing market research with database marketing', *Journal of the Market Research Society*, 39, 4, pp. 545–58.

Leventhal, B. and Moy, C. (2003) 'Opportunities to leverage the census for research and marketing', *Proceedings of the Market Research Society Conference*, London: MRS.

Macfarlane, P. (2003) 'Breaking through the boundaries – MR techniques to understand what individual customers really want, and acting on it', *Proceedings of the Market Research Society Conference*, London: MRS.

Murcott, A. (1997) 'The PhD: Some informal notes', unpublished paper. School of Health and Social Care, South Bank University, London.

Orton, S. and Samuels, J. (1988, 1997) 'What we have learned from researching AIDS', *Journal of the Market Research Society*, 39, 1, pp. 175–200.

Passingham, P. (1998) 'Grocery retailing and the loyalty card', *Journal of the Market Research Society*, 40, 1, pp. 55–63.

Silverman, D. (2005) *Doing Qualitative Research*, 2nd edn. London: Sage.

Recommended reading

Baez Ortega, D. and Romo Costamaillere, G. (1997) 'Geodemographics and its application to the study of consumers', *ESOMAR Conference Proceedings, The Dynamics of Change in Latin America*, Amsterdam: ESOMAR.

Baker, K. (2000) 'Date fusion', in Birn, R. (ed.) *The International Handbook of Market Research Techniques*, 2nd edition. London: Kogan Page.

Browne, N. and Keeley, S. (2004) *Asking The Right Questions: A Guide to Critical Thinking*, London: FT/Prentice Hall.

Dale, A., Arber, S. and Proctor, M. (1988) *Doing Secondary Analysis*, London: Unwin Hyman.

Dilly, R. (1995) *Data Mining: An Introduction*, http://www.pcc.qub.ac.uk/tec/courses/datamining/stu_notes/dm_book_1.html.

Hakim, C. (1982) *Secondary Analysis in Social Research*, London: Allen & Unwin.

Stoker, S. (1999a) 'Good data housekeeping', in *DM Direct*, August, www.dmreview.com/dmdirect.

Stoker, S. (1999b) 'Building an information warehouse', in *DM Direct*, December, www.dmreview.com/dmdirect.

Chapter 6

PLANNING AND CONDUCTING QUALITATIVE RESEARCH

Introduction

In Chapter 2 we looked briefly at the nature of qualitative research and the way in which it differs from quantitative research. The purpose of this chapter is to describe some of the methods used to collect or generate qualitative data, the applications of these methods, and what is involved in planning and conducting a qualitative research project.

Topics covered

- What is qualitative research?
- Observation and ethnography
- Interviews and group discussions
- Other interview-based approaches
- Online qualitative research
- Interviewing and moderating skills
- Designing the interview or discussion guide
- Semiotics and qualitative research

Relationship to MRS Advanced Certificate Syllabus

This chapter covers most of the material needed for Element 4 – Planning and Conducting Qualitative Research. The aims of this Element of the syllabus are to introduce you to key approaches to qualitative research and to a range of techniques for gathering qualitative data; to enable you to select and/or evaluate the appropriateness of a technique for a given research context; and to plan for the collection of qualitative data. This chapter is also relevant to Element 6 – Designing Data Collection Instruments. It includes material that should help you prepare an interview or discussion guide and it should equip you with basic knowledge of how to develop projective and enabling tools for data collection purposes.

Learning outcomes

At the end of this chapter you should be able to:

- understand what is involved in the main data collection methods used in qualitative research;
- choose the most appropriate method for a given research proposal;
- plan a qualitative research study;
- design an interview or a topic or discussion guide.

What is qualitative research?

As we noted in Chapter 2, qualitative research is about rich, detailed description, understanding and insight rather than measurement. It is both less artificial and less superficial than quantitative research and can provide highly valid data. It aims to get below the surface, beyond the 'top of mind', rational response. It tends to be sensitive to the wider context in which it is conducted; it is good at uncovering the subtleties and nuances in responses and meanings as a result. It is more flexible than quantitative research – it is less structured and allows for a less standardised approach, which can, if not monitored and controlled, threaten reliability. It is particularly suited to exploratory and descriptive research enquiries, and for researching complex issues.

Specialist interviewers, known as recruiters, are responsible for finding and inviting people to take part in qualitative market research. In academic and in some social research projects, the researcher responsible for the project may do the recruiting themselves. The approach to sampling, discussed in Chapter 8, and the sampling criteria to be used to choose the sample will be decided by the researcher responsible for designing the project. Either the researcher or a fieldwork manager will brief the recruiters to find people who match the criteria using the approach specified by the researcher.

Sample sizes in qualitative research are typically small. The number of interviews or groups or workshops conducted in a project will depend on the research objectives, the complexity of the topic, the sample requirements, the range of views needed, and the practicalities of time and cost. For example, to assess the effectiveness of a television advertisement, 8 to 12 in-depth interviews might be conducted alongside a quantitative advertising test; to understand the issues involved in adopting new technologies, you might need to complete 20 to 30 in-depth interviews with business executives; to understand the perspectives of those involved in a drug rehabilitation programme, it may be necessary to conduct 50 to 60 in-depth interviews; to guide the creative development of an advertising campaign, you might run two workshops. It would be unusual to conduct fewer than four group discussions on any topic – at least this number is typically needed to cover variations in sample and geographic locations; projects involving 10–12 groups are common.

THE ISSUE OF REPRESENTATIVENESS

With such small sample sizes and the use of purposive (rather than random) sampling methods, findings from qualitative research cannot be said to be representative in the statistical sense, and they are not meant to be so. The logic that underpins random or probability sampling (the logic that allows the quantitative researcher to choose a random sample from a population and have that sample represent the population with a known level of accuracy and precision) is not the logic used by the qualitative researcher when choosing a sample. This is not to say that there is no logic in how a qualitative researcher selects a sample; there is – or there should be. The relationship between the sample chosen and the wider population from which it is drawn should be made explicit by the qualitative researcher. The sampling approach used in any qualitative research study should be just as systematic and rigorous as that used in a quantitative study, and should be described just as openly as it would be in a quantitative study to enable clients and others to judge the reliability and validity of the research findings. We look at approaches to sampling in more detail in Chapter 8.

QUALITATIVE RESEARCH METHODS

A wide range of methods are grouped under the heading 'qualitative research methods' or 'qualitative methods of data collection'. This reflects the heritage of qualitative research – its roots in the social sciences, in particular in sociology, anthropology and, to a lesser extent, pyschology – as well as its application in these and other disciplines including geography, history and cultural studies, among others.

For many years, most commercial qualitative market research took the form of in-depth interviews or group discussions, including all the variations that those methods have to offer. More recently other methods – more often used in academic and/or social qualitative research – have become popular in the commercial sector. These include variations on observational and ethnographic techniques used in sociological and anthropological studies as well as the application of semiotics, the study of signs and symbols and how meaning is constructed and understood. In addition, the more traditional commercial interview-based methods – group discussions and in-depth interviews – have been developed into more collaborative and deliberative approaches such as workshops, panels and juries. These face-to-face, in-person methods have also be transferred to and adapted for use online, making online qualitative research a technique in its own right. We look in more detail at all of these methods below.

Observation and ethnography

Ethnography is a method or set of methods for studying and learning about a person or, more typically, a group of people, in their own environment over a period of time. It usually involves more than one method of data gathering: observation – watching and listening to what people say; and interviewing – asking questions. The researcher observes or participates or becomes 'immersed' in the daily lives of those being studied in order to get a detailed understanding of the behaviour, circumstances and attitudes of the group. The overall aim may be to achieve an holistic description of the group or set of people, or it may be to provide a detailed description of specific issues or situations or experiences within the wider setting.

While they are expensive and time consuming to conduct, ethnographic studies have a number of strengths:

- they give us insights that we may not be able to get through interviewing alone;
- they allow us to see the 'bigger picture' – the social and cultural context of the behaviour or activity in which we are interested;
- they allow us to see things from the point of view of the people involved;
- they allow us to hear people describe and explain things in their own words, in their own way;
- they allow us to see things happen – behaviour, activities and so on – in the setting and at the time they normally take place.

The extent to which the researcher is involved with the research participants – in effect, the role of the researcher – in an ethnographic study can vary from complete observer (performing what is often called 'simple observation') to participant observer (participant observation) to complete participant.

SIMPLE OBSERVATION

Simple observation involves watching and recording people and activity, for example in a supermarket, a bar, a café or a hospital waiting area, whatever setting is relevant to the research. If the researcher is present, he or she does not interact with those being observed but makes notes about the behaviour, about incidents, routines and body language (and might also record the activity). For example, in a bar, the researcher might note the demeanour and body language of people coming into the bar, the way in which the bar staff greet them, the time taken to choose a drink, the drink chosen, the seat chosen and so on. If the researcher is not present, the activity may be recorded and this record viewed and analysed later.

Observation allows the researcher to gather data on what people do rather than what they say they do. In order to understand why the respondent behaves in a particular way, the recording of the observation may be played back to the respondent as a reminder, and the researcher may ask about the activity, and the respondent's thoughts and feelings at the time. This technique, described as a 'co-discovery interview' (Griffiths et al., 2004), is used in Case study 6.2 below.

PARTICIPANT OBSERVATION

Participant observation is when the researcher is involved in or part of the activity or task being observed. The extent of participation may vary – the researcher may adopt the role of 'observer-as-participant' (Junker, 1960 and Gold, 1958 quoted in Hammersley and Atkinson, 1995), limiting the amount of involvement or engagement with the research subjects and focusing on observing; or the researcher may adopt the role of 'participant-as-observer', participating in the activities and the lives of the people being researched. In both cases, those involved are aware of the researcher and his or her role. The main difference between the two is the 'stance' of the researcher: in the 'observer-as-participant' role the researcher is relatively detached and remains at a distance from the subjects; in the 'participant-as-observer' role the researcher is less detached, more engaged and involved with the subjects. Accompanied shopping is an example of 'observer-as-participant' observation – the researcher goes with the respondent on a shopping trip, listening, observing and/or recording the subject's behaviour on audio or videotape, and making notes. The researcher may ask questions for clarification or understanding and to note the respondent's thoughts and feelings – collecting data relevant to the research objectives.

The researcher may adopt the role of 'complete participant'. In this case his or her role as a researcher is concealed from the subjects of the research. This type of research is sometimes known as 'covert observation'. The researcher joins (or is already a member of) the group under study, posing as an ordinary member but with the aim of conducting research. This approach is more common in academic (sociological and anthropological) research studies than it is in commercial social or market research. It is used to study secretive or 'hidden' groups (Renzetti and Lee, 1993), religious cults and criminal gangs, for example, or elite groups who are unlikely to let researchers in. While on the one hand this approach might be the only way to obtain data, and it offers a way of getting 'inside knowledge' untainted by the 'observer effect', which we look at below, it comes with some ethical drawbacks: the nature of the approach means that you cannot ask for informed consent before research begins. If you were planning such a study, you would in all likelihood be asked to submit your research plan to a research ethics committee or a human subjects research committee for discussion.

ETHICS AND OBSERVATION AND ETHNOGRAPHY

Conducting observational and ethnographic research raises a number of ethical issues – in particular in relation to informed consent, no harm to participants, anonymity and confidentiality – as well as issues to do with the data protection (audio and visual recordings of individuals are classed as personal data under the Data Protection Act 1998). Besides the rules set out in its Code of Conduct in relation to these issues, MRS publish *Qualitative Research Guidelines*. We set out the relevant key points and the rules from the MRS Code in Box 6.1.

Box 6.1 Professional practice and the MRS Code of Conduct: observation and ethnography

Guidance re ethnographic research:
1. Researchers should provide clients and sponsors of research with a clear account of any limitations involved in specific research projects.
2. Researchers should avoid situations where they could become vulnerable to accusations of misconduct (especially when working in respondents' homes) or where they became over-involved at an emotional level with the observed.
3. In accordance with the Data Protection Act 1998 and Rule A10 (see below), respondents must be told what will happen to any data gathered in the process of observation.
4. Researchers should inform respondents of the extended nature of ethnographic research at the point of recruitment before agreeing to participation and should be made aware of their 'right to withdraw' at any time.
5. Researchers should inform respondents (at the point of recruitment) of any activities they will be asked to engage in or undertake.
6. Researchers should inform respondents of the purpose and rationale for observation of their behaviour.
7. Where children and young people are to be the subject of observation, for instance where the Researcher is living with a family, the MRS guidelines relating to children's research should also be consulted, in particular in relation to the need to obtain checks from the Criminal Records Bureau.

Relevant rules:
A10 Members must take all reasonable precautions to ensure that Respondents are not harmed or adversely affected as a result of participating in a research project.
B2 All written or oral assurances made by any Member involved in commissioning or conducting projects must be factually correct and honoured by the Member.
B15 If there is to be any recording, monitoring or observation during an interview, Respondents must be informed about this both at recruitment and at the beginning of the interview. ▶

B47 Members must ensure that all of the following are undertaken when observation equipment is being used:
- Clear and legible signs must be placed in areas where surveillance is taking place.
- Cameras must be sited so that they monitor only the areas intended for surveillance.
- Signs must state the individual/organisation responsible for the surveillance, including contact information and the purpose of the observation.

Comment: Rule A10 of the Code requires Members to take all reasonable precautions to ensure that Respondents are not harmed or adversely affected as a result of participating in a research project. This may have particular pertinence in an ethnographic and observational setting. Issues to be considered are:
- *The need to be sensitive to the possibility that their presence may, at times, be seen as an unwarranted intrusion; here safeguards, and the ability to end the observation quickly, must be built into any ethnographic situation*
- *The need to be sensitive to the possibility that Respondents may become over-involved with them at a personal level*
- *The need to be sensitive to the possibility of 'observation fatigue'; again there is value in having the ability to end the observation quickly within any ethnographic situation.*

Guidance re recording:
1. The quality of the recorded image should be appropriate to meet the purpose of the surveillance.
2. Images must be retained no longer than is necessary.
3. Disclosure of recorded images to third parties must only be made in limited and prescribed circumstances and with the individual's consent.
4. Adequate security measures must be in place to ensure against any unauthorised processing, loss, destruction or damage to the data.
5. In accordance with Rule A1, Researchers who use CCTV must follow Security Industry Authority licensing requirements where applicable. For more information please see www.the-sia.org.uk.

Source: MRS Code of Conduct 2005. Used with permission.

THE OBSERVER EFFECT

Knowledge of being observed may alter the behaviour of those being observed to some extent (an argument used to justify the use of covert research). It is important to be aware of this observer effect and to plan to minimise it – at the design and fieldwork stage – and take it into account at the analysis stage. The main way of minimising it is to make the participants comfortable with the notion of being observed. Some ways in which you might do this, at various stages, are given below.

At the fieldwork stage:

- Briefing participants about the process and the end use of the data, being as transparent and open as possible (see below).
- Giving a general overview rather than a precise description of the purpose of the research – so as not to influence or bias participants' behaviour by alerting them to the activity that you want to observe.

■ Allowing time for participants to get used to the idea of being observed – by a camera or a researcher or both (after a period of time they may revert to their usual routines and behaviour).

■ Giving participants control of the observation – giving them the camera with which to film themselves, or having a camera that they can turn on and off.

■ Showing the participants your notes – to allay any fears about the sort of things you are writing about them.

At the fieldwork/analysis stage:

■ Asking them about things you have observed – to get their view about how typical such things are.

■ Showing them the film you have taken of them and asking for comment on or evaluation of the behaviour they see.

■ Observing them in a variety of settings and with different sets of people – to see if there is any variation in their behaviour or way of approaching things.

At the analysis stage it is important to recognise that the observer effect will have had some impact on at least some of the data you have collected.

■ Note when and where the observer effect occurs or is most prominent.

■ Think about why this might be the case.

■ Think about how relevant these effects are in relation to the research objectives.

USES

Case study 6.1 illustrates some of the uses of ethnography in market research; and Case study 6.2 shows how ethnographic techniques can be used in conjunction with more traditional qualitative research methods.

CASE STUDY 6.1

APPLICATIONS OF ETHNOGRAPHY

This case study illustrates some of the applications of ethnography to market research in order to produce a highly detailed and context-sensitive understanding of consumer behaviour and choice.

Why this case study is worth reading

This case study is worth reading for two main reasons: it gives examples of ethnography in practice in a variety of settings and for a range of product and services; and it illustrates what an ethnographic approach can offer the client.

The key words are: consumer experience, observing, role as researcher, objectives, invasion of privacy, open with respondents, contextual inquiry, natural context.

Retail navigation for a major bank

The objective of this research was to analyse the consumer's experience of navigating a novel type of bank branch targeted at investments rather than traditional types of banking services such as savings and loans. All of the physical and interpersonal elements of the branch were devoted to facilitating analysis, investigation and

▶

purchase of various investment products. Our research approach involved taking recruited participants through the branch and carefully observing how they interacted with and verbally reacted towards both the technology and people resources within the branch.

Guerilla ethnography or street research

This involves observing and talking with consumers in their natural habitats. The researcher commonly does not identify her role as a researcher nor does she formally state the objectives behind her interaction with consumers. Instead, through the normal course of chatting with fellow customers or sales personnel, an attempt is made to glean information about customer preferences, sales cues, consumer language etc.

The benefit of this approach is that the social distance and formal barriers between researcher and subject are broken down and interaction is more 'natural' and less subject to contrivance. The main objection expressed by critics, however, is the potential invasion of privacy and somewhat manipulative structure of interaction as well as the need to be absolutely open with the respondent.

Examples of the use of this type of study are to understand the impact of a new sales kiosk for cellular telephones and to assess sales associates' biases and predilections in recommending various telephone products and services. In the latter case, we presented various 'usage scenarios' – each linked to a prospective targeted segment – to sales people in a succession of stores. Their proposed solutions helped the client develop strategies for educating and motivating sales staff.

Contextual technology – user interface design

The term 'contextual inquiry' is often applied to this intensive ethnographic exploration of workplaces and home environments whose objectives are better to understand the needs and work processes around which technology can be woven. Another emerging use of ethnography in technology product development is to improve the computer–human interface and thereby enhance the usefulness, enjoyment and effectiveness of anything from software to websites. In their early stages, these research efforts tended to be laboratory based; however, the limitations of this rarefied context quickly became evident. The emerging preferred alternative is to go to homes and businesses to observe productivity and on-screen navigation in their natural context – on real consumer-purchased and customised machines. In this environment, consumers' expressed attitudes, observations of their interactions with computers as well as careful examination of surroundings, such as Post-It Notes attached everywhere and pen and paper resources coexisting with computers, become redolent with meanings and opportunities.

In other recent work, we have applied ethnographic approaches to designing home banking websites and in better understanding how business people utilise interpersonal, print and electronic resources while researching computer hardware and software they wish to purchase. In another study for a major manufacturer of office products, we spent time in business offices to learn about how secretaries and clerks use electronic and other resources in compiling reports. These studies yielded concepts and strategies for new product development and marketing communications.

Source: Adapted from Mariampolski, H. (1999) 'The power of ethnography', *International Journal of Market Research*, 41, 1, pp. 75–87, www.ijmr.com.

As Case studies 6.1 and 6.2 show, ethnography is useful in providing detailed and in-depth understanding of how and why people do things, in the context in which they do them – real behaviour, in real time, in context – and how they think and feel at the time of doing. It is a useful way of researching groups who may be hard to access using more traditional research methods. It is particularly useful in the exploratory phase of a project – when it is necessary to get to grips with an unfamiliar activity or process or setting. It is also a useful approach when we need to challenge the assumptions we make about everyday activities that can appear all too familiar, and when we need to see and understand things from the perspective of the respondent. It is useful in providing insight in situations where respondents might find it difficult to describe their behaviour. It is also useful for providing the context needed for understanding and interpreting other data. Observation and ethnography are, however, more time consuming and so more expensive than interviewing. The decision to use these methods should be determined by the objectives of the research, and by the practical constraints of time and budget.

UNDERSTANDING BINGE DRINKING

This case study sets out how ethnographic and traditional qualitative research techniques – observation, 'co-discovery interviews' and group discussions were used to reach an understanding of the phenomenon of binge drinking.

Why this case study is worth reading

This case study is worth reading for two main reasons: it describes how a project was conducted using a variety of ethnographic and traditional techniques; it describes the benefits of making and showing the ethnographic films and how these 'observations' were used within the project.

The key words are: friendship groups, filmed, co-discovery session, reconvened, soundtrack, stimulus, discussion groups, ethnographic films.

Introduction

Binge drinking has become an increasing issue for government policy, law and order, the medical profession and the drinks companies themselves. The client, a major drinks company, had run its own qualitative study using paired depths and had reached the conclusion that it would be very difficult to persuade 18–24-year-old young men in full-time work to drink more responsibly. So the task given to us was to see if we could find a solution.

Approaches

Friendship groups were recruited and filmed in two locations, one in the north of England and one in the south, on the Friday night. Filming began at the point where the participants left the house of the main subject and continued until the closing of the nightclub at the end of the night. The following morning a co-discovery session was held at the home of the subject and the friendship group reconvened to be interviewed about the night before using a rough cut of film. This session was edited down onto the soundtrack of each film to be used as stimulus within the research. ▶

For the next stage of the research four groups were recruited in London and outside Manchester, close to where the binge films had been made. Groups were made up of a combination of heavy drinkers consuming five or more pints a session and friendship groups who admitted to going out with the express intention of getting drunk. The binge films with the co-discovery interview as a soundtrack were used as stimulus in the discussion groups.

Usefulness of the films

Showing the films at the start of the groups created an impetus that drove the subsequent discussion. In the last group, two of the respondents were among the original subjects who had made the binge film and been through the co-discovery interview process – all those in this last group knew the town well, and many of them featured in the film. Showing them the film of a typical night out led into a comparison between the binge and other nights out in the town, how the town compared with other drinking destinations in the vicinity. There was an extended discussion about the violence that frequently accompanies the binge. We couldn't have raised these issues unless we had witnessed a brawl ourselves while filming. Using the film in conjunction with the discussion groups made it possible to raise related issues around the binge. The danger with a film viewed in isolation is that we lose the context of how the original participants would view it – which is why, even after the co-discovery interviews, there are often more follow up sessions with subjects than time allowed us here.

Another benefit of making the ethnographic films was that, because we chose to start filming at the respondent's house, we were able to define the binge in much wider terms than drinking in pubs and clubs. There was a danger that with a major drinks company as a client, the project would frame binge drinking in terms of what happened on licensed premises. But a lot of drinking happened before the subjects left home and went to the pub. They also frequently carried supplies with them to ensure that they could maintain the pace of the binge even when moving between venues or waiting to get served. Drinking stopped after the clubs closed – relatively little was drunk in the clubs because of the expense – and no drink was consumed at home afterwards.

By making films separately and prior to the groups we were able to study people's behaviour in a way that didn't run the risk of pre-conditioning or contaminating group respondents. And the ethnographic material proved very powerful later within the group discussion context.

Source: Griffiths, J., Salari, S., Rowland, G. and Beasley-Murray, J. (2004) 'The Qual remix', MRS Conference, www.mrs.org.uk.

Interviews and group discussions

Observation is often accompanied by interviewing (individuals, pairs or groups), as the case studies above show. As we saw in Chapter 2, what distinguishes qualitative interviewing from quantitative interviewing is the style of the interview. Quantitative interviews are standardised – the questions are worded in exactly the same way and asked in the same order in each interview – and most of the questions are structured rather than open ended and non-directive. Qualitative interviews (and in this we include group discussions, for ease of reference) are more like 'guided conversations' (Rubin and Rubin, 1995) or 'conversations with a purpose' (Burgess, 1984).

WHY CHOOSE A QUALITATIVE INTERVIEW APPROACH?

Qualitative research lends itself in particular to exploratory and descriptive research enquiries. You might choose to collect data using qualitative methods if the following apply:

- you want to find out about people's experiences, the way they do things, their motivations, their attitudes, their knowledge, the way in which they interpret things, or the meanings they attach to things;
- you want to (see and) hear people tell their own stories, in their own way, in their own words;
- you want in-depth accounts, detailed (idiographic) descriptions, context-rich data, an understanding of the issue, the processes or the behaviour;
- you believe that this is the best (or the only) way of getting the type of evidence you need to address your research problem, the best (or the only) way of finding out what it is you want to know.

Qualitative interviews or discussions are more flexible (Sampson, 1967 and 1996) than quantitative interviews. The interviewer (called a moderator or faciliator when taking group discussions) has the freedom to react to what the respondent is saying and adapt the interview accordingly. The questions that are asked can be altered, as can the order in which they are asked, and follow-up questions can be inserted if the respondent mentions something that the researcher would like to clarify or explore in greater detail.

The choice of interview (or discussion) as the method of data collection rather than observation, while driven to some extent by the nature and objectives of the research, often comes down to the practicalities of time and cost – it tends to be more cost effective. It is also more suitable when the objectives of the research are clearly defined, and when it is necessary to gather data from a greater range and number of people or settings. We look at the reasons why you might choose in-depth interviews or group discussions as your data collection method below.

IN-DEPTH INTERVIEWS

In-depth interviews are conducted by a qualitative researcher on a one-to-one basis with a respondent who has been chosen according to the agreed recruitment criteria for the project. As the name suggests, the aim is to explore a topic in depth, and most in-depth interviews will last from about 45 minutes to 2 hours, depending on the topic and what has to be covered. In most cases the researcher will use an open-ended interview approach. Interviews may take place in the respondent's home, workplace, central location or viewing facility. Typically the interview is recorded.

In-depth interviews are not an alternative to group discussions (see Box 6.2 below) – they generate different types of data. They are appropriate for more sensitive subjects, for understanding in detail without the views of the respondent being influenced by what members of the group say, or what other members of the group might think of them if they were to report a particular attitude or behaviour. Of course similar problems can arise in an individual interview situation but they are easier to read and disentangle when there is less contamination.

Box 6.2 Individual interviews or groups?

Choose in-depth interviews if:

- your topic is of a sensitive or intimate nature;
- you need to get detailed information on individual attitudes and behaviour;
- you need to get beyond the socially acceptable view;
- you need 'time-line' or longitudinal information (for example, to follow a decision-making process);
- your sample is difficult to find.

Choose group discussions if:

- you need to see a wide range of attitudes and opinions;
- you need to determine differences between people;
- you do not need minority views or views not influenced by the group;
- you want to understand social and cultural influences;
- you need to draw out creative thinking/solutions.

VARIATIONS ON THE IN-DEPTH INTERVIEW

There are several variations on the standard individual in-depth interview, including mini-depths, paired depths, triads and family interviews.

Paired depths (duos)

As the name suggests, paired depths are when two people are interviewed together. The pair may consist of two friends (see Case study 6.3); two family members – partners, siblings, fathers and sons; two work colleagues – whatever is suitable for the topic being researched. Paired depths are useful for two reasons. First, some people, particularly children and teenagers, find it less intimidating and embarrassing to be interviewed with someone rather than alone. Secondly, the research objectives of a particular study may mean that it is necessary to determine what goes on during a decision-making process that involves more than one person – for example, in buying a car. It may be important to find out who takes on what role, for example who is the purchase influencer and who is the buyer or the financier?

Triads (trios)

Triads involve interviewing three people simultaneously, and may be suitable for the same reasons as paired depths.

Family interviews

In-depth interviews are sometimes conducted with all or some of the family group, either together or separately, or in combinations. The purpose of family interviews is often to find out about elements of family life, decision-making patterns, rules and relationships governing food, clothes, holidays and leisure, for example.

Mini-depths

A mini-depth is a shorter version of an in-depth interview, lasting usually about 20 to 40 minutes, and is used to explore a specific, bounded topic.

TALKING TO TEENAGERS ABOUT SEX: PART 1

In this case study the researcher describes how and why a particular data collection method was chosen to gather data on a sensitive subject. (Case study 1.3 describes the background to the research and why it was commissioned; and Case studies 6.8 and 6.9 describe other aspects of the project.)

Why this case study is worth reading

This case study is worth reading for several reasons: it shows the links between the topics under research, the research objectives and the method of data collection; it describes the rationale for choosing in-depth interviews; it describes the mechanism for recruiting the pairs of respondents.

The key words are: groups, personal, in-depth, sensitive subjects, intimidating, younger respondents, trust, confidentiality, drawbacks, deeper exploration, balance, friend get friend pairs.

Introduction

The topics to be covered in this research project – sex, contraception and pregnancy – are personal, not subjects for group conversation. Moreover, in a group setting it is more tempting for respondents to exaggerate their sexual conquests. Equally, they may hide their true feelings and experiences. In-depth interviews are a more appropriate environment in which to discuss sensitive subjects. However, they can be intimidating for younger respondents. Many marginalised teenagers (the sample for the research project) have issues with trust and confidentiality in their lives. It is unrealistic to expect to build a trusting relationship with a marginalised teenager in a one-off in-depth interview. That having been said, there are also drawbacks in conducting communication strategy development research (which this was) in a series of one-on-one sessions with the same respondents over time. There is a need to balance the time taken to understand how people feel about a sensitive subject with the need to gather data to address the research objective – how to develop communication that has both impact and immediacy.

The method chosen: 'friend get friend' paired depth interviews

Friendship pairs formed the core of the research. The value of this method is that respondents feel comfortable in the presence of their friends and thus open up more easily. Secondly, their friends act as a safety net, challenging any false statements they may make and, in some cases, even volunteering information on behalf of their peers. People have a whole range of different friends. In order to provide a more sensitive environment for discussing attitudes to sex, one respondent was recruited and then asked to recommend the friend with whom they most felt comfortable discussing relationship issues. 'Friend get friend' pairs proved an open and constructive environment for in-depth discussion with at risk teenagers.

Source: Adapted from Cohen, J. (2005) 'Teenage sex at the margins', MRS Conference, www.mrs.org.uk.

Semi-structured interviews

Semi-structured interviews are a sort of half-way house between qualitative in-depth interviews and more fully structured quantitative interviews (Young, 1966 quoted in Sampson, 1967). They are often used in industrial and business-to-business research. The interview guide is more structured than is usual in qualitative research and interviews are carried out by interviewers trained in qualitative probing and prompting techniques but who are not necessarily qualitative researchers.

GROUP DISCUSSIONS

A standard group discussion or focus group is usually made up of 8–10 people (10–12 people in the United States) – small enough for a manageable discussion and large enough to have a range of views represented. Respondents are recruited for the group according to criteria relevant to the topic under investigation. A skilled qualitative researcher, known as a moderator or facilitator, guides the discussion. In some circumstances, depending on the nature of the topic and the objectives of the research, the group may consist of 6–8 participants, rather than 8–10. The smaller group allows the moderator to get a greater depth of response from group participants. Smaller groups are often used to research sensitive topics, or when the group consists of children or teenagers – smaller groups are less daunting for participants and allow the moderator to spend more time on each participant. A group usually lasts about an hour and a half to two hours (although in some countries, India for example, the group may happily continue for about four hours), giving enough time to explore a range of issues related to the research topic in some depth. Should it be necessary to research the topic in greater depth, the duration of the group may be extended. Groups usually take place in a central location, for example a meeting room in a hotel or, more commonly nowadays, at a viewing facility; some groups take place in the home of the person who recruited the respondents.

CASE STUDY 6.4

RESEARCHING SPIDER-MAN 2

Case study 2.2 described why Columbia Tri-Star Marketing Group needed to undertake research on the movie sequel, SPIDER-MAN 2 – to understand how best to market it. Here's what the first part of the research comprised.

Why this case study is worth reading

This case study is worth reading for several reasons: it describes a project in which group discussions – focus groups – were used; it gives details about the scope of the work – the sample, the number of groups, the geographic coverage; it describes the aims of the research and what was to be covered in the groups.

The key words are: focus groups, global health check, brand, territory, children, adults, 'off-targets', exploration, why.

Introduction

Prior to the creation of SPIDER-MAN 2's marketing campaign, the research agency, First Movies, was commissioned to undertake a 'global health check' for the SPIDER-MAN brand. This was done via a series of focus groups in the United Kingdom; Germany; France; Spain; Italy; Japan; and Australia.

The sample

In each territory, nine groups were conducted among children and adults, as follows:

Children
- 11–12 year old boys
- 11–12 year old girls
- 13–15 year old boys
- 13–15 year old girls

Adults
- 16–19 year olds
- 20–29 year olds
- 30–34 year olds who were pre-family
- Parents of at least one boy aged between 7 and 12 years
- 'Off-targets' who had not seen the first SPIDER-MAN film at the cinema, on video/DVD or on television.

Within each of the focus groups (with the exception of the off-targets), a minimum of two of each of the following were in attendance:

- Super-fans: those who had seen the first SPIDER-MAN film twice or more and who owned the video or DVD and who owned at least one piece of merchandise (specifically related to the film rather than the comic book)
- Fans: those who had seen the first SPIDER-MAN film at least once and who owned the video or DVD (but owned no merchandise)
- Non-committed: those who had seen the first SPIDER-MAN film once but had taken the movie experience no further (by not owning the video/DVD, or any merchandise).

What was to be covered

The focus groups therefore gathered together an extensive and comprehensive mix of cinemagoers who had seen the first film, allowing us to fully explore the key strengths of the brand and of the first movie, coupled with an exploration of any barriers facing the second instalment and potential traps facing the long-term health of the franchise. Through 'off-targets' we would understand why the first film had not been bought into and evaluate whether any mistakes could be avoided, potential viewers salvaged or, at least, to know who would be beyond the reach of even the most sophisticated marketing campaign and why.

Source: Adapted from Palmer, S. and Kaminow, D. (2005) 'KERPOW!! KERCHING!! Understanding and positioning the SPIDER-MAN brand', MRS Conference, www.mrs.org.uk.

DIFFERENT APPROACHES TO GROUPS

There are differences in how group discussions are conducted in Europe and in the United States. As we noted earlier, US groups tend to be bigger – 10 to 12 people rather than the 8 to 10 recruited for European groups. The interviewing style also tends to be different. Whereas

European groups tend to be less structured, with more open-ended, non-directive questions and more scope for the moderator to vary things, US groups are more likely to be structured, with little scope for the moderator to go beyond the questions listed in the discussion guide. Mary Goodyear (1996) describes the European style as 'conative', with an emphasis on exploring the topic, exploring respondents' inner feelings, and analysing the data as fieldwork is ongoing. She describes the US style as 'cognitive', focused on specific issues with an emphasis on collecting 'external' information.

VARIATIONS ON THE STANDARD GROUP DISCUSSION FORMAT

Mini-group

A mini-group, as its name suggests, is a cut-down version of a group, with usually about 4–6 respondents rather than 8–10. It lasts an hour to an hour and a half – rather than an hour and a half to two hours. Mini-groups are often used if the topic is a sensitive one, or if it is particularly difficult to recruit respondents.

Extended group

An extended group, again as its name suggests, lasts about four hours (and sometimes longer) rather than the usual one and a half to two hours. The extra time means that the topic can be explored in greater detail. A wide range of stimulus material can be examined and a variety of projective and enabling techniques can be used. The moderator may also devote a greater amount of time, in comparison to a standard group, to the group forming process, ensuring that the atmosphere created is relaxed and safe – this often leads to a greater level of disclosure from the group.

Reconvened group

A reconvened group is one that is recruited to take part in at least two discussions, usually separated by about a week. The first deals with the basics of the topic, explores the background to it and the more straightforward aspects of it. Participants are briefed on a task that is to be completed in time for the next meeting. The task might be to prepare something on a topic, for example, 'Can you live without . . . ?' The group reconvenes for the second discussion to impart their thoughts, feelings and experiences about the topic under investigation.

Friendship group

A friendship group, consisting of pairs or groups of friends or family members, is another version. This sort of group is often used when researching children or teenagers, or when examining a buying decision in which two or more people are involved (for example a mortgage or a car). For an example of the use of this approach, have a look at Case study 6.3.

GROUP PROCESSES

When people get together to form a group they tend to go through a number of different processes or stages. These stages have been described by Tuckman (1965) and Tuckman and Jenson (1977) as forming, storming, norming, performing and mourning and are useful in the context of research group discussions. They usually occur in this order, although some stages may be repeated during the discussion.

Forming

The forming stage of a group is the inclusion stage, and it is very important that the group passes through this stage if it is to function properly as a group. The moderator must explain the research, set out what is involved in the group discussion and get everyone to speak during the first few minutes. This helps respondents to get rid of their anxiety about speaking and contributing to the group, and allays their fears about being included and being a useful member of the group. It is also important that group participants talk to each other and not just to the moderator and so it can be very useful at the beginning of a group to run a warm-up or forming exercise. One way of doing this is to ask respondents to pair off and introduce themselves, then introduce each other to the group. Depending on the size of the group, this paired introduction can be expanded to groups of three or four.

Storming

Storming is the stage the group works through in order to establish how to relate to one another, to the moderator and to the task. At this stage respondents will be sizing each other up, testing the water, and trying to establish the boundaries of what is acceptable in the group. They might challenge the moderator, for example, or another group member. It is at the storming stage that you should be able to recognise (and should deal with) the dominant respondent(s) and the quiet respondent(s). Storming can happen later in the group when new tasks or new material are introduced. It is important at this stage that the moderator reiterates that all views, positive and negative, are valid and welcome and that he or she wants to hear from all participants.

Norming

Norming is when the group settles down, when respondents see that they have something in common with other members of the group. A sign that it has happened is when there is a general air of agreement, and when the atmosphere is noticeably relaxed. This is the stage at which the main work of the group can begin and so it is a good time to introduce or explain further the key tasks to be carried out.

Performing

The performing stage is when the work is done. It is the high-energy stage. When the group reaches this stage it is task oriented, co-operative and happy to get on with things. This is a good stage at which to introduce more difficult or complex tasks to the group.

Mourning

Mourning is the wind-down stage of the group. It is an important stage to work through so that participants can finish up and let go – of the task and the relationships that they have formed within the group. To make sure that this phase is worked through properly the moderator must signal the end of the group clearly and build in a wind-down period. If respondents are not given time to go through this stage they will not want to finish and/or they can feel used – they may be left with the feeling that the moderator wanted them to complete a task, get information from them and get rid of them. Signal the end of an hour-and-a-half-long discussion with about 15 to 20 minutes to go. With about 5 or 10 minutes to go, ask some winding-up questions, such as, 'Anything you'd like to say that you haven't mentioned?'

Other interview-based approaches

We live in an increasingly complex world and so the problems that researchers are asked to research are often complex (as many of the case studies in this chapter show). To cope with this change traditional methods of data gathering have been expanded, and reinvented, and less traditional methods – methods that are more common in academic social research and in government and public sector research – are becoming more popular in commercial market research. Ethnography, discussed above, is one example of this latter type; later in the chapter we look at another method, used for many years in commercial research but gaining increased popularity recently, semiotics. Here we look at three approaches that might be considered innovative takes on more traditional methods: workshops, panels and juries. What these three have in common – and what makes them different from conventional groups – is the extended amount of time available for generating the data, and reflecting on it; and the more collaborative or participative nature of the process. Case study 6.5 offers an example of a range of qualitative methods – standard group discussions, individual in-depth interviews, visits to places relevant to the research topic and workshops – in action and Box 6.3 below describes in some detail a workshop method referred to as 'collaborative inquiry'.

CASE STUDY 6.5

RESEARCHING THE MEDIA HABITS OF MINORITY ETHNIC GROUPS

This case study shows how a range of qualitative research methods including workshops were used in a project to explore in depth media use and attitudes to advertising among minority ethnic communities in Britain. More detailed findings in the form of a summary report can be found at the client's website (www.coi.gov.uk).

Why this case study is worth reading

This case study is worth reading for several reasons: it shows the link between the aims and objectives of the research, the sample and the methods used; it sets out the list of methods of data collection used; it describes the sample and how it was recruited.

The key words are: in-depth study, objectives, explore, workshops, standard group discussions, depth interviews, family visits, observe, community centre visits.

Introduction

In 2003 COI Communications, the UK government communications agency, commissioned a comprehensive, in-depth study of media use and attitudes to advertising among Britain's ethnic minority communities as part of a wider programme of research called the Common Good Research Programme (so-called because its findings were to be shared across all government departments and agencies). The aims of the Common Good Research Programme were:

■ To deliver fresh insight and inspiration to Government departments and their agencies;
■ To provide effective and practical information;
■ To be a long-term planning tool to assist in strategic, creative and media planning.

The objectives of the research among ethnic minority groups were to explore:

- Lifestyles, culture and feelings of identity;
- Media consumption and attitudes towards the media;
- Attitudes towards the representation of ethnic minorities in advertising;
- Information sources and delivery channels.

Methods used

The Common Good Research Programme aimed to uncover new insights and to go deeper than previous research among these communities. We wanted to know what people said about their media habits, but we also wanted to know what they did in the home and how families interacted in their day-to-day life. Thus, new methods were used and new target audiences included, to gain the maximum insight from the research. The project used entirely qualitative methods, comprising a mix of conventional and more innovative approaches:

- Two-hour workshops were the primary method used; these are similar to group discussions, but include a wider range of tasks and activities for respondents.
- Standard group discussions were used for respondents over 65, as we thought two hours would be too long for this group.
- Individual depth interviews were conducted among those who had recently sought information about a range of public issues (careers, schools, health, etc.).
- Family visits were conducted in order to explore media consumption in the home; these sessions lasted between two and three hours and took place in people's homes, videoing their media consumption patterns and observing their behaviour.
- Community centre visits were also conducted, to see how intermediaries such as advice workers actually used the Government information that they received. In addition to interviewing the workers, we also spent time observing the activities of the centre, taking photographs, and talking informally to centre users where possible.
- We also asked respondents to take photographs of their day-to-day lives and to fill out a media diary prior to attending the groups, interviews and workshops.

Sample

The sample covered the major visible ethnic minority communities in the UK, with a focus on those who had not been adequately covered in previous research, or who might have particular communications difficulties. Thus, the final sample covered:

- Indians, including Hindus and Sikhs;
- Pakistani Moslems;
- Bangladeshi Moslems;
- Chinese people, including Christians and Buddhists;
- Black Caribbean people, mainly Christians;
- Black African people, from a range of African countries;
- Young people of mixed race origin – from a range of mixed backgrounds.

The total sample comprised twenty-four workshops, four group discussions, fourteen depth interviews, four paired depth interviews, ten family visits and six community centre visits.

▶

Recruitment

Recruiting the sessions was a challenge, as some of these groups have been omitted precisely because of difficulties gaining access to the community. We did not use fieldwork agencies to do the recruitment on this project, as our experience is that they have difficulty accessing certain sections of the community – especially non-English speakers and more traditional Africans and Chinese people. We used specialist recruiters, many of whom were from an ethnic minority background themselves, to ensure that our sample was as representative as possible (for a fuller discussion of these issues, see Desai and Sills 1996, and Sharma and Bell 2002).

References

Desai and Sills (1996) 'Qualitative research among ethnic minority communities', *Journal of the Market Research Society*, 38, 3.

Sharma and Bell (2002) 'Beating the drum of international volunteering?', *Proceedings of the Market Research Society Conference*, London: MRS.

Source: Adapted from Desai, P., Roberts, K. and Roberts, C. (2004) 'Dreaming the global future – identity, culture and the media in a multicultural age', MRS Conference, www.mrs.org.uk.

WORKSHOPS

Workshops can be used to explore issues in detail, to solve problems and to come up with ideas and solutions using techniques such as brainstorming. Workshops tend to consist of about 15–20 people, sometimes more, and often include clients as well as consumers or those with an interest in the topic. They typically last at least two hours and may be run over the course of a day, lasting about six to eight hours. During the workshop session smaller sub-groups may break away from the main group to work on different aspects of an issue or problem. In Box 6.3 below, Roy Langmaid describes what he calls 'collaborative inquiry', a workshop approach that he views as an alternative to the traditional group discussion. Here he describes its use mostly in relation to the creative development process.

Box 6.3 Collaborative Inquiry

What is Collaborative Inquiry (CI)?
CI is best summarised as 'doing research with rather than on people'. In process terms it is encapsulated by the idea of 'asking people to build things rather than take them apart'.

Step One: Invitation and recruitment
The invitation needs to be more enticing than the standard focus group reminder postcard.

When judging the size and length of a CI session you need to bear a few things in mind:

1 The larger and longer your workshop the more data it will generate and the more likely you are to experience both repetition in the workshop itself and data overload afterwards. What level of depth, detail and repeat validity do you need?

2 You can get a lot more done if you enrol your client and agency planners and creatives in participating in the sessions. They can run sub-groups to follow up on their interests.

3 You need time and space for play as well as work if you are to build authentic permissive relationships.

4 You need to agree with your client and team how you will record the proceedings and how you will analyse and report on the data. (Langmaid & Andrews, 2003, Chapter 7.)

5 A usual length for a creative development session is one day. Generally we would pay respondents £100–£150 for their attendance and participation. We would also give them lunch!

Step Two: Setting up the method and process

Collaborative Inquiry is by nature participative and the entire team, including the respondents, must have some say on the agenda and topics. What they need to know from you, the project leader, is what is expected of them, what outputs you need, what resources are available in terms of materials and process, and how the work will be coordinated and timed. They also need to know your problem, relevant information about why you have the problem, what solutions you suggest, what you would like them to consider and how you will make that available to them.

Step Three: The multi-channel model in action

We have found it extremely useful to introduce the group to the idea that they live in a series of different worlds that might influence them in different ways. There is their own personal inner world, the world of self; the world of their intimate or family group; and the larger outside world reflecting issues that are local, national, international and global. To use this in workshops can allow greater access to the different channels of intra- and interpersonal communication that we all respond to in everyday life. All of these channels influence our perceptions and hence our choices.

Step Four: The creative development sessions

In a creative development session where there are a number of routes and executions to be explored, it is best to give respondents a choice of what they wish to work on. If you have four routes each focusing on a core idea about the brand, product or service, introduce each of these summarised in a few words and ask people to select the one which interests them most. You will get useful data just from watching how the group sorts itself and you can ask people why they chose a particular area once they have settled. Once they have selected an area of work ▶

there are a variety of processes you can use. In our work over the past few years we have used the following to explore creative ideas using the multi-channel approach:

Domain of the self

- Personal reflection/self-completion questionnaires;
- Telling a story or inventing a metaphor, symbol or icon for the brand;
- Art from within;
- One-to-one interviewing.

We have described the first three exercises in other places (Langmaid and Andrews, 2003). The fourth, one to one interviewing, can be really enlightening and efficient. Divide your workshop into pairs, including the client, agency and research team, then each pair member interviews the other to determine the key attributes determining their choices in the market under investigation. These attributes and their ranking are then recorded using self-completion sheets. This kind of workshop snapshot can then be used to create a Customer Value Map (Gale, 1994) that can provide an invaluable estimation of the relative weight of attributes like price, performance, brand image and advertising for a product area. This kind of value map can then be considered alongside the findings on the creative work. It provides a much-needed context for a qualitative inquiry, since it shows what is important to this group of consumers in this product area now.

In general to keep an account of the world of the self and personal reflections during the workshop we have found it useful to give each respondent a personal questionnaire that they will fill in privately at specific times during the workshop.

Domain of the family (small) group

Useful procedures here include:

- Standard discussion procedures – including showing advertising concepts, storyboards or animatics;
- Creating collages/mood boards;
- Designing symbols to express the creative ideas;
- Developing their own script along the lines of the favoured route.

This is familiar territory for qualitative researchers but recently we have been doing it differently. In one project respondents were invited to choose which area they wished to work on and then shown the creative executions from that area. This formed their primary task for the workshop – to discuss and comment on these executions. Later they saw all of the other preferred executions, presented to them by other sub-groups. Within these small groups, when reviewing the creative work, one of the tenets of CI is that you trust people to get on with the work without standing over them. So some facilitators leave their small group with the creative material and let them know they will return in twenty minutes to hear how they got on. Others prefer to work with the material and respondents interactively in the more classical style. You can also ask the respondents which way they would prefer to work – with you or without you.

Domain of the world – large group

This domain is represented by the large group in our model. Things you can do here include:

- Voting on preferred approaches as a community – followed by discussion of the vote;
- Presentation from sub groups followed by comments from the other groups;
- Enactments and story telling based on the creative ideas;
- Summaries and new information from the investigating team;
- Questions and concerns from anybody – especially the client and agency who are charged with taking the work forward;
- Film respondents presenting their work to each other to inform those back at the client/agency who cannot attend;
- Ask people to consider the day's work and let the community know what had most impact on them; how could the creative work change their buying behaviour, if at all?

One useful technique here is the go-round. Seated in a large group (numbering up to 35, any larger and it needs to be broken into two groups), each participant has a few moments to summarise their experience and tell the team what had the most impact on them during the day. This has the effect both of allowing the group to complete its work in a dignified and creative fashion and to complete the formal work of the session by taking a postscript from everyone.

References

Gale, B.T. (1994) *Managing Customer Value*, New York: Simon & Schuster.

Langmaid, R. and Andrews, M. (2003) *Breakthrough Zone*, London: Wiley & Co.

Source: Adapted from Langmaid, R. (2005) '21st century qualitative research', MRS Conference, www.mrs.org.uk.

PANELS AND JURIES

Qualitative data can be generated in more collaborative settings over extended periods of time – the extended workshop described by Langmaid in Box 6.3 is one approach. Other approaches include panels or juries. Qualitative panels and qualitative juries are made up of a number of individuals (around 20 for a panel and around 10–12, typically, for a jury). They meet at intervals and may stay together for an extended period (weeks or months – up to 12 months, or longer in some cases). The panel or jury may have a theme – consumer or community consultation, for example. At each session a topic relevant to the theme may be discussed. Participants may be briefed about the topic in advance of the session and/or topics may be revisited, allowing participants the chance to consider the evidence, examine possible options or courses of action, for example, and the chance to reflect on how they feel about these before discussing their views with, or presenting their views to, other panel or jury members. Case study 6.6 describes the use of a panel and in Box 6.4 Deborah Mattinson describes the citizens' jury model used in the UK.

KEEPING THE CONSUMER IN SIGHT: LEVI'S® YOUTH PANEL

In Case study 1.2 we saw the problems that Levi Strauss faced and how they overcame them to reinvigorate the research process and inspire the company to take action. In this case study we find out about one of the research tools they used – a qualitative consumer panel. The panel was put to use to address product design and development issues, among other things.

Why this case study is worth reading

This case study is worth reading for many reasons: it presents the rationale for use of the panel; it describes who the panel comprises, how they are recruited and how often data are collected; it shows the link between the sample and the research objectives; it highlights the contribution that information from the panel has made to the business.

The key words are: qualitative consumer panel, consumer typologies, quality, credibility, insight, contribution, trends, business forecasting, product lifecycle management, sponsorship activity, strategic agenda, trouble shooting, rapid response.

Introduction

The umbrella brand vision for Levi's®, the scary goal that serves as an inspirational rallying call across all organisational activity, is the intention 'to equip young people to change their world'. Jeans are clearly only one contribution to this overarching ambition. The first step was to build a process which would ensure that the business would never be able to let the consumer far out of its sight. The key tool was the Youth Panel. Initially, it was used as a source of illumination. Over time it became a powerful litmus test of innovation.

The make-up of the panel and how it is recruited

The panel is essentially a regularly refreshed, extremely select, qualitative consumer panel focused on the consumer typologies we believe exercise greatest influence on the dynamics of change within the casual apparel market – the Modernist and the Edge consumers, typologies derived from earlier research. The panel has been built up in each of the most fashion significant European cities (Berlin, Milan, Paris, Barcelona and London) and comprises between 50 and 100 of the most fashion forward youth you could hope to meet. We hand select them individually from the art/media/photographic schools of each city by stationing our most target friendly moderators in the bars, clubs, shops etc. they frequent. It is time consuming and expensive but it has revolutionised the quality and the credibility of the insight we are able to gather. To complement the trend setting consumers, and to ensure that we are equally exposed to the consumers from where the majority of our sales will flow, the panel also cover both Regular Guys and Regular Girls, often more surprising to the design team than the more fashion involved respondents.

The panel is convened twice a year to fit into the line development calendar ahead of the spring and fall line briefs for products. Meetings take place in environments selected to be sympathetic to the target rather than airport or audio convenient.

Contribution

In the past the contribution that research could make to the innovation process was dismissed for the usual rear view mirror reasons. Designers wouldn't waste time listening to mainstream consumers because they knew they had to aim ahead of the curve and there was no-one to talk to whose view on where the curve was going they would respect. The panel members, the environments we use, and the vocal support of the most senior management in the business has changed all that. We now get up to 15 people drawn from the brand and design teams attending each of the panel sessions and using the information, almost religiously.

Like all good tools the panel has come to serve a number of useful functions not all of which were envisaged from the outset. It provides perhaps the best indication the business has of how much momentum a particular trend has (left) in it, and therefore serves to guide both general business forecasting as well as specific product lifecycle management. It provides a continuous input into the company's sponsorship activity and plays an important troubleshooting role. Every second quarter the brand and design teams dedicate a day to working with the insights coming out of the panel. It helps set the strategic agenda and also enables some very effective and immediate troubleshooting. Products in line development have been dropped entirely based on panel feedback (previously unthinkable) and rapid response retail teams have been flown into Berlin the day after one of these events to address issues which were arising around the opening of the new opinion leading gallery store concept in Berlin.

Source: Adapted from Flemming from Thygesen and McGowan, P. (2002) 'Inspiring the organisation to act: a business in denial', MRS Conference, www.mrs.org.uk.

Box 6.4 UK citizens' juries

Here Deborah Mattinson describes the characteristics of the citizens' jury model used in the UK and gives an example of its application.

Introduction

Opinion Leader Research and the Institute for Public Policy Research have jointly developed the UK model in a series of juries. The UK model is being refined, but will tend to have these defining characteristics:

- The jury is made up of 12–16 randomly recruited ordinary members of the public, selected to match a profile of the local community.
- The jury is asked to consider a question or questions on an important matter of policy or planning. This may be local or national.
- The jurors sit for four days, with moderators. They usually receive a preliminary briefing session. ▶

- Jurors are fully informed about the question/s, receiving evidence and cross-examining witnesses. They can call for additional information and witnesses.
- Jurors can discuss the issues fully, interrogating witnesses, and deliberating amongst themselves in pairs, small groups, and in plenary session.
- On the final day, they draw their conclusions, which are compiled in a report.
- The jurors submit their report to the commissioning body, which is expected to respond.

Mini-case history: Cambridge and Huntingdon Health Commission

Issue: Health care rationing

Questions considered
- Should the public be involved in making decisions about health care?
- What criteria should be used to decide about health care decisions?
- When setting priorities, which is more important, quality or quantity?
- When setting priorities, which is more important: uncertain treatments for serious conditions, or effective treatments for minor ailments?
- Who should set priorities for health care, and at what level?

What did the jury do?
- Heard evidence from and interrogated:
  - medical and management staff;
  - patients;
  - the Royal College of Physicians;
  - a health economist.
- Called their own witnesses:
  - a local GP;
  - the Community Health Council.
- Deliberated in pairs, small groups, and plenary sessions.
- Received written evidence.
- Completed before and after questionnaires.
- Were involved in role playing/other projective techniques/exercises.
- Explored a number of case histories, offering 'real' examples of funding dilemmas.

Other applications

Successful public involvement programmes have considered issues ranging from the development of family friendly policies in government, through issues relating to town planning, to priorities for health care budgets. They have also explored more detailed policies for specific problems such as strategies for providing palliative care, and policies for dealing with severely mentally ill patients in the community. They have also been used to set guidelines for taste and decency in broadcasting and the use of genetic testing in setting insurance premiums.

Source: Adapted from Mattinson, D. (1999) 'People power in politics', *International Journal of Market Research*, 41, 1, pp. 87–95, www.ijmr.com.

Online qualitative research

Online qualitative research represents only a small proportion of all qualitative research conducted at present. It is, however, coming to be seen as a method in its own right and not just as an alternative medium for data collection. Research shows that data generated via online qualitative research is comparable to that generated in face-to-face discussions (Cursai, 2001; Balabanovic et al., 2003). In addition, while there are some limitations to the method (for example, loss of non-verbal communication), it offers many benefits on several fronts including the ability to research otherwise hard to reach groups; the ability to research sensitive topics; and the ability to generate (and simultaneously record) high quality data.

ONLINE QUALITATIVE RESEARCH TECHNIQUES

The most common online techniques are web-based group discussions; bulletin board groups; and email groups. Recruitment for online research can take place online (via 'pop-ups' or banners on websites or by email invitation, for example) or via traditional methods.

Web-based group discussions

A web-based group can be conducted in a specially set up chatroom in real time. This real time group, which seeks to replicate a traditional face-to-face group, is also known as a synchronous online focus group (SOFG). All participants – recruited in advance – log on and take part in a group discussion simultaneously. The group typically consists of between six and eight participants and the discussion may last between an hour and an hour and a half. The technology allows the moderator to communicate with the group and with individual group members. The client can observe the group output and can communicate with the moderator. Stimulus material can be shown. Depending on the complexity of the task and the number of participants, it is not uncommon to have two moderators. These sort of group discussions are more popular in the US than they are in Europe. In the US, where costs and travel time to groups can be substantial, this approach offers a cost-effective alternative (Walkowski, 2001).

Bulletin board groups

Another way of running a group discussion online is to use a bulletin board approach. As with SOFGs, participants are pre-recruited. This sort of online discussion – because it takes place at different times – is known as an asynchronous online discussion forum (AODF). Participants take part in a discussion at their convenience over an extended period of time. The discussion can run over several days, weeks or even months and involve a 'community' of 20–30 respondents. The moderator briefs respondents about frequency of viewing and responding to questions and comments, which can vary depending on the nature of the research and the duration of the discussion group.

The research-adapted bulletin board allows the moderator to structure and control the discussion. The format of the website used to host the discussion depends on the service or technology provider used. It is designed to facilitate an open-ended discussion between moderator and participants and between participants. Typically, the software includes tools that enable the moderator to design, post and modify the discussion guide; post new questions; monitor the discussion and respondents' participation in it; set up visual and audio stimulus material for participants to view on the main screen or in another window; and send out instructions and information to participants via email. It also includes tools that enable the respondents to click on headings in the discussion guide and post replies and comments to the questions under these headings; and it enables them to comment on or reply to contributions made by other participants. The technology allows the moderator to see who logs on when and for how long, and to track their comments and their viewing of the stimulus material. Case study 6.7 below gives examples of the use of this sort of online discussion.

CASE STUDY 6.7

NEW WAYS FOR NEW PRODUCTS: UNILEVER NPD RESEARCH ONLINE

This case study describes how asynchronous online discussion forums were used with great success in new product development research for an FMCG company.

Why this case study is worth reading

This case study is worth reading for several reasons: it is an example of online group discussions; it shows the fit between the method of data collection and the information needs or research objectives; it highlights the benefits of the approach; it shows how the method can be used with other data collection tools.

The key words are: AODFs, new product development, prolonged discussion, influence of others, open discussion, level of detail, group think, mix of respondent types, dynamics, honest, richly-textured explanations, interactive, community-based, characteristics of the Internet, enabling tool.

Introduction

Unilever wanted to explore new ways to involve consumers early on in the process of researching radically new ideas. A key concern was that really new or innovative ideas tend to be rejected too early in the new product development (NPD) process because consumers tend to immediately reject new, novel, or unfamiliar ideas. Asynchronous online discussion forums (AODFs) seem to be a way to explore consumer interest in such ideas early on in the process. Unilever recognised that new online methods (specifically the AODF approach) gave them the chance to have a prolonged discussion with consumers about these really new product ideas, and so they wanted to explore the potential of AODFs. To test the approach we conducted two AODFs with 30 participants in each. Each ran for a period of two weeks, during which time two very early-stage concepts were explored.

Outcome

The outcome was very positive. The study showed that acceptance did increase substantially during the course of the discussion. It seems that the extended time allowed for a more in-depth discussion about pros and cons. However, it would be wrong to conclude that these changes in opinions were due to time alone. The initial concept description did not fully address all the factors that were important in consumers' minds, and these had to be clarified during the course of the discussion. It is probable that the latter had just as much, if not more, impact on changes in perceptions than time alone.

Other benefits of the approach

The method proved to be useful for other reasons. First, it allows for an initial response from every respondent without the influence of others. After the initial response an open discussion is possible. Secondly, the level of detail and consideration of the responses contributed greatly to the concept development process. And finally, because a typical AODF contains more participants than a regular focus group, it increases the chances of finding 'concept supporters' which in turn contributes to a more open discussion, and reduces the risk of 'group think'.

The technique has been successfully applied in several projects. Because they facilitate a more iterative research approach, AODFs offer the possibility to improve the efficiency and effectiveness of qualitative NPD research. It is conceivable that NPD concept stimuli could be re-worked and fine-tuned during the life of the forum, and re-presented to participants later in the discussion – an approach considered by Unilever. It would be both logistically complex and expensive to replicate this approach using traditional face-to-face qualitative approaches.

Adapting the format

There are many other possible uses of AODFs. For example, the AODF could incorporate a diary-style data collection approach where respondents report back their day-to-day experiences and thoughts into the forum. Respondents could also be asked to complete various offline tasks/assignments during the life of the forum, to supplement the written exchange.

Conclusions

We found that AODFs match the performance of conventional groups in terms of measures of quality such as topic coverage, ability to access hard-to-reach information, and respondent animation. The AODF constitutes both a supportive and enabling tool for researchers, and an acceptable and enjoyable experience for participants. AODFs offer real opportunities for researchers to approach certain types of work in an entirely new way.

Source: Adapted from Balabanovic, J., Oxley, M. and Gerritsen, N. (2003) Asynchronous online discussion forums, MRS Conference, www.mrs.org.uk.

Email groups

Email groups are group interviews rather than group discussions. There is no direct interaction between group members; the interaction is with the moderator and with the moderator's account of the group's responses. In effect, they are more like one-to-one interviews operating in parallel. These 'moderated email groups' (a registered trademark of Virtual Surveys Ltd.) work like this (Comley, 1999; Adriaenssens and Cadman, 1999): the moderator emails questions to each of the group participants, between 10 and 20 per group, who send back their replies within an agreed time. The moderator collates and analyses these responses (often with input from the client) and produces a summary document, which is sent out to the group for comment. There may be a further wave of questions and interaction with the moderator, depending on the nature of the project and the time frame, which can be up to two or three weeks.

ADVANTAGES AND LIMITATIONS OF ONLINE QUALITATIVE RESEARCH

Online research is certainly suitable for researching those topics that relate to the Internet and the World Wide Web – online shopping or website evaluation, for example. It is also suitable when the population of interest is available via the Internet or the Web, and when you need to contact people whom you are unlikely to be able to reach in other ways – busy executives or online traders or members of online communities, for example. In addition, it has a number of practical advantages derived from its key characteristics:

- the people involved – participants, moderator and clients – do not need to be in the same place;
- depending on the method you use, the people involved do not need to be present at the same time;
- it offers anonymity to participants;
- the interaction is easily recordable;
- you can use sophisticated stimulus material; and
- the technology allows you flexibility in the design and execution of the research (e.g. showing different stimuli to different respondents).

In terms of place, there are a number of benefits. Online research sidesteps the logistical issues that you might face in trying to get people together in the one place for face-to-face groups – useful if the people you are trying to recruit to take part in research are members of 'elite' groups (lawyers, doctors, senior executives). In addition, with no need for participants, moderator or clients to travel, and no need to hire a research facility, it can offer savings in cost and time (although cost savings may be wiped out by the cost of IT equipment, set up and technical help, and savings in time may be eaten up by the increased set up and running time needed). From a sampling point of view, it means that you can conduct research with a geographically dispersed sample, and with low incidence samples – both of which may be too costly to do face to face. As we saw above, some forms of online qualitative research (AODFs) allow participants to take part in their own time. This also offers logistical benefits, and may allow you to attract people to take part who may not otherwise be interested in doing so because of the time commitment. With no pressure to respond immediately (as is the case in face-to-face groups and in synchronous online discussions), participants can take their time to compose and reflect upon their responses, and the moderator has more time to consider these responses. Research (Balabanovic et al., 2003) shows that responses tend to be detailed, and that this type of response is typical of all participants – not just a vociferous few, as might be the case in face-to-face groups.

From a methodological point of view, the anonymity of the medium offers a number of benefits allowing you to conduct research on sensitive topics that may be too embarrassing to discuss effectively in face-to-face groups. The anonymity and the remote feel offered by the online environment, coupled with the self-completion nature of the method (no interviewer is physically present with the respondent), engender a high level of honesty and openness from participants as well as a willingness to express extreme and less conventional opinions and a willingness to challenge other participants (Balabanovic et al., 2003). These features of the online environment also allow you to conduct research with diverse or heterogeneous samples, a set-up that can create tensions and a group dynamic that can be difficult to manage effectively in face-to-face research.

The fact that online research is based on written interactions can mean that it appeals to those who prefer to communicate this way, or find it more effective to do so. It can enable participants to consider, and even reflect on, their responses (and those of other participants) in a way that is not possible with verbal communication. As a result the data generated can be richer and more insightful – and more detailed and in-depth – than might be achieved with face-to-face groups. In addition, at the end of an online session you have a complete record of the interaction, ready for formal analysis. There is no time delay or added expense in transcribing the discussion, as is the case in face-to-face work.

What are the disadvantages? There are practical as well as methodological disadvantages. We look at the practical ones first. Online research can be expensive to set up and run. Although there are savings to be had over conventional groups in terms of travel and venue hire, as we noted above, the cost of equipment and technical support and the additional time needed to run an online project may outweigh these savings. With a reliance on technology, there comes the risk of the technology failing and the need to deal with that. The quality of the interaction with participants will be affected by the technological specification of each participant's equipment, in particular bandwith, upload and download speeds, and the availability of appropriate software as well as video and voice facilities. Also, as the volume of traffic on the Internet continues to rise, and to rise rapidly – driven to a large extent by the demand for video streaming and TV over the web – there is also the need to factor in the ability of the Internet to deal with this ever-increasing volume of traffic and to think about what that means for the design and execution of research projects. A further disadvantage is that the recruitment phase of a project can take longer than for traditional research methods – not only do you need to recruit participants but you also need to verify their email addresses and check if they can access the necessary website for the research. You need to prepare and upload the discussion guide and any stimulus material you plan to use, as well as preparing and sending out instructions to participants about how the process (and the software) works. You will be involved in 'fieldwork' over a longer period than would be the case with conventional research since online research tends to happen over an extended period.

The drawback most often cited in online research was the ability to recruit a representative sample of the target population. This was always less of a problem in qualitative research than in quantitative research since sample sizes in qualitative research are relatively small and notions of statistical 'representativeness' do not apply. With Internet access now so widespread, this concern has been banished almost entirely – although it is important in designing and planning a project to give it due consideration: it is still likely that there are people who do not have either access to the equipment or the skills needed to take part in online research. Another (still present) methodological disadvantage is that you have no way of verifying that the participants are who they say they are. Using traditional recruitment practices (face to face and telephone) is one way round this; another is to use a form of back-checking, telephoning respondents after a group session. Quality and consistency checks can also be made on the data themselves. Another drawback of online methodology is that in those methods that do not use a video-link you cannot see the people taking part, so you (and the participants) have no way of seeing, making use of or interpreting body language – which can lead to misunderstandings. Most online methods rely on written interactions between parties and while this has some advantages (noted above), it does mean that the quality of the interaction will depend on participants' ability to articulate their thoughts and feelings and to express these clearly in writing, and to do so in the limited time available. Having to think about things and then write them down produces a different sort of data than the sort you get when participants talk in face-to-face research. It is likely to be more considered, less spontaneous. Further, interaction between participants and between moderator and participants can be limited by comparison with face-to-face groups – because of the nature of the process and because of the limitations of the technology. Developments in software, however, are likely to mean that levels of interaction can be improved. Finally, there is the issue of client confidentiality and security – how to protect any commercially sensitive material that you might use in the fieldwork (product ideas, packaging or advertising mock-ups and so on) and how you deal with the 'disposal' of it in the virtual environment.

Box 6.5 Summary: advantages and disadvantages of online qualitative research

Advantages
- Useful if topic relates to virtual world
- Gives access to low penetration samples
- Gives access to hard-to-reach samples
- Gives access to geographically widely dispersed populations
- Can be a cost-effective alternative to conventional methods
- All participants have an equal chance to contribute
- Heterogeneous (mixed) groups are not a problem
- No group interactions to manage
- Can control interaction/influence of respondents
- Easy to keep to topic
- Suitable if a more structured approach is needed
- Have a verbatim record of the interactions
- Can show sophisticated stimulus material
- Can be flexible in approach and design, varying who sees what and when
- Can tackle sensitive topics
- Intimacy can be established more quickly compared to face-to-face groups
- Can elicit more extreme responses than face-to-face often allows
- Participants can answer at own pace, in own time
- Can get more considered, formal responses
- Respondents are less inclined to give socially desirable responses
- Can get more creative, imaginative, fantasy-driven responses.

Disadvantages
- Some groups may not be reachable via online research
- Verification of respondents difficult
- Respondents can adopt personas
- Interaction between participants is limited
- Interaction with moderator is limited – cannot always probe for detail and clarification
- Not being face to face – some communication lost
- Requires participants with computer literacy, typing skills and email access
- Requires moderator with computer literacy skills and ability to interpret responses
- May need more than one moderator to run efficiently and effectively
- Compatibility of software between moderator and participants required
- Administration and set-up can be difficult (recruitment, commitment, uploading materials)
- Time required can be longer than in traditional face-to-face groups
- Costs can be relatively high compared to traditional methods
- The risk of the failure of technology (in terms of slow speeds, risk of breakdown and security).

Interviewing and moderating skills

Of course doing in-depth interviews or 'moderating' or 'facilitating' group discussions or workshops is not just about asking questions and applying techniques – it is just as much, if not more so, about listening and observing, about building rapport with the research participants, and about managing yourself.

Much of what is communicated is communicated via tone of voice and body language. It is important that you listen not only to what is said but to how it is said – the words used, the pauses, the style of speech and the tone of voice, and the non-verbal cues of body language (Colwell, 1990). This gives you a fuller understanding of the meaning of what is said. This is easier said than done. During an interview or a group you are having a conversation with the respondent or respondents – asking questions, listening, asking the next question. You are also having a conversation with yourself, in your head. You are doing the following:

- thinking about how what the respondent has said or not said fits with the research objectives, or the ideas you have developed about the issue;
- deciding whether or not you should follow it up, or clarify, or move on;
- formulating the next question;
- watching the body language;
- taking account of the dynamics of the interview and what they mean for what should happen next;
- thinking about the time you have left and what else needs to be covered.

Box 6.6 NLP and qualitative research

Neuro-linguistic programming (NLP) is a technique that is applied in a range of fields including qualitative research. Developing a sensory acuity – being alert to what you are hearing and seeing and feeling – is one of the pillars of NLP practice. NLP also focuses on building and maintaining rapport for effective communication and on developing multiple perspectives in order to obtain the maximum amount of information and insight from an encounter. For these reasons it is a useful technique for qualitative researchers to have.

LISTENING

Despite this internal conversation, you must listen actively and attentively to the respondent and you must show that you are listening (in a non-judgemental, empathetic and respectful way) and show that you are interested in what is being said. To do this well:

- remove physical barriers between you and the respondent(s), if possible;
- make eye contact;
- lean slightly forward towards the respondent(s);
- keep a relaxed posture;
- use encouraging responses (nods, 'mm's).

Do not:

- use a desk or other object as a barrier;
- sit too close;
- stare or avoid eye contact or look away;
- look around the room or stare at the floor or at your discussion guide;
- look tense, anxious or ill at ease;
- look at your watch;
- fidget or make unnecessary movements;
- frown or look cross;
- yawn or sigh or make discouraging responses or use a discouraging tone of voice;
- interrupt.

BUILDING RAPPORT

The whole interviewing process can be a nerve-racking experience for respondents – meeting someone (or several people) they have never met before; being questioned and asked to talk about subjects that, sometimes, they may not even discuss with friends. It is vital that the researcher is able to put respondents at ease, and establish rapport – without rapport the quality of the interaction between interviewer and respondents (and the quality of the data) will be poor. Rapport is about getting the respondent's attention and creating trust. You can build rapport by actively listening, as described above, by giving the respondent your full attention and by showing the respondent that you are interested in understanding his or her perspective by going back over what was said. In addition, you can 'mirror' or 'match' – (subtly and genuinely) adopting aspects of the respondent's verbal and non-verbal behaviour – the pace and tone of speech, facial expression, posture, for example.

CASE STUDY 6.8

TALKING TO TEENAGERS ABOUT SEX – PART 2

This case study describes the approach taken to interviewing teenagers about sex, contraception and pregnancy as part of a study to help the government devise a strategy in relation to teenage pregnancy.

Why this case study is worth reading

This case study is worth reading for several reasons: it shows the link between the topic to be researched, the sample and the method; it describes how the researcher approached the interviews and the rationale for this approach; it shows how the interviews were structured and how the pre-task journals were used within the interview.

The key words are: transactional relationship, funnelling down the discussion, two-way relationship, marginalised teenagers.

Our approach

The approach to the research session itself was founded upon three principles:

- Building a transactional relationship;
- Funnelling down the discussion;
- Visual stimulus and sensitive projective techniques.

Building a transactional relationship

The aim is to build a trusting two-way relationship. The question is how. The research participants – marginalised teenagers – rarely have a voice and are almost never taken seriously. To expect to build a relationship based on bonds of trust and friendship in an hour long interview is unrealistic, particularly with teenagers who have often been let down. The participants know they have stuff to say that you need to know. That is why they are being paid: you pay, they talk, you listen. If you don't understand or you need more, you tell them. It's a transaction. And as with any transaction it only works if both parties get something real out of it.

For the moderator the deal is:

- You have to want to hear and listen to what they have to say – no agenda, no predetermined hypotheses.

For the respondent the deal is:

- They have to tell it like it is: no making it up, no pretending.

This simple transaction – this is what is expected of you and this is what you can expect of me – proved effective in creating a two-way relationship of equals.

Funnelling the discussion

The flow of the conversation was designed to put respondents at their ease by starting broad and becoming more personal and specific as the discussion progressed. This is a familiar research technique and was especially important here in generating productive discussion. Here is an outline flow of the discussion:

- Their world
- Relationships in their world
- Intimate relationships
- Sex
- Teen pregnancy
- Condoms and sexually transmitted infections
- Their sexual experiences
- Their use of contraception.

Typically the interview would start with a general conversation about their world, their lives, their homes, their interests, likes and dislikes. This was largely based on their pre-research journals (see Case study 6.9). It was important to show that both their views and their efforts were valued. It was a safe place to start, allowing them to expand on areas they felt confident and secure discussing. The journals were also designed to provide a springboard from that general conversation into a more focused conversation about relationships and people in their lives. Understanding the kinds of relationships they had with those they trust and what they can talk about to whom proved central to the development of the communications strategy that was the reason for the research. The flow from relationships to sex was relatively natural. In general, they were happy to talk about sex, attitudes to contraception and teen pregnancy as long as the subject had a natural place in the conversation.

Source: Adapted from Cohen, J. (2005) 'Teenage sex at the margins', MRS Conference, www.mrs.org.uk.

OBSERVING

To build and sustain rapport you need to observe as well as listen. You need to be aware of and sensitive to respondents' body language, including facial expression (Habershon, 2005), in order to interpret what they are saying correctly and in order to run the interview well. For example, you need to know whether the respondent understands the question or the issue, you need to know whether they are anxious or interested and so on. Body language will help tell you these things. The key elements of body language include the following:

- movements (of the head and other parts of the body, including hand gestures);
- facial expressions;
- direction of gaze (including eye contact);
- posture;
- spatial position (including proximity and orientation);
- bodily contact;
- tone of voice;
- dress.

If you are involved in international research, remember that gestures and body language may mean different things in different countries (Morris, 1994). In addition to observing respondents' body language you need to be aware of your own and the messages that it might be conveying to respondents.

MANAGING YOURSELF

It is important to think about your role in the interview process, about what assumptions you make about the people you are interviewing, and about the topic, and to make these explicit to yourself before fieldwork begins. An open mind and high degree of self-awareness are important ingredients in qualitative interviewing. At the outset of a study you should examine your own feelings and views on it. For example, ask yourself what assumptions you have made about the topic or what you think you might hear from respondents about it; examine what prejudices you have, what your views on it are; ask yourself how prepared you are to hear a view different from your own or to hear something shocking. Remember, part of your skills set as a qualitative researcher includes being able not to give your own opinion and not to appear judgemental.

Box 6.7 summarises the tasks of the qualitative researcher and the skills needed to carry out the role effectively; Box 6.8 explains some of the practical tasks involved in setting up and managing the research. It is widely accepted (Research and Development sub-committee on Qualitative Research, 1979) that the skill and experience of the qualitative researcher 'is the most important determinant of the value . . . of the study'.

THE ROLE OF THE ASSISTANT MODERATOR

In some circumstances an assistant moderator is involved in a group discussion (face to face or online). If, for example, there is a lot of material to cover or a lot of stimulus material to get through, it can be useful to have the help of an assistant, even if in face-to-face groups it is to take charge of the recording, the catering or the paper work. If the project is complex or the deadline is particularly tight it can be useful to have someone to take detailed notes – this can speed up the analysis process. The assistant moderator may be a trainee researcher and, besides the role in assisting or note taking, is there to learn. In some cases the discussion

Box 6.7 The job of the qualitative interviewer or moderator

Key tasks
- Understanding the research brief
- Choosing an appropriate research approach
- Briefing and liaising with recruiters
- Managing the fieldwork process
- Designing the interview guide
- Conducting the interview or discussion
- Creating an atmosphere in which respondents are willing to talk and share
- Listening attentively
- Relating what is being said to the research brief
- Deciding what to explore and in how much detail
- Deciding when to probe or challenge, ask for clarification, or summarise

Key skills (MRS Research and Development sub-committee, 1979)
- Personal capacity for empathy, sensitivity, imagination and creativity
- Ability to become involved and yet remain detached
- Articulate but a good listener
- Intellectual ability but common sense
- Capacity for logical analysis
- Conceptual ability and eye for detail
- Think analytically yet tolerate disorder
- Verbal skills
- Confidence to handle verbal presentations

Box 6.8 Practical aspects of qualitative data collection

Ethics and recruitment
As we noted above, specialist interviewers, known as recruiters, are responsible for finding and inviting people to take part in qualitative research. The recruiter is briefed by a fieldwork manager or by a researcher involved with the project and aims to find people who match the criteria specified. Guidelines for good recruitment practice are contained in *Qualitative Research Guidelines* published by MRS and available at its website (www.mrs.org.uk). These cover the ethical and legal issues that you need to take into account at this stage and throughout the qualitative research process. One of the key ethical and legal issues at the recruitment or sampling stage is getting informed consent. The MRS *Guidelines* offer advice and guidance on this and the MRS Code of Conduct sets out the 'rules' for its members. We note below what you should include in introducing your research to a potential respondent in order to get informed consent. You also need to remember that ▶

the documents created at this stage of the process – completed recruitment questionnaires, incentive and attendance lists – may include personal information that identifies respondents. You must protect this information, including taking steps to ensure that it is not used for any purpose other than that agreed at the time of data collection.

Incentives or participation fees

When participants are being recruited it is fairly common practice, especially in market research, to tell them that they will receive a 'thank you' payment or a participation fee. In being told of it up front, it is a form of incentive to attend (and is usually called an incentive). Anecdotal as well as research evidence suggests that this is a useful strategy – it saves money on sampling and recruitment costs by ensuring that those recruited will attend and avoids the need for excessive over-recruitment and rescheduling. Although the size of the incentive does not cover the total cost of taking part in a group, it shows participants that you value their time and realise the inconvenience they have experienced in attending. It is fairly common nowadays to find that people expect to be paid. According to the MRS Code of Conduct (clause B25), you must tell respondents who it is that is administering the incentive. Some clients or funders, however, particularly in social and academic research, do not have a tradition of paying attendance fees or incentives.

The venue

Qualitative research interviews are conducted in a variety of settings, including the recruiter's home, the respondent's home or workplace, a central venue such as a hotel, or in a specialised research venue. In the United States, most are conducted in these specialised venues, known as viewing facilities, and in Europe they are becoming more and more popular.

A viewing facility comprises a room in which the group or the individual sits (set up to look like someone's living room – although in the United States they have more of an office look) and an adjoining viewing room, where the client can sit to view the interview through a one-way mirror (and, depending on the facilities available, on a monitor – enabling the client to see close-ups of a respondent's face, for example, as well as the group as a whole). The equipment used to record the group is built in such a way that it is unobtrusive.

The choice of venue for the research will be determined by a number of factors, including the following:

- the availability and/or accessibility of a viewing facility or central venue;
- whether the client or funder wants to watch the discussions or interviews;
- the suitability of the venue for the topic under investigation or the type of respondents – for example, a study of household products among a sample of women may be more suited to a home environment; IT use among business people may be better suited to a more formal environment such as a viewing facility or a hotel;
- the type of interview – respondents in individual interviews can feel uncomfortable in a viewing facility, knowing that they are being observed;
- the need to record the research and/or transmit it (very often high quality recording is not possible anywhere but in a viewing facility);
- the need to provide a catering service for client and respondent (fieldwork often takes place at mealtimes, particularly evening mealtimes, and thus it may be necessary to conduct the research in a place that can serve food);

- the culture of the country in which the fieldwork is being done – in some cultures inviting people to a private home or to a viewing facility may not be appropriate;
- cost – hiring a viewing facility can add considerably to the cost of a project.

Whatever venue you choose for the research, make sure that respondents have no difficulty in getting to it (this may involve organising transport for them or ensuring that adequate parking facilities are available). Also make sure that the physical environment is comfortable – neither too hot nor too cold, with adequate lighting, that it is not noisy, has comfortable seats and so on. If necessary (and possible), rearrange the furniture so that there are no barriers between you and the respondent(s).

Ethics and observation

Wherever you conduct the research, even if it is online, if observers are present then you have an ethical responsibility to tell participants that they will be observed and you must tell them by whom and for what reason. Clause B15 of the MRS Code of Conduct states that, 'If there is to be any recording, monitoring or observation during an interview, Respondents must be informed about this both at recruitment and at the beginning of the interview' and B41 that 'Members must ensure that Respondents on attendance at a venue are informed about the nature of any observation, monitoring or recording and Respondents are given the option of withdrawing from the group/interview.' Clauses B21, B34, B37, B38, B39 and B40 reinforce this – among other details of the research, you need to tell respondents if the research is to take place in a viewing facility, whether or not observers are likely to be present and in what capacity, and whether the observer may know the respondent (which might arise in business or employee research). According to the MRS Code (B36), members must also inform observers about their ethical and legal responsibilities, not least in relation to confidentiality.

Ethics and recording of proceedings

Qualitative research – interviews, discussions or workshops – are usually recorded, with the respondents' permission, so that the material collected can be revisited (and transcribed) for detailed analysis. In most cases and in most settings an audio recording is made (tape, digital, MP3 format). If it is important to capture visually what took place – the dynamics or interactions in a group discussion, non-verbal communication, reaction to stimulus material – then the session will be recorded on DVD or downloadable video. Groups taking place in a viewing facility are almost always recorded; some viewing facilities can broadcast the group discussion live over the web so that those who cannot attend in person can watch it.

Again, there are ethical and legal issues to do with recording. As we noted above, Clause B15 of the MRS Code states that respondents must be informed at the recruitment stage that any recording may take place, and B41 reiterates this, noting that respondents have the right to withdraw from the group or interview. Audio and visual recordings are classed as personal data under data protection legislation. B9 in the MRS Code notes that if respondents have given consent for data to be passed on in a form which allows them to be personally identified (this would include recordings), then members must show that they have taken 'all reasonable steps to ensure that it will only be used for the purpose for which it was collected' and they must inform respondents 'as to what will be revealed, to whom and for what purpose'. B42 of the Code states that any material given to the client (including in a report or presentation) without the respondent's consent must be in an anonymised form. For example, the verbatim transcriptions made from the recordings must not contain anything that allows the respondent to be identified.

may be split between the moderator and an assistant moderator, with one maintaining the discussion and the other introducing new topics and handling stimulus material.

Designing the interview or discussion guide

The style of the interview or discussion guide (also known as the topic guide) – the equivalent of the quantitative researcher's questionnaire – varies from a simple list of topics that the interviewer plans to discuss or explore with the respondent to one that has more structure, with a series of questions listed under headings or topics. The style depends on a number of factors, including the following:

- the objectives of the research, for example an exploratory study may mean a less structured approach;
- the method of data collection – individual interview, group discussion or any of their variations – and whether face to face or online;
- the need for comparability between interviews or groups, for example if fieldwork is shared between a number of researchers or is conducted in a number of countries;
- the experience and knowledge of the interviewer – for example, an experienced researcher with an in-depth knowledge of the topic may find it easier to work from a topic guide, whereas a less experienced researcher might prefer to have a more detailed guide;
- the house style or preference of the researcher or client – some clients, for example, prefer a more detailed and structured guide.

Box 6.9 An example of an interview brief

Here is an example of the sort of brief you might get prior to fieldwork – to help you design the interview guide. It describes the background to the project – the reason the research is being conducted – and sets out the objectives of the research. It describes the sort of information you will need to get, in this case from mini-depth interviews.

Background

Centrail Station is a large railway station with local, national and international services. A private sector organisation manages the station and is responsible for leasing out retail units. The leases of three catering outlets are soon to come up for renewal. The management team sees this as an opportunity to review current provision. It has available to it key data about the financial performance of each of the catering outlets. In addition, however, the team wants to understand how station users view what is currently on offer. Armed with this information the management team believes that it will be better placed to make effective decisions about future provision.

Objective

The main objective for this exploratory stage of the research therefore is to get a better understanding for each of the outlets of the following:

- Who are the customers?
- Why do they choose that outlet?
- What do they want?
- What do they need?
- What do they feel they get at present from us?
- How do they feel about that?
- What do they think should be improved?

We need to carry out about 15 mini-depth interviews – lasting about 20 minutes – with customers of each of the three outlets.

Aim for a cross-section of different types of people at each outlet – men and women; a range of ages; people on their own; people in pairs or in groups, including those with children. If approaching a group, find out who chose the outlet they are in and interview that person. Be aware that people will be under a time constraint.

Interview coverage
We need to identify the main issues from the customers' point of view so that we have enough information from which to prepare an effective questionnaire for the quantitative stage of the research. You will need to draw up an interview guide to cover the following:

- Profile of customers: age group, gender, reason for being at the station, reason for travel, who travelling with, length of journey and so on.
- Explore why they are eating/drinking at the station, e.g. was it planned, not planned?
- Explore how the choice was made to eat/drink at that outlet: what was it they wanted, what other outlets were considered and why, who was involved in the decision, what are the perceptions of this outlet and the others considered and so on.
- Find out what meal type was chosen and why.
- Explore experiences/opinions of the outlet chosen, including the standard of service, the environment, the products on offer and those chosen, the price and so on.

QUESTIONING STYLE

The style of questioning used in qualitative research differs from that used in quantitative research (although many of the principles outlined in Chapter 9 Designing questionnaires can be applied to the design of questions and interview/discussion guides for qualitative research). Where most questions in a quantitative interview are closed or pre-coded, questions in qualitative data collection tend to be open ended and non-directive; projective and elicitation techniques are also used – we look at these in more detail later in the chapter. The style or model of interviewing most often used is called the 'psycho-dynamic' model – that is, it is 'based on the assumption that public statements may be rationalizations dictated by what respondents believe interviewers want to hear, or believe they "ought" to say' (Cooper and Tower, 1992). The aim of this style of qualitative interviewing is to get below the surface, beyond the rational response, to encourage respondents to talk in depth and in detail about their experiences, their attitudes and opinions and their thoughts and feelings (Cooper and Branthwaite, 1977; Cooper and Tower, 1992).

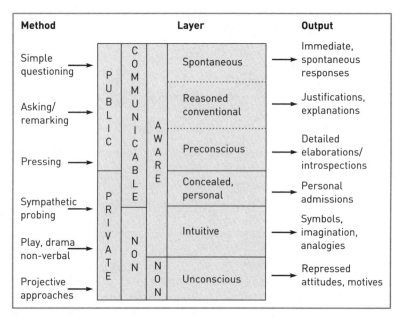

Figure 6.1 A qualitative interviewing model

Source: Cooper, P. and Tower, R. (1992) 'Inside the consumer mind: consumer attitudes to the arts', *International Journal of Market Research*, 34, 4, pp. 299–311, www.ijmr.com.

Open-ended and non-directive questions allow respondents to relate to the topic in their own way, to use their own language (and not that of the pre-coded response) with little or no direction in how to answer from the interviewer or moderator. Probing – using follow-up questions to clarify meaning or to encourage the respondent to answer in more depth or detail – for example, 'Exactly what happened next?' and 'Tell me more about that' – is used extensively. Closed or more precise questions can be used to establish clearly the context or ascertain particular facts – for example 'How much did you pay for it?' or 'How many times did you use it?' Prompting is another way of encouraging the respondent to answer: techniques include repeating the question or rephrasing it; using non-verbal cues – encouraging looks, nods of the head and pauses and silence, for example. It is important, of course, to keep a balance between encouraging the respondents to answer and leading them, or putting words in their mouths – for example 'I suppose you are sorry that you bought it'.

It is important in a qualitative interview or group discussion to listen to exactly how things are being said so that you can ask useful follow-up questions. Listen out for sweeping claims and generalisations, for example 'I always use that' or 'I would never buy that', and think of questions to challenge these claims in a gentle but probing way, such as asking 'Is there any exception?' or restating 'Never?' or 'Always?' Here are some more examples:

- *Response*: 'That's impossible' or 'I couldn't do that.' *Probe*: 'What makes it impossible?' 'What prevents you . . . ?' or 'What if . . . ?'
- *Response*: 'They must/should/need . . .' *Probe*: 'What would happen if they did not . . . ?'
- *Response*: 'That just doesn't work.' *Probe*: 'What doesn't work?'

Other useful questioning techniques include summarising and restating or reflecting what the respondent has said to clarify meaning, help increase understanding and build empathy, for example 'You feel upset about how they handled the problem.'

STRUCTURE OF THE INTERVIEW

The structure of the interview or group discussion is important. There should be a clear introduction and 'warm-up' phase and a clearly signalled ending or 'wind down', in line with the group processes of forming and mourning described earlier in the chapter.

The introduction

A clear introduction is vital – from an ethical point of view and in order to put the respondent(s) at ease. It is likely that they will be nervous (Gordon and Robson, 1980), and it is the interviewer's or moderator's job to allay any fears about what is involved and help the respondent relax. In the introduction you should do the following:

- say something about yourself (your name, the organisation you work for);
- tell respondent(s) about the topic and state the purpose of the research;
- tell the respondent(s) how long the interview is going to take;
- tell the respondent(s) about your role as interviewer or moderator (independent, there to guide the discussion or interview, and to listen);
- tell the respondent(s) how and why they were chosen;
- give assurances about confidentiality and/or anonymity;
- ask the respondents' permission to record the interview;
- tell the respondent(s) whether the interview is being observed and by whom and obtain their consent;
- tell the respondent(s) how the information will be used;
- let the respondent(s) know that their participation is voluntary and that they are free to leave and free to refuse to answer any questions;
- mention the 'ground rules' (that there are no right or wrong answers, that it is not a test, that it is the respondents' experiences, feelings, opinions you are interested in, that all views are valid, that they can talk to each other, that they do not have to agree with each other's views).

Box 6.10 Example of an introduction to an in-depth interview

'My name is [name] from [research organisation]. I am carrying out research on [topic]. The aim of the research is to [brief description]. It has been commissioned by [organisation]. The interview will last about an hour. All the information you give me will remain strictly confidential. Extracts from the interview may appear in the final report but under no circumstances will your name or any identifying characteristics be included. Your participation is entirely voluntary, you are free to end the interview at any time or decline to answer any of the questions.'

The main body of the interview

It is a good idea to start the interview with relatively straightforward, general questions or topics that respondents will find easy to answer or talk about – this helps create a relaxed atmosphere and helps establish rapport between interviewer and respondents. It is possible then to move on to more specific questions or more difficult topics. This technique is known as 'funnelling'. The content and order of the questions should, of course, always be guided by the research objectives of the project and there may be times when you need to take a different approach and jump straight to the main issue.

Here are the types of questions that you might ask in the body of the interview or discussion:

- *Broad, open-ended questions*: 'Tell me about shopping' or 'Tell me about a really satisfying shopping experience.'
- *Pressing and probing questions*: 'What do you particularly like/dislike about shopping?' 'You mentioned X. Tell me more about that.' 'What did you do about that?'
- *Questions narrowing in on particular topics or issues*: 'How did she react when you made the complaint?' 'What happened next?' 'What was the end result?' 'How does that compare to the way X handled it?'
- *Clarifying questions*: 'What exactly did you do then?' 'How did that make you feel?'
- *Summarising statements or questions*: 'You said that they sent you a letter of apology, explaining what the problem had been and offering you your money back. I get the impression that the apology meant the most to you.'

Box 6.11 Extracts from discussion guides

Example 1: Topic style group discussion guide

Subject: Customer satisfaction with problem handling and resolution for a utility company

Introduction
General attitudes towards the service and the service provider
Experience of any problems or areas of concern
Experiences of how provider dealt with problem(s)
Reaction to/feelings about how provider dealt with problem
Feelings about resolution of the problem (satisfied/dissatisfied – probe for detail)
Suggestions for improvement
Close

Example 2: Extract from a more detailed group discussion guide

Subject: Retail store development

Warm up
How often do you visit [type of shop]?
How do you decide which one(s) to visit?
Which do you really like going into? (Probe fully for reasons.)
Are there any you dislike visiting? (Probe fully for reasons.)

Attitudes to target shop
Check – have you ever visited X?
Have you ever bought anything from X?
When was that?

What did you buy?

What do you like/dislike about buying from the shop?

Explore – How would you rate it for the following:

- the range of products and brands;
- keeping the products you want;
- keeping the brands you want;
- prices (including offers);
- service (including staff attitudes, follow-up service);
- layout (including displays, lighting, signs, atmosphere/feel etc.);
- overall image?

What could X do to make you want to go there (more often)/buy more?

The wind down

It is important to signal the end of the interview or discussion – about 10 minutes before the end of an hour-long session, and about 15 minutes before the end of a one and a half to two hour session. Some useful wind-down strategies include presenting a summary of the main points and asking for final comments; asking respondents if there is anything that they have not said that they would like to say, or anything they have said and wish they had not; and asking what one thought or idea the respondent(s) would like the client to take from the session.

In putting together an interview or discussion guide, check that the questions:

- give you the information you want;
- are meaningful and relevant to respondents (and are within respondents' frame of reference);
- are in an order that helps the flow of the interview.

Box 6.12 Example of an in-depth interview guide

Here is the interview guide used to conduct individual in-depth interviews in a study to explore the decision of working adults to live in the parental home, and to understand the experience of living at home.

Background
Tell me a bit about yourself . . .

Age.
Work.
Education.
Relationship status.
Family.
Position in the family?

▶

Parents' lives.
Brothers and sisters.
How long living at home?
When did you move back/decide to stay?

The decision to stay at home
Tell me about your decision to live at home or stay at home . . .
How did it come about? Take me through that . . .
Calculated decision or just happen naturally?
Who influenced it?
Partner, friends, siblings, parents?
Encouraged or pressured?
What influenced it?
Do your friends live at home?
What were the pros and cons?
Economic, financial issues.
Commuting.
Plans for the future. . . . Move out or stay? Rent or buy? Saving to buy house, get married, travel . . .

Experience of living at home

How does it work? | Laundry
Take me through a typical week day . . . | Rent/money
You get up in the morning. . . . | **Set up – behaviour**
You come home after work . . . | Expectations – self, siblings, parents?
What about a typical weekend? | Rules
Set up – facilities | Breaking the rules
Use of rooms in house | Conflict
Access to/own a car | Resolving conflict
Set up – services | Relationships
Responsibilities | Decision making
Who does what for whom? | Support
Cooking | Commitment
Cleaning | Responsibility

Concluding
Sum up
Advantages
Drawbacks
Observations or recommendations to others thinking about staying at home/moving back home?
Any final thoughts you'd like to share, or that came up in the interview that you'd like to elaborate on?

Source: Adapted from Fleming, P., Ni Ruaidhe, S. and McGarry, K. (2004) '"I shouldn't be here": the experiences of working adults living at home'. Unpublished qualitative research project, MSc in Applied Social Research. Used with permission.

PROJECTIVE AND ENABLING TECHNIQUES

Projective and enabling techniques – indirect forms of questioning that are deliberately vague and ambiguous – are often used in qualitative research, and in particular in attitude research, to get beyond the rational response to the 'private' and the 'non-communicable' (Cooper and Branthwaite, 1977). The idea is that respondents will 'project' their ideas, feelings, emotions and attitudes in completing the task. In doing so, responses are elicited that respondents may not have been able or willing to give via direct questioning. It may be that, depending on the objectives of your research project, you will need to build the use of projective and/or enabling techniques into an interview or group discussion. It is likely that the best time to introduce them will be during the main body of the interview or group, when respondents are settled and at ease with the research situation.

Types of projective techniques

There are several types of techniques – techniques of association, completion, construction and expressive techniques. Examples are given in Table 6.1.

Table 6.1 Examples of projective techniques and their uses

Name	Description	Uses
Word association	Respondent asked for first word that comes to mind when given a particular word (spoken or written down).	To explore connections, get at language used, uncover product or brand attributes and images.
Picture association	From a large and varied collection of pictures respondents asked to choose which best suit a brand or a product or its users.	
Thought bubble completion	Respondents fill in what the person depicted in a drawing or picture might be thinking or feeling.	To uncover thoughts, feelings, attitudes, motivations and so on associated with different situations.
Sentence completion	Complete incomplete sentences, for example, 'If X [name of organisation] was really interested in protecting the environment it would . . .'	
Collage	Respondents create a collage from a pile of pictures; or a collage or picture board is compiled in advance of fieldwork.	To uncover a mood, an image or a style associated with a product, a service, a brand, an experience and so on.
Projective questioning	'What do you think the average drinker might think of this bar?'	To uncover beliefs, attitudes, feelings, ideas that the respondent may not want or be able to express directly.
Stereotypes	Develop a story about a person or a picture.	
Personalisation of objects/brand personality	'If this brand were a person, what would he or she look like? What would he or she do for a living? What type of house would he or she live in?'	
Mapping	Sort or group brands or organisations according to key criteria; sort again on a different basis.	To see how people view a market; to understand positioning; to identify gaps.
Choice ordering techniques	Given the ends of a scale, put brands or products where they fall along the scale.	To understand how people see a range of products or brands in relation to certain characteristics and in relation to each other.
Visualisation	Interviewer guides the respondent in thinking back to the last time he or she did X or tried Y, to visualise the scene in all its details.	To allow respondents to recall in detail an experience or a situation and to bring to mind thoughts and feelings about it.
Psycho drawing	Draw a brand or a process.	To bring to mind thoughts and feelings about a brand or a process that could not be articulated or were not top of mind.

UNDERSTANDING THE LIVES OF TEENAGERS

This case study describes the use of journals in a study among marginalised teenagers to help the government devise a strategy in relation to teenage pregnancy. The journals were given to respondents to fill in in advance of the main interview session – thus they were referred to as a 'pre task'.

Why this case study is worth reading

This case study is worth reading for the following reasons: it sets out why this particular approach was chosen; it describes how the task was set up; it notes how useful the journals were in generating rich, insightful data; it describes the end benefits to the client team.

The key words are: concrete examples, journals, pre group task, expectation, co-operative, enthusiastic, creativity, personalised notebooks, stickers, cameras, pictures, visual insight, hidden, powerful.

Introduction

Understanding the lives of teenagers was critical to the brief. This research was designed to find concrete examples of what teenagers think, feel and want. To this end, we asked participants to fill in journals. The journals focused on four areas:

- Their world: Shops, brands, music, TV, magazines, radio
- The people in it: Who they most care about, respect and admire; who they turn to for advice
- Them: Likes, dislikes, desires
- Hopes and fears: What they look forward to; what they want to be doing in ten years' time

To achieve enough journals to represent the lives of the teenagers in this sample the entire sample was asked to complete a journal. The expectation was that half would do so, of which a small proportion would be creative and imaginative. In fact, over 80 per cent of the sample completed journals and the vast majority of them were completed in style. That someone should care enough about their lives to pay them to put it down on paper was good for their confidence and their belief in the value of what they had to say. They expressed their lives and attitudes with flair and creativity.

Approach

The approach that we took to getting the sample to complete the journals was as follows:

- Stay close
- Keep it simple
- Make it visual
- Make it fun
- Make it cool
- Involve others.

Staying close

It is impossible to overstate the importance of recruiters staying close and providing support to respondents in order to generate high quality pre-research journals.

Simple, visual, fun and cool

The aim was to make participants feel, from the moment they first saw the pre task, that it was a fun challenge rather than a burden – designed to enable them to express themselves rather than something they might be made to do at school. To achieve this, they received personalised notebooks and sets of stickers printed with simple questions. Rather than giving them a rigid, predetermined order in which to complete their journal with allocated spaces for answers, the idea was to provide something more flexible and intuitive. The notebooks themselves were carefully chosen to ensure respondents felt good about the task, without being of such good quality or so cool that they didn't want to mess about with them. Written instructions were kept to a minimum.

Using pictures

All respondents were given cameras. There was some debate prior to fieldwork whether a Polaroid would be preferable to a disposable camera. Polaroids provide an instant picture which respondents can then put into their journals. The concern with disposable cameras was that respondents would be reluctant to take pictures, get them developed and then put those pictures into the journal. In the event, both Polaroid and disposable cameras were used and the pictures provided using disposable cameras were generally more revealing and more carefully considered.

Respondents were encouraged to rip things out of magazines and draw images in their diaries in order to give the diaries a real sense of them as people and how they felt. In many cases this was far more involving for respondents, and more interesting for us at the analysis stage, than the formality of photos.

Benefits to the client

One of the key benefits of respondent journals is that they provide a visual insight into the lives of people that would otherwise remain hidden. All involved with the client, the creative teams, strategic planners, media planners, PR consultants and the marketing teams and the government ministers can get a real sense of who the participants are and what matters to them. They have a visual reality that a PowerPoint presentation or written report simply cannot replicate. Because the journals were so powerful, the client made a significant commitment in terms of time and money to ensure that the most was made of them.

Source: Adapted from Cohen, J. (2005) 'Teenage sex at the margins', MRS Conference, www.mrs.org.uk.

Using projective techniques

When using projective techniques make sure that the technique you choose fits the research objectives. If you plan to use projective techniques in international research make sure that the techniques chosen are suitable for the particular culture. If you are conducting a multi-country study make sure that the technique used works in the same way in each country. Those suitable for multi-country work include collage (make sure that the pictures chosen are relevant to the country or market and check the meaning of signs, symbols and colours in each country); word association; bubble and sentence completion; mapping; and personification.

For a technique to work well it must be introduced at the right time, when respondents are relaxed and the interview or group is working well. The task should be simple and straight-forward: explain clearly and precisely exactly what is to be done. Make any instructions – whether it is to be done individually or in small groups, whether respondents can talk to each other during the task, whether they can ask questions, the amount of time available, what will be required at the end of the task and so on – as clear as possible. Reassure participants that it is not a test. As they work on the task, give them plenty of encouragement. Remind them when the time is coming to an end and reassure them that it does not matter if they have not finished. Invite them in turn to explain the end product to you (in an individual interview) or the group. Follow this up with a discussion about what conclusions they would draw from what has been done.

Semiotics and qualitative research

Semiotics is the study of signs and symbols (including words, images and music) and their use and meaning in all forms of communication. Kaushik and Sen (1990) describe, for example, how the colour yellow, which in India is associated with 'life-giving, auspiciousness and . . . vibrancy', used in a sunflower oil advertisement in India 'becomes the signifier that connects the goodness and the light quality of the cooking oil with the life and health-giving qualities of the sun's rays and the sun-kissed flowers'. Semiotics is used in qualitative research to explore, understand and interpret or 'decode' the meaning of signs and symbols, in particular those used in advertising, packaging and brand imagery, and is thus useful in gaining the cultural understanding necessary for developing effective communications, and in particular, cross-cultural communications (Harvey and Evans, 2001). Whereas interviewing aims to find out what people think – what their beliefs, attitudes and opinions are – and what they do – their behaviour – semiotics aims to find out, via the analysis of signs and symbols, what is going on in the surrounding culture – taking what Lawes (2002) calls 'an outside-in approach'. Since the meaning of signs and symbols changes over time, semiotic analysis is a useful way of under-standing what is 'lapsed' or out of date and what is up-to-date and 'emergent'. Also signs and symbols come to signify different things when put together with other signs and symbols. Lawes (2002) notes how 'purple is traditionally about royalty, especially when . . . teamed with gold. . . . However, when . . . used alongside . . . orange or shocking pink its meaning changes and it starts to be about having fun in a wacky kind of way'. This may be another reason for doing semiotic analysis – to understand what it is you are communicating.

As Case study 6.10 below shows, semiotics is often used alongside other forms of qualita-tive research. It can be used to 'decode' the content and meaning of advertising (Harvey and Evans, 2001) or packaging or other media communications (Clough and MacGregor, 2003) – your own and/or your competitors' – to understand what they might be communicating, in advance of group discussions or workshops. You might use this understanding to help structure the workshop, or design your discussion guide, or give you ideas for your analysis. Semiotics can also be used as a follow-up to more traditional qualitative research – to 'decode' what respondents have told you (Griffiths et al., 2004). This mixed method approach – 'informed eclecticism' as Spackman, Barker and Nancarrow (2000) call it – is becoming more common.

In addition, semiotics can be used as a stand-alone method. Alexander (2000) describes how it can be used to understand a brand and its context; Harvey and Evans (2001) show how it can be used to analyse and understand competitors' advertising in several cultures with-out the need for (expensive and time consuming) primary research. In fact, it is perhaps the

DEVELOPING A BRAND PROPOSITION FOR *THE MIRROR*

In Case study 3.1 we saw the business challenges faced by the British tabloid newspaper, *The Mirror*, and the research needed in order to tackle these challenges. In this follow-on case study we learn about the approach the client and its researchers took in addressing the research needs: 'a combination of semiotic analysis, and skilled qualitative work that utilised numerous Consumer Behaviour theories . . .'.

Why this case study is worth reading

This case study is worth reading for several reasons: it shows the link between the business problem, the research needs and the research approach; it gives an overview of the research project; it describes the research approaches used and the rationale for using them; it describes the development and use of a range of stimulus material; it is an example of semiotic analysis in action.

The key words are: semiotic analysis, consumer culture, creative stimulus, extended in-depth interviews, emergent themes, residual, dominant, mood boards, values, beliefs, own language, themes, concept, cultural values, attitudes, external environment, cultural web of meaning, behaviour, media, influence, scrapbook, discussion, collaborative.

Introduction

We needed to develop a new proposition for the brand – a proposition that took into account the colossal changes that had taken place in the lives of our core audience since *The Mirror*'s glory days.

Capturing the Zeitgeist – researching the future

The process we designed for this project involved the following steps:

- Semiotic analysis of UK consumer culture;
- Development of creative stimulus;
- Laddering-style extended in-depth interviews;
- Subsequent video interviews in respondents' homes.

Semiotic analysis of UK consumer culture

The main objectives of this semiotic analysis were to identify emergent themes in the broader cultural backdrop and to understand the direction and pace of change from residual to dominant, and then from dominant to emergent themes. The focus would be on themes of specific relevance to *Mirror* readers, and attention was specifically directed to understanding if being working class is represented as being significant in the media and in popular culture, and how this impacts upon relevant brands in the media category. Analysis was based upon a wide range of materials in the popular culture such as newspapers, magazines, websites, advertising, films, music and books. The semiotics team examined the approaches to such things as target, tone, icons, humour, environment, language, subject matter, music and working class heroes in these materials. Next we needed to understand how consumers reacted to these emergent themes. This required us to develop creative stimulus materials. ▶

Development of creative stimulus: stimulating future thinking

Researching the influence of changing cultural values is not an easy task as individuals are often not conscious of this influence. Stimulus was required that would enable consumers to visualise and react to the possible emergent themes and therefore help the research team to gain understanding of how these relate to *Mirror* readers. The stimulus needed to work at a level that would help us understand the deeper values and beliefs held by *Mirror* readers, and the direction and pace of change we might expect to see. It was vital that the stimulus materials left enough room for individuals to respond openly and in their own language. We used the themes identified by the semiotic analysis to create *stretch moodboards* in order to help us fulfil this objective. An example of one of the themes we used was 'Self Determination' based around the core proposition that 'Life today is more about thinking and acting for yourself'. Words and pictures were selected to stretch this proposition in different directions in order to avoid bias and to allow the research team to identify how *Mirror* readers were responding to different aspects of the concept.

The final piece of stimulus we developed was a comprehensive set of *celebrity photographs* including Royalty, sports personalities, politicians and showbiz celebrities. The aim of this stimulus was to understand the role of these opinion leaders in transferring meaning and thus forming values, beliefs and attitudes.

Researching culture, social class, values, beliefs, attitudes and behaviour

The research approach involved working with respondents to help them see the bigger picture or cultural web of meaning that is influencing their behaviour. In this way we hoped to understand the forces of change and the changing role of media within readers' lives. According to Engel, Blackwell and Miniard (1993) culture is passed from one generation to the next primarily by institutions such as family, religion, and schools. Early lifetime experiences, such as wars and the prevailing economic conditions, and the individual's peer group also transmit values. We believed that by focusing on each of these sources of values we would be able to help readers to articulate their own experiences of the process of cultural change as they had experienced it to date, prior to consideration of forecasted future change.

To understand the power of different sources of influence we asked our interviewees to create their own stimulus in the form of a *scrapbook with photographs* of things in their lives that they considered important, a family tree, their life story and a written description of a person who has strong influence on them. We opened the interviews with these scrapbooks and explored the significance of everything contained within them with our respondents. These items were used to stimulate discussion about the variety of influences upon the development of their values and beliefs in the past and in the present day.

Open and collaborative approaches with respondents allowed us to encourage projection into the future. We often used the past (as previously described by the interviewee) to achieve the sense of trajectory and to help our respondents perceive the process of cultural change as a means to projecting forward. Towards the end of the interview we explored the role of relevant stories picking up on themes that had emerged during the discussion. We also explored attitudes towards a wide range of celebrities to determine not only appeal but respect and values associated with different individuals.

The creative stimulus and the interview approach helped *Mirror* readers to articulate a strong sense of significant cultural change that has taken place during their lifetimes.

References

Engel, J.F., Blackwell, R.D. and Miniard, P.W. (1993). *Consumer Behavior*, 7th edn, Fort Worth, TX: The Dryden Press, pp. 65–116.

Source: Adapted from Clough, S. and McGregor, L. (2003) 'Capturing the emerging Zeitgeist: aligning *The Mirror* to the future', MRS Conference, www.mrs.org.uk.

most appropriate method to use if your aim is to understand communication in whatever form (rather than people's response to or opinions of the communication). It is also a useful technique in understanding likely future trends by uncovering the 'emergent' codes in a sector or culture and analysing developments in culture and communication taking place elsewhere. In Case study 6.11 we see how a semiotic analysis is carried out.

CASE STUDY 6.11

WHAT'S WRONG WITH TAKING THE BUS?

This case study explains how a semiotic analysis was done in order to find out what it is that puts people off taking the bus.

Why this case study is worth reading

This case study is worth reading for several reasons: it shows the link between the business problem, the research needs and the research approach; it gives a detailed guide to how the work was done; it is an example of applied semiotics in action.

The key words are: brainstorming, free associated, resource, themes, data searching, cultural evidence, culturally prominent, cultural background, materials, analysed, technical activity, dismantling, making sense, semiotic toolkit, similarities, differences, culturally available stories, target materials, formal activity, distinct set of tools, research procedure.

Introduction

The client had the idea that there are various prejudices and false beliefs around that discourage people from getting the bus. They wanted us to use semiotics to find out what these prejudices are and where they come from.

Stage 1

Stage 1 begins with a brainstorming session with the team. We free associated on buses – what kinds of things they are, who uses them, what sorts of things happen on buses. We drew on every resource we could think of: songs, jokes, TV entertainment, things in the news, personal experiences. We looked to see what our pool of ideas had in common and organised them into themes. Then we did some data searching to find out if there was any cultural evidence for these themes; were they just things we had made up among ourselves or were they recognisably part of the cultural world? ▶

While data searching we made a collection of pieces of text and images from a range of sources including the Internet, TV, newspapers, magazines and even the children's section of the local library. The set of themes we were looking for changed slightly as we grew more familiar with the cultural landscape. We discovered which themes were culturally prominent and rich in detail, and which ones were impoverished and more in the cultural background.

Stage 2

Stage 2 of the research process is where the collected materials have to be analysed. Semiotics can be a fairly technical activity; when you look at some piece of cultural material – a bit of advertising, say, or a news report – you have to come equipped with a set of tools for dismantling and making sense of what you see. Some of the things in the semiotic toolkit are as follows.

- Visual signs
- Linguistic signs
- Aural signs
- The implied communication situation
- Textual structure
- Information structure
- Visual emphasis
- Genre
- Binary oppositions and contrast pairs
- Communication codes.

The semiotic toolkit helps you think in an organised way about what you are looking at, and notice similarities and differences in the data within a category or sector. In the buses project, one of the themes that we noticed had to do with fear of crime. We collected some data – various stories and images that articulated this fear – and our stage 2 analysis using the semiotic toolkit revealed some interesting things about the nature of this concern.

If you look at culturally available stories about bus travel, the fear is of a specific type of crime – violent physical attack as opposed to pickpocketing, say, or deception. The stories about this type of attack share the same language . . . and they share some interesting narrative conventions. For instance, it's interesting to look at how teenagers are described in these stories. In a story taking place at the bus stop a teenager is more likely to be the victim than the assailant, but in stories where attacks happen on the bus, teenagers are the assailants while the victims occupy another category, akin to 'ordinary British citizens'.

Stage 2 where you deploy the semiotic toolkit is crucial. We did not just say to our client 'here are the prejudices and false beliefs you wanted to know about'. Because we had done some close analysis we were able to provide detailed insight into these culturally available themes and narratives. This was useful because it gave the client an idea of what they were up against, for instance, which of these 'prejudices' were most amenable to change.

Another approach

The bus client came to us with a fairly open brief along the lines of 'find out this about British culture'. On other projects the client asks a specific question to do with a particular piece of packaging or an advertising campaign or whatever. In such a case stages 1 and 2 are collapsed together. We analyse the materials in detail to see what we are dealing with but all the brainstorming and data searching goes on at the same time so that we can form an accurate impression of the cultural context in which the target materials are situated.

Whatever the details of the project, semiotics is always a formal activity with a distinct set of tools and a research procedure.

Source: Adapted from Lawes, R. (2002) 'De-mystifying semiotics: some key questions answered', MRS Conference, www.mrs.org.uk.

Somewhere (and everywhere) within the process of clarifying the problem to be researched, deciding that qualitative research is the best approach, identifying your target sample, choosing the most appropriate method(s) of data collection, designing your topic guide and doing the research, you will be thinking about the analysis of the data. We look in detail at analysis in Chapter 11.

Chapter summary

- There are two main ways of collecting qualitative data – observation and interviewing.
- The main advantage of observation over interviewing is that in an interview the respondent is recalling his or her behaviour whereas in observation the researcher sees it at first hand – without the filter of memory or selection.
- Less traditional methods – methods that are more common in academic social research and government and public sector research, for example, ethnography and semiotics – are becoming more popular in commercial research.
- Ethnography is a method or set of methods for studying and learning about a person or, more typically, a group of people, in their own environment over a period of time. It typically involves both observation – watching and listening to what people say; and interviewing – asking questions.
- The extent to which the researcher is involved with the research participants in an ethnographic study can vary – from complete observer (performing simple observation) to participant observer (participant observation) to complete participant.
- Ethnography can be expensive and time consuming to conduct but it is useful in providing detailed and in-depth understanding of how and why people do things, in the context in which they do them, and how they think and feel at the time of doing.
- Qualitative interviews have been described as 'guided conversations' (Rubin and Rubin, 1995). They are less standardised and more flexible than quantitative interviews. They use a more open-ended and non-directive approach.
- The choice of interview over observation will be dependent on the nature and objectives of the research and the practicalities of time and cost. Interviewing is more cost effective, and suitable when the objectives of the research are clearly defined, and when it is necessary to gather data from a range of people or settings. ▶

- The main forms of interviewing in qualitative research are the one-to-one in-depth interview lasting about one hour and the group discussion consisting of 8–10 respondents and lasting about one-and-a-half hours.

- Individual interviews are used if the topic is sensitive or intimate; if you need detailed information on individual attitudes and behaviour; if you need to get beyond the socially acceptable view; if you need 'timeline' information; or if your sample is difficult to find.

- Group discussions are appropriate if you need to see a wide range of attitudes and opinions; you need to determine differences between people; you do not need minority views or views not influenced by the group; you want to understand social and cultural influences; or you need to draw out creative thinking/solutions.

- There are variations on both the individual interview (paired depths, triads, for example) and the group discussion (mini-groups, extended groups, for example).

- Other interview-based data gathering approaches include workshops, panels and juries. What these have in common is the extended amount of time available for generating the data, and reflecting on it; and the more collaborative or participative nature of the process.

- Group discussions can be conducted online. There are three main approaches: synchronous online focus groups; asynchronous online discussion forums; and email groups.

- There are advantages and disadvantages to online data collection. Advantages include access to low penetration samples and widely dispersed populations; lack of problems associated with heterogeneous groups and group interactions; suitability if a more structured approach is needed; all participants have an equal chance to contribute, they can answer at their own pace and in their own time and responses can be more considered; and the anonymity can mean that you get fewer socially desirable responses. Disadvantages include loss of non-verbal communication and limited interaction between participants and with the moderator; it requires that participants are computer literate and have Internet access; time and costs can be high compared to traditional methods.

- The style of interview or discussion guide varies from a simple list of topics to one that has more structure, with a series of questions listed under headings. The choice depends on the objectives of the research, the need for comparability between interviews or groups, the experience of the interviewer and the house style of the researcher or client.

- Projective and enabling techniques – techniques of association, completion, construction and expressive techniques (indirect forms of questioning that are deliberately vague and ambiguous) – are used to get beyond the rational response.

- Listening and observing and the ability to build rapport with respondents, as well as questioning skills, are vital in qualitative interviewing. Other (related) skills include the capacity for empathy, sensitivity, imagination and creativity and the ability to become involved and yet remain detached.

- Semiotics is the study of signs and symbols and their use and meaning in all forms of communication. It is used in qualitative research to explore, understand and interpret or 'decode' the meaning of signs and symbols, in particular those used in advertising, packaging and brand imagery. It aims to find out, via the analysis of signs and symbols used, what is going on in the surrounding culture. It is often used alongside other forms of qualitative research.

Questions and exercises

1 Your client regularly commissions quantitative research, but has very little experience of the sort of insight that qualitative research can provide. Prepare a document that 'sells' qualitative research to this client. Include a section on the limitations as well as the benefits.

2 You are preparing to undertake a series of in-depth interviews on the same project and the same topic with two other colleagues. Each of you will be conducting six interviews. Describe and give a rationale for the steps you would take to ensure consistency of approach across all 18 interviews.

3 The interview or discussion guide has an important role to play in the quality of the data collected in qualitative research. Discuss.

References

Adriaenssens, C. and Cadman, L. (1999) 'An adapation of moderated e-mail focus groups to assess the potential for a new online (Internet) financial services offer in the UK', *Journal of the Market Research Society*, 41, 4, pp. 417–24.

Alexander, M. (2000) 'Codes and contexts: practical semiotics for the qualitative researcher', *Proceedings of the Market Research Society Conference*, London: MRS, pp. 139–46.

Balabanovic, J., Oxley, M. and Gerritsen, N. (2003) Asynchronous online discussion forums, *Proceedings of the Market Research Society Conference*, London: MRS.

Burgess, R. (1984) *In the Field: An Introduction to Field Research*, London: Allen Unwin.

Clough, S. and McGregor, L. (2003) 'Capturing the emerging zeitgeist: aligning *The Mirror* to the future', *Proceedings of the Market Research Society Conference*, London: MRS.

Cohen, J. (2005) 'Teenage sex at the margins', *Proceedings of the Market Research Society Conference*, London: MRS.

Colwell, J. (1990) 'Qualitative market research: a conceptual analysis and review of practitioner criteria', *Journal of the Market Research Society*, 32, 1, pp. 13–36.

Comley, P. (1999) 'Moderated email groups: computing magazine case study', *Proceedings of the ESOMAR Net Effects Conference*, London.

Cooper, P. and Branthwaite, A. (1977) 'Qualitative technology: new perspectives on measurement and meaning through qualitative research', *Proceedings of the Market Research Society Conference*, London: MRS.

Cooper, P. and Tower, R. (1992) 'Inside the consumer mind: consumer attitudes to the arts', *Journal of the Market Research Society*, 34, 4, pp. 299–311.

Cursai, C. (2001) 'A critical evaluation of face-to-face, interviewing vs. computer-mediated interviewing', *International Journal of Marketing Research*, 43, 4.

Desai, P., Roberts, K. and Roberts, C. (2004) 'Dreaming of the global future – identity, culture and the media in a multicultural age', *Proceedings of the Market Research Society Conference*, London: MRS.

Desai, P. and Sills, A. (1996) 'Qualitative research among ethnic minority communities', *Journal of the Market Research Society*, 38, 3, pp. 247–65.

Engel, J.F., Blackwell, R.D. and Miniard, P.W. (1993) *Consumer Behaviour*, 7th edn. Fort Worth, TX: The Dryden Press.

Fleming, P., Ni Ruaidhe, S. and McGarry, K. (2004) '"I shouldn't be here": the experiences of working adults living at home'. Unpublished qualitative research project, MSc. in Applied Social Research.

Flemming from Thygesen and McGowan, P. (2002) 'Inspiring the organisation to act: a business in denial', *Proceedings of the Market Research Society Conference*, London: MRS.

Gale, B.T. (1994) *Managing Customer Value*, New York: Simon & Schuster.

Gold, R. (1958) 'Roles in sociological field observations', *Social Forces*, 36, 3, pp. 217–23.

Goodyear, M. (1996) 'Divided by a common language: diversity and deception in the world of global marketing', *Journal of the Market Research Society*, 38, 2, pp. 105–22.

Gordon, W. and Robson, S. (1980) 'Respondent through the looking glass: towards a better understanding of the qualitative interviewing process', *Proceedings of the Market Research Society Conference*, London: MRS.

Griffiths, J., Salari, S., Rowland, G. and Beasley-Murray, J. (2004) 'The Qual remix', *Proceedings of the Market Research Society Conference*, London: MRS.

Habershon, J. (2005) 'Capturing emotions', *Proceedings of the Market Research Society Conference*, London: MRS.

Hammersley, M. and Atkinson, P. (1995) *Ethnography: Principles and Practice*, London: Sage.

Harvey, M. and Evans, M. (2001) 'Decoding competitive propositions: a semiotic alternative to traditional advertising research', *Proceedings of the Market Research Society Conference*, London: MRS.

Junker, B. (1960) *Fieldwork: An Introduction to the Social Sciences*, Chicago: University of Chicago Press.

Kaushik, M. and Sen, A. (1990) 'Semiotics and qualitative research', *Journal of the Market Research Society*, 32, 2, pp. 227–42.

Langmaid, R. (2005) '21st century qualitative research', *Proceedings of the Market Research Society Conference*, London: MRS.

Langmaid, R. and Andrews, M. (2003) *Breakthrough Zone*, London: Wiley & Co.

Lawes, R. (2002) 'De-mystifying semiotics: some key questions answered', *Proceedings of the Market Research Society Conference*, London: MRS.

Mariampolski, H. (1999) 'The power of ethnography', *Journal of the Market Research Society*, 41, 1, pp. 75–87.

Mattinson, D. (1999) 'People power in politics', *Journal of the Market Research Society*, 41, 1, pp. 87–95.

Morris, D. (1994) *Bodytalk: A World Guide to Gestures*, London: Jonathan Cape.

MRS Code of Conduct (2005), London: MRS (www.mrs.org.uk).

Palmer, S. and Kaminow, D. (2005) 'KERPOW!! KERCHING!! Understanding and positioning the SPIDER-MAN brand', *Proceedings of the Market Research Society Conference*, London: MRS.

Renzetti, C. and Lee, R. (eds) (1993) *Researching Sensitive Topics*, London: Sage.

The Research and Development Sub-Committee on Qualitative Research (1979) 'Qualitative research: a summary of the concepts involved', *Journal of the Market Research Society*, 21, 2, pp. 107–24.

Rubin, H. and Rubin, I. (1995) *Qualitative Interviewing: The Art of Hearing Data*, London: Sage.

Sampson, P. (1967 and 1996) 'Commonsense in qualitative research', *Journal of the Market Research Society*, 9, 1, pp. 30–8 and reprinted in 38, 4, pp. 331–9.

Spackman, N., Barker, A. and Nancarrow, C. (2000) 'Happy New Millennium: a research paradigm for the 21st century'. *Proceedings of the Market Research Society Conference*, London: MRS, pp. 45–53.

Tuckman, B. (1965) 'Developmental sequence of small groups', *Pyschological Bulletin*, 63, pp. 384–99.

Tuckman, B. and Jenson, M. (1977) 'Stages of small group development re-visited', *Group and Organizational Studies*, 2, pp. 419–27.

Walkowski, J. (2001) 'Online qualitative research for Motorola: lessons learned', *Proceedings of the Association for Qualitative Research/Qualitative Research Consultants Association*, Paris.

Recommended reading

Adriaenssens, C. and Cadman, L. (1999) 'An adapation of moderated e-mail focus groups to assess the potential for a new online (Internet) financial services offer in the UK', *Journal of the Market Research Society*, 41, 4, pp. 417–24.

Birn, R. (ed.) (2000) *The International Handbook of Market Research Technques*, 2nd edn, London: Kogan Page.

Bristol, T. and Fern, E. (1996) 'Exploring the atmosphere created by focus group interviews: comparing consumers' feelings across qualitative techniques', *Journal of the Market Research Society*, 38, 2, pp. 185–95.

Brooks, V. (2003) 'Exploitation to engagement: the role of market research in getting close to niche markets', *International Journal of Market Research*, 45, 3, pp. 337–54.

Chrzanowska, J. (2002) *Interviewing Groups and Individuals in Qualitative Market Research*, London: Sage.

Desai, P. (2002) *Methods Beyond Interviewing in Qualitative Market Research*, London: Sage.

Gabriel, C. (1990) 'The validity of qualitative market research', *Journal of the Market Research Society*, 32, 4, pp. 507–20.

Gordon, W. (1999) *Goodthinking: A Guide to Qualitative Research*, Henley-on-Thames: Admap.

Hammersley, M. and Atkinson, P. (1995) *Ethnography: Principles in Practice*, London: Routledge.

Harvey, M. and Evans, M. (2001) 'Decoding competitive propositions: a semiotic alternative to traditional advertising research', *Proceedings of the Market Research Society Conference*, London: MRS.

Kaushik, M. and Sen, A. (1990) 'Semiotics and qualitative research', *Journal of the Market Research Society*, 32, 2, pp. 227–42.

Kenyon, A. (2004) 'Exploring phenomenological research: pre-testing focus group techniques with young people', *International Journal of Market Research*, 46, 4, pp. 427–41.

Krueger, R. (1998) *Moderating Focus Groups*, London: Sage.

Lee, R. (1992) *Doing Research on Sensitive Topics*, London: Sage.

McPhee, N. (2002) 'Gaining insight on business and organisational behaviour: the qualitative dimension', *International Journal of Market Research*, 44, 1, pp. 53–70.

Marsden, P. (2002) 'What "Healthy-Living" means to consumers: trialling a new qualitative research technique', *International Journal of Market Research*, 44, 2, pp. 223–34.

Maughan, B. (2004) 'Investigator-based interviews', *International Journal of Market Research*, 46, 1, pp. 99–107.

O'Connor, J. and Seymour, J. (1993) *Introducing NLP*, London: HarperCollins.

Rose, J., Sykes, L. and Woodcock, D. (1995) 'Qualitative recruitment: the industry working party report', *Proceedings of the Market Research Society Conference*, London: MRS.

Rubin, H. and Rubin, I. (1995) *Qualitative Interviewing: The Art of Hearing Data*, London: Sage.

Sampson, P. (1985) 'Qualitative research in Europe: the state of the art and the art of the state', ESOMAR Congress, Wiesbaden.

Schlackman, W. (1984) 'A discussion of the use of sensitivity panels in market research', *Proceedings of the Market Research Society Conference*, London: MRS.

Sykes, W. (1990) 'Validity and reliability in qualitative market research: a review of the literature', *Journal of the Market Research Society*, 32, 3, pp. 289–328.

Valentine, V. (2002) 'Repositioning research: a new MR language model', *International Journal of Market Research*, 44, 2, pp. 163–92.

Chapter 7

COLLECTING QUANTITATIVE DATA

Introduction

Quantitative research is about collecting data from a relatively large sample or population in a structured and standardised way. In this chapter we look at the main methods of collecting such data – via interviewing (interviewer-administered and self-completion) and observation.

Topics covered

- Interviewing
- The role of the interviewer
- Face-to-face interviews
- Telephone interviews
- Self-completion methods
- Other data collection formats
- Observation

Relationship to MRS Advanced Certificate Syllabus

The material covered in this chapter is relevant to Element 5 – Planning and Conducting Quantitative Research. It should give you knowledge and understanding of the main techniques for gathering quantitative data. It should help you develop your ability to choose and your ability to evaluate techniques in relation to given research scenarios. It should also help you understand some of what it is you need to do in planning a quantitative research project – we look at other aspects in Chapter 8 on sampling, Chapter 9 on designing questionnaires and Chapter 10 on managing a project.

Learning outcomes

At the end of this chapter you should be able to:

- show awareness of the range of different methods of data collection used in quantitative research;
- understand the uses of each method;
- understand the limitations of each method;
- select the appropriate method or combination of methods for a given research proposal.

Interviewing

Quantitative data can be collected via interviews using standardised structured or semi-structured 'forms' – interview schedules or questionnaires and diaries. There are two ways of getting your sample to complete these 'forms'. You get the respondent to do it themselves – this is called 'self-completion'; or you get an interviewer to ask the questions, either in person face to face or via the telephone, and record the respondent's answers on the 'form' – this is called 'interviewer administered'. The option you choose will depend on a number of things. You will need to determine how suitable the method is for the following:

- the study and its objectives;
- the topic or issues under investigation;
- reaching the right sample;
- achieving the right numbers;
- the time and budget available.

For example, if you have a subject of a very sensitive nature a telephone or an online interview may be the best option as it offers the respondent a degree of anonymity and distance that a face-to-face interview does not. If you have a sample that is hard to reach in person – a sample of business executives, for example – a telephone, postal or email survey may be the best or only way of contacting them. If you need to show respondents stimulus material, for example an advertisement, or get them to try a product, a face-to-face approach may be the only feasible one. If you need to achieve a particular sample size you may decide against a postal survey or an email survey unless you are fairly sure that the return or completion rate (which can sometimes be hard to predict) will give you the numbers (and the sample) you need. If you are working to a tight budget you might consider a postal or online survey – with no interviewer costs it can be cheaper than a telephone or face-to-face survey. If you are working to a tight deadline a postal survey may not be appropriate – turnaround times are often relatively long – therefore a telephone or email survey might be considered.

Before we look in detail at the different methods of interviewer-administered data collection, it is first of all worth looking at the role of the interviewer.

The role of the interviewer

The interviewer has two jobs to do: contact people who match the recruitment or sample criteria of the survey and encourage them to take part in an interview, and administer the interview. This is a skilled job. It requires a high level of interpersonal skill, a sound understanding of the data collection and research processes, including responsibilities under data protection legislation as well as those set out in the relevant code of professional conduct, for example the MRS Code of Conduct or the ICC/ESOMAR Code of Practice. MRS publishes general guidelines for interviewers and guidelines relating to interviewing on specific types of projects including for example product tests. You can view these guidelines at the MRS website (www.mrs.org.uk). On the site you will also find a link to a set of health and safety guidelines for interviewers conducting work face to face.

THE EFFECT OF THE INTERVIEWER

Interviewers are not all the same and nor are respondents. An interviewer may react to or interact differently with different respondents, and respondents will react differently to different interviewers. Much research has been done on the effect an interviewer has on response rates and on the quality of data collected. There is evidence to show that appearance, age, gender, social grade, ethnic background, religion and attitude or personality have an effect on the interviewing process and on the outcome of the interview. This is not confined to face-to-face interviews. Research shows that respondents in telephone interviews make judgements about an interviewer's characteristics on the basis of his or her voice. To minimise the effects of interviewer variance interviewers are trained to carry out interviews according to the instructions provided and to do so in a professional, courteous and objective way.

UNIFORMITY OF APPROACH

A questionnaire will have been designed to gather data from a relatively large number of people that make up the sample or population under study. Due to the number of interviews needed it is likely that more than one interviewer will be involved in the data collection process. Uniformity or consistency of approach is a key aim in structured and standardised quantitative research – data must be collected in the same way across the sample and any possible bias or errors (part of the family of non-sampling errors) in asking questions or recording responses must be kept to a minimum. It is important therefore that each respondent is asked the questions on the questionnaire in exactly the same way. This means that the interviewer must read out instructions and ask the questions exactly as they appear on the questionnaire, and in the way that they were briefed to do (a change of emphasis on a word can change the meaning). With closed, pre-coded questions the interviewer selects or records the code that applies to the respondent's answer. For some questions, such as those with an 'other' code in the list of pre-coded responses, or where the respondent says 'Don't know' or 'Not sure', the interviewer may need to probe (depending on what it says in the briefing notes or instructions given during training). Where there are open-ended questions, questions that require the respondent to answer in their own words, the interviewer must record the answers verbatim. If probing is needed, to elicit a more detailed response, the interviewer must follow the specified probing/prompting procedure set out on the questionnaire or specified in training and in the briefing for the particular study. The interviewer must record the result of the probing/prompting.

All this means that the interviewer must be familiar and comfortable with the questionnaire and the interviewing process. Two things are vital here: interviewer training and project briefing. Questionnaire design also has a role to play: the person designing the questionnaire has a responsibility to the interviewer to ensure that the questionnaire is clear, logical, easy to follow and set out in such a way that makes it easy for the interviewer to record responses. We return to this in Chapter 9.

TRAINING

Typically training will have been provided by the research agency or fieldwork company for whom the interviewer undertakes work. This training will usually have involved one or two days of 'theory' in the classroom covering the following:

- how to find the right respondent;
- how to obtain and record information to determine the respondent's social grade;
- how to get the respondent to agree to an interview;
- explaining the nature of the interview and the time needed to conduct it;
- explaining about confidentiality, and the use of the personal details collected;
- the importance of asking questions and reading out instructions exactly as they appear on the questionnaire;

- the importance of coding pre-coded responses accurately;
- the importance of recording responses to open-ended questions verbatim or as close as possible;
- the extent of probing allowed or required and the manner in which probing is to be done (and how this should be recorded);
- how to use the data collection equipment;
- how to complete all paperwork accurately.

Office-bound training is followed by some practice interviews in the field under the supervision of a senior interviewer for face-to-face interviews, on the telephone with a supervisor or senior interviewer listening. Further on-the-job training takes place at regular intervals. Interviewers may be accompanied or listened to by a senior interviewer, supervisor or area manager from time to time to check on the quality of their work, especially if they are assigned a type of job of which they have little experience. This is part of the overall quality control procedure that is part of the management of a fieldforce. Fieldwork quality control also includes checking and monitoring the interviewers' completed work.

INTERVIEWER QUALITY CONTROL SCHEME

The Interviewer Quality Control Scheme (IQCS) was set up by MRS in 1978 to address the issue of quality in fieldwork. Now an independent legal entity, IQCS (www.iqcs.org) outlines a minimum standard for the quality of interviewers and interviewing in consumer, social and business-to-business research. Any company wishing to join the scheme must meet these minimum standards in a number of areas including recruitment, training, quality control (respondent and data validation), survey administration and office standards. The aim of the scheme is to assure clients that all data are collected to acceptable and ethical standards.

MRS ACCREDITED INTERVIEWER TRAINING

MRS has introduced a scheme of accreditation for interviewers. The aim of this scheme is to set national professional standards for interviewing and to provide a recognised qualification. To become an accredited interviewer, interviewers must complete a training scheme run by an accredited trainer – either an employer such as a research agency or a third party training provider who has achieved the Accredited Interview Training Scheme qualification. On successful completion of the training, the interviewer is awarded the MRS Certificate in Interviewing Skills for Market & Social Research.

INTERVIEWER BRIEFING

Interviewers are briefed in detail about the requirements of each particular job. The aim of briefing interviewers on each job is to ensure overall consistency of approach – by making sure that they understand clearly how to administer that particular questionnaire, and to address any concerns or questions that they may have about it. The briefing may be given by the client service or field executive or the supervisor or area manager, although it may sometimes involve the person commissioning the work (the client). Most briefings for telephone surveys take place face to face – mainly because the interviewers work from a central telephone unit and those involved with the project are usually on hand. In-person briefings for central location face-to-face surveys are common; those for street and in-home or at-work surveys often less so because of budget restrictions – it is expensive to gather together geographically dispersed interviewers and supervisors and client service or field staff. In such circumstances briefings are typically given by post, email or telephone. We look in detail at what is involved in a briefing in Chapter 10.

Face-to-face interviews

Depending on the nature of the survey, face-to-face interviews can take place in the respondent's home, in the street, in a central location, for example in a hall or in a shopping centre or mall, or at the respondent's place of work. Thus, if you need a quota sample of consumers, the interview is about product preferences and is likely to last no more than about ten minutes, you could recruit and conduct interviews in the street or in a central location such as a shopping centre. If, however, you are conducting a random sample survey on household spending that lasts up to 35 minutes, a face-to-face, in-home interview may be more appropriate.

STREET INTERVIEWS

Street interviews are conducted in busy streets, mostly in town centres where there is a lot of pedestrian traffic. The interviewer approaches people who seem to fit the sampling criteria, if the research is being conducted using a quota sample; if a random sample is required, the interviewer approaches the nth passer-by and requests an interview. Street interviews usually last no more than ten minutes – people will not stand around answering questions for any longer. The topic of the interview must be one that most people are content to talk about on the street. The amount of stimulus material that can be shown is limited.

MRS publishes a code of practice for interviewers working in town centre locations. It was put together to help ensure good practice so that town centres can continue to be used in sampling or the recruitment of people to take part in market research studies. A copy of the code can be downloaded from the MRS website.

SHOPPING CENTRE/HALL TESTS

The main advantage of interviewing in shopping centres or malls (or rooms or halls off busy shopping streets) compared to interviewing in the street lies in the comfort of the environment – interviewer and respondent are protected from the weather and the centre is traffic free. This allows a slightly longer interview, up to about 15 minutes. In addition, the layout of the centre may be such that it is possible to set out an interviewing station with tables and chairs at which to seat the respondent. As a result the shopping centre or hall may be used for what are known as 'hall tests' – longer interviews that would not be feasible in the street, lasting up to about 30 minutes. This format also allows scope for exposing the respondent to stimulus material – for example tasting a product.

Shopping centres and halls are private property and permission must be obtained in order to conduct fieldwork; a fee for their use is usually payable. Where necessary and relevant, interviews can also take place inside shops, but permission must again be obtained.

MRS publishes a checklist on its website of the sort of issues you need to address if you are planning on conducting a hall test which involves the testing of food or drink products. These include, for example, the following:

- Is the venue suitable and hygienic for the proposed test?
- Is the hall management happy for you to test out the products you are proposing to test (e.g. alcohol in church halls)?

CASE STUDY 7.1

INTERVIEWING IN GAY BARS

This case study describes how and why some of the fieldwork for a 1986 study of attitudes and behaviour in relation to AIDS was conducted in this non-typical venue.

Why this case study is worth reading

This case study is worth reading for several reasons: it shows the link between sample and fieldwork location; it highlights the issues of interviewing in a non-typical venue; it describes how the fieldwork was set up and managed in unusual conditions.

The key words are: gaining co-operation, type of interviewer, interviewing, central location, separate room, supervisor, research team, co-operation levels, refusals.

Introduction

We needed to interview homosexual men. We anticipated that we would have only limited success in locating this group by conventional methods. This was borne out in practice. It was therefore decided to attempt to sample them via known gay clubs and pubs. This raised major potential problems of gaining co-operation both from the owners and managers to set up interviewing facilities, and from clients to spend 40 minutes being interviewed when they had presumably gone out in the evening to enjoy themselves. It also posed problems of the type of interviewer to be used, given the nature of the locations and the time they were open (from midnight to 3am in some cases).

Bars often vary in their nature and clientele on different nights of the week, and thus care is taken to go on the same night out of the week on each occasion of visiting a particular bar. Interviewing is spread across the whole week and the day is selected in consultation with the manager, avoiding very quiet or exceptionally busy days. A team of three interviewers goes to each bar and sets up what is in effect a 'central location' system. Sometimes this is in a separate room; often it is in a corner of the bar. Respondents are recruited from the clientele and bought a drink at the end of the interview. Names are not taken. On the occasion of the first visit the team comprises one of the research team, plus a supervisor and an interviewer; on the second and subsequent visits a supervisor and two interviewers go along. Some of the executives and interviewers are men and some women; the supervisors are all women.

This aspect of the project succeeded beyond anyone's expectations. Of the initial sample only one club refused and subsequently we have had four more refusals. Although initially some managers said they would prefer only male interviewers, timing and other logistics meant this was not possible, and 'ordinary' interviewers have done the bulk of the work. Working in very unusual circumstances and in disco lighting and sound has been an eye-opening experience but refusals from those approached for interview are much lower than in conventional surveys. Often people queue to be interviewed and the co-operation levels are an indication of the seriousness with which the gay community in Britain is treating this problem. On any one evening the number of interviews obtained depends on the length of time the club is open, but it averaged about 14.

Source: Orton, S. and Samuels, J. (1997) 'What we have learned from researching AIDS', *International Journal of Market Research*, 39, 1, pp. 175–200, www.ijmr.com.

- Have you thought through the logistics of the hall test and what is going to happen in what way (before, during and after the hall test)? Is there sufficient space and are the facilities appropriate?
- Has access been considered? If you have refrigerated units, is the room you have hired on the ground floor and do the units fit through the doors? Are there sufficient plugs for any electrical appliances you may wish to use?
- If you need to use a kitchen, is it to the required standards and does it have all of the equipment you require (and are they clean and useable)?

IN-HOME INTERVIEWS

In-home interviews are conducted in the home of the respondent or on the doorstep. In-home interviews may be used for several reasons. It may be necessary to recruit the sample by going door to door to specific addresses (for example addresses chosen at random from a sampling frame such as the Electoral Register or the Postal Address File) or by going to specific areas or streets identified under a geodemographic classification system as containing the type of people likely to meet the sampling criteria. It may be that the home environment is the most suitable place for the interview – it may be necessary to refer to products used in the home or it may be a sensitive topic and the home may be the most relaxed environment for asking such questions. It may require the interviewer to record observations, for example the brand and model of washing machine or HD television – something that the respondent is unlikely to remember in detail. Interviewing in-home allows a longer interview to take place, usually about 45 minutes to an hour.

WORKPLACE INTERVIEWS

Workplace interviews are suitable when the subject matter of the interview is related to the respondent's work. The interview is conducted in the respondent's office or in a suitable meeting room or in a quiet area; somewhere, if possible, where interruptions – from the telephone ringing to people knocking at the door – can be kept to a minimum.

STRENGTHS OF FACE-TO-FACE INTERVIEWS

Face-to-face data collection has a number of advantages. The interviewer has the chance to build rapport with the respondent, which can help achieve and maintain co-operation and increase the quality of the data. Response rates can be relatively high in comparison to other methods. Face-to-face methods allow for a relatively high degree of flexibility in the interviewing process – the interview can last up to an hour; stimulus material can be used; complex questions can be explained and administered; and probing and prompting carried out. In central location or hall tests the environment of the interview can be controlled.

WEAKNESSES OF FACE-TO-FACE INTERVIEWS

There are some disadvantages with face-to-face data collection, particularly in relation to in-home interviews. It is relatively expensive and time consuming. It is difficult to cover remote or rural locations. Cluster sampling methods, which serve to reduce travel time and costs, risk introducing sample bias. Representativeness of the sample can be affected in other ways: interviewers may find it difficult to obtain interviews in higher income areas; they may be reluctant to interview in some (socially deprived) neighbourhoods, from a safety point of view, for example; indeed potential respondents in any neighbourhood may be unwilling to open the door to a stranger. Finding respondents at home (or at work) at a suitable time (and willing to take part) can be difficult. To overcome this it is often necessary (and almost essential for business-to-business interviews) to make an appointment with the respondent, either by telephone or in person, to set a suitable time, which further adds to the cost and the time needed for the survey. Interruptions from other members of the household or workforce or the presence of someone else in the room during the interview can impact on the quality of the data collected. There is a greater tendency in face-to-face methods for the respondent to give socially desirable responses – to appear in the best possible light. With quality control procedures at a greater distance than in telephone interviewing (where interviewers' work can be continuously monitored) there is greater scope for interviewer bias or cheating.

Box 7.1 Computer-aided data capture

Data can be captured and recorded electronically via a PC, laptop or handheld computer or personal digital assistant (PDA):

- CAPI – computer-aided personal interviewing;
- WAPI – web-aided personal interviewing;
- CATI – computer-aided telephone interviewing;
- CASI – computer-aided self interviewing;
- CAWI – computer-aided wireless interviewing.

In computer-aided methods the questionnaire (and the stimulus material), data entry and data editing and verification procedures are programmed into the computer. To start a new interview the interviewer calls a new questionnaire up on screen and enters responses into the computer using the keyboard or touch screen. The program is designed so that it automatically brings up the next question relevant to that respondent as soon as the response to the previous question is entered. All completed questionnaires are either stored in the computer's memory for later download or they are downloaded 'live' to a central computer at the agency's data processing centre. There are many advantages in using computer-aided methods.

Fieldwork management

- No printing of questionnaires required;
- Review of quotas and sample;
- Monitoring of interviewer performance and strike rates;
- Data on interview length;
- Electronic access to all questionnaires.

Use of stimulus material

- High quality images embedded in the questionnaire;
- Multi-media capabilities – can embed and play high quality video and audio material, can link to the web.

Data processing

- Checking and editing done automatically;
- No manual data entry – data downloaded to central processing;
- Interim results easily obtainable;
- Fieldwork to tabulation time greatly reduced.

Data quality

- Smooth flow of interview;
- Digital recording of verbatim responses;
- Automatic routing reduces errors;
- No separate data entry eliminates keying errors.

The main disadvantages are the capital investment required to buy and maintain the hardware and software and program the devices for data collection, storage and transmission; the cost of training and supporting interviewers and other staff in using the equipment; and the risk that the technology – the hardware or the software – will fail. For the 2010 Census in the United States, the government planned to use handheld wireless PCs to collect and transmit data from those who do not send in a Census return by post. In previous Census rounds this information was collected using pen and paper. But in April 2008 the government scrapped its plan for various reasons including: the complexities of programming the handheld devices, problems in testing, and issues of timing and cost. It reverted instead to the tried and tested pen and paper method to gather the non-returners' data.

Pilot testing is strongly advised in using any sort of computer-aided data collection for many reasons, not least that the hardware or the software can fail; even a simple mistake in the script (the programmed questionnaire) cannot be as easily rectified as it might be on a paper questionnaire once fieldwork begins. In some instances these risks may cancel out any potential benefits of using this method of data collection.

CASE STUDY 7.2

ASKING ABOUT CHILD ABUSE AND NEGLECT: FACE TO FACE OR NOT?

This short case study presents the rationale for the choice of method of data collection in a study into child abuse and neglect for the charity, the National Society for the Prevention of Cruelty to Children (NSPCC).

Why this case study is worth reading

This case study is worth reading for two main reasons: it explains the thinking behind the decisions about methods of data collection; it describes how the data collection process was structured.

The key words are: mode of administration, postal self-completion, complexity, sensitivity, face to face, privacy, confidentiality, honesty, computerised self-completion (CASI), questionnaire.

▶

What method?

Although some studies on the subject of child abuse and neglect have used postal self-completion methods of data collection, it was clear to us that a study of this importance, complexity and sensitivity required face-to-face contact between interviewer and respondent. However, we recognised the benefits offered by self-completion in terms of privacy, confidentiality and honesty of responses, particularly computerised self-completion. We therefore administered the most sensitive questions about experience of abuse using CASI (computer aided self-completion interviewing).

The questionnaire was introduced as being about 'experiences in childhood' and began by collecting some general background information about respondents' current circumstances and family background, before moving on to obtain some attitudinal information about child rearing. The second half of the interview addressed respondents' own experiences in childhood. Respondents completed this part of the interview themselves, reading the questions on the screen and typing in their answers. Thus they were able to provide information without the interviewer (or anyone else who might be present) knowing the questions asked or their answers. All sections were introduced with broad, general questions about aspects of care in childhood, gradually moving to more sensitive and detailed questions.

Source: Adapted from Brooker, S., Cawson, P., Kelly, G. and Wattam, C. (2001) 'The prevalence of child abuse and neglect: a survey of young people', MRS Conference, www.mrs.org.uk.

Telephone interviews

Most data collection via telephone interviewing is conducted from specialist telephone units or centres, most of which use CATI systems. Traditional telephone interviewing in which the interviewer records responses to questions on a paper questionnaire is, however, still used, for example for small scale business-to-business surveys or for multi-country projects where the budget or the time frame does not stretch to having an all language version of the questionnaire programmed into CATI. Telephone interviews typically last about 15–20 minutes, although if the subject matter is of interest to the respondent longer interviews are possible.

STRENGTHS OF TELEPHONE INTERVIEWS

Telephone interviewing, and especially CATI, has a number of advantages over face-to-face methods. A geographically dispersed sample (including those in remote and rural areas) can be obtained more easily. It may be the only way of reaching some populations – such as the business community. It is possible to use a pure random sampling approach rather than the cluster sampling approach that is common in face-to-face methods, thus reducing the chance of sampling error, and all at a greatly reduced cost because interviewer travel time is not an issue. A telephone survey may also make it easier to reach a wider spectrum of respondents – for example in socially deprived areas where interviewers may be reluctant to work and in higher income areas where access to homes may be difficult. It is possible to record digitally answers to open-ended questions in full. Greater quality control is possible (and so cheating is minimised), with interviewers being monitored 'live' rather than after the event, via back-checking. Clients and research executives can listen in, enabling them to get a feel for the findings.

It is relatively easy to monitor interview length and the time taken for individual questions – this can facilitate a dynamic or rolling pilot study and questions can be altered if necessary. It is also relatively easy to determine the strike rate and refusal rate and so monitor the sample and control quotas. Call-backs are easily managed so that bias towards those more often at home is reduced. Centralised, face-to-face briefings for interviewers are more common than on face-to-face projects, and supervisors and executives may be on hand to answer queries during fieldwork. Multi-country studies can be conducted from a central telephone unit, enabling greater control over administration and increased consistency. Telephone interviews offer respondents a greater degree of perceived anonymity than do face-to-face interviews. As a result, it is a useful method for collecting data on sensitive or intimate subjects, and it is useful in reducing social desirability bias. Telephone interviewing is faster than face-to-face interviewing – more questions can be asked in a shorter period of time and project turnaround times are faster. It can therefore be more cost effective than face-to-face interviewing.

WEAKNESSES OF TELEPHONE INTERVIEWS

There are some disadvantages. Although fixed line telephone ownership in the United Kingdom is almost universal this is not the case in other parts of the world – even among EU member states. Those who do not have a fixed line telephone are different from those who do; in the past and to some extent still, they are more likely to be from lower income households and they tend to be older or – more commonly now – they tend to be younger and own a mobile (cell) phone. This has implications for obtaining a truly random sample of these populations – not everyone has the same chance of being selected and not all of them are in the sampling frame or universe. This problem – of sampling error and bias – is exacerbated if the telephone directory is used as a sampling frame. Not all fixed line telephone numbers (and so individuals and households or businesses) are listed. In addition, standard directories do not list mobile telephone numbers, which further exacerbates the problem. The incidence of telephone answering machines, call screening, lines being used to access the Internet and more than one line per household add to the problems of access and sampling. The rise in the use of telemarketing has made people suspicious of bona fide telephone research and this has impacted on response rates.

In a telephone interview some of the benefits of social interaction and the chance to build rapport with a respondent are lost. It can be easier for the respondent to refuse an interview or end it early and harder for the interviewer to encourage the respondent to take part. Long and complex questions are best avoided. It is difficult to include stimulus material, although this can be overcome by sending material out to respondents in advance of the interview.

Box 7.2 Professional practice and the MRS Code of Conduct: research with children

The MRS Code of Conduct sets out rules in relation to data collection with two main aims in mind: to protect potentially vulnerable people and to strengthen the notion of public trust. To this end it has a number of rules in relation to research with children and young people:

B26 Consent of a parent or responsible adult (acting in loco parentis) must be obtained before interviewing a child under 16 in the following circumstances:
- In home/at home (face-to-face and telephone interviewing)
- Group discussions/depth interviews ▶

- Postal questionnaires
- Internet questionnaires
- Email
- Where interviewer and child are alone together
- In public places such as in-street/in-store/central locations (see exception under B27)

B27 Interviews being conducted in public places, such as in-street/in-store/central locations, with 14 year olds or over may take place without consent of a parent or responsible adult. In these situations Members must give an explanatory thank you note to the child.

Comment: Under special circumstances, permission to waive parental consent may be obtained, but only with the prior approval of the MRS Market Research Standards Board

B28 Where the consent of a parent or responsible adult is required Members must ensure that the adult is given sufficient information about the nature of the research to enable them to provide informed consent.

B29 Members must ensure that the parent or responsible adult giving consent is recorded (by name, relationship or role).

B30 For self-completion postal questionnaires, Members must ensure that:
- when it is known, (or ought reasonably to be known) that all or a majority of Respondents are likely to be under 16, these are addressed to the parent or responsible adult; and
- when it is known (or ought reasonably to be known) that all or a majority of Respondents are likely to be under 16, that all questionnaires carry a note or notice explaining that consent is required for all children to participate.

B31 For research administered electronically over the Internet, when it is known (or ought reasonably to be known) that all or a majority of Respondents are likely to be under 16, Members must ensure that Respondents are asked to give their age before any other personal information is requested. Further, if the age given is under 16, the child must be excluded from giving further personal information until the appropriate consent from a parent or responsible adult has been obtained.

B32 In all cases, Members must ensure that a child has an opportunity to decline to take part, even though a parent or a responsible adult has given consent on their behalf. This remains the case if the research takes place in school.

Source: MRS Code of Conduct 2005. Used with permission.

Self-completion methods

Self-completion surveys are one of the most cost-effective ways of collecting data, mainly because no interviewers are involved. They can be administered by post (the most common method) or electronically, via email or the web, or handed out in person. They can be included as part of a personal interview (as Case study 7.2 above shows) – to collect data on sensitive subjects, where the respondent might be embarrassed to provide answers to an interviewer; and in situations where it is not necessary to have an interviewer ask the questions, during a product or advertising test, for example. Diaries are a specialised form of self-completion survey – they can be used, for example, to gather data on respondents' product usage or eating or shopping habits. Self-completion surveys are an effective way of reaching people who would not otherwise take part in research – for example those in industry or busy professionals.

Self-completion surveys are an effective method of collecting data if you ensure that:

- the nature of the research and the topic are suited to this method of delivery;
- the topic is relevant and of interest to the target population;
- the method is a suitable way of reaching and achieving a response from the target population;
- the questionnaire is well designed – clear, easy to follow and easy to complete and a suitable length for the medium – and presented in a professional manner.

Success in encouraging response – on which the representativeness of the sample relies – depends on all of these. Before deciding to use this method it is worth asking whether the subject matter is interesting enough to the sample, and worth finding out (from the literature or from previous research) the response rate you might expect.

CASE STUDY 7.3

WHAT DO YOU DO ALL DAY? THE BBC WANTS TO KNOW

This case study describes the methods used to gather data about daily life in the UK in order to understand how people use their time and use the media.

Why this case study is worth reading

This case study is worth reading for many reasons: it gives details of the project plan including the sample; it links research objectives with choice of method of data collection – a diary and a questionnaire; it presents a rationale for using electronic over paper data collection for most of the sample; it describes the design of the script for the electronic diary; it gives details of the study's response rate; it describes the findings and their end use.

The key words are: objective, lifestyle questionnaire, diary, data, falling response rates, over-researched respondents, complexity, routing, data quality, personal digital assistants (PDAs), RDD (Random Digit Dialling), quotas, household, CATI script, helpline.

Introduction

The BBC Daily Life study has been carried out every five to ten years since the 1930s. The objective has always been to understand the UK public's time and media usage. As a public service provider the BBC strives to understand the needs of its audiences, and the BBC Daily Life project has played a key role in this. The basic principle is to ask respondents to list, throughout the day, all the activities they do. This is accompanied by a general lifestyle questionnaire that helps to categorise and segment the respondents. The scale and scope of the study has always been ahead of its time and the 2002/3 wave was no exception. Pioneering a technology new to market research at the time, this wave was groundbreaking.

Method

Initially the BBC planned to use a paper diary allowing participants to record media usage and other events soon after they did them. However, we live in an era of falling response rates and over-researched respondents. A diary covering all possible ▶

activities on a single or double page could prove daunting, so daunting both in terms of complexity and routing as to make data quality questionable. Early on in the design of the study personal digital assistants (PDAs) were considered as an alternative to traditional paper diaries, primarily because PDAs were:

- Portable – designed to be carried around making them ideal for completing a diary in 'real time'.
- Modern – the PDA had the potential to attract younger men who tend to be the least likely to participate in research.
- Programmable – the ability to route respondents through the diary was seen as a great advantage and would allow for more prompting and would streamline each time slot so the respondent would only need to see the screens applicable to them.

The project was piloted with a mixed methodology of 70 per cent PDA diaries and 30 per cent paper diaries. The pilot showed that this mixed methodology approach was justified. Although the PDA is a much more accurate method of data collection and has many advantages relating to routing and prompts, it was still important not to alienate those respondents who would either feel uncomfortable or nervous about using a PDA; these tended to be older respondents and those more fearful of technology in general. For this reason the final study used paper diaries for a sub-group of the sample (mainly the over 55s).

The design of the electronic diary 'script'

No 'off the shelf' software packages were capable of performing the functions on a PDA that a diary format necessitated. Most packages available at the time could not cope with the kind of complex routing that was required. Consequently TNS wrote a diary script from scratch in NSBasic. The end result was a user-friendly package that, very importantly, looked easy to complete. The electronic diary design was inspired by three central requirements:

- Respondent ease of use: it was essential that the diary looked easy to use.
- The BBC's specific data requirements: a real time data capture method was needed as well as the ability to prompt and route the respondent through various questions.
- Comparability with the accumulated industry knowledge: there have been numerous time use studies in the past and it was felt that comparability with these studies would be an important validation tool.

Project plan

The specifications for the study were as follows:

- Respondents were recruited using RDD (Random Digit Dialling).
- Quotas were set for recruitment on age, gender, working status, general ethnic origin, country of residence, level of technical ability and diary completion method.
- A maximum of one adult and one child could be recruited per household.
- Respondents were assigned either a paper or PDA diary based on their answers during the recruitment questionnaire in relation to their technical ability.
- Respondents were informed of the method of diary collection allocated by the CATI script at the end of the interview and were given the opportunity to refuse at that point based on their diary allocation.

- Diary completion method was split 70 per cent PDA and 30 per cent paper.
- PDA diary respondents were provided with a 24-hour freephone technical helpline to be used for any questions relating to the operation of the PDA.
- The diary covered three days and was split into 48 half hour periods per day, 144 time slots in total per respondent.
- Respondents also received a 24-page diagnostic questionnaire.
- Respondents received a £10 gift voucher for a completed diary and questionnaire.
- The study ran over four quarterly waves from October 2002 through September 2003.
- 5,212 respondents aged 4+ completed and returned the diary.

The respondent was called on the day prior to the commencement of their diary to check that the pack had arrived safely and that the respondent was still able to complete the diary the following day. The second call, scheduled for the day following the final day of their diary, checked that the respondent had finished the diary and was planning to return it. There would then be a seven day delay; if the PDA diaries still had not been returned a third round of calls began to chase the whereabouts of the PDA.

Response rates

At the recruitment stage the BBC was cited as sponsoring the study and this no doubt had a positive effect on not only acceptance rates but also completion rates. Fifty seven per cent of diaries dispatched were returned with useable data. Compared to a similar study (the Office of National Statistics Time Use Study 2000) with a net response rate of 45 per cent it is clear that the PDA methodology had a beneficial effect on response rates. Eighty six per cent of PDAs dispatched were returned. This is an important statistic in terms of financial viability. Looking to the future, a similar study could expect to dispatch an individual PDA on over eight separate occasions before it is lost.

Findings

The main challenge the BBC Daily Life study has faced is that the sheer scale of the database provides a massive opportunity but can also be intimidating to casual research users. In conjunction with Telmar, a media planning software service, considerable efforts were put into making the results database as user-friendly as possible whilst maintaining the exceptional variety of functionality necessary. By the time the final wave of data had been delivered the BBC Daily Life study had been integrated into the portfolio of research tools and data sources that the BBC regularly use to understand, target and profile their diverse audience, such as BARB (TV ratings data), RAJAR (radio audience ratings data), TGI (consumer profiles and media use data) and the PanBBC tracking study.

Conclusion

Daily Life is bringing the BBC closer to its audiences. It is a groundbreaking study that offers new, actionable insight into the way people live their lives in the 21st century and will form a key plank of the BBC's understanding of its audiences. But the BBC is not the only one making use of the study findings. JCDecaux, the outdoor advertising specialists, joined the study in the third wave and added some questions of their own to the self-completion questionnaire.

Source: Adapted from Holden, J. and Griffiths, G. (2004) 'The way we live now (Daily Life in the 21st century)', MRS Conference, www.mrs.org.uk.

TECHNIQUES TO INCREASE THE RESPONSE RATE

Other techniques or procedures that can help to increase the response rate in self-completion surveys include use of a personalised covering letter, sponsorship, pre-notification, reminders, incentives and, for postal surveys, a return envelope.

Covering letter or email

Postal, email and web questionnaires may be accompanied by a 'covering' letter or email, personalised if possible, as this has been found to increase response rates (Yu and Cooper, 1983). The aim of the letter is to do the following:

- explain the nature of the survey and why it is being conducted;
- explain why and how the recipient was chosen;
- reassure the recipient about the confidentiality and/or anonymity of the information they provide;
- state that participation is voluntary and that they can refuse to answer any question;
- give details of any incentive for completing the questionnaire (such as free entry to a prize draw);
- give details of the date by which the completed questionnaire should be returned;
- give details of how it should be returned (a pre-paid envelope is usually included).

Advance or pre-notification

Depending on the sample and the nature of the research, it may help to inform the sample in advance of the arrival of the questionnaire. This has also been found to improve the response rate (Yu and Cooper, 1983). Pre-notification can take the form of a letter, an email or a telephone call.

Sponsorship

It can be helpful in encouraging participation and response to include on the questionnaire or mention in the covering letter the name of the organisation sponsoring or involved in the research.

Reminders

In most postal, web and email surveys at least one reminder is sent – usually only to those who have not returned the questionnaire after a specific period of time. With postal surveys a reminder is usually sent after two to three weeks; with email or web surveys it depends on the time frame for the survey but a week is fairly typical. The reminder usually takes the form of a letter – carefully worded to encourage response and not deter it – and in most cases a second copy of the questionnaire is attached, in case the first one has been misplaced, destroyed or deleted.

Incentives

Incentives are used to encourage response and to thank respondents for the time taken to complete the survey. You can choose between pre-paid incentives (those presented upfront with the survey questionnaire) and those sent on receipt of the completed questionnaire; monetary incentives and non-monetary ones, for example a pen, a book, a copy of the research report and

BT: MEASURING CUSTOMER SATISFACTION BY POST

This case study describes the approach taken by BT, the British telecommunications company, to find out – among other things – what its residential customers and some of its non-customers thought about it at a time of rapid change in the telecoms market.

Why this case study is worth reading

This case study is worth reading for many reasons: it explains the client's need for research and describes the research objectives; it gives a rationale for the choice of postal over telephone data collection; it sets out decisions taken about the format of the questionnaire; it describes the content of the questionnaire; it describes how the survey was set up and managed; it describes what was done to elicit respondents' views about the survey and it summarises those views; it notes the reasons for non-response and discusses response bias.

The key words are: customer satisfaction, customer concerns and needs, response rate, questionnaire, mailing with bill, self-seal, reply paid, non-response, web-based version, impact, reminders, response bias.

Introduction

Here's the scenario BT faced at the end of 2001: it needs to launch Broadband. It wants to identify the early adopters of Broadband cheaply and effectively. Its new management also has a focus on customer satisfaction and listening to customer concerns and needs. It realises that customers are very tired of telemarketing. Why not mail the whole customer base and ask them about their customer satisfaction, what they think of BT, and how interested they are in Broadband and the other new products and services which BT has in the pipeline? The responses can be used for direct marketing, customer segmentation, improving customer satisfaction and generally understanding customer needs better. What could be more straightforward?

Approach

BT put together a team: Ogilvy One, a communications agency; Claritas, specialists in customer segmentation and geodemographics; and NOP, a research agency; and a dedicated internal team. What this team did was to send a questionnaire to the whole of BT's customer base. The research agency felt that a separate mailing would produce a better response rate than mailing the questionnaire with the normal BT bill – but had no real proof. The communications agency felt that a self-seal approach, that is, the questionnaire as a single piece of paper which could be sent out as a single piece and then re-folded and stuck down at the edges to form a reply paid returnable document was best for mailing with the bill – certainly the logistics of inserting a questionnaire and return envelope with the bill were pretty insurmountable. But was a self-seal approach the best for a separate mailing?

We 'tested' both self-seal and a standard approach, and with BT that meant we sent out 2.1 million of each! This formed the first phase of the programme. The response rate for the standard approach was twice that for the self-seal but in subsequent research with responders and non-responders, the self-seal design was never mentioned as a reason for non-response. We hypothesise that the main reason for the different response rate is   ▶

that the standard approach mailing appears less like direct mail (and therefore fewer are 'binned' automatically). But we don't know. For the next phase of the research, we did a one million test of including the self-seal questionnaire with the bill – and the response rate was quite a bit lower than for a separate mailing. The hierarchy of response rates achieved was follows: the standard mailing approach produced a response rate which was double that of the self-seal approach. The separate self-seal mailing produced a two and a half times better response rate than the self-seal questionnaire included with the BT bill.

The questionnaire

The questionnaire was kept as short and relevant to BT's current and future service offering as possible. It comprised:

■ Customer satisfaction with BT;
■ Use of telecoms, mobile telephony, Internet, TV services;
■ Interest in a list of future products and services;
■ Preferred channels of communication from BT;
■ Opt-out box.

Two open-ended boxes invited comments on how BT could improve the service the customer received from BT, and suggestions for future products and services. Customers were sufficiently engaged in the task to openly and honestly share their thoughts and suggestions in the verbatim boxes, and BT is using and acting on this information. No demographic, life stage or life style questions were asked. It took an average of 10 to 12 minutes to complete and was positioned as 'have your say in shaping BT Services and help Childline' [a donation of £1 was made to this children's charity for every questionnaire returned].

Other versions of the survey

A web-based version of the survey was offered as an alternative response mechanism. Customers with email addresses registered with BT.com were sent email invitations to complete the web-version and reasonable response rates were achieved from that particular set of customers. As an alternative to the mail version, however, very few customers chose to respond by web rather than by mail. After all, the paper version was simple and available – both important considerations for potential respondents. A large print version, braille version, a version that could be listened to (and responded to) on the web, and telephone response option were offered to those registered with BT as having sight difficulties. In addition, a Welsh language version of the questionnaire was sent to those who receive their BT bills in Welsh.

Call centre

A major consideration was how to deal with customers' queries regarding the mailings. We set up a special call centre to handle queries. We trained our interviewers and manned the phones to cover half a per cent of customers calling, and we set up processes for transferring any non-survey related calls directly through to BT – but hardly anyone called; the figure was closer to 0.03 per cent of those mailed.

Researching the effect of the survey on customers

BT wanted to be sure that the mailing was not irritating customers. One of the main criteria set by BT senior management was that the survey must be at least customer satisfaction 'neutral', that is, it must not have a negative effect on customer satisfaction. We also wished to understand what customers made of the survey. Research was conducted on the survey as follows:

- Group discussions were conducted (by an independent agency) with early versions of the questionnaire.
- A hall test (two locations) was conducted to check the questionnaire prior to any mailing.
- Follow-up telephone research was conducted (by an independent agency) of responders and non responders to each phase of the research.
- Questions were added to BT's ongoing Consumer measurement vehicle – the COS Monitor – to measure the effect of the survey.

All these research projects gave positive results:

- The group discussions showed that the overall concept was acceptable to customers – in fact many thought it was a 'good idea'.
- The hall tests showed that customers by-and-large understood and could complete the survey.
- The telephone research showed that those who recalled receiving the questionnaire generally reported that it gave them a more positive impression of BT (though quite high proportions did not recall receipt of the survey).
- The COS Monitor confirmed on an ongoing basis that the survey had a generally positive effect on customers' perceptions.

Non response

The majority of customers were sent the questionnaire with their bill, which was the lowest cost method, but which gave the lowest response rate. The main reason for non response was the questionnaire made no impact. Many customers did not even recall that they had received it. Where receipt was recalled, the reasons for non response were mainly non sinister 'couldn't be bothered/haven't got time' types of reasons. There was little expressed concern over the purpose of the survey. Reminders were not sent, because of the cost, but response rates could have been improved by the use of reminders. Most customers who recalled receipt of the questionnaire accepted the validity of BT trying to establish their views of BT, and at the same time asking about their interest in new services. Significant proportions of customers expect to be sold to as a result of the survey. Those who do not want follow-up calls or their data to be transferred into BT databases ticked the opt-out boxes provided, the remainder appear to be happy for the data to be used to improve services to themselves.

Response bias

It is always of concern as to whether such surveys actually give biased response. As far as we can tell there is a slight bias towards the more satisfied customers completing the survey – since these customers have a higher trust of BT it can be argued that they 'buy' the argument that BT wishes to know their views.

Source: Adapted from Macfarlane, P. (2003) 'Breaking through the boundaries – MR techniques to understand what individual customers really want, and acting on it', MRS Conference, www.mrs.org.uk.

entry in a prize draw. Case study 3.6 (Brennan, Hoek and Astridge, 1991) gives examples of incentives used in a postal study: of the incentives offered, a small monetary incentive with the first mailout proved most effective. There are ethical issues to consider in the decision to use incentives, and in the choice of what sort of incentive to use. We look at some of these issues in Chapter 10 and Case study 10.3 shows the decision-making process in the choice of incentive for a postal survey.

Return envelopes

For postal surveys a stamped or reply-paid envelope is usually included to encourage and facilitate response.

STRENGTHS OF SELF-COMPLETION METHODS

Postal, email and web surveys have a number of strengths. They are relatively easy to set up and administer, although email and web surveys do require specialist knowledge. They enable you to reach a widely dispersed population, and one that may not be amenable to research by other methods. They are an effective way of asking questions that need time for consideration or involve the respondent in checking or consulting documents. They are relatively cost effective as there are no interviewers to pay. And with no interviews they are free of interviewer bias or error. Also, having no interviewer, they offer respondents a high degree of perceived anonymity – which means that they are effective in collecting data on sensitive topics and for reducing the risk of social desirability bias.

WEAKNESSES OF SELF-COMPLETION METHODS

There are drawbacks to postal, web and email surveys. Although postal surveys in particular can be relatively cheap in comparison to other methods, the cost per completed interview, especially if a survey of non-responders is conducted, may be greater. Response rates vary – they can be as low as 10 to 15 per cent in postal surveys; web and email surveys can fare better (30–80 per cent). With a poor response rate, or one that is hard to predict, there is a chance that the sample will not be representative of the population: those who respond may differ from those who do not. The lower the response rate the less representative the sample. In addition, the sample is *self-selecting*. Although you might choose a sample relevant to the research and send questionnaires and reminders out to that sample, you have no control over who fills in the questionnaire (or how many do so). The recipient decides whether or not to take part; or may pass the questionnaire on to someone else, or someone else other than the intended recipient may complete it.

Another drawback to postal, email and web surveys is the lack of control over the data capture process, which has a knock-on effect in terms of data quality:

- The respondent can consult with others before answering the questions.
- Respondents may not answer all the questions they were supposed to or in the way required.
- You may get little detail in open-ended questions.
- There is no opportunity to probe or clarify answers – you must accept the response written in by the respondent.
- Questions requiring spontaneous answers do not work well.
- The respondent can skip ahead or indeed read the whole questionnaire before filling it in, so any 'funnelling' of questions and topics does not work.
- There is no opportunity to observe, for example, or to read body language or hear tone of voice.

> ## Box 7.3 Summary of strengths and weaknesses of self-completion methods
>
> **Strengths**
> - Easy to set up and manage
> - Cost – no interviewers to pay
> - No interviewer bias or error
> - Ability to reach a widely dispersed sample
> - Can ask questions that need considered answers
> - Can ask questions on sensitive topics
>
> **Weaknesses**
> - Poor response rates and so problems with representativeness
> - Reliant on availability of relevant and up-to-date sampling frame
> - Lack of control over data capture
> - Concerns about data quality
> - Not good for open-ended/complicated questions and instructions
> - Not always the most cost-effective route

ONLINE DATA COLLECTION

Data collection using the Internet offers many of the advantages of postal surveys. It can, however, be more expensive to commission. It also has most of the disadvantages of postal surveys. Sampling and representativeness of achieved samples are key issues and the suitability of the method for the population you wish to research must be considered in the light of these issues. The need for an accurate and up-to-date sampling frame is even more crucial than it is in other methods of data collection. Email, for example, does not tolerate wrong addresses. In addition, people tend to change ISPs and email addresses more often than they change postal addresses (and there is no easily accessible database of email addresses, as there is with postal addresses and telephone numbers). As Internet access, email use and web activity increase, it is important to bear in mind that the make-up of the population under study may be changing rapidly – samples drawn from even slightly out-of-date sampling frames may be unrepresentative. For many of these reasons, there has been an increase in recent years in – and widespread acceptance of – the use of online panels of pre-recruited potential respondents who can then be sampled to take part in surveys.

Web and email data capture offer advantages over the postal method not unlike those offered by CAPI and CATI over traditional paper data capture. Large-scale surveys are relatively easy to set up and manage. Response rates for email surveys can be monitored easily – for example there is automatic notification if an email is undelivered. (Response rates for web surveys are much harder to estimate.) Turnaround times from end of fieldwork to production of tables are fast compared to postal surveys: data (including verbatim responses) are captured directly, which also reduces data processing errors. You can show multi-media stimulus material (pictures, audio and video clips, websites). You can programme the software to skip automatically to relevant questions; and in web surveys you can control to some extent how much of the questionnaire the respondent sees before filling it in. In addition, you can set up the questionnaire in different languages and allow respondents to choose the language in which they wish to answer.

There are potential pitfalls, however. Surveys can take more time to set up and, for web surveys and panels especially, specialist skills are needed. Pilot studies are important, if not essential, in order to ensure that the questionnaire works in different computing environments and on different platforms – the browser type or screen size can affect the format of the questionnaire and thus how it looks to the respondent. It is also important in email surveys to take into account the size of the questionnaire file and the length of time it takes to download to the respondent's computer (this will depend on connection type and speed). From the sender's point of view in email surveys (and the receiver's, if the survey is being sent to one organisation or to those using the same server or ISP), it is crucial to think about what effect the size of the mailing and the likely size of return traffic will have on server capacity. If a large mailing is required it is best to spread it out over a period of time in order not to swamp the server. Some ISPs block mailings over a certain size and most organisations have firewalls to protect them against unsolicited mailings and viruses, which can stop large-scale mailings. It may therefore be necessary to encrypt the questionnaire or email in order to comply with security requirements.

Box 7.4 Things to think about when considering Internet data collection

Suitability, representativeness and quality of data issues
- How suitable is the population for this method of data collection?
- Can you achieve a sample that is representative of the population?
- Do you have a good quality, accurate and up-to-date sampling frame?
- What is the likely response rate?
- What about non-response bias?
- Can you survey the non-responders?
- How good is the recruitment process?

Technical issues
- How widespread is Internet access among your target population – what are the levels of PC penetration, Internet access, use of ISPs?
- Think of the respondent's set-up – the firewall, speed of connection, bandwidth, browser type and operating system.
- Think of the survey administrator's set-up – server capacity.

Design/layout issues
- Think of the respondents – you need to make it easy for them to complete and you need to keep them engaged with the subject.
- Keep it simple – remember download times and the effect of the browser type and screen size on layout.
- Keep the interview length to about 10 to 15 minutes.

Web and email methods are particularly popular in business-to-business and employee research – Internet access is almost universal among medium and large organisations and these methods are often the only way of reaching these populations. They are also effective in popular online business-to-consumer markets such as financial services, retailing (especially food, books and music) and travel services. For research among the general public, where sampling is more difficult and response rates poorer, online panels are the most popular approach.

WEB SURVEYS

Web surveys are conducted on the World Wide Web, usually at a specially designed private web address to which the sample is directed and/or given a password to access. Recruitment or sampling can happen in several ways. Traffic (people browsing the web) can be intercepted on a website – it is useful here to think of the analogy of the interviewer stopping people in the street – by alerting them via advertising banners, which scroll across the screen, or via 'pop-ups', which pop up on the screen (see Case study 3.3). This approach is sometimes referred

---

Box 7.5 Response rates in RAndom Web Interviewing

Here Pete Comley, Virtual Surveys, explains the difficulty in being able to give a single figure for the response rate in RAndom Web Interviewing.

One of the problems that bedevils research, and comparisons between techniques, is the lack of agreed definitions about what constitutes a response rate, and how two response rates relate to each other. This is particularly true with online research, where the rates often appear to be much lower than they are for offline surveys.

RAndom Web Interviewing (RAWI) cannot provide a single number which captures the response rate. The teaser pop-up that alerts the viewer has a response rate, and the invitation to take the survey has a response rate. In addition, some respondents will be screened out because they do not belong in the population (for example, it is not unusual to find some interviews being completed from other countries!).

This complexity is normally handled by reporting the different components to the response rate. The response rate to the invitation is the number of people taking part in the survey, divided by the number of people invited (ie those who clicked on the teaser ad). However, if there are a number of screenouts, for example on the basis of being under 16 or from the wrong country, then these should be allowed for in both the numerator and denominator. The response rate to the teaser ad is the number of people who click on the ad divided by the number of people shown the ad. Normally the ad serving company can supply data on how many times the average surfer saw the ad. In practice in the UK, we have found the response rates to the teaser question, that is, the pop-up, to be about 2 to 10 per cent, whilst the response rate amongst those invited to take the survey is typically 10 to 30 per cent. However, there are differences by country. In China for example, we often find response rates to the teaser question to be in excess of 10 per cent, whilst in the US the response rate to the teaser questionnaire is often closer to 1 per cent. Reading the respondents' survey comments, it is clear that pop-ups in the US are viewed more negatively than in most other countries and this probably accounts for some of these differences.

Source: Comley, P. (2003) 'Innovation in online research – who needs online panels?', MRS Conference, www.mrs.org.uk.

to as RAWI – RAndom Web Interviewing (Comley, 2003). Approaching potential respondents in this way – intercepting them or interrupting them as they browse or surf – means that you must limit interview time to about 5 or 10 minutes – any longer and the response rate falls off. Should you need respondents to complete a longer interview it is good practice to inform them of the length of time required and offer them the option of completing the interview at another time. Should they choose this option, they must provide an email address to which an encrypted link to the web survey can be sent. An alternative approach to conducting web surveys is to recruit a sample offline, giving them details – by telephone, post or email – of the web address at which the survey is posted. To achieve an acceptable response rate it is advisable to keep the interview length to no more than about 15–20 minutes. The questionnaire in all cases must be simple and straightforward – easy to follow and easy to fill in.

EMAIL SURVEYS

Email surveys are sent out to the respondent's email address with the survey questionnaire either embedded in the email or provided as an attachment. Pre-notification is important – email questionnaires sent to respondents who have not agreed to take part may be rejected, and the sender stopped from sending others. The sample may be notified about the survey by email, telephone or post. All the good practice recommended for a covering letter or email outlined above also applies here. The sample for an email survey may be recruited via traditional routes or via the web. As with web surveys, an interview length of about 15 minutes is recommended in order to achieve a reasonable response rate. And as with all self-completion data collection methods, it is essential that the questionnaire looks good and is easy to fill in.

ONLINE PANELS

Using an online panel is a useful way of conducting relatively cost-effective research in a relatively short period of time. The quality of data produced has been found in validation studies to compare favourably with that produced offline. The main concern with online panels is the quality of the sample: the degree to which it is representative of the relevant population; and the nature of the panel members – there is some concern that a relatively large proportion of panel members are 'professional respondents' belonging to several panels (Comley, 2003).

There are two main types of online panels: those that are recruited with a specific research purpose or task in mind – for example a customer satisfaction monitor with a panel representative of the population of those who shop online; and those that are recruited to work as a source of respondents for a range of research projects – for example a nationally representative sample of the population of those aged 18 to 65. Panel members can be recruited using traditional methods (telephone or face-to-face interview or via participation in other research) or online methods (for example, via sign-up pages advertised on banners or pop-ups or by email registration). Those recruited online may be contacted for a follow-up recruitment phase to verify that they are who they say they are. Online panels are a popular way of achieving a sample that represents a specific population, for example the representative sample of online shoppers and, with Internet access and use now more widespread, an increasingly popular way of recruiting broad, nationally representative samples that you can use for ad hoc research and tracking studies – the panel in effect becomes the population of interest and you recruit your sample from within the population of panel members.

Issues around keeping the panel together and minimising the attrition or drop-out rate are similar to those in traditional panels, although often more work is needed in building rapport and establishing the feeling of a community online. To this end it is essential to make sure that there are clear lines of communication between the panel members and the panel administrator, including telephone contacts as well as email contacts.

Box 7.6 The importance of panel size

Here Pete Comley, Virtual Surveys, explains why size matters in online panel research.

Small panels of 5,000 to 20,000 have proved useful to companies doing modest amounts of online research. This is particularly true where the panel has been constructed to match some specific research criteria, for example a sample of 10,000 people representative of 18–55-year-old citizens, can readily provide samples of 100 to 200, provided the screening criteria are not too demanding.

However, a small panel is unlikely to be of much help with ongoing projects such as tracking, or with a large volume of projects, or projects where the targets are harder to find. For example, with the panel comprised of 10,000 18–55 year olds, matched to the national population, we might expect 25 per cent [2,500] to be mothers of children under 16. A cereal tracking project, which might require 100 interviews per week, would require 4,800 interviews in a 48-week year. Given that response rates from quality panels are typically 20 and 50 per cent, this would require the 4,800 interviews to be conducted amongst 500 to 1,200 respondents, that is, repeat interviewing the same people up to ten times a year.

If large projects, harder samples, or tracking projects are going to be run in conjunction with panels, larger panels are required. I believe that a good size for a larger national panel is 100,000+ people if it broadly matches the national characteristics and 500,000+ if it tends to match the Internet's characteristics. For example with a sample of 100,000, one would expect to be able to interview buyers of specific types of snack food, users of the main fast food brands, drivers of the main categories of car (and owners of the main brands).

Source: Adapted from Comley, P. (2003) 'Innovation in online research – who needs online panels?', MRS Conference, www.mrs.org.uk.

Other data collection formats

In this section we look at two types of specialised data collection formats: panels and omnibuses.

PANELS

Panels are an example of a longitudinal research design (see Case studies 2.1, 3.4 and 7.5) – they are a way of collecting data from the same pool of individuals, households or organisations over time, either on a continuous basis (every day) or at regular intervals. The data can be used to monitor changes in the market, short-term changes – for example reaction to price changes or promotions – as well as long-term trends, such as in brand share. The data can also be used to examine ad hoc issues such as the effect of a new advertising campaign.

UNILEVER BESTFOODS: A PANEL FULL OF INSIGHT

In Case study 3.4 we learned the rationale that led Unilever Bestfoods Europe to choose a panel rather than an ad hoc approach to delivering its research needs. In this follow-on case study we find out how data from the panel provided insight into who consumers are and what they do as well as why they do it and allowed the client to build detailed profiles of consumers which could be used to gain insight in other work.

Why this case study is worth reading

This case study is worth reading for several reasons: it describes the business objectives, the research objectives and the research design, thus highlighting the links between them; it describes the advantages of using a panel design; it is an example of the use of a panel and the application of panel data; it describes the sample and gives the response rate; it sets out what was measured; it describes the end use of the data

The key words are: values, behaviour, business objective, research objective, panel, ad hoc study, sample, survey, response rate, weighted, nationally representative, questionnaire, diary, psychographic attributes, cluster analysis, segmentation.

Introduction

The Consumer and Market Insight Department at Unilever Bestfoods Europe started a research project to improve its understanding of consumer values and their influence on purchasing and consumption behaviour. The overall business objective was to anticipate future consumer potential, moving beyond understanding what had happened in the past. The business needed to understand why consumers did what they did, moving beyond who they are or what they actually did. This learning needed to be in a commercially valuable format such as measurable and accessible consumer segments.

The overall research objective was to develop an approach to grouping consumers, which could be applied to all activities, both at a strategic and operational level. Several criteria were agreed with the end clients of the study (both the sales and marketing departments):

- groups that were actionable (meaning they could be applied to New Product Development (NPD) projects, sales planning and execution, etc.);
- simple to understand and use (especially by non-data literate colleagues and external partner agencies);
- a broader consumer understanding beyond the current product categories;
- something to use throughout the whole business – brands and product categories;
- something to use in every market research process and methodology.

Approach

The key to the success of this project was the choice of methodology and data source. The ACNielsen Household Panel was used as the source of sample and data instead of collecting a separate dataset from an ad hoc standalone study. The advantages of this approach were:

- The consumer was measured as a complete holistic individual. All household grocery purchasing was recorded, not just a specific category.

- Data were grouped in many different ways – brand, category, variant, demographic (age, household size, etc).
- All measured at the same time without having to decide a priori which ones would be important to the analysis and understanding.
- Actual purchases were measured – not claimed or what the consumer could recall.
- It gave us a time-based measure of consumer purchase. Up to three years' past data were available to be analysed at any time.
- Future behaviour could be tracked on the same sample base without having to run a separate study.
- Direct measurable sales results could be determined from marketing activities – in general, specific account, or even at store level.

The sample

A total of 9,090 ACNielsen Homescan Panel members were eligible to be sent the Homescan Survey. The overall response rate to the survey was 83 per cent of households (i.e. 7,553 households). Of these, 5,773 households had 52 weeks continuous purchase history. This was the base used for the analysis of behaviour. The sample was weighted to be nationally representative on age, socio-economic, and regional representation. In addition, a sub-sample of 908 households completed an additional questionnaire which included a diary of food consumption and preparation over a two-week period within and outside the household.

What was measured

To understand what drives behaviour a questionnaire was developed to measure pyschographic attributes or values using specific statements and scales. For example, the value of recognition was measured in part with the statement, 'If I have done something I am proud of, I like others to know about it'. These data were combined with an understanding of who the groups were (demographics data) and what they did (purchase behaviour data).

Insight and useability

Significant insights were generated from this integrated understanding. A cluster analysis on the value-based variables was used to create the segmentation of the households. These groups or segments were found to be statistically robust and commercially viable – they were measurable, accessible and the profiles (based on demographic and other behavioural criteria) were distinct from each other.

Source: Adapted from Gibson, S., Teanby, D. and Donaldson, S. (2004) 'Bridging the gap between dreams and reality . . . building holistic insights from an integrated consumer understanding', MRS Conference, www.mrs.org.uk.

The panel is recruited to be representative of a particular population, for example all households in Ireland or subscribers to a particular ISP or owners of particular makes of car or all retail outlets of a particular type. As people (or units) drop out of the panel and the population from which the panel is drawn changes, new members are recruited so that the panel remains representative over time. This is particularly important in a new or rapidly developing market, for example users of mobile communication devices. Newly recruited panel members tend to behave differently from longer-established members. For this reason data from new members are usually excluded for their first few weeks on the panel.

Recruiting and maintaining panels is a relatively expensive business. Panel owners use a number of techniques to encourage panel members to stay with the panel and to prevent members dropping out before their time. Incentives include prize draws, competitions and reward points that can be redeemed against gifts. Panel newsletters are often used as a way of building on the community feeling of a panel as well as a way of keeping panel members informed.

Panels can be designed to gather all sorts of data. They are best for recording data about what, how many, how much – what people have actually done. Many panels are set up to gather information about market characteristics in order to determine things like brand share or media usage, details of TV viewing, radio listening, newspaper and magazine reading habits – what, where, when, how long for. Panels in which individual consumers are the respondents are called *consumer panels*. For example, there are panels of motorists and panels of mothers of babies and small children as well as panels representative of all households. Panels made up of a sample of retail outlets are called *retail panels* and are used to collect *retail audit* data such as stock held, brand coverage, rate of sale, promotions, price and so on in order to determine distribution and sales patterns of different brands, pack sizes by type of outlet, sales by location/region.

Capturing panel data

Data from panel members or panel outlets are collected using questionnaires, diaries and electronic and wireless devices, including bar code scanners and PDAs (see Case study 7.3 above). Consumer panel members recording grocery purchases, for example, used to do so in diaries; nowadays the same information is captured by scanners, handheld devices that read the black and white bar codes that appear on product packaging. The panel member scans each item purchased. The information captured by the scanner can be sent by the respondent down the telephone line via a modem to the agency's computer. Data from media panels measuring television viewing or radio listening are collected using electronic meters attached to the television or radio. Retail panel data are often collected by an interviewer who visits the store and counts and records, either on paper or in an electronic notebook, the number of items on the shelves and in storage, and checks delivery dockets for items received in the period since the last audit.

Accuracy of panel data

Recruiting and in particular maintaining the representativeness of a panel can be difficult to achieve. The data can be weighted to bring the sample more in line with the population characteristics. Other errors that can affect panel data apart from sampling error include pick-up errors, when the respondent (or the data collector in a retail audit) omits to record or scan in an item, which can be accounted for when making estimates of market size in a process similar to weighting the sample to population estimates.

Omnibus surveys

Omnibus surveys are surveys that are run by research agencies on a continuous basis. Clients can buy space on these surveys to insert their own questions – they are usually charged an entry fee and a fee per question that covers fieldwork and standard data analysis. They can be used to generate continuous or longitudinal data by repeating the same questions in each round, or they can be used to gather cross-sectional data on an ad hoc basis – to collect data on specific issues as the need arises.

Depending on the number of questions included, using an omnibus survey can be very cost effective – fieldwork costs are shared and set-up time is minimised because of the ongoing, pre-set nature of the survey. The law of diminishing returns, however, kicks in at about 8 to 10 questions – it is likely that for this number of questions a customised survey is just as cost effective.

The omnibus may survey a representative sample of the general public or it may target a more specialised population or group. For example, omnibus surveys are run among samples of general practitioners, motorists, teenagers, older people, Internet users, European consumers and independent financial advisers.

Omnibus surveys are usually conducted face to face or by telephone. Nowadays (almost) all use computer-aided interviewing (CAPI or CATI). Respondents are recruited anew for each round of an omnibus survey using random or quota sampling techniques. Many omnibus surveys take place weekly, some twice weekly and others once every two weeks. Sample sizes vary: for general public omnibus surveys the sample is usually around 1,000 respondents per week but can be up to 3,500; for more specialised target groups it may be 500 every two weeks. To achieve a robust sample of a low incidence target group, for example hearing aid users, may mean that questions are included on more than one round of the omnibus. Turnaround times – from close of fieldwork to delivery of the tables – is often a matter of two to three days, if the data are captured electronically (using CAPI or CATI) and if there are few open-ended questions to code; for international work it is about two weeks.

Variations on the omnibus survey

A variation on the omnibus survey is when the agency designs the questionnaire, collects the data on a continuous basis or at regular intervals, processes the data and sells it on in whole or in part to whichever client wants it. None of the data is confidential to a particular client

---

Box 7.7 Advantages and disadvantages of omnibus surveys

Advantages
- Cost effective
- Available at short notice
- Speed of delivery of results
- Good for collecting data from low incidence groups
- Produce robust, quality data
- Results confidential to client who inserted the questions

Disadvantages
- Position effects – at beginning or end of interview, subjects tackled before your questions
- Not good for gathering open-ended data, or if probing necessary
- Not cost effective if more than 8 to 10 questions

since all the questions were included by the agency itself. An example of this type of continuous survey is the British Market Research Bureau's (BMRB) Target Group Index (TGI) which collects data on consumer purchases and media habits.

A tracking study is a survey that runs on a continuous basis with a fresh sample each time but in this case the client designs the questionnaire and so the data collected are confidential to the client. The syndicated tracking study is a variation on this. Several clients interested in the same product field or topic commission a continuous study. The questionnaire includes questions common to all clients – all clients see data on these – each client has some space in which to ask their own questions, for which only they see the data.

Observation

Structured observational techniques can be used to collect quantitative data. Observations can be made and recorded by researchers or fieldworkers on a paper or electronic data collection instrument designed for the purpose. Collecting data in a retail audit, for example, is a form of structured observation, as is mystery customer research, outlined below. Observation can be done electronically without the presence of a researcher – using closed circuit television, for example; television-viewing meters are also a form of electronic observation, as are the scanners used in shops to record purchases in the store's database.

Box 7.8 Professional practice and the MRS Code of Conduct: observation equipment

The MRS Code of Conduct sets out the following rule in relation to the use of observation equipment:

B47 Members must ensure that all of the following are undertaken when observation equipment is being used:
- Clear and legible signs must be placed in areas where surveillance is taking place.
- Cameras must be sited so that they monitor only the areas intended for surveillance.
- Signs must state the individual/organisation responsible for the surveillance, including contact information and the purpose of the observation.

Source: MRS Code of Conduct 2005. Used with permission.

As we noted in Chapter 6, the main advantage of observation over interviewing is that it enables us to record actual rather than reported behaviour. This was a benefit noted in Case study 5.1 where data captured at the box offices of arts venues proved insightful in understanding the behaviour of arts attenders – more insightful than that reported via survey questionnaires. The main disadvantage of observational data is that in most cases we are unable to determine the reason for the behaviour. To overcome this, interviewing is often used in conjuction with observation.

MYSTERY CUSTOMER RESEARCH

The aim of mystery customer or mystery shopping research is to collect data in order to give feedback to an organisation on the quality of its services. Mystery customer research involves a trained observer posing as an everyday customer. The 'respondent' is a member of staff of the organisation being researched or 'mystery shopped'. The observer goes through the

---

Box 7.9 Professional practice and the MRS Code of Conduct: mystery shopping

The MRS Code of Conduct sets out the following rules in relation to mystery shopping:

B43 For mystery shopping of a Client's own organisation, Members must take reasonable steps to ensure that:
- the Client's employees have been advised by their employer that their service delivery may be checked through mystery shopping;
- the objectives and intended uses of the results have been made clear by the employer to staff (including the level of reporting if at branch/store or individual level);
- if mystery shopping is to be used in relation to any employment terms and conditions, that this has been made clear by the employer.

B44 Since competitors' employees cannot be advised that they may be mystery shopped, Members must ensure that their identities are not revealed. Members must ensure that employees are not recorded (e.g. by using audio, photographic or video equipment). This applies in all instances where employees cannot or have not been advised that they could be mystery shopped.

B45 Where there is mystery shopping of Client's agents or authorised distributors (as well as any organisations which are responsible to a compliance authority), Members must ensure that:
- the employees to be mystery shopped have been advised by their employer and/or regulator that their service delivery and/or regulatory compliance may be checked by mystery shopping; and
- the objectives and intended uses of the results have been made clear by the employer and/or regulator (including the level of reporting if at branch/store or individual level); and
- if mystery shopping is to be used in relation to any employment/contractual/ regulatory terms and conditions this has been made clear by the employer and/or regulator.

B46 Members must take reasonable steps to ensure that mystery shoppers are fully informed of the implications and protected from any adverse implications of conducting a mystery shopping exercise.
Comment: For example, they must be made aware by the Member that their identity may be revealed to the organisation/individual being mystery shopped if they use personal cards to make purchases, loan arrangements etc. and credit ratings may be affected.

Source: MRS Code of Conduct 2005. Used with permission.

customer experience, asking the sort of questions a real customer might ask. As soon as the mystery customer research exercise is complete the mystery researcher fills in details of the experience on a questionnaire. For a personal visit the information recorded might include, for example, length of time in the queue; number of service points or tills open out of the total available; details of the greeting and exchange with the member of staff; handling of questions; information or advice offered and so on. For a telephone mystery shopping exercise the information recorded might include number of rings before the phone was answered, length of time on hold, as well as information on the exchange between shopper and staff member.

Box 7.10 Improving validity and reliability in mystery customer research

Here Morrison, Colman and Preston offer suggestions for how the accuracy of mystery customer research can be improved.

The demands of memory
There are potential threats to the accuracy, validity and reliability of mystery customer surveys. Some of these arise from the memory demands placed on the assessors (the mystery shoppers or mystery customers), who normally record the attainment or non-attainment of various standards that they have observed some time after making the relevant observations.

Suggestions for minimising errors of memory
Omissions and distortions of memory can arise at all three stages of the memory process: encoding, storage, and retrieval. In the light of this, a review of findings from cognitive psychology suggests a number of steps that could be taken in designing and carrying out mystery customer surveys to minimise errors arising from memory failures:

■ To reduce the memory burden on assessors, it might be possible to restrict their task to checking the attainment of personal and interactive standards of service delivery – for example, 'Was I served within two minutes?', 'Did the bank teller smile?' rather than checking whether the impersonal and relatively fixed, 'physical' standards were attained – for example, 'Were the toilets in working order?', 'Was the company logo prominently displayed?' This would reduce the memory demands, thereby helping to minimise errors arising from memory.

■ It is essential that recording of observations should take place during or immediately after the visit to reduce the problems of decay and reconstructive memory distortion. Recording should probably be done in writing and the questions on the assessment forms should be carefully designed to give maximal retrieval cues and above all to minimise the use of suggestive or leading questions.

■ It may be possible to reduce memory problems by using event recorders. These are small devices that can be carried in one's pocket. The assessors' memory task would then be restricted to remembering what standards to check and in what order to check them.

■ Assessors should be encouraged to make their visits at a time of day when they are alert and not tired and when the ambient lighting gives them the best chance of seeing what needs to be seen.

- Video recordings of a few typical service encounters, including common problems and difficult distinctions, may be useful for training future mystery customers and establishing common standards.
- The training of assessors should include a suggestion that, if they have difficulty remembering certain details while filling in an assessment form, they should try shutting their eyes and vividly imagining themselves back in the place where their observations were made [visualisation]. In addition, assessors should attempt to retain a neutral emotional state throughout the assessment visit and when recording the results.
- Assessors should be warned about the problem of social pressure and the tendency to prefer giving favourable reports rather than unfavourable ones, especially if the people working in the target establishments seem pleasant or easy to empathise with. They should also be encouraged to assess each establishment objectively on its own merits rather than consciously or unthinkingly making direct comparisons between different establishments.
- The standards that form the basis of mystery customer surveys should be as objective as possible. For example, 'Was I served within two minutes?' is completely objective, but 'Was the bar tidy?' or 'Was the shop tidy?' requires a subjective judgement, which is likely to undermine the reliability and validity of a survey. The client should be asked wherever possible to specify exactly what they mean by, for example, 'tidy', 'clean', and so on, to enable objective standards to be defined.
- Buyers and users of mystery customer research should establish a 'best practice' protocol for conducting mystery customer surveys. Changes in procedure can have unpredictable and unknown effects on the validity and reliability of the findings.
- Further research is required into the optimal design of assessment forms for recording observations, the effects of gender, age, and other demographic assessors factors on the reliability of assessment, and most importantly of all, on the reliability and validity of mystery customer surveys in general.

Source: Adapted from Morrison, L., Colman, A. and Preston, C. (1997) 'Mystery customer research: cognitive processes affecting accuracy', *International Journal of Market Research*, 39, 2, pp. 349–61, www.ijmr.com.

Chapter summary

- Quantitative data can be collected via interviewing and observation using standardised structured or semi-structured 'forms' – questionnaires and diaries.
- The method of data collection chosen depends on its suitability for achieving the research objectives; the topic or issues under investigation; its ability to reach the sample and achieve the right numbers; and the time and budget available.
- The interviewer has a vital role to play in collecting good quality data. Interviewing is a skilled task requiring a high level of interpersonal skill and a sound understanding of the data collection process. ▶

- Data can be captured and recorded electronically. The questionnaire, data entry, editing and verification procedures are programmed into the computer. There are advantages from fieldwork management to data processing – fieldwork to tabulation time is reduced and data quality is enhanced. The main disadvantages are the capital investment and training required.

- Face-to-face interviews can take place in the home, in the street, in a central location or at the respondent's place of work, depending on the nature of the survey. Face-to-face data collection has a number of advantages over other methods. It enables the interviewer to build rapport with the respondent, which has positive effects on data quality; and it allows for a degree of flexibility in the interviewing process. It is, however, relatively expensive and time consuming; cluster sampling methods, which serve to reduce travel time and costs, risk introducing sample bias; with quality control procedures at a distance there is greater scope for interviewer bias or cheating.

- Telephone interviewing, especially CATI, has a number of advantages over face-to-face methods. Geographically dispersed and other samples that are hard to reach can be obtained more easily; it is possible to use a random sampling approach, thus reducing sampling error; greater quality control is possible with interviewers being monitored 'live'; and it is faster and more cost effective. There are some disadvantages related to sampling and representativeness, including the increased incidence of mobile rather than fixed line phones and telephone answering machines, call screening, lines being used to access the Internet and more than one line per household.

- Self-completion surveys – postal, email and web – are effective if the topic is relevant and of interest to the target population and the method is a suitable way of reaching the target and achieving a response. Response rates may be increased by the use of a personalised covering letter, sponsorship, pre-notification, reminders, incentives and, for postal surveys, a return envelope. They are easy to set up and manage, can be cost effective as there are no interviewers to pay, and are suitable for reaching widely dispersed and otherwise hard to reach samples. Web and email surveys offer the advantages that come with electronic data capture. All methods, however, can suffer from poor response rates and thus problems with representativeness; and there is lack of control over data capture.

- Panels are a way of collecting data from the same pool of individuals, households or organisations over time, either on a continuous basis (every day) or at regular intervals. The data can be used to monitor changes in the market over time.

- Omnibus surveys are run on a continuous basis. Clients buy space to insert their own questions for an entry fee and a fee per question that covers fieldwork and standard analysis. They can be used to generate continuous or longitudinal data by repeating the same questions in each round, or they can be used to gather cross-sectional data.

- Structured observational techniques can be used to collect quantitative data, in person or electronically. Mystery customer research is an application of personal observation; television-viewing meters are a form of electronic observation.

Questions and exercises

1 A colleague is planning to conduct a survey among a sample of female university students on a sensitive health topic. He is considering the following methods of data collection:

(i) face to face;
(ii) telephone;
(iii) email.

(a) Discuss the advantages and disadvantages of each of these methods for this survey.

(b) Recommend the method of data collection that you believe is most appropriate, giving reasons for your choice.

2 Your client is a small organisation with a very limited research budget. It needs to gather information to help it target its core services (aimed at men aged 25–55) more effectively.

(a) Discuss the strengths and limitations of using an omnibus survey to gather the information needed.

(b) What other method(s) of data collection would you recommend? Give reasons for your choice.

3 For the past eight years your organisation's annual employee satisfaction survey has been administered by post. With the vast majority of the workforce now on email your boss has asked you to examine the issues involved in administering future rounds of the survey via email. The next round is due to take place in three months' time.

(a) Outline the issues involved and discuss the advantages and disadvantages of email data collection for this survey.

(b) Recommend which method of data collection should be used in the forthcoming round of data collection, giving reasons for your recommendation.

4 Your client commissions at least three ad hoc surveys every year, among the same target population. You believe that their research needs might be better served by setting up an online panel rather than recruiting a fresh sample of respondents for each of their ad hoc surveys. Prepare a short report outlining the advantages and limitations of the online panel approach versus multiple ad hoc surveys.

References

Brennan, M., Hoek, J. and Astridge, C. (1991) 'The effects of monetary incentives on the response rate and cost-effectiveness of a mail survey', *Journal of the Market Research Society*, 33, 3, pp. 229–41.

Brooker, S., Cawson, P., Kelly, G. and Wattam, C. (2001) 'The prevalence of child abuse and neglect: a survey of young people', *Proceedings of the Market Research Society Conference*, London: MRS.

Comley, P. (2003) 'Innovation in online research – who needs online panels?', *Proceedings of the Market Research Society Conference*, London: MRS.

Gibson, S., Teanby, D. and Donaldson, S. (2004) 'Bridging the gap between dreams and reality . . . building holistic insights from an integrated consumer understanding', *Proceedings of the Market Research Society Conference*, London: MRS.

Holden, J. and Griffiths, G. (2004) 'The way we live now (Daily Life in the 21st century)', *Proceedings of the Market Research Society Conference*, London: MRS.

Macfarlane, P. (2003) 'Breaking through the boundaries – MR techniques to understand what individual customers really want, and acting on it', *Proceedings of the Market Research Society Conference*, London: MRS.

Morrison, L., Colman, A. and Preston, C. (1997) 'Mystery customer research: cognitive processes affecting accuracy', *Journal of the Market Research Society*, 39, 2, pp. 349–61.

Office of National Statistics (2000) *The UK 2000 Time Use Survey*, www.statistics.gov.uk/TimeUse/default/asp.

Orton, S. and Samuels, J. (1997) 'What we have learned from researching AIDS', *Journal of the Market Research Society*, 39, 1, pp. 175–200.

Yu, J. and Cooper, H. (1983) 'A quantitative review of research design effects on response rates to questionnaires', *Journal of the Market Research Society*, 20, 1, pp. 36–44.

Recommended reading

MRS publishes a range of Guidelines on data collection, all of which are available at the MRS website (www.mrs.org.uk). These aim to interpret and expand on the MRS Code of Conduct in relation to data collection and MRS recommends that they are read alongside its publications (also available via the website) on the use of databases and on the Data Protection Act.

Moser, C. and Kalton, G. (1971) *Surveys in Social Investigation*, 2nd edn. Aldershot: Dartmouth.

Sparre, M. and Steen, J. (2000) 'Advantages of conducting employee research on the Internet: a case study', *Proceedings of the ESOMAR Net Effects Conference*, Dublin: ESOMAR.

Wissing, A. (2000) 'Using the Internet to measure advertising effectiveness', *Proceedings of the ESOMAR Net Effects Conference*, Dublin: ESOMAR.

Chapter 8

SAMPLING

Introduction

In this chapter we look at the ideas behind sampling and the issues involved in developing a sampling plan and choosing a sampling technique.

Topics covered

- Developing a sampling plan
- Sampling theory
- Probability or random sampling methods
- Semi-random sampling
- Non-probability sampling methods
- Sampling in qualitative research

Relationship to MRS Advanced Certificate Syllabus

The material covered in this chapter is relevant to Element 3 – Selecting a Sample. It should help you understand and learn how to apply the key principles in sampling, and it should help you understand how to develop appropriate sampling plans for given research scenarios.

Learning outcomes

At the end of this chapter you should be able to:

- demonstrate knowledge and understanding of sampling theory and practice;
- develop and implement an appropriate sampling plan;
- understand the implications of the sampling plan for data accuracy and generalisability of research findings.

Developing a sampling plan

Sampling is about selecting, without bias and with as much precision as resources allow, the 'items' or *elements* from which or from whom we wish to collect data. In market and social research projects these elements are usually people, households or organisations, although they may be places, events or experiences. Drawing up a sampling plan is one of the most important procedures in the research process. It involves the following:

■ defining the target population;
■ choosing an appropriate sampling technique;
■ deciding on the sample size;
■ preparing sampling instructions.

Box 8.1 Sampling units and sampling elements

The elements of the sample – the people, the organisations – may be 'contained' in a *sampling unit*. For example, imagine you are commissioned to gauge the attitudes of the general public to a range of social issues. To achieve the sample you decide to use a sample source (a *sampling frame*) that provides you with details of households. You select a sample of households from this sampling frame and from each household you select an individual. In this case the household is a sampling unit and the individual is the sample element. You may have decided, on the other hand, to select a sample of individuals directly, and not from within households. In this case the individual is both the sampling unit and the sample element.

DEFINING THE POPULATION

In research terminology the term 'population' has a broader meaning than its common usage in reference to human populations of particular countries. In a research context it refers to the 'universe of enquiry' or – put another way – to the people, organisations, events or items that are relevant to the research problem. It is important to define the population of interest as precisely as possible. Any flaws in the definition of the population will mean flaws in the sample drawn from it.

For example, if you are investigating the health and social welfare needs of older people, then you might say that older people are the population of interest. But what do you mean by 'older people'? What age limits do you impose? For the lower age limit, do you use retirement age, for example 60 years of age for women and 65 for men? Or do you have one lower age limit for both sexes? Should you impose an upper age limit or not? Do you include only older people living independently in the community or do you include those living in sheltered or residential care accommodation or those in nursing homes or hospitals? If you decide that it is only those living independently in the community, how do you define that? Should you include those living in the home of a relative or only those living in their own home?

The way in which the population is defined depends on the issues the research aims to address. If, for example, the study of the health and social welfare needs of older people has been commissioned to help develop policy in relation to community health initiatives, you

Box 8.2 Examples of criteria used in defining the population

Organisations and employees

- *Type of organisation* – for example private sector (privately owned or stock market listed), public sector or not for profit; those selling mainly to consumers or mainly to other businesses or both; or those selling to more than one country or to one country only.
- *Geographic area* – for example all organisations with a head office (or any office) in a particular region or country.
- *Market or industry sector* – for example all organisations in the financial services sector or those in the financial services sector selling to private individuals only.
- *Size of organisation* – for example in terms of annual turnover or number of employees.
- *Type of experience and/or time* – for example all organisations involved in an Initial Public Offering (IPO) on the stock market in the last financial year.
- *Type of department or office within the organisation.*
- *Job title or role or responsibilities of an individual employee.*
- *Type of experience of an employee* – for example all those receiving merit pay awards or promotions in the last six months.

Households and people

- *Geographic area* – for example all households within a particular region or country or telephone area code.
- *Demographic profile* – for example age, sex, social class, presence of children.
- *Geodemographic profile* – those living within a particular geodemographic cluster or type of residential neighbourhood.
- *Time* – for example all those visiting a pharmacy between 10 am and 1 pm on weekdays; all those who bought a new car in the last three months.
- *Type of experience and/or time* – for example women who gave birth in the last six months in a private hospital; regular users of brand X.

may decide that those in residential care, nursing homes or hospitals are not part of the relevant population. In defining the population, think of the aims of the research.

Target population and survey population

Moser and Kalton (1971) make the distinction between the *target population* and the *survey population*. The target population is the population from which the results are required; the survey population is the population actually covered by the research. As Moser and Kalton point out, in ideal circumstances the two should be the same but, for practical reasons, they may not be. For example, people or organisations in places that are remote or difficult to access using a face-to-face survey, such as those on islands, may not be included in a survey population. In a survey of older people's health and social welfare needs it may be difficult to get permission to interview those living in sheltered or residential accommodation. So, although you may have identified them as part of the target population, they may be excluded for the sake of expediency from the survey population.

If there is a difference between the target and the survey population, to avoid misrepresentation of the research and its findings it is important that the difference is made clear to all involved with the research and in any documents relating to the research.

Census or sample?

Once the population is clearly defined you must decide whether to collect data from every member or element of that population (usually referred to as a *census*) or from a representative sub-set or *sample* of it. In most market and social research the population of interest is too large for a census to be practicable, either in terms of the time it would involve or the cost. There are some circumstances, for example research among members of a professional body or employees of an organisation, where the population may be small enough, and accessible enough, for a census to be feasible. In other cases it may be necessary or desirable to collect data from all elements of a population (see Macfarlane, 2003, Case study 7.4). For example, in research to help with a decision about changes in working practices it may be important (and politic) to ensure that all employees' attitudes and opinions are surveyed.

There are other disadvantages in conducting a census besides those of time and cost. The level of non-response may mean that the results are less representative than might have been achieved with a well-designed sample of the same population. Furthermore, the size and scope of the census undertaking may result in an increase in the amount of non-sampling error as scarce administrative, field and data processing resources are stretched to the limit. In the end, a census may deliver data of poorer quality than a well-designed sample. Some of the cost and time savings that arise from using a sample rather than a census could be directed to reducing non-response and non-sampling error.

The argument for using a well-designed sample rather than a census rests on two issues: on the practical issue of the time and cost involved in administering it; and on the methodological issue of the ability of a sample to be *representative* of the population (to deliver *external validity*). By 'representative' we mean that the results provided by the sample are *similar* to those we would have obtained had we conducted a census. Of course it is unlikely, no matter how carefully we choose a sample, that it will deliver results that match exactly the values in the population. Sampling theory tells us that a sample design is sound if it delivers results each time it is repeated that *on average* would have been achieved with a population census. Producing representative results is an important aspect of actionable research. It would be pointless if a study of a sample of older people's health and social welfare needs could not be used to generalise about the health and social welfare needs of *all* older people; or if, from a study of the brand preferences of a sample of 18–24 year olds we could not make reliable and valid inferences about the brand preferences of *all* 18–24 year olds.

SAMPLING TECHNIQUES

How do you design a sample that is representative of the population from which it is drawn? It is important to restate what we mean by 'representative'. When a sample is representative of the population it should deliver results close to the results we would have obtained if we had surveyed the entire population. The results are not biased in any way – the sample estimates of the characteristics we set out to measure (for example the incidence of cinema attendance among 16–24 year olds) closely match the value of these characteristics in the population. So what kind of sampling technique produces a representative sample?

Types of sampling technique

There are two categories of sampling techniques:

- random or probability sampling;
- purposive or non-probability sampling.

Random or probability sampling is where each element of the population is drawn at random and has a known (and non-zero) chance of being selected. The person choosing the sample has no influence on the elements selected. The random selection process should ensure to some extent that the sample is representative of the population. There are certain conditions that need to apply, however, for random selection to produce a truly representative sample:

- For true randomness in the selection process to take effect the sample size must be at least 100.
- The population should be homogeneous or well mixed – if it is not (if it is stratified or layered in any way or there is a tendency for similar elements within it to cluster together) a simple random selection process may not deliver a truly representative sample.
- The sampling frame, which represents the population from which the sample is chosen, must be complete, accurate and up to date.
- Non-response must be zero or, put another way, all those selected as part of the sample must take part in the research.

Of course, in real-world research situations, the last three conditions may not hold. We come back to this in more detail later.

The theory that underpins probability or random sampling allows us to calculate how accurately a sample estimates a population characteristic and how likely or probable it is that the sample estimate lies within a certain range of the population characteristic. This leads us to the concepts of sampling distributions, sampling error, standard error and confidence intervals, to which we return in more detail in the section on sampling theory.

In *non-probability sampling* there is no random selection process, and we do not know what probability each element has of being selected because the person choosing the sample may consciously or unconsciously favour or select particular elements. So how do we ensure that the sample chosen in this way is representative of the population? We address this issue when we look in detail at non-probability sampling methods later in the chapter. Suffice to say at this stage that quota sampling, the method of non-probability sampling most widely used in market research, can produce results that closely resemble those that would have been achieved with a probability sample.

In qualitative research, notions of *statistical* representativeness do not apply because of the small sample sizes involved. But representativeness is still an important goal and later in the chapter we look at ways in which sampling in qualitative research sets out to achieve this.

Choosing a sampling technique

How do you decide which type of sampling technique to use? For qualitative studies, which in most cases involve relatively small sample sizes, non-probability techniques are the most suitable. We look at various approaches to sampling for qualitative studies, including theoretical or judgement sampling, 'lurk and grab', list sampling, snowball sampling, and piggy-backing or multi-purposing, later in the chapter. The decision about which technique to use in a quantitative study is more complicated. It will be influenced by both methodological issues, such as the nature and aims of the study, and by practical concerns, including the nature and accessibility of the study population, the availability of a suitable sampling frame, and the constraints of time and budget.

THE SAMPLING DECISION IN A CONSUMER TELEPHONE SURVEY

This case study from Network Research and Marketing Ltd sets out the sampling decision in a consumer survey that is to be conducted by telephone.

Why this case study is worth reading

This case study is worth reading for many reasons: it illustrates the decision-making process involved in choosing a sampling approach; it highlights the link between the aim of the research, the sampling approach chosen and the method of data collection; it describes the sampling approach; it deals with the issue of 'representativeness'.

The key words are: aim, sampling units, households, representative, telephone households, list, random sample, random digit dialling, blocks, seed sample, digit plus 1, biases, original database, directory sample, fixed sampling interval, random start, listed, non-listed, estimate, non-listed households, analysis stage, weight, differences in the incidence, probability of selection, sampling plan, overrepresent.

The survey

The aim of the survey is to produce a comprehensive overview of consumers' use of product X. The sampling units are households (in the United Kingdom). It is crucial to the aims of the research that the sample is representative of all telephone households. A problem arises in terms of how to achieve a representative sample, however, because there is no list of all domestic telephone numbers commercially available: telephone directories (or their electronic equivalent) do not contain non-listed numbers – the sample drawn would not therefore be representative of all telephone households.

The sampling options

A random sample could be drawn using random digit dialling. This involves dialling numbers at random within 'blocks' of numbers that are known to be issued. A disadvantage of this method, however, is that it results in many calls being made to numbers that do not exist or that are fax or business numbers. Another approach might be to use telephone numbers from previous surveys or from commercial databases as a 'seed' sample. New numbers are created for the sample by adding one (known as 'digit plus 1') to the original number. A potential problem with this method, however, is that there may be biases in the original database from which the sample was drawn, and these are carried over into the new sample.

The method chosen

This problem can be avoided by using a directory sample combined with 'digit plus 1'. The first step is to select a representative sample of private households from the telephone directories for the whole of the United Kingdom using a fixed sampling interval from a random start point in each area directory. This will give us a representative sample of all households whose numbers are listed in the directory. Instead of calling the selected households, this sample is used as the 'seed' sample to create new numbers to call by adding one to the final digit of each telephone number. Thus the number generated by the random selection from the directory, say, 0123 123456 will become 0123 123457. This will ensure that the numbers called will include non-listed numbers as well as listed ones. These households should be similar in location and type of household to the number originally selected but will still underrepresent non-listed numbers in areas where non-listed numbers are particularly prevalent (Foreman and Collins, 1991).

During the interview the respondent is asked whether his or her number is listed or non-listed. This enables us to estimate, for each directory area, the proportion of non-listed households. At the analysis stage a weight may be applied to each household (if necessary) to correct for any differences in the incidence, and therefore the probability of selection, of non-listed numbers within each directory area.

This sampling plan should produce a reasonably representative sample of private telephone households. It is, however, worth noting the following:

- it will not represent any mobile telephone-only households; and
- it may overrepresent households with two or more land lines since these have a greater chance of being selected (this is a problem with all of the common methods of selecting domestic telephone samples).

Initial calls will be made to the selected 'digit plus 1' numbers during evenings and weekends in order to avoid overrepresenting households where people are at home during the day. It may be that households with only one line and who are heavy Internet users may be difficult to reach. The only practical solution to this problem is to ensure that subsequent calls are made at different times of day and on different days of the week.

References

Foreman, J. and Collins, M. (1991) 'The viability of random digit dialling in the UK', *Journal of the Market Research Society*, 33, 3, pp. 219–27.

Source: Network Research and Marketing Ltd. Used with permission.

In deciding what sampling technique to use, think first of all about the nature and aims of the study. If the purpose of the research is exploratory and not conclusive (that is, neither descriptive nor explanatory), in other words if it is not necessary to obtain highly accurate estimates of population characteristics in order to make inferences about the population, then a non-probability sample is appropriate. If, on the other hand, it is necessary to obtain measurements from the sample of known accuracy or precision (in order to make statistical inferences or generalisations from the sample to the population), then a probability sampling technique should be used.

Random sampling, however, does not always produce more accurate estimates of population characteristics than non-probability techniques. In fact, in certain circumstances, non-probability (quota) sampling may provide a more representative sample. Where there is little variability within a population, that is when the population is homogeneous, a non-probability sample can be effective in achieving a representative sample; with a great deal of variability in the population a random sample is likely to be more effective. When the non-sampling error (errors arising from question wording, interviewer bias, recording error, data-processing error) is likely to be greater than the sampling error, non-probability techniques may be just as good at producing a representative sample.

THE SAMPLING DECISION IN A SURVEY OF 16 YEAR OLDS

Here we see how a review of the Young Life and Times Survey, a survey of social attitudes among young people, led to a decision to switch from a sample of 12–17 year olds derived from a household sample to an independent sample of 16 year olds only, the approach that has been used since.

Why this case study is worth reading

This case study is worth reading for many reasons: it illustrates the decision-making process involved in choosing a sampling approach, including what alternatives were considered; it describes how the researchers got access to a suitable sampling frame; it describes the sampling approach in detail; it gives details of the response rate and the mode of completion of the survey. Further information including survey questionnaires, datasets and examples of how the data were used can be found at www.ark.ac.uk/ylt/.

The key words are: same household, adult survey, rationale, methodology, responses, linked, response rate, age-range, parental permission, questions, suitable, population of interest, sampling frame, schools, household sampling, robust sample, Child Benefit Register, getting access, drawing the sample, data protection, personal data, survey team, letter, unique identifier, questionnaire, prize draw, pre-stamped return envelope, fieldwork period, phone, online, post, reminder, mode.

Introduction

From 1998–2000, the Young Life and Times (YLT) Survey recorded the attitudes of young people aged 12–17 years living in the same household as an adult respondent to the Northern Ireland Life and Times Survey. YLT involved a paper questionnaire containing a sub-set of questions from the adult survey, and one complete module of particular relevance to young people. One rationale for this methodology was that the responses of the adult and those of the younger respondents could be linked and subsequently analysed.

However, by 2000, the response rate had dropped from 74 per cent (in 1998) to 62 per cent. In addition, while many researchers were using the data from the adult and young people's surveys separately, few were actually making use of the link. In the light of this, in autumn of 2001 the YLT team undertook a review of the future and format of the Young Life and Times Survey. The review consisted of three strands:

- a review of other surveys of young people and in particular, their sampling metholodogies;
- a review of postal and online surveys;
- a discussion forum, involving users and potential users of the surveys from the academic and voluntary sectors.

The outcomes of this review were that there was unanimous support for having some sort of Young Life and Times Survey. Having a time series component was useful, especially when monitoring the impact of policies on young people's attitudes. However, the link between the adult and young person's survey was not seen as important and so a standalone Young Life and Times was seen as acceptable. The age-range of respondents was an issue. In particular, interviewing younger people (under 16 years) requires parental permission. There was a concern that questions suitable for 17 year olds were not always suitable for 12 year olds (and vice versa) and that this was restrictive. Finally, consultation with young people themselves, in terms of developing question themes and/or interviewing was suggested. Consultation was also thought to be important for 'selling' the survey to young people.

Population and sample: deciding on a sampling frame

Thus, in 2003, the YLT team planned to run a revised version of the survey, among 16 year olds only. The population of interest therefore was all 16 year olds living in Northern Ireland. The question was how to find a sampling frame for this group. We ruled out using schools as a way of sampling for several reasons including the following:

- Not all schools would agree, and only particular types of schools might participate;
- The problem of privacy among pupils;
- The effect of having a teacher in the room;
- The omission of pupils excluded from school.

While there are also problems associated with household sampling (for example, the exclusion of young people not living in a private household and parental influence on response), on balance this may be the best methodology for obtaining a more robust sample.

The sample frame

We knew that every child is eligible for Child Benefit, a government benefit for people bringing up children. The Child Benefit Register contains information on all children for whom Child Benefit is claimed. This Register would be a very useful sampling frame for our population. Getting access to it was now the issue. The Child Benefit Register was maintained by the Social Security Agency (SSA) of the Department for Social Development (DSD) in Northern Ireland, who kindly agreed to facilitate drawing the sample. We decided to approach all young people who celebrated their 16th birthday in February of that year, accounting for approximately 2000 young people. However, in 2004, while DSD still maintained the database, the responsibility for the payment of Child Benefit transferred to Inland Revenue. Thus, it was necessary to negotiate access to this Register from Inland Revenue. This process of negotiation took five months, culminating in the preparation of an explanatory memorandum relating to the Tax Credits (Provision of Information) (Evaluation and Statistical Studies) (Northern Ireland) Regulations 2004.

Sample selection

With access now available, we were able to select all those young people who celebrated their 16th birthday during February 2004. However, under data protection regulations relating to use of personal data, the survey team could not contact these young people directly. Thus, all documentation relating to the survey was processed by an independent research organisation.

Each eligible young person received a letter from DSD inviting him or her to take part in the survey. The initial letter was addressed to the relevant person and provided an introduction to the survey. It also explained the role of DSD in the project and ▶

confirmed that the YLT project team did not have access to names and addresses of the young people in the sample. This letter contained a unique identifier (with a check letter) under the address, which was highlighted as 'Your identification number'. A non-personalised letter from the university project team provided more information about the survey, including the aims of the project, the three possible methods of completing the questionnaire, and details of a prize draw of £500 for which all respondents completing the questionnaire were eligible. The pack also contained a paper questionnaire and a pre-stamped return envelope.

Fieldwork

The fieldwork period lasted from 25 August to 24 September 2004. While every eligible young person received a paper questionnaire, each was able to choose one of three methods for completing it.

1. They could take part by phone, having quoted their identification number and check digit.
2. They could complete the questionnaire online – quoting their personal identifier to enter that part of the Young Life and Times website.
3. They could complete the paper questionnaire that was sent to them in the initial pack and post it back in the pre-stamped envelope.

After one week, a reminder postcard was sent out to addressees who had not made contact of any kind.

Response rate

1,983 questionnaires were sent out. 824 completed questionnaires were received, representing a response rate of 41.6 per cent. The response rate in subsequent years has been as follows: 2005 – 40 per cent (total sent 2,049); 2006 – 39 per cent (total sent 1,973); and 2007 – 33 per cent (total sent 1,925).

Besides sending a copy of the questionnaire directly to each sample member, each was offered the chance to complete the questionnaire online or via the telephone. The most popular mode of completion was paper with between 95 and 98 per cent choosing this option over the period 2004 to 2007. Telephone was the least popular (fewer than one per cent chose it). The popularity of online completion varied: it was two per cent in 2004; four per cent in 2005 and 2006; and five per cent in 2007.

Source: Paula Devine, Research Director, ARK, Queen's University Belfast, written for this book.

In terms of the practicalities, if there is no suitable sampling frame from which to select the sample, then random methods are not feasible. We look at sampling frames in more detail later. In addition, probability sampling, especially for face-to-face research, can be difficult, time consuming (not only in terms of drawing the sample but in conducting the fieldwork) and expensive; it is more straightforward and easier to manage in a telephone survey. If time and budget are limited in a face-to-face study, it is likely that a non-probability method such as quota sampling will be used. We look in more detail at various random or probability and non-probability techniques later in the chapter.

Box 8.3 Applications of sampling techniques

Probability or random sampling

- Descriptive and explanatory (conclusive) research enquiries
- Surveys conducted to provide accurate estimates of sales, market share, usage, incidence of behaviour or attitudes (for example employment, household spending, social and political attitudes or opinion)
- Telephone surveys

Non-probability sampling

- Exploratory research enquiries
- Surveys conducted to provide guidance, for example on product/service design and development, advertising development
- Qualitative research studies
- Street interviewing and hall tests
- Absence of a suitable sampling frame
- Hard to reach or inaccessible populations

CHOOSING A SAMPLE SIZE

The sample size is the number of elements that will be included in the sample. The size of the sample is important, particularly in terms of the precision of the sample estimates, but on its own does not guarantee that the results will be accurate or unbiased; the way in which the sample is chosen (the sampling technique used, the sampling frame) will affect this.

Deciding on the sample size involves thinking about the nature and purpose of the research enquiry, and the importance of the decisions to be made on the basis of the results. In exploratory research the sample size (for qualitative or quantitative methods) may be relatively small in comparison to that used in a conclusive study. In conclusive research enquiries the aim is often to provide precise estimates of population characteristics (also called population parameters) – for example the proportion of 25–34 year olds using brand X. The sample size therefore needs to be big enough to provide such estimates. The research may be commissioned to provide conclusive evidence that, for example, a greater proportion of 16–24 year olds compared to 25–34 year olds prefer brand X, and to provide that evidence with a certain degree of confidence that the findings are an accurate reflection of the situation in the wider population. The sample size in this case needs to be large enough to provide the evidence with the specified degree of confidence. If we know the level of precision required of the sample estimates, or the size of the confidence level or interval required, we can work out the sample size needed to achieve these. We look at this in more detail later, in the section on sampling theory.

It is also important to consider the way in which the findings will be analysed. We may need to look at (and compare) the findings among particular sub-groups within the sample, for example particular age groups, or organisations of different sizes or in different industry sectors. It is therefore important to consider how big these sub-groups need to be in order to provide precise estimates of their characteristics and to allow robust analysis. Also, we need to think about the type of analysis needed – if, for example, we plan to use multivariate statistical techniques, we need to think about what implications this has for sample size. In planning the sample it is helpful to know the incidence in the population of any groups of interest, as this may affect the decision about the overall sample size and the choice of sampling technique. Finally, and arguably in practice the most important factor in the choice of sample size, we must take into account the time, budget and other resources available. Generally speaking, for any given sampling approach, the bigger the sample size the greater the cost.

PREPARING SAMPLING INSTRUCTIONS

Once a sampling approach and a sample size have been agreed it is important to set out how the actual sampling process is to be conducted. This will involve drawing up a sampling plan that should include the following:

- the definition of the target and/or study population;
- the sample size required;
- the sampling method to be used, including the way in which the units and elements are to be selected;
- details of the sampling frame, if one is available.

Box 8.4 Sample details from the Life and Times Survey 2006

- Target population: men and women aged 18 and over in Northern Ireland
- Required sample size: 1,230
- Sampling frame: Postal Address File (PAF)
- Sampling units: households
- Sample elements: individuals aged 18 and over; eligible individuals at the selected address chosen randomly using next birthday rule
- Sampling technique: to ensure adequate representation in areas of lower population density, Northern Ireland was stratified into three areas and using a simple random sampling approach addresses were selected from each of these areas
- Number of sampling units selected: 2,162 selected in order to provide reserve addresses
- Number of sampling units in scope: 1,987 (175 were found to be vacant, derelict or commercial properties)
- Sampling/data collection procedure: pre-selected addresses; advance letter notification; CAPI and self-completion
- Number of calls: interviewers to make five calls or to have received a refusal or other information confirming that an interview would not be obtained before being given a reserve address
- Response from 1,987 addresses: 1,230 interviews; 479 refusals; 227 non-contacts; and 49 others, giving a response rate of 62 per cent

Source: Adapted from Devine, P., Technical Notes (http://www.ark.ac.uk/nilt/datasets/technotes.html). Used with permission.

CHECKING THE SAMPLE ACHIEVED

As the fieldwork progresses the sample is monitored to ensure that the units and elements selected meet the sample criteria. Once sampling and fieldwork are completed, the sample achieved is checked to ensure that it matches the sample requirements. If any discrepancies are found (high rates of non-response, under- or over-representation of particular elements and so on) it will be necessary to address them (for example by conducting further sampling and fieldwork, or statistical manipulation). It is also important to check key sample statistics against the relevant population parameters, if that information is available (for example from a recent census) or against sample statistics from other surveys. This serves as a validation check on the representativeness of the sample.

Sampling theory

Before discussing the details of the various sampling techniques we need to look at the theory that underpins probability sampling. This is important because it will help you to understand better a number of related issues, including those of precision, accuracy and bias, and the rationale behind confidence intervals and inferential statistical tests.

TERMINOLOGY

First of all we need to introduce some more terminology. The things that we want to talk about in the population, for example the proportion of 18–24 year olds who drink brand A, or the average income of a particular group, are known as *population parameters*. The corresponding figure derived from the sample is an estimate of this population parameter and is known as a *sample statistic*. For example, in a survey of the brand preferences of 18–24 year olds, the proportion who drink brand A is the sample statistic, or the estimate of the proportion who drink brand A in the population. Here is another example: you are conducting a survey among organisations in the financial services sector to determine the average pay of women. The average obtained from the sample is called the sample statistic. It is an estimate of the population parameter, the unknown value of average pay among women in the wider population of financial services organisations.

The purpose of a survey may be to provide such estimates. The important thing to remember is that the findings provided by a sample are only *estimates* of the population values. Statements based on findings from a random or probability sample are always *probability statements*. We cannot make claims about the value of population parameters based on sample data with absolute certainty. What we do is rely on an effective sample design to ensure that the sample estimates accurately reflect the population values *most of the time*, and with a known *margin of error*. This brings us to sampling theory.

SAMPLING DISTRIBUTION OF THE MEAN

You are interested in knowing the weekly food spend of single person households in Sweden. You select a sample at random from the population of all single person households and from the sample data you note the average (or mean) of the particular value that interests you – weekly spend on food. You then select another sample at random and note the value of weekly food spend from this sample. You continue this process ad infinitum; you plot the value of the average weekly spend on food from each sample on a graph. Once you have plotted this value

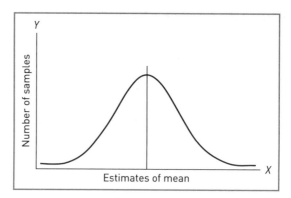

Figure 8.1 Sampling distribution of the mean

for your infinite samples you should have a graph like the one in Figure 8.1, the bell-shaped curve of a normal distribution. This graph is known as the *sampling distribution of the mean*.

Sampling variability

The graph shows that each sample does not produce the same value: a range of samples produces a range of values for the same measure (in this case the average weekly food spend). This variation is known as *sampling variability*. In real-world research, however, we do not take repeated samples from a population to measure a value; usually we take only one sample and we estimate the population value on the basis of this one sample. But given the amount of variability between samples that the sampling distribution shows, how can we know how accurately our sample measure reflects the true population value? We can do this with a fairly simple calculation – called the *standard error of the mean* – from one randomly selected sample made up of at least two sampling units.

Standard error of the mean

The standard error of the mean is a measure of the variability within the sampling distribution – the variability or spread in the values of the measures we have taken from each sample. It is the standard deviation of the sampling distribution. We can use it to measure the probable accuracy or precision of a particular sample estimate. To work out the standard error of the mean we need to know the standard deviation of the population (S) and the size of the sample (n). There is a small complication – it is very unlikely that we will know the value of the population standard deviation. In its place we use the standard deviation of the sample (s).

From the information needed to calculate the standard error of the mean we can see that what it measures – the precision of a sample estimate – depends on two things: sample size and the level of variability in the population, which is measured by the standard deviation. It makes sense that these two factors have an impact on precision. If you think about sample size, it makes sense that a bigger sample will deliver results that are more precise. The formula for calculating the standard error shows the relationship between precision and sample size: to increase the precision of an estimate by a factor of two – in other words, to halve the standard error – you need to increase the sample size by a factor of four. It also makes sense that variability within the population will have an impact on the precision of a sample estimate. If, for example, there is very little variability – say, for example, that the average weekly food

> ## Box 8.5 Formula for calculating the standard error of the mean
>
> For numerical data:
>
> $$\text{Standard error } (\bar{x}) = \frac{s}{\sqrt{n}}$$
>
> For % data:
>
> $$\text{Standard error } (p\%) = \sqrt{\frac{p\%(100 - p\%)}{n}}$$

spend of all single person households in Sweden is €200, then the standard deviation and the standard error would be zero. We can say that the sample provides a precise estimate of the population value. If, however, the average weekly food spend varies from, say, €50 to €500, the standard deviation will be relatively large and so will the standard error. As a result, the sample will provide a less precise estimate of the population value.

CONFIDENCE INTERVALS

You saw in Figure 8.1 that the sampling distribution of the mean closely resembles a normal distribution. In fact, the larger the sample, the closer the sampling distribution will be to a normal distribution. The normal distribution has a number of useful properties that can be applied to sampling. It is symmetrical in shape, with 50 per cent of observations or measures lying above the mean and 50 per cent lying below the mean. If we divide the normal curve up into segments delineated by standard deviations, we find that about 68 per cent of all observations lie within 1 standard deviation either side of the mean; 95 per cent lie within 2; and 99 per cent are within 2.6 standard deviations.

If a sampling distribution closely resembles a normal distribution then we can use the properties of the normal distribution to obtain some very useful information about our sample estimates. The first thing we need to do is to convert the standard deviations into standard errors. This allows us to say that 95 per cent of our sample estimates lie within 1.96 standard errors of the population mean; and 99 per cent lie within 2.58 standard errors. To put it another way, we can say that a sample mean or sample statistic has a 95 per cent chance of being within 1.96 standard errors of the population mean or the true mean; or a 99 per cent chance of being within 2.58 standard errors.

Calculating the accuracy of the sample estimate

An example makes all this a bit less abstract and a bit more real: imagine that you have completed your survey on weekly food spend among single person households in Sweden. You have found that the average weekly spend is €250. The first question you ask is, how accurate an estimate is this of the population value? In other words, how big is the standard error? To work this out you need to know the standard deviation and the size of the sample.

The first step in working out the standard deviation is to calculate the variance (which is a fairly simple measure of the spread of values within the sample). To do this, you subtract the

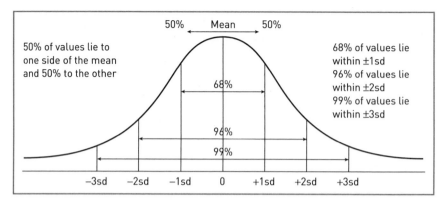

Figure 8.2 Normal curve with standard deviations

Table 8.1 Symbols for population and sample values

Value	Population	Sample
Mean	μ	x̄
Proportion	π	p
Variance	σ² or S²	s²
Standard deviation	S	s
Size	N	n

sample mean from each of the individual observations, which in this case are amounts of money spent on food. Next, you square each of the deviations from the mean (to get rid of any negative values), then add them all up and divide by the sample size. This last figure is the variance of the sample. Take the square root of the variance to get the standard deviation. To calculate the standard error, divide the standard deviation by the square root of the sample size. The calculations are slightly different if you have proportions or percentages rather than means, for example if you want to look at the proportion of buyers of brand A in the sample.

Box 8.6 Formulae for variance and standard deviation

Using means

$$\text{Variance } s^2 = \frac{\sum (X - \bar{X})^2}{n}$$

$$\text{Standard deviation (s)} = \sqrt{s^2}$$

Using percentages

To calculate the standard deviation using percentages:

$$\text{Standard deviation (s)} = \sqrt{\frac{p\%(100 - p\%)}{n}}$$

Table 8.2 Calculations involved in determining the standard deviation

Sampling unit Household	Observation (x) Weekly food spend (€)	Sample mean (x̄) Average spend (€)	Deviation from the sample mean (x − x̄)	Square of the deviations (x − x̄)²
1	247	250	−3	9
2	253	250	+3	9
3	247	250	−3	9
4	248	250	−2	4
5	259	250	+9	81
6	242	250	−8	64
7	250	250	0	0
8	252	250	+2	4
9	244	250	−6	36
10	258	250	+8	64
Total	2,500		Total	280

Of course, you would use a computer program to calculate these figures – in a real research project it would not be practicable to calculate them by hand. From the formulae, however, you can get some idea of the underlying logic. The second column in Table 8.2 shows the weekly food spend from the ten households in the sample (in reality, of course, the sample would be much bigger). Column three shows the average spend across all ten households; column four shows the deviation of the actual spend from the average spend; and the final column shows the square of that deviation.

The sum of the squared deviations – the total of the figures in the final column of Table 8.2 – is 280. To calculate the variance you divide by the sample size, which in this example is 10. The variance therefore is 28. The standard deviation, that is the square root of the variance (28), is 5.29. The standard error, which is the standard deviation (5.29) divided by the square root of the sample size (3.16), is 1.67. What does this figure tell you? You can say that you are 68 per cent confident that the true (population) value of average weekly food spend lies within the range €250 ± €1.67 (the mean plus or minus 1 standard error). In other words, you are 68 per cent confident that the average weekly spend among the population is somewhere between €248.33 and €251.67. You can say that you are 95 per cent confident that it lies within the range 250 ± 1.96 standard errors (1.96 × 1.67) – that is, between €246.73 and €253.27. You can be 99 per cent confident that it lies within the range 250 ± 2.58 standard errors (2.58 × 1.67), that is, between €245.69 and €254.31. These limits on the range of a value are called *confidence limits*. The size of the difference or the margin of error is called the *confidence interval*.

You can look at this another way – in terms of the probability that the claims you make about your findings are correct. This is where significance levels come in. If you claim that the average weekly food spend among the population lies somewhere between €246.73 and €253.27, the probability that you are right in this assertion is 95 per cent (the confidence limit is 95 per cent). There is a 5 per cent or 1 in 20 chance that you are wrong (this is known as the significance level). If you want to make sure that there is less chance that your assertion is wrong, say, 1 in 100 or 1 per cent chance (a greater significance level), you are setting a wider confidence interval, which means the margin of error will be larger.

In conducting a piece of research you may want to specify at the outset how precisely you want the sample measures to reflect the population values – in an opinion poll, for example. In other words you may want to specify the confidence limits and the margin of error that will be acceptable. For example, in the survey of weekly food spend among single person households, you may want to set the confidence limits at the 95 per cent level (the level most commonly used in market and social research) and you might want the estimate of average weekly spend to be accurate to within €1 of the population values. The question is, what sample size do you need to achieve this? The formula for calculating the sample size is given in the example in Box 8.8.

Box 8.7 Significance levels and the risk of error

What are significance levels?

Significance levels are the level of probability at which you accept that a difference is statistically significant or real – that is, that it is not due to chance. They are sometimes referred to as the p or α (alpha) value. The level of significance is the point at which the sample finding or statistic differs too much from the population expectation for it to have occurred by chance – the difference cannot be explained by random error or sampling variation and is accepted as a true or statistical difference. Decisions about whether a null hypothesis is accepted or rejected are based on these significance levels.

Which significance level to use?

The three significance levels used most often are the 5 per cent or the 0.05 level of probability (sometimes written as $p = 0.05$ or $p <= 0.05$); the 1 per cent or 0.01 level; and the 0.001 or 0.1 per cent level. At the 5 per cent significance level there is a 5 per cent probability or a 1 in 20 chance that the result or finding has occurred by chance. This is the lowest acceptable level in most market and social research projects. At the 1 per cent significance level you are setting a higher standard by saying that there is a 1 per cent or 1 in 100 probability that the finding has occurred by chance. The 0.1 per cent level indicates that there is a 1 in 1,000 probability that the finding has occurred by chance. As the significance level falls, in other words, the more confident you can be in the results (the confidence level is greater). So in using significance levels to judge results, you are giving a probability that the results are sound and at the same time saying that there is a chance that they may not be. The significance level you choose will depend on the amount of risk you are prepared to tolerate in drawing the wrong conclusions from the research. If, for example, the research involves evaluating a product, it might be best to set the significance level at $p = 0.001$, as the impact on the client's business of launching a product that might be rejected 5 per cent of the time (if $p = 0.05$) could be costly.

Type I and Type II errors

Every time you make a decision to accept or reject a null hypothesis you risk making an error. There are two types of error – Type I or α (alpha) and Type II or β (beta) errors. If you make a Type I error you reject the null hypothesis when in fact it is true and you should have accepted it. An example of a Type I error is when an innocent person is found guilty. You make a Type II error when you accept the null hypothesis when in fact it is false and should have been rejected. A Type II error is when a guilty person is acquitted.

The chance of committing a Type I error is no greater than the level of significance used in the test (which is why the significance level is sometimes called the alpha value, the value associated with an alpha error). If you use the 5 per cent level you can only make a Type I error 5 per cent of the time. You can reduce the probability of making a Type I error by setting the significance level at 1 per cent or 0.1 per cent. If you drop the significance level (in effect increasing the stringency of the test and raising the confidence limits to 99 per cent or 99.9 per cent) you increase the chances of making a Type II error.

In setting significance levels, therefore, you need to reach a compromise between the types of error. If making a Type I error (accepting as true something that is really false) is deemed worse than making a Type II error (accepting something that should be rejected and is not), then you should set the significance level low (say 0.1 per cent). If, however, the risks associated with a Type II error are greater, then it might be best to set the significance level at 5 per cent. To lower the risk of either type of error arising, you increase the sample size.

Box 8.8 Calculating the sample size for a given level of precision

The 95 per cent confidence interval means that the sample estimate will lie within
 1.96 standard errors of the mean. So $1.96 = z$
The standard deviation of the sample is 5.29. So $s = 5.29$
The margin of error we want is € ±1. So $d = ±1$ where $d =$ the confidence interval
 required

Formula for working out sample size:

$$n = \frac{z^2 s^2}{d^2}$$

$$= \frac{(1.96 \times 1.96) \times (5.29 \times 5.29)}{(1 \times 1)}$$

$$= 107.5$$

$$= 108 \text{ (rounded up to the nearest whole number)}$$

So you need a sample of 108 to ensure that you can be 95 per cent confident that our estimate of average weekly food spend is within €1 of the population value.

In research we deal with percentages as well as averages. To work out the sample size necessary to ensure that a particular percentage is within an acceptable margin of error, the formula is similar. For example, in the survey of weekly food spend, imagine that you asked whether people had bought fresh fruit. You expect that about 60 per cent will have done so and you want a confidence interval of ±2 per cent and a confidence level of 99 per cent. The calculation is shown in Box 8.9.

Box 8.9 Sample size calculations using percentages

Confidence interval $d\% = \pm 2$ per cent
Standard error for 99 per cent confidence level $z = 2.58$
Estimate of percentage being measured $p = 60$

Formula

$$n = \frac{z^2 p\%(100 - p\%)}{d^2}$$

$$= \frac{(2.58 \times 2.58) \times 60(100 - 60)}{2 \times 2}$$

$$= \frac{15,975.36}{4}$$

$$= 3,993.84$$

If you were to reduce the confidence level from 99 per cent to 95 per cent, what effect would this have on the sample size needed to achieve the same confidence interval of ± 2 per cent? Lowering the confidence level would mean that a sample of 2,305 would deliver a ± 2 per cent confidence interval. If you were to reduce the confidence interval by half to ± 1 per cent, keeping the confidence level the same, what would this mean for sample size? You would need a sample size of some 9,220 – in other words, to halve the confidence interval you need a fourfold increase in sample size.

In deciding on sample size it is not just the total sample that is important; you need also to think about the size of sub-groups within the main sample. For example, it may be crucial to the research objectives to examine the views of women and men separately, or to look at regular users of a service or occasional users. You need to make sure that these sub-samples are large enough to allow you to comment at the chosen confidence level and within an acceptable confidence interval.

Caveat – For ease of explanation, all of the above is based on the use of a simple random sampling approach. Most sample designs in real-world market and social research are more complicated than this, with the result that calculating margin of error and confidence intervals is also more complicated. We have also made assumptions about using standard deviation of the sample rather than the standard deviation of the population.

Probability or random sampling methods

A random or probability sample is one in which each member of the population has a known and non-zero chance of being selected. There are several kinds of random sampling methods, from the fairly straightforward simple random sampling approach to the more complex cluster sampling methods.

SIMPLE RANDOM SAMPLING

Simple random sampling works like this: imagine we have a population of 1,000 (denoted $N = 1,000$). The population might consist of people or organisations, whatever is relevant to the research investigation. Before making any selection from the population, we know that each item in it has a 1 in 1,000 chance of being selected. Once an item is selected as part of the sample we do not return it to the population. This is known as *sampling without replacement.* The reason for using sampling without replacement is to make sure that no item (a person or organisation, for example) is chosen more than once. In a market or social research survey we would not (usually) interview the same person twice. This makes simple random sampling slightly different from the sampling associated with probability theory, which is sampling with replacement. In this 'unrestricted random sampling' approach (Kish, 1965) a selection is made from the population and that item is replaced before the next selection is made.

There are two main ways of selecting a simple random sample. The first will be familiar to anyone who has watched numbers being selected in a lottery game. Each item in the population is represented by a ball. All balls are placed in a drum, thoroughly mixed, and a sample of them is drawn at random. The second method of simple random sampling involves numbering each item in the population, from 1 to N. A sample is drawn at random by selecting numbers from a random number table or by generating a random number using a computer program.

SYSTEMATIC RANDOM SAMPLING

Systematic random sampling is a variation of simple random sampling. The items in a population are numbered from 1 to N and arranged in a random order. We decide what size of sample we need (n) and we work out what is known as the sampling interval (k) by dividing the population size (N) by the sample size (n). We select every N/n item from the randomised list of the population. For example, say we have a population of 6,000 and we need to draw a sample of 200. We calculate the sampling interval to be 30 (6,000/200) and starting at a random point between 1 and 6,000 (N) in the list we select every 30th item from the list until we get the required sample size of 200. The reason that this method is referred to as *systematic* random sampling is because a system is in operation for selecting the sample and using the system means that the sampling interval and the randomly chosen starting point on the list will determine which items in the sample are selected. For example, if our random start point is 37, then using the sampling interval of 30 the next item to be selected will be 67, and the item after that will be 97, then 127 and so on until all 200 sampling units are selected. So each item selected is dependent on the previous item. In simple random sampling there is no such dependence – each item is selected independently of all other items in the population.

The results produced by a systematic random sample will be very similar to those produced by a simple random sample if the list used to generate the systematic sample is randomised. If, however, the list is ordered in some way – for example names in alphabetical order, employees in order of their staff grade, or students ranked in order of examination results – then a systematic sample may produce a better sample because it will ensure a spread of sample units from right across the list. The only problem that might arise is if the list has an inherent pattern or is sub-divided into categories. For example, if users and non-users of a service are listed alternately on the list, an even-numbered sampling interval will miss odd-numbered items. Or if items on the list are grouped in some way, depending on the size of the groups and the size of the sampling interval, some groups may be missed out or under-represented. As a result, the systematic approach may not deliver a good sample.

For practical reasons it may not be possible to use either simple random sampling or systematic random sampling. In many market and social research situations lists of the target population may not be available. Where they are available population size may make it difficult to number all of the items, although with computerised lists and databases this is less of a problem that it was in the past.

STRATIFIED RANDOM SAMPLING

Stratified random sampling is one of the most widely used methods of sampling in research. In sampling a population for a market or social research project it is very likely that we know something about that population which we can use to improve the quality of the sample and the precision of the results derived from it. For example, in a population of employees, we may know which staff grade each holds. We can use this information to make sure that employees from each staff grade are properly represented in the sample. To do this we must divide the population into the relevant groups or strata, for example all who belong to staff grade 1, all who belong to grade 2, all from grade 3 and so on. In this case staff grade is what we call the *stratification factor*. Which stratification factor to choose will depend on what you believe to be most relevant to the research objectives. From each of the strata we choose the required sample size – using a simple random or a systematic random sampling approach.

Proportionate and disproportionate stratified sampling

If you choose the sample from within each stratum using a systematic sampling approach and you select sample units from each stratum in proportion to the size of the stratum, this is known as *proportionate allocation*. Using the same sampling interval for each stratum will produce a proportionate allocation to the strata and achieve a *stratified sample with proportionate allocation*. Put simply, this means that in the sample the strata are represented in the same proportion as they appear in the population.

If for some reason you want to over- or under-represent particular strata in the sample, then you use *disproportionate allocation*. For example, it might be important to examine the views of a low incidence group within the population. The best way of achieving a robust sub-sample for analysis is to make sure that the group or stratum is over-represented in the sample in comparison to the population. To achieve such a *disproportionate stratified sample* you use a different sampling interval for each stratum. An approach known as *optimum allocation* is common in business-to-business research, where sampling units – the organisations – vary in size and you want to ensure that you include a greater proportion of the larger organisations. The sampling fractions for each size of stratum within the population (for example, the small, medium and large organisations) are calculated to provide the best sample (with the lowest sampling error for a given cost) using the statistical theory of optimum allocation. You might end up sampling 1 in 40 small organisations; 1 in 20 medium sized; 1 in 10 large organisations and 1 in 5 very large organisations.

CLUSTER AND MULTI-STAGE SAMPLING

Populations can often be divided up into groups. The national population is easily divided up into administrative areas, states or regions, electoral constituencies, wards and postcode areas, for example; organisations have departments and so on. We can make use of these natural *clusters* in a sampling strategy. It is also possible, if no natural clusters exist, to create a cluster by, for example, imposing a grid on to a map.

In a study of attitudes to the redevelopment of a park among the population of a large town, you might first select a sample of the electoral wards (administrative districts made up of a relatively small number of streets) that make up the town. You could then draw a sample of households from within each of the selected wards. This is an example of a cluster sample – the households, the sampling units, are clustered together in wards. You could add further stages before selecting individuals for interview. You could select particular streets within each ward.

Box 8.10 Selecting individuals: the next birthday rule and the Kish Grid

Where there is more than one eligible person for interview, and to ensure that each has a roughly equal chance of selection, individuals can be selected using the 'next birthday rule', choosing the individual with the next birthday, or by using a Kish Grid.

Table 8.3 Example of a Kish Grid

Serial number of contact	Number of eligible individuals					
	1	2	3	4	5	6 or more
1	1	2	1	4	3	5
2	1	1	2	1	4	6
3	1	2	3	2	5	1
4	1	1	1	3	1	2
5	1	2	2	1	2	3
6	1	1	3	2	3	4
7	1	2	1	3	4	5

A sampling approach in which you first of all select a sample of groups such as an electoral constituency or a department, and then go on to select a sample from within each group, is known as *multi-stage sampling*. The first stage groups are known as *primary sampling units* or *PSUs*. If the units within each of the PSUs are clustered together, the sample is known as a *cluster sample*. But it is not necessary in multi-stage sampling to begin with clusters – the first stage groups may be widely dispersed.

Using clusters of the target population and selecting a sample from within each cluster is often a more cost-effective approach than that of simple or systematic random sampling where the sample may be more widely spread. The interviewer travel time needed to complete a set number of interviews in a cluster sample is usually much less. There is a disadvantage with multi-stage sampling. The standard error is greater than if a simple random or a stratified random sample were used. At each stage of a multi-stage sample we are introducing sampling error and, as a result, sample estimates may be less precise than those from a single stage probability sample.

Sampling with probability proportional to size (PPS)

It is possible, even very likely, that PSUs (for example electoral constituencies, or organisations) will vary greatly in size. In a random selection of these PSUs each has an equal chance of being chosen. For example a small PSU, say a small organisation with 50,000 customers, has the same chance of being selected as a large organisation in the same market with 100,000 customers. This could lead to an unrepresentative sample. If both the large and the small organisations were chosen as PSUs, then at the second stage sampling any one of the smaller organisation's 50,000 customers has a greater chance of being selected than any one of the 100,000 in the larger organisation. You could overcome this by using the same sampling interval for both sizes of organisation. For example, with a sampling interval of 500, we would achieve a sample of 100 from the smaller organisation and a sample of 200 from the larger one. Again, this may not be satisfactory since we may not achieve a robust enough sample size for analysis of different sub-groups of customers from the smaller organisation. You could use disproportional allocation, in the manner outlined above.

Another solution is to use sampling with *probability proportionate to size* or *PPS*. Using this approach, the PSUs are chosen in proportion to their size. So, for example, the larger organisation, at twice the size of the smaller one, would have twice the chance of selection. At the second stage of the sampling process the same number of items is chosen from each PSU. This means that overall the chance of any item being chosen is the same, regardless of the size of the PSU to which it belongs. So, in our example, each customer has the same chance of selection.

The advantage of using PPS is that it delivers a sample with a smaller standard error (or greater precision) than does a simple random sample of PSUs followed by second stage sampling with a constant sampling interval. Although the larger PSU is more likely to appear in the sample using PPS, the number of second stage units taken from it are fixed, so its 'members' are unlikely to dominate in the total sample. The only drawback with this approach is that in order to set the probability proportional to size we need to have accurate and up-to-date information about the size of the PSUs.

Box 8.11 Professional practice and the MRS Code of Conduct: sampling

Use of Client Databases, Lists and Personal Contact Details

B7   Where lists of named individuals are used e.g. Client databases, the list source must be revealed at an appropriate point in the interview, if requested. This overrides the right to Client anonymity.

Respondents' Rights to Anonymity

B8   The anonymity of Respondents must be preserved unless they have given their informed consent for their details to be revealed or for attributable comments to be passed on.
      Comment: Members must be particularly careful if sample sizes are very small (such as in business and employee research) that they do not inadvertently identify organisations or departments and therefore individuals.

B9   If Respondents have given consent for data to be passed on in a form which allows them to be personally identified, Members must:
      ■ demonstrate that they have taken all reasonable steps to ensure that it will only be used for the purpose for which it was collected and
      ■ fully inform Respondents as to what will be revealed, to whom and for what purpose.

B10   If Respondents request individual complaints or unresolved issues to be passed back to a Client (for example, in customer satisfaction research), Members must comply with that request. The comments/issues to be passed back to a Client must be agreed with the Respondent and must not be linked back to any other data or used for any other purpose without the explicit consent of the Respondent.

Source: MRS Code of Conduct 2005. Used with permission.

SAMPLING FRAMES

In order to choose a random sample you need a sampling frame. A sampling frame can be a database, a list, a record, a map – something that identifies all the elements of the target population. Examples used for selecting samples of the general public include the Electoral Register, the Postal Address File, or the Child Benefit Register cited in Case study 8.2. Customer databases – those belonging to the client, for example – are now also commonly used as sampling frames in market research. To use a database for research purposes the database owner must register with (notify) the Office of the Information Commissioner under the terms of the 1998 UK Data Protection Act (see Chapter 1). In addition, the use of a customer database raises ethical issues in relation to the privacy of those who appear in it. The MRS Code of Conduct (see Box 8.11 below) sets out rules for how researchers should deal with this.

To be effective as a sampling frame, to allow you to draw a sample that is representative of the population, it must be accurate, complete and up to date. The famous and much quoted example of the consequences of using an inappropriate sampling frame (the poor response rate, 22 per cent, also played a part) is that of the *Literary Digest* 1936 opinion poll. The magazine's poll predicted that in the United States presidential election Alf Landon would beat the incumbent Franklin Roosevelt by a landslide. In fact Roosevelt won a second term by the largest majority in history. The poll sample of 10 million was drawn from two sources: car registrations and telephone listings. Remember, the year was 1936, the effects of the Depression were still much in evidence. Choosing a sampling frame that over-represented the relatively well off (those who could afford cars and telephones) and under-represented the relatively poor section of the electorate produced a biased sample.

In terms of practicality, the sampling frame must be easily available, convenient to use, and contain enough information to enable us to find the elements listed on it. Kish (1965) identifies four main problems with sampling frames: missing elements; clusters of elements; blanks or foreign elements; and duplication.

Missing elements

Missing elements are elements that belong to the population but do not appear on the sampling frame. It can often be difficult to detect whether a sampling frame has missing elements. An incomplete sampling frame will mean that the sample derived from it will not be representative of the population. One way round this is to look for another source of information about the same population and compare and/or combine the two. For example, a list of dentists may be obtained from a subscription list to a professional association or to a journal or magazine. If it appears to be incomplete – some dentists may not subscribe – the list could be checked against the listing of dentists given in the telephone directory.

Clusters of elements

A sampling frame may list elements not as individuals but as groups or *clusters of elements*, for example individuals at the same address. In our dentist example, rather than listing individual dentists, the sampling frame might list dental practices. A dental practice may be one dentist or it may be several dentists. How do we treat this? We have a number of options:

■ Include all the dentists from the cluster in the sample. *Drawback* – dentists in the same practice may be similar in attitudes, age and so on.
■ Choose one at random from the cluster. *Drawback* – this means that all elements of the population do not have an equal chance of selection.

- Take a sample of all the clusters in the sampling frame, list all the elements of each one and take a random sample from this list. *Caution* – need to take a large enough sample of clusters and an appropriate sampling interval to ensure that each of the elements in the final sample comes from a different cluster.

Blanks or foreign elements

An element may be included in a sampling frame that does not belong there. Such elements are known as *blanks* or *foreign elements*. The incidence of blanks or foreign elements may be relatively high in a sampling frame that is out of date. For example, between the compilation of the sampling frame and its use individuals listed may have died, retired, left the country, or no longer be eligible to be considered as part of the target population. The sampling frame may cover a wider population than the population of interest and so contain elements that are not relevant to the target population. For example, a subscription list for a dental journal may be a useful sampling frame from which to draw a sample of dentists but it may also include non-dentists, such as dental equipment sales people, dental technicians or dental nurses.

The best way of treating blanks or foreign elements when drawing a sample is to omit them and continue selecting sample units in the appropriate way. A substitution of the next item on the list is not a suitable way of dealing with them. That approach means that an item next to a blank or foreign element has two chances of being selected, once in its own right and once as a replacement for a blank or foreign element.

Duplication

An element may be *duplicated* in a sampling frame, appearing more than once. For example, in a subscription list, an individual may appear twice if he or she subscribes to two or more products. Duplication is relatively easy to deal with when the sampling frame is held electronically. A *de-duplication* program is run which eliminates the recurrence of an element.

Box 8.12 Dealing with non-response

Non-response error occurs when those included in the sample do not respond. This is an important issue in research – it can lead to serious concerns about the representativeness of the sample and so the validity of the data. If the responders and the non-responders to a survey differ, the data – the sample estimates – will be biased.

The main causes of non-response are refusals and 'not at home'. Refusal rates can be reduced by good questionnaire design and good research administration (including training and briefing of interviewers, pre-notification and follow-ups, use of appropriate incentives and so on). There are two main approaches to managing 'not at homes': varying the times at which contacts are made (weekends and weekdays, daytime and evening) and making 'call backs' or return visits. Non-response can also be addressed by providing substitutes or replacements for the non-responder. Taking a sample of the non-responders (and using the results to project to all non-responders) can help in understanding the differences between respondents and non-respondents and the final sample may be adjusted accordingly.

EXAMPLES OF SAMPLING FRAMES

For selecting samples of households and members of the general public, the most commonly used sampling frames in the United Kingdom include the Postal Address File (PAF) and the Electoral Register. Several commercial organisations specialise in designing samples from the PAF and the electoral register. Sources of sampling frames for business-to-business research include Census of Employment List (UK) and commercial directories such as Kompass (www.kompass.com), Dun and Bradstreet (www.dnb.com) and, in the United Kingdom, the Yellow Pages (www.yell.co.uk).

Semi-random sampling

In all of the sampling methods described above, the interviewer is not involved in selecting a subject for interview or observation – the sample performs this task and the interviewer's job is to get hold of that subject. This can be an expensive process, especially in face-to-face surveys. Generating the sample, a detailed list of addresses for each interviewer to visit, and completing the fieldwork can be time consuming and expensive. One way of reducing the time and cost involved without giving the interviewer greater discretion in selecting locations, households or individuals (and thus introducing selection bias) is to use a *semi-random* sampling procedure known as *random route sampling* or *random walk*. This method does not involve the time and expense incurred in drawing a full random sample from a sampling frame. A list of random starting addresses is selected using a multi-stage stratified random sample, for example to ensure a mix of urban and rural locations or towns of varying size. Each interviewer is given one random address at which to conduct the first interview (and instructions for choosing which individual to select within that household). Along with the random starting address the interviewer is given a set of instructions for selecting subsequent addresses at which to interview.

As with random sampling methods, no substitutes for the chosen subject are allowed and a number of call backs may be necessary to achieve an interview. This may mean that there is little difference in fieldwork costs. In order to achieve cost savings call backs may be scrapped in favour of a quota-based approach. We will look at quota sampling next.

Non-probability sampling methods

It is not always possible or feasible to use probability sampling methods. The time and cost involved may be prohibitive, a sampling frame may not be available, or the type of research may not require it. In this section we look at the alternatives to probability sampling – *non-probability sampling* methods. With non-probability sampling the interviewer or observer has some control over the selection of elements for the sample. We do not know what chance any item has of being selected and we cannot use probability theory to make inferences about a population based on the sample or make calculations about precision of sample estimates.

QUOTA SAMPLING

Quota sampling is perhaps the most widely used sampling technique in quantitative market research. In most markets the researcher or the client will have extensive knowledge of the target population, especially on key variables or characteristics. This knowledge will have been derived from primary and secondary sources, including customer databases, geodemographic

Table 8.4 Example of independent quota controls

Characteristics	Proportion in the target population %	Number necessary for sample of 400
Age		
18–34	30	120
35–54	35	140
55+	35	140
Gender		
Male	48	192
Female	52	208

or national census data and other research. This information is used to design a sampling framework that will reflect the make-up of the population on these key characteristics. For example, the research might require a nationally representative sample of the adult population of the United Kingdom in terms of age, gender and socio-economic group. A sampling framework or *quota* based on these characteristics can be drawn up. Quotas are allocated to interviewers and the interviewers' task is to select the individuals who fit the characteristics set out in the quota.

In designing a quota sample we have two options. We can have an independent quota or an interlocking quota. In an independent quota the interviewer is free to select anyone who fits a particular quota criterion, independent of any other criteria. There is no instruction to obtain, for example, specific numbers of male respondents within a particular age band, or a specific number of women in each socio-economic group. Within the age quota 18–34, for example, we assume that individuals will be chosen at random but the interviewer could choose women and not men. Since this may lead to an unrepresentative sample it is likely that the interviewer will be instructed to select a 'spread' of the sexes within each age group, and a spread on socio-economic group. An example of a sample with independent quota controls is given in Table 8.4. The advantages of independent quota controls are that they are easier to set, easier for the interviewer to achieve and so less expensive in comparison to a sample with interlocking quota controls. The disadvantage is that, in leaving the interviewer so much leeway in the selection process, a representative sample is not always achieved.

When the interviewer is asked to find an individual who meets several of the quota controls in combination, for example so many women within each age band and within each SEG, the quota is known as an interlocking quota. An example of an interlocking quota is given in Table 8.5. Designing an interlocking quota sample is more difficult than designing an independent quota, and it can be more difficult and time consuming for interviewers to achieve. It may, however, limit selection bias, and so give more control over the composition of the final sample and a greater chance of the sample being representative of the population.

In setting quotas for consumer surveys, the population characteristics most often used include age, gender, social class, region, working status, and characteristics directly appropriate to the research study, for example buyers or non-buyers of a particular product or brand. In a study

Table 8.5 Example of an interlocking quota control

	Age 18–34		Age 35–54		Age 55+	
	Male	Female	Male	Female	Male	Female
Buyers	30	30	50	60	30	25
Non-buyers	20	20	50	40	20	25
Total	50	50	100	100	50	50

in which organisations rather than people are the sampling units the quota controls may include organisation type or sector, size (number of employees or turnover), or region.

The quality of a quota sample will depend on two factors: the degree of randomness, or extent of bias, with which the interviewer makes selections (which can be influenced by interviewing training, clear briefing instructions, variation in interviewing times and locations); and how accurate and up to date is the information on which the quota controls are based. In choosing which characteristics to use in setting quota controls it is important to think of the research objectives and to choose characteristics that are relevant to these. In many ways quota sampling resembles stratified sampling – on the basis of what we know about the population we are able to divide it up into strata and determine what proportion we need in each stratum to ensure that the sample represents the population. The main difference between stratified sampling and quota sampling lies in the choice of individuals (or items) to fill the quota. In a stratified random sample these items are chosen at random and the interviewer's task is to interview them, even if this means completing a number of call backs. A substitute is not accepted if the specified individual is not available. In a quota sample the characteristics of individuals (or items) are specified by the quota but a particular individual is not specified. The interviewer's task is to interview someone (anyone) who fits the quota criteria, not a particular individual chosen at random. If a person is not available for interview call backs may be made but it is more likely that the interviewer will look for someone else more readily available or easier to find to fill the quota. In other words, with a quota sample the choice of the final sampling unit is not random.

A variation on 'pure' quota sampling suitable for use when in-home interviewing is needed is random location sampling. It is a form of quota sampling that aims to reduce bias by minimising interviewer discretion about where to interview. It combines elements of random sampling (in particular, multi-stage sampling) and quota sampling – in order to garner the 'advantages' of both (Crouch and Housden, 2003): the randomness (and objectivity) of probability sampling; and the cost effectiveness, speed and ease of management of quota sampling.

It works something like this:

- You have a list of geographic areas (for example, the 'small areas' from the UK Census output areas).
- You may want to stratify this list by geographic region or by neighbourhood type using a geodemographic classification system (see Chapter 5) in order to ensure representativeness.
- From this list you select a random sample of areas.
- You choose sampling points within each of these small areas.
- You give each interviewer a list of all addresses that fall within that sampling point.
- You give each interviewer instructions about the number of people to interview during the fieldwork period as well as a set of quota controls setting out whom to interview (the quota controls might be based on age, working status, gender and chosen to be in line with/ representative of the profile of the area).
- The interviewer can use all of the allocated addresses to achieve the quota. However, when an interview is completed at a particular address, the dwellings within two doors either side are not to be used.
- You may want to instruct the interviewers to work at certain times of the day/week in order to maximise the chance of interviewing working people.

The strengths of this approach are as follows:

- You can use a sampling frame that covers an entire geographic population.
- You can design the sample and set the quota controls using knowledge of the population from the Census and from a geodemographic classification system.

- You can set the quota controls to achieve representativeness on the quota control criteria within the sampling points you choose.
- You can aim to reduce bias by restricting the interviewer's choices of respondent to the selection of an address within an allocated area.
- You can reduce bias towards those not working (that is, those more likely to be at home when an interviewer calls) by varying the fieldwork times appropriately.
- You can ensure the approach is well executed by preparing detailed interviewer instructions and giving a comprehensive briefing.
- It is cost effective – there is relatively little travel time since interviewers work in a small area.

The weaknesses of the approach are as follows:

- It is not a random sample so none of the characteristics of a random sample will apply:
  - you will not be able to work out the sampling error;
  - you will not be able to get a fine degree of accuracy of measurement from the data;
  - you cannot apply confidence limits to the data;
  - if you use inferential statistical tests on the data (which it is not entirely appropriate to do) you will need to interpret the findings with some care.
- While the sample may be representative of the wider population on the variables set out in the quota, it may not be representative on other key variables (it is impossible to judge what biases may exist in terms of other variables).
- The method is better suited to sampling in urban areas with a high density of addresses at which to attempt to get an interview; in rural areas it can be more time consuming.

In other words, the decision to use this method represents a trade-off between cost and methodological rigour. Since it is a non-probability rather than a probability method, it cannot deliver a sample that is representative of the population with a known level of accuracy and precision. It is, however, likely to be more cost effective than random sampling and with care taken in choosing and executing the sample, bias can be reduced. An example of random location sampling in use is given in Case study 8.3 below.

Research has been carried out in which the results obtained by random sampling and quota sampling have been compared and found to be different (Marsh and Scarbrough, 1990). Many research organisations, however, argue (from experience) that quota sampling can produce a quality, representative sample, especially if care is taken to limit bias at the final selection stage. To this end particular care is taken to ensure that hard-to-find individuals, for example those at work, those who travel a lot, are included in the sample. While a well-designed probability or random sample should be representative of the target population in all aspects (because of randomness), a well-designed quota sample may only be representative of the population in terms of the characteristics specified in the quota. It may be unrepresentative in other ways. With probability samples we are able to estimate representativeness; with quota sampling we are not able to estimate representativeness, or even gauge the possible biases that exist.

Quota samples have a number of points in their favour which account for their popularity in market research. In comparison to probability methods they are relatively quick and inexpensive to set up and administer. Call backs can be avoided, saving on interviewer travel time and expenses. A quota sample is often a more practicable alternative if a sampling frame does not exist. However, if a research project demands that results be underpinned by statistical theory, probability sampling is the only choice.

SAMPLING THE GENERAL PUBLIC AND GAY MEN

Here Orton and Samuels describe the sample design for their investigation into public knowledge, attitudes and behaviour in relation to the disease AIDS, research commissioned by the UK Government in relation to its programme of public education and publicity.

Why this case study is worth reading

This case study is worth reading for many reasons: it describes two sampling 'operations' to achieve two samples from two different universes; it explains the decisions (and outcomes) in choosing particular sampling approaches; it offers an example of a sample design suitable for a repeated cross-sectional study; it describes a form of random location sampling; it describes over-sampling and explains why it was done; it contains examples of the use of purposive sampling in reaching a hard to find population.

The key words are: sample design, replication, universe, sampling operations, oversampling, age, sex, area, population, random location sampling, probability proportional to, sampling points, number of interviews, matching, ACORN, Census Enumeration Districts, sample stratification, sampling fluctuations, Address List, quota, controls on age and sex, sub-group size, standard error, optimum efficiency, disproportionate sampling, snowballing, confidentiality, sampling frame, gaining co-operation, purposive sampling, matched samples.

Introduction

Our task was to develop a sample design which would be capable of *replication* over an unknown number of waves of interviewing. The universe for investigation was the general public and groups at high-risk particularly homosexuals and young people. The design adopted comprised two independent sampling operations: one for the general public, which oversampled young people and within which it was hoped to obtain a sample of covert homosexuals, and the second a sample of overt homosexuals (i.e. people who had, in the terminology, 'come out' and hereinafter called the 'gay' sample). We describe the design of each sample below.

The general public

The aim in designing the sample for the general public was to oversample the young and covert homosexuals. While it would be possible to ask people's age at the contact stage we did not feel we could ask whether a person was homosexual. We therefore attempted to meet the requirements by adopting a sampling scheme which oversampled men, the young, and certain types of area as follows:

■ On the question of age, we restricted the survey to people aged 18–64. We realised that many people over 65 would still be sexually active but we felt that, with the level of resources available, more would be gained by increasing the numbers of young people. We accepted that people under 18 were both sexually active and at risk, but the subject matter was exceptionally sensitive and we believed there would be problems in obtaining permission to interview and then obtain reliable data from younger people. Within the age-range 18–64 we oversampled younger people such that half were 18–34 and half 35–64, i.e. an oversampling of about 50 per cent. ▶

- On the question of sex, men were known to be massively more at risk than women and thus we opted for three-quarters of our sample to be men, again an oversampling of about 50 per cent.
- On the question of area, we considered a number of options. We rejected oversampling of London because, although the incidence of AIDS is much greater there, there would be a sufficient sub-sample in any reasonably sized national sample. We rejected undersampling rural areas because, although the incidence of AIDS is very low, they only contain 10 per cent of the population and for political reasons it was necessary to have a national sample. However, in the hope of increasing the number of homosexuals in the sample, we sampled areas with probability proportional to the percentage of households that are all adult males under 65.

The key features of the detailed research design were that it maximised the number of sampling points and emphasised the matching of sampling points between waves. The number of sampling points was maximised by restricting the number of interviews to the minimum viable interviewer assignment. This was one afternoon and two evenings (the emphasis on the evening being required because of the oversampling of men).

The design for selecting and matching sampling points was a sophisticated variant of random location sampling developed by BMRB and known by us as 'Rolling ACORN'. The detailed design was as follows:

(i)   An initial selection of 40 sampling points was made. Each point was a Census Enumeration District (ED) containing, on average, 150 households.

(ii) The selection of 40 points was made by computer after stratification of the C110,000 EDs in England and Wales by ACORN type within Standard Region. (ACORN is a geodemographic classification system increasingly used in preference to other possible social class indicators for sample stratification.)

(iii) Areas were selected with probability proportional to number of households comprised of all adult males under 65.

(iv) Following the initial selection of 40 areas (Set A), the computer then selected other sets of areas (B, C, D, etc.) each element of which was matched with an individual area within Sample A. Thus we have a very closely matched sample of 40 very small geographic areas. Each survey takes place in two of the sets areas, and the design allows for each set to be used on two successive waves.

(v)   The first time a set of areas is used interviewers are restricted to the odd-numbered houses and the second time to the even-numbered houses.

(vi) The pattern for the research programme is therefore:

Wave 1	Wave 2	Wave 3	Wave 4
Ao	Be	Ce	De
Bo	Co	Do	Eo

(vii) Thus at any wave one half of the areas are exactly the same as those used the previous wave, and one half the same as those used on the next wave. This ensures a very high degree of matching indeed, and reduces the influence of chance sampling fluctuations on the results. Moreover, if results look 'odd', the two halves of the sample can be inspected to discover if anything is unusual.

(viii) The interviewer is supplied with an Address List listing the streets and numbers (or house names) where she is allowed to interview. She is given a quota of nine interviews to obtain with controls for sex and age. (No social class quota is set because the area selection controls for social class.) The quotas lead to oversampling of men vis-à-vis women, and of 18–34 years old relative to 35–64 years old – in each case by about 50 per cent.

The design worked out extremely well in practice. It produced samples that are very closely matched between waves of interviewing, not only on demographic characteristics but also on various other measures which we would not expect to change in the short term, despite increasing publicity, but which may be important determinants of attitude. For example, the proportion claiming to know an injecting drug user has been 6 per cent on each occasion, the proportion claiming to know a homosexual has varied only slightly between 33 per cent and 36 per cent, and we have observed remarkably consistent results on our question on personal sexual orientation.

Another aspect of sample design that worked extremely well is oversampling of young people with the aim of increasing the numbers in sample who have had multiple sex partners. We had no direct evidence on which to base our decision as to the extent to which we should oversample the under 35s – the decision for 50 per cent oversampling was typical of the way researchers make such decisions, i.e. on the basis of hunch and intuition and the minimum desirable sub-group size for over 35s!

In practice we were surprised by the success of our guesstimates. Had we had prior knowledge of the number of different partners within age bands, and thus been able to design a sample measuring the standard error to optimum efficiency, we would have done almost exactly the same level of disproportionate sampling!

Homosexuals

We have been much less successful in our second aim of increasing the number of covert homosexuals. We attempted to do this via a 'snowballing' method. At the end of the interview, we asked all those people who said they knew a homosexual whether they would ask that person whether they would be willing to be interviewed. For this purpose we provided a letter stressing confidentiality, and a reply letter and envelope which did not refer to AIDS. The intention was that the snowball sample from one wave would be interviewed on the next wave. However, only 4 per cent agreed to pass the letter on at Wave 1 and only two people were interviewed via this route at Wave 2.

We tried a second tack at Wave 2. Here we asked our gay bar sample [see below] whether they knew gay people or bisexuals who did *not* go to gay bars nowadays whom we could contact. Twenty-four per cent said they did but the route proved only marginally more fruitful in yielding interviews. We therefore abandoned this approach. We are thus left with the homosexuals we have located naturally within our main general public sample.

The gay bar sample

The vast majority of AIDS cases in Britain at the time occurred among homosexual men. We anticipated that we would have only limited success in locating this group by conventional methods, which was borne out in practice. It was therefore decided to attempt to sample them via known gay clubs and pubs. This raised major potential ▶

problems of gaining co-operation from owners and managers to set up interviewing facilities. There were also the more 'mundane' sampling problems of a sampling frame and matching between waves!

We enlisted the help of the Terrence Higgins Trust (an AIDS-related charity named after Britain's first victim). Gay clubs and pubs vary widely in their nature: from leather bars to country pubs, from lavishly appointed discos to places with no furniture at all. Similarly their clientele varies too. Using a list of gay clubs and pubs in the publication *Gay Times* a purposive sample of 10 bars (Set A) was selected to cover different parts of the country and different types of bar. We then proceeded to select matched samples of bars purposively (Set B, C, etc.). The samples were then 'rolled out' in a manner akin to the general public sample.

At Wave 1 interviewing took place in Set A only, at Wave 2 in Sets A and B, at Wave 3 in Sets B and C, and at Wave 4 in Sets C and A again (as it was exactly one year later). Bars often vary in their nature and clientele on different nights of the week, and thus care is taken to go on the same night out of the week on each occasion of visiting a particular bar. Interviewing is spread across the whole week and the day is selected in consultation with the manager, avoiding very quiet or exceptionally busy days.

Source: Adapted from Orton, S. and Samuels, J. (1997) 'What we have learned from researching AIDS', *International Journal of Market Research*, 39, 1, pp. 175–200, www.ijmr.com.

Sampling in qualitative research

In qualitative research sample sizes are generally small and so probability theory and notions of statistical representativeness do not apply. But, as we noted earlier, this does not mean that representativeness is not important. Neither does it mean that selecting a sample is not a rigorous or systematic process.

In choosing a sample for a qualitative research study it is important, as in a quantitative study, to define clearly the target population. It is crucially important to define clearly what relationship the sample has with this population. For example, the sample may aim to be broadly representative of the wider population in terms of key characteristics such as age, gender and social class but it will be difficult, if not impossible, to achieve a truly representative sample with a small sample size. In many cases true representativeness is not the aim. The sample may be chosen to encapsulate a range of characteristics relevant to the topic under study, or to provide a detailed view of behaviour, experiences or events that are seen in the wider population. As in the quantitative research context, it is important to think back to the research objectives and ahead to the analysis and interpretation of the findings. Choosing sample units or elements on the basis of their relevance to the research problem, the analytical framework or the explanation you hope to develop is known as theoretical sampling. The best-known version of this sampling approach is that developed by Glaser and Strauss (1967).

THE SAMPLING PROCESS

Once you have defined how your sample relates to the population you must decide how you are going to select members of it. In qualitative market research sampling is usually referred to as *recruitment* and the specially trained interviewers who undertake it are known as *recruiters*.

Recruitment can take a number of forms: the choice will depend largely on the nature of the sample – who the people are, where they are and/or where you might find them, and what information you have on them already.

Usually a grid or matrix or a detailed list is drawn up identifying the types of people or organisations relevant to the research. For example, they might be defined in terms of demographic characteristics (age, gender, social class, working status and so on) or they might be defined in terms of usage of a particular product or service, or in terms of their attitude or experience of an event – whatever is relevant to the aims of the research. A combination of factors may be used to describe the target population and so the sample required. Care should be taken not to over-specify, however, as this is usually unnecessary and can make recruitment difficult and expensive.

If necessary, a *recruitment* or *screening questionnaire* can be used and recruiters are asked to find individuals who match the recruitment or sample criteria. The recruitment question-naire may be administered face to face by contacting people at home or on the street, or at a specific place where the incidence of those likely to fit the recruitment criteria is relatively high. Recruiting at a specified site is another form of convenience sampling, sometimes known as *outcropping* or 'lurk and grab'. For example, if we were looking for church-goers, we would recruit near a church, perhaps at the time of a service. The recruitment questionnaire may also be administered by telephone or by post. Telephone or postal contact is often used if a sampling frame of the target population, for example a business directory or database, is available. The client may provide a list of possible contacts or you may have your own list, built up through knowledge of the market or subject area (in both cases this raises issues in relation to data protection, and the owner of the list should be registered, if in the UK, under the 1998 Data Protection Act). Using lists or sampling frames in recruitment is sometimes referred to as *list sampling*. The quality of the sample will depend to some extent on the quality of the sampling frame. Using a network of contacts and asking these contacts to refer you to others is known as *network sampling* or *snowball sampling*. This method is useful if a list or sampling frame is not available, or if the sample is difficult to find, for example a low incidence or low visibility group. A disadvantage is that you may end up with a sample made up of people with similar characteristics. *Piggy-backing* or *multi-purposing* is another way of recruiting or identifying a sample. At the end of a study respondents are asked if they would be willing to be recontacted to take part in further research. They are contacted again at the recruitment stage of the new study to check their willingness to take part and their suitability. This sampling strategy is useful if individuals are expensive or difficult to find.

CASE STUDY 8.4

FINDING TEENAGERS AT THE 'MARGINS'

This case study describes how the research team gained access to a hard to reach population – teenagers 'at the margins'.

Why this case study is worth reading

This case study is worth reading for the following reasons: it highlights issues in sampling hard to reach groups; it is an example of network sampling; it describes ethical issues related to the topic of the research and the target group.

The key words are: teenagers at the margins, recruitment network, recruiters, codes of conduct, sensitive, parental/guardian consent, commitment, close relationship, experts. ▶

Introduction

To develop an effective communications campaign strategy on teenage pregnancy, the UK Government Department of Health through the Central Office of Information (COI) commissioned research into teenage attitudes to sex and contraception. Teenagers 'at the margins' – a particularly high risk group – were the target audience and so the target population for the research.

The sample to be drawn from this population was to include boys and girls of a broad range of ages but with a core of 11- to 17-year-olds. It had to include those teenagers identified as being most at risk including:

- those from social grades DE;
- those from high risk areas (from urban inner city estates to rural seaside resorts);
- the sexually active and non-active;
- teenage parents;
- 'looked after' children;
- teenagers from minority ethnic groups.

Even with considerable experience recruiting lower income respondents, we soon found that our existing recruitment network was not going to do the job. We used the recruiters closest to the margins within our existing network to find and train recruiters from 'lower income' backgrounds. In other words, recruiters recruited new recruiters closer to the margins. Those new recruiters then went on to recruit respondents.

New recruiters were given clear guidance regarding appropriate codes of conduct. All recruiters were briefed on appropriate and sensitive ways to approach respondents. Furthermore, the importance of the application of parental/guardian consent for all potential respondents was impressed on recruiters. No respondents were allowed to take part in the research without the requisite parental/guardian consent. The success of the project was in no small measure due to the enthusiasm and commitment of this dedicated recruitment team. In addition, the close relationship between recruiter and respondents enabled us to overcome some of the particular challenges of recruiting teens to discuss the sensitive area of teenage sex.

The specific recruitment of 'looked after' children and teenage mothers required the involvement of experts and professionals in those fields. Within Local Education Authorities there are dedicated teams who work with 'looked after' children and teenage mothers, and who were instrumental in recruiting those willing to take part in the research.

Source: Adapted from Cohen, J. (2005) 'Teenage sex at the margins', MRS Conference, www.mrs.org.uk.

Ethical issues

There are several ethical issues that you need to consider at the sampling and recruitment stage. The first of these is the nature of the population from which you plan to draw the sample: for example, are you planning to interview children or those in other 'vulnerable' groups (see Case study 8.4 above), for instance those with learning difficulties or those involved in illegal activities? You will need to think carefully about how you plan and manage your research in these cases, in particular in gaining informed consent and in ensuring that no harm comes to participants as a result of taking part in the research. There are other issues relating to data protection: if you plan to record the group or interview then you will need to ask potential participants for their consent in writing at the recruitment stage. Also, if you know that someone – a client or colleague – will be observing the discussion or interview then again you must ask for the potential participant's permission in writing at this stage. A set of good practice guidelines, covering issues relating to data protection and recruitment, are contained in the *Qualitative Research Guidelines* (2006) published by MRS at www.mrs.org.uk.

Box 8.13 Professional practice and the MRS Code of Conduct: sampling in qualitative research

Here are the MRS 'rules' that are relevant at the sampling and recruitment stage of a project:

A1 Research must conform to the national and international legislation relevant to a given project including in particular the Data Protection Act 1998 or other comparable legislation applicable outside the UK.

A3 Members must act honestly in dealings with Respondents, Clients (actual or potential), employers, employees, sub-contractors and the general public.

B2 All written or oral assurances made by any Member involved in commissioning or conducting projects must be factually correct and honoured by the Member.

B15 If there is to be any recording, monitoring or observation during an interview, Respondents must be informed about this both at recruitment and at the beginning of the interview.

B17 Respondents must not be misled when being asked for co-operation to participate in a research project.

B19 Members must ensure that Respondents are able to check without difficulty the identity and bona fides of any individual and/or their employer conducting a research project (including any sub-contractors).

B21 Members must ensure that all of the following are clearly communicated to the Respondent:
- the name of the interviewer (an Interviewer's Identity Card must be shown if face to face);
- an assurance that the interview will be carried out according to the MRS Code of Conduct;
- the general subject of the interview;
- the purpose of the interview;
- if asked, the likely length of the interview;
- any costs likely to be incurred by the Respondent.

B34 At the time of recruitment (or before the research takes place if details change after recruitment), Members must ensure that Respondents are told all relevant information as per rule B21 and:
- the location of the discussion and if it is to take place in a viewing facility;
- whether observers are likely to be present;
- when and how the discussion is to be recorded;
- the likely length of the discussion including the start and finish time; and
- the Member, moderator and/or research agency that will be conducting the research.

Source: MRS Code of Conduct 2005. Used with permission.

Sample size

Although sample sizes in qualitative studies are usually small, they should be large enough to give you the information you need to address the research problem clearly and unequivocally, and large enough to include sub-groups of relevance to the topic and to allow you to make meaningful comparisons. In choosing the sample size you should be guided by your experience (or the experience of others) in similar types of study or in similar areas or markets. One approach (common in social and academic research) is to take a 'rolling' or dynamic sample – in other words to sample until you reach 'theoretical saturation' (Bertaux and Bertaux-Wiame, 1981), until you are seeing or hearing nothing new in the data.

Chapter summary

- Sampling is about selecting, without bias and with as much precision as resources allow, the 'items' or elements from which or from whom we wish to collect data. In market and social research projects these elements are usually people, households or organisations, although they may be places, events or experiences.

- Drawing up a sampling plan is one of the most important procedures in the research process. It involves defining the target population, choosing an appropriate sampling technique, deciding on the sample size and preparing sampling instructions.

- There are three main approaches to sampling – probability or random sampling, semi-random sampling and non-probability sampling.

- Random sampling approaches include simple random sampling, systematic random sampling, stratified random sampling and multi-stage and cluster sampling. Sampling or probability theory underpins random sampling.

- Sampling frames are used from which to draw random samples. A sampling frame can be a database, a list, a record, a map – something that identifies all the elements of the target population. To be effective as a sampling frame, to allow you to draw a sample that is representative of the population, it must be accurate, complete and up to date. It must be easily available, convenient to use, and contain enough information to enable you to find the elements listed on it. Problems with sampling frames arise as a result of missing elements, clusters of elements, blanks or foreign elements, and duplication.

- Sample size is the number of elements included in the sample. It is important in terms of the precision of sample estimates but on its own does not guarantee that the results will be accurate or unbiased; the way in which the sample is chosen (the sampling technique used, the sampling frame) will affect this. Choice of sample size depends on the nature and purpose of the research enquiry, the importance of the decisions to be made on the basis of the results, and the analysis requirements (particularly of sub-groups within the sample). It needs to be large enough to provide the evidence with a degree of confidence in the findings. If the level of precision of the sample estimate or the size of the confidence level or interval required is known, the sample size can be calculated to achieve these. Time and budget constraints are also a factor in the choice.

■ Quota sampling is the most commonly used non-probability sampling method and is employed widely in market research. Information on key characteristics in the target population is used to design a sampling framework that reflects the make-up of the population on these key characteristics. The quality of a quota sample depends on the degree of randomness with which the interviewer makes selections and on how accurate and up to date is the information on which the quota controls are based.

■ A well-designed probability or random sample should be representative of the target population in all aspects (because of randomness); a well-designed quota sample may only be representative of the population in terms of the characteristics specified in the quota – it may be unrepresentative in other ways. With probability samples we are able to estimate representativeness; with quota sampling we are not able to estimate representativeness, or even gauge the possible biases that exist.

■ Non-probability sampling techniques are used in qualitative research – samples are typically small and notions of statistical representativeness do not apply. Representativeness is an important goal nevertheless and selecting a sample for qualitative research should be a rigorous and systematic process.

Questions and exercises

1 Discuss the contribution that the following make to the quality of the data gathered in quantitative research:

(a) sampling approach

(b) response rate.

2 (a) Compare and contrast the following two sampling approaches:
   (i) stratified random sampling
   (ii) quota sampling.

(b) Your client, a government body, wants to do research to help it come to a decision about a controversial policy issue. It is likely that whatever decision is made it will come under heavy scrutiny. It is important therefore that the findings of the research are representative of the wider population. Which of the two sampling approaches would you recommend to your client? Give reasons for your choice.

3 You are planning to do qualitative research among mothers with children under the age of 4 to explore the decision to either return to work or not return to work.

(a) Describe three approaches that would be suitable for recruiting or drawing a sample from this population, outlining the strengths and limitations of each approach.

(b) Which approach would you recommend? Give reasons for your answer.

References

Bertaux, D. and Bertaux-Wiame, I. (1981) 'Life stories in the bakers' trade', in Bertaux, D. (ed.) *Biography and Society: The Life History Approach in the Social Sciences*, London: Sage.

Cohen, J. (2005) 'Teenage sex at the margins', *Proceedings of the Market Research Society Conference*, London: MRS.

Crouch, S. and Housden, M. (2003) *Marketing Research for Managers*, London: Butterworth-Heinemann.

Foreman, J. and Collins, M. (1991) 'The viability of random digit dialling in the UK', *Journal of the Market Research Society*, 33, 3, pp. 219–27.

Glaser, B. and Strauss, A. (1967) *The Discovery of Grounded Theory*, Chicago, IL: Aldine.

Kish, L. (1949) 'A procedure for objective respondent selection within the household', *Journal of the American Statistical Association*, 44, pp. 380–87.

Kish, L. (1965) *Survey Sampling*, New York: Wiley.

Macfarlane, P. (2003) 'Breaking through the boundaries – MR techniques to understand what individual customers really want, and acting on it', *Proceedings of the Market Research Society Conference*, London: MRS.

Marsh, C. and Scarbrough, E. (1990) 'Testing nine hypotheses about quota sampling', *Journal of the Market Research Society*, 32, 4, pp. 485–506.

Moser, C. and Kalton, G. (1971) *Survey Methods in Social Investigation*, London: Dartmouth.

Orton, S. and Samuels, J. (1997) 'What we have learned from researching AIDS', *Journal of the Market Research Society*, 39, 1, pp. 175–200.

Recommended reading

Birn, R. (ed.) (2000) *The International Handbook of Market Research Techniques*, 2nd edn., London: Kogan Page.

Bock T. and Sergeant, J. (2002) 'Small sample market research', *International Journal of Market Research*, 44, 2, pp. 235–44.

Foreman, J. and Collins, M. (1991) 'The viability of random digit dialling in the UK', *Journal of the Market Research Society*, 33, 3, pp. 219–27.

McIntosh, A. and Davies, R. (1970 and 1996) 'The sampling of non-domestic populations', *Journal of the Market Research Society*, 12, 4 and 38, 4, pp. 429–46.

Marsh, C. and Scarbrough, E. (1990) 'Testing nine hypotheses about quota sampling', *Journal of the Market Research Society*, 32, 4, pp. 485–506.

Mason, J. (2004) *Qualitative Researching*, 2nd edn. London: Sage.

Moser, C. and Kalton, G. (1971) *Survey Methods in Social Investigation*, London: Dartmouth.

Qualitative recruitment: Report of the industry working party (1996) *Journal of the Market Research Society*, 38, pp. 135–43.

Chapter 9

DESIGNING QUESTIONNAIRES

Introduction

The purpose of this chapter is to introduce the principles of questionnaire design. We look at why questionnaire design is important; we examine the process of planning a questionnaire, including the need to address specific issues that relate to different types of questionnaire and data collection method; and finally we look briefly at the concepts of validity and reliability in the context of questionnaire design.

It is useful to consider what we mean by the term *questionnaire*, as its use varies. Some, in particular those involved in social research, use the term questionnaire to describe the self-completion format used in postal, web and email surveys. The structured and semi-structured data collection instruments used in interviewer-administered surveys, they refer to as *interview schedules*. In market research, however, the term questionnaire is generally used to describe any data collection instrument used in quantitative research or at the recruitment stage of qualitative research, regardless of whether it is self-completion or interviewer administered. This wider definition is the one that will be used here. Decisions about content, structure, wording, order of questions and layout are important to the design of both formats, self-completion and interviewer administered.

Many of the issues we look at in this chapter are relevant to the design of *interview guides* or *discussion guides*, the less structured data collection tools used in qualitative research. So, although the focus of this chapter is the design of questionnaires, the issues raised and the processes discussed may be of some use to those designing guides for qualitative data collection.

Topics covered

- The importance of good design
- The questionnaire design process
- Question content
- Question wording
- Question structure
- Asking questions on attitudes
- Question order

- Layout and appearance
- Questionnaire length
- Pilot study

Relationship to MRS Advanced Certificate Syllabus

The material in this chapter is relevant to Element 6 – Designing Data Collection Instruments. It should help you develop the knowledge and skills to enable you to work out the information needs of a project and prepare a suitable set of questions with which to collect that information.

Learning outcomes

At the end of this chapter you should be able to:

- understand the principles of questionnaire design;
- develop an instrument for the collection of valid and reliable data.

The importance of good design

Good design matters. Quite simply, effective research and quality data depend on it. This means that not only should it be effective in addressing the research objectives – collecting valid and reliable data to address the research problem clearly and unambiguously – but it should also be suited to the practical tasks of data collection and data processing and analysis. The questionnaire has a huge role to play in helping the interviewer gather and record data accurately and effectively, and in helping the respondent provide accurate, complete and reliable data. It must be a workable, user-friendly tool for the interviewer, the respondent and the data analyst. It also has a role to play in representing research, and the research industry, to the wider world. Many of these issues are touched upon in Case study 9.1 below.

CASE STUDY 9.1

BARCLAYS BANK: MONITORING BRAND HEALTH

This case study presents the reasons why a questionnaire underwent a major redesign and what happened as result.

Why this case study is worth reading

This case study is worth reading for several reasons: it highlights the importance of designing a questionnaire not only with the research objectives in mind but also with respondent and interviewer experience in mind; it illustrates the benefits of using CAPI; it gives examples of useful techniques; and it illustrates the benefits of running pilot studies.

The key words are: brand and advertising tracking, brand health monitor, role of interviewers, interview quality, in-home interviews, interview length, repetition, pen-CAPI, flexibility, routing, patterned response, self-completion, open-ended questions, confidentiality, recruitment process, pilot, brief, debrief, respondent evaluation, follow-up depth interviews, incentives, reward, satisfaction, enjoyment rating, impact of technology, sponsor.

Introduction

Early in 1999 Barclays Bank decided to review their brand and advertising tracking work, with the objective of establishing a consistent framework across business divisions. There were concerns at the time within the research industry that the role of interviewers in the research process was being neglected, resulting in a detrimental effect on the information collected. Barclays felt there was an opportunity to draw these elements together and, with their appointed agency, to develop a new survey addressing both interviewer and respondent issues while providing a sound basis of understanding from which the business could make strategic decisions. The result was the Barclays Brand Health Monitor (BHM). The findings discussed here are drawn from experiences during the development of the BHM and from experimentation within the first four months of its use.

Creative questionnaire design

Barclays considered what information was essential, and removed what would be 'nice to know' – the priority being *quality* (in terms of both the process and the information collected) rather than *quantity*. The aim was to get an interview length of under 30 minutes, an acceptable length for an in-home interview, and to avoid the common pitfall of repetition, frequently cited as a source of frustration to interviewers and respondents alike. Subsequent feedback from interviewers was very positive.

What we did

We stressed confidentiality, provided respondents with a genuine estimate of interview length and identified the nature of the interview during the recruitment process.

The interview was to be administered via pen-CAPI technology without the use of stimulus material beyond that which could be displayed on screen. This in itself is perceived as a benefit to interviewers – they do not have to co-ordinate multiple stimuli during the interview and can focus on asking the questions, thus streamlining the entire process. We found that use of pen-CAPI greatly increased flexibility in terms of routing and the variety of techniques it was possible to incorporate, but careful attention needed to be given to the layout of each screen.

We used a mix of techniques to measure brand image, the main objective of which was to provide the respondent with variety in style of questioning and hence avoid any lapse into complacency and 'patterned response'. We created, for example, some self-completion sections which required the respondent to use the CAPI machine to answer sections of the questionnaire (including confidential classification questions) themselves. We used a number of open-ended questions to allow respondents to express their views, including two open questions at the end where respondents have the opportunity to say what they think of the interview itself and make any additional comments pertaining to the subject-matter.

Pilot testing

An extensive pilot study was undertaken in a hall environment. Although the survey itself would take place in-home, this gave the team (client, research agency and advertising agency) the chance to brief and debrief interviewers and to observe the interview process. A second pilot study was conducted in-home when issues arising ▶

from the first pilot had been addressed. Reaction to the second pilot, from interviewers and respondents, was extremely positive.

Conclusions

Our assessment of respondent reaction to the Brand Health Monitor, during development and subsequent to its launch, has reassured us that many of the steps taken to improve the interview experience for respondents have proved successful. Benchmarked against other surveys of comparable length and methodology, but outside the financial arena, the BHM has achieved enhanced enjoyment ratings. This, despite the general preconception that financial surveys may be 'dull' or difficult to administer. Initial qualitative assessment among interviewers has suggested they too appreciate that the questionnaire has been designed effectively in comparison to other studies although there remain calls for further streamlining, particularly where respondents' perceptions of less familiar brands appear to be stretched. We found that interview length, if properly managed, is less of an issue to respondents than it is to interviewers.

Source: Adapted from Miles, K., Bright, D. and Kemp, J. (2000) 'Improving the research interview experience', MRS Conference, www.mrs.org.uk.

Box 9.1 Professional practice and the MRS Code of Conduct: questionnaire design

With its central role in the research process, the MRS Code of Conduct, as you might expect, has much to say in relation to questionnaire design. At key points within this chapter we list the relevant clauses from the Code. You may also find it useful to read the MRS Questionnaire Design Guidelines (2006) which you can download from the MRS website (www.mrs.org.uk/standards/quant.htm). Here are three of the general rules of the MRS Code of Conduct (2005) that apply to various aspects of the research process including questionnaire design:

A1   Research must conform to the national and international legislation relevant to a given project including in particular the Data Protection Act 1998 or other comparable legislation applicable outside the UK.

A3   Members must act honestly in dealings with Respondents, Clients (actual or potential), employers, employees, sub-contractors and the general public.

A10 Members must take all reasonable precautions to ensure that Respondents are not harmed or adversely affected as a result of participating in a research project.

Source: MRS Code of Conduct 2005. Used with permission.

QUESTIONNAIRE DESIGN AND DATA QUALITY

There are many ways in which error can creep into the research process; a poorly designed questionnaire can open the floodgates to it. Here are some of the ways in which this can happen and the sort of problems that arise as a result:

- A poorly designed questionnaire can result in an unpleasant experience for the respondent and a poor perception of research and the research industry, which can in turn lead to an unwillingness to take part in future research.
- A poor introduction or presentation of the research can lead to high levels of non-response and problems with representativeness of the sample.
- Poorly conceived questions not measuring what they claim to measure mean the data collected are not valid.
- Unsuitable or irrelevant content – questions that lie outside the respondent's frame of reference, or which relate to subjects about which he or she has little or no knowledge, or which rely too heavily on the respondent's memory to provide accurate answers, will produce inaccurate and unreliable data.
- Poorly worded questions (using ambiguous, vague, difficult, unusual or technical language) can be misunderstood, misinterpreted or interpreted differently by different people and will lead to unreliable and invalid data.
- A badly structured questionnaire (difficult, sensitive or personal questions appearing too early, before sufficient rapport has been established) can result in refusals to answer or complete the questionnaire.
- Poor question order may result in order bias, or contamination of later responses by earlier questions.
- Long, boring or repetitive questions may result in a loss of interest in answering or produce inaccurate responses.
- A questionnaire that is too long can lead to respondent fatigue, loss of interest and thus poor quality data; too short and it may mean that there is no time to build rapport.
- Inadequate or poorly written interviewer or respondent instructions can result in response and recording errors.
- Poor layout can lead to errors in recording and data processing.

Box 9.2 Validity and reliability

A way of understanding what these concepts mean is to think about the measurement of temperature (Kirk and Miller, 1986). We have two thermometers: we put the first thermometer into boiling water and each time it reads 82°C – it gives a reliable measurement (it is consistent) but not a valid one (it is not measuring the true temperature of the water); each time we place the second thermometer into the boiling water the readings vary around 100°C – this thermometer gives a valid measurement but an unreliable one (each time we get a different value).

Validity

We looked at the concept of internal and external validity in Chapter 3, in the context of research design. Internal validity is also an important concept in questionnaire design. In this context it refers to the ability of the specific measures or questions used in the research to measure what they claim to measure. There are three types of this 'measurement' validity:

▶

- *Construct validity* is about what the question is measuring. It has to do with how it was constructed. Why did we choose to build the question in that way? On what concept is it based?
- *Content validity* is about the suitability of the question to measure the concept that it claims to measure. It is more subjective than construct validity.
- *Criterion validity* is about how well a new measure or question works in comparison to a well-established one, or how well a question works in relation to other questions that are considered meaningful measures of the characteristic or attitude being studied.

Reliability

Reliability refers to the consistency of research results. If we repeat the research, or if different interviewers undertake the fieldwork, will we get the same results? Perfect reliability relies upon the same conditions pertaining each time we repeat the research, which is, of course, very unlikely in real-world situations (we have to accept as reliable results that vary within certain limits). In designing questions and putting together a questionnaire, and briefing and training interviewers in how to administer it, it is important to bear in mind that we are aiming for reliable data. There are several methods for assessing the reliability of questions – the 'test/retest' method, the alternative forms method and the split-half method:

- The *test/retest* method – since reliability is about the extent to which a question will produce the same result when repeated under the same conditions, one way of ensuring it is reliable is to test it and then retest it on the same subjects in the same way. There are a number of difficulties with this approach (associated with the fact that the retest is not independent of the original test) that cloud the issue of reliability. There are problems associated with the following:
  - reassembling the same sample and creating the same conditions – for example, in the time between the test and the retest something may have occurred that leads respondents to change their views;
  - asking the same questions of the same respondents on more than one occasion; respondents may have lost interest, with the result that their responses differ, or they may recall their answers from the original test and repeat them exactly.
- In the *alternative forms method* two different but equivalent versions of a question are administered simultaneously to the same people. Responses are examined to determine if the two measures are correlated. A high correlation would show that the two measures are measuring the same thing. Designing an equivalent question, however, is difficult, and so we have the problem of understanding how much of the difference between the two is due to unreliability or to the differences between them.
- The *split-half method*, a type of alternative forms test, is the most widely used test of reliability. It does not assess stability of a question over time, as does the test/retest method, but rather it assesses the internal consistency of the research. It involves splitting the sample into two matched halves and applying the alternative measures to each half. The results from each are checked using a correlation technique.

QUESTIONNAIRE DESIGN AND THE RESPONDENT

Interviewing is a social process. Regardless of how structured the questionnaire or the interview format, the interviewer and the respondent interact. Even with a self-completion questionnaire there is an interaction, albeit with an invisible researcher. The interview is a sort of conversation, one in which the respondent is a willing, interested and able participant. The questionnaire should facilitate this process, not get in the way of it. In designing the questionnaire you therefore need to think about how to begin this conversation, what words to use, what order to present the questions in and how to bring it to a close. Introductions are given in Box 9.3 (your own organisation or your client may have a standard introduction that is modified to suit each project). The introduction is clearly important in establishing the 'ground rules' for the interview – in particular, for covering the key ethical and professional Code of Conduct issues relating to anonymity or confidentiality; voluntary participation and informed consent (including transparency); and no harm to participants. Relevant rules from the MRS Code of Conduct are also quoted in Box 9.3.

Box 9.3 The importance of a good introduction

A good introduction is crucial to getting and maintaining the respondent's participation. It sets the tone of the interview. It should set out clearly the nature of the research, the topic or topics under investigation and the time needed to complete it. It is important that the introduction mentions these things not only for the dynamics of the interview but in order to establish informed consent, one of the key ethical principles in research practice. The introduction in a telephone interview in these days of call centres and telemarketing is even more important in gaining the respondent's co-operation. It should mention why the respondent was chosen for the research and how the respondent's telephone details were obtained. In all types of interview the respondent should be assured of the bona fides (good faith) of the interviewer and the research organisation, and of the confidentiality of the information supplied. The interviewer should inform the respondent that they can refuse to answer any question or withdraw from the interview at any time and, if they wish it, that all or part of the information they give will be destroyed at once.

Introduction to a telephone survey among a business sample

'Good morning/afternoon. My name is [name] from XYZ Research – we are one of the leading research companies in Europe. We are conducting research on [topic]. The research has been commissioned by ABC Services, who plan to publish a report on the findings. As an organisation involved in this field, we are interested in talking to you. We obtained your details from [source]. The interview will last about 20 minutes. The answers you give me will be treated in strictest confidence; your name or the name of your organisation will *not* be disclosed. When the research is finished we will send you a copy of the published report.'

▶

MRS Code of Conduct and questionnaire introductions

B7 Where lists of named individuals are used e.g. Client databases, the list source must be revealed at an appropriate point in the interview, if requested. This overrides the right to Client anonymity.

B15 If there is to be any recording, monitoring or observation during an interview, Respondents must be informed about this both at recruitment and at the beginning of the interview.

B17 Respondents must not be misled when being asked for co-operation to participate in a research project.

B18 A Respondent's right to withdraw from a research project at any stage must be respected.

B21 Members must ensure that all of the following are clearly communicated to the Respondent:

- the name of the interviewer (an Interviewer's Identity Card must be shown if face to face);
- an assurance that the interview will be carried out according to the MRS Code of Conduct;
- the general subject of the interview;
- the purpose of the interview;
- if asked, the likely length of the interview;
- any costs likely to be incurred by the Respondent.

B22 Respondents (including employees in employee research) must not be unduly pressurised to participate.

Source: MRS Code of Conduct 2005. Used with permission.

QUESTIONNAIRE DESIGN AND THE PERCEPTION OF RESEARCH

The questionnaire is at the front line of research – it is what the general public understands research, particularly market research, to be about. The questionnaire and the interviewer who administers it are ambassadors for the research industry. An interviewer should never be in the position of having to administer (or a respondent to answer) a poorly designed questionnaire. With declining response rates, the onus is more than ever on the researcher to prepare a questionnaire (or discussion guide) that is clear and easy to understand and easy to administer or fill in. It should cover issues that are relevant to the respondent and it should be designed to maintain the respondent's interest throughout. The task of completing the questionnaire should not be burdensome to the respondent in any way, either in terms of the time needed or the difficulty or sensitivity of the topics covered.

The research experience should serve to bolster the credibility of the research industry and the high standards and professionalism it espouses. Effective questionnaire design can help to ensure that we do not 'spoil the field' for future research. We look at question wording and question order and how to bring the interview to a close later in the chapter.

Box 9.4 The contribution of good design

To data quality:
- delivering valid and reliable data;
- minimising non-response – encouraging and maintaining participation;
- minimising error – question error, response and recording error, and data processing error.

To the interviewer's task:
- making the task as straightforward as possible;
- minimising questioning and recording errors.

To the respondent's experience:
- getting and maintaining interest in and willingness to participate;
- making it an enjoyable experience;
- making it as easy as possible.

The analyst's task:
- making data processing and analysis accurate and efficient.

To the perception of research:
- raising the profile of research;
- enhancing the professionalism and credibility of research;
- increasing the goodwill of the general public towards research.

The questionnaire design process

Questionnaire design follows on from a thorough and rigorous examination of the research problem and a clear understanding of the nature of the evidence needed to address it. Decisions about question content, wording and order are the end result of a process that considers the following:

- *What is the research problem?*
  - Background to the problem
  - Definition of the problem
  - Research objectives
  - Use to which data will be put.
- *What type(s) of evidence is needed to address it?*
  - Exploratory
  - Descriptive
  - Causal or explanatory.
- *What ideas, concepts, variables are we measuring?*
  - Content
  - Definitions and indicators.
- *What type(s) of data is appropriate?*
  - Qualitative
  - Quantitative.

- *From whom are we collecting the data?*
  - Nature of the target population or sample.
- *What method of data collection is most suitable?*
  - Observation
  - Interviews
  - Interviewer administered or self-completion
  - Face to face or telephone; email, web or postal.
- *Where will the data be collected?*
  - In the street/shopping centre
  - At respondent's home
  - At respondent's place of work.
- *How will responses be captured?*
  - Pen and paper
  - Computer
  - Audio- and/or video-recording.
- *What are the constraints?*
  - Time
  - Budget.
- *How will the responses be analysed?*
  - Computer
  - Manually.
- *How will we ask the questions?*

OVERVIEW OF THE PROCESS

The aim of the questionnaire design process is to convert the research objectives into meaningful questions and assemble the questions into an effective and workable questionnaire. There are several stages:

- clarifying what it is exactly that you need the questions to measure;
- wording the questions;
- deciding on the types of question and the response format;
- putting the questions into an effective and logical order;
- designing the layout;
- testing out a draft version;
- revising the draft and agreeing a final version.

Question content

The purpose of a questionnaire is to collect data – valid and reliable data that can be used to address the research problem. The first task in designing a questionnaire or discussion guide therefore is to clarify the research objectives – the information requirements – and agree what exactly it is that the questions need to measure.

If the research objectives are not clear it is important to spend time clarifying them. You cannot design an effective questionnaire without being crystal clear about exactly what information it has to deliver. Some exploratory research may be needed to understand the subject area from the point of view of the target population (often different from how the researcher or the client might see it) and to uncover the language used to talk about the issues. This exploratory work might involve a review of secondary data sources (previous research on the topic, for example) and/or formal or informal qualitative research. The nature of the exploratory phase, and the extent of it, will depend on the topic and your familiarity with it and the time and resources available.

> ## Box 9.5 Professional practice and the MRS Code of Conduct: design
>
> B2 All written or oral assurances made by any Member involved in commissioning or conducting projects must be factually correct and honoured by the Member.
> B3 Members must take reasonable steps to design research to the specification agreed with the Client.
> B4 Members must take reasonable steps to design research which meets the quality standards agreed with the Client.
> B14 Members must take reasonable steps to ensure all of the following:
> - that questions are fit for purpose and Clients have been advised accordingly;
> - that the design and content of questionnaires are appropriate for the audience being researched;
> - that Respondents are able to answer the questions in a way that reflects the view they want to express;
> - that Respondents are not led towards a particular answer;
> - that answers are capable of being interpreted in an unambiguous way;
> - that personal data collected is relevant and not excessive.
>
> *Source*: MRS Code of Conduct 2005. Used with permission.

STANDARD QUESTIONS

As well as questions that relate directly to the research objectives, you will almost certainly need questions to determine eligibility to take part in the survey and the characteristics or circumstances of those who do. In a consumer or social survey these classification questions might include questions on age, marital status, working status, social class, total household income, housing tenure and so on. In a business-to-business survey they might include questions on type of organisation, job title, number of employees and so on. In addition, in consumer surveys in particular, you might also have questions on awareness (of products, services, brands, advertising), buying behaviour, usage and satisfaction, for example. For these commonly asked questions there is often a standard format and so no need to design them anew each time. Using standard or consistent questions not only makes questionnaire preparation easier (and, since these questions are tried and tested, more effective) but it is essential to use a standard format should you wish to compare responses to these questions across surveys conducted in different time periods, or even on different topics. It is also essential should you wish to combine or fuse data from different surveys. Research and client organisations may have their own 'standard' versions – check before designing your own. Some examples are given in Box 9.6. Question 6 (Q. 6) is to determine working status: the interviewer asks the question, showing the respondent a prompt or 'show card' on which possible responses are listed. Standard versions of a range of demographic questions used in government surveys have been developed by experts at the UK's Office of National Statistics. They can be inspected at its website (www.statistics.gov.uk).

Box 9.6 Examples of standard questions

Marital status
Q. 4 Marital status **CODE FIRST TO APPLY**

Single (never married)	1
Married	2
Living as married	3
Separated	4
Divorced	5
Widowed	6

Working status
Q. 6 Which of these descriptions applies to what you were doing last week, that is in the seven days ending last Sunday? **SHOW CARD**
IF ON HOLIDAY OR TEMPORARILY SICK ASK WHAT THEY ARE USUALLY DOING

Working part time	1	Go to Q. 6a
Not working (seeking work)	2	
On a Government Training Scheme	3	
On ACE (Action for Community Employment)	4	
Retired	5	
Working full time	6	
In full-time education	7	Go to Q. 7
Looking after the home	8	
Permanently sick or disabled	9	
Not working (and not seeking work)	10	
Caring for elderly or disabled person full time	11	
Other (Write in)	12	
Q. 6a How many hours a week do you normally work in your job?		

Source: ARK. Northern Ireland *Life and Times Survey 2001*, www.ark.ac.uk/nilt. Used with permission.

Awareness, purchase and usage
Q. 2 Which of these brands of X [**SHOW CARD**], if any, have you ever heard of?
Q. 3a Thinking about the last time you bought [product], which brand did you buy?
Q. 3b Which brand or brands do you buy most often?
Q. 4 Next time you need [product] how likely or unlikely are you to buy brand X?

Definitely will	1
Probably will	2
Might or might not	3
Probably will not	4
Definitely will not	5
Don't know	8

Screening and eligibility questions

It may be that, for reasons of client confidentiality or because you believe that certain groups of people may not be typical or representative of the target group, you want to exclude those involved in a similar or related area to that being studied. For example, in an advertising pre-test for a hair shampoo, you may want to exclude those who work in the hair care or beauty products industry as well as those who work in marketing, advertising, public relations or journalism. You may also need a series of questions to determine if the person contacted is eligible to take part in the research. For example, if you need to interview representatives of organisations whose customers are primarily the general public (the consumer market) rather than other businesses (the business-to-business market), you will need to include a question to establish this. Some examples are given in Box 9.7.

Box 9.7 Examples of screening and eligibility questions

Q. A. Do you or anyone in your household work in any of these occupations?
SHOW CARD

Market research	1	
Advertising	2	**CLOSE**
Journalism	3	
Public relations	4	
Marketing	5	
Petrol or oil company	6	
Motorists' shop or garage	7	
None of these	8	**CONTINUE**

Q. 1 I am working on a survey among motorists. Do you have a current driving licence for a car?

Yes	1	**CONTINUE**
No	2	**CLOSE**

Q. 2 Is there a car in your household that is available for you to drive?

Yes	1	**CONTINUE**
No	2	**CLOSE**

Designing questions for some topics may seem to be, or may even be, fairly straightforward. The topic might be familiar, or you might be using standard or tried and tested questions from previous studies. There are, however, some things that are more difficult to measure, and many things that are more difficult than they at first appear. In such cases much work is needed to clarify the meaning and define clearly what is to be measured so that there is no ambiguity about what the question you design is measuring (and how the response to it is interpreted).

CLARIFYING THE MEANING: CONCEPTS, DEFINITIONS AND INDICATORS

Being clear about what is being measured (the concept or the variable) means agreeing a definition of the concept or variable. This should happen before the questionnaire design process begins (it is a good idea to do it at the problem definition and research design stage) so that it is clear what the question needs to measure. For example, think about something simple such as the age of the respondent – are you measuring the respondent's age at the time of the interview or at last birthday? Take another example, the housing status of the respondent. Do you want to know the respondent's housing type, that is whether the type of dwelling he

CASE STUDY 9.2

WHAT DO YOU MEAN, ANTI-SOCIAL BEHAVIOUR?

The client wanted to know about anti-social behaviour on buses but how do you define the 'intangible concept' of anti-social behaviour for use in a questionnaire? Here the researchers explain how they did it.

Why this case study is worth reading

This case study is worth reading for several reasons: it shows why having a working definition of the 'thing' the client wants to find out about is important in the questionnaire design and data collection process; it shows what was involved in the process of arriving at a definition; and it shows the link between the concept – the 'thing' the client wanted to 'measure' – and concrete examples or indicators of it.

The key words are: comprehensive definition, alternative definition, concrete examples, working definition, final definition, approved, questionnaire, ideal, clarity, context, subjective, tested, 'other' option.

Introduction

Drawing up a comprehensive definition of anti-social behaviour would serve three purposes:

- Explain what anti-social behaviour refers to when used in any questionnaire.
- Form the basis of a pre-coded list, for when respondents are asked to state spontaneously which types of activities on buses or at bus stops they perceive as being anti-social.
- Form the basis of a prompted list, for when respondents are asked which different types of anti-social behaviour they have actually experienced.

Defining anti-social behaviour

What anti-social behaviour is is a matter of debate among experts. The Crime and Disorder Act 1998 defined anti-social conduct (which includes speech) as those actions or behaviours that take place 'in a manner that caused or was likely to cause harassment, alarm or distress to one or more persons not of the same household [as the defendant]'. An alternative definition was drawn up based on information in the UK Government Home Office Review of Anti-Social Behaviour Orders (London School of Economics and Political Science, 2003). This review noted 17 different types of behaviour including harassment, noise, drunk and disorderly, threats and throwing missiles. It stated that defining anti-social behaviour in this way was not wholly ideal as certain definitions lacked clarity in a practical context as they were not necessarily independent of the context in which they occurred (e.g. a certain level of noise may be acceptable in one area but not in another).

Using concrete examples

While we accepted that this definition was not beyond criticism, we felt that the overall approach of prompting respondents with concrete examples of anti-social behaviour was the correct one for this study. In particular, there was the concern that a subjective and open approach may end in results that reflected popular or media hype about anti-social behaviour rather than actual experience of specific behaviour.

Testing a working definition

A working definition of anti-social behaviour listing certain individual types of relevant behaviour was drawn up. It was tested in a rigorous manner. First, bus drivers and bus company management staff were asked to discuss the types of behaviour they considered anti-social on buses or at bus stops. Secondly, care was taken in the pilot interviews to ensure that those answering the questionnaire were able to outline any 'other' options that they had not had the chance to mention, with the possibility that frequently mentioned answers could be added to the prompted list. As a result it was decided to include an 'other' option as part of the questionnaire not only when asking respondents what types of activity they perceived as anti-social but also when asking them to detail the types of anti-social behaviour they experienced. In this way respondents were given room to include any types of behaviour they considered anti-social and did not fit in the existing definition. Thus while a subjective approach (i.e. not prompting respondents at all with elements of anti-social behaviour) had originally been rejected, a small element of this approach was incorporated within the question wording.

Agreeing a final definition for the quantitative research

At the end of this process the following final definition of anti-social behaviour relating to buses and bus stops was approved:

'Anti-social behaviour is defined as behaviour that threatens the physical or mental health, safety or security of individuals or causes offence or annoyance to individuals. For the purposes of this particular study this definition includes:

- harassment and intimidating behaviour that creates alarm or fear, towards bus drivers and/or other passengers, including verbal or physical abuse
- drunken and abusive behaviour towards bus drivers and/or other passengers
- assault of bus drivers and/or other passengers
- vehicle crime such as vandalism, graffiti, throwing missiles or other deliberate damage to buses or bus company property
- dumping litter or rubbish on buses
- conflicts or racist abuse/incidents
- engaging in threatening behaviour in large groups at bus stops or on buses
- smoking of cigarettes or illegal drug taking on buses or at bus stops.'

This definition was included in all questionnaires (after any spontaneous questions concerning the definition of anti-social behaviour) to ensure that each respondent understood what types of behaviour were covered when the questionnaire mentioned anti-social behaviour. A shortened version was also used as the pre-coded list for the question asking respondents to define anti-social behaviour and as the prompted options when asking for experience of anti-social behaviour.

Source: Adapted from Granville, S., Campbell-Jack, D. and Lamplugh, T. (2005) 'Perception, prevention, policing and the challenges of researching anti-social behaviour', MRS Conference, www.mrs.org.uk.

or she lives in is a detached house or an apartment, for example; or do you want to know about housing tenure, that is whether the house is owned (on a mortgage or outright) or rented (from a local authority, a housing association or a private landlord)?

Concepts and conceptualisation

In some cases it is relatively easy to decide what is to be measured and relatively easy to reach an agreed definition; in other cases it is not so easy. Think, for example, how you might meaningfully measure the incidence of sexism. Before deciding how, you need to define what you mean by the term 'sexism'. You need a nominal or working definition of the fairly abstract concept of sexism and you need to specify a set of more concrete 'indicators' of it. This process of moving from the abstract to the concrete is known as conceptual ordering or conceptualisation.

Box 9.8 Cultural barriers and the harmonisation of research data

Graham Mytton, BBC World Service, describes some of the issues involved in defining key indicators for cross-cultural use.

Terms like 'household', 'occupation' and the demographic indicators of education, social class and income level are a problem to define in a way which can be compared across cultures. In Northern Nigeria, for example, where people can live in large extended family compounds, what does 'household' mean? If such a compound or *gida* is to be defined as a household it will be an important factor in making comparisons with household data from elsewhere where households may be defined differently. Different interpretations of some words used in questionnaires can be problematic. Precise terms may not be understood in the same way. Even periods of time such as a week, a month or a year may have different lengths. The day may begin not at midnight, but at dawn or dusk. Collecting data on age can be a major problem. The practice of knowing one's birthday, or even birth year, is certainly not universal. One way is to try to work out the person's age by finding out events which happened at key times in the respondent's life. Can he or she remember independence or the start of the civil war or certain floods, volcanic eruptions or other events? Were these before or after puberty?

Source: Adapted from Mytton, G. (1996) 'Research in new fields', *International Journal of Market Research*, 38, 1, pp. 19–31, www.ijmr.com.

Definitions

So how do you arrive at a working definition? You could, for example, using formal or informal qualitative research, ask members of the target group what sexism means to them; you could check what definitions others have used (via a search of secondary sources). Whichever method you use, the outcome should be a clear specification of exactly what it is you are going to measure with the question or set of questions you construct and exactly what you mean when you use a particular word or phrase to describe that concept (or variable). The nominal definition of sexism might be something like 'the view that one sex is inherently superior to the other and/or that particular roles or tasks are suited to one sex or the other'.

Indicators

Once you have a clear and agreed definition of the concept the next step is to develop a set of concrete 'indicators' of it. These indicators will be used in designing the question or set of questions to measure the concept. To get from the abstract concept to the concrete indicators of it you may need to think about the 'dimensions' or aspects of the concept. You might decide that really you are interested in the gender stereotyping dimension of sexism (the view that particular roles or tasks are suited to one sex or the other). You might go further and specify that you are interested in gender stereotyping in relation to home or family duties or in relation to work and job roles, or both. In making these sorts of decisions you would refer back to the research objectives and the question of why you are interested in measuring the incidence of sexism in the first place. You might be interested in measuring the incidence of gender stereotyping in relation to work in order to design equality awareness courses for employees, for example. So how do you develop indicators of gender stereotyping? Again a review of the relevant literature and/or exploratory qualitative research can be useful. The indicators in relation to work roles might include a view that men are more suited to jobs with a physical aspect, or less suited to jobs involving children. A question from the Life and Times Survey 2000 (reproduced in Box 9.9) shows the sort of question that you might design based on your indicators.

The task does not end with the design of the question. The next step is to think about how to interpret the responses to the question. What pattern of response would indicate or could be interpreted to mean that the respondent tends to gender stereotype? You might first of all make explicit which roles you regard as traditionally male and traditionally female. For example: firefighter, soldier in 'front line' action and priest or minister – male; and childminder, midwife, staying at home to look after the children and secretary – female; and primary school teacher

---

Box 9.9 A question of roles

Q. 2 For each of these jobs, please say whether you think it is appropriate for men only, for women only or appropriate for both men and women.

	Appropriate for men only	Appropriate for women only	Appropriate for both women and men	Don't know
Childminder	1	2	3	8
Firefighter	1	2	3	8
Primary school teacher	1	2	3	8
Midwife	1	2	3	8
Soldier in 'front line' action	1	2	3	8
Staying at home to look after the children	1	2	3	8
Priest or minister	1	2	3	8
Secretary	1	2	3	8

Source: The Life and Times Survey 2000. Used with permission.

Box 9.10 Pursuing the meaning

The more structured the enquiry (and the more structured the data collection instrument), the more important it is to be rigorous in pursuit of the meanings we attach to the things we are measuring. In a structured (quantitative) project we design a set of questions that cannot be easily modified in the course of data collection. With a less structured (qualitative) project we may start off with several sets of meanings or dimensions of a concept. The purpose of the research may be to understand the meanings that the respondents place on these, or it may be to refine and define these further, either as an end in itself or for feeding into the next stage of a more structured piece of research. Whatever the purpose, we must start off with clear definitions of the concepts that we are measuring before we can formulate the questions, otherwise the data we get from the questions might be ambiguous at best and meaningless at worst.

– both. You might then devise a scoring system or scale so that a higher score indicates a stronger tendency to gender stereotype (assigning traditionally male jobs as appropriate to men only and traditionally female jobs to women only) and a lower score indicates a weaker tendency. In reporting on the incidence of gender stereotyping you should make it clear to the audience or reader not only how you defined the concept and how you measured it, but also how you analysed and interpreted the data. This is important as you could almost certainly come up with a different set of findings about gender stereotyping if you used a different definition, a different set of indicators and a different way of analysing and interpreting the data.

Now that we know what we want to measure we have to think about how best to word the questions. We need to turn the concepts and variables we identified into meaningful, objective questions that measure what we want them to measure. In addition, we want to design questions that the respondent is willing and able to answer.

Question wording

What you are trying to achieve in wording a question is to ensure that you get valid and reliable data. To this end, each question should be worded so that the following hold:

- it measures what it claims to measure;
- it is relevant and meaningful to the respondent;
- it is acceptable to the respondent;
- the respondent (and the interviewer) understand it;
- it is interpreted in the way in which you intended;
- it is interpreted in the same way by all respondents;
- it elicits an accurate and meaningful response;
- the meaning of the response is clear and unambiguous.

Achieving all of this is far more difficult than it might at first appear, even for seemingly simple, straightforward questions, as the two examples in Box 9.11 show.

Box 9.11 What are you asking me?

Put yourself in the respondent's place. On first hearing or reading the two questions below you might think that they are fairly straightforward (if somewhat intrusive in the case of the first one). But as you start to think about your answer you might wonder, 'What exactly are you asking me?'

Q. How much money do you earn?

■ What do they mean by 'earn'? Money earned in employment or money earned on investments or from social benefits or a total amount earned regardless of the source? What if I'm not working, say I'm retired or unemployed. Does this mean I have no 'earnings'?

■ To what time period does this apply? Do they want to know how much I earn in a year, a month, a week? Do they want to know my earnings in the last calendar year, the last financial or tax year or the year up to the date of the interview? Do they want to know earnings before or after tax or other deductions?

If it is personal income that you want to find out about, you might consider asking the question like this (from the 2003 Life and Times Survey):

Q. 29 What is your <u>personal</u> income <u>before</u> tax and national insurance contributions? Please just give me the number on the card.

SHOW CARD
INCLUDE ALL INCOME FROM EMPLOYMENT AND BENEFITS

Under £3,000 per annum (less than £60 per week)	1
£3,000–£3,999 per annum (£60–£80 per week)	2
£4,000–£6,999 per annum (£80–£135 per week)	3
£7,000–£9,999 per annum (£135–£195 per week)	4
£10,000–£14,999 per annum (£195–£290 per week)	5
£15,000–£19,999 per annum (£290–£385 per week)	6
£20,000–£25,999 per annum (£385–£500 per week)	7
£26,000–£29,999 per annum (£500–£580 per week)	8
£30,000–£39,999 per annum (£580–£770 per week)	9
£40,000+ per annum (more than £770 per week)	10
I do not wish to answer this question	11
(Don't know)	98

Q. Do you have a personal computer?

■ What do they mean by 'personal computer'? A computer that I personally own? Or are they referring to a type of computer, for example a desktop computer or a laptop or a handheld computer?

■ What do they mean by 'you'? Me personally, or the household or family unit in which I live or the organisation for which I work?

■ What do they mean by 'have'? Do they want to know whether I own a PC or have access to one or the use of one? Do they mean at work or at home?

VAGUELY WORDED QUESTIONS

The examples in Box 9.11 highlight some of the problems that can arise when questions are vaguely worded and not specific enough. In seeing the responses to such questions, would you be confident in knowing what it was you had measured? In hearing or reading a question, the respondent must be able to understand precisely what it is you are asking about. To achieve this you may need to provide clear and precise definitions of words or terms. It is usual for the definition to appear first, followed by the question. See the examples in Box 9.12. As well as definitions of terms, you may also need to specify a reference period. You might, for example, want to know whether respondents visit the cinema often, sometimes, rarely or never; whether they visit several times a week, about once a week and so on; or you might want to know the actual number of visits they make on average in a month; or the actual number of visits they made last month. For questions about use or behaviour that occurs frequently, a shorter reference period is usually more suitable; for use or behaviour that happens less frequently, a longer reference period is more appropriate. In asking about usage or behaviour during a particular time period, a week for example, you need to decide whether it is appropriate to ask about 'in the last week' or 'last week', or 'last week, that is, the seven days ending last Sunday'. In deciding on reference periods the degree of precision may depend on the aims of the survey, the type of usage or behaviour you are asking about and what the respondent can be reasonably expected to remember. The question – the definition or description of the topic or terms used, the question itself and the instructions to the interviewer – should be complete so that the interviewer does not have to use his or her own words or interpretation to explain the question to the respondent.

Box 9.12 Examples of definitions and reference periods

Q. Apart from special occasions such as weddings, funerals, baptisms and so on, how often nowadays do you attend services or meetings connected with your religion?

Q. Do you have a long-standing illness, disability or infirmity? By long-standing I mean anything that has troubled you over a period of time or that is likely to affect you over a period of time?

Q. Some people have extra family responsibilities because they look after someone who's sick, disabled or elderly. May I check, is there anyone living with you who is sick, disabled or elderly whom you look after or give special help to (for example, a sick or disabled or elderly relative, wife, husband, partner, child, friend)?

Q. Financial services play an important role in all our lives – credit, hire purchase, loans, mortgages, insurance and so on. Thinking first of all of people in their fifties and up to retirement age, which of these two statements comes closest to your own view?
SHOW CARD

Source: The Life and Times Survey and the National Centre for Social Research. Used with permission.

Q. May I just check, thinking back to the **last** general election – that is the one in 2005 – do you remember which party you voted for then, or perhaps you didn't vote in that election?
IF YES: Which party was that?
IF NECESSARY SAY: The one where Tony Blair won against Michael Howard.

Source: Adapted from The Life and Times Survey and the National Centre for Social Research. Used with permission.

OTHER PITFALLS

There are other potential pitfalls in question wording besides vague and incomplete questions. Others to be avoided include the following:

- Questions using words, jargon, technical language or abbreviations unlikely to be familiar to the target population:
  - Q. Have you initiated any major refurbishments in the place where you reside?
  - Q. Now thinking hypothetically, if you were in charge of fiscal policy, which of the following options would you implement?
  - Q. How would you rate the performance of the UNHCR?
- Questions using words or phrases that are difficult to pronounce or read out:
  - 'In an anonymous form'.
- Double-barrelled questions – asking two questions in one:
  - Q. Do you like using email and the web?
  - Q. Did you find the article interesting and informative?
  - Q. Would you like to be rich and famous?
- Negatively phrased questions:
  - Q. Public speeches against racism should not be allowed. Do you agree or disagree?
  - Q. Do you agree that it is not the job of the government to take decisions about the following?
- Long or convoluted questions:
  - Q. Have you personally, in the last months, travelled abroad on holiday (not including visits to friends and relatives) for a stay of four days or more?
- Questions which overtax the respondent's memory:
  - Q. How many hours of television did you watch last month?
  - Q. List the books you have read in the last year.
- Leading questions:
  - Q. Do you always buy the most expensive brand?
  - Q. To what extent do you agree that the service is meeting your needs?
  - Q. Do you agree that it is right that your organisation makes donations to political party X?
- Questions using sensitive or loaded 'non-neutral' words:
  - Q. What do you think of welfare for the poor?
- Questions that make assumptions:
  - Q. How often do you travel to France?
  - Q. When did you stop beating your wife?
- Questions with overlapping response categories:
  - Q. How many hours did you spend in the library yesterday?

0 to 1 hour	1
1 to 2 hours	2
3 to 4 hours	3
4 to 6 hours	4
More than 6 hours	5
Don't know	8

- Questions with insufficient response categories:
  - Q. How do you travel to work each day?

By car	1
On foot	2
By bus	3
On a bicycle	4

In addition, if you need to ask hypothetical questions and want to avoid running the risk of getting meaningless, hypothetical data you need to give as much detail and context as you can within the question. The question, 'Would you like better quality public services?' for example is likely to elicit a 'yes' answer from most respondents. If instead you include material within the question that allows respondents to think themselves into the situation you are asking about, you are more likely to get meaningful data. Some examples of questions that ask about hypothetical situations are given in Box 9.13 below.

It is important to maintain the respondent's interest throughout the questionnaire. One way of losing that interest is to ask irrelevant or unnecessary questions. Questions should be relevant to the research objectives (if not, they should be excluded) and relevant to the respondent's situation or experience, and on a subject that he or she can reasonably be expected to answer accurately. If a question is irrelevant to a particular subset of respondents routing instructions should be used to ensure that they are not asked the question. Including too many questions on topics that are boring or not of concern to the respondent should be avoided in order to maintain interest.

Box 9.13 Vignette or scenario style questions

Q. I am now going to ask about a few hypothetical situations. I would like to remind you that there are no right or wrong answers, only opinions.

You are queuing up at a small post office. It is near closing time or last post collection. A person with a speech impairment is taking a long time to be served as they are speaking very slowly. How would you feel? **SHOW CARD. CODE ALL THAT APPLY**

	Yes	No
Annoyed, irritated	1	2
Threatened, frightened	1	2
Suspicious, dubious	1	2
Nervous, anxious	1	2
Uncomfortable, embarrassed	1	2
Surprised, shocked	1	2
Curious	1	2
Worried of adverse reaction/offending person	1	2
Sorry for the person	1	2
Understanding, genuinely concerned	1	2
Fine, would not bother me	1	2
Other	1	2
None of these	1	2
Don't know	1	2

Q. What, if anything, would you do? **CODE ALL THAT APPLY**

	Yes	No
Complain to member of staff immediately	1	2
Leave/go to another Post Office	1	2
Leave/come back another day	1	2
Politely ask another member of staff if they could open another window to serve	1	2
Nothing, keep waiting	1	2
Ask Post Office staff if I could help out	1	2
Ask person being served if I could help out	1	2
Other	1	2
Don't know	1	2

Source: The Life and Times Survey 2003. Used with permission.

Box 9.14 The importance of a good translation

In translating a questionnaire it is important to ensure that the words used mean the same thing in the languages used. To achieve this, it is not only necessary to understand the language but also to understand the wider cultural context and the context of the research topic within that country. This understanding should help you to find the words or phrases that give you the meaning you want. If possible, get a native speaker who is living in, or has recently been living in, the country to do the translation. As well as words and meaning, check the conventions on using scales (they may be interpreted in different ways in different countries) and asking demographic questions (social grading varies). Back-translation – retranslating into the original language – is advisable, especially in studies where consistency (and comparability) across countries is important. A native speaker of the original language should also do the back-translation. Even when words or phrases are back-translated they may miss the meaning of the original; it may be that there is no word in the language for something that needs to be translated. Consistency, although worth aiming for, may be elusive – it is certainly harder to attain than you might at first imagine.

QUESTIONS ON SENSITIVE TOPICS

If not handled properly – clearly worded, in the right place on the questionnaire, the question and the answer recorded without embarrassment on the part of the interviewer – questions on sensitive or embarrassing topics can lead to refusals – refusals to answer the question or to continue with the interview, or refusal to take part in the first place. What is judged to be intrusive, embarrassing or sensitive varies enormously; and what is a straightforward issue to the researcher may be a particularly sensitive issue to the respondent, and vice versa (Lee, 1992). Subjects that tend to be sensitive to most people and in most cultures include money, voting, religion, sexual activity, criminal behaviour, and use of alcohol and drugs. One way of handling responses to sensitive questions in a face-to-face interview is to ask respondents to fill in the answers on the questionnaire themselves on the screen or on a separate self-completion sheet as in Case study 9.5. Alternatively, show cards, from which the respondent reads out a code for his or her response, can be used, as in Case study 9.3. (The relative anonymity of a telephone or online interview often makes these approaches unnecessary.)

Social desirability bias

Questions on some sensitive topics are susceptible to a form of response bias known as *social desirability* or *prestige bias*. According to Sudman and Bradburn (1983) there are three areas of questioning in which socially desirable responses, and in consequence over-reporting, occurs: questions about being a good citizen; being a well-informed and cultured person; and fulfilling moral and social responsibilities. So, for example, it might arise in questions about completing accurate tax returns, driving to the speed limit, using your vote, frequency of visiting museums and art galleries and going to the theatre, giving to charity and recycling waste. Prestige bias can also affect answers to questions about age, occupation, income, and cleanliness and grooming. The flip side of social desirability, in which there is likely to be under-reporting rather than over-reporting, occurs in relation to issues such as illness, alcohol consumption, sexual activity and socially undesirable behaviour such as criminal activity and use of illegal drugs.

In designing questions to avoid this type of bias you need to make it just as easy and painless for the respondent to give the low prestige answer as it is to give the high prestige answer. This can be done in the same way as questions about sensitive topics – via a self-completion questionnaire, or using show cards or shuffle packs from which the respondent reads the relevant code. Another way is to ensure that the question is presented in such a way that all answers are allowable and equally acceptable, or that the respondent has a valid escape route. Some examples are given in Box 9.15 (see Brace and Nancarrow, 2008, for further examples and how they fare in practice). As with sensitive topics, the more anonymous methods of data collection – telephone and self-completion (postal or online) – may be better suited to collecting this type of information.

Box 9.15 Examples of techniques to overcome social desirability bias

Q. 1 Talking to people about the general election on . . . , we have found that a lot of people didn't manage to vote. How about you – did you manage to vote in the general election?

IF NOT ELIGIBLE/TOO YOUNG TO VOTE: CODE 'NO'.

| Yes, voted | 1 | Ask Q. 1a |
| No | 2 | Go to Q. 2 |

Source: British Social Attitudes Survey. Used with permission.

Q. 19 Some people say that even if they are a bit prejudiced it doesn't affect how they actually talk to people from minority ethnic groups; other people say that it does affect their interactions. How about you? Would you say that your interactions with people from minority ethnic groups are affected by how you feel or not? **SHOW CARD**

Always	1
Sometimes	2
Never	3
(Don't know)	8

Source: *The Life and Times Survey*, 2006. Used with permission.

Q. 30 What is your *personal* income before tax and national insurance contributions? Please just give me the number on the card.

SHOW CARD [Income bands plus 'I do not wish to answer this question'. The interviewer can code 'Don't know' but this response is not on the show card.]

INCLUDE ALL INCOME FROM EMPLOYMENT AND BENEFITS

Source: *The Life and Times Survey*. Used with permission.

CASE STUDY 9.3

HOW DO YOU ASK THAT?

This case study highlights the questionnaire design issues that arose in researching AIDS and shows how they were successfully resolved. Some interviews took place in gay bars (see Case study 7.1) and some took place in the respondent's home.

Why this case study is worth reading

This case study is worth reading for many reasons: it shows questionnaire design in action – it shows what was done and why; it illustrates some key techniques and gives a rationale for their use; it discusses the impact of questionnaire design and interviewing technique on data quality (and on the interviewer and respondent experience of taking part in research).

The key words are: length, respondent fatigue, sensitive, embarrassing, inhibited, respondent, interviewer, interviewing environment, confidentiality, progression, hurdles, coded shuffle packs, quality control, structure of questionnaire, random order, code checking, literacy, grid, self-completion booklets, quality of data, wording of questionnaire, instructions, honesty, valid data.

Introduction

Questionnaire design for this project faced the 'normal' problems of balancing comprehensiveness against length and respondent fatigue. It also faced the much more difficult task of eliciting highly sensitive information from potentially inhibited respondents. For purposes of comparison it was highly desirable that the same

▶

questionnaire could be used for both the general public and gay samples. Although it was anticipated from qualitative work reported elsewhere (Siddall et al. 1987) that the latter would be relatively uninhibited in discussing sexual matters, in February 1986 no such assumption could be made about the general public. There were also the problems of inhibition in relation to other people present during the interview, or to the interviewer herself.

Thus the key issues were:

- How to accommodate the very different interviewing environments ('gay bar' v 'Englishman's castle').
- How to minimise inhibitions vis-à-vis eavesdroppers (either a friend in the bar or a wife or husband at home).
- How to minimise inhibitions vis-à-vis the interviewer and enable the respondent to give honest answers to very personal and sensitive questions.

There are, of course, problems with all questionnaires but they applied *a fortiori* in this case. In tackling them we built on our experience and the accumulated wisdom of survey research. Little in our approach was entirely new but we do believe it represents an impressive and valuable case history in collecting sensitive data.

The three basic tools, which we subsequently discuss, were:

- Confidentiality
- A progression of hurdles in the interview which, when cleared, moved the respondent on to increasingly more sensitive or personal subjects
- The use of coded shuffle packs and prompt aids for the vast bulk of the questions.

Confidentiality

Interviewing in gay bars we take no names and addresses [see Case study 7.1]. For the in-home interview of the general public we assure respondents of confidentiality and say that there is no need to take names and addresses. However, at the end of the interview we ask whether the respondent would be willing to be re-interviewed on a similar subject. About 80 per cent agree and in these cases it is 'natural' to take names and addresses, but they are written on different forms and posted to us separately from the interviews. These are used to conduct our normal quality-control backchecking procedures. Letters are left with respondents as a reassurance at the end of the interview. Whilst these procedures are valuable for the respondent, we also believe they are valuable for the interviewer in reassuring *her* of the confidentiality and contributing to a confident approach to her task. In all cases, both at bars and in homes, interviewers are instructed to try to obtain the interviews with respondents on their own. This happens in about 60 per cent of interviews with the general public and 75 per cent of interviews in gay bars.

Clearing hurdles

The general structure of the questionnaire is one of progressive hurdles, moving to evermore sensitive subjects, starting with fairly innocuous questions about general health hazards and ending up with detailed questions on sexual behaviour in quite explicit terms – for example whether they have engaged in anal intercourse, with or without a sheath, in the last three months.

The actual coverage of the questionnaire is as follows.

Spontaneous beliefs about health hazards.
*Awareness of AIDS in context of seven other diseases.
*Rating of eight diseases for how common or rare they are, how serious for people who catch them, degree of respondent knowledge, extent of threat to health of nation, personal concern about catching.
*Spontaneous and prompted knowledge of ways of catching AIDS, and the people at risk, and ways of reducing risk.
*Attitudes to AIDS.
Ease of obtaining information about AIDS.
*Reactions if relative caught AIDS.
Source of information about AIDS.
Advertising recall.
*Attitudes to advertising.
Awareness of and reaction to leaflets.
*Attitudes to homosexuality.
Whether know homosexual.
Blood donation and reasons for lapsing.
Media exposure.
Demographic and other classification.
*Heterosexual behaviour questions.
*Men only: sexual orientation and homosexual behaviour questions.
Willingness to be re-interviewed.

The question areas marked * are administered by shuffle packs (or self-completion) which is our most important tool.

Shuffle packs and booklets

BMRB interviewers are familiar with the use of shuffle packs and sorting boards in conventional surveys. We believe they have many advantages over the more frequently used methods of using a prompt card with a scale on it and the interviewer reading out the attitude battery or self-completion scales. For example:

- They enable the concepts to be presented to each respondent in a unique and random order.
- They give respondents time to read and consider each statement and when they see the pattern of their answers to make minor adjustments.
- They are much faster in administration.
- Respondents are more involved and less likely to become fatigued.
- They are less tiring for interviewers who also have time for code checking and thought-gathering.

In the present case they have one further overwhelming advantage – they enable the communication of sensitive information on potentially very embarrassing subjects, without either the respondent or the interviewer having to say any words that might inhibit them.

We realised it would be critical to train respondents. This is done at the very early stages. They are asked to sort a set of eight cards each with a name of a disease and a number printed on it into those they have heard of and those they have not. The ▶

interviewer then asks for the numbers only. Moreover her questionnaire only has numbers on it, so even if names are given she has to ask for the numbers before she can code. (The code that she has to ring is the same as the number on the card which greatly speeds up the process.) The cards for the diseases the respondent has heard of are then shuffled on three occasions. After each shuffle he has to sort them into categories on a different board to show respectively how common they are, how serious it would be for someone who caught them and how much he feels he knows about each. After this series of questions the respondent understands what to do with each subsequent shuffle pack as it is handed to him. He gets on with the task and knows that at the end he will be required to call out the numbers in response category order.

Having carried out a large number of interviews ourselves, we can vouch for the fact that at the end the interviewer has virtually no idea of the respondent's views on anything – it is genuinely confidential. Moreover, when anyone else is present they too are only hearing an exchange of numbers. In addition, the process of training the respondent helps rapport and interaction with the interviewer.

The system speeds up the process of coding while allowing the respondent time to consider each answer. There are on occasion difficulties with literacy of some respondents, but these are far outweighed in our view by the absence of respondents mishearing attitude statements. Indeed we do not believe a method of verbal administration of attitude batteries would have been possible in the disco type conditions in many of the gay bars. . . .

Altogether seven question areas with 118 pieces of information are covered by different coloured shuffle packs and similarly coloured sorting boards, compared with only 30 questions (plus classification) obtained by standard question and answer methods, with or without prompt cards. These techniques take us through most of the questionnaire and classification leaving only the questions on sexual behaviour.

For those who qualify we then have a self-completion booklet which asks in very considerable detail about sexual behaviour in the last three months and twelve months – numbers of partners, types of sexual activity indulged in, sex with bisexuals, prostitutes, drug injectors and so on. These booklets are handed over to respondents together with an envelope into which they are placed after completion, sealed, and handed back to the interviewer.

Because of the known outspokenness of the gay community from the qualitative work it was felt that detailed sexual behaviour would probably be obtainable from all the gay sample. However, for the general public we restrict the booklet to those who claim to have had two or more heterosexual partners in the last year (we thus avoid, for example, asking older monogamous people about their sexual activity with their only partner).

Quality of the data

Although we have taken very great care with the approach and *wording* of our questionnaire, it is difficult to be sure whether people end up telling the truth or not (as it is in all survey research). At the end of the interview the interviewers are asked to assess the respondent's honesty. Typically, 75 per cent of the general public and about 85 per cent of the gay sample are coded as 'very honest' and virtually everyone else as 'quite honest'. We also ask respondents how worthwhile they feel it has been to give their time to being interviewed. About 80 per cent of the general public and over 90 per cent of gays say that it has been 'extremely' or 'very' worthwhile.

References

Siddall, J., Stride, C. and Sargent, J. (1987) 'Are you homosexual, heterosexual or bisexual? If so, you could develop AIDS', *Proceedings of the Market Research Society Conference*, London: MRS.

Source: Adapted from Orton, S. and Samuels, J. (1997) 'What we have learned from researching AIDS', *International Journal of Market Research*, 39, 1, pp. 175–200, www.ijmr.com.

Question structure

Two further considerations in designing questions are whether you want to offer respondents a choice of answers or whether you want them to provide their own answers; and how you want to record the response.

OPEN QUESTIONS

In an open or free response question the respondent gives the response in their own words. For example, 'What is it about X that makes you say that?'. The respondent in a personal interview gives the answer verbally to the interviewer, who notes it down (or in a telephone interview or qualitative interview might record it); in a self-completion interview, the respondent writes or types the answer into the space provided on the questionnaire. The responses to open questions can be 'pre-coded' or listed in the questionnaire (a list which the respondent does not see). The interviewer records the response or responses that correspond(s) to the respondent's answer. If the answer is not on the list, the interviewer records it under 'Other', which is usually accompanied by the instruction 'Write in' or 'Specify'.

Box 9.16 Examples of open questions

Not pre-coded
Q. What can you remember about the last TV advertisement you saw for X?
RECORD ANSWER BELOW.

Q. 14a Have you ever felt that you were not treated as well as you might have been by people in the financial sector because of your age? [Closed question leads in.]

Yes	1	Ask Q 14b
No	2	Go to Q 15
(Don't know)	8	

Q. 14b In what way were you not treated well? ▶

Pre-coded

Q. Which brands of instant coffee can you think of? Any others?

	First mentioned (One code only)	*Other mentions (Multi-code)*
Café Noir	1	1
Kenco	2	2
Nescafé	3	3
Maxwell House	4	4
. . . etc.	5	5
Other (Write in)	8	8
None	9	9

Numeric

Q. How many people do you manage or supervise? **ENTER NUMBER.**

Numeric pre-coded

Q. How many people do you manage or supervise?

None	1
1–4	2
5–9	3
10–15	4
16–20	5
21–24	6
25 or more	7
Don't know	8

The main advantage of open questions is that they can make respondents feel more at ease and more in control – a feeling that the interviewer or researcher wants to know exactly what they think and is not making them select a pre-formulated response. For this reason it is useful to include open questions early in the questionnaire, or at the start of a new topic, to help build rapport. In addition, open questions allow us to see a wide range of responses, rather than the more limited ones we might get using a prompted response question; we then have those responses in the words used by the respondent. An open-ended format also offers the chance in personal interviews to probe for more detail. From a design point of view open questions can be easier to word than closed questions.

As to the disadvantages, open questions require more of the respondent, the interviewer and the data processing provider and so are more time consuming and more costly to use. The respondent has to articulate a response; and the interviewer (the respondent in a self-completion format) has to record it word for word. Sometimes detail or meaning can be lost in this process – the respondent, not wanting to write or type things out in full, may shorten sentences or abbreviate words; the interviewer may not be able to write or type as fast as the respondent talks. From the responses, the data processing department has to build a code frame, which can be expensive and difficult to do well.

CLOSED QUESTIONS

A closed question offers the respondent a choice of answers. The alternatives may be read out or shown on a card (known as a show card or prompt card). In a self-completion questionnaire the respondent may be asked to tick a box corresponding to the answer, or underline or circle the response.

Box 9.17 Examples of closed questions

Q. I am going to read out some things that other people have said about X. Using this card **[SHOW CARD]**, could you tell me to what extent you agree or disagree with each statement?

	Strongly agree	Agree	Neither agree nor disagree	Disagree	Strongly disagree	Can't choose
Are a company you can trust	1	2	3	4	5	8
Have friendly, helpful staff	1	2	3	4	5	8
Care more about the environment than other companies	1	2	3	4	5	8
And so on	1	2	3	4	5	8

A version suitable for a telephone interview, using a slightly different scale:

Q. To what extent do you agree or disagree with the following statements about X? Please rate each statement from 1 to 5 where 1 means you 'Strongly disagree', 3 means you are 'Indifferent' and 5 means you 'Strongly agree'.
[1 = Strongly disagree; 2 = Disagree; 3 = Indifferent; 4 = Agree; 5 = Strongly agree]

Q. And thinking about your knowledge of health matters in general, would you say that, compared with other people, you know . . . **READ OUT** . . .

More than other people,	1
About the same as other people,	2
Or, less than other people about health matters in general?	3
Other WRITE IN	4
Don't know	8

Closed questions can be relatively easy to administer – they take up less time than open questions and do not involve interviewer or respondent in recording detailed responses. They also make the data processing task relatively easy. The main disadvantage is that they can be difficult to formulate well, and poorly formulated questions can result in poor quality data. In addition, using a closed question means that we lose some sensitivity in measurement – what the respondent actually said is not recorded and there is no way of analysing the 'real' response. Too many closed questions in succession can be boring and repetitive for the interviewer to ask and for the respondent to answer, which also has a negative effect on data quality.

Box 9.18 Examples of response scales

Behaviour – buy or try
Definitely would
Probably would
Might/might not
Probably wouldn't
Definitely wouldn't

Rating

Very good	Much better
Good	A little better
Fair	About the same
Poor	A little worse
Very poor	Much worse

Preference
Prefer R
Prefer Q
Like both equally
Dislike both equally

Opinion

X treated much better	Strongly agree	Strongly in favour
X treated a bit better	Agree	In favour
Both treated equally	Indifferent	Neither in favour nor against
Y treated a bit better	Disagree	Against
Y treated much better	Strongly disagree	Strongly against

Frequency

I always . . .	I sometimes . . .	I never . . .

Extent

No interest at all									A great deal of interest
1	2	3	4	5	6	7	8	9	10

Response 'scales' are a form of closed question often used to measure attitudes, as we will see below. Scales are also used to measure such things as preference, likelihood to buy and satisfaction. The choice of scale and response format will depend on your information requirements, the level of sensitivity that you need in measuring the issue under investigation and the suitability for the method of data collection.

PROBING AND PROMPTING

Probing is the term used to describe the follow-up questions that sometimes accompany open questions. The purpose of these probes is to obtain a more detailed or more fully considered answer from the respondent. Typical probes include 'What else?', 'Why do you say that?' and 'What is it about X that makes you say that?' Probing instructions or questions are usually included in the questionnaire (or script) and the interviewer is clear about when and how to apply them. It is important for reliability of the data that each interviewer applies and asks them in the same way. An example of a more specific probe is given in the question sequence in Box 9.19. Prompts are used to elicit responses to closed questions. The interviewer asks the question and follows it up by reading out or showing to the respondent, on a prompt or show card, a list of possible answers.

Box 9.19 Examples of a probe and prompt

Q. 13 Generally speaking, do you think of yourself as a supporter of any one political party?

Yes	1	Go to Q. 15
No	2	Ask Q. 14
(Don't know)	8	

Q. 14 Do you think of yourself as a little closer to one political party than to others?

Yes	1
No	2
(Don't know)	8

Q. 15 **IF YES AT Q. 13 OR Q. 14**: Which one?

IF NO/DON'T KNOW AT Q. 13: If there were a general election tomorrow, which political party do you think you would be most likely to support?

Source: British Social Attitudes Survey. Used with permission.

Asking questions on attitudes

Attitudes are 'the market researcher's favourite measurement' (Sampson, 1980). We are interested in them for their own sake and for the way in which they relate to motivation, intention and behaviour – for what they tell us about what people think and feel, and for what they tell us about how people intend to act. A study of attitudes helps us understand people's view of the world, how individuals and groups of people differ from each other; and, because they help us understand what influences and motivates people's intentions to act, attitudes are useful in studying behaviour and understanding the ways in which we might influence it.

Attitudes are complex and difficult to research. In setting out to design research and craft questions to gather data on attitudes it is important to be as clear as possible about what it is we need to know. As Tuck (1976) explains, it is important to research attitudes towards specific events and not attitudes to generalities.

Box 9.20 Attitudes and related concepts

Definitions of the concept 'attitude' vary but there is general agreement that holding an attitude about something means that we are predisposed or likely to respond in a particular way when we encounter the object and/or the circumstances related to that attitude. We can have attitudes about almost anything, from the mundane and everyday – frozen food or fabric conditioner – to the more serious – drug taking or religion. The attitudes we hold may reflect how we think and feel about it (so they are related to beliefs and feelings), and may influence what our intentions might be or what we might do in relation to it in certain circumstances (so they are related to action or behaviour). They may therefore provide us with a framework for responding to, and coping with, the stimuli we face in everyday situations.

Where do attitudes come from?
We acquire attitudes in different ways and can classify them loosely according to their source or the influences on them:

- *physiological and psychological* – from biogenic, psychogenic and learnt needs and wants, and the motivation to satisfy them;
- *sociological* – from the culture and the society in which we live, from its traditions, its myth and folklore;
- *social psychological influences*, for example from the groups we belong to – primary groups such as the family, and secondary groups such as a club or society, an interest group or political party.

This classification suggests that, depending on their source, attitudes might have different properties. Those that are related to or arise from our innate needs and our personality may be more deep-rooted, more stable and less likely to be susceptible to change than those we have acquired from our day-to-day experience. Social psychologists (Oppenheim, 2000) have given labels to different 'types' of attitudes:

- the more superficial and the more likely to change they call 'opinions';
- the less superficial and less likely to change are referred to as 'attitudes';
- the more deep-rooted and the more immutable are called 'values' or 'basic attitudes';
- the most deep-rooted and most enduring are attitudes that are a part of personality.

In market and social research we collect data about all of these types of 'attitudes': for example, people's opinions about events and issues, about products and brands – things that are likely to change as a result of experience, media coverage or advertising; issues connected to value systems and to personality, which are less likely to change (political and social attitudes, attitudes to money). We approach these investigations in different ways: generally speaking, we use quantitative techniques to measure the more superficial opinions and attitudes; and we use qualitative techniques to explore and analyse the less superficial, more deep-rooted.

How do attitudes relate to needs, wants, motivation, goals and behaviour?

Every human being has physiological or biogenic **needs** (for food and water, for example) and psychogenic needs (for self-expression, for example). These needs are innate. We also have learnt or secondary needs, related to our personality, our experiences and the society or culture in which we live (for example the need for approval or achievement). Needs can be expressed as **wants** (you have a need to quench your thirst, you want to drink water).

Needs and wants are the basis of **motivation** – we are motivated to fulfil our needs and wants. Motivation is the concept that links needs and wants to action: having a need or a want may motivate us to act in order to fulfil or satisfy that need or achieve that want.

Many social scientists believe that attitudes are an indication of a predisposition to act or behave, and so can be used to understand, if not explain or predict, **behaviour**. At the same time it is recognised that there is no automatic link between holding an attitude to an object and taking action in relation to it. A range of intervening factors may affect both the attitude and the behaviour. For example, situational factors such as economic circumstances (you may hold positive attitudes to organic food but not buy it because it is too expensive), mood, the physical or social environment in which you find yourself (you might prefer to dress casually but if everyone else at work dresses formally you may do so, too) can have an effect. Other factors, such as the strength or depth of the attitude or its relationship to other attitudes, may dictate whether we act and the way in which we act on an attitude. It is accepted that two people can hold identical attitudes, arrived at in different ways, and that they can behave in entirely different ways. While knowing a person's attitude does not allow us to predict whether they might take a particular action, it might tell us something about their pattern of behaviour.

Goals are the outcomes we seek by taking action: our behaviour can be said to be goal directed. Several different goals or outcomes may be available that would satisfy a particular need or want. Attitudes arise from and can influence our needs, the motivation to fulfil these needs and the goals or outcomes we seek.

It is difficult to word questions to gather factual data or data about behaviour; it is even more difficult to design questions on attitudes, which, as we have seen, are not factual, in a way that achieves both validity and reliability. Capturing the essence of an attitude is almost impossible using one question or one statement: it is unlikely that we will be able to capture the complexity of the attitude, so it will lack validity; and it is unlikely that one question or statement will deliver consistent results – respondents tend to be more sensitive to the wording and the context of attitudinal questions compared to factual questions – so it will lack reliability. It is therefore unwise to measure an attitude using a single question or statement. Research shows that we can improve the validity and reliability of attitude measurement by using banks of questions or 'attitude statements' combined in an attitude scale. Validity may be improved if the question, the statements and the response sets used are designed to encompass the complexity of the attitude, and the context of it. Reliability may be improved because issues of question wording and context may be cancelled out across the range of statements. These improvements depend, of course, on ensuring that the question wording is sound, the response set is appropriate and all of the statements used reflect or measure elements of the underlying attitude.

DESIGNING QUESTIONS ON ATTITUDES – SOME TECHNIQUES

Designing questions to gather data on attitudes consists of two parts: designing and choosing the list of attitude statements or the 'item pool' for the particular attitude variable; and choosing the response format.

Designing evaluative and descriptive attitude and belief statements

According to Oppenheim (2000), an attitude statement 'is a single sentence that expresses a point of view, a belief, a preference, a judgement, an emotional feeling, a position *for or against* something [italics original]'. The list of statements to be included in an attitude scale should be grounded in an in-depth understanding of the subject area. A study of previous research or a review of the relevant literature on the subject are good starting points. Depth interviews and group discussions among the survey's target group are invaluable – they allow us to examine the nature and complexity of the attitudes, to determine what exactly it is we want to measure, what the indicators should be, and to understand the language respondents use to express the attitudes in question.

Once a list has been generated each of the statements on the list should be carefully worded following the good practice guidelines set out above. You should ask the following:

- Is each statement clearly worded?
- Is each statement unambiguous?
- Are any statements too long?
- Does each statement contain one issue only?
- Is the list balanced – that is, are there roughly equal numbers of positive and negative items?
- Are the statements in a random order?

We look at some examples below. Further examples can be found in Life and Times Survey questionnaires (1998–to date) available at www.ark.ac.uk/nilt/quests/.

Item analysis

The item pool generated from a review of the relevant literature, through qualitative research and pilot testing, should offer a valid measure of the attitude in question. We need, however, to check that this is the case by conducting what is known as item analysis. Item analysis helps to determine which statements are indeed the most valid measures of the attitude – in other words which ones are the best to use in the scale. We have no external, measurable 'output' of the attitude against which to assess each of the attitude statements. What we do therefore is to examine how well each individual item correlates with the rest of the items in the pool, based on the assumption that the whole item pool is the best measure of the attitude in question. We calculate what is called the 'item-whole' correlation: the correlation, or strength of association, between each item and the rest of the items in the pool. (A statistical or data analysis package should be able to do these calculations for you.) Items that correlate poorly with the rest of the pool, those with low correlation coefficients, are excluded from use in the scale on the basis that they do not measure the attitude measured by the other items. The item-whole correlation can be carried out on the results of a pilot study; those items with low correlation coefficients are excluded from the final questionnaire, and so the final attitude scale. Alternatively, you can include the full item pool on the survey and calculate the correlations based on responses from the whole sample, and exclude the low correlations from the scale at the analysis stage.

The response format

Assembling an item pool is common to most scaling techniques. The techniques, however, vary in the way in which items are chosen, phrased and scored to suit particular response formats. A detailed account is beyond the scope of this book; instead we focus on one response format – the Likert Scale, which is the one you are most likely to come across. The main concern in choosing items for a Likert Scale is that all the items should measure aspects of the same underlying attitude – in other words a Likert Scale should be unidimensional. A further consideration is that neutral items and those at the extremes of the attitude continuum should be avoided. The response format on the Likert Scale consists of five points: 'Agree strongly', 'Agree', 'Neither agree nor disagree', 'Disagree' and 'Disagree strongly'. (Few researchers, however, use the Likert Scale in the way Likert intended – most use the Likert five-point response format and construct a scale from the responses.) A 'Don't know' response is added to the end of the scale, which, although not offered to the respondent, gives the interviewer a way of recording the response if it does arise.

You may find in your list of attitude statements that you have some positively phrased statements and some negatively phrased ones. Make sure that you are consistent in how you score or analyse these. If, when constructing your attitude scale, you decide that a high score means a positive attitude, score the positive statements 5 for 'Agree strongly' to 1 for 'Disagree strongly' and score the negative statements 5 for 'Disagree strongly' to 1 for 'Agree strongly'. This can be confusing to do on the questionnaire, where it is best that the response set for each statement uses the same number code; you may have to make this an instruction for data processing.

Once you have decided on the attitude statements and the response format, pilot the question and examine respondents' reactions to each of the statements. Check whether they answer at the extremes of the scale or the middle of it, or whether they answer 'Don't know'. This information should tell you whether your attitude statements are working or not. You want respondents to recognise the statements as something they would say themselves, or something that someone they know might say. You should begin to see a pattern, with respondents falling into different groups according to their responses. What you do not want is a large proportion of respondents choosing the middle response, 'Neither agree nor disagree', or saying 'Don't know' – rather you want them to choose the 'Agree' or 'Disagree' responses; this indicates that the statements are differentiating between respondents.

An example

Consider the example in Box 9.21 – it is a question from the 1999 Life and Times Survey conducted in Northern Ireland by the University of Ulster and Queen's University Belfast. A full version of the questionnaire and the data derived from this question can be downloaded

Box 9.21 Attitudes to citizenship education

Q. 17 There has been a lot of talk recently about teaching 'Citizenship' in secondary and grammar schools in Northern Ireland. This could include classroom discussions on things like politics and human rights in Northern Ireland. Some people are against the idea of teaching this in schools while others are very much in favour.

How much do you agree or disagree with the following statements? **SHOW CARD**

	Strongly agree	Agree	Neither agree nor disagree	Disagree	Strongly disagree	(Don't know)
It isn't the job of schools to teach children about politics and human rights	1	2	3	4	5	8
It's about time schools started to openly tackle such difficult issues	1	2	3	4	5	8
Teaching children about politics and human rights at school is just trying to brainwash them	1	2	3	4	5	8
I doubt whether the people teaching this kind of thing would do it fairly	1	2	3	4	5	8
Our children will never be effective members of society unless we allow them to learn about human rights and politics when they are young	1	2	3	4	5	8
Schools should be a place where children are able to get away from the political problems of Northern Ireland	1	2	3	4	5	8
Teaching about human rights and politics at school will help young people become active members of their own communities	1	2	3	4	5	8
Teaching about human rights and politics at school runs the risk of encouraging children toward extreme political views	1	2	3	4	5	8
Discussions about politics and human rights will help children understand why other traditions in Northern Ireland feel hard done by	1	2	3	4	5	8
Discussions about politics and human rights at school will be too painful for a lot of children who have personally suffered during the Troubles	1	2	3	4	5	8

Source: The Life and Times Survey 1999. Used with permission.

from the Life and Times website at www.ark.ac.uk/nilt. The question is designed to measure attitudes to the teaching of citizenship in schools for children aged 11–18. It has two components:

- the list of attitude statements or items, for example 'It isn't the *job* of schools to teach children about politics and human rights';
- the fixed responses of the five-point Likert Scale, 'Strongly agree' to 'Strongly disagree'.

The attitude statements in the list were chosen to ensure that they are measuring aspects of the one underlying attitude. Extensive exploratory research was conducted, which involved a review of the literature on citizenship and education and attendance at conferences as well as a series of in-depth interviews with experts, opinion leaders and those in the target population. The survey questionnaire was pilot tested.

Reading the attitude statements you will see that some take a positive view (in favour) of teaching citizenship and others take a negative view (against it). Each response has a code assigned to it on the questionnaire, from 1 for 'Strongly agree' to 5 for 'Strongly disagree', regardless of whether it is positive or negative. At the data processing stage these codes are transformed into scores, so it will be important that on the data processing specification the list of statements is scored consistently, with, say, a high score denoting a favourable attitude and a low score a less favourable attitude. Once the scores have been assigned consistently across the statement list a total score can be calculated for each respondent across all the statements. This is the respondent's score on the *attitude scale*. It is a summary measure of the respondent's attitude to citizenship education, as measured across the list of attitude statements.

Building the scale

Say for this example that we score the favourable attitude statements from 5 = Strongly agree to 1 = Strongly disagree and the unfavourable attitudes 5 = Strongly disagree to 1 = Strongly agree. The possible range of scores on this attitude scale, excluding Don't knows, ranges from 10 (a score of 1 on each of the ten statements) to 50 (a score of 5 on each of the ten statements): these are the extremes of the scale. This type of scale is known as a linear scale. A score of 11 or 45, for example, means little except to indicate that those scoring 45 are at the more 'favourable to citizenship education' end of the scale and those with a score of 11 are at the less favourable end. The respondent's score on the attitude scale indicates the strength of their attitude to the particular subject or variable, in this case 'citizenship education' in schools. But the scores are more meaningful, and more useful, when used to compare the responses of different groups. For example, we might want to examine differences in attitude according to social class or – particularly relevant to Northern Ireland – religion (asked at Q. 22 on the survey). To compare attitudes we could, for example, work out the mean score for the Protestant respondents in the sample, the mean score for the Catholic respondents and the mean score for other groups, such as those with no religion. We might find that these mean scores are different and conclude that one group is more positive about education for citizenship than the other; or we might find that the mean scores on the scale are the same, indicating that attitudes to citizenship education may not be dependent on the respondents' religion. Below in Box 9.22 is an example from the Life and Times 2003 survey, this time about attitudes to older people. You will see that in this example there is no mid-point answer on the Likert Scale.

OTHER SCALES

The examples given in Boxes 9.21 and 9.22 are examples of a linear scaling technique. As you have seen, it can be time consuming (and therefore expensive) to construct, and so may not suit every situation. Here we look briefly at two other types of scale: a semantic differential scale and a rank order scale.

Semantic differentials

The semantic differential (Osgood et al., 1957) is a seven-point bi-polar rating scale (although some use a ten-point scale) with the extremes of the scale denoted by adjectives that are opposite in meaning (see Box 9.23). For example, a semantic differential might be strong and weak, or masculine and feminine, or active and passive, or rich and poor. A scale appropriate to the objects being assessed is developed and the respondent is asked to rate a series of objects (brands, for example) using the scale. Work by Osgood et al. (1957) shows the semantic differential to be a valid and reliable measure. It is important, though, that the elements of the scale are carefully chosen. Pilot work (a review of secondary research, qualitative exploration

---

Box 9.22 Attitudes to older people

Q. 5 For each of these statements about older people, I would like you tell me if you agree strongly, agree slightly, disagree slightly, or disagree strongly

	Agree strongly	Agree slightly	Disagree slightly	Disagree strongly	(Don't know)
Older people are admired and respected by young people	1	2	3	4	8
People in their 50s should give up work to make way for younger people	1	2	3	4	8
Older people are too set in their ways and ideas	1	2	3	4	8
Older people are not willing to listen to young people's views	1	2	3	4	8
Older people should stand up more actively for their own rights	1	2	3	4	8
Older people and young people should mix together more often socially	1	2	3	4	8
All older people should be given reduced prices for things like gas, electricity, telephone and transport	1	2	3	4	8
These days older people are much younger in their ways	1	2	3	4	8
Society doesn't recognise the contribution many older people are still able to make	1	2	3	4	8

Source: The Life and Times Survey 2003. Used with permission.

and quantitative testing to determine relevant factors) is extremely useful in this regard. It is also important to ensure that the adjectives used to describe the ends of the scale really are opposites. The statements should be rotated or randomised in some way to avoid order bias. The ratings for each object can be averaged across the sample and can be used to compare the perceptions held by different types of respondent to a particular object – a brand or service or organisation, its image or its attributes, for example.

Box 9.23 Examples of semantic differentials

Please tick one box for each scale

Very trustworthy							Not at all trustworthy
Modern							Old-fashioned
Unfriendly							Friendly
Reliable							Not reliable

Ranking

We can also measure opinion or attitudes to an object by asking respondents to rank a set of attitudes or opinions relevant to the object. For example we might ask, 'What, in your opinion, are the most important causes of homelessness among men in London? Please choose the five causes which in your view are the most important and number them from 1 to 5, where 1 = the most important.' Or, 'Which of these companies, in your opinion, produces the best quality products? Please choose no more than five companies and number them 1 to 5, in order of quality.' By ranking, we get an idea of the way in which a person evaluates an object on a set of criteria. One important thing to bear in mind about ranking is that we cannot say anything about the distance or intervals between the rankings. In effect, we are creating an ordinal scale and we cannot make the assumption that the distance between the intervals on the scale is equal (unlike the linear scale, in which we do assume that they are equal). For example, in rating the quality of products, it may be that first place company C rates a long way ahead of second place company A but that company B is a very close third to company A. In constructing a ranking question we must take care to ensure that the instructions are clear and unambiguous, so the respondent is clear about the basis on which to compile the ranking, and the list of items to be ranked should be limited to about ten – any more makes the task difficult to manage, for the respondent and the researcher. In addition, the criteria on which we ask respondents to rate an object must be meaningful. For completeness, it is important to include 'Other' and 'Don't know' categories in the list of criteria. As with the scores on the semantic differential, we can average the rank scores across the sample, and we can count how many first place rankings a particular criterion received, how many second place and so on, for each criterion.

Paired comparisons

Paired comparisons are a form of ranking – the respondent is presented with two objects and asked to choose between them. This approach is used in product testing, when the respondent is asked, for example, to choose between two products on the basis of taste or appearance. To get a rank order measurement from a series of objects, say a group of six products, we must present each pair combination to the respondent. This can make the use of paired comparisons for creating rank order scales unwieldy – with 6 items there are 15 pairs $[0.5 \times N(N-1)]$; with 8 items there are 28 pairs; with 10 items there are 45 pairs and so on.

In designing any rating scale the guidelines that pertain to question wording should be followed. Particular attention should be paid to the wording of instructions, to ensure that they are clear and easy to follow. Relevant information should be given as to the context of the required rating (for example thinking about how you use this product) and the aim of the rating scale. The rating criteria or attitude statements, the elements of the scale, should be relevant to the object being rated, should mean the same thing to all respondents and should be within the respondent's frame of reference. The response categories should be relevant to the purpose of the question – a Likert format, a semantic differential or a rank order, for example. A decision also needs to be made about the number of steps in the scale, which can vary from three to ten, and you must also decide whether or not there should be a midpoint – a neutral, 'neither/nor' category.

PROBLEMS WITH SCALES

You need to be aware of the 'error of central tendency' – the tendency for respondents to avoid using the extreme of the scales. This can be counteracted to some extent by ensuring that the extremes do not appear too extreme, or by combining the two (or three, depending on the number of steps in the scale) top categories at each end of the scale at the data processing stage.

Another common problem with rating scales is the 'halo effect': in responding to items on a scale a like or dislike for the object being rated may influence a respondent's rating. This may be overcome to some degree by designing the questionnaire so that the rating scales are spaced apart. Another manifestation of the halo effect is a sort of automatic response syndrome, which can occur if the scale is laid out in such a way that all the positive scores line up on one side of the page and all the negative ones line up on the other, or if all the statements or items in the scale are positive or all of them are negative. If the respondent notices this pattern, there may be temptation to reply automatically, without really thinking about the answer. The solution is to include in the list positive and negative statements, and, if using a semantic differential scale, to make sure that the positive ends of the scale are not on the same side.

Another common problem is that of logical error. This type of error occurs when the respondent gives a similar rating to an object on attributes or attitudes that he or she thinks are somehow related. A way of overcoming this is to ensure that such attributes or attitudes do not occur close together on the rating scale.

GRIDS

If you want to understand how respondents describe or evaluate a product, service or brand – useful in understanding how the consumer perceives the market or the brand, and what effect marketing activity has on the perception of brands, for example – rating products or services against a set of criteria can be useful. An association grid, which allows the respondent to choose which statements are associated with particular brands, is a useful way of collecting a lot of information quickly and allows scope for analysing the data in a variety of ways, from calculating the proportion of the sample who associate a particular statement with a brand or product, through comparisons of the profiles of each brand across all the statements to more complex multivariate mapping techniques.

To measure the 'attitude' towards an object, a product or service, for example, the first step – as with the attitude scale – is to develop a set of evaluative or descriptive statements designed to reflect attitudes or beliefs about the object. Descriptive attitude statements can relate to particular properties of a product, service or brand, perhaps those that have been emphasised in marketing or advertising activity. Evaluative attitude statements relate to more opinion- or attitude-based characteristics, such as 'reliable', 'good quality', 'suitable for children'. Research has shown (Bird and Ehrenberg, 1970) that evaluative measures discriminate more effectively between users and non-users of a brand than do general descriptive measures, which may be worth bearing in mind.

Before choosing the statements it is therefore important to be clear about what it is you are measuring and the purpose to which the findings will be put. Are you collecting information on attitudes and beliefs – asking respondents to evaluate a list of products or brands – in order to see how people distinguish between different products, services or brands? Or are you collecting information on attitudes and beliefs in order to determine preference, or likely choice when it comes to buying or using the products, services or brands? Or both? The end use of the data should determine the choice of criteria: the thing to remember here is that those statements that distinguish between products may not necessarily be the same as those that are used to make preference or purchase decisions or those that underlie an attitude (Bird and Ehrenberg, 1970). What is important to remember in using this approach is to determine the relevant or salient beliefs about or characteristics of a product, service or brand or list of brands. If you are assessing a range of brands it is important to include attitudes and beliefs that are salient to each of the brands. Using salient beliefs will help you write much better attitude and belief statements and will give you a more sensitive understanding of the market. One way of obtaining a list of salient attitudes and beliefs is to get respondents in the target market to list (without prompting) the characteristics or attributes of a service, product or brand and their opinions of it, and to use these to develop a set of evaluative or descriptive statements (a list of 10 or 12 is manageable). Remember, in designing the statements and the questions, be specific, and put them in context.

Quantitative methods are particularly suitable for collecting data on attitudes when a less detailed understanding is required. If the measures used are grounded in solid qualitative work it is likely that they will be reasonably valid measures; if well designed they can produce reliable (repeatable and consistent) measures, which can be used in statistical analysis (in cluster and factor analysis, for example). In the course of developing attitude questions, however, there is a tendency to oversimplify and so risk losing much of the richness and detail and even some of the understanding of the nature of the attitude. Using scales and rankings can mislead us into thinking that attitudes fall on a continuum, with positive at one end and negative at the other, which may not be a useful or valid way of thinking about attitudes at all.

Box 9.24 Example of a grid

	Brand L	Brand M	Brand N	Brand O	Brand P
Pleasant tasting	1	1	1	1	1
Makes you drowsy	2	2	2	2	2
Quick to take effect	3	3	3	3	3
Easy to take	4	4	4	4	4
Suitable to use throughout the day	5	5	5	5	5
Treats all the symptoms of a cold	6	6	6	6	6
Effective	7	7	7	7	7

Box 9.25 Examples of views and belief statements

Here are examples of statements used in a quantitative study to understand the views of General Practitioners (GPs) to the prescribing of pain killers (analgesics). The statements were developed from previous work – in the case of the GPs' views about patients, from qualitative research; in the case of the GPs' personal beliefs, from work done on other projects in other countries.

GPs' views about patients
I like my patients to be involved in their own treatment
Patients are much more demanding these days
Some of my patients know what best relieves their own pain
I hope my patients don't return within the month
I always start my patients on mild analgesics
Most patients feel cheated if I don't prescribe for them
I always start my patients on generic analgesics
Analgesia is not a high interest area for me

Five point response scale: Disagree strongly = 1.0/Agree strongly = 5.0

GPs' personal beliefs
I tend to judge people in terms of their success
Over the years my beliefs and values have not changed *very* much
Getting ahead in the world depends on whether you were born rich or poor
I try to get my own way regardless of others
All the rules and regulations nowadays make it difficult for me to get on in the world
I enjoy getting involved in new and unusual situations

Five point response scale: Disagree strongly = 1.0/Agree strongly = 5.0

Source: Adapted from Hurrell, G., Collins, M., Sykes, W. and Williams, V. (1997) 'Solpadol – a successful case of brand positioning', *International Journal of Market Research*, 39, 3, pp. 463–80, www.ijmr.com.

REVIEWING THE QUESTIONS

Once you have designed a set of questions, before going any further it is useful to review them against the relevant research objectives and, if necessary, amend them. For each draft question, ask:

- Does it give me the information I want?
- Does it answer my research objectives?
- Is the purpose of the question clear?
- Is it really necessary?
- What assumptions have I made in this question?

In addition, check whether the questions are suitable for the target group, for the method of data collection and for how the data are to be analysed.

Box 9.26 Seeing the answers, rewording the questions'

At the first wave of our data collection (Wave 1) our question for number of heterosexual partners was 'How many *different partners* of the opposite sex have you had in the last twelve months?' We specifically chose the wording to distinguish 'partners' from number of 'occasions'. From our own interviewing and the results it was obvious that a proportion of people interpreted this question to mean 'different from my usual partner'. There was therefore a tendency to undercount by one. The question was reworded for Wave 2 to exclude the word 'different'.

Source: Adapted from Orton, S. and Samuels, J. (1997) 'What we have learned from researching AIDS', *International Journal of Market Research*, 39, 1, pp. 175–200, www.ijmr.com.

Target group

Is the target population made up of adults or children, consumers or business people? Review the wording of the questions to ensure that the vocabulary used is suitable for the respondents; review the response format to ensure that respondents will have no difficulty answering the questions; and check to make sure that the questions and answers make sense.

Method of data collection

In a telephone interview, where the respondent cannot see the interviewer or the questionnaire, prompts or scales must be read out, and instructions on how to use them must be clear. To prevent confusion and misunderstanding it is best to avoid long questions, long scales and long descriptions.

For self-completion methods much depends on how the questionnaire looks – it must be visually appealing (for example, a postal questionnaire should not, for example, look too thick or feel too heavy; the text in a web survey should be large enough to read easily) and should create a positive first impression. It should reflect the professionalism of the research organisation. With no interviewer present there is no chance to clarify the meaning of questions or instructions. The questionnaire must look easy to fill in and be easy to fill in. For this reason most questions will be pre-coded – to make the process relatively easy. Open questions can be used to allow respondents to comment on, explain or add to the responses given at closed questions. The questions and the instructions must be written in clear and unambiguous language; the routing must be easy to follow. Because the respondent can read the whole questionnaire it is not possible to use unfolding techniques or pre-coded lists for unprompted questions. Without an interviewer present it is also more difficult to establish and maintain interest. The topic and the questions should be of interest to the respondent and relevant to him or her. If they are not, the respondent may not complete the questionnaire or may give it to someone else whom they think will be able to answer the questions.

CASE STUDY 9.4

JUST CHECKING: AN INFORMAL PILOT TEST

A survey of a school meals service was conducted using self-completion questionnaires to gather data from staff, primary school pupils, post-primary school pupils and parents. The following examples are from the pilot stage of the questionnaire for primary school pupils, and in particular, the problems identified by Sam, the 7-year-old son of a member of the survey design team.

Why this case study is worth reading

This case study is worth reading for one reason: it shows the value in testing a questionnaire on its target audience, highlighting how questions can be read and interpreted differently by different people (in this case – the adult questionnaire designer and the 7-year old target group respondent).

What the respondent saw

The first problem that Sam, our junior researcher, picked up was an ambiguity in the question wording:

Q. What do you have for breakfast? Put a tick in each square if you have that food for breakfast.
Respondents were given a list of items to tick (multi-response):

Cereal	☑
Toast	☑
A cold drink	☑
A hot drink	☑
Fruit	☑
Hot food	☑
Biscuits or crisps	☑
I don't eat breakfast	☐

Sam ticked all boxes except the last one. When questioned on this by his mother, who knew that he didn't have all of these items for breakfast, he pointed out that theoretically, these were all breakfast foods, and so it was valid to tick them all. Thus, the question was changed to 'What do <u>you</u> have for <u>your</u> breakfast'. Put a tick in each square that says if you have that food for breakfast.

The second problem that Sam identified was an error in the response codes. Respondents were given a list of questions relating to the practical aspects of school dinners, and asked to tick a box relating to each statement – Yes, No, Sometimes. For most questions, these response items were appropriate, for example:

Q. When you have school dinners does the food taste nice?
Q. Do you get enough to eat?
Q. Does the food look nice?
Q. Is the dining room clean and tidy?
Q. Is the dining room too small?

Sam pointed out that the response item 'sometimes' was not appropriate for the final question 'Is the dining room too small?' as the dining room did not change size. Thus, this response item was deleted for this question.

Source: School dinners project survey team, Queen's University Belfast. Used with permission.

Box 9.27 Examples of a self-completion layout

Q. Which of the following types of business does your company deal in? PLEASE TICK ALL THAT APPLY.

Mortgages	☐
Pensions	☐
Life insurance	☐
Health insurance	☐
Motor insurance	☐
Holiday/travel insurance	☐
Investment/savings schemes	☐
Portfolio management	☐
Other	☐

PLEASE TICK AND WRITE IN THE TYPE OF BUSINESS

Q86. And have you yourself ever done any of these things? Please tick one box in each row

	No	Once	A few times	Many times	Can't remember
Used illegal drugs	☐1	☐2	☐3	☐4	☐5
Smoked tobacco	☐1	☐2	☐3	☐4	☐5
Drunk alcohol	☐1	☐2	☐3	☐4	☐5
Used solvents to get high	☐1	☐2	☐3	☐4	☐5
Had sexual intercourse	☐1	☐2	☐3	☐4	☐5
Stopped eating although you were hungry in order to lose weight	☐1	☐2	☐3	☐4	☐5

Source: ARK. *Young Life and Times Survey*, 2007 [http://www.ark.ac.uk/ylt/2007/YLT07quest.pdf]. ARK www.ark.ac.uk/ylt

For examples of self-completion and interviewer-administered questionnaires among samples of adults and young people, see the ARK/Life and Time website www.ark.ac.uk/nilt/about/. You can download these questionnaires and have a look at the data they generated. There is also information on how the surveys were conducted and examples of how the findings were written up.

Data analysis

Think about how the data are to be analysed and seek the advice of the person responsible for the data processing. The data entry and analysis software to be used may dictate the layout of the questionnaire and the way in which questions are coded.

Question order

Now that you have a set of questions that you believe address the research objectives, the next task is to put them into an effective and logical order. Remember that the interview is a conversation and to keep the respondent's interest and co-operation it must make sense; there should be no jarring non sequiturs or illogical jumps between topics. The questionnaire should create a positive impression of the particular piece of research and of research in general. The order of the topics and questions is also important in enabling the interviewer to establish and build rapport with the respondent. Asking questions on difficult or sensitive topics too early in the interview can destroy rapport and lead to withdrawal from the interview or refusal to answer particular questions; or when answering the respondent may not feel comfortable enough to give accurate replies, so data quality is compromised (see Case study 9.3). The order of questions can impact on the interviewer's confidence that the questionnaire will work in practice – and research has shown that a confident interviewer will have greater success in achieving interviews.

In deciding on the order of questions it is useful to draw up a flow chart. From a list of draft questions, group together the questions that relate to each topic. Each group or set of questions is a module. Put these modules into an order – straightforward, non-challenging topics first, more difficult or sensitive topics, including classification questions on age, income and so on towards the end. To help the flow of the questionnaire it is useful to include a brief introduction to each module. For example, on the Life and Times 2001 questionnaire the module on Culture, Arts and Leisure is introduced like this: 'The next questions are about culture and the arts, and the things people do in their leisure time.' Also, in terms of the flow of the questionnaire, you need to think about the balance between the types of questions: too many closed questions or attitude scales together can be boring and repetitive for interviewer and respondent and will adversely affect the quality of the data.

Once you have decided on the order of modules you need to decide on the order of questions within each module. Moving from general questions to more specific ones – the funnel approach – is effective. Again, more difficult or sensitive questions should appear later. Bear in mind that earlier questions may bias response to later ones. For example, ask unaided or spontaneous awareness questions before asking aided or prompted awareness ones; ask about usage and behaviour before asking about attitudes. In asking respondents about a relatively long list of items – brands, for example, or image or attitude statements – fatigue can set in, influencing the quality of responses to items at the end of the list. A way of randomising this effect across the sample is to rotate or randomise the order in which you present the items. This can be done automatically in computer-aided interviewing and by using randomised tick starts in pen and paper interviewing.

Remember, if a question module or an individual question is not relevant to a respondent, make sure you include routing instructions that take the interviewer or the respondent to the next relevant module or question.

Layout and appearance

The layout or appearance of the questionnaire may seem unimportant but needs to be considered for several reasons. In a self-completion format the questionnaire must be laid out so that the respondent understands what is required and can fill it in easily. An interviewer-administered questionnaire must be set out so that the interviewer can read it easily, follow the routing and record the respondent's answers accurately. In adding in interviewer instructions the convention is to use capitals and bold text, as you can see in the examples here; question text and answers are in lower case, not bold. Routing instructions should appear opposite the question codes, as shown in the examples used here, and where appropriate, above the question (for example, **IF YES AT Q. 13 OR Q. 14 ASK:** Which one?). As we noted above, layout is also important from a data processing point of view and should take into consideration the requirements of the data entry and analysis software.

In finalising a questionnaire, have it checked thoroughly by a fieldwork expert and by a person involved in data processing. In particular, it should be proof-read to ensure that routing and coding instructions are clear and accurate; that there is enough space to record and code answers (and, on paper questionnaires, enough space for coders to write in codes); for manual data entry that the codes (and column numbers, if used) are where the data entry person would expect to find them. (We look at the process of questionnaire approval in Chapter 10.)

Questionnaire length

The questionnaire must be long enough to cover the research objectives; the right length to meet the research budget (the longer the questionnaire, the greater the cost); and the right length to suit the choice of data collection method. The recommended maximum length for an in-home face-to-face questionnaire is about 45 minutes to an hour; for a telephone interview it is about 20 minutes; and for a street interview about 5 or 10 minutes. It must also be of a length that allows the interviewer time to build up rapport with the respondent. On the other hand, it should not be so long that the task of completing it is burdensome, or so long that the respondent is unwilling to take part at all. Besides affecting co-operation rates, the length of the questionnaire has been shown to affect the quality of the data collected, with poorer quality data collected towards the end of a long interview, as the respondent tires of answering questions.

Pilot study

It can sometimes be difficult to assess objectively how a questionnaire or a discussion guide in which you are involved will work – being so close to it you tend to make too many assumptions. Conducting a pilot study is an invaluable way of testing it out – it will show what questions are difficult, which ones give the type of answers you were expecting and so on. A pilot is especially useful if a questionnaire is a new one and not a repeat of a previous job or similar to other questionnaires you have used with a similar sample (or if the discussion guide is on a topic that is fairly new to you). Although relatively expensive and time consuming to conduct, in the end a pilot study can save time and money by delivering a questionnaire (or discussion guide) that is efficient in collecting good quality data. Pilot studies are crucial in multi-country projects to ensure that the questionnaire has been adapted to suit the language and culture in which it is to be used. The results of the pilot tests in each country should be compared to ensure that the questions are measuring the same things, that they are gathering equivalent data.

CONDUCTING A PILOT STUDY

The pilot study can be conducted at any stage in the development of the questionnaire – from the conceptualisation stage (to explore the meanings of concepts and understand the language used by the target audience) to the fully developed draft (to check if it delivers the information it is designed to deliver). The style of the pilot interview will depend on how well developed the questionnaire is. Pilot interviews undertaken in the early stages of development might take the form of an informal qualitative in-depth interview. Those undertaken with a more fully formed questionnaire are likely to resemble a formal quantitative interview (in the first instance face to face, then using the method of data collection intended for the final version).

Regardless of the style of the pilot or the stage at which the draft is being piloted, it is a good idea that you, the person involved in designing the questionnaire or discussion guide, conduct some of the pilot interviews. This can be invaluable in developing your questionnaire design skills as you hear and see for yourself how your questions work (or do not work!) with a real respondent. Once the questionnaire is close to the final draft stage interviewers from the fieldforce conducting the survey should do some pilot interviews. It is invaluable to get feedback from experienced interviewers as well as relatively new ones – each will have a different view of the interview process and the effectiveness of the pilot questionnaire. A relatively new interviewer will have insights into the way the questionnaire works from the interviewer's point of view – if it is easy to follow, if instructions are clear and so on; the more experienced interviewer will have insights into how it works from the respondent's point of view; and both will give you feedback on timing and overall manageability of the interview. If a full-scale, proper pilot study is not possible, ask some people you work with who are not directly involved in the project (and if possible who are in the target population) to do pilot interviews with you.

HOW DO WE DO IT? FINDING OUT ABOUT CHILD ABUSE

This case study looks at the issues involved in designing, pilot testing and administering a questionnaire on a very sensitive topic – child abuse. It is interesting to compare the mode of administration of some of the more sensitive questions in this survey (CASI – computer-aided self interviewing) with that used almost 15 years earlier in Case study 9.3 (shuffle packs). The survey used a random probability sample and a total of 2,869 interviews were achieved throughout the UK, a response rate of 69 per cent. A separate booster was conducted to enhance the number of respondents from minority ethnic groups so that differences between the groups could be explored.

Why this case study is worth reading

This case study is worth reading for several reasons: it illustrates the process of questionnaire design; it highlights the issues faced in designing a survey on a sensitive and complex topic; it describes the structure of the questionnaire and the interview; it describes pilot tesing; it describes the use of two forms of data collection within one interview (interviewer-administered and self-completion); it describes what respondents thought of the interview.

The key words are: sensitive subject, rapport, trust, definitions of abuse, question loops, CAPI, self-keying, complexity, piloting process, CASI, qualitative interview, honest, embarrassment, prevalence of abuse, unethical, objective measurement, self-defined measurement.

Introduction

In designing the questionnaire we had to address a number of specific issues:

■ The need for a questionnaire which was clear and concise, yet allowed time for the interviewer to build a rapport and feeling of trust with the respondent, prior to the most sensitive questions being asked.
■ The need to account for the numerous ways in which abuse can manifest itself, in order to minimise the risk of failing to identify abuse, and to enable the construction of flexible definitions of abuse to aid comparison with other surveys using alternative definitions.
■ The need to capture data on hugely complex experiences, using 'question loops' incorporating questions to define the nature of the abuse, the victim's age, its frequency and duration, the relationship with the abuser, the effects, involvement of officials etc. Such complex questionnaire design meant that CAPI was essential.
■ The need for the most sensitive questions to be self-keyed directly into the laptop computer. This required questions and response codes to be phrased in very simple terms, using very simple keying methods, because the consequences of making errors and becoming 'stuck' could be embarrassing for respondent and interviewer alike.

Pilot studies

Given the extreme sensitivity of the subject matter and complexity of the questionnaire design, the piloting process took on particular importance. A first pilot resulted in significant improvements to the questionnaire. A second pilot identified further improvements. Because of the very narrow age band eligible, the pilots were conducted at central venues, with respondents recruited in the street and incentivised. After completing the CASI interview each pilot respondent took part in a qualitative interview in which they were questioned on their feelings about the survey. In particular, we asked whether some questions were too sensitive to be asked, whether they felt they could be completely honest in responding, and whether they might feel embarrassed completing the survey in their own home. Some respondents did report a degree of embarrassment and feeling upset at the explicit nature of some of the questions, but we were reassured by the fact that respondents consistently understood why such questions needed to be asked and the importance of providing a candid response.

▶

At the time of setting up the pilot survey we did not know what the prevalence of abuse would be, and had to consider the possibility that we would find no pilot respondents who had experienced abuse. This would have left large numbers of the most sensitive questions untested. Consequently we contacted a number of charitable organisations providing services to young adults with social problems, such as homelessness and drug addiction. This enabled us to conduct additional special pilot interviews at hostels and day centres.

Administering the questionnaire

The questionnaire was introduced as being about 'experiences in childhood' and began by collecting some general background information about respondents' current circumstances and their family background, before moving on to obtain some attitudinal information about child rearing. The second half of the interview addressed respondents' own experiences in their childhood. Respondents completed this part of the interview themselves, reading the questions on the computer screen and typing in their answers. Thus they were able to provide information without the interviewer (or anyone else who might be present in the room) knowing the questions asked or their answers. All sections were introduced with broad, general questions about aspects of their care in childhood, gradually moving to more sensitive and detailed questions on family relationships; amount of supervision and freedom; physical care; verbal, physical and violent treatment; bullying and discrimination; emotional or psychological treatment; and sexual experience.

Responses which indicated that the young people may have had abusive or potentially abusive experiences were followed up in detail with those respondents. The questions themselves did not define abuse and neglect. Instead, respondents were asked whether or not they had experienced any of a range of behaviour towards them (some of them positive, some negative). If they had some of the more negative experiences, they were asked a number of further questions to put that experience in context. At the end of each section, the respondents were asked if they considered the treatment they received to have been child abuse. This provided both a flexible, 'objective' measurement of abuse and, importantly, a self-defined measurement of abuse.

Source: Adapted from Brooker, S., Cawson, P., Kelly, G. and Wattam, C. (2001) 'The prevalence of child abuse and neglect: a survey of young people', MRS Conference, www.mrs.org.uk.

The pilot interviews should be conducted face to face (regardless, in the case of a questionnaire, whether the final version is designed for the telephone or as a self-completion sheet) with members of the target population. A face-to-face interview enables the interviewer to observe and note the respondent's physical reaction to the questions. In order to get a clear picture of how a survey questionnaire works conduct at least about 12 interviews. (For a discussion guide, a relatively new qualitative interviewer should conduct about three or four pilot interviews; with more experience, one or two interviews might provide the necessary insight.) One approach is to conduct the interview as you would a 'real' interview, making notes on how the respondent reacts to the questions. At the end of the interview you might go back over each question, asking the respondent for comments. Alternatively, you can ask the respondent to comment on each question as it is asked. You may even give the respondent a

Box 9.28 Pilot checklist

In conducting a pilot study, here are some things to think about:

- *Clarity of purpose.* Did the questions measure what they are supposed to measure? How did the respondent interpret the questions? Were the questions relevant to the respondent? Were they meaningful to the respondent?
- *Wording of the questions.* Were any questions too vague, unclear or ambiguous, loaded or leading? Did any use unfamiliar or difficult words, ask about more than one thing, use a double negative? Were any too long or convoluted?
- *Question content.* Were there any questions that discouraged the respondent from completing the questionnaire, or that were embarrassing for the interviewer to ask or the respondent to answer?
- *Type of questions.* Was the balance right between open and closed questions? Was the use of each type appropriate? Were the scales used suitable?
- *Response alternatives.* Were the response alternatives full and complete? Was the list too long?
- *Order of question modules and questions within modules.* Did the questionnaire flow smoothly from question to question and from module to module? Did the order seem logical to the respondent and the interviewer? Did anything seem odd or discordant? Were more sensitive topics in the right place? Was there any evidence of order bias or order effects?
- *Layout/appearance of the questionnaire.* Was it suited to the method of data collection? If self-completion, did the respondent find the instructions clear and easy to follow? If interviewer administered, how easy or difficult was it? How easy or difficult was it to record responses?
- *Length.* How long did it take to complete? What were interviewers' and respondents' perceptions of the length? Was it too long, too short, about right?

copy of the research objectives for evaluation of the questions. It can be useful to record pilot interviews and listen to them again.

REVIEWING AND REVISING

When the pilot study is complete, it is useful to think through how you would analyse the responses. Check the data against the research objectives to see whether you are getting the sort of information you need. For a quantitative project, it is worth preparing a coding frame based on the responses to the questions, editing the questionnaires, entering the data and producing a hole count. This allows you to check for any inconsistencies in logic or in coding that might hamper data processing. Make the necessary changes to the questionnaire or discussion guide that the pilot work suggests. If they are substantial it may be worthwhile conducting another pilot study with a new set of respondents. Finally, it will also be worthwhile to run a short pilot study using the data collection method that is to be used in the main study, in order to identify any problems that may be related to the method of data collection.

CASE STUDY 9.6

IT HAS TO CHANGE: FINDINGS FROM A PILOT STUDY

Following a comprehensive face-to-face briefing on the Life and Times Survey, which included practice or 'mock' interviews, 60 face-to-face pilot interviews were carried out by the interviewers who would go on to conduct the full survey. Some of the suggested changes are shown below. The pilot also highlighted the need to include additional questions and to remove others (either because they were not delivering valid data or they were too sensitive). It also gave valuable information on the time needed to complete the survey and each of the question modules within it. You can download the version of the questionnaire used in the full survey from the Life and Times website www.ark.ac.uk/nilt/2001/quest01.html.

Why this case study is worth reading

This case study is worth reading for one reason: it gives examples of the sort of changes suggested by a pilot study including changes to the wording of some questions, additions to pre-coded lists, and changes to the order of question modules.

Change: pre-coded list

From Section 2A: Health issues

In the pilot, quite a few respondents said that they would go to a pharmacist for advice. This was added to the pre-coded list and the show card.

Q. 1a Thinking about the health problem or health issue which was most important for you, where did you go to find information or advice about this?
SHOW CARD [but not for pilot]
CODE ALL THAT APPLY

	Yes	*No*
A doctor or other health professional	1	2
A friend or relative who is a health professional	1	2
Another friend or relative	1	2
Someone who practises alternative medicine	1	2
The Internet	1	2
Books	1	2
Leaflets	1	2
Telephone helpline	1	2
A support group	1	2
Pharmacist	1	2
Other (WRITE IN)	1	2
Don't know/Can't remember	8	

Change: question wording

From Section 2A: Health issues

To reflect everyday usage, 'illness' replaced 'condition' and, to avoid embarrassment and to show greater sensitivity towards the respondent, mention of specific illnesses (heart disease and cancer) were removed.

Q. 2 Suppose you go to your GP with chest pains and he or she tells you that you may have a serious *condition* [replaced with illness] *like heart disease or cancer* [removed]. The GP makes arrangements for you to have further tests. In the meantime, would you try and get more information yourself on what might be the matter or would you probably rely on the doctors to give you the information you need?

Change: order of question modules

From Section 3: Political attitudes

Interviewers found that not enough rapport had been established at this stage of the interview to enable good quality data to be collected on political attitudes. As a result this question module was moved to later in the questionnaire.

Change: response items

From Section 4: Education

In the pilot several respondents replied that 'everyone should be treated equally'. This was added to the question's response items.

Q. 14 Some people say that particular groups of unemployed people should be given extra help with free training courses and courses to get them back to work. Are you in favour or against giving extra help like this to *lone mothers*? **SHOW CARD**
(a) And what about *ex-prisoners*?
(b) *People in their fifties who are out of work*?
(c) *People in their twenties who are out of work*?

	Strongly in favour	In favour	Neither in favour nor against	Against	Strongly against	Don't know	Everyone should be treated equally
Lone mothers	1	2	3	4	5	8	6
Ex-prisoners	1	2	3	4	5	8	6
People in their fifties	1	2	3	4	5	8	6
People in their twenties	1	2	3	4	5	8	6

Source: The Life and Times Survey Team and Research and Evaluation Services (fieldwork provider). Used with permission.

Chapter summary

- The questionnaire is the instrument used to collect data. Effective research and quality data depend on a well-designed questionnaire. It must be effective in addressing the research objectives – collecting valid and reliable data to address the research problem clearly and unambiguously – and it must be suited to the practical tasks of data collection and data processing and analysis. It also has a role to play in representing research, and the research industry, to the wider world.

- Questionnaire design follows from a thorough and rigorous examination of the research problem and a clear understanding of the nature of the evidence needed to address it.

- Designing questions for some topics may be fairly straightforward. The topic might be familiar, or you might be using standard or tried and tested questions from previous studies. Standard questions are essential if comparisons are to be made between surveys and if data from different surveys are to be fused. Some things are more difficult to measure, and many things are more difficult than they first appear. Much work is needed to clarify the meaning and define clearly what is to be measured so that there is no ambiguity about what the question is measuring and how the response to it is interpreted.

- Careful attention must be paid to question wording, to question structure (open-ended or closed-response formats), to the order of question modules and questions within the modules, to the length of the questionnaire and its layout.

- Attitudes are of interest to social and market researchers for their own sake and for the way in which they relate to motivation, intention and behaviour.

- Attitudes are difficult to research in a way that achieves validity and reliability – they are complex, multi-faceted and may be dependent on particular circumstances; we may be unaware that we hold them and we may find it hard, or be unwilling, to articulate them.

- Capturing an attitude is almost impossible using one question or one statement: it is unlikely that we will be able to capture the complexity of it, so it will lack validity; and it is unlikely that one question or statement will deliver consistent results – respondents tend to be more sensitive to the wording and the context of attitudinal questions compared to factual questions – so it will lack reliability.

- The validity and reliability of attitude measurement can be improved by using banks of questions or 'attitude statements' combined in an attitude scale. Validity may be improved if the question, the statements and the response sets used are designed to encompass the complexity of the attitude, and the context of it. Reliability may be improved because issues of question wording and context may be cancelled out across the range of statements.

- Designing questions to measure attitudes quantitatively consists of two parts: designing and choosing the list of attitude statements or the 'item pool' for the particular attitude variable; and choosing the response format. The most common approaches include linear scaling techniques, semantic differential scales and rank order scales.

- Be aware of the sources of error in the design of scales – the error of central tendency, the 'halo effect', automatic response syndrome and the problem of logical error – and take steps to overcome them.

- An association grid allows respondents to choose which statements they associate with particular brands and is a useful way of collecting information quickly. It allows scope for analysing the data in a variety of ways, from calculating the proportion of the sample who associate a particular statement with a brand or product to comparisons of the profiles of each brand across all the statements to more complex multivariate mapping techniques.

- A pilot study is invaluable in determining whether or not you are asking the right questions in the right way.

Questions and exercises

1 Discuss the contribution of questionnaire design to each of the following, illustrating your answer with examples:

   (a) Data quality.

   (b) The respondent's experience.

   (c) The interviewer's experience.

2 Your organisation sells goods to other organisations. It has been running a customer satisfaction survey using telephone interviews for several years but has noticed that over the last two rounds of the survey the response rate has declined.

   (a) Discuss the possible reasons for the decline in response.

   (b) Suggest the steps you would take to increase the response rate, giving a rationale for any suggestions you make.

3 Describe the steps you would take to ensure that the interviewers working on your face-to-face survey are well prepared. Give reasons for the steps you suggest.

4 Start collecting examples of questionnaires from as many sources as you can (the ARK/Life and Times website mentioned above is a good place to start). For each questionnaire in your collection, ask yourself the following:

(a) What information does the questionnaire aim to collect?

(b) At whom is it aimed?

(c) Is it for self-completion, or would an interviewer fill it in?

(d) What types of questions are used?

(e) How is the questionnaire set out?

(f) Is it easy to fill in?

(g) Did you understand the questions?

(h) How long did it take you to complete?

(i) What sort of questions come first?

(j) Are the questions in a logical order?

(k) Were any of the questions sensitive or too personal?

(l) Would you feel anxious about what might be done with the information you give?

References

ARK, Northern Ireland Life and Times Survey. ARK. www.ark.ac.uk/nilt.

Bird, M. and Ehrenberg, A. (1970) 'Consumer attitudes and brand usage', *Journal of the Market Research Society*, 12, 3, pp. 233–47.

Brace, I. and Nancarrow, C. (2008) 'Let's get ethical: dealing with socially desirable responding online', *Proceedings of the Market Research Society Conference*, London: MRS.

Brooker, S., Cawson, P., Kelly, G. and Wattam, C. (2001) 'The prevalence of child abuse and neglect: a survey of young people', *Proceedings of the Market Research Society Conference*, London: MRS.

Granville, S., Campbell-Jack, D. and Lamplugh, T. (2005) 'Perception, prevention, policing and the challenges of researching anti-social behaviour', *Proceedings of the Market Research Society Conference*, London: MRS.

Hurrell, G., Collins, M., Sykes, W. and Williams, V. (1997) 'Solpadol – a successful case of brand positioning', *Journal of the Market Research Society*, 39, 3, pp. 463–80.

Kirk, J. and Miller, M. (1986) *Reliability and Validity in Qualitative Research*, Newbury Park, CA: Sage.

Lee, R. (1992) *Doing Research on Sensitive Topics*, London: Sage.

Miles, K., Bright, D. and Kemp, J. (2000) 'Improving the research interview experience', *Proceedings of the Market Research Society Conference*, London: MRS.

MRS Code of Conduct (2005) (www.mrs.org.uk)

Mytton, G. (1996) 'Research in new fields', *Journal of the Market Research Society*, 38, 1, pp. 19–31.

Oppenheim, A. (2000) *Questionnaire Design, Interviewing and Attitude Measurement*, London: Continuum.

Orton, S. and Samuels, J. (1997) 'What we have learned from researching AIDS', *Journal of the Market Research Society*, 39, 1, pp. 175–200.

Osgood, C., Suci, G. and Tannebaum, R. (1957) *The Measurement of Meaning*, Urbana, IL.: University of Illinois Press.

Sampson, P. (1980) 'The technical revolution of the 1970s: will it happen in the 1980s?', *Journal of the Market Research Society*, 22, 3, pp. 161–78.

Siddall, J., Stride, C. and Sargent, J. (1987) 'Are you homosexual, heterosexual or bisexual? If so, you could develop AIDS', *Proceedings of the Market Research Society Conference*, London: MRS.

Sudman, S. and Bradburn, N. (1983) *Asking Questions*, San Francisco, CA: Jossey-Bass.

Tuck, M. (1976) *How People Choose*, London: Methuen.

Whitehead, C., Stockdale, J. and Razzu, G. (2003) *The Economic and Social Cost of Anti-Social Behaviour: A Review*, London: London School of Economics and Political Science.

Recommended reading

Ajzen, I. and Fishbein, M. (1980) *Understanding Attitudes and Predicting Social Behaviour*, New Jersey: Prentice-Hall.

Bird, M. and Ehrenberg, A. (1970) 'Consumer attitudes and brand usage', *Journal of the Market Research Society*, 12, 3, pp. 233–47.

Converse, J. and Presser, S. (1986) *Survey Questions: Handcrafting the Standardized Questionnaire*, London: Sage.

Duffy, B. (2003) 'Response order effects: how do people read?', *International Journal of Market Research*, 45, 4, pp. 457–66.

Madden, M.J., Ellen, P.S. and Ajzen, I. (1992) 'A comparison of the theory of planned behavior and the theory of reasoned action', *Personality and Social Psychology Bulletin*, 18, 1, pp. 3–9.

MRS (2006) *Questionnaire Design Guidelines*, London: MRS.

Oppenheim, A. (2000) *Questionnaire Design, Interviewing and Attitude Measurement*, London: Continuum.

Payne, S. (1951) *The Art of Asking Questions*, Princeton, NJ: Princeton University Press.

Sudman, S. and Bradburn, N. (1983) *Asking Questions*, San Francisco, CA: Jossey-Bass.

Tuck, M. (1976) *How People Choose*, London: Methuen.

Yu, J., Albaum, G. and Swenson, M. (2003) 'Is central tendency error inherent in the use of semantic differential scales in different cultures?', *International Journal of Market Research*, 45, 3, pp. 213–28.

Part III **GETTING ON AND FINISHING UP**

Chapter 10

MANAGING A RESEARCH PROJECT

Introduction

In Chapters 3 and 4 we looked at the process of starting a research project – defining the problem, preparing the brief and writing the proposal. We now pick up the process again, moving on to what happens once the research has been commissioned. The aim of the chapter is to take you through what is involved in running a research project, from organising fieldwork to organising and specifying data processing and checking the data. The detail of what to do with the data – how to analyse them and present or report them – is covered in the remaining chapters, Chapters 11 to 14.

Topics covered

- Making it happen
- Organising fieldwork
- Checking the viability of the data collection tool
- Briefing interviewers and recruiters
- Organising data processing
- Overview of the analysis process
- Checking and reporting progress

Relationship to MRS Advanced Certificate Syllabus

The material covered in this chapter is relevant to almost the whole syllabus: it should help you see the links in the chain from the brief and proposal stage of a project through to the production of the data; it should help you understand better the role of the various people involved at each stage; and it should give you an understanding of how to manage a project.

Learning outcomes

At the end of this chapter you should be able to:

- understand and manage the day-to-day requirements of a project;
- brief the fieldwork supplier;

- brief interviewers and recruiters;
- conduct a pilot study;
- organise data processing;
- prepare a data processing specification;
- check data tables.

Making it happen

It is important that what was requested in the brief and what you promised in the proposal and in discussion with the client is turned into an effective research plan that is carried out efficiently. There may be practical concerns that you could not have anticipated when you wrote the proposal. For example, the client may have requested changes that affect the cost and/or the design; your preferred fieldwork dates might clash with a major holiday period among the target population; the length of the interview or the agreed sample size may have implications for fieldwork and data processing. The role of the research executive at this stage in the process (Box 10.1) is to communicate what is needed to those who can make it happen. In other words, you need to talk to the fieldwork supplier, the data processing and analysis supplier and other members of the research team. You need to ensure that everyone involved with the project is clear about what is required. Much of the thinking about the research design and the research plan will have been completed at the proposal stage, and the feasibility of it will have been discussed with field and data processing suppliers; the task now is to turn the thinking into action.

Box 10.1 Running a project: the research executive's role

Once a project gets under way the research executive becomes the pivotal person in the research team. The research executive is responsible for liaising with those who commissioned the research and those who are involved in executing the fieldwork and processing the data. The level of responsibility or autonomy will depend on seniority and experience. The tasks will include the following:

- administering the project on a day-to-day basis, checking progress, answering queries from field, DP, the client;
- making contributions to discussions about questionnaire/discussion guide design;
- laying out the questionnaire/discussion guide;
- briefing and liaising with the fieldwork supplier on the set-up of fieldwork;
- preparing interviewer or recruiter briefing notes;
- briefing and liaising with the DP supplier about the questionnaire script, coding and data processing;
- liaising with the client about preparation and delivery of stimulus material;
- checking the accuracy of data tables;
- listening to tapes and preparing transcripts and notes;
- interpreting the data;
- preparing presentations and draft reports;
- liaising with the client about progress, meetings, presentation and report.

PROJECT MANAGEMENT: LOOKING AT THE BIGGER PICTURE

It is perhaps worth at this point stepping back from what are the day-to-day tasks and taking a look at the bigger project managment picture and what is involved in that.

Project start: client to agency

In the first instance the client tells the researcher the following, usually in the form of a written brief:

- what the end product of the research must be (the information needs, the research objectives, the outputs);
- what the project resources are (in effect, the budget);
- the time constraints;
- the risks – which are acceptable and which are not.

Once the agency has taken on the project, these four things become the responsibility of the project manager. Depending on the size and scope of the project, the project manager may be an independent consultant/researcher supplier or the director, associate director or senior research executive within a research agency or consultancy.

The role of project manager

The role of the project manager is therefore to:

- Understand the aims and specific objectives of the project.
- Understand the constraints (time, money, risk etc) of the project.
- Draw up a risk management strategy (a plan for handling what can go wrong).
- Draw up a project workplan that will achieve the aims and objectives within the constraints.
- Understand what has to be done – identify the work tasks.
- Allocate clear and well-defined roles to team members.
- Monitor and review progress.
- Adjust the project workplan when necessary.
- Keep all involved in the project informed of progress.

Identifying the risks or pitfalls

Here are some of the likely risks that you may encounter during the life of a research project:

- Not having a clear and accurate definition of the business and/or research problem.
- Failing to understand client brief/client research needs.
- Being given an unrealistic budget and/or timings.
- The client changing his or her requirements once the project has been commissioned.
- Not having enough staff to run the project.
- Not having the right key skills and/or knowledge within the project team.
- Choosing the wrong research design.
- Setting unrealistic targets (e.g. for the sample).
- The client failing to meet requests (e.g. for sample lists, stimulus material).
- The breakdown of the agency/client relationship.

Having a risk management strategy means that you identify the likely risks in advance and that you work out a plan to prevent or control them.

Project management tools

There are two main types of project management tool: the type that helps you work out the most effective project plan; and the type that helps you communicate the plan to all those involved. You have already come across several of these in Chapter 4: the research proposal – in effect this is an early project plan, making clear to the client and to the project team members what is involved in the project; the project start meeting – a meeting at which the project manager briefs the project team in detail about the project and how it will run and answers any questions about key issues including roles, responsibilities and timings; the project timetable, which sets out key dates or milestones in the life of the project and may take the form of a critical path analysis chart, a project evaluation and review technique (PERT) chart, or a Gantt chart (see the example in Chapter 4); a costing schedule or grid showing the budget available for each part of the project. Other useful project management tools include the sampling plan (see Chapter 8) and the briefing documents you will see in this chapter.

Communication

The key element in running a project well is effective communication. A good project manager should help all involved to do the following:

- understand the project and its aims and objectives;
- understand how these aims and objectives are to be achieved;
- understand their role in achieving these aims and objectives.

In addition, the effective project manager will share information with the client and with those involved in different aspects of the work on how the project is progressing in relation to the aims and objectives.

Leadership

Part of what is involved here is leadership – the process by which we influence others to achieve a goal. To be a good leader you should:

- know your own job;
- be familiar with the tasks of others involved in the project;
- ensure that all involved understand what must be achieved;
- support them to achieve it;
- set an example;
- take responsibility for your actions – if things go wrong, assess the situation, take action and move on – do not blame others;
- make sound and timely decisions;
- keep everyone informed;
- use the full range of resources available to you.

Managing resources

Project resources are typically time and money – money in this case being the project budget assigned by the client at the briefing stage and allocated to various tasks by the researcher or agency when preparing the proposal and planning the work. Once a project plan and a project team are in place there is a job to do in managing time and money effectively, ensuring that all tasks and activities undertaken are moving you towards achieving the aims and objectives of the project.

Managing the budget

You may not always be in charge of the entire project budget but you may have responsibility for part of it – and you will certainly be responsible, if not accountable, for the part of it that has been assigned to the task that you have been given. For example, this might be the design of the questionnaire, the analysis or the preparation of the report or presentation. Here are some useful things you can do to help you get to grips with and manage the budget:

- If you are the project leader, inform team members about the budget allocated for their tasks.
- If you are a team member, ask about the budget allocated to your tasks.
- Find out how long key tasks take or have taken in the past (make use of information on costs of previous – similar – jobs to cost this job).
- Be clear about where the costs in your part of the project lie and be clear about how you or your project manager reached them.
- Agree a realistic budget for the work requested.
- Assess and discuss the risk of overruns and, if possible, agree a contingency.
- Inform your project leader and/or the client about the costs involved in additional work requests.
- Monitor your spend against the budget set.
- If you detect an overrun or you think a budget overrun is likely, assess the situation and take appropriate action as soon as possible.

Managing your time

In the context of managing your time on a particular project, some useful approaches include the following:

- Prepare a list of the tasks you need to complete each day.
- Prioritise – list and then tackle the tasks in order of importance.
- Acknowledge when a task has been completed.
- Assign or delegate tasks where appropriate.
- Get on with what you have to do.

We look briefly at time management again at the end of the chapter in terms of managing your overall workload – it is, of course, likely that you will be working on more than one project at once.

Organising fieldwork

Typically the first step, once a job has been commissioned and the details agreed with the client, is to brief the fieldwork supplier in detail about what is required.

BRIEFING FIELD

When preparing the proposal you will have discussed the feasibility of the research design with the fieldwork supplier. The fieldwork will have been costed based on assumptions about the incidence of the target sample in the wider population; ease of identifying or approaching the target sample; the nature and length of the interview and the number of interviews that an interviewer could achieve in one shift (the strike rate); and the total number of interviews needed. Now that the proposal has been accepted it is important to confirm the details, including fieldwork start and finish dates, with the field supplier and to discuss any changes that may have been made to the original plan which may affect cost, timing or level of staffing needed. The fieldwork supplier should be clear about exactly what is required before the fieldwork is booked. The questions you will need to be able to answer about fieldwork are given in Box 10.2. This is not an exhaustive list – questions will arise that are specific to types of projects, for example a product or advertising test, and to individual projects.

Box 10.2 Preparing a briefing for field

- What type of job is it? What is the research design?
- Is it an ad hoc project or is it continuous? Does it consist of phases? For example, an exploratory qualitative phase followed by a quantitative survey?
- What methods of data collection are involved? Qualitative or quantitative or both? Group discussions or accompanied shopping? Face-to-face or telephone interviews?
- What research locations are needed? If more than one country, how is this to be managed?
- What equipment is needed (e.g. computer workstations)?
- What is the target population? What is the incidence in the general population?
- What type of sampling procedure is to be used?
- What sample size is required?
- Is there a suitable sampling frame?
- How long is the questionnaire or discussion guide?
- What stimulus material or test product is needed? Who is to provide it?
- What is the turnaround time from start of fieldwork to delivery of data?
- Have similar jobs been done in the past? What did we learn from those?
- If it is a repeat of a previous job, what implications does this have, for example in terms of the questionnaire or the recruitment screener, the use of sampling points or fieldwork locations, or particular interviewers?
- Is there to be a face-to-face interviewer briefing session (with client service and the client)?
- Will the client be attending or observing/listening to fieldwork?
- How will completed questionnaires or data files be transferred to the data processing supplier?

For a multi-country project or one that involves international fieldwork, to avoid any misunderstandings it is important that the briefing is as detailed and thorough as possible. The number and detail of the briefings you give may depend on how the fieldwork is to be organised. If it is to be undertaken by a local supplier in each country you may need to prepare separate, specific briefings, ensuring that you are consistent across countries if data are to be compared or combined. If it is to be co-ordinated centrally by one supplier one main briefing document may suffice, with perhaps some notes about special requirements by country.

SHELL INTERNATIONAL: CENTRAL VERSUS LOCAL

In this case study Rosemary Childs of the oil company, Shell International, describes her approach to international research.

Why this case study is worth reading

This case study is worth reading for several reasons: it is an example of how a multinational corporation approaches international research; it examines two main approaches – buying research centrally and buying it locally – and gives the benefits and disadvantages of each; it outlines the responsibilities of the co-ordinator and the suppliers in the research process; it highlights the links between elements of the research process and the importance of understanding the client's needs and the research task.

The key words are: research buying centrally or locally, rules, frameworks, consistency, value, risk, downsides, local context, common core, centrally co-ordinated, marketing perspective, research perspective, sensitive, local suppliers, cultures, insight.

Introduction: setting rules or frameworks

Many companies run their research buying centrally or locally around a set of fairly strict rules and frameworks (even prescribing questions to be asked). This ensures a high level of consistency in coverage and an ease of access to the findings from different countries at the analysis stage, and the value of these cannot be overstated. However, in my view, there are downsides too, in that by being prescriptive you risk preventing the local researchers from thinking about the issue under research, and also you may be applying an approach that is sub-optimal and simply not suitable to the local context. You risk losing some of the sensitivity of the customer understanding you are aiming to collect.

Identifying common elements

My own approach has been not to aim for a set of 'rules' or prescribed questions but rather to identify the areas where research is required and to develop with colleagues in the operating companies a common core of elements to be included within these.

Responsibilities in centrally co-ordinated studies

Where it is beneficial to do so (for reasons of speed, cost, use of proprietary techniques or specialist research suppliers, or complex or unfamiliar techniques, or if a centrally driven marketing initiative is to be researched), centrally co-ordinated studies are run. In these we work with a common supplier, at least for the design, co-ordination and analysis/interpretation of the research. We look to our co-ordinating suppliers to manage this process in the optimal way. They need to have fully understood the task, both from a marketing perspective and a research perspective, in order to give the best advice, choose the most suitable local fieldwork suppliers, and design the approach that will best suit the countries and cultures concerned. It is their responsibility to ensure that the local analysis is sensitive and insightful and that the overall interpretation is a fair reflection of the picture emerging from across the countries. ▶

Using local suppliers: the rationale

Even in centrally co-ordinated studies it is sometimes preferable to use the usual local supplier to conduct the fieldwork, under the briefing, vigilance and guidance of the co-ordinator. This has the advantage of securing a valuable element of ownership within the local [Shell] operating company. It is also appropriate where fieldwork is being locally funded. In a couple of instances we have switched from our local supplier to work with one recommended by the co-ordinating agency in the interests of project flow and effective communication, and to maximise the sensitivity and understanding that is carried through the process. Where the co-ordinating agency has a local contact with which it is used to working, the 'learning curve' is less steep and both parties have more time to concentrate on the project itself, rather than having to learn how to work together effectively.

Source: Adapted from Childs, R. (1996) 'Buying international research', *International Journal of Market Research*, 38, 1, pp. 63–6, www.ijmr.com.

Once all the issues have been discussed and agreed with the fieldwork supplier you need to agree timings and contact details. It is useful to include the following information in a document, which you can circulate among all those directly involved in managing the project:

Summary of key dates for:
- delivery of the final approved version(s) of the questionnaire or recruitment screener;
- delivery of interviewer or recruiter briefing notes;
- interviewer/recruiter briefing session (if appropriate);
- attendance at fieldwork (if appropriate);
- arrival/dispatch of stimulus or other material;
- start of fieldwork;
- close of fieldwork;
- availability of data to the data processing supplier.

Contact details of the person:
- with day-to-day responsibility for the project;
- to whom completed questionnaires or data files should be sent.

GETTING ACCESS TO THE TARGET POPULATION

When fieldwork is to be conducted at a particular site, say an airport or in a particular store, it is necessary to get the permission of the site owner. Gaining access to a sample for most consumer market research projects is, however, relatively easy. Access is fairly open, there are no barriers, and so contacting potential respondents is relatively straightforward (whether they consent to take part in the research is, of course, a different matter). In other types of research, however, particularly in business-to-business and social research, the sample or population can be more difficult to access. Some populations can be 'hidden' or they may be of such a low incidence in the general population that they are hard to reach. The ability to get access to a particular group therefore has implications – for costing, planning and conducting research – and so should not be overlooked. Case study 10.2 below illustrates some of the issues involved.

When potential respondents belong to a vulnerable or relatively hidden group – drug users, the homeless, children, for example, or to a powerful 'elite' group – such as business executives, members of the medical and legal professions, politicians – access can be difficult (see the MRS Code of Conduct and the relevant Guidelines at www.mrs.org.uk). For many elite groups it can be severely limited or even closed. It is often necessary in such cases to get past a 'gatekeeper', a person who protects access to the potential respondent. Negotiations with a gatekeeper may be lengthy and time consuming, and may even be fruitless. It may be necessary to use a sponsor, someone whom the target population respects and trusts, who can allay any suspicions about the research, someone who can recommend the research organisation and help 'sell' the idea of being involved in research to the target group. For example, in his research among executive directors, Winkler (1987) used the Institute of Directors, a professional body representing company directors, as a sponsor in organising group discussions.

CASE STUDY 10.2

FINDING GAY MEN

This short case study shows how researchers got access to a hard to find sample.

Why this case study is worth reading

This case study is worth reading for two main reasons: it is an example of a strategy used to find a hard to reach population; it describes the issues involved.

The key words are: conventional methods, gay clubs and pubs, gaining co-operation, interviewing facilities.

Where and how?

At the time [1986] the vast majority of AIDS cases in Britain had occurred among homosexual men. We anticipated that in conducting our survey we would have only limited success in locating this group by conventional methods. This was borne out in practice.

It was therefore decided to attempt to sample them via known gay clubs and pubs. This raised major potential problems of gaining co-operation both from the owners and managers to set up interviewing facilities, and from clients to spend 40 minutes being interviewed when they had presumably gone out in the evening to enjoy themselves. We enlisted the help of the Terrence Higgins Trust (an AIDS-related charity named after Britain's first AIDS victim) in sample selection and gaining co-operation.

Source: Adapted from Orton, S. and Samuels, J. (1988, 1997) 'What we have learned from researching AIDS', *International Journal of Market Research*, 39, 1, pp. 175–200, www.ijmr.com.

ORGANISING STIMULUS MATERIAL

Many projects, qualitative and quantitative, involve showing material to respondents – for example advertisements, photographs of products or packaging or the products themselves. Think about what stimulus material is needed for the project and discuss with the client who is going to supply or prepare it. For example, if you are researching a new product, the client will need to provide the material; if, however, you are researching an existing product it may be easier for you to shop for it yourself. Make sure that whoever is supplying the material is aware of the fieldwork deadlines so that the material arrives at the fieldwork site or with the fieldwork co-ordination unit in time to be dispatched to interviewers or moderators.

DECIDING ON AN INCENTIVE

As we saw in Chapters 6 and 7, it is common practice in market research to offer an incentive to potential respondents to either encourage them to take part and/or to thank them for taking part. Some people – particularly those in academic social research – do not have a tradition of paying incentives. Anecdotal as well as research evidence suggests it can be useful to offer an incentive: it can save money on sampling and recruitment costs by ensuring that those approached are likely to take part and complete what is asked of them – for example, turning up to a hall test or completing a product test or filling in a self-completion questionnaire – and so it can avoid the need to over-sample and/or rescheduling interviews. Although the size of the incentive does not cover the time the respondent will devote to the research task whatever it is, it does show to some extent that you value his or her time and contribution. In deciding whether or not to offer an incentive, and what type of incentive to offer you must bear in mind the nature of the sample, the nature of the research task (what are you asking the sample to do and how long will it take?) and what is ethically, legally and practically viable to offer. Case study 10.3 below illustrates the decision-making process in choosing an incentive for a postal survey among telecoms users and Box 10.3 shows what the MRS Code of Conduct has to say about incentives.

CASE STUDY 10.3

WHAT'S THE INCENTIVE?

In a large-scale postal survey among its residential customers, non-customers and new customers, the project team for this BT customer satisfaction research gave some consideration to the choice of incentive.

Why this case study is worth reading

This case study is worth reading for several reasons: it describes the thinking underlying the decision about what sort of incentive to offer; it shows the client's and the agency's ideas on the issue; it gives a rationale for the choice of incentive; it describes the effect of the incentive.

The key words are: options, regulatory and practical reasons, prize draws, bill discounts, charity donation, easily communicated, blackmail, disincentive, response rate.

The incentive issue

The issue of incentives was hotly debated during the set-up of the project. Most options had to be rejected for regulatory or practical reasons. Thus neither huge prize draws nor individual discounts on the BT bill could be offered. A donation to charity for each return received was quickly determined as the best option. £1 donation per completed survey seemed to be the most sensible, easily communicated incentive.

It is known that donations to charity can be seen as a two-edged sword – some respondents resent the implication of emotional blackmail. Also, if the charity is not to their liking, it can be a disincentive. The research agency recommended a choice of four charities to cover the full range of likely interests (a health charity, children's charity, old person's charity and animal charity). The published literature suggests that offering a choice can improve the response rate. However, the client, BT Group, had recently decided to focus its charity efforts on a single charity, Childline, and it was determined that all proceeds from the survey would go to Childline. The proposition was tested in early group discussions and hall tests (prior to the postal survey) and proved to be sound. Childline is a charity that appears to be universally acceptable to all age groups and social classes. That said, there is some evidence that the response rate was slightly higher among the young and among women, as a result of the £1 to Childline incentive. However, this was not a bad thing as the young generally have a poorer opinion of BT, and therefore to achieve a good response from this group was helpful to BT's marketing community.

Overall, the incentive was shown by the follow-up research to have had a significant effect on the response rate.

Source: Adapted from Macfarlane, P. (2003) 'Breaking through the boundaries – MR techniques to understand what individual customers really want, and acting on it', MRS Conference, www.mrs.org.uk.

Box 10.3 Professional practice and the MRS Code of Conduct: incentives

B25 Where incentives are offered, Members must clearly inform the Respondent who will administer the incentive.

Comment: Incentives need not be of a monetary nature to be acceptable to a Respondent as a token of appreciation. With the Client's permission, an offer to supply the Respondent with a brief summary report of the project's findings can sometimes prove a better alternative encouragement to participate in a research project. Other alternatives are for example:

- *Charity donations*
- *Non-monetary gifts*
- *Prize draws (for Prize draws the rules, as detailed in the MRS Prize Draws Guidance Note, must be adhered to.)*

Source: MRS Code of Conduct 2005. Used with permission.

Checking the viability of the data collection tool

You will have designed a questionnaire with the research objectives in mind, one that contains questions that are measuring what you think they are measuring and which will collect the kind of evidence you need to address the research problem. It is important to have fieldwork experts (field executive, interviewers and respondents) check it from a data collection and fieldwork management point of view; and a data processing expert check it from a data processing and analysis point of view. The same is largely true for a discussion or topic guide for group discussions and for an interview guide for qualitative in-depth interviews. Besides having it checked by the client to ensure that it will gather the evidence needed to address the research objectives, it is very useful to have it checked by an experienced qualitative researcher – someone with a lot of fieldwork or moderation experience.

CHECKING IT OUT WITH THE FIELDWORK SUPPLIER

Have the questionnaire (or discussion guide) approved by a fieldwork expert before it goes to the client for approval (and before it goes into the field). (The equivalent of the 'field' executive in qualitative research is someone with experience as a moderator or interviewer in the type of research you are planning.) Get field to check it as soon as you have what you think is a reasonable draft version. Leaving it too close to the fieldwork start date or until you have agreed a final version with the client may mean that you have little or no time to make any changes. The consequences of this could be costly and embarrassing – you may have to delay fieldwork, and your reputation may suffer. The field executive examines the questionnaire with the respondent and the interviewer in mind:

- Is the questionnaire the right length for achieving the strike rate on which the costing and timings are based? (If not, questions will need to be removed or modified, or the job recosted and timings renegotiated to reflect the lower strike rate.)
- Is it likely to overburden the respondent? Are all the questions necessary? Do they require too much effort of the respondent? Might they overtax the respondent's memory?
- Do the questions make sense? Are they clear and unambiguous?
- Is the language suitable for the sample? For example, will all the respondents in a business survey understand the jargon or technical/business language used? Will younger respondents grasp the meaning of the rating scales?
- Is the balance of questions right? Are there too many dull and repetitive questions? If you are using a grid, an image grid for example, it is advisable to keep the number of statements to about 12, otherwise both respondent and interviewer will be bored and data quality may be affected.
- Is the content relevant to the sample? Are the questions or topics within the respondent's frame of reference? Will the respondent be able to articulate an answer?
- Is the order or flow of questions logical, with no unexpected jumps or changes of subject?
- Are instructions to respondents and/or to interviewers in the right place?
- Are instructions to respondents and/or to interviewers easy to follow?
- Has the questionnaire (the program in computer-aided questionnaires) been set up so that order bias is minimised, for example by using tick starts or by rotating the start order in lists and grids?
- How many versions of the questionnaire are there? What are the differences between the versions and how are they to be administered?
- Is the self-completion questionnaire or form laid out clearly so that it is easy for the respondent to fill it in?
- For paper questionnaires, are the page breaks in convenient places?

CHECKING IT OUT WITH DP

The questionnaire must also be checked and approved for data processing by a DP expert. It is good practice to do this as soon as you have a final draft that has been checked and/or piloted by the fieldwork specialist. There is no point asking DP to check it if there is a possibility that field might tell you that some questions will not work, for example. The DP executive will ensure that the questionnaire is coded correctly – that it contains all the information necessary to turn completed questionnaires into tables – and that it is set out in a way that makes coding and data entry as efficient as possible. If the questionnaire is to have several versions, aim to get the main version checked and approved before creating other versions. This will save you having to make changes to all versions of the questionnaire.

FINALISING THE QUESTIONNAIRE

It is important that the final version of a questionnaire is checked and approved for use by the client, by field and by DP. A questionnaire in particular may change a lot during the design process. It is useful to have a fresh pair of eyes check it, as those previously involved may be too used to it. If this is not possible create a checklist of comments and suggested changes, changes made throughout the design process, and refer back to this list to make sure that all of them have been implemented correctly. In addition, make a final check to ensure that the questionnaire or discussion guide addresses the objectives set out in the brief, and that each question is measuring what you think it is measuring. With a questionnaire, make sure that it meets the standards set out in Chapter 9. Check that all the necessary administrative and instructional details are correct:

- project number;
- space to record serial numbers and interviewer numbers;
- all questions and parts of questions numbered correctly;
- all routing instructions complete and easy to follow;
- interviewer and/or respondent instructions complete and easy to follow;
- all codes correct;
- all versions correct.

Translations

On international projects the questionnaire or discussion guide should be translated once you have approval of the original version (from field, data processing and the client). To make the translation process as efficient as possible try to ensure that a native speaker with a sound knowledge of research prepares the first translation of the questionnaire or discussion guide, and the back-translation.

Box 10.4 The role of the co-ordinator in multi-country research

Michael Wilsdon, Apex International Research, deseribes the role of a co-ordinator:
   The co-ordinator's role is analogous in many ways to a project manager in, say, the construction industry, controlling bought-in services from a range of sub-contractors, and with overall responsibility from Day 1 to completion. The role combines the functions of research buyer and research supplier. For the end user, the final client, the co-ordinating agency is the supplier; for the fieldwork and other sub-contractors, the co-ordinating agency is their client.
   A fairly typical selection of operational matters with which the co-ordinating manager has to deal are:

- *Cultural diversity* – for example creating an image battery that will work in Britain, Spain, Thailand and Taiwan; careful questionnaire development and close collaboration with the local supplier are needed before fieldwork begins.
- *Language problems* – most are dealt with by correct translation routines but hazards can emerge.

▶

- *Sampling* – most suppliers have an adequate system of achieving representative consumer samples but these sometimes come unstuck in the execution; there are problems of imposing a sampling method that the supplier does not normally use.
- *Fieldwork organisation* – the variety of ways of organising interviews, even within Europe, is a problem for the co-ordinator seeking a degree of uniformity in – for example – interviewer briefing.
- *Data preparation and entry* – it is wise to have data preparation and entry done by the local research agencies; the co-ordinator prepares the multi-country code book and writes the edit program with all the right logic checks and provides clear and detailed instructions.

Source: Adapted from Wilsdon, M. (1996) 'Getting it done properly: the role of the co-ordinator in multi-country research', *International Journal of Market Research*, 38, 1, pp. 67–71, www.ijmr.com.

Briefing interviewers and recruiters

The instructions that appear on a questionnaire are there to show the interviewer around the questionnaire, and to show where the respondent should be probed or prompted. Most questionnaires will also be accompanied by a set of more detailed interviewer briefing notes and in some cases the field and client service executives and the client may run a face-to-face briefing. We look at both in this section.

WRITING INTERVIEWER BRIEFING NOTES

The aim of these briefing notes is to give the interviewer a greater understanding of the purpose of the research, the questionnaire as a whole and the specific questions or topics within it. Briefing notes may include information under the following headings:

- *Introduction and background to the research* – An introduction to the research that may include a summary of the research objectives.
- *Contents of the interviewers' work pack* – A list of the contents of the work pack. The nature of this list will depend on the nature of the research (product or advertising research, attitude survey, recruitment screener) and the method of data collection (telephone, face to face, CATI, CAPI). It may list, for example, 'Thank you' letters or notes for respondents, incentives, stimulus material or show cards, a quota sheet, address lists or area maps, questionnaires, contact record forms, return of work forms, pay claims.
- *Importance of the briefing notes* – A short statement emphasising the importance of reading the notes and being familiar with the questionnaire before starting fieldwork.
- *Fieldwork location and sampling area (if appropriate)* – Details of the geographic area in which the interviewer or recruiter must work, for example a particular postal district or town.
- *Sampling practice or procedure* – Details of how the sample is to be drawn, for example use of Kish Grids or random route, random digit dialling, details of quota controls, if appropriate, for example in terms of age, sex and social class.
- *Details of specific eligibility criteria* – A description of the type and range of respondents needed. For example: 'The respondent must be a domestic user of the service and not a commercial or business user; the respondent should be the person mainly or jointly

responsible for making decisions about telephone and Internet Service Provider services and paying the telephone and ISP bills.'

■ *Details of how to present the research to potential respondents* – A description of the research and information on the length of the interview and a reminder about confidentiality, anonymity and data protection issues and guidance on how to handle queries about the research, for example the end use of the research, the client's name, contact details of the fieldwork supplier.

■ *Detailed questionnaire instructions* – A question-by-question guide to the questionnaire or screener. This should include (as appropriate) the use of show cards, stimulus material or self-completion elements, and a reiteration of questionnaire instructions including routing and skips, instructions for probing and clarification, and recording of answers verbatim, details of questions that are multiple response and those that are 'one code only'. There should be instructions for checking and editing the questionnaires at the end of each interview.

■ *Any ethical, legal or Code of Conduct/Code of Practice issues* – A note on, for example, data protection and the need to be open about the purpose of the survey and the need to establish informed consent. Or, for example, if the sample comprises children, details about the need for obtaining informed consent from the parent or responsible adult, while at the same time making sure the child has the chance to decline to take part.

■ *Details of incentives for participants* – A description of the incentive, and how it is to be delivered, for example whether it is included in the work pack or is being mailed out, details of when the respondent should expect to receive it.

■ *Fieldwork timings* – Details of when to begin fieldwork and when to complete it.

■ *Return of work arrangements* – Details of how the completed work should be returned, to whom and by what date.

■ *Project management issues* – Contact details of the person responsible for handling any queries that might arise, for example eligibility of particular respondents, difficulties in filling a quota, queries about a particular question or topic.

■ *Thanks* – A note of thanks for accepting the project should be included.

In addition, if interviewers are out in the field conducting fieldwork on their own, training and briefing will need to cover the issues of risk and safety. This includes, for example, identifying and addressing risk of physical harm or physical threat or psychological harm (as a result of what is disclosed during an interview, see Box 10.7 below for an example) and the risk of causing physical or psychological harm to others as well as the risk of being in a situation where one is open to accusations of improper behaviour. Safety when working is the joint responsibility of employer and employee. Organisations employing interviewers have a duty of care to them under health and safety at work legislation and should therefore have policies in place to address these issues with procedures and guidelines. A useful source of further information is *The Code of Practice for the Safety of Social Researchers* published by the Social Research Association (2001) (www.the-sra.org.uk).

Below in Box 10.6 is an extract from a set of briefing notes for a social and political attitude survey, the *Life and Times Survey*, which has been conducted on an annual basis in Northern Ireland since 1998. Survey interviews are conducted face to face in the respondent's home using CAPI and CASI. A copy of the questionnaire to which these notes relate, the 2004 questionnaire, can be downloaded from the Life and Times website, www.ark.ac.uk/nilt. These notes should give you an idea of the sort of thing that briefing notes address – the type of background explanation that can be useful to interviewers. They provide information to interviewers about the nature of the survey and about how the data they collect will be used. They also highlight important ethical issues about the conduct of research.

Box 10.5 Professional practice and the MRS Code of Conduct: fieldwork

At this stage of the research process – planning and conducting fieldwork – the focus of the MRS Code of Conduct is on the rights of respondents and thus on what those planning the fieldwork and those conducting it must do in this regard. Reading the rules below you will see that the emphasis is on the following ethical principles – voluntary participation, no harm to participants, informed consent, anonymity/confidentiality and transparency (see Chapter 1 for detail). There are, in addition to the rules below, specific rules in relation to research with children and specific rules for various sorts of data collection method – observation, mystery shopping and qualitative research, which we looked at in Chapters 6 and 7.

B15 If there is to be any recording, monitoring or observation during an interview, Respondents must be informed about this both at recruitment and at the beginning of the interview.

B16 Members must not knowingly make use of personal data collected illegally.

B17 Respondents must not be misled when being asked for co-operation to participate in a research project.

B18 A Respondent's right to withdraw from a research project at any stage must be respected.

B19 Members must ensure that Respondents are able to check without difficulty the identity and bona fides of any individual and/or their employer conducting a research project (including any sub-contractors).

B20 For telephone and face-to-face interviews, calls must not be made to a household (local time) before 9am weekdays and Saturdays, 10am Sundays or after 9pm any day, unless by appointment.

B21 Members must ensure that all of the following are clearly communicated to the Respondent:
- the name of the interviewer (an Interviewer's Identity Card must be shown if face to face);
- an assurance that the interview will be carried out according to the MRS Code of Conduct;
- the general subject of the interview;
- the purpose of the interview;
- if asked, the likely length of the interview;
- any costs likely to be incurred by the Respondent.

B22 Respondents (including employees in employee research) must not be unduly pressurised to participate.

B23 Members must delete any responses given by the Respondent, if requested, and if this is reasonable and practicable.

B24 Recruiters/interviewers must not reveal to any other Respondents the detailed answers provided by any Respondent or the identity of any other Respondent interviewed.

Source: MRS Code of Conduct 2005. Used with permission.

Box 10.6 Extract from 'Notes for interviewers: Life and Times Survey 2004'

The *Life and Times Survey* is the leading independent source of information on what Northern Ireland people think about a wide range of social and political issues. Carried out annually by the University of Ulster and Queen's University since 1998, the survey is relied upon by policymakers in government and academics in universities when looking at attitudes to important social and political issues. The questionnaire to which these notes refer is at www.ark.ac.uk/nilt/quests/.

General points
This is largely a survey of attitudes so there will always be questions where the respondent really doesn't know or doesn't have a view about a particular topic. While we don't want you to *offer* the 'Don't know' option in any of the questions, it is quite acceptable to code 'Don't know' answers to attitude questions, rather than try and force the respondent to choose one of the other answer codes.

Section 1: Introductory questions
These are general questions that are meant to provide an easy lead-in to the main body of the questionnaire. They are almost identical to those in previous years.

Section 2: Men's life and times
While most people in the UK could probably make a reasonably good attempt at describing what 'women's issues' are – most would still find it very difficult to comprehend what 'men's issues' are, what they might include or, indeed, why we should even be bothered about this question in the first place. But the world of local men and boys is still, definitely, at the edge of our understanding. There is very little scientifically rigorous, academic research into males' needs, issues, values, attitudes and life experiences . . . This module is funded by the Office of the First Minister and Deputy First Minister. We have worked closely with both them and the Parents' Advice Centre in the design of these questions.

Section 3: Grandparenting and family life
Last year the Life and Times Survey ran a module looking at the extent of prejudice against older people and whether or not older people were being actively discriminated against. This year we look at another aspect of life for older people and are interested in the extent to which older people 'contribute' both socially and economically to the fabric of our daily lives. For example, in their role as grandparents, some older people contribute quite extensively to the economy by providing childcare for grandchildren. In more general terms, the extent to which older people contribute to family life and kinship networks, and the extent to which they provide a rescue service at times of family breakdown and for childcare needs is of great interest to researchers. The module also includes a set of questions for all respondents (whether they are grandparents or not) on whether they are involved in 'caring' for a family member or someone else outside the family. Again we are primarily interested in the extent to which *older* people are increasingly involved in ▶

caring for spouses and other relatives. Overall, the key social policy interest for this module is in the ways in which older people support their families, the services they provide, the money they save the State and their own feelings about their role. The module is funded by *Atlantic Philanthropies* who have embarked on a major programme on ageing and ageism in Ireland, North and South.

Section 4: Community relations
These questions are funded by the *Community Relations Unit* within the Office of the First Minister and Deputy First Minister. The first 16 questions have been asked before and will be familiar to many interviewers. They cover general questions about whether community relations are improving or not, as well as attitudes to mixed marriages. The second part of the module covers attitudes to the flying of flags and the extent to which work and local environments are perceived as 'neutral spaces'.

Section 5: Countryside and farming
One of the key topics to be covered this year is attitudes to the countryside and farming in Northern Ireland. We have been working closely with academics at Queen's University in developing this module. Agriculture is a very important part of the life and economy of Northern Ireland, but the BSE and Foot and Mouth crises have affected farmers very badly in recent years. The module asks the general public about their views on farming, and the countryside in general. In particular, given the problems facing farmers in the last few years, should farmers be taking on new roles? The results of the survey will inform public and policy debates, such as the reform of the Common Agricultural Policy. The study will also provide benchmark and monitoring data for Northern Ireland against which change in attitudes over time towards the countryside can be measured. These questions are funded jointly by the Economic and Social Research Council and the Ulster Farmers' Union. The press release which announces the launch of NILT 2004 highlights this module in particular.

Section 6: Political attitudes
The opening questions in this module are standard questions that have been used on NILT for many years now. However, the majority of the module covers an entirely new area focusing on the legacy of 'the Troubles'. There has been much discussion in recent years over whether Northern Ireland should have some sort of 'Truth Commision' – an inquiry where everyone would have to tell the truth about the conflict. These questions are designed to assess whether the public thinks that we should have a Truth Commission, what it should look like if we did have one, and who should run it. We are working closely with academics at the University of Ulster on this module and the results will be used both in academic papers, and to feed into the more public debate around this issue. So far, nobody has assessed public opinion quite as extensively as this. Note that there are a number of questions at the end of this module asking respondents about their own experiences as 'victims' of the Troubles. We have supplied you with leaflets to leave with all respondents which give the telephone numbers of various 'helplines' for victims. While the questions do not probe for details about individual experiences, it is nonetheless possible that some people might be upset answering these questions and we do not want to leave people without some kind of support – if this is the case.

As always with this module, it is important to stress the role of the two Northern Ireland universities in ensuring that there is *independent* and *publicly available* information about political attitudes in Northern Ireland.

Section 7: Background

This is largely the same as last year's survey and again includes the question on 'sexual orientation' – that is, whether people would describe themselves as heterosexual, homosexual, or bisexual. This question has worked well for several consecutive years now and it is encouraging that other surveys are also beginning to include the question routinely. However, it is important that you understand exactly why we are asking the question, so that you can address any concerns that the respondent may have.

Legislation introduced in Northern Ireland now requires that public sector bodies review their efforts to help bring about equality between all sections of society. An important aspect of the new law is that it covers equality between people of different sexual orientations. Therefore, we now ask about sexual orientation for the same reason that we have always asked people what religion they are, and whether or not they have any disabilities – so that we know that the views and experiences of all groups of people are properly represented in the survey . . .

Data protection issues

You will notice that the survey formally asks respondents if they understand the purpose of the survey and agree to take part. We must obtain this 'informed consent' in order to abide by the terms of the Data Protection Act.

You must be completely open about why we are doing the survey. The survey is used *mainly* for research purposes at universities in Northern Ireland and beyond. However, we also make the results publicly available on the Internet so that everyone with an interest in public opinion can refer to them. In fact the biggest users (after university researchers and the government) are journalists, students and school children. The survey is now well recognised as an authoritative and independent source of statistical information on Northern Ireland. It is important that people understand that the results are only ever made available in an *anonymised* form.

Source: The Life and Times Survey Team at the University of Ulster and Queen's University Belfast (2004). Used with permission.

GIVING AN INTERVIEWER BRIEFING

Sometimes it is necessary to run a face-to-face briefing session for interviewers and/or supervisors to discuss issues around sampling and recruitment as well as interviewing and the interviewer–respondent relationship. These sessions may involve the client, the field executive and the client service researcher. The client or the client service executive briefs the interviewers about the background to the project, explaining the need for the information and the use to which it will be put. Particular features of the product, service or brand that is the subject of the research may also be described. The field executive and/or the client service executive briefs the interviewers about the specifics of recruitment or sampling, how to get access to respondents, and how to introduce the research. They will demonstrate how to administer the questionnaire by reading out each question or by setting up a mock interview. Interviewers and/or supervisors conduct a pretend interview themselves in order to familiarise themselves with how the questions work, and to get used to handling stimulus material. Supervisors can repeat the briefing session with interviewers in their fieldwork location. Besides briefing the fieldforce, a personal briefing session is a good way of demonstrating to the client the rigorous and quality-conscious approach adopted by the supplier.

Box 10.7 Example of a briefing on a sensitive subject

Below the researchers discuss the interviewer briefing session for a research project on the sensitive subject of child abuse and neglect. (See also Case study 9.5 in which the authors discuss pilot testing the questionnaire for this project.)

Interviewer briefing
Though the research agency's interviewers are used to conducting surveys on health, crime and other sensitive subjects, the issue of child abuse is possibly the most sensitive subject of all. This sensitivity relates not only to the interviewer/respondent relationship, but potentially to the interviewers themselves. We were aware from the beginning that, with several hundred interviewers working on the survey, it was likely that the subject matter would raise difficult personal issues for some.

The briefings therefore included a session introducing the subject of child abuse, placing it in its historical and contemporary context. We were deliberately explicit in briefings about the fact that it was likely that, in the room of 20–30 people, one or more may have personal experience of abuse. The client, the National Society for the Prevention of Cruelty to Children (NSPCC), had supplied us with helpline information to be left with respondents but asked us to make it clear to interviewers that this service was also available to them if required.

It is standard practice to include an examination of the questionnaire at interviewer briefings. In this case we took particular care to make sure that it was thoroughly examined, as we wanted all interviewers to be absolutely clear about the nature of the questions, in both the interviewer-completed sections and the self-keyed sections. At the end, we assured interviewers that there was no compulsion to work on this project if they did not feel comfortable with the questions.

Source: Adapted from Brooker, S., Cawson, P., Kelly, G. and Wattam, C. (2001) 'The prevalence of child abuse and neglect: a survey of young people', MRS Conference, www.mrs.org.uk.

Organising data processing

In this section we look at the four key tasks in relation to quantitative data processing:

- checking and editing questionnaires;
- coding;
- specifying the output from data processing;
- checking the output.

In a research agency these tasks are typically the responsibility of the data processing executive or analyst and the research executive. Some of the material presented here assumes an understanding of the basics of data analysis – in particular, an understanding of how data from a questionnaire are translated into data tables and an understanding of those data tables, sometimes known as cross-tabulations or cross-tabs. If some or all of this is unfamiliar to you then we recommend that you read Chapter 12.

CHECKING AND EDITING QUESTIONNAIRES

To ensure good quality, data questionnaires are typically checked and edited, first of all in the field, and then again back at the office. Have a look at Chapter 12 for detail on the sort of errors and inconsistencies that the checking and editing process aims to eliminate.

Checking and editing in the field

The process should begin as soon as possible after a questionnaire is completed. It should be checked to ensure that each question relevant to the respondent has been asked and a response coded and that no elements of the interview are missing, for example a self-completion sheet or a page from the questionnaire. Checks should be made to ensure that routing instructions have been followed correctly (particularly important for self-completion questionnaires). In computer-based data collection these sorts of checks are typically built into the program and so are handled automatically; paper questionnaires are checked by the interviewer or fieldwork supervisor or by an office-based editor. In addition to checking the completeness of the questionnaire, the quality of responses should be examined. For example, responses to open-ended questions should be reviewed in order to ensure that probing was conducted in the manner set out in the briefing notes or instructions. Checks should also be made to ensure that the respondent was eligible to take part in the research and the sample composition should be monitored on an ongoing basis and checked at the close of fieldwork, to ensure that the original sample specifications have been met. If they have not, the fieldwork supervisors can arrange for the completion of additional interviews. Editors and 'back-checkers' make further quality control checks as questionnaires are returned from the field or downloaded to the data processing server. Most organisations conduct a '100 per cent verification', that is, all codes on all questionnaires are re-entered and the original entry and re-entry sets checked against each other.

If your project involves paper questionnaires discuss with the field executive and/or make a note in the interviewer briefing notes about the sort of checks you want done. For projects involving computer-based data capture check that the program contains the necessary checks; if you also want manual checks carried out specify this in the interviewer briefing notes.

Dealing with inadequate or incomplete data during data processing

You may need to give the data processing team instructions about how to handle whatever errors or inconsistencies remain in the data on completion of fieldwork. Inadequate or incomplete data can be dealt with in a number of ways. Incomplete questionnaires or those containing poor quality data can be excluded from analysis. Removing cases from the sample, however, biases the findings (the cases removed may differ significantly in profile from other cases) and if this course of action is taken the procedure should be clearly documented and the effect on the sample checked. It can be appropriate, particularly when large amounts of data or vital elements of a case are missing; and it may have a limited effect if the total sample is large and the number of cases removed relatively small. Another option is to recontact respondents to obtain the missing data or clarify responses. This can be relatively straight-forward but to be effective it should be done as soon as possible, to ensure that the time lapse does not influence the response. If possible, the respondent should be recontacted or reinter-viewed using the same method of data collection as was used originally. Since it may not be advisable to remove a case from the sample or possible to recontact a respondent, missing data may be dealt with during data processing, in ways outlined in Chapter 12: assigning a code to the missing value; performing a pairwise deletion; or imputing a value. If missing values remain at the end of the fieldwork checking and editing process, tell the data processing department how you would like them to be treated. Decide which option is most appropriate and include details on the data processing specification (DP spec).

The data processing specification is the document that sets out the way in which you want the data from the questionnaires to be handled and in what format you want the output presented. For those questionnaires that include open-ended questions you also need to set out the way in which responses to these questions are handled or coded. We look at both of these below.

CODING

Coding is the process by which responses from open-ended (non-pre-coded) questions, sometimes called 'verbatims', are analysed and labelled, and given a numeric code so that they can be counted by the analysis program. A coding brief sets out how you want these data handled and a coding frame or code frame provides instructions about how open-ended questions are to be processed.

Preparing a coding brief

To write a good quality coding frame you need first of all to review the background informa-tion on the issue or research topic – this will help you to understand and interpret the responses given on the questionnaire, which can sometimes be ambiguous or unclear. If you are researching a particular market it is a good idea to familiarise yourself with the technical language or jargon that respondents might use as well as the key issues in that market. If the focus of the research is a particular product range it is worth having a look at the products or brands, even using or tasting them. If the research is about the quality of service provision find out what the key drivers are. If it involves advertising it is worth reviewing the advertisements so that you understand to which advertisement or brand a respondent is referring. If you are not directly involved with the nitty-gritty of the coding process then ensure this material is available to the coders. You may want to summarise this information in a coding brief, in which you could also include a draft coding frame, listing what you think might be important codes, to ensure that the coders are aware of the key issues to look for in the verbatims.

Sometimes respondents may not give the answer to a question when you ask it but at a later stage in the interview, in answer to another question. To ensure that no information is lost you can ask the coders to check for this (by reading through the entire questionnaire) and 'back-code' such responses to the relevant question. It may also be important in terms of the objectives of the project to get an understanding of each respondent's overall reaction to the research topic (for example an advertisement, a product, a service or a social issue). To do this the coders must read the whole questionnaire and code or classify each respondent according to their response, for example in terms of a positive, negative or neutral reaction. It is often important that the detail given at open-ended questions is preserved. You may want to ask for verbatims to be extracted and preserved whole, labelled with key (demographic) data so that you can see what type of respondent said what. Whatever your coding requirements make sure that they are clearly set out in the coding brief.

If the project is a multi-country one in which findings are to be compared on a country-by-country basis it is important to work closely with coders to produce a good quality master coding frame, one that can be used in preparing tables for all countries in the study. The master frame should be built using verbatim comments from questionnaires from all countries, with interpretation and clarification provided by those working in each country. Differences will remain but if frames were developed separately for each country comparisons would be more difficult to make.

Preparing 'extractions'

As questionnaires are returned from the field, responses from each of the open-ended questions and each of the questions with an 'other – please specify' response are extracted and listed, question by question, as individual response items. (This process can be done automatically in a CAPI or CATI system.) For example, a respondent gives the reason for staying with the same utilities provider at the moment as 'I have had no trouble with them and I do not know the track record of other suppliers.' This statement is broken up into its two elements, 'no trouble with them' and 'do not know the track record of other suppliers', each of which is listed in the extractions. The process of extraction continues until the content of what is being extracted does not change – until saturation point is reached and further extraction is not showing new content. A list of 'extractions' from the source material forms the basis of a draft coding frame for each question.

From draft coding frame to final coding frame

The next step is to group together similar responses. For example, in Box 10.8 several extractions refer to knowledge or lack of knowledge about other suppliers. Once grouped together these responses can be examined for differences in meaning, in particular shades of meaning that may need to be distinguished to meet the research objectives. For example, from the list of extractions in Box 10.8, 'I want to find out more about the competition' suggests an active attitude or intention, and it may be important for the client to know what proportion of the sample say that; 'I do not know the track record of other suppliers' suggests inertia; and it may be important to make the distinction between these. On the other hand, it may be that this difference is not important and that both statements could be coded as 'current lack of knowledge about competitors'. Each group of extracted responses should be examined in this way and a code written to represent them. These codes are listed question by question in a draft coding frame, which is approved by the research executive and, in some cases, the client. This draft is used to code the responses from the entire sample. As coding progresses it may be that some responses do not fit into a particular code. These responses are listed as queries and a 'query listing' is sent with the draft coding frame to a query coder with specialist knowledge of the topic or to the client service executive responsible for the survey. If the queries cannot be accommodated in an existing code, a new code may be created. If, in the judgement of the query coder or the research executive, the response is unlikely to occur in many cases, or is of limited interest to the research objectives, it may be placed in an 'other' category. The draft coding frame is updated, and the coding process continues, with perhaps several updates to the frame as queries arise, until all responses from the sample are coded. The final coding frame is used in the data processing program.

Box 10.8 From extractions to coding frame

The question
Q. 'Why have you chosen to stay with your current [utilities] supplier at the moment?'

The list of extractions
I have had no trouble with them.
I want to find out more about the competition.
I do not know enough about other suppliers.
I am waiting to see what happens.
I am too unwell to make a decision.
I cannot be bothered to change.
They have always been my supplier.
I feel safe with them.
I don't think I'd save any money.
I do not know the track record of other suppliers.
The hassle factor.
Other suppliers may not be reliable.
They did a good job fixing a problem.
Better the devil you know.
I have not got around to finding out about the others.
The price difference is not big enough.

The coding frame
Haven't thought about it.
Want to wait and see how things develop.
Satisfied with service provided by current supplier.
Don't feel that others would offer better service.
Satisfied with the price charged by current supplier.
Don't think that there would be any financial saving.
Poor perception of other suppliers.
Don't know enough about other suppliers.
Other.

PREPARING A DATA PROCESSING SPECIFICATION

There are a variety of ways in which data from a questionnaire can be processed. The purpose of the DP spec is to set down clearly, unambiguously and in detail exactly how you want it done. Most organisations have their own house style, perhaps a pro forma on which you write in your requirements. A clear, well thought out DP spec helps DP process the job quickly, accurately and efficiently. In preparing a specification you need to think about how you plan to use the output. This will inform the nature of the output you ask for and its structure. It is therefore important to have completed your analysis plan beforehand. Getting a detailed set of cross-tabulations is relatively easy and it is often quicker to ask for all questions on the questionnaire to be tabulated against every demographic, geodemographic, attitudinal or behavioural variable – in fact any variable you think might be useful as an explanatory variable. Resist the urge to do this – be selective in specifying cross-tabulations, asking only for those tables that are relevant to your analysis plan.

The questions that a DP spec must address include the following:

- What is the job about?
- Who is the client?
- What type of survey is it?
- Are there different versions of the questionnaire?
- What are the deadlines?
- Who wants the tables?
- Is the job/questionnaire the same as or similar to a previous one?
- What output is required? Cross-tabulations, descriptive statistics, inferential statistics, multivariate analysis?

You need to be clear about what it is you want so that you can communicate it clearly to others. Talk to the executives in the DP department or DP bureau in order to get an idea of what is possible – in terms of time, money and output.

Background briefing

To give the data processing executive an idea of the context of the project and the objectives of the survey, a DP spec should contain information on the background to the project. An example is given in Box 10.9. Alternatively, you can give the DP executive a copy of the project brief. This information will enable the DP executive to understand the job better and to make suggestions about processing and analysis options.

Box 10.9 Example of the first page of a DP specification

Background to the survey

The client is conducting a review of the organisation's business strategy in order to produce a new draft business plan. The organisation is currently the main supplier in a market that has changed relatively little in the past ten years or so. Its key products and services have a market share of about 80 per cent. A new competitor, however, has recently entered the market and, although its market share is still relatively low, the client is concerned. Adoption of new technology, which was slow to take hold in the client's market, has gathered pace in the last year and most of the client's target market is now online, connected to the Internet. This presents opportunities for the client – the organisation is considering delivering some of its products and services via this channel. It also presents a threat – market intelligence shows that two competitors have a range of online products and services that are likely to threaten the market for the client's own products and services. As part of the business review and planning process the client wants to assess customer satisfaction with its products and services, and determine interest in delivery of its products and services via the Internet. ▶

Timings

A telephone survey (CATI) is to be conducted among a sample of 400 of the organisation's target market. A copy of the final version is attached. The datafile will be available when fieldwork closes on 24 April. The coding frame will be finalised by 1 May. The research executive needs the tables on 10 May. The tables are due to go out to the client on 15 May. The presentation is scheduled for 25 May with the report a week later. Please contact Joe Bloggs at 0123 345 678 when the tables are ready. Thanks for your help.

General instructions

- Title of the survey and client's name to appear on all pages.
- Tables to be numbered.
- Questions including question numbers to appear in full on each table.
- Rows and columns to be labelled.
- Column percentages to be calculated.
- All tables to be based on total sample including 'Don't knows' except if stated otherwise.
- No weighting is needed.

In a multi-country study cross-tabulations should be designed with the analysis plan in mind. If the aim of the research is to compare data on a country-by-country basis, tables should be set out with each country as the top break, rather than producing a separate set of tables for each country. You may need to decide whether the data should be weighted to reflect market size or population size. Also, consider whether each country will want to see data on their country in isolation or compared to all others. Consider too whether you need to produce tables in different languages.

Cross-breaks or top headings

Specifying how you want variables such as age or social class to appear on the tables is relatively straightforward. For example, on the questionnaire the categories of the 'Age' question may have been 18–24; 25–34; 35–44; and 45–54 and this may be how you want them to be presented in the tables. You would therefore include on the analysis spec the instruction, 'Age × 4 – as questionnaire' – in other words, the age variable split into four categories, as it appears on the questionnaire. For other variables the instructions may be less straightforward and are likely to need a written or visual explanation. For example, you may want responses from a question with an Agree/Disagree scale like this:

Strongly agree	5
Agree	4
Neither agree nor disagree	3
Disagree	2
Strongly disagree	1

to appear as a top break in the tables like this:

Total agree (codes 4 or 5) – all those saying 'Agree' or 'Strongly agree'.
Total disagree (codes 2 or 1) – all those saying 'Disagree' or 'Strongly disagree'.

It is important in designing the banner heading to think of the layout and appearance of the final tables. How many headings can fit across the page without looking untidy, squashed or hard to read? If the top breaks amount to more than one page, decide how you want them split and group them into meaningful sets. The order in which top breaks appear can help in reading the tables. Often it is the demographic breaks – age, sex, class and so on – that appear next to the total column. It may be more useful to have others first, such as heavy users, medium users and light users.

In addition to looking at responses to questions by the demographics or the main banner heading, you may want to see summary tables for grid questions. Summary tables are those in which the brands, for example, used in the grid appear across the top (as the column variable) and the statements appear down the side (the row variable). You may want to show the responses to several questions on one table, for example 'Heard of', and below it on the same table 'Buy now', for ease of comparison. You may want to combine the values of a variable into a summary code or overcode – for example, 'Very satisfied' and 'Fairly satisfied' to 'Totally satisfied', or a set of responses that lists 'Likes' about a service to 'Any likes'. It may be appropriate for most tables to be based on the responses of the total sample but there will be occasions when you may want some tables to be filtered on a different base, for example 'Those who buy now', or 'Those who have heard of the brand'. Remember, a filter applies to a whole table so be careful not to confuse a filter and a top break – a top break is just the column heading.

Box 10.10 Example of a set of top breaks

Q. 1. In total, how many cars are there in your household?

	Total	Gender Male	Female	Age group <25	25–34	35–44	45+	Marital status Single	Married	Accommodation House	Flat	Other
	1505	798	707	322	409	299	475	862	643	1002	471	32
	100%	100%	100%	100%	100%	100%	100%	100%	100%	100%	100%	100%
Number of cars:												
0	156	53	103	102	48	6	–	97	59	5	130	21
	10%	7%	15%	32%	12%	2%	0%	11%	9%	0%	28%	66%
1	1013	559	454	121	349	226	317	674	339	690	314	9
	67%	70%	64%	38%	85%	76%	67%	78%	53%	69%	67%	28%
2	275	151	124	99	10	52	114	91	184	249	26	–
	18%	19%	18%	31%	2%	17%	24%	11%	29%	25%	6%	0%
3	55	31	24	–	2	14	39	–	55	54	1	–
	4%	4%	3%	0%	0%	5%	8%	0%	9%	5%	0%	0%
4+	6	4	2	–	–	1	5	–	6	4	–	2
	0%	1%	0%	0%	0%	0%	1%	0%	1%	0%	0%	6%

Summary and inferential statistics

Think about what summary statistics you want to appear on the tables. For questions with rating scales you may want the mean score; for arithmetical variables, for example annual turnover or number of employees, you may want the mean, the median and standard deviation.

If you need a mean score, think about how it should be calculated. For example, if the rating scale ran from +2 to −2, will the mean score be calculated using this scale, or should it be changed to +4 to +1 to make comparison with other data easier, or to fit with the convention used by the client? If you are working with data derived from a random sample then you may want to indicate which values or variables should be tested for statistical significance (and at what level of significance). Give details if you need any further analyses, for example a factor analysis or cluster analysis.

Box 10.11 How to prepare a DP spec

Example: Questions from Life and Times Survey 2000, self-completion questionnaire B

A copy of the questionnaire from which these questions are taken can be downloaded from www.ark.ac.uk/nilt/quests/

Q. 3 Are you the person responsible for doing the general domestic duties – like cleaning, cooking, washing and so on – in your household?

The question's response format is:

Yes, I am mainly responsible (1).

Yes, I am equally responsible with someone else (2).

No, someone else is mainly responsible (3).

DP instruction

Q. 3 by main set of top breaks. Tabulate as questionnaire (codes 1 to 3) and include summary code for Mainly or Equally responsible (codes 1 or 2).

Base: Total sample (all answering).

Appearance of table

Title: Responsibility for doing the general domestic duties

Respondent mainly responsible

Respondent equally responsible with someone else

Someone else is mainly responsible

Summary: Respondent mainly or equally responsible

No answer.

Q. 4 From the following list, please circle one number from each item to show how important you personally think it is in a job. How important . . . [list of items follows].

The question's response format is an importance scale:

Very important (1), Important (2), Neither/nor (3), Not important (4), Not important at all (5), Can't choose (8).

DP instruction

Q. 4 Importance scale for each of the eight items in the question by main set of top breaks. Tabulate scale as on questionnaire (codes 1 to 8) and include summary codes for Total important (codes 1 or 2) and Total not important (codes 4 or 5).

Mean score (based on values 1 to 5 where 1 = Very important).

Base: Total sample (all answering).

Appearance of table
Title: Importance rating of job security
>   Job security
>   Very important
>   Important
>   Neither important nor unimportant
>   Not important
>   Not important at all
>   Can't choose
>   Summary: Total important
>   Summary: Total not important
>   Mean score excluding 'Can't choose'.

DP instruction
Also need summary table for Q. 4 – the same layout as above but this time with the item statements as top breaks.

Base: Total sample (all answering).

Appearance of table
Title: Summary table of importance rating re aspects of job

	Job security	High income	Good opps	Interesting job
Very important				
Important				
Neither important nor unimportant				
Not important				
Not important at all				
Can't choose				
Summary: Total important				
Summary: Total not important				
Mean score				

Q. 8 Suppose you were working and could choose between different kinds of jobs. Which of the following would you personally choose?

The question's response format is:

(a) I would choose . . .   Being an employee (1)
                             Being self-employed (2)
                             Can't choose (8).
(b) I would choose . . .   Working in a small firm (1)
                             Working in a large firm (2)
                             Can't choose (8).
(c) I would choose . . .   Working for a private business (1)
                             Working for the government or civil service (2)
                             Can't choose (8).

DP instruction
Q. 8 Each part (a to c) by main top breaks. Tabulated as questionnaire.

Base: Total sample (all answering).

For Q. 8b and Q. 8c separate tables again by main top breaks and tabulated as questionnaire but this time based on those saying 'Being an employee' (code 1 at Q. 8a).

Appearance of table
As above.

CHECKING THE OUTPUT

Data tables must be checked for accuracy before they are sent to the client or used to prepare the presentation or report. Typically, two people will check them – the data processing executive or analyst and the client service or research executive. Each will check them from a different perspective. The DP executive will, for example, check the holecount to make sure that the program has delivered the right tables with the correct bases, filters and weighting, that the statistics requested are complete, and that the tables are laid out properly and are readable. The client service executive will check whether the tables meet the specification as set out – in terms of layout, statistics, bases, filters and weighting – and will check whether the data make sense in the context of his or her knowledge of the project topic.

Box 10.12 Standard checks on tables

- Is the total sample as expected? In other words, have all responses been included?
- Does the demographic profile match the profile of the sample or the quota controls?
- Are the headings on the tables correct (project number, name, dates, client name, table title and so on)?
- Is the set of tables complete? Did you ask for a table of contents? (If so, check off all the tables against your specification and against the questionnaire.)
- For the main top breaks – are the cross-breaks or top break headings correct?
- Are the top break totals correct?
- For each table check the following:
  - that the base size is correct;
  - that the question has been handled in the way set out in the specification, e.g. filtered on the correct base;
  - that summary statistics – means, etc. – have been calculated correctly;
  - that summary codes (overcodes) are correct (that they do not total less than any item contained in the overcode);
  - that the data look right – if there are any unexpectedly high or low numbers, check them thoroughly.

Checking data derived from different versions of the questionnaire

If there are several versions of a questionnaire it is important to check in detail those tables that are derived from the questions that vary across the versions. For example, a code on one version of the questionnaire may not mean the same thing on another version. In producing a table based on all versions the program must define what each code means in all versions. There is a chance for error to creep in here, so it is worth checking a holecount for each version to determine the frequency of response on each one.

If you have a top break that is derived from a question rather than the classification data, for example 'Use brand X nowadays', it is worth checking to ensure that it is based on the right total. To do this you need to go to the question from which it is derived, for example 'Which of these brands do you use nowadays?' and check that the number of people answering

Table 10.1(a) Brand use nowadays: incorrect version

	Total	Use brand X nowadays
Brand use nowadays	%	%
Brand X	56	100
Base: All responding	(600)	(226)

Table 10.1(b) Brand use nowadays: correct version

	Total	Use brand X nowadays
Brand use nowadays	%	%
Brand X	56	100
Base: All responding	(600)	(336)

'Brand X' matches the number you have in the top break. In Table 10.1(a) 56 per cent or 336 of the total sample use brand X, therefore the top break based on 226 is wrong. The version in Table 10.1(b) is correct.

Checking top breaks based on summary codes or compound variables

Check too that top breaks which are combined from different questions, or are summary codes, are correct. In the example below, 75 interviews were conducted in each country; countries were grouped together into regions as follows:

- Central and Eastern Europe (450) – Czech Republic, Slovakia, Poland, Romania, Hungary, Russia;
- Asia Pacific (375) – Japan, South Korea, Malaysia, Singapore, Australia;
- Nordic (225) – Norway, Sweden, Finland;
- Southern Europe (300) – Spain, Portugal, Italy, Greece.

Table 10.2(a), however, shows the total sample to be (1,275) rather than (1,350); and the total for the Central and Eastern Europe (CEE) top break is (375) rather than (450). A quick check found that Russia had been left out of the CEE top break.

Table 10.2(a) Regional data: incorrect version

	Total %	CEE %	S Eur %	Nordic %	Asia Pac %
Central and Eastern Europe	33	100	–	–	–
Southern Europe	22	–	100	–	–
Nordic	17	–	–	100	–
Asia Pacific	28	–	–	–	100
Base: All responding	(1,275)	(375)	(300)	(225)	(375)

Table 10.2(b) Regional data: correct version

	Total %	CEE %	S Eur %	Nordic %	Asia Pac %
Central and Eastern Europe	33	100	–	–	–
Southern Europe	22	–	100	–	–
Nordic	17	–	–	100	–
Asia Pacific	28	–	–	–	100
Base: All responding	(1,350)	(450)	(300)	(225)	(375)

Table 10.3(a) Age group: correct version

Age group	Total %	18–34 %	35–54 %	55+ %
18–24	10	40	–	–
25–34	15	60	–	–
35–44	16	–	50	–
45–54	16	–	50	–
55–64	33	–	–	77
65+	10	–	–	23
Base: All responding	(608)	(152)	(194)	(262)

Table 10.3(b) Age group: incorrect version

Age group	Total %	18–34 %	35–54 %	55+ %
18–24	10	24	–	–
25–34	15	76	–	–
35–44	16	–	–	–
45–54	16	–	100	–
55–64	33	–	–	77
65+	10	–	–	23
Base: All responding	(608)	(249)	(97)	(262)

Tables 10.3(a) and (b) also show where it is possible for errors to occur. Table 10.3(a) is correct – all the cells are based on the right proportion of the sample. Table 10.3(b) shows how it might go wrong. The 35–44 age group has been included in error in the 25–34 age group.

Checking repeat data

If your data are repeat data, for example from a panel or tracking study or a dipstick monitor, do not assume that because the previous set of tables were correct this new set will be too. Check them as thoroughly and in the same way as you would a new set. In addition, make sure that the tables have the correct fieldwork dates, and that any changes to the questionnaire since the tables were last run have been included (for example new questions added, old ones deleted, changes to codes as a result of new brands being added to a brand list or new statements to an image grid). Check that any changes in the data, any differences since the last fieldwork period, are explainable in the context of market activity.

An overview of the analysis process

We look in detail at analysing qualitative data in the next chapter, Chapter 11, and at quantitative data analysis in Chapters 12 and 13. Below, however, we have set out a summary of what is involved. You will of course have been thinking about the analysis as you have worked on the project. In taking the client brief and designing the research to address the client's business problem you will have thought ahead to what the research might produce; if you conducted any secondary or exploratory research or if you were involved in any of the fieldwork, you may well have formulated some ideas about what the findings might be. Now that you have your accurate set of tables from your quantitative study and/or your transcripts, recordings and notes from your qualitative research you are ready to start on the more formal, systematic stage of the analysis. Remember, the data as you see them now are in their raw form – in Andrew Ehrenberg's (1982) lovely phrase, they are 'untouched by the human mind' – they are not findings. You have to work through and with the data to draw out the findings and get at the 'story'.

Here is a summary of the sort of things you need to do (whether or not your data are qualitative or quantitative in nature):

- Review the client's problem, the research problem and the research objectives.
- Review the data and get to know them bearing in mind the research problem and research objectives.
- Plan out your overall approach to the analysis: are you going to take a 'top down' approach – that is, working with an idea of what the story (the 'big picture') is and looking for the detail in the data to support or refute it; or are you taking a 'bottom up' approach – that is, immersing yourself in the detail of the data and working up to developing the 'big picture'? You may find that you end up using both approaches in a sort of back and forth or iterative way.
- If there are any ideas or hypotheses that you want to explore or test out in the data, write them out.
- Once you are familiar with the data, select only those parts of it that are relevant to addressing the research problem.
- Think about ways of organising and reducing the mass of data to make it as workable as possible.
- Work through the data, doing some informal analyses – e.g. highlighting interesting numbers, extreme values, anything unexpected, writing summaries of the key themes or issues emerging.
- Continue working through the data (keeping the research problem in focus at all times), manipulating or structuring it in a way that helps you bring out or test your ideas and the emerging 'story' – e.g. re-working relevant data into summary tables, preparing charts or diagrams that summarise the data and make the findings stand out, building in comparisons with other relevant data, where appropriate.
- Look for other data that support the story that is emerging and continue to develop it.
- Don't jump to conclusions too early – be prepared to let go of some of your ideas if they are not supported in the data.
- Check that the detail of the findings fits the 'big picture' and/or that the big picture explains or accounts for the detail of the findings.
- Use your common sense to assess how credible your findings are in the light of what you know already about the problem being researched and its wider (business) context.

Checking and reporting progress

As we mentioned at the beginning of the chapter, during the life of a project you will be expected to liaise with and answer queries from the fieldwork organiser, coders and the data processing supplier, other members of the research team and the client. You therefore need to make sure that you are well briefed about the project so that you can handle queries in a confident and professional manner and keep all members of the project team informed and up to date with progress. You may find it useful to attend a fieldwork session, to hear and/or see for yourself how respondents react to a request to take part in research, how they respond to the questions or the stimulus material, and how the interviewer handles an interview. The experience will help you to answer questions about coding, for example, and will give you insights into the data that you might otherwise miss simply by looking at the tables or reading the transcripts. It will help you build up a greater understanding and appreciation of the data collection process and should help to improve your questionnaire and discussion guide design skills. It is also worthwhile spending some time working with the data processing supplier, in particular, in checking, editing and coding questionnaires. Reading through an entire record of an interview will give you greater insight into how the respondent views the issue under investigation than you may get seeing the data in tables aggregated by question.

LIAISING WITH THE CLIENT

As soon as the client agrees the proposal and gives the go-ahead for the research, plan the fieldwork and data processing schedule with your suppliers and work out a detailed project timetable listing key delivery dates. There are two examples of timetables in Chapter 4 (Figures 4.2 and 4.3) that you might find useful in designing your own. Discuss and agree this timetable, making amendments where necessary, with the client. If, as the project progresses, some of these dates will not be met, tell the client as soon as possible, explaining the reasons why. Try not to set deadlines that you know you are unlikely to meet; if possible (and it is not always possible) build in some contingency time, in case fieldwork takes longer than anticipated, for example. Make sure that the client is clear about what is happening, when it is happening, what output to expect, and what input is expected of him or her, for example agreement of the final questionnaire or dispatch of stimulus material. Keep the client up to date with regular progress reports, formal or informal, depending on the nature of the project, your relationship and what you agreed in the proposal.

MANAGING YOUR TIME

At any one time you may be dealing with four or five different projects, all at different stages of the research process. For example, you may have just been briefed on one job and may need to start preparing a proposal; another job has just gone into field and you need to start thinking about developing an analysis plan; yet another job might be at the report-writing stage. It is important to prioritise this work and manage your time effectively so that you have enough time to do each part of each job well, and meet external and internal deadlines (DP specs and so on). One way of doing this is to plan out your projects on a workplan chart, with key dates highlighted and preparation time built in. Have a look again at the workplan examples in Chapter 4; you could adapt these to suit your own project. Alternatively, as we noted at the beginning of the chapter, you could list in order of priority all the tasks you must complete each day and each week and tackle them accordingly.

Recording and monitoring time

Recording and monitoring the time and costs associated with a project – filling in and analysing time reports – is important. If you are involved in costing a project you can use information in the time report system to see how long various aspects of similar projects took. To be useful, however, the information in the time report system must be accurate and up to date – hence the need for accurate and timely completion of the dreaded time sheets. The information in the time report system is also useful in workload planning – those managing the work can assess how busy people are (utilisation rates) and use this information to assign projects, decide on staffing levels and determine if there is a need to develop new business. The information is also useful in reviewing individual projects, to assess how time spent on the project compares with the original costing or the fee charged to the client.

If a project took longer than the original costing suggested it is important to know why, so that any pitfalls may either be avoided on future jobs or built into the costing. There are many reasons why a project might go over budget, including the following:

- poor communication or briefing leading to tasks taking longer than expected or having to be redone;
- a client asking for more than was anticipated, for example extra reports or meetings;
- a change in the nature of the project after the original costing that was not addressed at the time;
- a sample that was harder to achieve than anticipated;
- the need for extra analyses to understand the research problem.

Although clients are not charged for proposals, time spent on proposals – even those that are unsuccessful – should be recorded so that you can work out the time and cost involved in generating new business and incorporate this into the costing structure.

Chapter summary

- What was requested in the brief and promised in the proposal and in discussion with the client must be turned into an effective research plan that is carried out efficiently. The role of the research executive is pivotal in this in briefing the fieldwork, data processing and analysis suppliers and other members of the research team.
- The research executive's role also includes the following:
  - administering the project on a day-to-day basis, checking progress, answering queries from field, DP, the client;
  - making contributions to questionnaire/discussion guide design;
  - ensuring the questionnaire/discussion guide is suitable and ready for fieldwork and analysis;
  - preparing interviewer or recruiter briefing notes;
  - preparing a coding and an analysis specification;
  - checking the accuracy of data tables;
  - listening to tapes and preparing transcripts and notes;
  - liaising with and reporting progress to the client.
- Project management involves clear communication, sound leadership and effective management of risk and resources.
- A range of project management tools can be used to manage a project effectively including project plans, timetables and briefing documents, and meetings.
- International and multi-country research can be centrally co-ordinated or handled locally. The aim should be to achieve consistency across markets without losing any sensitivity in understanding particular markets. The role of co-ordinator is analogous to that of project manager, liaising with both the client and the local suppliers.
- A skill of the researcher is to manage the time effectively so that all internal and external project deadlines are met, and all elements of the project are carried out to a high standard.

Questions and exercises

1 Describe the key stages involved in the following:

(a) Preparing a project to go 'into the field'.

(b) After fieldwork has been completed.

2 Your client is planning research that involves a quantitative survey in four countries: the US, Australia, India and China. The client is unsure whether to brief four in-country agencies to conduct the work or to brief one agency in Australia to co-ordinate the whole project and has asked you for advice.

(a) Describe the advantages and limitations of each approach.

(b) Which approach would you recommend? Give reasons for your choice.

3 Describe the stages in a project at which it is important to do the following, giving reasons for your answers:

(a) Inform the client.

(b) Consult with the client.

References

Brooker, S., Cawson, P., Kelly, G. and Wattam, C. (2001) 'The prevalence of child abuse and neglect: a survey of young people', *Proceedings of the Market Research Society Conference*, London: MRS.

Childs, R. (1996) 'Buying international research', *Journal of the Market Research Society*, 38, 1, pp. 63–6.

Ehrenberg, A. (1982) *A Primer in Data Reduction*, London: Wiley.

Macfarlane, P. (2003) 'Breaking through the boundaries – MR techniques to understand what individual customers really want, and acting on it', *Proceedings of the Market Research Society Conference*, London: MRS.

MRS Code of Conduct (2005), London: MRS (www.mrs.org.uk).

Orton, S. and Samuels, J. (1988, 1997) 'What we have learned from researching AIDS', *Journal of the Market Research Society*, 39, 1, pp. 175–200.

SRA (2001) *The Code of Practice for the Safety of Social Researchers (2001)*, London: Social Research Association.

Wilsdon, M. (1996) 'Getting it done properly: the role of the co-ordinator in multi-country research', *Journal of the Market Research Society*, 38, 1, pp. 67–71.

Winkler, J.T. (1987) 'The fly on the wall of the inner sanctum: observing company directors at work', in G. Moyser and M. Wagstaffe (eds), *Research Methods for Elite Studies*, London: Allen Unwin.

Recommended reading

Hornsby-Smith, M. (1993) 'Gaining access', in Gilbert, N. (ed.), *Researching Social Life*, London: Sage.

Ibeh, K. and Brock, J. (2004) 'Conducting survey research among organisational populations in developing countries: can the drop and collect technique make a difference?', *International Journal of Market Research*, 46, 3, pp. 375–83.

Kumar, V. (2000) *International Marketing Research*, Upper Saddle River, NJ: Prentice-Hall.

Simmons, S. and Lovejoy, A. (2003) 'Oh no, the consultants are coming!', *International Journal of Market Research*, 45, 3, pp. 355–71.

The US Army Leadership Field Manual (2004), New York: McGraw-Hill.

Chapter 11

ANALYSING QUALITATIVE DATA

Introduction

In this chapter we look at ways of analysing and making sense of qualitative data, converting a mass of raw data – notes, recorded interviews, group discussions or workshops, transcriptions of interviews – into meaningful findings.

Topics covered

- What is qualitative data analysis?
- Planning the analysis
- Doing the analysis
- Using computers in data analysis

Relationship to MRS Advanced Certificate Syllabus

The material covered in this chapter is relevant to two elements of the syllabus: Element 4 – Planning and Conducting Qualitative Research and Element 7 – Analysing Data. Gathering and analysing qualitative data are very closely linked – interwoven almost – and in this chapter we touch on some of things you would do at the gathering stage as well as covering in detail what you do at the main analysis stage. The material in this chapter should help you understand the links between the research objectives, the data gathering process and the data analysis choices you need to make, and should help you build the skills and knowledge you need to analyse data and to evaluate the data analysis approach adopted by other researchers.

Learning outcomes

At the end of this chapter you should be able to:

- understand how to approach qualitative data analysis;
- understand and evaluate the findings from qualitative research;
- undertake and manage the qualitative analysis process.

What is qualitative data analysis?

Qualitative data analysis is part mechanical – handling and sorting the data – and part intellectual – thinking about and with the data. In the same way that we look for patterns and relationships in quantitative and numeric data, we examine qualitative data for patterns, themes and relationships. The process of analysis is not a discrete phase undertaken once fieldwork is completed, rather it is ongoing from the very start of the research and a lot of the ideas about what you think is going on in the data will occur to you during fieldwork. It is once fieldwork is over, however, that you get the chance to organise the data, sort through them, think about them and with them, and pull together 'the findings'.

Box 11.1 Introduction to analysis

In 1993 an MRS Working Party (called the A to B Group) investigated the way in which clients and researchers see analysis. Here Sue Robson and Alan Hedges describe some of the key findings and conclusions. It serves as a useful introduction to qualitative analysis.

The client view
On the whole analysis is taken for granted – most clients generally assume researchers do what is necessary; and assume it is competently done. They see it largely as a matter to be left to the researcher's professional standards (insofar as they have a definite view, which is not always the case).

Is analysis important? Some think analysis *is* important. They argue that:

(a) relying on memory can be fallible and limited;
(b) thorough analysis is necessary for reliability and validity;
(c) working over the material maximises productivity and avoids waste;
(d) it is important to go back and reinterpret earlier sessions [findings from fieldwork] in the light of what has been learned since they were done.

Some think analysis is *not* particularly important. However, after they had spent time discussing the issue during the group sessions [organised by the Working Party] many clients felt that on closer inspection analysis seems more important than they had assumed.

Some ideas about analysis
The following were among the more positive ideas sometimes suggested by individual participants:

(1) Analysis ought to begin with the brief.
(2) It needs clear objectives.
(3) It needs to be systematic and structured.
(4) But on the other hand it shouldn't be mechanistic.
(5) It is not to do with numbers and percentages – not just counting heads.
(6) It is primarily a mental activity – brains and not just processes are important.

(7) Insight is important – it should not just be 'paper shuffling'.

(8) The main skill is distilling the essence of a lot of material.

(9) Many are doubtful about the role of computers (actual or potential).

(10) Ideally analysis should be done between [fieldwork] sessions, so that it steers the development of fieldwork.

A problem of resources

Many clients pointed out that analysis takes time, whereas real-world deadlines are often short. The timing of a tight top-line debrief often prevents serious analysis. Analysis is also sometimes seen as expensive, and the economics may work against it. Some feel that researchers should *say* if they need more time/money to do the job properly – and the view was that they do *not* usually say, they accept the given constraints.

Different clients, different approaches

Different types of client tend to take different approaches. At one extreme are often the advertising agency planners, who tend to look for ideas rather than evidence; creativity rather than reliability; and very fast feedback. At the other extreme some public sector clients usually seem to put a premium on thoroughly digested evidence; reliability and accountability; and full written reports. Other clients tend to fall somewhere between these extremes – and of course requirements may vary from job to job.

The researchers' view

Despite the broad experience of the 'sample', there was in fact much common ground. The analysis process was described as two interlocking, interacting processes: data handling and 'thinking' (or interpreting). The use of the word 'data' makes qualitative researchers uncomfortable at times but no one could identify a better shorthand description to cover all the interviewing experiences collected when running groups or interviewing individuals.

Data handling covers the processing, organising and structuring of the evidence collected in order to make sense of it, and draws inferences and conclusions from it. Data processing can start before any physical handling occurs, since the way the data are processed will relate to the research objectives, the method of interviewing, the questions asked, the order of exploring topics in the discussions and so on.

Thinking is, obviously, the important mental process whereby the researchers draw conclusions from all they have experienced from the moment they were briefed on the project. Sometimes qualitative researchers find that this process does not stop at the verbal presentation stage (or even after the report has been written!). At every stage of the project, the researcher is creating hypotheses about the research, perhaps on the basis of thinking about what respondents have said and incorporating interim conclusions into the next group or interview, or on the basis of reflecting about whether or not what respondents have said is really credible, or whether to approach the next discussion group or interview differently – change the order, ask different questions, change the stimulus material, etc.

So, whereas the data handling process is really a means to an end, the thinking process encompasses the end goal of the project. Nevertheless, the two go hand in hand. The qualitative practitioners agreed that, whatever form of data handling is chosen, it is the best means available of structuring the buzz of confusion that ▶

typifies human interaction and articulation. Without the discipline of this process, there is a danger that there will be insufficient to think about and so valuable insights and connections will be lost. There is also the danger that the result – the presentation and report – will be thin, will lack substance. A thorough approach to data handling makes the project outcome richer, more substantive, altogether more productive.

To sum up

Some of the key conclusions the majority of qualitative researchers came to were:

■ analysis is important;
■ analysis requires more than just memory alone;
■ analysis involves revisiting the data with one's brain engaged;
■ analysis is a thoughtful and creative process;
■ analysis involves the need for judgements about the data;
■ (thorough) analysis is the interaction of 'brain and material'.

Our conclusions

The points below cover the main issues that should be in a Good Practice Guide and give suggestions of the standards that should be adhered to:

1. The need for analysis will vary with the problem set, the size and type of project. The analysis method adopted will also vary with the personal style of the researcher(s) working on the project.
2. Nevertheless there is a need for an analysis stage and this should be handled professionally, just as should be every other stage of the project.
3. Analysis should include: recording all groups/interviews with good quality equipment; going back over those recordings ('re-visiting'), by listening and/or by reading transcripts done by self/other; spending time re-evaluating the tapes/transcripts by writing notes, or by restructuring the data onto analysis sheets – small or large, with or without coloured pens; spending time thinking on what it all means, i.e. interpreting the findings and making judgements.
4. While it is not possible to give an exact definition of the time required, again certain guidelines can be offered: it commonly takes three times fieldwork time to revisit the data thoroughly, resulting in the requirement of a good amount of time being allowed between the end of fieldwork and the verbal debrief. Project size and complexity varies and so does the opportunity to listen to tapes while finishing off the rest of the fieldwork. But based on the experience and judgement of a good many qualitative researchers, one can expect one week minimum between end of fieldwork and debrief on small to medium projects, with obviously more time being needed for large or complex projects.
5. When debriefs are required immediately or very shortly after fieldwork, clients and researchers should carefully weigh up the pros (mainly speed of decision-making) and the cons (a loss of quality, productivity, richness and reliability).
6. More discussion generally between clients and researchers on the importance/ relevance of an analysis stage would be beneficial.

Source: Adapted from Robson, S. and Hedges, A. (1993) 'Analysis and interpretation of qualitative findings. Report of the Market Research Society Qualitative Interest Group', *International Journal of Market Research*, 35, 1, pp. 23–35, www.ijmr.com.

APPROACHES TO ANALYSIS

Analysis of qualitative data is difficult and time consuming. There are no standard techniques or clearly defined procedures – there are many different approaches. Most researchers have their own way of doing it – and since little has been written about how it is done, particularly in commercial market research, there are no common guidelines. Denzin and Lincoln (1994) refer to qualitative research as 'bricolage', the art of adapting and using a variety of materials and tools, and to the qualitative researcher as a 'bricoleur', someone who is skilled in the use and adaptation of the tools. Qualitative data analysis is one area of qualitative research where this 'bricolage' approach is very much in evidence. Techniques for conducting qualitative research and analysing qualitative data have been drawn from a range of disciplines within the social sciences, in particular from social anthropology and sociology. The approach you might take in analysing qualitative data depends on a range of factors and their interaction. These include your background and training, for example in science, social science or humanities; in psychology, sociology or anthropology; in the rational or emotional schools of qualitative research; in a particular paradigm or method such as semiology, hermeneutics, symbolic interactionism, ethnomethodology or discourse analysis. The approach may also depend on the following:

- the way your mind works to sort and think about things (influenced by your learning style, your training and perhaps the left brain/right brain split);
- your level of experience;
- your level of knowledge in the area under investigation;
- the availability of relevant theories or models;
- the type of project (groups, depths, workshops; face to face, online);
- the nature of the research enquiry – exploratory, descriptive, explanatory or a combination of these;
- the subject matter and how respondents approach it;
- the end use of the research;
- the resources available – time, money and number of people.

With so many factors having a potential influence it is not surprising that qualitative data analysis is idiosyncratic – there are almost as many approaches to it as there are researchers.

Box 11.2 Analytic induction

The approach known as analytic induction (AI) works something like this. You have defined the research problem and have some ideas about what you are looking for. From this, and using your understanding of the issues and the background to the problem (what you know from other research as well as gut feeling and intuition), you develop working hypotheses about the matter under investigation. You start fieldwork and throughout it you are thinking about how what respondents are telling you fits with your initial ideas and hypotheses. You keep questioning this, asking whether you need to amend or expand the hypotheses, modify your ideas about what is happening, explore some issues in greater depth, get more examples of things that fit with and do not fit with your hypotheses and so on.

Inductive and deductive reasoning

There are, however, some common principles based on deductive and inductive reasoning. In a deductive approach we speculate up front, in advance of fieldwork, about what it is we think we will find and we set out in the research to test this theory or hypothesis or idea. We design the research and approach the analysis in a way that allows us to do this. We move from the general to the specific in deductive reasoning – from an idea or general hypothesis or theory about what might be happening to specific observations to see if what we expect is actually happening. This approach is common in quantitative research and among some qualitative researchers (Katz, 1983) who refer to it as 'analytic induction'.

In qualitative research the tendency is to use induction rather than deduction. Using this approach means that we do not go into the fieldwork to test out assumptions or existing theories or ideas. Data are collected and from the data we identify general principles that apply to the subject under study – we move from the specific to the general – theory building rather than theory testing. One such well-documented approach, grounded theory, is outlined in Box 11.3.

As you might imagine, it is difficult to use a purely inductive approach in practice. It is difficult to keep out all other ideas and to have a completely open mind when tackling a problem. It is likely that you will have some knowledge of the product field or area under investigation, or at least some understanding of general patterns of behaviour and attitudes (from previous research or the literature). Thus in real-world research analysis it is an iterative process involving both inductive and deductive reasoning. Ideas and hypotheses emerge from the data and are tested out within the data; you might revise or change them, collect more data in which to test and develop ideas and so on.

Box 11.3 Grounded theory

Grounded theory is the approach to analysis of data described by Glaser and Strauss (1967) and later by Strauss and Corbin (1998). In the grounded theory approach data are examined using the 'constant comparative method' in order to identify themes and patterns; concepts and codes are developed in order to summarise what is in the data. These concepts and codes are used to build propositions, or general statements, about relationships within the data. The codes and propositions are tested out in the data to make sure that they hold up, to make sure that they fit the categories to which they were assigned and that the propositions help to explain what is being studied. 'Theoretical sampling' is used to select new 'cases' (respondents) that might help develop the emerging concepts, propositions and theory.

Although grounded theory is often cited, particularly in academic research, as the approach taken in analysis, there is evidence (Bryman and Burgess, 1994) that few use it in its entirety in the way that Glaser and Strauss and Strauss and Corbin describe. Citing the grounded theory approach is more likely to mean that the analysis is 'data driven' rather than meaning that the specific approach, for example the coding procedures, the use of the constant comparative method or theoretical sampling, is followed exactly.

A word of caution is appropriate here. We all have biases – ways of thinking, opinions and attitudes, ideas about the research and what we might find before we start. These might come from our life experience and general knowledge as well as from work on projects in the same area, from briefing documents and background reading and so on. It is important that these are not allowed to skew the analysis and interpretation of the data or limit it in any way. Your own thinking about the issue may mean that you see only what you want to see, or only what fits with your view of the problem. It is important in qualitative research and in analysis to think about alternative hypotheses, to be open to different ways of looking at and interpreting the evidence, and to question and challenge what we see or think we see in the data. At the outset of a project, therefore, it is important to examine what you 'know' or assume, what preconceptions you might be bringing to the fieldwork and analysis. Before going into the field think through how you feel about the topic. Ask yourself: What do I think about the advertising? What attitudes do I have about this issue? Make these explicit, articulate them, challenge them and then leave them to one side as much as possible.

This approach, however, does not rule out the use of existing theories or models. A good theory or model can be an invaluable aid to analysis – it can be used to help develop and expand your thinking; it can speed the analysis process by giving it a framework and thus a coherence; it can suggest questions to ask and lines of enquiry to follow; and it can provide ideas for developing typologies. Used alongside a systematic testing out of ideas in the data – looking for evidence that supports them and evidence that refutes them – a model or theory can help produce a more robust analysis (see Case study 11.1). In choosing a model or theory you need to examine how well founded it is – use those that are well researched and empirically based.

In analysing qualitative data remember the following:

- keep an open mind;
- do not jump to conclusions too early;
- separate how you see the issue from how respondents see it (to avoid imposing your views and ways of thinking on the data);
- do not force the data to fit with what a theory or model suggests.

THE AIM OF ANALYSIS

Regardless of the approach, however, the aim of analysis is the same – to extract meaningful insights from the data and to produce valid and reliable findings that help to answer the research problem. To achieve this, analysis should be disciplined and rigorous. This does not mean that it should be entirely mechanical or prescriptive. It does mean that it should be thorough, consistent and comprehensive, systematic without being rigid, and open to the possibilities and insights that emerge as a result – intuition and creativity are a vital part of it.

The aim of this chapter is to set out some general guidelines for analysing data in a way that leads to valid and reliable findings. For ease of description the process is broken up into stages:

- Planning the analysis and developing a strategy.
- Doing the analysis:
  - organising the data;
  - getting to know the data;
  - getting to grips with what is going on;
  - making links, looking for relationships;
  - pulling together the findings.

In the real-life, untidy world of qualitative analysis, however, these activities often do not always exist as distinct phases – parts of each phase may be taking place at any one time. Rather than moving from one stage to the next in a neat progression it is more likely that bits of each stage will be repeated over and over again as you move through the data. What is presented here is not a prescription for qualitative data analysis but a guideline or set of techniques that you may find useful in getting to grips with your data and discovering your own approach to analysis.

Planning the analysis

In this section we look at what needs to be done before the main stage of analysis – post-fieldwork – begins. In other words, what do you need to be thinking about during the early stages of the project?

AT THE RESEARCH DESIGN STAGE

Although the main phase of analysis happens at the tail end of fieldwork, that is not where it begins. Analysis really does start from the moment you get the brief and start thinking about the problem. Box 11.4 is a checklist designed to help you think through what implications

---

Box 11.4 Thinking forward to the analysis

The problem
- Are you clear about the issues involved? Is the problem clearly defined?
- Is your task to explore, describe, explain or evaluate?
- What output is expected? How will the findings be used?
- What, if any, are your working hypotheses or ideas?
- Is there any previous research or relevant literature that might be helpful?

The sample
- Whom do you need to interview? How many?
- Have you identified different types of respondent?
- What implications will this have for your analysis? Do you expect to see different responses from different types of respondent? Will it be useful to compare responses among similar groups of respondents and between different groups?

The method
- What method have you chosen? Observation? Depth interviews? Group discussions?
- How will this affect the analysis process?

The questions
- What topics are to be covered in the interview or discussion?
- What questioning techniques will you use? Will you use projective or enabling techniques?
- What implications do these questions have for the analysis?

each bit of the research process and each decision has for the analysis. There is no substitute for clear, thorough thinking at this early stage. The process of analysis will be less painful and the outcome of much better quality if you spend time at the front end understanding the research problem and its implications for analysis. This may involve reviewing any relevant literature on the research topic, or reviewing the findings of other research projects on the same or similar topics. The aims and objectives of the research drive the research design and the choice of sample, method and questions, and all of this will determine the analysis strategy. Thinking about these things at an early stage will often give you a way into the analysis, a way of tackling it, helping you to develop both a strategy and a framework for interrogating the data and presenting the findings.

AT THE FIELDWORK STAGE

There is a huge overlap between fieldwork and analysis in qualitative research. You collect data, think about them all the while and collect more – perhaps using a slightly amended discussion guide or reworked stimulus material as fieldwork sheds light on the issues. The whole time your thinking about the issues is developing: ideas, hunches and insights will pop up, hypotheses will emerge that you might want to test out or explore further.

Fieldnotes

For this reason it is worth keeping a fairly detailed log of thoughts and insights as they occur to you during fieldwork. Write them down as soon as possible – you may not remember them when it comes to the main phase of analysis. Sit down as soon as possible after an interview or group or workshop is over and 'braindump' all your thoughts, feelings, ideas, impressions and insights in as much detail as possible. If you are working with a colleague review the fieldwork session together in detail as soon as possible after it is over and make detailed notes. If you have client observers talk to them – ask them what they thought and note down what

> **Box 11.5 Summary so far**
>
> - Think about and plan how you are going to tackle the analysis when you plan the research.
> - Think about and evaluate what is going on while you are doing the fieldwork – what you are hearing and seeing and sensing.
> - Braindump all your thoughts as soon as possible afterwards.
> - Make detailed notes or maps about what is emerging, what picture is beginning to build up; write down any particularly relevant or interesting quotations.
> - Ask yourself what was unexpected or surprising; examine and challenge your own assumptions.
> - Think of questions to ask of the data, comparisons that might be useful.
> - Consider what issues need to be explored in greater depth, what new areas you need to probe.
> - Consider what implications these early findings have for further fieldwork, and for analysis and interpretation, and make changes if necessary.

they say. Write down what you think are the key themes, relevant quotations, things that you might want to explore or think about in more detail later, anything that was said that you did not expect, for example. In other words make a note of anything that occurs to you that you think might be useful when the analysis process is in full swing. Make sure to clarify what are impressions and inferences and what are facts or more concrete observations (Boulton and Hammersley, 1996).

It is also useful at the end of an interview or group to write up a summary of the main points made by the respondent or by the group under each of the topics or questions on the interview guide or on a 'contact summary' form (Miles and Huberman, 1994). Another useful approach is to 'mind map®' them (Buzan and Buzan, 2003). Use whichever approach you think will help settle and fix things in your memory and will be useful later in the analysis. Having a summary record of some sort will help you think about and develop ideas about the data and decide on an analysis strategy. It may also be a useful reference source or guide when it comes to writing up the findings in detail. These notes, summaries and/or maps can be particularly useful if more than one person is involved in the fieldwork, and if more than one person is to be involved in the analysis. Other members of the team can read them in order to get to grips with data across the whole sample.

DEVELOPING AN ANALYSIS STRATEGY

Having thought through the research problem and completed some of the fieldwork you will have in your head – and in your notes – the basis of an analysis strategy, or plan for tackling the analysis. It is worth formalising this plan, making it explicit, especially if you are relatively new to qualitative research. It is easy to feel overwhelmed by the amount of data you have collected, and by the thought of having to find a way through them. The possible lines of enquiry in most qualitative studies are numerous, and time and resources are limited. The analysis strategy should set out a way of approaching the data, and in doing so calm your fears about the size and complexity of the task and ensure that you tackle it in a systematic and rigorous way. A strategy that has been developed to suit the aims and requirements of the research should help you make the most of the time and resources available by prioritising your lines of enquiry. But having a strategy in place does not mean that you have to stick rigidly to it, whatever the data throws up – it can and should be adapted and modified to fit the circumstances.

In putting together your analysis strategy it is useful to think about the following:

- What are the practical considerations?
  - How many are going to be involved in the analysis?
  - Is the client or sponsor to be involved in the analysis process?
  - How long do you have for analysis?
  - Are you going to work from transcriptions, tapes or notes or a combination?
  - Will you be using a computer analysis package?
- What are the research considerations?
  - What decisions are to be taken on the basis of the research findings?
  - How detailed does the analysis need to be?
  - What outputs are required? Presentation, summary report, full report?
  - Are the findings to be published?
- How are you going to tackle the task?
  - By country?
  - Interview by interview or group by group?
  - Question by question?
  - By respondent type?

There is no one way of developing a strategy – one approach is to use the research brief or the research proposal (if there is one). Start by writing down the big research questions that you have set out to answer – the objectives of the research. List the questions and the types of respondents that might help throw light on each of these and write down what it is you will be looking for in the data generated by the questions and the respondents that will help you address the research objectives. This is your analysis strategy.

MARRYING THEORY AND DATA TO GET A CLEARER VIEW

Here Diarmaid O'Sullivan describes how he used theory to help him develop his analysis.

Why this case study is worth reading

This case study is worth reading for several reasons: it is a first-hand account of how someone tackled the analysis of a project; it describes the issues encountered in analysing the data; it gives an example of how the use of ideas and theory from elsewhere helped the researcher develop his thinking.

The key words are: strategy, data, interview guide, question by question, story, emerging, tapes, transcripts, summary, notes, key topics, literature, culture, theory, culture shock, acculturation, framework, coherent, added layer.

Introduction

My initial strategy in analysing my data (from 11 in-depth interviews with overseas social workers working in Ireland) was to follow the structure of my interview guide, question by question. There was a beginning, middle and end, taking respondents from thinking about working in Ireland – their first experiences of working here to their future plans. It made sense to look at the data in this way, too. I had divided the 'story' emerging from the data into two areas: (1) all the processes that went on before making the move to Ireland; and (2) experiences of working in Ireland: first impressions, the induction period, supervision, colleagues, clients, future plans.

Analysis

I listened to the tapes of the interviews and before preparing full transcripts, I wrote up a summary of each interview, building in the notes I had made at the time of the interview. These interview summaries served as a very useful guide to the whole interview and enabled me to pull out a number of key topics related to the working environment in which respondents found themselves. These included:

- The lack of structure in Irish social work
- Induction into social work in Ireland
- Supervision
- Interaction with colleagues
- Interaction with clients

While I now had a set or list of topics, I had no way of drawing the experiences of all respondents together, as not all respondents had the same experiences or unanimous views on these topics.

▶

Following a suggestion by my research supervisor I began reviewing the literature on culture and its effects. It soon became apparent to me that what many of the respondents had experienced when coming to work in Ireland initially was culture shock. It was clear that the idea of culture shock and the process of acculturation as described by Hofstede (1984, 1991) would help me understand and explain what was going on in the data I had collected – it would help me tie all the respondents' stories together within a framework.

In particular, Hofstede's dimensions of culture, in particular the values of power distance and uncertainty avoidance, helped me to question the data and understand the experiences and feelings respondents were describing in a more coherent way. The notion of culture shock and the theory or process of acculturation gave me a framework within which I could explore and explain how non-Irish social workers felt when they came to work in Ireland.

Comparing the power distance and uncertainty avoidance scores for Ireland with those for the country of origin of each respondent helped me understand more fully, for example, the uneasy or unfamiliar nature of the boss/subordinate relationship many respondents described. Power distance informs us, among other things, about the relationship between subordinate and boss. In large power distance cultures, from which most respondents came, there is a considerable gap between boss and subordinate with a culture of direction-giving from the boss. In small power distance cultures like Ireland there is a limited dependence of subordinates on bosses and a preference for consultation between the two, that is, interdependence between the boss and the subordinate. Not surprisingly, perhaps, some respondents felt that their supervisors in Ireland were too young and inexperienced to offer them adequate supervision and that they did not give them the sort of support they expected: many reported a lack of regular supervision and some commented that it lacked structure.

The notion of uncertainty avoidance informs us about a culture's tolerance for the unpredictable. Ireland has a lower score on the uncertainty avoidance index than the countries of origin of many of the respondents, indicating a more comfortable relationship with the unpredictable. In describing their experiences, many respondents appeared to note this – commenting on, for example, the lack of structure and lack of clear guidelines which they felt characterised social work in Ireland.

Conclusion

Hofstede's theory helped me to transform a list of 'complaints' and issues in relation to work practices in Ireland into a coherent story about culture shock and the process of acculturation among foreign social workers working in Ireland. The theory allowed me to question the data in ways I had not thought of. It enabled me to infuse my analysis with an added layer of understanding and explanation, mindful at all times to avoid 'explaining away' respondents' experiences. Without it I just had respondents' perceptions about a list of issues.

References

Hofstede, G. (1984) *Culture's Consequences*, London: Sage.
Hofstede, G. (1991) *Cultures and Organizations – Software of the Mind*, London: HarperCollins.

Source: O'Sullivan, D. (2008), written for this book.

As your analysis and your ideas develop you might find (through a search of secondary data sources) that there is a body of knowledge that supports them or that will give you ideas and alternative ways of looking at the data. You might find this knowledge in previous reports of research on your topic or in the literature about the substantive topic you are investigating – for example there may be well-developed models and theories from management science, marketing science, psychology, consumer behaviour, sociology or anthropology, for example. It can often be worthwhile to make use of these models and theories – they can help you to structure the analysis, suggesting lines of enquiry, and will help you to develop your thinking. They should not be overlooked as a source of inspiration and help but neither should they be used uncritically.

Doing the analysis

The main stage of analysis usually begins when fieldwork is more or less completed. There are five main steps in this part of the process:

- organising the data;
- getting to know the data;
- getting to grips with what is going on in the data;
- making links, looking for relationships;
- pulling together the findings.

ORGANISING THE DATA

Organising the data involves sorting out all the materials you need in order to get on with the analysis. Depending on the size and complexity of the project, and the way in which you like to work, you may well have accumulated a lot of 'raw materials' – a pile of recordings from interviews or group discussions; fieldnotes; transcriptions of the taped interviews; and notes about respondents' interpretations of enabling and projective exercises and copies of the output of these exercises.

It may help you to declutter your mind in readiness for the in-depth analysis process if you spend some time sorting this material into files or folders, labelling it, and generally making it easy to retrieve. It is particularly useful at this stage to make several copies of transcripts – an unadulterated master copy, a copy for cutting and pasting (if that is how you like to work), and a copy on which to make notes. Once this sorting and filing is complete you can review your field notes, listen to (or watch) your tapes or recordings, read through the transcripts and prepare how you plan to tackle the analysis.

Common reactions of novice researchers at this stage are panic and anxiety – about the mass of data and how to get started. In all likelihood you will have more thinking done than you realise, and sorting and organising your data, reviewing your notes, reading transcripts and talking to colleagues about the data will help sort things out in your mind. Do not put off getting started – look back at your analysis strategy and get stuck in. It can be a laborious process – and you must approach it in a systematic way – but you will soon find that when you engage your brain with the data that things fall into place, and a story will start to emerge.

GETTING TO KNOW THE DATA

It is a good idea in the early stages of your qualitative research career (if time and teamwork considerations permit) to prepare your own transcripts. Not only will you learn a lot about

Box 11.6 The analysis audit – part 1

Introduction: Making the process explicit

People approach the analysis of qualitative data in many different ways. Over the past few years I have worked with around 180 trainee researchers on 60 or so different projects. Below, and at relevant points throughout this chapter, are what I have found to be the most common tasks in analysing data. You might find them useful in helping you move through your analysis or you might find them useful in auditing or reviewing what you have done as you approach the end of your analysis. I have broken the tasks up into stages but since the process of analysis is not always linear or sequential – it is usually iterative and sometimes sort of circular – you may find yourself working back and forth between tasks and stages, repeating some of them as you go. You may not do all of them all of the time – and some of them you may never do. It will depend on you, your previous experience or training and how you like to work, on the type of project and on the analysis or reporting needs. I've used 'interview' throughout to refer to any data gathering method.

Taking it in – Part 1 During and shortly after fieldwork

- You do the interview – you hear and/or see and/or feel some of the data.
- You make notes at the time of the interview and/or shortly afterwards.
- You discuss the interview with the client/observer/colleague.
- You prepare a full written summary of what went on in the interview.
- You think about what went on in the interview – thoughts/ideas occur to you.
- You listen to or watch the recording of the interview – you hear/see/remember more data.
- You prepare a transcript – a full written account of the interview (with notes about non-verbal stuff).
- You make notes about what you saw and/or heard and/or felt and/or thought.
- You summarise the findings from each interview in note form or as a list.
- You summarise the findings from each interview as a map or diagram.
- You list questions about the data.
- You note ideas that occur to you.

You may find at this stage of the process that one or other of the following statements describes how you feel:

A. When you finish the interviews and/or read the transcripts you feel that you sort of understand or can see the big picture but are unclear about how the details fit in.
B. When you finish the interviews and/or read the transcripts you feel that you sort of understand or can see the details but are unclear about the big picture.

Taking it in – Part 2 After fieldwork is completed

You might find yourself working in a team with at least one other researcher or with a client, in which case it is likely that you will share your data and your ideas. If, however, you are working on your own it is very useful to find someone with whom you can share your ideas, someone who will act as a sounding board. Make sure, of course, that in sharing data you observe your ethical and data protection responsibilities, and MRS Code of Conduct rules (if they apply to you).

■ You share your recordings and transcripts with other team members or with clients.
■ You circulate your notes to other team members or clients.
■ You listen to/watch recordings or other team members' interviews.
■ You read the transcripts of interviews completed by other team members.
■ You read other team members' notes about their interviews.
■ You prepare your ideas about what you think is going on in the data on your own.
■ You brainstorm ideas in a group session.
■ You take notes during the discussion or brainstorm session.
■ You talk to the team about your interviews and what you found.
■ You listen to others talking about their interviews.
■ You discuss your ideas with other team members or clients.

your interviewing technique but it will give you the chance to get into the data, to get to know it thoroughly. If you are not able to do this make sure you listen to or watch your recordings and read through the transcripts (which someone else will have prepared for you) in full. Make notes as you do this, putting faces to words, noting how things were said, what was not said, what interpretations occur to you as you go through, what ideas strike you and so on.

Although you go into this more intensive phase of analysis with some ideas, feelings and impressions about what is going on, and perhaps some ideas about what it all means, it is important not to jump to conclusions too early. You may find that until you listen to your recordings or read through the transcripts that the interviews or groups you conducted all merge into one in your mind. There is a danger that you misremember things, or give some things more importance in your mind than was actually the case. You need to protect against the selectivity and decay of your memory (see Box 7.10). This is why notes made at the time are particularly important – they are more reliable than notes made some time after field-work – and why listening to or viewing the recordings of the interviews is so important. When reading your notes and transcripts and listening to or watching your recordings, write down any analytic ideas and impressions that occur to you and make a note about testing them out right across the data to see if they hold up. You will need to go back through all of the data systematically and read, listen to or watch them closely to make sure that you see the whole picture, not just the bits that stuck in your mind. Test your ideas out by looking at and comparing data from different types of respondents. Do not get too attached to ideas too early – you may have to ditch them as the analysis develops. Keep your mind open throughout the process to the possibility of new or alternative explanations and new ideas.

GETTING TO GRIPS WITH WHAT IS GOING ON

This is the 'pulling apart' stage of the analysis. Once you have read your notes and transcripts and listened to/watched the recordings, and looked at the data by respondent, by type of respondent or by topic, you will start to notice patterns and themes. You will see that some things crop up a lot, or at least more than others, that there are discernible patterns in attitudes, behaviour, opinions and experiences. You may notice patterns in the way in which people express themselves about an issue and the language they use to describe things. Record all of these – in a notebook, on the transcripts, on your data analysis sheet, in the computer program – whichever you use.

Coding and summarising

To understand fully what is going on you need to dissect the data, pull them apart and scrutinise them bit by bit. This involves working through the data, identifying themes and patterns and labelling them or placing them under headings or brief descriptions summarising what they mean. This process is known as categorising or coding the data. Later in the process, when you have a thorough understanding of all the elements, you can link the data – all the coded segments – together again.

This coding process is not just a mechanical one of naming things and assigning them to categories, it is also a creative and analytic process involving dissecting and ordering the data in a meaningful way – a way that helps you think about and understand the research problem. Coding is a useful 'data handling' tool – by bringing similar bits of data together (Miles and Huberman, 1994) and by reducing them to summary codes you make the mass of data more manageable and easier to get to grips with, enabling you to see what is going on relatively quickly and easily. The process of developing codes and searching for examples, instances and occurrences of material that relate to the code, ensures that you take a rigorous and systematic approach. Codes are also a useful 'data thinking' tool. The codes you develop – and the way you lay them out – allow you to see fairly quickly and easily what similarities, differences, patterns, themes, relationships and so on exist in the data. They should lead you to question the data and what you see in them. The coding process can help you develop the bigger picture by bringing together material related to your ideas and hunches, thus enabling you to put a conceptual order (Strauss, 1987) on the data (moving from specific instances to general statements) and to make links and generate findings.

Generating codes

But how do you generate these codes in the first place? Where do they come from? You can use the topics or question areas from your discussion or interview guide (without reference to the data) as general codes or headings. For example, you might have asked respondents to describe their ideal airline flight – you could have a general code called 'ideal flight' and during the coding process bring together all the descriptions from across the groups or interviews under this code or heading, as follows (although in a live project each extract would be labelled with respondent details):

Ideal flight

'Good films, plenty of leg room, decent food. You're sitting on your own for six or eight hours, you want those things.'
'You want to feel appreciated by them. You don't want to be treated like a number.'
'Plenty of airmiles that I can use to go on holiday.'
'Nothing to annoy you – no one in front of you in the check-in queue, no delays, a seat with plenty of leg room and no one sitting beside you, decent food, clean toilets and not having to wait around for ages before your bags arrive.'
'Comfort and decent entertainment – that's it.'
'The service – the feeling that they're there to serve you.'
'There's never a queue at check-in – it's hassle-free . . .'
'A reserved car parking space, close to the terminal, that's free.'

'An efficient service from check-in right through to collecting your luggage.'

'Speed at the check-in, and not having to be there really early.'

'Comfort and plenty of room – and no one sitting beside you, that's great.'

'A fully reclinable chair and plenty of room around you.'

'Being left alone to get on with some work.'

'A good entertainment system – good head phones, comfortable ones, and your own little screen.'

'No delays or hassles – simple things like that.'

'Being able to get off the plane feeling great, not uncomfortable and exhausted.'

Box 11.7 The analysis audit – part 2

Sorting and processing the data

There are several ways in which you might tackle this – I've called them 'bottom up' and 'top down'. You might use one or other, depending on how your brain works and on the type of project it is, or you might use a mix of both, in a sort of iterative, back and forth approach.

Order 1 – Bottom up

- You think about what individual respondents said/did not say.
- You examine the words and phrases they used.
- You note the frequency/strength with which things were said.
- You examine how they said things as well as what they said.
- You look at the context in which they said it.
- You think about what they meant.
- You think about what these things were examples of.
- You create headings or codes or categories to label or describe things.
- You make notes of these headings or codes in the transcript.
- You highlight or colour code these bits of the transcript.
- You cut and paste bits of the transcript under these headings, creating a new document or section for each heading.
- You build up a 'code frame' or list of headings.

Order 2 – Sort of top down

- You have in your mind a list or set of ideas or concepts or headings.
- You create a 'code frame' based around these.
- You go through the transcripts looking for examples of each of these.
- You make notes of these headings or codes in the transcript.
- You highlight or colour code these bits of the transcript.
- You cut and paste bits of the transcript under these headings.
- You go through the material under these headings.
- You think about what individual respondents said/did not say.
- You examine the words and phrases they used.
- You look at the context in which they said it.
- You note the frequency/strength with which things were said.
- You examine how they said things as well as what they said.
- You think about what they meant.

Remember during this coding some people may have talked about a particular topic or answered a question later or earlier than the topic was mentioned, so you may need to search the data record for all incidences of it.

Rather than imposing codes from outside the data you can go into the data (a bottom up, data driven approach) and see what words or terms or concepts respondents use to describe things and use these as the codes. Remember that different people may use different language to describe the same thing so make sure that you look for this.

The coding process

The coding process itself can also be tackled in a number of ways, and different researchers will have different approaches – using pen and paper or computer. A relatively easy way of doing it if your transcripts are available in a word-processing package is to create a new document for each heading, topic or code. As you work through your transcript, cut out sections of text that relate to the code and paste them into the document you have created to represent that code. In this way you can build up a store of relevant material related to that particular code or topic. Take care to label the source of each bit (respondent details, fieldwork details, place in transcript) that you cut so that you know the context from which it came, and can refer back to it if necessary. And remember that one bit of data or text may fit under more than one heading or code. You could, alternatively, go through the transcript and label bits of text *in situ*, before gathering the same or similarly labelled bits in one place or under one heading.

It is likely that you will make several – at least two – coding 'passes' through the data. At the first pass you might keep the codes fairly general and keep the number to a minimum. For example, you might have identified four or five key themes in your data or you may have divided it up under several topic areas. As you work through the data a second time you can divide these big, general codes into more specific ones. In the 'ideal flight' example you might, on a second coding pass, pull apart all the aspects respondents include in their ideal flight and code or group these under headings such as 'emotional aspects' (feelings of well-being and so on), 'physical aspects' (leg room and so on), 'facilities available' or 'service'. In this second pass you might group your data extracts under each of the relevant codes as follows (note that some appear in more than one category, either because the respondent said more than one thing and you want to maintain the quotation in full or because in some cases it is not clear in which category to include them):

Emotional aspects

'You want to feel appreciated by them. You don't want to be treated like a number.'
'Nothing to annoy you – no one in front of you in the check-in queue, no delays, a seat with plenty of leg room and no one sitting beside you, decent food, clean toilets and not having to wait around for ages before your bags arrive.'
'Being left alone to get on with some work.'
'No delays or hassles – simple things like that.'

Physical aspects

'Good films, plenty of leg room, decent food. You're sitting on your own for six or eight hours, you want those things.'
'Nothing to annoy you – no one in front of you in the check-in queue, no delays, a seat with plenty of leg room and no one sitting beside you, decent food, clean toilets and not having to wait around for ages before your bags arrive.'
'Comfort and decent entertainment – that's it.'

'Comfort and plenty of room – and no one sitting beside you, that's great.'

'A fully reclinable chair and plenty of room around you.'

'Being able to get off the plane and feeling great, not uncomfortable and exhausted.'

Facilities

'Good films, plenty of leg room, decent food. You're sitting on your own for six or eight hours, you want those things.'

'Plenty of airmiles that I can use to go on holiday.'

'Nothing to annoy you – no one in front of you in the check-in queue, no delays, a seat with plenty of leg room and no one sitting beside you, decent food, clean toilets and not having to wait around for ages before your bags arrive.'

'Comfort and decent entertainment – that's it.'

'A reserved car parking space, close to the terminal, that's free.'

'A good entertainment system – good head phones, comfortable ones, and your own little screen.'

Service

'Nothing to annoy you – no one in front of you in the check-in queue, no delays, a seat with plenty of leg room and no one sitting beside you, decent food, clean toilets and not having to wait around for ages before your bags arrive.'

'The service – the feeling that they're there to serve you.'

'There's never a queue at check-in – it's hassle-free . . .'

'A reserved car parking space, close to the terminal, that's free.'

'An efficient service from check-in right through to collecting your luggage.'

'Speed at the check-in, and not having to be there really early.'

'Being left alone to get on with some work.'

'No delays or hassles – simple things like that.'

Alternatively, you can code the other way round – coding everything that occurs to you as you pass through the data the first time and use the second or third pass to structure or revise these more detailed codes. There is no right or wrong way – do what feels best for you and for the data.

During the coding process do not rule out the possibility that bits of data may have multiple meanings or a meaning different from the one that you are assuming. Always check out the context of comments in order to learn more about the meaning of what was said; it may also be useful to go back to the recording. Stay open to new ideas and new ways of looking at and coding the data. Try not to jump to conclusions or close off avenues of enquiry. Do not think of the codes you have created as static or fixed – they can be expanded, split apart or even discarded if they no longer seem useful or if they do not work.

Once you have bits of data together under a heading or code the next step is to compare all the bits – looking for similarities and differences between them. This will help you refine the codes, making them more specific, and it will also help you achieve a greater understanding of the data. You might do this during the second pass at coding, or even at a third pass, depending on the time available and the level of detail and depth you need to achieve with the analysis.

At this stage you may want to extract some verbatim comments – quotations or vignettes, extended story-like quotations that illustrate a typical experience or event (Miles and Huberman, 1994) – for use in the presentation or report of the findings. In selecting these make sure that you do not oversample the responses of the more articulate respondents. You may want to choose a range of responses that illustrate a particular phenomenon, attitude, feeling or experience,

> ## Box 11.8 Approaches to coding and analysis: variations by technology
>
> - *Pen and paper*: use a different coloured pen to highlight or underline comments that relate to each topic or theme; cut out verbatim comments from the transcript and paste them together with other comments relating to that topic or theme on to a separate sheet of paper.
> - *Word processor*: use the word-processing package to highlight comments using different colours or different fonts for different topics or themes; cut and paste relevant sections of the transcriptions under headings or themes on a separate page or into a separate document.
> - *Qualitative data analysis package*: there is some variation, depending on the package, but in summary once you have imported transcripts, you can use the software to label sections of text that relate to particular topics and themes with relevant headings or brief descriptions (codes), sort and retrieve passages of texts labelled in the same way, look for links and connections and patterns within the data, prepare maps and diagrams, build theory.

putting together a sort of database of quotations. Make sure in removing them from the transcript that you provide enough context so that the meaning is clear, and ensure that they are labelled with the relevant respondent details.

During and after this 'dissection' stage you will start to see links and connections between bits of data. The next step is to put things back together again in the light of the understanding you have achieved via the dissection. The summary version of the data – the coding scheme – can make it easier to see links, connections and relationships in the data.

MAKING LINKS AND LOOKING FOR RELATIONSHIPS

You should now have a very good grasp of your data. A 'story' should be emerging, and it is likely that you will have some tentative ideas or explanations about what is going on. As you have read through and/or listened to your data and as you have coded them you will have made notes about links between different themes or codes that overlap and you will have been asking questions of the data, testing out ideas and looking for relationships. For example, you might ask, 'Does the description of an ideal flight vary between frequent and less frequent flyers or those who usually fly club class and those who fly first class?', 'Is it only users who think *x*, or do non-users hold the same view?', 'Is it younger women who say that or is it all women?' or 'Is it life stage rather than age or demographics that might explain a particular pattern?'. You may be able to develop typologies, categorising respondents in terms of similarities in their characteristics. You might be able to isolate several types of business flyer, for example, characterised by frequency of travel and attitude or delight in the experience; or different types of homeless people, characterised by the length of time they have been homeless and their feelings about their situation. The questions you ask of the data and the way you develop the data will be driven by the research objectives.

As you make links and connections, or see relationships, think about what might explain them and think about more than one explanation. Once you have generated some possible explanations start looking for evidence to support your ideas and interpretations as well as evidence that might not support them. At this stage you may well still be coding the data – and making the codes more detailed or refined. At the same time you may also find that you can move from the specific codes you developed to more abstract concepts and from these concepts to a greater degree of generalisation about what is going on in the data.

Box 11.9 The analysis audit – part 3

Thinking about what's going on

Words and meaning:
- You look for common words and phrases.
- You look at the context of words to try to get an understanding of the respondent's meaning.
- You try to think of alternative meanings in a phrase.

Frequency, strength and consistency of response:
- You examine the data to find out how common particular responses were.
- You examine the data to determine if there was a range of response in relation to a particular topic or question.
- You note how diverse or how similar the responses were.
- You note how strongly opinions or attitudes or beliefs were expressed.
- You examine how consistent opinions or attitudes or beliefs were.

Piecing it together
At this stage one or other of these statements might describe how you feel . . .

A. You feel that you need to get to grips with all the detail in order to form the big picture.
B. You feel that you need to get an idea of the big picture in order to see how the details fit in.

- You look to see if your codes or categories or headings occur in all the transcripts.
- You amend your code frame accordingly as you examine all transcripts.
- You pull together all examples from all transcripts under these codes or categories.
- You add headings into the body of the transcripts.
- You compare and contrast individual cases (respondents, groups).
- You summarise the headings or codes.
- You create a diagram or map or flow chart linking the codes or headings, showing how they relate to each other.
- You create a grid or a table (an analysis sheet) using the main codes or headings to show how response varied or did not vary across the sample.
- You make detailed notes about what you find out about each heading or code.
- You make summaries about what you find out about each heading or code.
- You re-read the transcripts thinking about only one or two headings or codes (or themes or ideas) at a time.
- You form ideas or hypotheses about what might be going on in the data.
- You test these ideas or hypotheses within the data.   ▶

- You go back through your recordings or transcripts or notes looking for evidence to support your ideas or hypotheses.
- You go back through your recordings or transcripts or notes looking for evidence that refutes your ideas or hypotheses.

Linking and connecting
- You look at the codes or categories or headings you have created.
- You look for patterns.
- You look for links or connections or relationships between them.
- You link things – codes, headings – together.
- You brain dump all your ideas.
- You map out your ideas or your codes or headings.
- You order the ideas or codes or categories or headings.
- You go back and forth through the data checking and testing your ideas and hypotheses.
- You formulate and test new hypotheses.
- You look for or find outliers or anomalies.
- You map out pathways or processes.
- You create vignettes that illustrate typical behaviour or experiences.
- You create typologies.
- You write up a summary of the findings.
- You revisit the literature.
- You seek out more literature.
- You use theories or models you found in the literature to explore or question your data further.
- You use theories or models to help you explain your data.

Using charts, diagrams and maps

Using diagrams, tables, flow charts and maps to sort and present data can help you think and can help to uncover or elucidate patterns and relationships. Some people can think in and/or express ideas better in pictures and diagrams than they can in words. Reducing data to fit a diagram or table or mapping things out can focus the thinking on the relationships that exist in the data (see Figures 11.1 and 11.2). The most suitable format will depend largely on what it is you are trying to understand. A perceptual map may be useful in showing how different brands lie in relation to each other and key brand attributes. Figure 11.3 shows an example.

A flow chart might be suitable to show a detailed chronology of events, for example the events leading to homelessness or a move to a hostel or shelter, or the steps involved in investment planning. A table might be useful for summarising the reactions of different groups or types of respondents to particular stimulus material – product concepts, for example, or mood boards. An example is given in Table 11.1. Key comments about each concept can be written in for each respondent.

PULLING TOGETHER THE FINDINGS

As you work through your data – immersing yourself in them, pulling them apart and building them up, questioning, testing out ideas and hypotheses – you are likely to reach a point

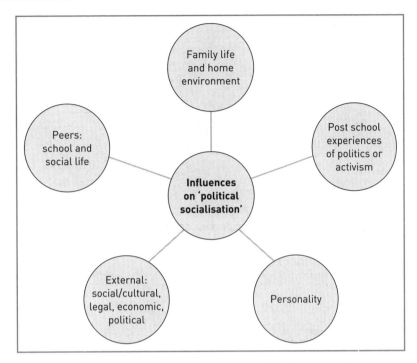

Figure 11.1 Diagram summarising key influences on political socialisation

Source: Adapted from Beattie, D., Carrigan, J., O'Brien, J. and O'Hare, S. (2005) ' "I'm in Politics Because There's Things I'd Like to See Happening." ' Unpublished project report, MSc in Applied Social Research. Used with permission.

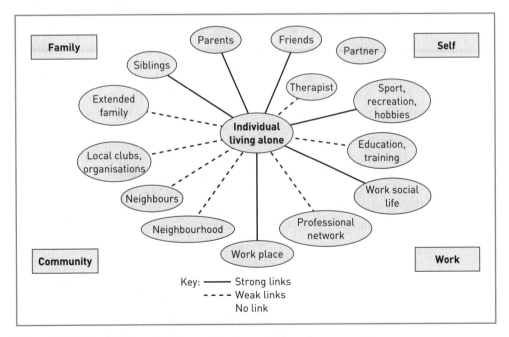

Figure 11.2 Map of respondent's social support network

Source: Breslin, G., Comerford, F., Lane, F. and Ó Gabhan, F. (2005) 'On and Off the Treadmill: A Typology of Work – Life Integration for Single Workers Aged 35–44'. Unpublished project report, MSc in Applied Social Research. Used with permission.

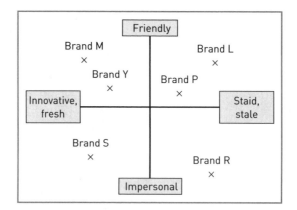

Figure 11.3 Example of a perceptual map

Table 11.1 Data analysis summary table

Concept code	Younger respondents (15–18 years) Comments			Older respondents (19–24 years) Comments		
	R1	R2	R3	R1	R2	R3
1						
2						
3						
4						

where suddenly it all seems to fit together and make sense or produce a story. Here are a few ways of helping this along. When all of the data and ideas are in your head it can be useful to take a break from the analysis, to let things ferment, to give things time to 'gestate'. Go and do something unrelated – sleep, exercise, cook or listen to music – and you may find you have that 'eureka' moment. Another way is to talk about the findings out loud to someone not directly involved in the project. All they have to do is sit and listen and perhaps ask a few questions. Often in trying to articulate the ideas in your mind in order to speak them out loud and explain them to someone else you make connections or see a picture that you have not seen before. The other person can help by asking questions so that you have to explain your thinking and reasoning. They may ask questions that you have not asked yourself, which may help further. Yet another way is to read the literature relevant to your project, whether it is the original briefing notes or a journal article on the same topic. This may spark off fresh ideas, suggest further lines of questioning or help you make a useful connection.

MANAGING YOURSELF

In Chapter 6 we noted how important it is to think about your role in the interview or data gathering process, about what assumptions you make about the people you are observing or interviewing, and about the topic; we noted how important it is to make these explicit to yourself before fieldwork begins so that you go into fieldwork with an open mind and high degree of self-awareness. You should take yourself through the same process of self-examination at the analysis stage, too – especially at this point, when you do not want to let your assumptions, prejudices or views intrude on your interpretation of the data. Throughout

Box 11.10 Professional practice and the MRS Code of Conduct: analysis and interpretation

Here are the rules that you need to keep in mind when pulling together your findings (in Chapter 14 we present those relevant to presenting and reporting):

B49 Members must ensure that research conclusions disseminated by them are clearly and adequately supported by the data.

B52 Members must allow Clients to arrange checks on the quality of fieldwork and data preparation provided that the Client pays any additional costs involved in this.

B57 Members must ensure that when interpreting data they make clear which data they are using to support their interpretation.

B58 Members must ensure that qualitative reports and presentations accurately reflect the findings of the research in addition to the research practitioner's interpretations and conclusions.

Source: MRS Code of Conduct 2005. Used with permission.

Box 11.11 The analysis audit – part 4

Pulling together the findings: Things that help

Sharing, not sharing
- Sharing the process with others (i.e. working in a group).
- Working on your own.

Talking, writing, reading, drawing/visualising
- Talking about it out loud – to yourself and others.
- Writing out your ideas, writing out summaries.
- Reading things over – transcripts, notes.
- Reading the literature or write-ups of other research.
- Mapping things out or drawing diagrams.

Taking a 'stance'
- Being totally immersed in the data.
- Remaining detached.
- Taking different subjective perspectives – your own, the client's, the respondents', the literature, the outsider's.

Leaving it to gestate in your paraconscious/subconscious
- Leaving it alone and not thinking about it.
- Doing something else entirely – sleeping, exercising, cooking, listening to music, doing nothing.

the analysis process (which of course overlaps with data gathering in qualitative research) make a conscious effort to examine and make explicit to yourself your own feelings and views on the topic; challenge your own way of thinking and feeling about it. Remember, one of your skills as a qualitative researcher is to be aware of your 'stance' in relation to the topic and the data, and to be able to stand back and not to impose your own opinion, and to remain non-judgemental. This applies just as much to the analysis and interpretation stage of the process as it does to the data gathering stage. An extension of this skill is the ability to take

---

Box 11.12 The analysis audit – part 5

Checking, verifying, developing
- You think about what the connections and the patterns mean:
  1 in the context of the individual interview;
  2 in the context of the whole sample;
  3 in the context of the theme or concept or idea;
  4 in the context of the big picture, the overall story.
- You re-read the transcripts for a holistic view.
- You discuss the findings with team members and others (clients).
- You re-read the literature.
- You seek out more literature.
- You compare your findings with what is set out in the literature.
- You question your findings further having read the literature.
- You go back and forth between the literature and the data.
- You go back and forth through the data checking out your ideas and hypotheses in the data.
- You check whether your assignment of things to codes or categories or headings still makes sense.
- You think about what assumptions you might have made.
- You question whether there could be alternative explanations or interpretations.
- You think about whether the detail really does fit with the big picture.
- You think about whether the big picture really does explain or capture all the detail.

'Completing' it
- You are able to see or explain the big picture.
- You are able to fit all the details into the big picture.
- You are able to present the overall picture and relate key details back to the overall picture.
- You feel that you have explained or accounted for any conflict or lack of fit or discontinuity.
- You feel that you have moved forward towards a more complete understanding of the issues, the problem.
- You are able to map or set things out in a series of sequential steps.
- You are able to see a narrative or a coherent story in the data.
- You feel that you have 'completed the circle', 'tied the story together', arrived at a 'best fit', found an 'internal logic'.

another perspective, to see things as others might see them – all the time being aware that this is what you are doing.

During the whole of the analysis process it is important that you bear in mind the objectives of the research – do not lose sight of them as you become immersed in the data. It can be helpful after you complete the coding stage to start writing things down in some detail and, as you do so, to be constantly asking yourself how it all ties in with the research objectives. As soon as you have the story or the elements of the story clear in your mind, go back again to the research objectives. Think about what light the evidence you have uncovered sheds on the research objectives. Think about what implications the findings have – what is the 'So what?' of each of the insights the research has produced?

It is also useful to think about the quality of your findings:

- How plausible are they?
- Do they make sense?
- Are they intuitive or counter-intuitive? Surprising or what you might expect?
- How much evidence is there to support them?
- How credible and plausible is this evidence?
- How does it fit with evidence gathered elsewhere – from other research in this area, from theory, from the literature?
- Have you thoroughly examined the data for disconfirming evidence?
- Have you checked that other explanations do not fit the data better?
- Have you accounted for contradictions, oddities or outliers?
- Have you introduced any bias?
- Have you given more weight to what the more articulate in the sample have said at the expense of others?
- Have you been systematic and rigorous in looking for evidence and taking into account all views and perspectives?
- Are you seeing in the data what you want to see?
- Are you overinterpreting things?
- Is there anything you might have missed?

Using computers in qualitative data analysis

There is no computer program that will perform the task of data analysis for you. There are, however, many programs that can be used for the more mechanical aspects of the process including storing and managing data, searching for and retrieving text, coding and mapping or charting data. There are also programs that can be used for theory building, linking concepts and categories. In addition to software for analysing text there is also available a range of software for analysing audiovisual data (a description of this is, however, beyond the scope of this book).

Computer-aided qualitative data analysis software is popular in academic research, in some larger scale applied social research projects and in large scale public consultation exercises, not least because it allows an audit trail through the researcher's analysis process, which may be essential for peer review of the work or for scrutiny if the findings are to be used in policy making. Use of such software tends to at least imply a systematic approach, added rigour in the analysis process, and a transparent and traceable route through the data (but note that most of these benefits come from how the researcher uses the software rather than from the software itself).

Use of analysis software in commercial market research is still relatively limited: a recent survey (Rettie, Robinson, Radke and Ye, 2007), with a relatively low response rate, estimated that fewer than one in ten market researchers used it. The main reason for lack of use of such software in commerical research is mostly down to lack of time – most market research projects work to very tight turnaround times and using specialist software to analyse the data can be time consuming. In addition, most packages rely on full transcripts of interviews or discussions, which are not always produced in commercial research – again because of time and often budget pressures. Using the packages effectively and efficiently also requires training. Finally, there is some scepticism about what such software brings to the process (beyond data management).

There is available a wide range of qualitative data analysis software with a wide range of features and functions. In summary, the main functions in most packages are 'search and retrieve' facilities; coding and labelling facilities; note-making facilities; content analysis; and visual mapping and charting. The levels of complexity of these functions will vary depending on the package. For example, in terms of the search and retrieve function you may be able to do a key word or phrase search in context (KWIC); or a key word search that allows you to use alternative words with similar meanings; searches that produce a key word index, a word frequency count and/or a word frequency table; and searches that allow you to look for and verify whether there are relationships between concepts or themes. Some software packages also offer artificial intelligence features and data mining type operations (discovery and verification, 'if . . . then' classification rules).

Qualitative data analysis packages are a good way of storing and handling data and making analysis accessible. They allow you to change how you think about the data, reworking coding schemes as new insights emerge, revisiting segments of the data quickly and easily. As you work through the data you can record all your thinking about it (the way you might make notes in the margin of a transcript, for example). They allow you to see all the bits of data plus the whole – you can move back and forward in order to see the context of extracts. The search and retrieve functions allow you to interrogate the data more easily and so more thoroughly than you might with paper transcripts – and thus enable you to achieve a more in-depth understanding of the data and have greater confidence in your findings.

Ultimately, of course, any package is only as good as your own thinking and analysis skills. Do not think that by simply going through the procedures set out in the program you will end up with a good piece of analysis. The program will only carry out your instructions; it does not think for you. It will help you do the things you would normally do, and enable you to do them in more detail, more often and more thoroughly.

If you are thinking of using an analysis program it is advisable to have a good grasp of the principles of analysis before you start as well as an awareness of how you think about and approach the analysis task – in general and in relation to the specific project you are working on – as this should influence which program you choose. You should bear in mind that despite your analysis skills there is quite a steep learning curve with most programs. In addition, do not forget that most require full transcripts, which are time consuming to prepare – and factor this in. Once familiar with a program, however, you may save time in the labour-intensive tasks of sorting, organising and coding the data. This is particularly true if you are working on a large project or have a complex mass of data to analyse. With smaller projects – Morgan (1998) suggests the cut-off point is six groups or less – it may not be worth the bother.

An excellent website should you want further detailed information is the CAQDAS Networking Project site, http://caqdas.soc.surrey.ac.uk/. It includes reviews of the most popular software packages.

Box 11.13 Professional practice and the MRS Code of Conduct: data storage

During the analysis process it is important that you keep the promises you made to the participants when you collected the data. This is likely to mean that you must preserve the anonymity of the participants and the confidentiality of the data they gave you – to this end you must keep the data secure and allow access only to those working on the project – and you must use the data only for the purposes you described to the participants at the outset. The MRS Code of Conduct sets out the following rules of relevance here:

B35 Members must ensure that completed recruitment questionnaires, incentive and attendance lists, or any other research information which identifies Respondents are not passed to Clients without the explicit permission of the Respondents; and Members must take reasonable steps to ensure that the documents are used only for the purpose agreed at the time of data collection.

B42 Members must ensure that any material handed to Clients or included in reports, without consent from Respondents, is anonymised, e.g. transcripts containing verbatim comments and projective material.
Comment: Special care must be taken when the universe is small, as in the case of some business to business research studies.

B62 Members must take reasonable steps to ensure that all hard copy and electronic lists containing personal data are held securely in accordance with the relevant data retention policies and/or contractual obligations.

B63 Members must take reasonable steps to ensure that all parties involved in the research are aware of their obligations regarding security of data.

B64 Members must take reasonable steps to ensure that the destruction of data is adequate for the confidentiality of the data being destroyed. For example, any personal data must be destroyed in a manner which safeguards confidentiality.

Source: MRS Code of Conduct 2005. Used with permission.

Chapter summary

■ Qualitative data analysis involves looking for patterns, themes and relationships in the data. It is an ongoing process that begins at the start of a project and continues during fieldwork. The main work is, however, done at the end of fieldwork.

■ It is a difficult and time-consuming task. There are no standard techniques or clearly defined procedures – there are many different approaches. Techniques are drawn from a range of disciplines within the social sciences, in particular from social anthropology and sociology. The approach individual researchers take depends, among other things, on their background and training. ▶

- The aim of analysis is to extract meaningful insights from the data and produce valid and reliable findings that help answer the research problem. Analysis should be disciplined and rigorous, systematic without being rigid, and open to the possibilities and insights that emerge as a result – intuition and creativity are a vital part of it.

- One approach to analysis is the inductive approach – to collect data and from the data identify general principles that apply to the subject under study, moving from the specific to the general – theory building rather than theory testing. Grounded theory is an example of this approach.

- It is difficult to use a purely inductive approach in practice as it is likely that you will have some knowledge of the product field or area under investigation. In real-world research analysis is an iterative process involving both inductive and deductive reasoning. Hypotheses and ideas emerge from the data and are tested out within them.

- It is important in approaching fieldwork and analysis to be aware of your biases – ways of thinking, opinions and attitudes, ideas about the research and what you might find before we start. These should not be allowed to skew the analysis and interpretation of the data or limit it in any way. Throughout the analysis process keep an open mind, do not jump to conclusions too early; separate how you see the issue from how respondents see it.

- A good theory or model can be an invaluable aid to analysis, helping to develop and expand thinking; speed the process by giving it a coherence, suggesting lines of enquiry to follow and providing ideas for developing typologies. In choosing a model or theory examine how well founded it is – use those that are well researched and empirically based. Do not force the data to fit with what a theory or model suggests.

- The process of analysis involves organising and sorting the data, getting to know the data in detail, thinking about them and with them, pulling them apart to understand them and fitting them together, making links and looking for relationships, to produce 'the findings'.

- In the real-life world of qualitative analysis these activities do not always exist as distinct phases – parts of each phase may be taking place at one time. Rather than moving from one stage to the next in a neat progression it is more likely that bits of each stage will be repeated over and over again as you move through the data.

- The process of coding or labelling the data is an important analytical tool. It not only helps summarise the mass of data but it enables the researcher to think with the data and uncover patterns, themes and relationships.

- Using diagrams, tables, flow charts and maps to sort and present data can help you think and can help to uncover or elucidate patterns and relationships.

- Findings and the evidence on which they are based should be checked and tested in the data in a thorough and systematic way.

- There are many specialist computer programs for the analysis of qualitative data. The programs help with the storage, sorting, searching and retrieval of data; some facilitate theory building. The quality of the analysis produced can be greater in depth and detail but is dependent on how the researcher uses it, not on the software itself.

Questions and exercises

1 Outline the key steps in the qualitative analysis process.

2 You are working on a project with two other researchers. Each of you has conducted six in-depth interviews. You are the lead researcher.

   (a) Prepare a briefing document for the team outlining how you plan to tackle the analysis.

   (b) Describe the steps you would take to ensure that the analysis of the data is thorough and consistent.

3 Discuss the value of each of the following to good quality data analysis:

   (a) Making notes at the time of fieldwork.

   (b) Preparing full transcripts.

   (c) Listening to recordings of fieldwork.

   (d) Watching recordings of fieldwork.

   (e) Making use of theory.

References

Boulton, D. and Hammersley, M. (1996) 'Analysis of unstructured data', in Sapsford, R. and Jupp, V. (eds) *Data Collection and Analysis*, London: Sage.

Bryman, A. and Burgess, R. (eds) (1994) *Analyzing Qualitative Data*, London: Routledge.

Buzan, T. and Buzan, B. (2003) *The Mind Map® Book*, London: BBC Worldwide.

Denzin, N. and Lincoln, Y. (eds) (1994) *Handbook of Qualitative Research*, London: Sage.

Glaser, B. and Strauss, A. (1967) *The Discovery of Grounded Theory*, Chicago, IL: Aldine.

Hofstede, G. (1984) *Culture's Consequences*, London: Sage.

Hofstede, G. (1991) *Cultures and Organizations – Software of the Mind*, London: HarperCollins.

Katz, J. (1983) 'A theory of qualitative methodology: the social science system of analytic fieldwork', in Emerson, R. (ed.) *Contemporary Field Research*, Boston, MA: Little, Brown.

Lewins, A. and Silver, C. (2006) *Choosing CAQDAS Software*, CAQDAS Networking Project: http://caqdas.soc.surrey.ac.uk.

Miles, M. and Huberman, A.M. (1994) *Qualitative Data Analysis: An Expanded Sourcebook*, London: Sage.

Morgan, D., quoted in Krueger, R. (1998) *Analyzing and Reporting Focus Group Results*, Chapter 8, p. 93, London: Sage.

Rettie, R., Robinson, H., Radke, A. and Ye, X. (2007) 'The Use of CAQDAS in the UK Market Research Industry', in *Advances in Qualitative Computing Conference Proceedings*, http://caqdas.soc.surrey.ac.uk/conference/conference07.htm.

Robson, S. and Hedges, A. (1993) 'Analysis and interpretation of qualitative findings, Report of the Market Research Society Qualitative Interest Group', *Journal of the Market Research Society*, 35, 1, pp. 23–35.

Strauss, A. (1987) *Qualitative Analysis for Social Scientists*, Cambridge: Cambridge University Press.

Strauss, A. and Corbin, J. (1998) *Basics of Qualitative Research*, London: Sage.

Recommended reading

Buzan, T. and Buzan, B. (2003) *The Mind Map® Book*, London: BBC Worldwide.

Casey, M. (1998) 'Analysis: honoring the stories', in Krueger, R. (ed.) *Analyzing and Reporting Focus Group Results*, London: Sage.

Ereaut, G. (2002) *Analysis and Interpretation in Qualitative Market Research*, London: Sage.

Lewins, A. and Silver, C. (2007) *Using Software in Qualitatve Research: A Step-by-Step Guide*, London: Sage.

Miles, M. and Huberman, A.M. (1994) *Qualitative Data Analysis: An Expanded Sourcebook*, London: Sage.

Ritchie, J. and Spencer, L. (1992) 'Qualitative data analysis for applied policy research', in Burgess, A. and Bryman, R. (eds) *Analyzing Qualitative Data*, London: Routledge.

Robson, S. and Hedges, A. (1993) 'Analysis and interpretation of qualitative findings, Report of The Market Research Society Qualitative Interest Group', *Journal of the Market Research Society*, 35, 1, pp. 23–35.

Strauss, A. and Corbin, J. (1998) *Basics of Qualitative Research*, London: Sage.

Taraborelli, P. (1993) 'Becoming a carer', in Gilbert, N. (ed.) *Researching Social Life*, London: Sage.

Wells, S. (1991) 'Wet towels and whetted appetites or a wet blanket? The role of analysis in qualitative research', *Journal of the Market Research Society*, 33, 1, pp. 39–44.

For those interested in computer-aided qualitative analysis, the main applications are reviewed at the CAQDAS website, http://caqdas.soc.surrey.ac.uk.

Chapter 12

ANALYSING QUANTITATIVE DATA 1

Introduction

The aim of this chapter is to introduce you to the basics of quantitative data analysis. We look at what you need to think about in planning the analysis; we look briefly at how data get to be data; we introduce you to four types of data analysis; we look at one of these types – univariate descriptive analysis in some detail (the other three we look at in Chapter 13).

Topics covered

- The purpose of data analysis
- Planning the analysis
- Understanding data
- Types of data analysis
- Univariate descriptive analysis

Relationship to MRS Advanced Certificate Syllabus

The material in this chapter is relevant to Element 7 – Analysing Data. This element covers approaches and techniques for the analysis of primary and secondary quantitative data. The material in this chapter should lay the foundations for developing a sound understanding of quantitative data analysis. It should help you to develop the skills and knowledge to enable you make the links between research objectives of a project and the data analysis choices for that project, and it should give you an understanding of how to plan your approach to the analysis of your quantitative data.

Learning outcomes

At the end of this chapter you should be able to:

- understand the purpose of analysis;
- understand the need to plan the analysis;
- understand quantitative data;
- understand what data analysis is;
- understand what is meant by data reduction;
- conduct univariate analysis of quantitative data.

The purpose of data analysis

The purpose of data analysis is to extract meaningful insights from data and to produce valid and reliable findings that help to answer the research problem. The research which produced the data will have been done with a purpose, an aim, in mind – for example, to advance knowledge about how people use a particular product or service, or to gauge reaction to a new advertising campaign. The process will have been something like this: the client identified a business problem; it was determined that information was needed in order to decide what action to take in relation to this problem; research objectives were stated; questions were formulated, asked and answered; data were produced. The next stage in the process is the analysis of those data: it is not an independent, stand-alone stage but rather part of the bigger process of helping to shed light on the client's problem. As we noted in Chapter 10, data in raw form – the dataset you see at the end of the data collection and data processing stage – are not findings, they do not speak for themselves: they are 'untouched by the human mind' (Ehrenberg, 1982). The job of analysis is to work through and with the data to draw out the findings and get at the 'story'. Analysis is a disciplined and rigorous process. It should be thorough and systematic but it should not be an entirely mechanical business, although the mechanical part – working through data tables, running statistical tests and so on – is essential and does form a large part of it.

You will in all likelihood go into the analysis stage with some fairly solid ideas about what you are looking for. This is the nature of quantitative research. You will have chosen to do quantitative research – to collect quantitative data – because you had a clear idea about the concepts that you wanted to 'measure', the questions that you wanted to address and/or the hypotheses you wanted to 'test'. In fact, you will have done a lot of your thinking about the analysis when you translated the research objectives from the client's brief into a research design, in particular when you decided on your sample – who and how many – and when you decided what questions to ask on the questionnaire, and how to ask them. Research is, after all, a process with all the stages linked, dependent on each other. The quality of the latter stage of the process – where we are now with the analysis of the data – is dependent on the quality of the earlier stages, namely, the problem definition and research design stages. The outcome of the analysis will be of much better quality (and much easier to manage) if you spent time ensuring that the client's business problem was clearly defined and that the research needed – as set out in the research objectives – would indeed deliver evidence (data) that would help the client address the business problem. If you did all that, it is likely that you now have sound, relevant data. So what do you do now?

Planning the analysis

The next thing you do is to go back in time and review – reacquaint yourself with – why the research was conducted, what it set out to achieve. You have three documents that are very valuable to you at this stage: the research brief; the sampling plan; and the questionnaire. The research brief – what the client asked you to do – gives you the 'big picture'; it tells you what the client's business problem is and what information he or she needs to do something about it (the research proposal, if there is one, should also tell you this). You must not lose sight of this: as you do the analysis you must keep asking of every 'finding', 'So what? What does this mean for the client?'. In tackling the analysis you are looking for information in the data – meaningful insights – that will allow the client to make an 'informed' decision. You might find it helpful to print out a summary of the client's problem and the research objectives and stick it above your desk so that it is in view at all times throughout the analysis process.

Box 12.1 Seeing the big picture: reviewing the brief

- Why is the research needed?
- How are the findings to be used? What does the client want to do?
- What are the research objectives? What are the research questions?
- Was the aim of the research to explore, describe, explain and/or evaluate?
- What, if any, are the working hypotheses or ideas?
- What light does previous research or relevant literature cast on the problem?
- *What does all this mean for your analysis plan?*

So, while the brief gives you the big picture, the sampling plan and the questionnaire give you the detail. The sampling plan tells you who you need to look at – which groups or types of people. The questionnaire is in effect a map or index of the data – it tells you 'what' you have. You can use both in conjunction with the brief to plan out how you will tackle the analysis. However, do not use them without the brief – if you do, you run the risk of losing your focus on the big picture. We saw in Chapter 10 how you use the questionnaire to spec out the data tables, and we noted how easy it is to ask for – and to get – a set of tables for all the questions on the questionnaire, every question tabulated against every demographic, geodemographic, attitudinal or behavioural variable. This approach is tempting – it will give you most of what you need. But it will also give you lots of stuff that is irrelevant. Taking this approach you risk being overwhelmed by the mass of data that you get, the sheer number of tables generated. And it really only serves to delay the decision about who and what to look at and how to go about the analysis. In preparing a DP specification you do need to have thought out what is you want, what is relevant to the brief and how you plan to use the data. It is worthwhile, therefore, for the sake of your sanity as well as your timetable and your budget – because both will be limited – to decide on a line of enquiry, an analysis strategy or plan that will take you through the mass of data in a systematic and rigorous way. A strategy that meets the requirements set out in the brief – that addresses the research objectives – will make the whole analysis task much more efficient and productive. But remember, a strategy is not set in stone – it is likely that the data will throw up some interesting findings and it is perfectly acceptable to wander off your strategy to investigate these. By the time you finish your analysis, however, you should see – or feel that you have an understanding of – the big picture and how the details fit in to that big picture.

As your analysis progresses, so will your thinking about the issues and you might find it useful to re-visit any relevant secondary data sources – previous research, your initial background or secondary research for this particular study, the existing body of knowledge (including theory) on the area or topic you are investigating. This may well give you ideas that help you develop your thinking and your analysis – for example, you may find it useful to look at well-developed models and theories from management science, marketing science, consumer behaviour, or even sociology, psychology or anthropology, which can be a source of inspiration and help but should of course not be used uncritically.

The next step in the analysis process is to get to know the data, to start working through it and reorganising it to suit your purposes. I say 'reorganising' it because the raw data that you get at the beginning of the analysis process is structured and organised as a result of being collected in the structured way that is a feature of quantitative research. In the section below we look at how the data are transformed into data from responses on the structured questionnaire. We move on from there to look at some of the terminology and ideas used in quantitative analysis before turning to look at some useful basic analysis techniques that will help you get to grips with what is going on in the data.

Understanding data

The process of quantitative data analysis involves sorting, organising and summarising data collected via the questionnaire in a way that aids interpretation and reporting of findings, and ultimately helps the client decide what to do in relation to the business problem. Before we go into detail about the approaches and techniques of quantitative data analysis it is first of all worth looking at how we get from the answers (mostly words) of the questionnaire to the numeric counts – the numbers – that you see in a data table. In other words, how do we come to the data – how are responses to a questionnaire translated from 'responses' into 'data'?

CONCEPTS, QUESTIONS AND VARIABLES

Quantitative researchers often talk about 'measuring', saying things like, 'This question was designed to measure . . . '. 'Measuring' in this context can be taken to mean gathering data on whatever the relevant 'thing' is – the thing that the client in the brief has asked you to collect data on. It could be factors involved in the decision about which mobile phone to buy; it could be your level of income; it could be the level of your financial capability; it could be your attitude to global warming. In Chapter 9 on designing questionnaires, we saw that this 'thing' can be something as relatively straightforward as marital status or it can be something less straightforward, more difficult to ask as – or to convert to – a question; for example, sexism or attitude to global warming. We saw in Chapter 9 that to get to a valid and reliable question about sexism we had to start with an examination of the concept of sexism; we had to agree a definition of sexism and agree what dimension of it we were really interested in measuring – the dimension relevant to the particular research project – and we had to establish what outward indicators would be appropriate to use in measuring it. Finally, we designed the question. This process is sometimes known as 'operationalising' the concept. But the task didn't really end with the design of the question – we had to decide what response format we would use, and we had to think about how we might later interpret the responses to the question. So back at the questionnaire design stage you were thinking ahead to the analysis – and making sure that the question you designed linked back to the 'thing' that the client asked you to measure.

Also at the questionnaire design stage you will have made a decision about the response format and this will have an impact on the sort of analysis you can do. For example, say that you have included the question, 'What was your age on your last birthday?' and you have decided to record the age of the respondent in years rather than recording it in bands. Deciding to record age in this way gives you scope within your analysis to calculate, for example, the mean (average) age of the sample, the spread of ages and the standard deviation. You could not do this sort of analysis if you had recorded age in bands. Should you later find it useful or convenient, however, you can turn this numeric scale of age into bands, for example, grouping them as follows: 18–24 years; 25–34 years; 35–44 years; and 45 and over. With other questions you will have little or no choice in the response format you use – for gender, for example, you are restricted to using two categories, men and women. This is all about a thing called level of measurement, which we look at in more detail below.

At the analysis stage the conventional practice is to refer to the questions you designed as variables and to refer to the responses as values of the variable. We also look at this in more detail below.

The important things to note at this point are the connection between questions and variables, and the link back to the concept or thing that you set out to measure; and the link between your choice of question/response format and its impact on what you can do in your analysis.

Cases, variables and values

A complete individual unit of analysis is called a case. Typically, one questionnaire – the record of an interview with one respondent – is one case. If you have a sample of 300 completed questionnaires you have 300 cases. To identify each individual case a unique number – a serial number – is assigned. In a sample of 300 each questionnaire would be numbered, from 001 to 300. For each case, or questionnaire, the individual bits of information (questions or parts of questions) are called variables, and the answers the respondent gives to these questions are called values.

Have a look at the first question in Box 12.2 below. Respondents were asked about changes in their household income over the last year or so. The variable has been labelled HINCPAST (an abbreviation of household income over the past year); the respondent's answer – Fallen behind; Kept up; Gone up by more; or Don't know – is the value of the variable. If you were to answer in response to this question that your household's income had gone up by more than prices, you or the interviewer would 'code' the number 3. This process of assigning a number to a response is called coding. Coding means that data captured in a non-computerised form – answers marked or written on a questionnaire – are converted into number values that a computer analysis package can recognise and use. It is likely that you will need to prepare a codebook describing the codes for all the variables from your questionnaire. Have a look at Box 12.3 below.

Box 12.2 Response codes example

Q. Looking back over the *last year* or so, would you say that your household's income has . . . **READ OUT** . . .

Fallen behind prices	1
Kept up with prices	2
Or gone up by more than prices	3
(Don't know)	8

Q. How old were you when you completed your continuous full time education?

15 or under	1
16	2
17	3
18	4
19 or over	5
Still at school	6
Still at college or university	7
Other – write in	8
(Don't know/Can't remember)	98

Table 12.1 Data entry grid for ten fictional respondents to the Life and Times 2006 Survey

Int No			Serial No				Q1		Q2	Q2a			Q3	Q4	Q5	Q6
1	2	3	0	0	1	0	0	4	1	1	2	2	3	1	1	1
1	2	3	0	0	1	1	3	9	2	–	–	–	5	2	2	1
1	2	3	0	0	1	2	2	4	1	2	1	1	3	1	1	2
1	2	3	0	0	1	3	1	2	1	1	1	1	3	1	1	1
1	2	3	0	0	1	4	1	9	2	–	–	–	4	2	2	1
1	2	3	0	0	1	5	0	0	1	2	2	1	4	2	1	2
0	0	7	0	0	1	6	1	1	2	–	–	–	2	2	1	1
0	0	7	0	0	1	7	0	8	2	–	–	–	2	1	1	1
0	0	7	0	0	1	8	1	5	1	1	2	1	2	1	1	2
0	0	7	0	0	1	9	0	9	1	1	2	2	1	1	1	1

DATA ENTRY OR 'KEYING IN'

In order for an analysis program to receive and understand data from the questionnaire the data must be in a regular, predictable format. For most datasets the data usually appear in a grid arrangement – this will be familiar to you if you have ever used a spreadsheet such as Microsoft Excel or if you have an analysis package such as SPSS for Windows. The grid is made up of rows of cases and columns of variables. Each case makes up a line or row of data and the variables appear as columns of number codes. The purpose of data entry is to convert the answers on the questionnaire into a 'line of data' that the analysis program will accept and recognise.

Table 12.1 is an illustration of how these lines of data and columns of codes would look for the answers given to Q. 1 to Q. 6 on the Life and Times 2006 questionnaire by ten respondents. The first three columns of numbers are the interviewer's identity number; the next four columns are the unique serial number or case number of that particular questionnaire – both are on the front page of the questionnaire. The subsequent columns represent the responses to Q. 1, Q. 2 and so on in sequence up to Q. 6. (You can download the questionnaire from the Life and Times website (www.ark.ac.uk/nilt/2006/quest06.html) and check what responses the codes represent on the questionnaire.)

You can see from this grid how each variable or question has been coded. Numeric data entered by the interviewer, for example in response to Q. 1 'How long have you lived in the town (city, village) where you live now?' appears as it is. The respondent with serial number 0010, for example, has lived for four years in a small city or town (Q. 3 code 3) and this has been coded 04 in the grid; respondent number 0011 has lived for 39 years in the same farm or home in the same country (Q. 3 code 5) as now; respondent 0015, who has lived where they live now for less than a year, has been coded 00, following the instructions on the questionnaire.

Where the information you want to code is not a numeric value, Q. 2 to Q. 6 in the Life and Times example, the response is entered using the number code assigned as the label for that response (the value of that variable). So, for example, responses to Q. 2 'Have you ever lived outside Northern Ireland for more than six months?', 'Yes' and 'No', are coded as 'Yes' = 1 and 'No' = 2. (Note that for questions that the respondent is not eligible to answer, a blank – or a space or a zero – is entered in the grid.) Remember, however, that although the code for these questions is a number it has no arithmetic value.

These number codes are what you or the data entry program transfer from the questionnaire into the analysis program in a process known as *data entry* or *data input* or *keying in*. Besides allowing you to enter numeric codes, most packages also allow you to enter alphanumeric codes – codes that use letters as well as numbers. Codes that use letters are called *string* variables. You might want to use a string variable to enter a brand name, for example, or to transfer responses to open-ended questions verbatim rather than coding the response in numeric form.

Box 12.3 Preparing a codebook

If you are transferring data from your questionnaire into an analysis package – SPSS, for example – then you need to prepare what is called a codebook. The codebook lists the variables from the questionnaire. Each variable is assigned its own unique variable name and each value of the variable is assigned a numeric code. We saw how this was done above with the example in Box 12.2. In the first question in Box 12.2 respondents were asked about changes in their household income over the last year or so. This variable has been labelled HINCPAST, an abbreviation of **h**ousehold **inc**ome over the **past** year. The rules for naming variables for SPSS state that each name must be unique – no two variables can have the same label; the label must begin with a letter; it can be up to 64 characters long; it must not include words that are used in SPSS commands; it must not use any non letter or non number characters (e.g. ^ * ~ : ; . and so on). Check the naming rules for whatever package you are using – and whatever version of SPSS. The values of the HINCPAST variable are the answers offered (or not) to the respondent – this was a closed question: Fallen behind; Kept up; Gone up by more; or Don't know. On the questionnaire each of these responses was assigned a number – a numeric code. This is the coding instruction: it tells the analysis package that this HINCPAST variable has four possible values only – 1, 2, 3 and 8 – anything else and an error will be flagged. What happens if you have an open-ended question? As we saw in Chapter 10, the coding process for open-ended questions works as follows: responses are extracted and listed as individual response items – extraction continues until the content of what is being extracted does not change and no new content is seen; the list of 'extractions' is used to develop a draft coding frame of unique responses, each of which is assigned a numeric code. This draft coding frame is used to code the responses from a portion of the sample. At the end of this pilot test phase it is amended if necessary. It is then listed in the codebook and used to code responses from the entire sample. The codebook together with the questionnaire form a sort of map of the final entered dataset.

With computer-aided data collection (CAPI, CATI, CASI and so on) there is no separate data transfer or data entry phase; the responses are captured – entered – electronically and verified almost simultaneously. The data capture program alerts the interviewer or the respondent if a response is not within the bounds allowed by the question. Data collected on a paper questionnaire, however, must be transferred – 'entered' – into an analysis package. This is done either manually (responses keyed into the data entry program) or electronically (responses read by a scanner or optical mark reader).

In compiling the table for the first question in Box 12.2 above, the analysis program will count the number of times across the sample (the total number of cases) that each response code has been entered or coded. It will count the number of respondents who said 'Fallen behind prices' or code 1; the number who said 'Kept up with prices' or code 2; the number who said 'Gone up by more than prices' or code 3; and the number who said 'Don't know'. Typically, these frequency counts will be converted to a percentage, calculated on the most suitable base for that particular question, all answering or total sample, for example. You can ask in your data processing specification or when you write the table specification that both the percentage and the frequency count or raw number appear on the table.

If you use or are interested in using the analysis package SPSS then you might find it worthwhile to have a look at the dataset from the 2006 Life and Times Survey at the website www.ark.ac.uk/nilt/datasets/teaching/index.html. This is a dataset in the form of an SPSS datafile. It has been developed as a teaching and learning aid for quantitative data analysis, as Box 12.4 below explains.

Box 12.4 Life and Times Survey 2006 Teaching Dataset

A special Teaching Dataset in the form of an SPSS datafile has been developed from the 2006 Northern Ireland Life & Times (NILT) Survey by ARK, a social and political archive. It contains over 150 variables and gives the answers of all 1,230 respondents to the NILT2006 Survey. The scope of the Dataset from such a large-scale representative and contemporary sample means that it is a useful resource from which to learn and from which to gain experience in analysing 'real world' data. The Dataset has been modified from the original NILT2006 dataset to enhance its capacity as a teaching and learning tool and to make it easier to use:

- The data are taken mainly from the 'Community Relations' and 'Political Attitudes' modules of the survey, along with data based on the general background questions asked of each respondent. This allows you to develop an overview of the scope of the data while retaining the capacity for carrying out a variety of analyses.
- The dataset has been subjected to a secondary cleaning process to simplify its structure, remove anomalies that could confuse the novice and make it in general more 'user friendly'.
- Each variable is identified as either nominal/categorical, ordinal, or 'scalar' (interval/ratio) to help you use data that is appropriate for a given analysis procedure.
- Each variable that comes directly from a question in the interview has the question number in its label. You can view or print the complete questionnaire from the website www.ark.ac.uk/nilt/2006/quest06.html and so you look at the exact question wording and response options that respondents were given.
- ARK derived additional 'scalar' variables that greatly increase the scope for using parametric statistical procedures such as correlation or regression.

Source: ARK and the Northern Ireland Life and Times Survey Team (2006), University of Ulster and Queen's University Belfast. Used with permission.

LEVELS OF MEASUREMENT

You will have noticed from the above descriptions of the use of numbers as codes that numbers do not always mean the same thing. In all cases they describe or measure something but they can represent different types or levels of measurement. Sometimes they represent numeric quantities, years lived where you live now, for example, or age or number of people in the household, or the price paid for a product. Sometimes they are merely symbols, for example, where 1 = 'Yes' and 2 = 'No' in Q. 2 in the Life and Times questionnaire. In the context of quantitative data analysis it is important to understand what level of measurement a number represents. There are four levels: nominal, ordinal, interval and ratio. Data at the nominal or ordinal levels are known as categorical or non-metric data; data at the interval or ratio level are known as continuous or metric data. Interval and ratio numbers are also known as cardinal numbers.

Nominal scale numbers

At the nominal level of measurement numbers are used to classify or label (name) things. Other symbols would be just as suitable but numbers are used because they are familiar and easy to understand. When they are used in this way numbers have no arithmetic meaning or value. In an analysis context sex or gender is a nominal variable – we have assigned the number 1 to represent male and the number 2 to represent female; 'ever lived outside Northern Ireland for more than six months' is also a nominal variable with 15 'Yes' for those who have; and 25 'No' for those who have not. These numbers have no other meaning than that – it would be meaningless to add them together.

Ordinal scale numbers

At the ordinal level of measurement numbers represent a category and indicate that there is a relationship between the numbered items. In other words there is an order or ranking or sequence to the numbers. House numbers on a street are ordinal numbers; your position in a race or birth order in your family – first, second, third and so on – are ordinal rankings. An example of an ordinal level variable would be opinion ratings or preference ranking in a product test: first preference; second preference and so on. An ordinal number does not represent a real amount, so, as with nominal scale numbers, arithmetic is not meaningful.

Interval scale numbers

At the interval level of measurement numbers represent numeric values, so arithmetic is meaningful. The numbers in an interval scale are ordered and the intervals between the numbers are of equal size. Temperature is measured on an interval scale. The main feature of an interval scale is that there is no absolute zero: negative amounts mean something. For example, minus 5°C is a meaningful number. Income is an example of an interval level variable – it is possible to have a negative income if one has debts, for example.

Ratio scale numbers

Ratio scale numbers have the same properties as interval scale numbers – they have a rank order, there are equal intervals between numbers, arithmetic is meaningful – but on the ratio scale there is an absolute zero. Zero on a ratio scale means that there is nothing there, whereas on the interval scale zero might mean 'low' or 'very low'. At the ratio level of measurement it is impossible to have minus numbers. Examples of ratio level variables would be elapsed time, weight, the number of times an item has been used or the number of children in a household.

But why does all this matter?

In research you will come across variables at all four levels of measurement. Interval and ratio level variables can be manipulated using a range of mathematical and statistical procedures – because they represent numeric amounts and because arithmetic is meaningful with these types of numbers. We noted this earlier when we looked at recording age in years. Nominal and ordinal level variables, on the other hand, because they do not represent numeric amounts, are not suitable for precise methods of analysis. (This is the case if we were to record age in bands.) So, in order to determine what type of analysis is appropriate, and the type of statistical test to use when testing hypotheses, it is important to be able to recognise what kind of number or variable you have. Different tests are suitable for different levels of measurement. We look at how to choose the relevant test in the next chapter.

EDITING AND CLEANING THE DATASET

As the data are being entered on a case-by-case basis they can be edited or cleaned to ensure that they are free of errors and inconsistencies. Such checks should be carried out by interviewers and field supervisors during fieldwork and by editors when paper questionnaires are returned from the field (we looked at this briefly in Chapter 10). With computer-aided data capture this process is incorporated into the data capture program. During the editing and cleaning process missing values, out of range values, and errors due to misrouting of questions are sorted out and the data are checked for other inconsistencies.

Missing values

If a response has been left blank it is known as a 'missing value'. Missing values can occur for all sorts of reasons – the question may not apply to the respondent, the respondent may not know the answer or may refuse to answer, or the interviewer may have inadvertently forgotten to record a response. It is important to deal with missing values so that they do not contaminate the dataset and mislead the researcher or client. One way of dealing with the possibility of missing values is at the questionnaire design stage and at interviewer training and briefing sessions. In a well-designed questionnaire there will be codes for 'Don't know' and 'No answer' or 'Refused'. Interviewers should be briefed about how to handle such responses and how to code them on the questionnaire. It is also possible to avoid missing values by checking answers with respondents at the end of the interview or during quality control call backs.

If missing values remain, a code (or codes) can be added to the data entry program that will allow a missing value to be recorded. Typically a code is chosen with a value that is out of range of the possible values for that variable. Imagine that for some reason a respondent to the Life and Times Survey did not answer, or the interviewer did not ask for or record, a response to Q. 3 'Would you describe the place where you live as . . . ?'. The values or response codes for this question range from 1 = 'big city' to 5 = 'farm or home in the country'; you could assign a missing value code of 9 for 'No response'. If you know in more detail why the information is missing – for instance 'Doesn't apply', 'Refused to answer', or 'Don't know', and this is not already allowed for on the questionnaire, you can give each of these a different missing value code – 'Doesn't apply' could be 96; 'Refused to answer' could be 97; 'Don't know' could be 98; and 'Missing for some other reason' could be 99. There are other ways of dealing with missing values. One extreme approach, known as casewise deletion, is to remove from the dataset any case or questionnaire that contains missing values. This approach, however, results in a reduction in sample size and may lead to bias, as cases with missing values may differ from those with none. A less drastic approach is the pairwise deletion in which only those cases without missing values are used in the table or calculation. This too will affect the quality of the data, especially if the sample size is relatively small, or if there is a large number of cases with missing values.

An alternative is to replace the missing value with a real value. There are two ways of approaching this. You could calculate the mean value for the variable and use that; or you could calculate an imputed value based on either the pattern of response to other questions in the case (on that questionnaire) or the response of respondents with similar profiles to the respondent with the missing value. Substituting a mean value means that the distribution of the values for the sample does not change. We are assuming, however, that the respondent gave such a response when of course the answer given may have been more extreme. If we substitute an imputed value we are making assumptions and risk introducing bias.

Inconsistencies, routing errors and out of range values

Other data cleaning issues involve resolving problems that arise due to inconsistent answers, routing instructions not followed correctly, extreme answers and answers that are not valid or are outside the range of possible answers. For example, if at Q. 2 in the Life and Times Survey a respondent answered, 'No' (they have not lived outside Northern Ireland for more than six months), this respondent should not be asked Q. 2a but should skip to Q. 3. Only those answering 'Yes' at Q. 2 are eligible to answer Q. 3 – all others should be filtered out. If a respondent answers 'No' at Q. 2 and goes on to answer Q. 2a, the 'skip' or routing instruction has not been followed correctly and the answers at Q. 2 and Q. 2a are inconsistent. This should not happen in a CAPI survey such as the Life and Times, where the routing is handled automatically by the data capture program. Data collected via CATI, CAPI, CASI, CAWI or web-based methods are subjected to such checks automatically as data are entered – built-in editing programs and logic checks should highlight any such problems, if programmed correctly. The program alerts the user (the interviewer or the respondent) to inconsistent answers, skips to the appropriate question and can be programmed to refuse an answer or code that is out of range. Further checks on the accuracy and consistency of the data can be made at the next stage of the process, when the data are available in the form of a frequency count or 'holecount'. For example, if 406 respondents out of a total of 1,100 say that they have bought goods over the Internet, have 406 replied to a later question to which they are directed about the type of goods they bought?

Once the data have been entered, edited and verified they are in a form that can be manipulated and analysed.

It is typically the case that data collection and data processing and analysis are done by the same supplier. Nevertheless there are some circumstances in which an organisation or an individual will have collected data and, not having the staff or the skills or the software to process and analyse it, may ask an outside contractor to do this on their behalf. Box 12.5 below contains an example of the reply to this sort of request. You may find it useful in that it gives an overview of what is involved in the data analysis process, including issues to do with data security.

Box 12.5 Example of a proposal for data entry, analysis and reporting

The client designed and carried out a postal survey and now wants data from the completed questionnaires entered, analysed and a report written.

Key words are: survey, data, postal, transferred, analysis package, findings, report, approach, timings, costs, experience, questionnaires, closed questions, open-ended questions, data tables, data set, editing, verification, cleaning, coding, data entry, verbatims, independent variables, aggregate, cross-tabulated, confidentiality, data security.

Overview

Catville Community Safety Forum, a group within Catville Local Council, has collected data via a Community Safety survey administered by post. The data were collected from two groups in the Catville district: business owners and residents. As we understand it from your brief, you would like these data transferred to a data analysis package and the findings from the data analysed and written up in a report. The purpose of this proposal is to set out our approach to this, the timings and costs involved and our relevant experience.

Terms of reference

As we understand it, you have consulted with Catville residents and businesses via a survey to identify their experiences and fears of crime and anti-social behaviour. The aim of this research was to help you identify key areas for action and so inform the Community Safety Strategy for the Catville district. At present you have two sets of completed questionnaires, returns from a postal survey among the two groups – business owners and residents. Each questionnaire contains 25 closed questions and five open-ended questions. You require two main tasks to be completed:

Task 1

Convert the data from the questionnaires into data tables. This will involve the following:

- set up of a dataset for each of the sectors surveyed;
- data transfer from the two sets of questionnaires (730 residents' questionnaires and 69 business questionnaires);
- editing, verification and cleaning of each dataset;
- coding and data entry of the open-ended questions;
- preparation of verbatim comments from these open-ended questions;
- design and running of two sets of tables based on each of the datasets using relevant 'profile' or independent variables.

Task 2

Analysis and interpretation of the two sets of data and preparation of a report covering both groups of respondents. As you note in the brief, the report should identify the fears, concerns and experiences by business sector, type, size and location for the business respondents and by key demographic variables for the residents' sample. The qualitative information gathered from the open-ended questions in each questionnaire should also be analysed and written up in the report.

Proposed outputs

On completion of the project you would receive two datasets containing all the information gleaned from each of the questionnaires in aggregate form. You would also receive a set of tables for each of the sectors you have surveyed. These tables would consist of responses to all of the questions on the questionnaire cross-tabulated with the profile or independent variables you have identified for that group. The qualitative information in the open-ended questions would be coded and analysed to draw out content and meaning. This information would be presented in the data tables and verbatim comments gleaned from these questions would also be used to illustrate points made in the report.

We would welcome the chance to discuss with you the possibility of setting the findings from your research into the wider context of other research conducted on similar topics at a national level. We feel that this would be valuable to the decision-making process.

Details of the project team

The project team for this work would be Ray Orbis, Senior Data Processing Executive, and Caroline Mali, Senior Research Executive. They have worked together on many similar projects, most recently on a similar project for Dogville District Town Planning Service. Ray would be in charge of data processing through to preparation of the data tables – in other words all of Task 1. Ray has ten years' experience in data processing and analysis. He has considerable experience in running similar projects. Caroline would be responsible for Task 2 – interpreting the findings and writing the report. Caroline has ten years' experience in research practice on a wide variety of projects.

Table 1 Draft schedule with costs

Date	Task	Cost
W/c 9 November	Client to send questionnaires for data processing	
10/11 November onwards	Editing and coding	£1,100
	Data entry and 100% verification (includes cleaning)	£1,100
	Set up of two datasets: programming for data entry and programming for designing, running and producing tables	£1,400
	Preparation of verbatim (qualitative) comments from open-ended questions	£500
W/c 16 November	Write up of reports for each dataset	£1,500
W/c 30 November	Delivery of written report	
	TOTAL PROJECT COST	**£5,600**

Costs and timings

Table 1 gives a breakdown of the costs and timings involved in each of the elements of the project. Without an exact start date for the project it is difficult to be precise about a completion date. We do, however, understand that time is of the essence and we would aim to work with you to meet your deadlines.

This cost is exclusive of sales tax, which would be charged at the appropriate rate. The cost remains current for two months from today.

▶

Information on confidentiality and data security procedures/policies

As members of the professional body, MRS, we adhere to the Society's Code of Conduct on confidentiality and data security. The Code incorporates the key principles of the Data Protection Act 1998. Details of this can be found on the MRS website – www.mrs.org.uk. Questionnaires will be stored securely during data processing and will only be available to those involved in that element of the task. Once data are transferred to an analysis package questionnaires will be returned to you. All data files and tables will be stored securely. No information will be disclosed to those not involved in the project.

We understand that Catville Community Safety Forum will remain the owner of all the data and any subsequent databases and reports. Following completion of this piece of work, we would hand over all data and other relevant documents to Catville Community Safety Forum.

Types of data analysis

With the data entered and cleaned we are now back at the start of the analysis stage proper. This is the point in the process where – if you are the research executive – you come back into a project: you will probably have been involved in the project design and set up and in the design of the questionnaire but it is less likely that you will have been involved in gathering or processing the data. You may, however, have been involved in preparing an analysis specification, a written request to the data processing and analysis executive setting out the sort of analysis that you want done and how you want the dataset and the data tables to look, which we covered in Chapter 10. What we turn to now is how to do the analysis.

The purpose of your research project has been to answer questions, questions raised by the client in wanting to explore, describe, count, explain, understand or evaluate an issue or problem relevant to his or her business or situation. You are now at the point of being able to answer these questions (if, of course, the research questions were indeed relevant to the research problem and if you chose an appropriate research design with which to address them). Data analysis is the process by which you answer these questions. There are four main types of analysis (Blaikie, 2003):

- univariate descriptive analysis;
- bivariate descriptive analysis;
- explanatory analysis;
- inferential analysis.

THE CASE FOR INFERENTIAL ANALYSIS

You may in the course of a project use one or more, even all, of these types of analysis. The case of inferential analysis is, however a special one: the decision to use this type of analysis depends largely on what type of sampling approach you used – that is, whether you used probability (random) or non-probability (non-random) sampling. As we saw in Chapter 8, one of the reasons for using a probability or random sample is that you want to generalise from the sample to the population – you want to be able to estimate whether what you see in the sample (for example, the characteristics of your product's buyers or relationships between age and product usage) exists in the population from which the sample was drawn. If you have this sort of sample and you want to make these sort of inferences (and other things are in place, including a reasonably high response rate), then you will want to do inferential analysis. If you do not have this sort of sample then this type of analysis is not appropriate, although it is often used. Smith and Fletcher (2004) note that it may be used but with limitations on how the data are interpreted. We will come back to this in Chapter 13 when we look at inferential analysis, along with bivariate descriptive and explanatory analysis, in more detail. We now look at what the first of these four types of analysis – univariate descriptive analysis – involves.

Univariate descriptive analysis

Univariate descriptive analysis is analysis that describes one variable. It is a fairly basic but very useful and informative type of analysis, the purpose of which is often to help you get to know the data. In essence, it involves summarising or describing responses using frequency counts and frequency distributions, and calculations known as summary or descriptive statistics – measures of central tendency (also known as 'averages') and measures of spread or variation.

FREQUENCY COUNTS

A frequency count is a count of the number of times a value occurs in the dataset, typically the number of respondents who gave a particular answer. For example, we want to know how many people in the sample are very satisfied with the level of service provided by Bank S. A frequency count – a count of the number of people who said they are very satisfied with Bank S – tells us this.

The first data you might see is a frequency count for each of the values of a variable in the dataset (this used to be known as a 'holecount', a term that harks back to the use of punched cards in analysing data). It can be useful to run a holecount before preparing a detailed analysis or table specification as it gives an overview of the responses to a question, allowing you to see the size of particular sub-groups within your sample, what categories of responses might be grouped together, and what weighting might be required. For example, say we have asked if respondents are users of a particular Internet banking service. The holecount or frequency count will tell us how many users we have. We can decide if it is feasible to isolate this group – to look at how the attitudes, behaviour or opinion of Internet customers compares to those of non-Internet customers, for example.

It can also be useful to look at a graphical display of frequency in what is known as a frequency distribution chart: this is where you plot the range of values on the x-axis (the horizontal axis) of the chart and the frequency of response to each value on the y-axis (the vertical axis). As Figure 12.1 below shows, this type of display allows you to see quickly and easily the spread of values for a particular variable.

Frequency distribution charts are also a useful way of describing the shape of a distribution of continuous or metric variables. If the distribution is symmetrical (for example, like the normal distribution which takes the form of a bell curve), half of all values will lie below the mean and half above it. There is no 'skewness' in either direction; the mean, the mode and the median take the same, or roughly the same, value. When a distribution is skewed it is off-centre or asymmetrical, with more values or observations falling to one side of the mean than the other and the mean, the mode and the median will not have the same value. If the distribution is positively skewed a greater proportion of values will lie above the mean than below it; negative skewness means that a greater proportion lie below the mean than above it.

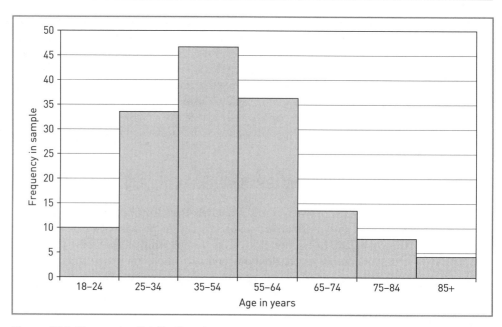

Figure 12.1 Frequency distribution chart

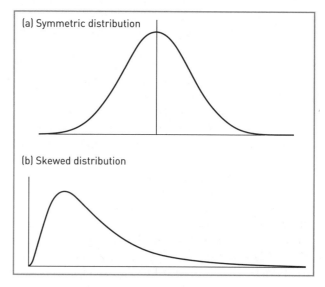

Figure 12.2 A symmetric and a skewed distribution

Raw numbers, proportions, percentages and ratios

A frequency count is usually expressed in raw numbers, telling us, for example, that 36 respondents are Internet customers; it does not tell us, however, what proportion or percentage of the total sample this number represents. It can be useful to reduce frequencies to proportions or percentages – it allows us to compare data between groups (for example, the proportion or percentage of men who are Internet customers compared to the proportion or percentage of women). The proportion is the relative incidence of occurrence expressed as a proportion of 1.00 – it is the frequency of occurrence divided by the total number of cases; the percentage is the relative incidence of occurrence expressed as a proportion of every 100 cases – in other words, it is the frequency of occurrence divided by the total number of cases then multiplied by 100. The proportion of Internet customers in this example is 0.12 (36 divided by 300); the percentage of Internet customers is 12 per cent.

Ratios are a useful way of comparing the relative size of two groups. Say that you have divided your sample into users of the leading brand and users of all other brands. It might be useful to summarise how the size of each of these groups compare. So say that you have 450 users of the leading brand and 150 users of all other brands. The ratio of the leading brand to other brands is 450:150, that is, the number in the largest category divided by the number in the smallest category, which works out at 3 to 1. So we can say that for every three users of the leading brand there is one user of another brand.

Graphical displays

We noted above how useful it can be to look at graphical displays of frequency. There are other charts that are also useful – pie charts, bar charts, histograms and line graphs. In choosing a suitable chart format you need to consider the type of data you have. For categorical data (variables at the nominal and ordinal level of measurement) the most suitable formats are pie charts and bar charts; for continuous or metric data (variables at the ratio and interval level of measurement) the most suitable formats are histograms and line graphs. We look at each of these types of charts below.

Pie charts

If you want to show how the whole of something divides up into parts a pie chart is useful. For example, if you want to show the breakdown of support for the political parties in an election (a nominal level variable), a pie chart is a reasonable way of doing this. Each segment or slice of the pie will represent the proportion of the sample which supports that party (see Figure 12.3). The slices should be ordered logically in a clockwise direction. If you want to highlight a particular segment you can 'explode' that segment, removing it slightly from the rest of the pie. Pie charts are not a good choice of format if you have a lot of categories in your variable (more than four or five segments make the chart look messy and can be difficult to read). Although two pie charts side by side are sometimes used to demonstrate the relative

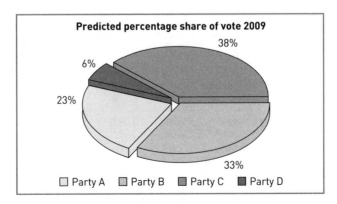

Figure 12.3 Example of a pie chart

breakdown of two sets of data or 'wholes', having to move back and forth between pies to compare segments can be hard work.

Bar charts

Bar charts and histograms are often confused. Use a bar chart when the data are nominal or ordinal (categorical variables, non-metric data); use a histogram when the data are interval or ratio (cardinal numbers, metric data, continuous variables). The horizontal or x-axis of the bar chart in Figure 12.4 is used to display the categories; the vertical or y-axis is used to display the frequency or number of observations or responses in each category – the height of the bar represents the frequency. The categories or bars should be ordered in a way that draws out the meaning or the finding. Figure 12.4 shows what percentage of the sample associates each attribute with brand L.

There are several ways of displaying bar charts. The bars can be displayed vertically, as well as horizontally. Two or more sets of bars can be displayed on the one chart, with each set clustered or grouped together, for example to show the responses of the sample to different brands as in Figure 12.5 (a) and (b). A bar can be divided up into sections, with each section representing measurements that relate to each other in some way. Figure 12.6 shows a stacked bar chart with one section showing the percentage who rate the brand effective and the other showing the percentage who 'buy nowadays'. In this example each component of the bar represents the proportion of the total sample giving that response; Figure 12.7 shows a component bar chart in which the total bar represents the whole sample and each component represents the percentage or frequency of that particular response.

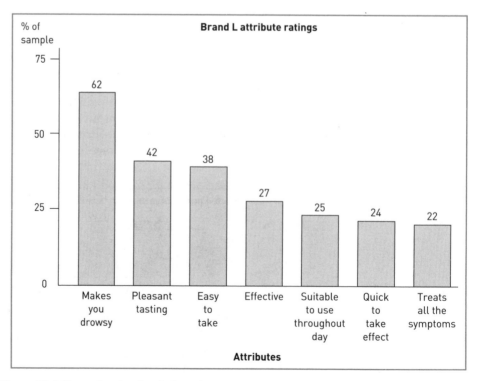

Figure 12.4 Example of a simple bar chart

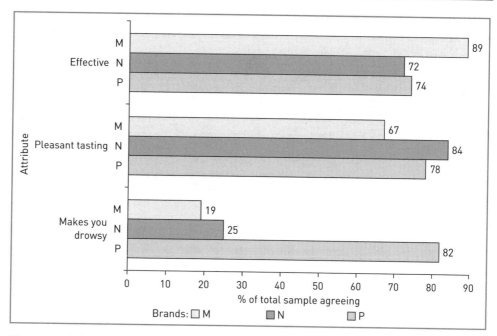

Figure 12.5(a) Example of a horizontal 'grouped bars' bar chart

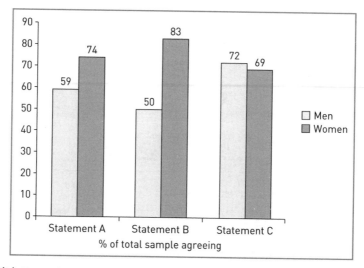

Figure 12.5(b) Example of a vertical 'grouped bars' bar chart

Histograms

A histogram looks like a bar chart without the spaces in between the bars. The reason there are no spaces, the reason the bars are touching, is because the histogram is displaying continuous data at the interval or ratio level of measurement – age bands, for example, or income groups – and not data that can be grouped in discrete categories, such as male and female or social class. The width of the bar represents the size of the interval covered by the band or group

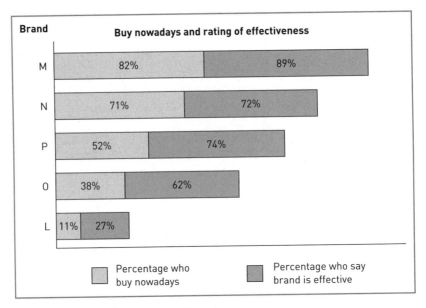

Figure 12.6 Example of a 'stacked bars' bar chart

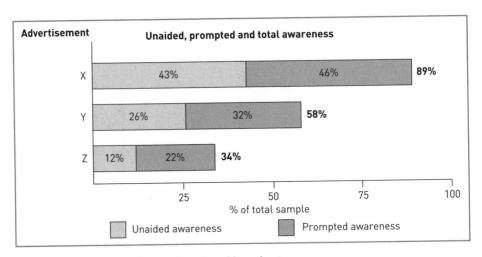

Figure 12.7 Example of a 'component bars' bar chart

of responses and so the area of each bar on the histogram is proportional to the frequency of responses for that group (see Figure 12.8).

Line graphs

Data that can be displayed on a histogram can also be shown as a line graph or line chart by drawing a line that joins the midpoints of the histogram bars. This sort of chart is also sometimes known as a frequency polygon.

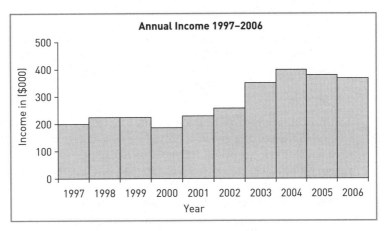

Figure 12.8 Example of a histogram

Choosing the scales for charts and graphs

Besides taking care to choose the right format, care should be taken when deciding on the scales for the x- and y-axis in charts and graphs. If the vertical or y-axis is exaggerated in scale in relation to the x-axis, the effect will be to pull the graph or chart upwards and make increases over the length of the x-axis seem bigger than they might otherwise appear. If, on the other hand, the y-axis is compressed, differences over the length of the x-axis may appear flatter than is the case. Tufte (2001) has examined many cases, investigated the geometry and the aesthetics of shape and, taking the advice of Tukey (1977), recommends a shape that is wider than it is tall. He cites as benefits the ease of reading along the horizontal and of labelling on an extended horizontal axis.

SUMMARY OR DESCRIPTIVE STATISTICS

Another way of looking at the shape of the distribution, without having to plot a chart or graph, is to calculate a number – a summary or descriptive statistic – that will give you the same or similar information. There are two sets of such statistics: measures of central tendency (sometimes called measures of location) and measures of variation (sometimes called measures of dispersion or measures of variability).

Measures of central tendency

A measure of central tendency is more commonly known as an average. It is a single figure used to represent the average of a distribution or group of values. It anchors or locates the distribution on a scale of all its possible values. There are three 'averaging' statistics: the mean, the mode and the median. As we shall see below, knowing the level of measurement of your variable is important in deciding which of these to use.

The mean

The mean or arithmetic mean is the average most often used. However, it can only be used on data of at least interval level of measurement. To calculate it you add together all of the values in the sample and divide by the total number of values. For example, to work out the mean number of children in households in the sample you add together the number of children in every household in the sample and divide by the total number of households.

The mode

The mode is the most frequent response. It requires no calculation except a frequency count of all values to see which is the most commonly occurring. It can be used on data of any level of measurement. It is possible to have more than one mode in any distribution.

The median

The median is defined as the middle value when all the values are arranged in order. It can be used on all types of data except nominal level data. It has the same number of values or observations above it as it has below. If there is no one middle value – if you have an even number of values, for instance – to work out the median you take the mean of the two middle values.

Properties of the mean, the mode and the median

Each of these three averages has particular properties. The mean differs from the mode and the median in that all the values in the distribution are used in calculating it. It is an arithmetical calculation and it can be used in further calculations. It can, however, produce an 'impossible' value, for example 2.3 children per household, and because all values are used in its calculation outliers (extreme values) can distort its value. The median, on the other hand, is not an arithmetically derived calculation, it cannot be used in further calculations but it will usually produce a real value and it is not affected by extreme values. The mode, in referring to the most frequently occurring response, takes no other value into account, cannot be used in further calculations and always produces a real value.

So when do you use the mean, the mode or the median? Use the mean when:

- you need a statistic that is widely understood;
- you want to take into account the influence of all values, even the outliers;
- you need a statistic that you can use in further calculations;
- you do not need a 'real' value;
- your data are at the interval or ratio level of measurement.

For example, the mean is used for working out average household income or average spend or the average age of users of a service.

Use the median when:

- you want an average that is not affected by outliers;
- you do not need the average to calculate further statistics;
- the middle value has some significance;
- you want a more realistic representation of the average;
- your data are interval or ratio level.

The median can be used, for example, to describe the average breakdown rates of washing machines or in other cases where outliers might distort the value of the arithmetic mean. It can also be used to track changes in attitudes, when you want to follow changes to the middle value on an attitude scale.

Use the mode when:

- you do not need any further statistics based on the average;
- you are interested only in the most frequent value;
- your data are numerical (interval or ratio) or non-numerical (nominal or ordinal).

The mode is used when it is interesting to quote the most frequent response, for example the price that most people said they were willing to pay, or the most frequently cited ISP.

Box 12.6 Manipulating variables

After an initial inspection of the data using frequency counts and frequency distributions you may find that some variables or values of a variable are not in a form that is useful for further analysis. It is possible to change the variables or values by recoding them or manipulating them to create new variables. For example, say you asked a question about holiday destinations and you received a long list of responses. You may decide that it would be more useful to recode them into smaller groups, say by country or by continent. Remember, too, that if a variable is at the interval or ratio level of measurement you can use arithmetic functions to create a new variable based on the values of the original variable or variables. For example, perhaps you asked respondents to give their average monthly spend on their mobile phone and now you find that recoding this spend variable into annual spend is more appropriate to your analysis needs. Or say you have two variables – number of adults in the household and number of children in the household. You do not, however, have a variable for the total number of people in the household. You can create this variable via the analysis program by adding the value that represents the number of adults in each household to the value that represents the number of children in the same household for each case in the dataset.

Measures of variation

The average tells us something about where the middle of a distribution is but it does not tell us about the range of values. For this we need a second group of statistics called measures of variation. The range and the standard deviation are the most commonly used measures of variation. Again, as we shall see below, knowing the level of measurement of your variable is important in deciding which measure of variation to use.

The range

The range is the difference between the highest value in the distribution and the lowest value. It is suitable for use with data at the metric level (interval and ratio variables). It is a useful way of determining the scope of the distribution, the range over which the values are spread. The bigger the range, the bigger the spread in values; the smaller the range the more tightly clustered the values. For example, you might be interested in establishing the range of prices paid for service A. The range is, however, a fairly crude measure because one outlier can have a huge effect on it. Consider the example in Figure 12.9. The distributions are identical save for one value. This one number increases the range from four to ten. To calculate the inter-quartile range you divide the distribution in four and the interquartile range is the difference between the third quartile and first quartile. It is the measure of dispersion equivalent of the median. It is a more stable statistic than the range.

The variance and the standard deviation

The standard deviation is a statistic that summarises the average distance of the values from the mean. Like the range, the bigger the standard deviation the greater the variation or spread

Price paid for car cleaning service at nine outlets in two regions, A and B	
Prices in €	
Sample A: 10, 11, 11, 12, 12, 13, 13, 13, 14	Range: 14 – 10 = 4
Sample B: 10, 11, 11, 12, 12, 13, 13, 13, 20	Range: 20 – 10 = 10

Figure 12.9 The effect of an outlier on the range

in the sample or distribution. It is a more robust calculation than the range because in calculating it we use more of the values of the distribution – not just two, as with the range. The first step is to work out the mean. Once you know the mean you subtract each value in the distribution from the mean – in effect working out how far each one is from the mean. These figures – some are below the mean (and so are minus numbers) and some are above it – are known as the deviations from the mean. In order to get rid of the minus numbers from the calculation the deviations are squared. These figures are known as the squared deviations. The next step is to add all these values together – giving us the sum of the squared deviations. You then divide the sum of the squared deviations by the total number of values or observations – this is the mean of the squared deviations, also known as the variance. To get the standard deviation you take the square root of the variance, in effect removing the squaring that you applied earlier. Thus the standard deviation is a summary statistic that tells you the amount of variation around the mean of the distribution.

The standard deviation is a useful statistic, particularly when used alongside the mean. For example, you are comparing service A and service B. The mean price paid for A and B was the same at €79. The standard deviation in the price paid for service A is greater, however – €22 compared to €14. This tells you that while the average prices are the same the price of A is more variable than the price of B. The next step in your analysis might be to check why this variation exists (what might explain it) – is it due to a sub-group of service A providers charging more, or to one or two providers charging a lot more? However, for the standard deviation to be a reasonably sound indicator of spread, the distribution it describes must be a normal (bell curve) distribution.

THE STORY SO FAR

In terms of analysis you now have a reasonable armoury with which to explore the data: frequency counts and percentages will tell you how many gave each answer; and the measures of central tendency and variation will tell you about the average and the spread of the whole group of answers. At this level of analysis, however, you are looking at only one variable and/or one value at a time, hence the name of this type of analysis – univariate. There is only so much of the story that you can tell using this type of analysis. In most research projects you will need to compare the responses of different groups of people – men and women, younger and older people, buyers and non buyers and so on – to see if there are patterns, to examine whether or not relationships exist between variables: gender and buying behaviour, age and financial capability, and so on. You will want to answer questions such as: Are those with different demographic profiles more or less likely to buy product X? Is there a relationship between age and mobile phone use? Are women more likely to visit a general practitioner than are men? To answer these sorts of questions – and to take us towards explanatory and in some cases inferential analysis – we need bivariate descriptive analysis; in other words, we need analysis that involves examining the relationships, associations, including covariance and correlation, between two variables. We look at these sorts of analyses in the next chapter.

Chapter summary

- The purpose of data analysis is to extract meaningful insights from data and to produce valid and reliable findings that help to answer the research problem.

- Analysis is a disciplined and rigorous process. It should be thorough and systematic but it should not be an entirely mechanical business, although the mechanical part – working through data tables, running statistical tests and so on – is essential, and does form a large part of it.

- Research is a process with all the stages linked and so dependent on each other: the quality of the analysis is dependent on the quality of the earlier stages in the process, namely, the problem definition and research design stages.

- Preparing or planning analysis means reacquainting yourself with why the research was conducted and what it set out to achieve. Three documents are very valuable here: the research brief; the sampling plan; and the questionnaire. Review the research brief to get a clear view of the 'big picture', and the sampling plan and the questionnaire to be clear about what is in the dataset.

- Decide on a line of enquiry, an analysis strategy or plan, that will take you through the data in a systematic and rigorous way so that you do not become overwhelmed during the analysis process. Your strategy or plan should be designed to meet the requirements set out in the brief.

- Data are transferred from a questionnaire to an analysis package in a process known as data entry (or keying in). This process is handled automatically in computer-aided data capture.

- Once entered the data are checked and edited – missing values, out of range values and errors due to misrouting of questions are sorted out and the data are checked for other inconsistencies.

- A complete individual unit of analysis is called a case. Typically, one questionnaire – the record of an interview with one respondent – is one case. The individual bits of information on the questionnaire (questions or parts of questions) are called variables and the answers the respondent gives to these questions are called values.

- Data exist at several levels of measurement: nominal, ordinal, interval and ratio. Data at the nominal or ordinal levels are non-metric data; data at the interval or ratio level are metric data. To determine what type of analysis is appropriate, and the type of inferential statistical test to use, it is important to be able to recognise what kind of data you have.

- There are four types of data analysis: univariate descriptive analysis, bivariate descriptive analysis, explanatory analysis and inferential analysis.

- Inferential analysis is largely dependent on data generated from a random sample (with a reasonably high response rate).

- Univariate descriptive analysis is analysis involving one variable at a time.

- Frequencies counts, frequency distributions, percentages, ratios, measures of central tendency (mean, mode and median) and measures of variation (range, standard deviation) are all examples of univariate descriptive statistics. ▶

- A frequency count is usually expressed in raw numbers. It is useful to look at percentages as well as raw numbers – a percentage gives the relative proportion or incidence of occurrence per 100 cases. It is usual in expressing percentages to specify whether or not they include or exclude those who said 'Don't know' or 'No opinion'. Deciding how to handle such responses will depend on the aims of the question.

Questions and exercises

1 Define what is meant by the following terms:

(a) variables;

(b) levels of measurement;

(c) missing values.

2 Download the Life and Times 2006 main survey questionnaire from http://www.ark.ac.uk/nilt/2006/main06.pdf. Determine the level of measurement of each of the variables in Section 2 Community Relations and Section 6 Political Attitudes. You can check your answer in the Teaching Dataset at www.ark.ac.uk/nilt/datasets/teaching/index.html.

3 (a) Describe what is meant by the following, giving examples of when you might use each one and what it contributes to your understanding of the data: (a) measures of central tendency; and (b) measures of variation.

References

Blaikie, N. (2003) *Analyzing Quantitative Data: From Description to Explanation*, London: Sage.

Ehrenberg, A. (1982) *A Primer in Data Reduction*, London: Wiley.

Smith, D. and Fletcher, J. (2004) *The Art and Science of Interpreting Market Research Evidence*, Chichester: Wiley.

Tufte, E. (2001) *The Visual Display of Quantitative Information*, Cheshire, CT: Graphics Press.

Tukey, J. (1977) *Exploratory Data Analysis*, Reading, MA: Addison Wesley.

Recommended reading

Birn, R. (ed.) (2000) *The International Handbook of Market Research Techniques*, 2nd edn. London: Kogan Page.

Callingham, M. and Baker, T. (2002) 'We know what they think, but do we know what they do?', *International Journal of Market Research*, 44, 3, pp. 299–335.

Clegg, F. (1991) *Simple Statistics*, Cambridge: Cambridge University Press. A clear and accessible book on descriptive and inferential statistics.

Ehrenberg, A. (1982) *A Primer in Data Reduction*, London: Wiley. A classic text introducing statistics and data analysis.

Oldridge, M. (2003) 'The rise of the stupid network effect', *International Journal of Market Research*, 45, 3, pp. 291–309.

Pallant, J. (2004) *SPSS Survival Manual: A Step-by-Step Guide to Data Analysis Using SPSS Version 12*, 2nd edition. London: Open University Press.

Smith, D. and Fletcher, J. (2004) *The Art and Science of Interpreting Market Research Evidence*, Chichester: Wiley.

Chapter 13

ANALYSING QUANTITATIVE DATA 2

Introduction

The aim of this chapter is to introduce you to a range of approaches and techniques for analysing primary or secondary quantitative data. In Chapter 12 we looked at the early stages of data analysis – from planning through to data entry and on to basic univariate descriptive analysis. We now move on to look at the techniques of bivariate descriptive analysis, explanatory and inferential analysis, and data reduction. The aim is to show you what is available, when it is appropriate to use and how to 'read' it and write it up. In this chapter we do not cover all of the techniques or statistical tests that are available – only the ones that you are most likely to come across or might need to use in everyday market and social research projects; and for those we do cover, we do not examine their inner workings (for that you will need a statistics textbook and we recommend a few at the end of the chapter). It is rare nowadays that you would need to work out any of these techniques or tests by hand – you will either request them from a data analyst or statistician or run them yourself using an analysis package such as SPSS. Nevertheless for some of the more common ones we do offer a very brief overview of how they work to help you develop your understsanding of them.

Topics covered

- Bivariate descriptive analysis
- Data reduction
- Looking for patterns and relationships
- Explanatory analysis
- Inferential analysis

Relationship to MRS Advanced Certificate Syllabus

The material in this chapter is relevant to Element 7 – Analysing Data. The aim of Element 7 is to cover the main approaches and techniques for the analysis of primary and secondary quantitative data. Some of the material presented in this chapter goes beyond the requirements of the Advanced Certificate but it should help you to develop the skills and knowledge to enable you to choose appropriately and/or evaluate these approaches and techniques.

Learning outcomes

At the end of this chapter you should be able to:

- understand when and how to do bivariate descriptive analysis;
- understand the concept of data reduction and how and when to use it;
- understand what is involved in explanatory analysis;
- understand when and how to do inferential analysis;
- understand and evaluate the findings from quantitative research.

Bivariate descriptive analysis

In Chapter 12 we looked at univariate descriptive analysis, the sort of analysis that allows you to describe or examine the characteristics of one variable at a time – for example, the proportion or percentage of the sample that owns a pay-as-you-go mobile phone (the variable here is type of mobile phone owned); the average (mean) number of texts sent per month (the variable here is number of texts sent per month); the average (mean) length of a call (the variable here is length of calls). Bivariate descriptive analysis, as the name suggests, takes us to two variables, e.g. age and number of texts sent per month, and allows you to determine if there are similarities or differences between the values of one variable in relation to the values of the other variable. It allows you to describe (and measure the strength of) the relationship or association between the two variables. So, in terms of age and number of texts sent per month, bivariate descriptive analysis would mean that you look at the number of texts sent per month – grouped into categories – by age, grouped into categories, as Table 13.1 shows. You can see from the table that there are differences: a greater percentage of people in the younger age group send more texts per month than do people in the older age group. On the basis of this analysis you might say that there is a relationship between age and texting.

The sorts of things that clients often want to know from the research they commission are frequently things like this: who – what group of people – is most likely to use or buy my product or service; how often do key segments of my target market use my product or service? To continue the mobile phone example, the client might want to know more about phone use among the younger age group, for example whether there is a difference in the average number of texts sent per month between 18–34 year olds with a pay-as-you-go phone and 18–34 year olds with a contract phone.

We saw other examples of the sort of things that clients want to know in many of the case studies throughout the book. For example in the McDonald's case study (Case study 1.1),

Table 13.1 Number of SMS (text) messages sent per month and age

Q. 7 Number of SMS text messages sent per month	Age	
	18–34 years %	35–54 years %
None	0	5
1–30	7	36
31–60	20	43
61–90	28	14
91 or more	45	2
Don't know/not sure	–	–
Base:	(400)	(400)

McDonald's wanted to know who was leaving the brand, and what different types of customers thought of its food; Levi Strauss (Case study 1.2) wanted to know who was – and who wasn't – buying its jeans; the executives at *The Mirror* newspaper (Case study 3.1) needed to know what type of people read its paper. Bivariate descriptive analysis allows you to get this sort of information for the client.

So bivariate descriptive analysis allows you to look at similarities or differences, and it allows you to examine relationships between variables. It also allows you to go a step further. If, for example, you find that as age increases then number of texts per month falls, you can say that age and number of text messages per month are associated or related. You can put this another way: you can say that age is a good predictor of number of text messages sent per month. If you know what age group a person is in, you can predict what volume of text messages they might send in a month. Here's another example: you find that sales of milk shakes rise as temperature rises; you can say that sales of milk shakes and temperature are associated (or related). You can also put this another way: you can say that temperature is a good predictor of milk shake sales. Here's another example: if your analysis shows that 'working class' people are more likely than others to buy newspaper X and that 'middle class' people are more likely to buy newspaper Y, then you can say that social class is a good predictor of type of newspaper bought. If you know what social class a person belongs to, then you can predict what newspaper they might buy.

To get to grips with bivariate descriptive analysis there are a number of concepts and a bit of terminology that you need to master (these are also useful in relation to explanatory and inferential analysis):

- ideas and hypotheses;
- cross-tabulations and cross-breaks or top breaks or banner headings;
- the dependent and the independent variable;
- bases and filtering; and
- weighting.

We look at each of these below in some detail.

IDEAS AND HYPOTHESES

You will see from what we have discussed above that you may go into this sort of analysis to explore or check out ideas and hunches (from, for example, your background research or your literature review or your understanding of consumer behaviour) and things that are of interest and relevance to the client's information needs and to the research objectives. These ideas are sometimes called hypotheses. In planning your analysis – in going back to the client brief and in reviewing the sample and the questionnaire – ideas or hypotheses may have occurred to you which you noted down in your analysis plan with a view to following up in the data. It is likely that as you work through the analysis, other ideas will emerge: make sure to keep a log of these as you work through the data. Blaikie (2003) points out the difference between these sorts of hypotheses and the use of hypotheses in inferential statistical tests – where you have a random sample and a high response rate and you want to make generalisations from your sample data to your population. You formulate a statistical hypothesis to find out whether the characteristic of interest or the relationship that you see in your sample data can be expected to exist in the population. If you have data from a non-random (non-probability) sample, for example a quota sample, then you have no use for statistical hypotheses but you can of course still formulate ideas to examine in the data.

Case study 13.1 below gives examples of two hypotheses examined in the data from a survey about the incidence of anti-social behaviour on buses and at bus stops. The hypotheses

ANTI-SOCIAL BEHAVIOUR: WHO EXPERIENCES IT?

Here are two of the hypotheses researchers tested in a study to understand experiences of anti-social behaviour on buses or at bus stops.

Why this case study is worth reading

This case study is worth reading for several reasons: it shows the sort of ideas the researchers wanted to test out in the data; it is an example of the use of bivariate descriptive analysis, examining the relationship between two variables (age and experience of anti-social behaviour, and gender and anti-social behaviour); it shows that the perceptions that the researchers had going into the analysis – that older people and women were more likely to experience anti-social behaviour – were not supported by the survey data.

The key words are: hypotheses, perception, relationship.

Introduction

Results from the survey showed that most of those who had ever travelled by bus (70 per cent) had experienced some form of anti-social behaviour on buses or at bus stops. We wanted to know what types of people were more likely to experience it. We formulated the following hypotheses to investigate this further.

Hypothesis 1 – Experience of anti-social behaviour on buses or at bus stops is related to age

Perceptions of the relationship between age and experience of anti-social behaviour on buses and at bus stops are complex. Many assume that older people may be more likely to be the victims of anti-social behaviour or, at least, may be more affected by it, while others assume that young people are more likely to be the perpetrators. Among those who had ever travelled on a bus, younger respondents were more likely to have ever experienced anti-social behaviour on a bus or at a bus stop than older respondents. About three-quarters of those aged 12–18 years (76 per cent), 19–24 (76 per cent) and 25–39 (77 per cent) years claimed to have ever experienced at least one type of anti-social behaviour on a bus or at a bus stop, compared to only 59 per cent of those aged 60 or over.

Hypothesis 2 – Experience of anti-social behaviour on buses is related to gender

There is a widespread perception that men tend to be both the victims and perpetrators of crime more than women. Experience of anti-social behaviour was slightly higher among men (73 per cent) who had ever travelled by bus than among women (67 per cent) although this was not a statistically significant difference. No significant differences were seen between genders in terms of experience of individual types of anti-social behaviour, although men were more likely than women to have experienced drunken behaviour (45 per cent vs. 34 per cent), smoking cigarettes on buses (43 per cent vs. 33 per cent) and graffiti (28 per cent vs. 20 per cent).

Source: Adapted from Granville, S., Campbell-Jack, D. and Lamplugh, T. (2005) 'Perception, prevention, policing and the challenges of researching anti-social behaviour', MRS Conference, www.mrs.org.uk.

Table 13.2 Likelihood to upgrade mobile phone handset in next three months

Q. 7 Likelihood to upgrade handset in next three months	Age	
	18–24 years %	25–34 years %
Very likely	26	8
Fairly likely	40	17
Fairly unlikely	20	28
Very unlikely	8	40
Don't know/not sure	6	7
No answer	–	–
Base size:	(180)	(280)

are examined using bivariate analysis. The case study also shows the sort of feedback you can give to the client from this sort of analysis.

CROSS-TABULATIONS

The most common way of doing bivariate descriptive analysis is to use a cross-tabulation of one variable or set of variables or questions against another – in other words, by inspecting data laid out in a grid or table format like the one in Table 13.1. This is known as a cross-tabulation. It is the most convenient way of reading the responses of the sample and relevant groups of respondents within it. The convention in preparing a cross-tabulation is to use what you think is the independent or explanatory or predictor variable (see Box 13.2 below) as the cross-break or column variable and to calculate percentages within this variable. This means that percentages are read down the column variable and the responses of different groups can be compared side by side for each value.

Table 13.2 is another example of a cross-tab: the variable 'likelihood to upgrade mobile phone handset in the next three months', which is split into four categories (or values of that variable) plus a 'don't know' and a 'no answer' is tabulated against the variable age, which is split into two groups – 18–24 year olds and 25–34 year olds. The size of this cross-tab or table is determined by the number of categories that each variable has: this table contains 12 'cells' – the variable used in the top break has two categories; the variable used as the 'stub' has six categories. Each cell contains a percentage (and sometimes a raw number or frequency count). Using this table we can compare, side by side, the responses of younger and older people. We can see from the data in the table that 26 per cent of the younger age group (18–24 years) say they are very likely to upgrade their handset in the next three months; among the older age group (25–34 years) the figure is 8 per cent. From this data, you might say that there is a relationship between age and likelihood to upgrade in the next three months.

How to read a cross-tabulation

Each column in the table is based on the total number of people in that particular group, and this is determined by the number of people who gave that answer (or group of answers) to the question or questions from which it is derived. For example, the column 18–24 years is based on all those in the sample belonging to that age group, a total of 180 people – denoted by the figure in brackets at the bottom of the column and labelled in the stub on the left as 'base size'. We know that 40 per cent of this group say they are fairly likely to upgrade their handset in the next three months. With a base size of 180, we therefore know that 72 people aged 18–24 are fairly likely to upgrade. If you add up the responses in each of the columns you will find that each comes to 100 per cent. When it is possible to give only a single response to a question – in this case, likelihood to upgrade – the column percentages in a cross-tab should add up to 100. Due to rounding of proportions it may sum to slightly more or less than 100. If, however, you were able to give more than one answer to a question, for example, 'Which of the following social networking websites have you ever used?', the column percentages may add up to more than 100 because respondents may have used several different social networking websites.

Including 'Don't knows' in calculating percentage figures

You will come across questions that, where appropriate, have offered respondents 'Don't know' or 'No opinion' answer options. It is usual in expressing percentages to specify whether or not they include or exclude those who said 'Don't know' or 'No opinion'. (The number and percentage of those who 'Refused to answer' may be reported on the table.) Deciding how to handle such responses will depend on the aims of the question. It may be important to report how many respondents say 'Don't know' or 'No opinion' – for example if we are asking respondents about their likelihood of adopting new working practices in the next year, or – as in Table 13.2 above – the answer 'Don't know' may be a genuine answer telling you that there are people who do not know how likely or unlikely they are to upgrade their handset. On the other hand, including those who say 'Don't know' or 'No opinion' may obscure or distort the findings. Consider the data presented in Tables 13.3 and 13.4 below. At first inspection it appears that a smaller proportion of 'light users' is satisfied with the service provided, especially when compared to those who are 'medium users' – but almost three out of ten 'light users' have answered 'No opinion'. If we repercentage the figures in the table excluding the 'No opinion' group, and so including (or basing the table on) only those who expressed an opinion, a different interpretation emerges: there is no difference in rating between medium and light users. Deciding which way to report data will depend on the context. In most cases it can be useful to report both the percentage who said 'Don't know' or 'No opinion' and the proportion split between responses excluding 'Don't know' or 'No opinion'. It is also worth

Table 13.3 Including 'No opinion'

Q. How satisfied or dissatisfied are you overall with the service provided by your telephone company?

	Heavy users %	Medium users %	Light users %
Very or fairly satisifed	76	65	52
Very or fairly dissatisfied	16	23	19
No opinion	8	12	29
Base:	(200)	(200)	(200)

Table 13.4 Figures repercentaged excluding 'No opinion'

Q. How satisfied or dissatisfied are you overall with the service provided by your telephone company?

	Heavy users %	Medium users %	Light users %
Very or fairly satisifed	83	74	73
Very or fairly dissatisfied	17	26	27
Base:	(184)	(176)	(142)

bearing in mind that people in some cultures are more likely than others to give 'Don't know' as an answer. If you are analysing and reporting multi-country data then you will need to be aware of this and take it into account – at the questionnaire design and fieldwork briefing stages as well as at the analysis stage.

COMPILING A SET OF CROSS-TABULATIONS

In the examples above we see only one variable tabulated against one other variable. It is unusual – except perhaps in a presentation document or in a report – to see tables like this. It is more common to see a cross-tab with an array of variables in the 'top break' or 'banner'. The choice of variables to include in the top break (those that define the columns) should be made with the objectives of the research in mind. The variables commonly used fall into four groups: demographic and geodemographic, attitudinal and behavioural.

Demographic variables include age, sex, class, working status, region; geodemographic variables are composite variables that include location and demographic measures. If the research objectives involve determining the profile of users of a product or service, for example, or finding out whether different groups vary in terms of their attitudes or opinions, then it will be worth including the relevant variables as a top break. Attitudinal variables describe attitudes, for example liberal or conservative social attitudes, or attitudes to health, or level of satisfaction with a service or product. Behavioural variables describe behaviour or usage, for example users of Internet banking services or frequent buyers of ground coffee or those who visit a gym at least once a week. Looking at the data through the eyes of those with different attitudes or who behave in different ways can help us understand what motivates or influences different

Box 13.1 Example of a cross-tabulation using demographic variables

Q. 10. In total, how many cars are there in your household?

		Gender		Age group				Marital status		Accommodation		
	Total	Men	Women	<25	25–34	35–44	45+	Single	Married/ living as married	House	Flat	Other
	1505	798	707	322	409	299	475	862	643	1002	471	32
	100%	100%	100%	100%	100%	100%	100%	100%	100%	100%	100%	100%
Number of cars:												
0	156	53	103	102	48	6	–	97	59	5	130	21
	10%	7%	15%	32%	12%	2%	0%	11%	9%	0%	28%	66%
1	1013	559	454	121	349	226	317	674	339	690	314	9
	67%	70%	64%	38%	85%	76%	67%	78%	53%	69%	67%	28%
2	275	151	124	99	10	52	114	91	184	249	26	–
	18%	19%	18%	31%	2%	17%	24%	11%	29%	25%	6%	0%
3	55	31	24	–	2	14	39	–	55	54	1	–
	4%	4%	3%	0%	0%	5%	8%	0%	9%	5%	0%	0%
4+	6	4	2	–	–	1	5	–	6	4	–	2
	0%	1%	0%	0%	0%	0%	1%	0%	1%	0%	0%	6%

types of people and can help us build up a picture of the dynamics of a market. Are those with liberal social attitudes more or less likely to favour government funding of religious schools than those with conservative social attitudes? Are those who are concerned about their health more likely to buy organic food than those who do not worry about their health? What other drinks do frequent buyers of ground coffee buy? What is it about the service that Internet banking customers receive that makes them more likely to be satisfied with their bank than traditional account customers?

As we noted in Chapter 10, getting a set of cross-tabulations is relatively easy, and it is often quicker to ask for all questions on the questionnaire (that is, all variables) to be tabulated against every demographic, geodemographic, attitudinal or behavioural variable – in fact any variable you think might be useful for your bivariate descriptive or explanatory analysis. Resist the urge to do this – be selective in specifying the variables for the top break in your

Box 13.2 The dependent and the independent variable

In formulating ideas and hypotheses and talking about relationships between variables we often designate one variable as the dependent variable and the other as the independent variable. This suggests that we know the direction of influence – that we know which variable influences which other variable. Very often this is based on our prior knowledge of the subject area (from well-established theories, for example) or on previous research or on findings from exploratory research.

The dependent variable is the one that we predict will change as a result of the other – for example, satisfaction is dependent on type of banking service used. The independent or explanatory variable is the one that we think explains the change in the dependent variable – the level of satisfaction is explained by the type of banking service used. When we ask, 'Are those who are concerned about their health more likely to buy organic food than those who do not worry about their health?' we are suggesting or hypothesising that the purchase of organic food is dependent on or influenced by attitudes to health; or, put another way, we believe that attitude to health might explain likelihood to buy organic food. Attitude to health is the independent variable and propensity to buy organic food is the dependent variable. Similarly, when we ask, 'Is age related to likelihood to upgrade mobile phone handset in the next three months?', the dependent variable is likelihood to upgrade and the independent or explanatory variable is age. In other words, our hypothesis is that age might predict (or even explain) likelihood to upgrade handset in the next three months. We use this thinking about variables to design cross-tabulations – to make the decision about what should appear in the banner heading or cross-break – since it is traditional that we look at responses to questions by the variables that help us look for and describe relationships and think further about things like influence – and it helps if we can compare the responses of different groups or types of people side by side in the cross-tab. But do remember that in deciding that a variable is the independent variable you are making assumptions and if you suggest that it is the *cause* of a relationship or a difference you have gone too far. We come back to the idea of cause and influence in the section below on explanatory analysis.

cross-tabulations and ask only for those tables that are relevant to your analysis plan, otherwise you risk being overwhelmed by the volume of data you have and your analysis may lose focus. Remember the adage, 'data rich, information poor'. Take an orderly and systematic approach. If questions arise that you cannot answer with the tables you have, think about what other tables or analyses might help and make a note to run those next.

USE OF BASES AND FILTERING IN TABLES

Each table is usually based on those in the sample eligible to answer the question to which it relates. Not all questions are asked of the total sample, however, and analysis based on total sample is not always relevant. For example, in a survey of the use of e-commerce, we might ask all respondents whether or not their organisation uses automated voice technology (Q. 7, say). Those who say 'Yes' are asked a bank of questions (Q. 8a to Q. 8f) related to this; those who say 'No' are filtered out and routed to the next relevant question (Q. 9). When the data tables are run it would be misleading to base the tables that relate to these questions on the total sample if the purpose of the table is to show the responses of users of the service. The tables should be based on those who were eligible to answer the questions, in other words those saying 'Yes' at Q. 7. The tables for Q. 8a to Q. 8f that relate to automated voice technology are said to be based on those using automated voice technology (those saying 'Yes' at Q. 7). The table that relates to Q. 7 is said to be based on the total sample. In designing tables it is important to think about what base is relevant to the aims of your analysis.

If you have a particularly large or unwieldy dataset and you do not need to look at responses from the total sample, 'filtering' the data, excluding some types of respondents or basing tables on the relevant sub-sample can make analysis more efficient and safer. For example, your preliminary analysis of data from a usage and attitude survey in the deodorants market involved an overview of the total sample. Your next objective is to examine the women's deodorant market. In the interests of efficiency and safety, it may be worthwhile to have the tables rerun based on the sub-set of women only.

LABELLING TABLES

Cross-tabulations should be clearly laid out and easy to read – it makes the whole task of thinking about the findings much easier. Each table should have a heading that describes the content of the table, and should contain the question number to which it refers and, in full or in summary, the question(s) or variable(s) on which it is based. The base on which percentages are calculated should be clearly shown and it should be indicated whether percentages are based on the column or the row variable or both.

WEIGHTING THE DATA

Weighting is used to adjust sample data in order to make them more representative of the target population on particular characteristics, including, for example, demographics and product or service usage. The procedure involves adjusting the profile of the sample data in order to bring it into line with the population profile, to ensure that the relative importance of the characteristics within the dataset reflects that within the target population. For example, say that in the usage and attitude survey the final sample comprises 60 per cent women and 40 per cent men. Census data tell us that the proportion should be 52 per cent women and 48 per cent men. To bring the sample data in line with the population profile indicated by the Census data we apply weights to the gender profile. The over-represented group – the women – are down-weighted and the under-represented group, the men, are up-weighted. Multiplying the sample percentage by the weighting factor (Table 13.5) will achieve the target population proportion. To calculate the weighting factor divide the population percentage by the sample percentage. Any weighting procedure used should be clearly indicated and data tables should show unweighted and weighted data.

Table 13.5 Applying a weighting factor

Group	% of the sample	% in target population	Weighting factor
Women	60	52	0.87
Men	40	48	1.20

CASE STUDY 13.2

WEIGHTING FOR HOUSEHOLD SIZE

Here we look at how weighting is used to compensate for disproportionate household size in a random sample survey.

Why this case study is worth reading

This case study is worth reading for two main reasons: it shows why weighting is needed; it shows how weighting is done.

The key words are: respondents, two-stage process, random sample, households, individual, next birthday, chance, selected, varying probability, disproportionate household size, data, weighted, weight factor, applied.

Introduction

Identifying respondents for the Northern Ireland Life and Times Survey is a two-stage process. Firstly, a random sample of households is obtained from the Postal Address File. Secondly, one individual is randomly selected from each household (the person with the next birthday). Consequently, this means that a person living alone in a household has a 100 per cent chance of being selected for interview. In contrast, a person living in a five-person household has a 20 per cent chance of being selected.

The weighting

Thus, to compensate for these varying probabilities due to disproportionate household size, the data are weighted. The weight factor for each respondent is calculated based on the number of adults aged 18 or over living within their household, and the total number of adults interviewed. This weight factor is applied when analysing individual data. However, it is not applied when analysing the data based on the household, for example, household tenure, as this applies equally among all people living within the household.

Source: Paula Devine, Research Director, ARK, Northern Ireland Life and Times Survey Team. Used with permission.

Data reduction

Data reduction is the process of reducing the mass of data to something that is more manageable (and more meaningful). The term data reduction is used a lot and can refer to different things. It can be something as simple as calculating the mean or standard deviation for a variable (univariate descriptive analysis) or it might involve recoding variables (e.g. age in years to age groups) or getting rid of variables – 'noise' – from your cross-tab if they are not useful or relevant to your research aims. It also takes in more complicated procedures such as creating scales or indices based on responses to a range of questions (e.g. measuring attitudes); some researchers also include factor and cluster analysis under the heading of data reduction. Below we look at what you might do with the more basic data reduction techniques as you work through your analysis.

AT THE HOLECOUNT/FREQUENCY COUNT STAGE

As we noted in Chapter 12, you may get the chance to look at a holecount or frequency count of the data. If you do, you will be able to make an early impact on data reduction by reviewing the frequency counts and frequency distributions at each question for the total sample. You will be able to make decisions about recoding variables: which categories of which variables might be usefully be combined together, e.g. number of visits to your GP in the last year – should you present this as 0, 1, 2, 3, 4 and so on or does the distribution (coupled with your own knowledge) suggest that it would be better to present it as 0, 1–3, 4–6, 7–9, 10+? You will also be able to make decisions about the viability of key variables as top breaks for your cross-tabulations – e.g. are the base sizes big enough and/or robust enough to view separately in a column? Can you look at responses from Chief Financial Officers separately from those of Chief Operating Officers or might you be best to combine them into a larger group of all C-suite executives?

AT THE UNIVARIATE DESCRIPTIVE ANALYSIS STAGE

You can summarise the mass of data with the relevant descriptive statistics (averages and measures of spread or variation). These are especially useful with scale questions such as likelihood to buy as they give you one number that tells you the average score for the whole sample or the whole sub-group and one number that tells you the amount of variation.

AT THE BIVARIATE DESCRIPTIVE ANALYSIS STAGE

Having reviewed the research objectives (and refreshed your mind about the client's business problem), and having perhaps seen the raw data of the holecount, you are likely now to have a good idea about variables you want to use as top breaks and how you want the data for each question to appear in the cross-tab. We looked at this in Chapter 10 on preparing a DP specification. It is at this point in the process that you should resist the urge to ask for everything by everything – all the demographic, geodemographic, attitudinal and behavioural variables in your top break or banner against the answer to every question on the questionnaire. You now have enough information about your data to be selective – and you need to be selective so that you do not lose sight of the big picture. Choose only to run tables that are relevant to your research objectives with only the relevant top breaks and the relevant recoded variables and summary statistics. Don't worry if you do not look at every single piece of data generated by the survey. Focus only on what you need to know. The rest is there if you need to go back to it. A final data reduction issue to consider at this stage is whether you are happy for the analysis program to round off column (and row) percentages to the nearest whole number or whether you need them calculated to one or two (or more) decimal places. This will depend on the type of data you have and on your research objectives. With data reduction in mind, whole numbers might be the way to go with a footnote on the table or in the report to indicate that this is what has been done.

Once you have your cross-tabulations and you have examined them and have come to some idea about the story that is coming through, you may want to edit them to allow that story to emerge more clearly. This editing process may involve getting rid of columns or rows of data that do not tell you anything; labelling or relabelling the table and/or the columns to draw attention to key findings; re-ordering the columns so that the findings stand out – e.g. re-ordering the age groups to run from left to right in order of interest in the product; repercentaging the table on a more relevant base, e.g. changing it from total sample to those who bought the product or used the service (see above for how to handle 'don't know' responses in a table). We look at some of these operations in Chapter 14 in the context of presenting tables in presentations and reports.

Box 13.3 An example of the data reduction process

Imagine you were commissioned by the government to investigate perceptions of healthcare among the adult population. You are now planning the analysis, thinking about what you need to get from the data and how you can best go about it. This example is based on real questions asked in a real survey. You can download the survey questionnaire from www.ark.ac.uk/nilt/2006/main06.pdf and the topline datatables from www.ark.ac.uk/nilt/2006/Healthcare/index.html. Should you want to explore this data further, you can also download the entire dataset from www.ark.ac.uk/nilt/datasets/index.html.

The aims of the analysis
The basic aims of your analysis are as follows:

- To describe levels of satisfaction with how the NHS and its various parts are run nowadays.
- To describe the level of support for the idea that the NHS should be available only to those on lower incomes.

You need to describe the levels of satisfaction and the level of support among the total sample (that is, the adult population as a whole); you also want to determine if there are specific groups within the population with different views.

The questions
The questions that are of relevance are the following:

Q1   All in all, how satisfied or dissatisfied would you say you are with the way in which the National Health Service is run nowadays?

The response format was a five-point – from very satisfied to very dissatisfied plus 'Don't know'.

Q2   From your own experience or from what you have heard, please say how satisfied or dissatisfied you are with the way in which each of these parts of the National Health Service runs nowadays. First, local doctors or GPs? National Health Service dentists? Being in hospital as an in-patient? Attending hospital as an out-patient?

The response format was the same five-point response scale used in Q1 above.

Q3   Are you yourself covered by a private health insurance scheme, that is an insurance scheme that allows you to get private medical treatment?

The response options were 'Yes' and 'No'.

Q5   It has been suggested that the National Health Service should be available only to those with lower incomes. This would mean that contributions and taxes could be lower and most people would then take out medical insurance or pay for healthcare. Do you support or oppose this idea?

The repsonse format was a four-point scale plus 'Don't know'.

Q7   Please think back over the last 12 months about how your health has been. Compared to people of your own age, would you say that your health has on the whole been . . .

Excellent/Good/Fair/Poor/Very poor/Don't know.

Q8   Do you have a long-standing illness, disability or infirmity? By long-standing I mean anything that has troubled you over a period of time or that is likely to affect you over a period of time?

The response options were 'Yes' and 'No'.

Q8a   Does this illness or disability limit your activities in any way?

The response options were 'Yes' and 'No'.

IF YES TO BOTH Q8 AND Q8a DO NOT ASK Q8b

Q8b   Have you ever had a long-term illness that affected your activities?

The response options were 'Yes' and 'No'.

First step in the data reduction process
You review the questionnaire (and the brief) and, taking into account your knowledge of the subject area, you decide that – from the array of demographic, attitudinal and behaviour variables available (for a list, see http://www.ark.ac.uk/nilt/2006/Background/index.html) – it will be most useful to include the following variables only (a mix of demographic 'background' variables and 'situation' variables) as top breaks in your cross-tabulations:

- Age
- Gender
- Presence of children

▶

■ Social grade
■ Presence of illness or disability (Q8)
■ Presence of private health insurance (Q3)
■ Self-rating of health (Q7).

These will allow you to examine differences between, for example, older and younger respondents; men and women; people with children and those without; those with a long-term illness and those with none; those who say they are currently in good health and those who say not; those with private health insurance and those without.

The next step in the data reduction process
You review a holecount/frequency count or percentage tables for the total sample to check accuracy of data and to see if the size of the categories within each of your chosen top break variables is sufficient to be viable as a top break. As a result of this you decide to do the following data reduction tasks:

■ recode the range of variables to obtain one variable for social grade;
■ recode presence of illness/disability and whether illness/disability affects activities into one variable;
■ recode self-rating of health into three categories;
■ prepare tables with column percentages rounded to nearest whole number;
■ display the appropriate descriptive statistics (average, spread) on the tables for the scale questions, Q1, 2 and 7.

You now have the following groups in your top break – representing a total of 22 including the total sample column (about the most you can get on one page):

■ Age: six bands – 18–24; 25–34; 35–44; 45–54; 55–64; 65+
■ Gender: men and women
■ Presence of children: yes and no
■ Social grade: AB; C1C2; DE
■ Presence of illness or disability: none; illness/disability not affecting activities; illness/disability affecting activities
■ Presence of private health insurance: yes and no
■ Self-rating of health: excellent/good; fair; poor/very poor.

Once you see the cross-tabulations you will be able to do the following:

■ Describe the response for the total sample on the relevant questions, for example – Q1 Satisfaction with the way in which the National Health Service is run nowadays:

Total sample (1,200)	%
Very satisfied	6
Quite satisfied	36
Neither satisfied nor dissatisfied	13
Quite dissatisfied	25
Very dissatisfied	19
Don't know	1

- Determine the response for each sub-group for each relevant question, e.g. Q1 Satisfaction with the way in which the National Health Service is run nowadays by age:

Group	%	%	%	%	%	%
	18–24 (168)	25–34 (168)	35–44 (226)	45–54 (240)	55–64 (180)	65+ (220)
Very satisfied	6	3	5	5	7	11
Quite satisfied	49	39	30	27	29	46
Neither satisfied nor dissatisfied	22	12	11	11	13	9
Quite dissatisfied	16	29	28	35	25	17
Very dissatisfied	7	16	27	22	26	16
Don't know	1	1	0	0	1	1

- See the variability in response between sub-groups of a variable: for example, a greater percentage of the youngest and oldest age groups say they are very or quite satisfied with how the NHS is run nowadays; the age group with the greatest percentage of people saying they are dissatisfied (either quite or very) is the 45–54 years group.

The next steps
After a further round of data reduction – purging the noise from these cross-tabs – getting rid of all unnecessary data; restructuring the tables – e.g. combining the response codes for 'very satisfied' and 'quite satisfied', and those for 'quite dissatisfied' and 'very dissatisfied'; re-ordering the columns into a logical sequence; labelling the tables accurately and meaningfully, and so on – the next step is to look in more detail for patterns and associations or relationships between variables.

DATA DISPLAY AS DATA REDUCTION

Data display is a technique in its own right and it is also a form of data reduction – following the Chinese proverb, one picture is worth ten thousand words. When you want to display bivariate data, scatterplots, line graphs and bar charts are appropriate. These can be used to see if there is some relationship between two variables. Scatterplots (see Figure 13.1) are often produced as the first step in looking for associations or relationships prior to running a correlation or a regression. You can also use pictograms, network diagrams or flow charts, maps, spidergrams – whatever usefully, accurately and clearly illustrates the data.

Looking for patterns and relationships

We noted earlier that bivariate descriptive analysis is about describing the relationship or association or connection between two variables and, we noted very briefly, that it is also about measuring the strength of that association. How do you do this? This is what we look at next.

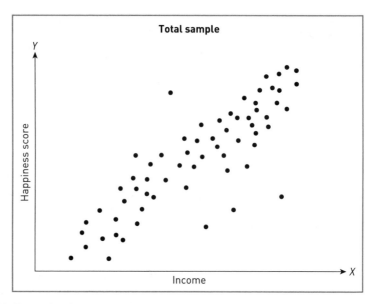

Figure 13.1 Example of a scatterplot

You may have come across the term, *measures of association*. Like *measures of central tendency* (the mean, the mode and the median) and *measures of dispersion or variation* (the range, the standard deviation), a measure of association is a *summary statistic*: a single number that tells you something – in this case about a relationship or association or correlation between two variables. One of the most important things to remember about measures of association is this: a measure of association will tell you whether there is or is not a relationship between two variables; it will *not* tell you which variable influences which variable. Think back to Chapter 3 and the sections on covariance, correlation and causation: just because there is a relationship or an association between two variables does not mean that that relationship is a *causal* relationship, that one causes the other. The two variables might *co-vary*, that is, one might follow the other – a change in X is accompanied by a change in Y – advertising spend increases, sales increase. It might be that X and Y – ad spend and sales – are strongly correlated. But it is possible to observe covariation and correlation *without there being any causal relationship between X and Y at all*. For example, the correlation between advertising spend and sales may be *spurious* (that is, not causally related at all); it may be that the correlation you see is the result of another variable, an *extraneous* (or confounding) variable (competitor activity, for instance). So telling you that there is a relationship or an association between two variables is the limit of this sort of analysis. We will come back to the idea of influence and the idea of controlling (or removing) a confounding variable later in the chapter.

At the most basic level what a measure of association tells you is that there is either a positive relationship between your two variables, a negative relationship between them or no relationship at all between them. A positive relationship is one where if you increase the value of one variable, you increase the value of the other one – put another way, a high 'score' on one variable is associated with a high score on the other variable: e.g. advertising spend increases, sales increase. A negative relationship is one where if you increase the value of one variable, you decrease the value of the other, or a high score on one variable is associated with a low score on the other variable: e.g. the older you are, the less likely you are to upgrade your phone handset.

As with measures of central tendency and measures of variation, there are several measures of association. Choosing which one to use, as with those other measures, depends largely on the level of measurement of your variables: nominal and ordinal (also called non-metric or categorical variables) and interval or ratio (metric or continuous) variables. For many people this a dreaded task. Box 13.4 below contains a very basic guide to helping you choose the most appropriate measure but we strongly recommend that you seek advice from a dedicated statistics text.

Box 13.4 Basic guide to choosing a measure of association

Variable 1	Variable 2	Conditions	Measure of association
Nominal	Nominal	Each variable with at least three categories	Cramer's V, standardised contingency coefficient
Nominal	Nominal	Each variable dichotomous, e.g. Men/Women	Phi coefficient
Nominal	Ordinal	Each variable with at least three categories	Cramer's V, standardised contingency coefficient
Nominal	Ordinal	Each variable dichotomous	Phi coefficient
Ordinal	Ordinal	Ordered categories	Kendall's tau-b, gamma
Ordinal	Ordinal	Ordered items with small samples	Spearman's rho
Metric	Nominal	Nominal variable is a dichotomy (or can be dichotomised)	Pearson's r (also known as Pearson's product-moment correlation)
Metric	Nominal	Metric variable recoded to ordinal	Pearson's r
Metric	Ordinal	Ordinal variable dichotomous (or can be dichotomised)	Pearson's r
Metric	Ordinal	Metric variable recoded to ordinal	Kendall's tau-b, gamma
Metric	Metric		Pearson's r

As we mentioned at the beginning, the aim of this chapter is not to impart detailed knowledge of the inner workings of these statistical measures – for that you will need a statistics textbook (and we offer some suggestions at the end of the chapter). Rather the aim here is to give you an understanding of when you might use them and why, and what the result tells you. However, to give you some idea of what underlies some of these measures of association we look in a little more detail at some of the most commonly used ones: those that are based on a version of the chi square contingency coefficient; and Pearson's r.

CHI SQUARE AND THE CONTINGENCY COEFFICIENT

Just to recap, you will have made the decision to use a measure of association because in the course of your bivariate descriptive analysis you want to check to see if there is a relationship between two variables. You are using a variation of the contingency coefficient because the two variables you are investigating are categorical (either nominal or ordinal).

The contingency coefficient is derived from *chi square* (χ^2). But what is chi square? Chi square is a measure of association, a statistic, that computes the frequency distribution it expects to see between two variables if there were no association between them and it compares these expected frequencies (E) with what is observed (O) – it takes the squared differences between the observed (O) and the expected (E) frequencies, and divides them by the expected frequency (E) for every cell in what is called the contingency table. The first step in working out the chi square statistic is to create such a table – a cross-tabulation – using raw numbers (not percentages). The greater the difference between the expected (E) and the observed (O) frequencies in the table, the larger the chi square statistic and the larger the chi square, the stronger the association between the variables.

The chi square test produces a *contingency coefficient*, which has a range of values between 0 and 1, and tells us the strength of the association between the variables: 0 indicates no association and 1, a perfect association. If you get a figure of 0.07 then you know that the association between the variables is very weak indeed; if you get a figure of 0.67 then you know that the association is fairly strong.

But how – and why – do you go from chi square to contingency coefficient? The why first of all: the size of the chi square statistic can be influenced by the size of the totals in the contingency table; so to get rid of this effect we change the chi square into the contingency coefficient. This is done by dividing the chi square statistic by the total of the sample size (n), (the total number in the table) plus the chi square statistic, then taking the square root of this figure. Now you have C, the contingency coefficient. It may be that you need to compare contingency coefficients from tables of different sizes (2 × 2 tables or 5 × 2 tables, for example). If this is the case then you need to *standardise* the contingency coefficient. You do this by dividing the contingency coefficient by its upper limit, the biggest possible value of the contingency coefficient for the size of table you have. You work out the upper limit for your table by subtracting 1 from the number of rows in your table and dividing that number by the number of rows; you do the same calculation for the number of columns; then you multiply these two numbers and take the quadruple root. (If your table is square, that is, if you have the same number of rows and columns, subtract 1 from the number of rows, divide that number by the number of rows and take the square root of that.)

THE PHI COEFFICIENT, CRAMER'S V, GAMMA AND KENDALL'S TAU-*B*

Another coefficient you might come across (as we noted in Box 13.4 above) is the phi coefficient (φ). This gives the strength of association in 2 × 2 tables. To work it out you divide the chi square statistic by the sample size (the total number in the table) and take the square root of it. You interpret this number – the phi coefficient – in the same way that you interpret the contingency coefficient – its values for 2 × 2 tables range from 0 to 1. Cramer's V is another measure of association – it is also a variation of the contingency coefficient and gives the strength of the association between categorical variables in tables larger than 2 × 2 with values ranging from 0 to 1.

Goodman and Kruskal's gamma is a measure of association that can be applied to variables at the ordinal level of measurement. What this measure does is to see if there is a consistent pattern in the data in relation to the two variables of interest, e.g. is level of educational attainment consistently associated with higher levels of income? What gamma does is to compare every pair of respondents in the sample to determine if their position on each of the variables of interest is concordant or discordant – so checking for the presence or absence of the consistent pattern (it does not, however, take into account pairs with the same score on each variable and if there are lots of these then the gamma statistic will underestimate the strength of the

> # Box 13.5 An example of a 2 × 2 contingency table
>
> Imagine that you want to see if there is an association between gender and participation in sport. Your hypothesis is that participation in sport is related to gender (the null hypothesis is that there is no relationship). You might even go so far as saying that the dependent variable is participation in sport and the independent variable, gender. The cross-tabulation of these two variables would look as shown in Table 13.6.
>
> **Table 13.6** Participation in sport by gender
>
> | Participation in sport | Gender | | Total |
> |---|---|---|---|
> | | Men | Women | |
> | Yes | 296 | 202 | 498 |
> | No | 104 | 198 | 302 |
> | Total | 400 | 400 | 800 |
>
> To determine if there is a relationship between these two variables the most appropriate measure to use is the phi coefficient (chosen on the basis that you have two nominal variables, each of which have dichotomous categories).

relationship between the variables). What gamma produces is a measure of association in the range −0.1 to +0.1. A limitation of gamma is that it can find only linear relationships whereas phi and the contingency coefficient can detect all kinds of relationships (linear/curvilinear, symmetric/asymmetric). Kendall's tau-*b* is also suitable for use when both variables are ordinal – and it is particularly suitable if your contingency table is square (4 × 4, 5 × 5 and so on). In doing its calculations, unlike gamma, tau-*b* does include the 'tied' pairs.

Caution: If you decide to use the contingency coefficient in any of its varieties then you must make sure that you have sufficient numbers (frequencies) in each of the cells of your contingency table (the cross-tabulation).

SPEARMAN'S *RHO*

Finally, before we move on to look at associations between metric variables, it is worth mentioning Spearman's rank order correlation coefficient, also known as Spearman's *rho*. You would use this measure if you have data that can be ranked, e.g. scores on a Likert Scale or position in class based on examination results. If you think that the notional differences between positions in your rank order are not equal then you might decide to use *Kendall's tau* instead of Spearman's *rho*.

PEARSON'S *R*

If you have two metric or continuous variables, for example temperature and sales of soft drinks, life expectancy and income, or years in education and earnings, and you want to establish if there is an association or relationship between them, the most appropriate measure to use is Pearson's *r* – also known as Pearson's product moment correlation or the correlation coefficient. The first stage in establishing whether there is a relationship may be to plot the values of the variables on a scatterplot – this will show visually any pattern that might exist in the data. You can judge linearity, homoscedasticity, whether or not there are any outliers (see Box 13.6) and whether or not there is a relationship – and if so, if it might be positive or negative. A line of best fit through the data can be calculated mathematically. The statistic associated with this calculation is r – the correlation coefficient. It tells us the strength of

---

Box 13.6 Things to consider when interpreting measures of association and influence

The following is a list of things that you need to be aware of as having an effect on the statistics you get from measures of association. For detailed information on them, consult a statistics textbook.

Linearity: a linear or a non-linear relationship

Some measures of association and influence work on the assumption that the relationship between the two variables of interest is a straight line – that is a linear relationship. You will get an idea of the nature of a relationship if you plot the values of one variable against the values of the other. If you can draw a straight-ish line through the points on the plot (either from bottom left to top right or from top left to bottom right) then you may have a linear relationship; if not, then it may be a curvilinear relationship. Sometimes it may be hard to tell (and this of course may be a finding in itself). If there is a curvilinear or non-linear relationship between the variables then some of the measures of association (e.g. Pearson's r) may – in doing its calculations and giving you a number – underestimate the strength of the relationship.

Outliers

We saw in Chapter 12 the effect that an outlier – an extreme value – can have on one of the measures of central tendency, the mean. Outliers can also have an effect on the output of a measure of association, especially – again as we noted in Chapter 12 – if the sample size is small. It is good practice to check the data for outliers – it is sometimes the case that extreme values turn out to be errors either in recording or in keying in the data.

Normality – the spread of values or scores

The values or scores on each variable should ideally be normally distributed – that is, if you produced a histogram or bar chart of them then the profile would be bell-shaped. Also, it is worth checking the spread of the distribution of your variables – it will influence test results if one is widely dispersed and the other skewed.

Homoscedasticity

Homoscedasticity, also called the homogeneity of variance, is where the variation in the values or scores of one variable is similar to the values or scores on the other variable. If you plot the values of each variable then the distribution of points on the plot should look like an oval (a bit like a very elongated rugby ball) if you have homoscedasticity; if not, then your measure may underestimate the strength of the relationship between the variables. You need your data to conform to homoscedasticity if you are using Pearson's r or regression.

association between the two variables. The value of r ranges from -1 to $+1$, where -1 tells us that there is a strong negative correlation between the variables (for example, as the price of X rises, sales of X fall); $+1$ tells us that there is a strong positive correlation (for example, the greater the income the greater is life expectancy); when r is zero it means there is no linear relationship between the two variables. If the value of r is -0.82, say, then you can say that there is a very strong negative relationship between the variables. If you square r you get what is denoted as R^2. This is called the *coefficient of determination* and tells us the proportion of variation in one variable that is explained by the other. Put another way, it is a measure of the overlap or commonality between the variables. For example, if r is $+0.2$ we have a fairly weak positive correlation, say between temperature and sales of soft drinks; if r is $+0.7$ then R^2 is 0.49, which tells us that 49 per cent of the variation in sales is explained by temperature, or that the temperature gives us a 49 per cent chance of predicting sales of soft drinks.

So Pearson's r is very useful in itself. It is also very useful in that it forms the basis of other useful analysis techniques including partial correlation, which is an extension of Pearson's r and allows you to control for the effect of a 'confounding' variable; multiple regression, which is a technique for exploring the ability of a set of variables – independent variables – to predict an outcome or (metric) dependent variable; and cluster analysis for which the patterns of correlations in a set of variables are summarised and searched for clusters or groups of simliar scores. When it is used to look at a relationship between two variables, Pearson's r is sometimes referred to as a *zero-order correlation coefficient*. This term is used to denote its bivariate rather than its multivariate use, which we will come back to later in the chapter. It is also worth noting that it is possible to test the statistical significance of the relationship between the variables as measured by r. We'll come back to this later, too.

THE LIMITS OF BIVARIATE ANALYSIS

What happens when you want to look at the relationship between more than two variables at one time? Three variables are manageable within a cross-tabulation. In fact a third variable can clarify the analysis by further explaining the relationship between the original variables. For example, in an examination of employment patterns among young people aged 18–34 we find by cross-tabulating employment status by sex (Table 13.7) that, among other things, a similar proportion of men and women are in full-time employment. We are interested in going further and determining if employment patterns among men and women vary by age. To do this we split the two groups on the age variable into men aged 18–24 and men aged 25–34 and women aged 18–24 and women aged 25–34. This new table, Table 13.8, reveals that while the proportions of men and women aged 18–24 in full-time employment are similar, proportions among the older age group are different – a smaller proportion of women compared to men are in full-time employment. A possible explanation for this finding is that women in the 25–34 age band may have children and that this is the reason they are not working full

Table 13.7 Employment status by sex

Q. 25 Employment status	Men %	Women %
Full time	68	62
Part time	16	30
Unemployed	11	5
Other	4	2
No answer	–	1
Base:	(250)	(250)

Table 13.8 Employment status by age within sex

Q. 25 Employment status	Men		Women	
	18–24 %	25–34 %	18–24 %	25–34 %
Full time	64	72	67	58
Part time	17	16	24	35
Unemployed	13	9	3	6
Other	6	3	4	1
No answer	–	–	2	–
Base:	(112)	(138)	(120)	(130)

time. To explore this further we could compare employment patterns among women in each group with children and those without.

But this sort of analysis only takes us so far. We are really only looking at relationships between two variables – we need, for example, to be able to look at the effects of a third variable. In addition we have yet to take into account the notion of influence in relationships between variables. So we move on now to look at influence and to what is involved in explanatory analysis.

Explanatory analysis

We noted above that although we can see that there is a relationship or an association between two variables we cannot say anything about – we cannot infer – cause. We can offer some predictions with caveats (warnings) but that is about it. We do go a bit further in that we tend in analysing survey data in cross-tabs to label some variables (or at least to use them in the role of) as independent variables (also known as explanatory or predictor variables) and to label others as dependent or outcome variables. Those we put into the independent category and use as top breaks tend to be demographic (e.g. age, gender, working status), geodemographic (e.g. neighbourhood type) and behavioural (e.g. use nowadays, visited in the last month) – and sometimes attitudinal (e.g. scores on an attitudes to the environment scale) variables. In doing this we are certainly saying something about *direction of influence*: when we look at a relationship between two variables and put one of them in the role of explanatory or predictor variable and one in the role of outcome variable, we are saying that the values of the outcome variable are influenced or explained by or can be predicted by the values of the explanatory/predictor variable. But when we make statements like this in a report or presentation of the findings of a survey we are not explaining a relationship between the variables, we are showing only that we have identified something that might be involved in it. It may be the beginning of explanatory analysis but it is some way from offering a conclusive explanation.

RESEARCH DESIGN AND EXPLANATORY ANALYSIS

Think back to Chapter 3 and research design: what contributes to your ability to develop causal explanations from your data are the decisions you made at the research design stage. You might remember from Chapter 3 that the sort of research enquiry that you needed was one that would allow you to rule out rival explanations, come to a conclusion – an enquiry that would help you to develop causal explanations. The characteristics of this sort of research are those that allow you to do the following:

- look for the presence of association, covariance or correlation;
- look for an appropriate time sequence;
- rule out other variables as the cause;
- come to plausible or common-sense conclusions.

So what can you do if you have data from a cross-sectional design, typically in the form of an ad hoc or one-off survey? This is probably the most common design in marketing and social research. With a cross-sectional design, and this is something that distinguishes it from experimental research design, you rely on there being differences within the sample to allow you to make comparisons between different groups (whereas in experimental design you create them by manipulating the independent variable to see if it causes a change in the dependent variable – and in an experiment you can control the time sequence). In a cross-sectional design, having specified the relevant sample and asked the relevant questions, you look in the data for relationships and associations or correlations between variables (bivariate descriptive analysis) and you try (with explanatory analysis) to establish *causal direction*. What you cannot do is *prove cause*. So you might say that the extent of your explanatory analysis from cross-sectional data in particular will be limited.

You can go further than just look to see if there is a relationship or an association between two variables. For example, you can see that sales of brand A increase if advertising spend is increased, or that income is greater among those with higher levels of educational attainment. You can check out whether there is a direct relationship – the change in Y (sales of product A) is 'caused' directly by X (ad spend on brand A) – or whether there is an indirect relationship – in the link between X and Y there may be an intervening variable or variables that produce the change in Y. Occupation may be the intervening variable through which educational attainment and income are related. This falls under the heading of multivariate analysis. You can use a technique known as partial correlation to look at this – we'll come back to it later. If you had had an experimental design you could examine *in isolation* the effect of the independent or explanatory variable on the dependent variable because in an experimental design the effects of other variables have been removed or *controlled* to allow you do this. But experimental designs are artificial, not often appropriate for the sort of things that clients want to know and in an experimental design it is not always possible to isolate or account for the complexity of variables in real-life marketing and social research 'problems'. So even if you had gone with an experimental design you would need to be wary about the extent to which a causal relationship is said to be proven. So you can examine and to some extent rule out other variables as the 'cause' with data from your cross-sectional design. Now we turn to the time sequence issue. Again with a cross-sectional design you are limited – you have collected your data at one point in time – so it may not be possible to unravel the time sequence that would give you evidence in relation to establishing cause. A longitudinal design would help you here since it collects data from the same sample over time but this design can be difficult to run, expensive and time consuming and so may not suit the client's needs on those grounds.

So, in summary, we are saying here that your ability to offer causal explanations via explanatory analysis of the sort of data that you collect in market and social research projects is limited. You can talk about influence, and any comments you make about direction of influence will be based on assumptions.

BIVARIATE EXPLANATORY ANALYSIS

As with measures of association, choosing which technique to use to examine influence depends largely on the level of measurement of your variables. Box 13.7 below contains a very basic guide to helping you choose the most appropriate measure but once again we strongly recommend that you seek advice from a dedicated statistics text. Measures of influence can be split into two types: symmetric and asymmetric. Symmetric measures assume that no direction of influence between the two variable is implied; asymmetric measures assume that there is a direction of influence (that one variable is the explanatory or predictor variable and the other is the outcome variable). Since here we are interested in direction of influence and will usually be able to label one variable as explanatory and the other as outcome, we look only at the asymmetric measures.

Box 13.7 Basic guide to procedures for measuring influence

Predictor variable	Outcome variable	Conditions	Measure
Nominal	Nominal		Lambda
Nominal	Ordinal		Lambda
Ordinal	Ordinal		Somer's *d*
Metric	Metric		Bivariate regression
Nominal	Metric	Recode metric variable to ordinal	Lambda
Nominal	Metric	Use means (means analysis)	Eta
Nominal	Metric	If nominal is dichotomised and metric is multichotomous	Bivariate regression
Ordinal	Metric	Recode metric variable to ordinal	Lambda
Ordinal	Metric	Use means (means analysis)	Eta
Ordinal	Metric	If ordinal is dichotomised and metric is multichotomous	Bivariate regression
Metric	Nominal	Recode metric to ordinal	Lambda
Metric	Ordinal	Recode metric to ordinal	Somer's *d*

For the detail of how these statistical measures work and more information on the conditions in which they can be used you will need a statistics textbook. Below we offer only a very brief look at them.

Goodman and Kruskal's lambda

Lambda (λ) is a measure that can be used to predict the value of one nominal variable from another, when one variable is labelled the explanatory or predictor variable and the other the outcome or dependent variable. The value of the lambda statistic varies (the higher it is, the greater the influence of one variable on the other) but it does not indicate the direction of the relationship between the variables – to work that out you have to look at your cross-tab. You may find from this inspection of the tables that there appears to be a relationship between the variables but your lambda statistic says that there is not. In interpreting lambda, therefore, you need to be aware that it is not a very sensitive test.

Somer's *d*

Somer's *d* is a measure that can be used to predict the influence of one ordinal variable on another ordinal variable. It works in a similar way to one of the measures of association we saw above, gamma. The number that you get at the end of your Somer's *d* calculation will have a sign (positive or negative) that tells you the nature of the influence of one variable on the other.

Bivariate regression

Bivariate regression is also known as linear regression or Ordinary Least-Squares (OLS) regression. To use it both your variables must be metric. It works on the assumption that the relationship between the variables is linear – that an increase in one will be associated with an increase (i.e. a positive relationship) or a decrease (negative relationship) in the other – and that the value of one changes at the same rate as the value of the other. If, for example, you are looking at the relationship between income and happiness, a regression analysis will give you information that will allow you to predict a person's score on the happiness scale if you know his or her income. This is a useful sort of analysis to do if you have only limited information about your sample and you need to make predictions in order to make decisions. The idea of regression relies on the notion that you can fit a straight line (the line of best fit) through a plot of the values of one variable (the independent or explanatory or predictor variable on the x-axis – the horizontal) against the other (the dependent or outcome variable on the y-axis – the vertical). Regression describes the influence of one variable on the other by telling you about the line of best fit through the data. The equation of the straight line describing a positive relationship between the variables is $y = bx + a$ where x is the explanatory variable and y is the outcome variable, b is the slope (the angle) of the line through the data points, and a is the point where the line crosses (intersects with) the y-axis. (The calculations involved in working out b are similar to those used to work out Pearson's r.) The values that you get for b is

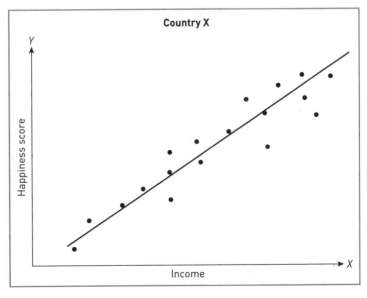

Figure 13.2 Example of a scatterplot showing a line of best fit

dependent on the values of the variables you used to calculate them. You get a more useful statistic (as we saw earlier with the contingency coefficient) if you standardise b. To do this you translate it into a z score and from there you calculate beta (β), the standardised version of b. What you then find in your bivariate regression is that β (also known as the regression coefficient R) has the same value as Pearson's r. The regression coefficient in bivariate regression (it varies from −1 to +1) tells you the extent to which the explanatory or predictor variable influences or accounts for the outcome or dependent variable.

The next step is get a measure of how well the regression line fits the data (since the same line could be arrived at for a different set of data). Put another way, we need to know how much of the variation between the two variables is explained by the line of best fit through them. This next bit will be familiar if you have used Pearson's r: to find out how much variation is explained by the line, you square the regression coefficient R to get R^2. This tells you how much – what proportion – of the variance is explained by the explanatory or predictor variable.

Next you might want to know how well the regression line explains or predicts the values of the outcome variable (y) given the values of the explanatory or predictor variable (x). What this means really is that you want to know more about the data points that lie off the regression line – those that lie along it are the ones explained by the regression coefficient; the ones that lie to either side of it are the unexplained ones – the ones the line does not fit. This will tell you something about the unexplained variance. You know quite a lot about these off-the-line data points since you know that in effect where they should be on that line. So what you can do is work out the difference between where they should be on the line (if the line was a perfect fit through all the data points) and where they actually are. This is the measure of error there is in predicting the value of the outcome variable y from the value of the explanatory or predictor variable x. It is also known as the residual. You take these deviations (some will be above the line and some below, so some will be positive and some negative in value), you square them (to get rid of the negative signs) and then add them all up. To be able to use this statistic in comparison with others, you standardise it to produce what is called the *standard error of the estimate*. It is analogous to the standard deviation of the mean (see univariate analysis) in that it tells you how dispersed things are around the regression line: the bigger its value, the more dispersion; the smaller the value, the less dispersion.

So now you know quite a lot about the relationship between your two variables: you know whether there is a relationship or not – say, this time between age and happiness; if there is one, you know whether it is positive or negative – say that it is a positive relationship, older people tend to have higher happiness scores than younger people; you know the extent to which your explanatory variable influences the outcome variable – say that R is 0.7 (so there is a strong relationship between age and happiness) and so R^2 is 0.49 or 49 per cent, which means that 49 per cent of the variation in happiness scores is explained by age; you can also describe the extent of the unexplained variation between them. So age and happiness are related to some extent. The older you get the more likely you are to say that you are happy. But the data show that age does not explain everyone's happiness score – so you might think that it is not just influenced by age but there are other factors involved. So you look elsewhere in your data to see what else might influence it. You have several other variables that you think might have an effect on your happiness score: your self-rated health, for example, or a rating of your stress level, or a rating of the current nature of your close relationships, or level of disposable income. The next bit of analysis that you might do is a multiple regression – to look at the influence of these other variables on happiness, all with a view to explaining what it is that makes people (your employees, your customers) happy. We look briefly at this later in the chapter.

A point to remember when interpreting your regression statistics is that outliers – extreme values – may affect the result. Inspect your data to see if there are outliers, check that they are not errors and, if not, think about what they mean in terms of your findings. For some of the other things that you need to bear in mind when interpreting regression and other measures, look back at Box 13.6 above.

Regression with dummy variables

There is a form of regression analysis (there are whole books dedicated to it) that you can do if your explanatory variable is a dichtomous nominal variable (e.g. gender – male/female – or yes/no or presence of something/absence of it) or one that can be dichotomised (you might also be able to dichotomise the categories of an ordinal variable) and your outcome variable is metric. So you may need first of all to manipulate your nominal or ordinal variable so that each of its categories becomes a dichotomy – for example, to present it in such a way that each is a yes or a no, the presence of something or the absence of it. If you allocate a code of 0 for no/absence and 1 for yes/presence then you have in effect created a metric (interval level) variable – a dummy variable – and you can then run a regression analysis.

MULTIVARIATE EXPLANATORY ANALYSIS

You will know from your own experience that, while it is useful to look at the relationships and associations and influences between two variables, things in the real world are never that simple – there is usually a complex pile of variables involved in explaining and predicting. As a result you need analysis techniques that allow you to look at more than two variables at a time.

For example, imagine that you have looked at the relationship between advertising spend and sales and you see that there is a relationship (they co-vary) – as ad spend increases, sales increase. It turns out that they are fairly strongly correlated and that ad spend does influence sales – to some extent. But remember it is also possible to observe covariation and correlation *without there being any causal relationship between ad spend and sales at all*. The correlation between the two may be *spurious* (that is, not causally related at all); it may be that the correlation you see is the result of another variable or variables – an *extraneous* (or confounding) variable (competitor activity, for instance) or an *intervening* variable or a *moderating* variable. To investigate this you move into the realm of multivariate analysis. Remember above we mentioned that examining the relationship between two variables is sometimes called zero-order correlation. When you bring in a third variable to the mix it becomes first-order correlation; bringing in a fourth variable makes it a second-order correlation.

Partial correlation

Partial correlation, as we noted above, is an extension of Pearson's product-moment correlation *r*. You use it when you think that there might be another variable exerting an influence over your two variables. Partial correlation allows you to 'control' (statistically) for the effects of this third variable. In essence, it allows you to get rid of, or remove, the effects of it so that you get clear sight of the relationship, the correlation, between the other two variables. To use partial correlation to do this, all of your variables must be at the metric level of measurement and the data must conform to the assumptions of linearity, normality and homoscedasticity (see Box 13.6 above). The results of the partial correlation will give you Pearson's *r* for the relationship between the two variables without taking into account the effect of the third

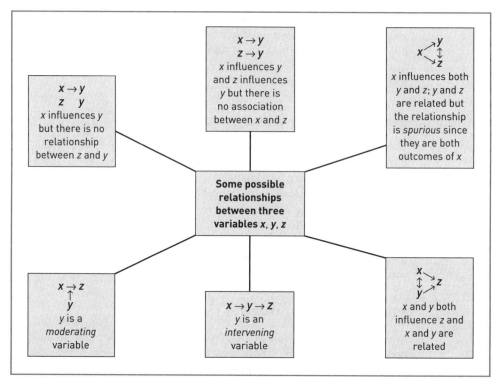

Figure 13.3 Relationships between three variables

variable (that is, the zero-order correlation) and the value of r controlling for the effects of the third variable (the partial correlation). The difference between the two values of r will tell you what sort of effect controlling for the third variable had on the relationship between the two variables of interest. If the two values are similar – that is, the difference between them is small – then you can say that the third variable had little effect: that the relationship that you see between the two variables is not due to the influence of the third variable. If the difference between the two values is fairly large, however, then you can say that the third variable does have some influence or effect.

Multiple regression

Multiple regression is one of the most commonly used techniques in multivariate explanatory analysis. It allows you to investigate the relationship between one (metric level) dependent or outcome variable and two or more explanatory or predictor variables (which can be metric or categorical – if it is categorical then the type of regression analysis you do is called logistic regression). Regression allows you to make predictions about the dependent variable based on what you know about the explanatory variables. It also tells you what contribution each of the explanatory variables makes in relation to the outcome variable. It allows you to evaluate the influence of each of your explanatory variables by controlling for the influence of the others. So what you get is an understanding of the separate or independent influence of each explanatory variable, plus their total influence on the outcome variable. The underlying principles of multiple regression, which we will not go into here, are similar to those of bivariate or linear regression. There are a number of assumptions that need to be met in order to use multiple regression and have faith in what it tells you: you need a fairly large sample size (at least 100); you need to check that your explanatory variables are not highly correlated (a phenomenon known as multicollinearity); you need to check that you do have 'singularity' (that is, that one of your explanatory variables is not a combination of any of the others); you need to take appropriate action to deal with outliers (e.g. removing them, re-scoring them); and you need to check the distribution of the values of your variables – do they conform to the rules of linearity, normality and homoscedasticity?

There are several types of multiple regression – standard, hierarchical and stepwise. For further details on these and on other aspects of multivariate analysis you'll need to consult a specialist textbook such as Tabachnick and Fidell (2006). Logistic regression is the sort of regression analysis you do when your explanatory variable is either categorical or metric and your dependent or outcome variable is dichotomous. The result will tell you which of the two categories your respondent belongs to. If you have more than two categories in your outcome variable (i.e. it is not dichotomous) then you would use logit logistic regression.

Analysis of variance

You use analysis of variance (ANOVA) if you want to find out if there is a relationship between a metric outcome variable and a categorical explanatory variable. For example, you may be interested in the price variations in a product by outlet type, or variations in income by social class or by gender, or differences in crime rates in different types of cities. ANOVA compares the amount of variation between the categories of the explanatory variable with the amount of variation within them. For example, say you want to examine the price variations on a brand of whisky in independent outlets and in multiple or large retailers. Using ANOVA will tell you the amount of variation in the price of the whisky *across* the different types of outlet and the variation in price *within* each type of outlet. If there is a greater variation between the outlet types than within each type we can say that there is a relationship between price and type of sales outlet. MANOVA, multiple analysis of variance, takes ANOVA a stage further and allows you to compare between groups across two or more outcome variables.

OTHER TECHNIQUES

There are of course lots more techniques available for the explanatory analysis of data. The ones we have looked at above are referred to as dependence techniques: they examine the relationship between one or more dependent variables. There is another set of techniques called interdependence techniques. *Inter*dependence techniques are those that look at the *inter*relationships between a pile of variables with no assumptions about which one influences which. The aim in using these techniques is to see how a set of variables relate to each other, to see what they might have in common and to reduce their number from many to a few – factors, clusters or dimensions (which is why some people refer to them as data reduction techniques).

We look briefly at three of these sorts of techniques, those that are popular in market and social research – factor analysis, cluster analysis and multidimensional scaling. (It is worth noting that Harris, 1981 argues that cluster analysis should not be categorised as an interdependence technique but should be in a category of its own.) Factor analysis and cluster analysis are particularly popular in market research because of the role they play in market segmentation. Segmentation is about identifying the size and nature of useful sub-groups within a market so that marketers have a clearer understanding of who their customers are and as a result can target their products or services at these groups (thus making for a more efficient use of the marketing budget). As we noted in previous chapters (and in relation to the decision about what top breaks to use in your cross-tabs), the sort of data that you might use for your segmentation study – the sorts of variables that might first of all go into your factor analysis – are demographics, geodemographics, attitudes, behaviour (customer/consumer) and situation. You might have collected this data on a survey designed for this purpose, or you might just happen to have these variables and decide that you can do a segmentation study or these variables might exist in a secondary dataset or customer database.

Factor analysis

The aim of factor analysis is to reduce or summarise a large number of variables into a smaller set of factors. The analysis does this by looking for patterns in the data – correlations between all of the variables in the particular set of data on the basis of bivariate relationships. For example, in a study to evaluate customer perceptions of the service provided by a telecommunications company, respondents were asked to rate the organisation on 16 different attributes. The factor analysis examines the relationships between all of these attributes and summarises or reduces these to a smaller set of factors that tell us what is driving perceptions of the service. If you want to gauge the nation's financial capability, you do qualitative work to get an idea of the dimensions that make up financial capability and from this you prepare a set of, say, 36 atttitude statements for your survey questionnaire. You administer the survey and as part of your analysis plan you run a factor analysis on those 36 attitude statements to see if it is possible to reduce them to a smaller set of factors – an eight factor solution say – that will still adequately represent the sample. You could then use these derived factors as the basis for your cluster analysis to see if it would produce a set of clusters that would describe people in terms of their financial capability. This in turn would help you target your advertising or information campaign to address the needs of each of these cluster groups.

Factor analysis is also widely used in, among other things, product testing research, to determine which features of a product drive preference, and market segmentation studies, to identify factors on which to group or cluster respondents. The aim of factor analysis is not to explain or predict. The sort of variables you need for a factor analysis are metric variables but a lot of factor analysis is done using categorical (ordinal) variables.

Cluster analysis

The aim of a cluster analysis is to divide a sample (of at least 100) into distinct, homogeneous groups or clusters. Each cluster will contain respondents with similar characteristics or values on particular variables; each cluster will be different from all other clusters (you sometimes see them described as an homogeneous cluster – the people or items in a particular cluster will be similar to each other; the clusters will be different from each other). Attitudinal data are often used to build the clusters. For example, clusters can be developed based on social and political attitudes, or based on attitudes to the adoption of new technology in an organisation. The analysis identifies a number of distinct clusters in the sample by analysing the relationships between the variables and each cluster is given a name that reflects its most important attribute. Respondents should fall into one particular cluster; the output of the analysis gives details of the proportion of the sample that falls into each one and the proportion of variation in the sample accounted for by each cluster.

Cluster analysis can be used simply to generate clusters in order to describe groups within the data (see for example Gibson, Teanby and Donaldson (2004) in Case studies 3.4 and 7.5) which marketers can then target. It can also be used to reduce data into more manageable and meaningful units; the clusters can be used as cross-breaks in further analysis. Cluster analysis is often used to help understand the make-up of a particular market and the needs and preferences of segments within that market. For example, a cluster analysis based on questions about the range or repertoire of brands bought will help identify what types of consumers buy what group of brands and may help determine if there is a gap in the market which a new brand might fill. Case study 13.3 below gives a detailed example of cluster analysis in practice.

It is possible to get factor analysis and cluster analysis confused: the key thing to remember is that factor analysis is about grouping variables together and cluster analysis is about grouping people or things together. For more detailed insight into the working of cluster analysis and its applications in retailing and in business markets, it is worth reading Blamires (1995) and Blamires, Ray and Askew (1997).

VONS SUPERSTORES: TARGETING LOCAL NEEDS

This case study gives an example of the application of cluster analysis in designing grocery stores to meet the needs of local shoppers.

Why this case study is worth reading

This case study is worth reading for several reasons: it is an example of cluster analysis in action; it shows the process – what goes on before the cluster analysis and what happens with the findings; it shows the usefulness of the demographic profile and of sales data; it shows how 'targeting' works.

The key words are: demographic profile, cluster analysis, scanner data, store clusters, store identities.

Introduction

Vons is a grocery superstore chain with shops on the West Coast of the United States. Each of its stores' range and decor is tailored to its catchment area, based on broad groupings of the company's outlets which relate customer profile to store performance. How did it do this? The how is explained below.

Demographic profile of the catchment area

Vons commissioned a demographic profile of the catchment area of each store. A correlation analysis carried out on this data against store performance variables showed that three key demographic variables differentiated between the company's outlets: in order of importance – income; age; and ethnicity.

Cluster analysis

A cluster analysis of Vons stores was then carried out based on the variables. Twelve groups were identified although for practical purposes these were merged into the following five:

(i)   High Hispanic/low income
(ii) Moderate to high Hispanic/moderate to high income
(iii) High Anglo American/low income
(iv) High Anglo American/moderate to high income
(v)   Average.

▶

Management input

Managers of the individual stores commented on their own store's classification and its profile: while conscious of the need for a 'scientific' approach, retailers respect the 'gut reaction' which historically guided retailing and that can only come from years of experience and contact with the customer.

Sales data and shelf space allocation

For each Vons store cluster, the scanner in each store provided weekly sales data for every product. Using a space management system, shelf space was allocated to every product for each store cluster, taking account of the size of the stores and the available shelf space. This involved some products disappearing from certain clusters. These space allocations were refined with reference to the merchandising department. The buying team was consulted for its views on and approval of the ranges being put forward for the various store clusters.

End result and further action

This exercise has given Vons five clear store identities with product ranges and space allocation to suit the catchment area profile of the stores. Maintenance of the range and merchandising is now an ongoing process taking into account seasonality, competitors' activity and new product launches as well as individual product sales performance. Having successfully managed the transition from one to five retailing formats, Vons has since developed two completely new store concepts, Tianguis and Pavilions, targeted at specific groups, based on the same research and analysis approach.

Source: Adapted from Johnson, M. (1997) 'The application of geodemographics to retailing: meeting the needs of the catchment', *International Journal of Market Research*, 39, 1, pp. 201–24, www.ijmr.com.

Multidimensional scaling

Multidimensional scaling (MDS) is a mapping technique (sometimes called a perceptual mapping technique). You would use MDS if you wanted to see how key aspects of peoples' perceptions or ratings or opinions sit in relation to one another. Conjoint analysis and correspondence analysis are examples. The aim of correspondence analysis is to produce a map showing in two dimensions how variables and items relate to each other. To use correspondence analysis your data must be derived from an association matrix: a grid of image or attribute statements (ordinal or metric) by a list of, say, supermarket brands, marques of car or brands of beer, for example. The variables (the statements) and the items (the brands) are shown as points on a map. From the map it is possible to say something about the relationship between the items and the attributes, and so the positioning of items or brands in relation to the attributes and to each other. The analysis determines what proportion of variation between the items is accounted for by the dimensions included. Correspondence analysis is useful in understanding markets, how they are segmented, how consumers perceive brands, how effective advertising has been in positioning a brand, or where there might be a gap that a new product could fill.

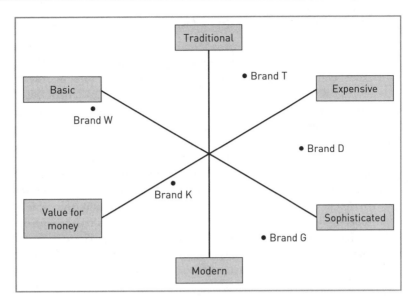

Figure 13.4 Example of a perceptual map

Inferential analysis

If you have data from a random (probability) sample, and you achieved a response rate of at least 65 per cent (to help ensure representativeness of the sample) then it is appropriate to use inferential analysis. If your data are based on a quota sample or if you achieved a poor response rate then it is not advisable to use inferential analysis – although some (Smith and Fletcher, 2004) say that you can, but exercise caution.

Why would you want to use this sort of analysis anyway? The reason is that when we talk about the findings from a sample we want to generalise – we want to talk about our findings in terms of the population and not just the sample. We can do this with some conviction if we know that our sample is truly representative of its population. You can of course use the other approaches to analysis that we described above on your random sample data – you are not limited to doing only inferential tests on them. You should not ignore measures of association and influence.

Even with a random sample, however, there is a chance that it is not truly representative. As a result we cannot be certain that the findings apply to the population. For example, we conduct a series of opinion polls among a nationally representative sample of voters of each European Union member state. In our findings we may want to talk about how the opinions of German voters compare to those of French voters. We want to know if the two groups of voters really differ. We compare opinions on a range of issues. There are some big differences and some small differences. Are these differences due to chance or do they represent real differences in opinions that exist within the population? We use inferential analysis – and the statistical tests and procedures that are part of it – to tell us if the differences are real rather than due to chance. But we cannot say this for certain. The tests tell us what the probability is that the differences could have arisen by chance. If there is a relatively low probability that the differences have arisen by chance then we can say that the differences we see between the samples of German voters and French voters are *statistically significant* – real differences that are likely to exist in the population and not just in the sample we have studied.

WHAT SORT OF TEST? PARAMETRIC AND NON-PARAMETRIC TESTS

When you consult a statistics textbook or an SPSS manual you will come across tests described as parametric and non-parametric. Very briefly in Box 13.6 above we noted that there are some conditions or assumptions which you need to fulfil in order that particular techniques will work to give you a valid test result. For example, you need the distribution of the variable in your population to be normal (normality). When you are comparing sample data from two different populations you may need the variance – the spread of values – to be the same in each. When these conditions are fulfilled you can use a test from the parametric group. When these conditions are not met then you use a test of the non-parametric kind. Sometimes you may not be able to check whether or not the conditions are fulfilled. To make things slightly more complicated, there is the issue of the level of measurement to take into account. If you have metric level variables (sometimes called continuous variables) there is a good chance – depending of course on what the population characteristic is that the variable is measuring – that it will be normally distributed within the population. If, on the other hand, you have a categorical variable then there is less chance of satisfying the normality condition – in which case it is best to choose a non-parametric test.

SIGNIFICANCE LEVELS, CONFIDENCE LEVELS AND CONFIDENCE INTERVALS

As we saw in Chapter 8, the question then arises: at what point or level of probability do we accept that a difference is statistically significant or real? The significance level is the point at which the sample finding or statistic differs too much from the population expectation for it to have occurred by chance – the difference cannot be explained by random error or sampling variation and is accepted as a true or statistical difference. At the 5 per cent ($p = 0.05$) significance level there is a 5 per cent probability or a 1 in 20 chance that the result or finding has occurred by chance. You can express it another way – as the confidence level, in which case it is 95 per cent. Stated this way it tells people how confident you are about your population estimate based on your sample statistic or data. This is typically the lowest acceptable level in most market and social research projects. You will also hear about 'confidence intervals'. The confidence interval is the range of values around the sample value within which you expect the population value to lie. The extremes of the confidence interval are referred to as the confidence limits. For example, you might see opinion poll data stating that 45 per cent ±3 per cent of the population were going to vote Republican in the US presidential election. The ±3 per cent are the confidence limits for that value. The higher the level of confidence, the wider will be the confidence interval. In other words, the more confident you are about your sample value, the less precise it will be (it will have a wider confidence interval). As we mentioned in Chapter 8 on sampling, you can reduce the confidence interval and maintain a high confidence level if you increase the size of your sample. This is not often done as conducting research with large samples is time consuming and expensive, and the trade-off between precision and price may not be worth it. (Also, with a larger sample you run the risk of introducing a greater level of non-sampling error.) See Box 8.8 for how to calculate sample size to achieve a given level of precision.

SIGNIFICANCE TESTS

When you are doing bivariate descriptive and bivariate explanatory analysis there are tests you can use to determine (to estimate) if the relationships – the associations, the correlations, the influences – that you see in your sample can also be expected to exist in the population from which the sample was drawn. These tests are often referred to as significance tests. To run a significance test you set out the nature of the relationship between the two variables in a hypothesis. Because you cannot prove an empirical assertion but you can disprove it, you test the null hypothesis – the hypothesis of no difference. If the significance test tells you that you can reject the null hypothesis then you can accept the alternative or research hypothesis; if you fail to reject the null then you cannot accept the research hypothesis. We set out the procedure for hypothesis testing below.

Procedure for hypothesis testing

- Formulate a specific research hypothesis (for example, that there is a difference in men's and women's attitudes to the environment).
- State the null hypothesis (for example that there is no difference in men's and women's attitudes to the environment).
- Set the significance level.
- Choose the appropriate significance test.
- Apply the test and get the test statistic.
- Interpret the test statistic (determine the probability associated with it or the critical value of it).
- Accept or reject the null hypothesis.
- State the finding in the context of the research hypothesis and the research problem.
- Draw conclusion.

Type I and Type II errors

We looked at the concept of Type I and Type II errors in Chapter 8 on random sampling but it is worth recapping here now we are at the sharp end of the analysis. Every time you make a decision to accept or reject a null hypothesis you risk making an error. There are two types of error – Type I or α (alpha) and Type II or β (beta) errors. If you make a Type I error you reject the null hypothesis when in fact it is true and you should have accepted it. An example of a Type I error is when an innocent person is found guilty. You make a Type II error when you accept the null hypothesis when in fact it is false and should have been rejected. A Type II error is when a guilty person is acquitted. The chance of committing a Type I error is no greater than the level of significance used in the test (which is why the significance level is sometimes called the alpha value, the value associated with an alpha error). If you use the five per cent level you can only make a Type I error five per cent of the time. You can reduce the probability of making a Type I error by setting the significance level at one per cent or 0.1 per cent. If you drop the significance level (in effect increasing the stringency of the test and raising the confidence limits to 99 per cent or 99.9 per cent) you increase the chances of making a Type II error.

In setting significance levels, therefore, you need to reach a compromise between the types of error. If making a Type I error (accepting as true something that is really false) is deemed worse than making a Type II error (accepting something that should be rejected and is not), then you should set the significance level low (say 0.1 per cent). If, however, the risks associated with a Type II error are greater, then it might be best to set the significance level at five per cent. To lower the risk of either type of error arising, you increase the sample size.

WHAT TEST?

It is important to choose the correct test for the data otherwise you risk either ending up with a test result and a finding that are meaningless or you miss an interesting and useful finding.

First of all you, ask yourself whether the hypothesis you are testing is directional or non-directional, that is, are you predicting the direction of influence of one variable on the other? If you are then you need to run a one-tailed test (think of it as looking in only one direction, the direction you specified). If you are not predicting the direction of influence in your hypothesis then you need to run a two-tailed test (think of it as looking in both directions). The next thing you need to ask yourself is what are you testing for – a difference or a relationship?

A DIFFERENCE OR A RELATIONSHIP?

Hypothesis testing can be applied to test differences or to test associations or relationships. You might want to test the difference between means or proportions or percentages or rankings. For example, you may want to find out whether the average price independent retailers charge for product X is significantly different from that charged by multiple retailers; or you may want to find out if the mean number of breakdowns reported by owners of brand X washing machines is really different from the mean number reported by owners of brand Y machines; or you might want to find out if the proportion of students achieving a first class honours degree differs significantly between university A and university B. Alternatively, you might want to test for associations or relationships – for example you may want to know whether there is a relationship between use of your product or service and gender – is it more likely to be used by men than women? Next you need to check the level of measurement of the data involved.

Box 13.8 Examples of one and two sample tests

A one sample test

Z and *t* tests are used to determine whether the mean of the sample differs significantly from the mean of the population. For example, a survey shows that the average annual income of those holding an Internet account with bank X is €60,000; the average annual income of all of bank X's customers is €42,000. Do those holding Internet accounts with the bank really earn more or is the difference caused by chance? The research hypothesis (H_1) is that those holding Internet accounts have a greater annual income than the population of the bank's customers. The null hypothesis (H_0) is that there is no difference in annual income between the sample of Internet account holders and the population of the customers of the bank. To test the null hypothesis – to determine if there is a significant difference between the sample of Internet account holders and the population of the bank's customers – we use a *z* or a *t* test. To use a *z* test, besides the information we have already, we need to know the standard deviation of the annual income of the bank's customers. If this is not available, or we cannot work it out, we can use a *t* test. The calculations in the *z* and the *t* test produce a value. Using standard normal tables – statistical tables based on the normal distribution – the probability of getting the particular value produced by the test can be determined. This probability level is compared to the significance or probability level you set for the test (for example, *p* is 0.05). If it is greater than this value we must accept the null hypothesis; if it falls below this value we can reject the null hypothesis (that there is no difference) and accept the research hypothesis that there is a difference. We can say that the difference is statistically significant at the 5 per cent significance level. In other words there is a 1 in 20 chance that it is not a real difference and a 95 per cent chance that the difference is real and that the mean annual income of Internet account customers is significantly greater than the mean annual income of the bank's customers.

The end result of most tests is a statistic. This statistic is not meaningful in itself. For it to tell us anything about the difference it has tested we have to compare it against a set of possible values (given in a set of tables specially derived for that test statistic) at a given level of probability.

A paired or related samples test

For example, the client would like to say that his product is better rated than the product of his competitor. You design a blind paired comparison product test. Each respondent rates the client's beer and the competitor's beer. Half the sample tries the client's beer first and half tries the competitor's beer first. Respondents are asked to rate each on a score of one to ten. This is an example of a related samples or paired samples situation and so a related t test such as the Sign test or the Wilcoxon T test would be appropriate.

THE DATA: WHAT LEVEL OF MEASUREMENT?

As we noted above, for interval and ratio level – that is, metric data, you can use a parametric or a non-parametric test, depending on how precise or powerful you need the test to be in detecting differences at any given level of significance. Parametric tests are the more powerful – power refers to the test's efficiency or precision in detecting differences. Parametric tests are more powerful because they make Type II errors on fewer occasions – they are more discriminating than non-parametric tests. They have, however, greater restrictions on their use. As we saw above, besides being suitable for metric data only, the data must be normally distributed. For non-metric data you are restricted to using non-parametric tests. Non-parametric tests are relatively free of any conditions on their use and are suitable for use on data at any level of measurement. The downside is that they lack precision or statistical power.

Finally, you need to check whether the data you are testing are derived from one sample or two and, if two, whether the samples are related or unrelated.

ONE SAMPLE OR TWO AND UNRELATED OR RELATED?

When we talk about one sample what (see Box 13.8) we mean is that we are comparing the statistic – the mean or the proportion or percentage from a sample – against a known population parameter or standard. For example, we know the incidence nationally of reported violent crime; we want to determine if the incidence in a particular city is significantly different. We have two unrelated or independent samples when we have two groups that are not related in any way – the values of one group have no effect on or no relationship to the values of the second group. For example, we want to know if there is a significant difference between Japanese and German organisations in the proportion of their profits reinvested for research and development. The two samples – Japanese organisations and German organisations – are unrelated. We are dealing with related samples (sometimes called paired samples), for example, when we ask a group or a sample of respondents to rate product S and product R. We may calculate the mean score for product S and the mean score for product R but the same respondents are involved in each one, so, although we have two groups, they are not independent of each other.

Box 13.9 Basic guide to inferential statistical tests

Type of analysis: testing for *difference* or *association/relationship*?

If testing for *difference*:
Are the data categorical/non-metric or continuous/metric?

- If non-metric: from one sample or two or more samples?
- If one sample: chi square and binomial for goodness of fit.
- If two related samples: Sign test, Wilcoxon test and chi square.
- If two unrelated samples: Mann-Whitney *U* test, chi square, Kruskal-Wallis, ANOVA.
- If metric: from one sample or two or more samples?
- If one sample: *z* test and *t* test (parametric); Mann-Whitney *U* or Wilcoxon test (non-parametric).
- If two or more unrelated samples: *z* test, *t* test, ANOVA and *F* test.
- If two or more related samples: paired *t* test.

If testing for *association*:
What is the level of measurement of the dependent or outcome variable and the independent or predictor variable?

- If both the outcome and the predictor variables are categorical/non-metric: chi square, contingency coefficient, Cramer's V, Kendall's tau-*b* (and others).
- If the outcome variable is continuous and the predictor variable is categorical: ANOVA (F test).
- If both the outcome and the predictor variables are continuous: regression and correlation (bivariate regression – *t* test for Pearson's *r*; multiple regression – *F* test for R).

END NOTE

It is worth noting that even if the differences or the associations that you see in your data are statistically significant they may not necessarily be meaningful in relation to your research objectives. Looking at this the other way round, meaningful findings may not turn out to be signficant. You should always interpret your findings in the light of your research objectives and in relation to addressing the client's problem.

Chapter summary

- Data exist at several levels of measurement: nominal, ordinal, interval and ratio. Data at the nominal or ordinal levels are non-metric data or categorical; data at the interval or ratio level are metric data. To determine what type of analysis is appropriate, it is important to be able to recognise what kind of data you have.

- Bivariate analysis involves two variables; multivariate analysis involves more than two variables.

- Cross-tabulations or data tables are used to facilitate bivariate and multivariate analysis – they are the most convenient way of reading the responses of the sample and relevant groups of respondents within it. The independent or explanatory variable typically appears as the column variable and the dependent or outcome variable as the row variable, allowing responses of different sub-groups to be compared side by side.

- Tables may be based on those in the sample eligible to answer the question to which it relates. Not all questions are asked of the total sample, however, and analysis based on the total sample may not always be relevant. In such cases tables may be filtered – based on the responses to a particular question rather than on the total sample.

- Weighting is used to adjust sample data in order to make them more representative of the target population on particular characteristics and to ensure that the relative importance of the characteristics within the dataset reflects that within the target population.

- The aim of explanatory analysis is to help explain or predict the relationship between one variable and another (bivariate) or between one variable and another set of variables (multivariate).

- There is a range of techniques available under the heading 'explanatory analysis'. Choice of technique depends largely on the level of measurement of the variables involved.

- There are multivariate techniques that are not about explaining and predicting but that are about looking for the interrelationships between variables with no assumptions about which is the explanatory variable and which is the outcome variable. These techniques are sometimes called interdependence techniques and include factor analysis and cluster analysis.

- Factor and cluster analysis are popular in market research and are put to use in market segmentation studies.

- Inferential analysis – the use of inferential statistical tests – should be confined to data from samples drawn using random sampling techniques with a high (more than 65 per cent) response rate.

- The aim of inferential analysis is to be able to generalise from the sample to the population from which the sample was drawn.

Questions and exercises

1 For a project that you have worked on or are about to work on, describe the research objectives and, using those objectives as a framework, describe the sort of analysis you did or plan to do.

2 Describe what is meant by the following terms, stating the value of each in understanding data:

   (a) bivariate descriptive analysis;

   (b) explanatory analysis; and

   (c) inferential analysis.

References

Blaikie, N. (2003) *Analyzing Quantitative Data: From Description to Explanation*, London: Sage.

Blamires, C. (1995) 'Segmentations techniques in market research: exploding the mystique around cluster analysis', *Journal of Target Marketing, Measurement and Analysis for Marketing*, 4, 2, pp. 62–73.

Blamires, C., Ray, A. and Askew, P. (1997) 'Electronic data capture: taking advantage of a new era', *Proceedings of the Market Research Society Conference*, London: MRS.

Gibson, S., Teanby, D. and Donaldson, S. (2004) 'Bridging the gap between dreams and reality . . . building holistic insights from an integrated consumer understanding', *Proceedings of the Market Research Society Conference*, London: MRS.

Granville, S., Campbell-Jack, D. and Lamplugh, T. (2005) 'Perception, prevention, policing and the challenges of researching anti-social behaviour', *Proceedings of the Market Research Society Conference*, London: MRS.

Harris, P. (1981) 'Recent developments in the multivariate analysis of market research data', *Proceedings of the Market Research Society Conference*, London: MRS.

Johnson, M. (1997) 'The application of geodemographics to retailing: meeting the needs of the catchment', *Journal of the Market Research Society*, 39, 1, pp. 201–24.

Smith, D. and Fletcher, J. (2004) *The Art and Science of Interpreting Market Research Evidence*, Chichester: Wiley.

Recommended reading

Blaikie, N. (2003) *Analyzing Quantitative Data: From Description to Explanation*, London: Sage.

Birn, R. (ed.) (2002) *The International Handbook of Market Research Technques*, 2nd edn. London: Kogan Page.

Callingham, M. and Baker, T. (2002) 'We know what they think, but do we know what they do?', *International Journal of Market Research*, 44, 3, pp. 299–335.

Clegg, F. (1991) *Simple Statistics*, Cambridge: Cambridge University Press. A clear and accessible book on descriptive and inferential statistics.

Ehrenberg, A. (1982) *A Primer in Data Reduction*, London: Wiley. A classic text introducing statistics and data analysis.

Rowntree, D. (2003) *Statistics Without Tears: A Primer for Non-mathematicians*, London: Allyn and Bacon.

Smith, D. and Fletcher, J. (2004) *The Art and Science of Interpreting Market Research Evidence*, Chichester: Wiley.

Tabachnick, B. and Fidell, L. (2006) *Using Multivariate Statistics*, 5th edn. New York: Allyn & Bacon.

Chapter 14

COMMUNICATING AND REVIEWING THE FINDINGS

Introduction

The final stage in the research process involves, on one side, communicating the findings of the research in the context of the problem or issue to which they relate and, on the other, reviewing what is presented to you. Findings are communicated via an oral presentation or a written report or both. The purpose of this chapter is to give you some guidance on how to communicate the findings clearly, accurately and effectively in a presentation or a report, and to set out guidelines for reviewing the output.

Topics covered

- Communicating the findings
- Preparing and delivering a presentation
- Writing a report
- Presenting data in tables, diagrams and charts
- Evaluating the quality of research

Relationship to MRS Advanced Certificate Syllabus

The material covered in this chapter is relevant to Element 8 – Reporting Research Findings. It should help you to think about the output or end results of a research project in terms of the end user's needs, the application of the research findings to the original research problem and ultimately the client's business problem, and to plan and design the reporting accordingly. It should help you make the links between the original business problem (Element 1 and Chapters 1, 3 and 4); the research problem and the research objectives (Element 2 and Chapters 3 and 4); and the findings (Element 9 and Chapters 11 and/or 12 and 13).

Learning outcomes

At the end of this chapter you should be able to:

- communicate the findings of research via an oral presentation and a written report;
- review the quality of the output.

Communicating the findings

It is obvious but worth saying nevertheless that research is a pointless exercise if the findings are not disseminated in some way. The two most common methods of disseminating the findings are via an oral presentation and a written report. Both a presentation and a written report are prepared for most projects. In some projects findings may be written up for publication in journals and books. Presentations and reports are important to the research process for several reasons:

- as a means of crystallising the thinking about the research findings;
- as a channel for communicating and disseminating the findings;
- as a way of influencing and persuading the client in a course of action;
- as a way of selling the skills and expertise of the researcher.

Presentations are also important because they offer a chance for two-way communication to take place – they give the client and the researcher an opportunity to discuss the findings and explore their implications. Reports too have their own particular strengths. The report brings together in one document the detail of the research project – from the original definition of the problem to the findings and implications – and so acts as a record for the work completed. Many of those who read the report or attend the presentation will not have been involved at any other stage of the project – the presentation or the report *is* the project for them. In commissioning further work the client or the client researcher may look back at a report or presentation document as a way of evaluating the quality of the research and the quality of the research supplier. It is worth bearing in mind the point made by Parsons (2004) in Box 14.3 below. The document that you leave with the client at the end of a presentation is typically a copy of the slides used to illustrate your oral presentation. Think about how well this document – without your verbal commentary – conveys the story of the research findings. You may want to include a written version of your verbal commentary within this document. It can add considerable value to it.

The written report can precede or follow the presentation. If a full and detailed presentation of the findings and their implications is made the client may feel that a full report is not necessary and may opt for a summary report, sometimes called a management summary report. Alternatively, the client may prefer a full report in advance of a presentation, in order to get to know the data, the findings and the implications. A presentation may or may not follow. Some clients prefer a draft report in advance of the presentation, using the presentation to discuss and debate the implications, and the action to be taken; following the presentation the researcher prepares a final report to reflect the discussion and to record the conclusions reached. Presentations and reports are sometimes delivered during the course of a project. In large-scale or multi-stage projects the researcher may present interim findings, findings from the exploratory qualitative stage, for instance, or the results of the quantitative pilot study, with the aim of getting input or sharing ownership or simply updating the project team.

COMMUNICATION

Before looking in detail at what is involved in preparing presentations and writing reports it is worth thinking about the art of communication. What is communication about? What does it involve? The aim of communication is to transmit 'stuff' – data, information, knowledge, ideas – in order to inform or influence or persuade. It involves four components:

- the sender or a source, the originator of the message;
- the message;
- the channel or the medium of delivery;
- the receiver or the audience.

To deliver effective communication, whether it is a presentation or a report, it is important to understand the role of these four components and their interaction. You need to know what you want to say, you need to be clear what the message is, you need to know the audience and how that message relates to the audience and why it is important to them. The aim is to match the message with the audience, and make use of the sender or source and the channel to enhance the delivery of it. More specifically, in a research context, you need to make research 'come alive . . .' (Biel, 1994).

PLANNING A PRESENTATION OR REPORT

In planning a presentation or writing a report the first step is to think about what you want to achieve. What is the purpose of it? Why did the client commission the research in the first place? What was the problem they came to you with? What help are they expecting the research to give them?

The objective

Focus on the client's needs, think yourself into their shoes. What end result do you want to achieve? What do you want the client to do as a result of what you have said or written? Do you want, for example, the client to tailor their service provision to suit the needs of customers better? How do you do that? What evidence did the research provide about this? Did it provide insight into what customers need and want? Perhaps you want the client to choose Ad A rather than Ad B for their new advertising campaign. How do you do that? Show how and why Ad A works more effectively at communicating brand values than Ad B?

Box 14.1 A new sort of presentation?

Based on research, Niven and Imms believe that the traditional 'delivery' style of debrief is an ineffective way of connecting with clients. Instead they advocate a more participative approach that is:

- interactive;
- sensitive to the context of the project, the stage in the marketing process and the overlap with existing data and knowledge;
- better designed to meet the learning needs of the client rather than simply delivering research findings;
- uses more collaborative skills;
- still fits with the genuine needs of clients to be informed, to understand and to be able to go forward to make sound business decisions.

Source: Adapted from Niven, A. and Imms. M. (2006) 'Connecting with clients: Re-thinking the debrief', MRS Conference, www.mrs.org.uk.

Always approach the presentation or report with the client's needs in mind. Think of it in terms of taking the audience or the reader on a journey from where they are with their problem to where you – as a result of the research findings – want them to be. At the end of the presentation or the report the audience should be clear about what action is needed, about what the next steps are. Do not approach a presentation or report by thinking about how much data you can pass on in the time or space available. Data are not what the client is interested in. They are interested in information and knowledge, evidence to help them make better decisions. The content of the presentation or the report should be driven by the end result, the objective, and not by the pile of data the research has produced. Develop the message in order to meet the objective of the presentation. Aim to deliver to the client the relevant findings and the implications of the findings for their business. You do not want the client saying 'So what?' at the end of the presentation or report. You must think of the 'So whats' during preparation so that at the end of the presentation or the report the client is clear about what action to take.

Clearing up assumptions

To do this effectively you need to know the client's needs, you need to know the nature of the decision-making process and the decision-making environment. You need to know the audience. So think about what you really know and what you are assuming you know. Think again about why the research was done, about how the findings are to be used, about the decision the client has to take, about what is going on in the client's mind. Think about the assumptions you are making about all of this. What problems or issues is the client facing? What attitudes or opinions do they have about the research, about the problem, about the decision to be made? What do they know about research practice or research techniques? Will there be people in the audience with different perspectives? If in doubt, ask these questions before or as you are preparing the presentation or report. You need this information in order to be able to craft the message to fit the audience and achieve your objective. Remember, the presentation meeting may be the only chance you get to talk to the client team, and it may be one of the rare times that the client team, together in one place, have to talk to each other about the research findings and their implications. The onus is on you to use this time – theirs and yours – to maximum effect.

The audience may be a diverse lot and there may be underlying political currents. Try to find out what these might be. If this is not possible, just be aware that everyone in the room may not be thinking along the same lines or may not be envisaging the same outcomes. You may need to decide whom you most need to influence, and aim the presentation or report and

Box 14.2 Who is the audience or the reader?

- How big will it be?
- Who are they?
- Where are they?
- How senior are they?
- How familiar are they with research?
- How familiar are they with the problem?

target the message at that person or group of people. You may even need to prepare separate reports or give separate presentations to meet the needs of different audiences.

Preparing and delivering a presentation

You know the audience – you have done your background research on who will be present – how do you design the presentation to get them interested and keep them interested?

THE MEDIUM

The source of the message is you and the channel or the medium of delivery is the visual aids. The choice of medium will affect the way in which the message is received – it may enhance the delivery of the message or it may even get in the way of the message. It can add to or detract from the credibility of the source and the message. Your choice of visual aids will depend on three things: the setting (the type and size of the room and the audience); availability of the equipment; and your own preferences.

CASE STUDY 14.1

SEEING IS BELIEVING: CONSUMER VIDEOS

It is important that those who commission research get as much benefit from it as possible. This case study shows how this can be done using an innovative approach to disseminating the research findings.

Why this case study is worth reading

This case study is worth reading for several reasons: it illustrates the limitations of the traditional approach and the advantages of a more innovative one; it describes what was done and why; it describes the outcome.

The key words are: consumer insight, written reports, traditional debriefs, segmentation exercise, data heavy, bring to life, impact, engaging, memorable.

Introduction

Consumer insight is often communicated in written reports, with lots of facts and figures and the occasional verbatim quotation. As issues get more complex, consumers more sophisticated and users more diverse, traditional debriefs, pen-portraits and presentations, do not do the data justice, nor do they do the audience justice. Imagine if you could watch a TV documentary about each of the consumer typologies you have identified, in which you could see the rich, colourful complexity of the consumers' lives you need to understand – a sophisticated 'slice of life' research-based video. So how might this work?

What Van den Berghs did

In 1998 Van den Bergh (VdB) Foods conducted a study among British consumers about their habits and attitudes to life and cooking. As part of the study, VdB did a segmentation exercise to divide consumers into seven attitudinal groups. This would ▶

form the basis of future brand and new product development. This quantitative study was critical to the business and formed the basis of understanding how consumers operate in their environment – beyond simple product usage.

Reporting back

They achieved part of this understanding through the efforts of the quantitative research agency who delivered robust, high quality data that was useful for the immediate research literate audience within the marketing department. However, this was in the standard form – data heavy and full of charts and pen portraits.

Expanding the audience, taking the message further

The challenge was to communicate complicated and detailed information in a way that could be used and understood by everybody. We had to do something creative without losing the integrity, quality and robustness of the information. VdB with ?What If! Television came up with an approach that would make the data understandable and useable by a number of different audiences within and outside the company. The purpose was not to replicate the research conducted but to bring to life what had been learnt, to visualise a difficult set of data. It was essential to create interest in the information, and a desire to understand and learn more. The plan was to do a one-off video. However, this video proved so useful that VdB are now creating a library of consumer videos that show how consumers' lives are changing over time. Together they form a powerful combination of both breadth and depth of information.

Why it works

- **It's simple**: It simplifies a very complicated set of data and charts. It allows users to see similarities and differences between the groups of people, and sparks off debate about them. Suddenly everybody 'gets it' and the data has more impact.
- **It's real life**: The power of seeing someone real, in their home, and with their family is engaging, memorable and emotive – you get comments like 'Oh my God! Did they really do that?'
- **It helps creativity**: Within VdB, with a common understanding of its consumers, everybody is able to take *their* knowledge forward and have new ideas. This creates an environment for finding new insights that the dry data alone would not have delivered.

Source: Adapted from Walter, P. and Donaldson, S. (2001) 'Seeing is believing', MRS Conference, www.mrs.org.uk.

Choice of visual aids

Choose the method which best allows you to communicate your message to that particular audience in the particular venue. Low technology methods such as handouts, flip charts or slides can be just as effective in the right situation as high-tech methods such as a multimedia presentations, including the sort of films described in Case study 14.1 above.

Although handouts are easy to prepare and offer a permanent record of the material presented, they are low in impact as a main presentation tool. If they are handed out to accompany the presentation they can distract the audience's attention. They are perhaps best given to the audience when the presentation ends. Flip charts are most suitable for very small audiences.

They are easy to prepare but can have little impact with a large audience or in a big room (especially if the writing is small and unclear).

Slides are easy to prepare on a word processor or presentation software package and most venues have the equipment needed to display the charts (a screen, a projector and/or a computer). They can have high impact if well designed – for example, not too much text, text of a readable size, a background that enhances rather than detracts from the text – but they can be difficult to use well. Get lots of practice so that you are comfortable using this approach. If you are bringing your own projector or an electronic copy of your presentation to load onto the venue's PC or indeed you are bringing your own laptop computer, then make sure that the facilities can cope; and remember equipment can fail so it is always wise to have a contingency plan – a set of paper charts, for example – for such circumstances.

Chart design

In designing individual charts or slides think about the way in which people assimilate information: some prefer numbers, some words, others pictures and diagrams. It is a good idea in any presentation (and in a report) to use a combination – to break up the style, to ensure that the presentation does not become monotonous. Make sure, however, that the choice is suitable to the material (see Chapter 12).

Integrate your visual aids into the presentation. Remember, they are only aids; they are not the presentation, so do not let them dominate it. Do not put a full script of your presentation on to the charts. This will take the focus of the audience's attention away from what you are saying. Use the visual aids to emphasise and enhance the story and the message, to draw

Box 14.3 The art of storytelling

Here James Parsons argues for oral story telling with slides used as back-up props only.

Microsoft's presentation software PowerPoint is a marvellous, extremely useful blank slate for presenting images. It is a highly versatile canvas, and the conventions of organisation, abbreviation and hierarchisation are not embedded in the medium. The only features embedded are sequentiality and landscapeness – features that emphasise its value as a visual tool.

Perhaps the way forward is to use this medium as a visual prop to a fine verbal spiel; perhaps new practitioners could be taught the art of telling a good story, enthralling, inspiring and engaging their audience rather than fighting against their charts, then departing the meeting, for the disseminated document to wend its way around the audience's organisation unaccompanied by its presenter.

It's worth thinking about how we can engage more with our audience through the quality of our verbal delivery. A key challenge is to revisit the arts of clear, concise, well-argued oral communication, backed up with involving and engaging visual props with concise, written documents for dissemination.

Source: Adapted from Parsons, J. (2004) 'PowerPoint is not written in stone: Business communication and the lost art of storytelling', MRS Conference, www.mrs.org.uk.

attention to key elements of it. Point out what the audience should look for on your charts or handouts and talk around them.

CONTENT AND STRUCTURE

Edit the content ruthlessly. Present only those data or findings that shed light on the issue. Think about ways of presenting the material that clarify your argument or your interpretation – using two-sided arguments, or summaries, repetition and reinforcement, by citing evidence from other data sources or other research you have conducted, for example. Structure the presentation in a way that is relevant to the project or the client. For example, you might want to start with an overview or summary of the findings and move on to the detail, or start with the conclusions and then show the evidence that supports the conclusions.

Think about the order in which you present the main findings. Remember that you need to keep the audience's attention – build the story so that it leads clearly to the most import-ant finding or implication. If bad news is to be delivered talk about the good news first – this generally tends to help the audience accept the bad news and the overall message. Include signposts or placeholders in the presentation so that the audience knows where the story is going and can make links between different bits.

PREPARATION AND PRACTICE

Make sure that you are well prepared. Know your material inside out. Do a timed practice run. Ask some colleagues to sit in, watch and listen, ask questions and give you feedback. In particular, ask them to give you feedback on:

- audibility;
- tone of voice;
- pace/speed;
- body language;
- audience connection;
- handling of visual aids;
- quality of visual aids;
- mastery of the material;
- ease of following the logic of the presentation;
- signposting;
- timing;
- illustration of points made;
- opening and closing;
- handling of questions and discussion.

If you cannot get a practice audience run through the presentation on your own out loud any-way. Having to say it out loud means you take fewer short cuts than when you run through it mentally. Just hearing your own voice speak the words out loud is very helpful in judging what works and what does not – for example where your links between sections or your line of argument are weak.

Think of the sort of questions that your presentation might raise. Depending on your role and the type of presentation, you should prepare yourself to address two types of ques-tions: technical or methodological questions; and questions about your interpretation, your recommendations or your insight or wisdom about the issue or its wider business or social context.

THE LOGISTICS

Check how much time has been allocated for the entire presentation meeting, for the presentation itself, for discussion time, and for other items, and tailor the presentation accordingly. Do not let the volume of data you have dictate the length of the presentation. People will not concentrate for much longer than 45 minutes. Time the presentation and cut back as necessary. If you have been allocated 45 minutes, design the presentation to last about 30 minutes – you may be slowed down by interruptions or questions or by a late arrival delaying the start of the meeting but you will be expected to finish on time anyway. In making the presentation shorter than the allotted time you give yourself some leeway should such situations arise.

Check the technical details – make sure that the room in which you are presenting has the equipment you need and that the room layout and size is suitable for the audience and the method of delivery. Make sure you are comfortable with the equipment and that if anything breaks down or does not work you or someone with you knows how to put it right. Have a back-up set of slides or a presentation document – if the equipment fails you can at least run through a paper version of the presentation.

Settling in

Arrive at the presentation venue in plenty of time to give yourself a chance to get settled and organised and to familiarise yourself with the room (you may want to rearrange the seating to suit your needs). Make sure that the room is neither too cold nor too hot – an overheated room can send people into lethargy and a cold room can make them fidgety and unable to concentrate. You will probably be a bit nervous, most people are. The adrenalin generated will help you perform. Try to relax by slowing down your breathing. Think positive thoughts – you are well prepared, you have practised, you have a good story to tell. Your nerves will probably disappear as soon as you get into your stride, and once you get into the flow of the presentation.

Getting started

Put your watch or your phone on the desk or podium in front of you so that you can check your time easily and unobtrusively. Wait until everyone is settled. Find out if everyone can hear you and see your slides. Make the necessary adjustments if they cannot, then begin. Make a conscious effort to speak slowly and clearly. It is very easy when you are nervous to talk too fast, and in a higher pitch than normal. Be aware of the tone of your voice – try to vary it, make it conversational rather than monotonous. Remember, you are aiming to establish and maintain a connection with the audience, to get their attention and maintain their interest in what you are saying – not how you are saying it. Keep your body language open and friendly. Look at the audience, make eye contact with all of the people in your audience, to include them in what you are saying. Try not to talk when looking down at any notes you might have or at your PC and do not turn your back on the audience. Try to avoid making gestures that might distract people, for example tapping or playing with a pen or a pointer, putting your hands in and out of your pockets, pacing up and down or rocking back and forward, or playing with jewellery. If you are using a laptop and a presentation software package you can call up notes on the screen; you may have notes on the podium or desk. Do not read these notes verbatim – use them as a guide only, as an aide-memoire – in reading them out your voice may sound monotonous. Talk *to* the audience, not *at* them.

If some audience members' first language is not the same as your own make sure that you speak clearly, avoid using too many idioms and ensure all your main points are clearly set out on your charts or handouts. Most people using a second language may find it easier to follow written materials than speech.

GETTING INTEREST: THE OPENING

How do you get people interested and motivated enough to listen to your presentation (or read your report)? This should be relatively straightforward if you have thought your way inside their heads – if you have designed the presentation to target the needs of the audience. People are more likely to remember messages that interest them and that are relevant to their needs. A good opening is important – you need to establish a connection with the audience. The main purpose of the opening is to prepare the ground, to set the scene, to get the audience ready for the message. You can use the opening to relax the audience. Tell them something they already know – use the opening to tell them why there was a need for the research, for example. If you have reviewed the background to the issue move on to demonstrate, for example, the gap in knowledge and how the research findings will address it. Another way of opening is to acknowledge the options available, or the difficulties involved in the client's decision. You can follow this with a statement of how you think the research findings will help. Research findings are often full of stories and anecdotes; using one of these can be an interesting and engaging way of starting the presentation. Choose one that ties in well with your overall message, or one that gets the audience to think in a different way about the issue, a way they may not have considered.

Depending on the audience and the nature of the project, it might be useful to describe the research methodology, including a description of the sample, but keep this brief. It is unlikely that many people will be interested in a lot of methodological detail at this stage. They are there to hear the findings and although the methodological details give them an understanding of the validity and reliability of the research it is not appropriate to go into detail by starting with something that may be unfamiliar or difficult to understand. Keep it simple – do not risk losing the audience by overwhelming them or boring them with methodological detail. Also, be wary of saying anything contentious, it may be too distracting at such an early stage and cause the audience's attention to wander. However, do say something contentious if you need to challenge the audience's thinking about the topic.

Whatever opening you use make sure it captures the audience's attention and prepares the way for the main focus of the presentation. Give a map of the presentation – an outline of the structure of the presentation, the issues or findings that you will deal with – so that the audience knows what is involved and where the presentation will take them. There are some housekeeping tasks that can be dealt with here too. Tell the audience how long the presentation will last, whether you will take questions during it or at the end; and let them know whether you are providing handouts, so that they can decide whether or not to take notes.

KEEPING INTEREST ALIVE

Once the presentation is under way you need to work at maintaining the audience's interest and your connection to them. All elements of the presentation should contribute to this. You know yourself from attending presentations and lectures why your attention sometimes wanders. Here are some of the most common problems – make sure in preparing and delivering your presentation that you avoid them.

The structure and content of the message

- You lose track of where the presentation is going.
- You lose track of the relevance of the content.
- The content is dull and uninteresting.
- It is hard to follow and difficult to understand.
- It is not clear what particular findings you should be focusing on, what the important elements are and what is padding or just 'nice to know'.

The source: the presenter

- Speaks in a monotonous voice.
- Reads from a script or from notes.
- Distracts you by fiddling with clothing or jewellery.
- Does not engage the audience with appropriate eye contact or body language.
- Talks down to the screen or to notes rather than to the audience.

The medium: the visual aids

- The charts are not in the right order.
- There are problems with the equipment.
- The text on the charts is difficult to read.

BRINGING THE PRESENTATION TO AN END

Signal clearly to the audience that the presentation is coming to an end. In most research presentations the end involves a summary and some concluding remarks and/or recommendations. Summarising the main points of the message – in effect restating the main message or the key issues in short form – can help consolidate the audience's awareness and understanding of the issues. Conclusions should be based on the evidence you have included in your presentation; do not introduce new material at this stage. If appropriate to the project and the setting, make recommendations for future action. This may just mean clarifying the next steps, suggesting further research, inviting audience members to contact you for further analyses or queries about the findings, or even arranging a meeting to evaluate the research or the research contribution to the project. Make sure to finish on time. If you are running over time skip some of the detail of the findings and move to the ending.

THE DISCUSSION/QUESTION AND ANSWER SESSION

In many presentations the discussion or question and answer session begins when the presentation ends. When answering questions take your time, do not rush to give an answer. Do not be afraid of pauses – they often seem longer to you than they do to the audience – do not rush to fill the silence. Repeat the question in order to clarify your understanding of what is being asked, in case some people may not have heard it, and to give yourself some thinking time. If someone from your organisation is attending the presentation ask them to note down the questions asked and the comments made so that you can follow them up if necessary. When you answer a question address the entire audience, not just the questioner. Keep the answer to the question relevant – do not use it as an opportunity to talk about something that has just come into your head. If someone wants to know something in detail that may not be relevant to the whole audience, or not wholly relevant to the main issue, tell them that you will talk to them about it at length at the end of the meeting.

GETTING FEEDBACK

Once the presentation is over ask colleagues and clients for feedback; think about what you did well and what you would do differently, or what you could improve on.

Writing a report

Although the medium is different, the aim in writing a report is the same as the aim in giving a presentation – to communicate the results of the research clearly and effectively. Plan out the report in detail. Before starting to write be clear about what you want the report to achieve. Why is it being written? What is the objective of the report? Who are the readers? What do they expect to read? What do you want to tell them or get them to do as a result of reading the report? It is essential to do this. As the examples in Box 14.4 below show, asking these questions upfront may well dictate the content, language, layout and presentation of your report.

Box 14.4 How shall I put it? Examples of how to get the message across

Here are examples from three sets of researchers on ways of making research findings more accessible and – as a result – more widely used.

1 Paying attention to language and medium

In a project among a sample of people with learning difficulties the research team wanted to find ways of reporting and disseminating the findings that would be accessible to the people they interviewed. Here are the solutions they suggested:

■ All reports are to be produced in two formats: the first is a summary report written in plain English using pictures to aid comprehension; the second is a more detailed report, as accessible as possible while including technical details.
■ In addition to more conventional routes such as published documents on paper and the Internet, consider holding conferences, seminars and discussion groups with stakeholders and interested parties. In this way the findings can be further discussed and stakeholders have some input to any decisions taken as a result of the findings.

Source: Adapted from Emerson, E., Malam, S., Joyce, L. and Muir, J (2003) ' "Nothing about us without us". Meeting the challenges of a national survey amongst people with learning difficulties', MRS Conference, www.mrs.org.uk.

2 Paying attention to style and packaging

The style magazine

The insight we gather is only as good as its application. And it only gets applied right when it is properly absorbed. We attached great significance to finding the right medium to convey the message to best effect. The inspiration came by thinking about the internal audience as any media planner would its external audience. When were we most likely to find a slice of their attention? Easy – on planes, trains and sofas. The bibles of the fashion industry are style magazines so we needed to package our knowledge as a style magazine. 'YP' was born and is now in its sixth edition with a print run of over 500. It's a simple tool but it means everybody who needs to be close to the consumer has an accessible bag-sized reminder of where the market is moving and what the key challenges are for the brand (Levis®).

Source: Adapted from Flemming from Thygesen and McGowan, P. (2002) 'Inspiring the organisation to act: a business in denial', MRS Conference, www.mrs.org.uk.

3 Paying attention to the time and the place

The mini-newsletter in the lavatory – and the right to reply!
An idea that still makes us chuckle was introduced by a fast-moving consumer goods company. They wanted people in the marketing department to read more about the research results but were realistic about how little time people had in which to do it. So they decided to create a mini-newsletter and to put it in exactly the place they felt people had the most time and opportunity to read it. They hung it behind the door in the toilets! Simple, effective, and they have now gone on to provide Post-It notes and a pen for people to write notes and thoughts in reply to questions raised, and to leave them stuck to the door!

The laminated fact sheet on the desk
An executive had pulled together a neat summary of 'The key things you should know about our customer', gleaned from a range of research projects. They produced something eye-catching and punchy on A4 paper. But they knew that in that state, printed on paper, it would just get put in a pile and be forgotten. So they laminated it, and left one on every desk that they felt appropriate. The result – it was suddenly transformed from just an interesting sheet of paper into something more official looking, more permanent, and clearly meant to be kept and referred to. It tended to be pinned to the partitions between desks, and other staff who saw it came to the research department to see if they could have one. The result was that the messages from the research got through.

Source: Adapted from Wills, S. and Williams, P. (2004) 'Insight as a strategic asset – the opportunity and the stark reality', *International Journal of Market Research*, 46, 4, pp. 393–410, www.ijmr.com.

Once you have established the objective of the report and the audience for it you will have some idea of the content, format and style that is suitable. Now start writing.

PREPARING AN OUTLINE

It can be helpful to prepare a report outline – a map of what is to be included in the report (see Figure 14.1). Collect all the data and information you need and write down all the main ideas, issues, key findings, interesting facts. Do not pay too much attention to order or style – just get it all together in one document or on one large sheet of paper. Read through it all

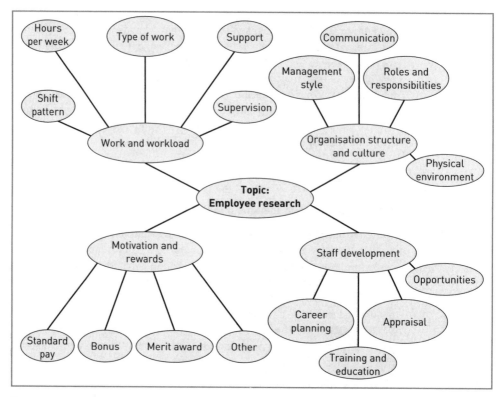

Figure 14.1 Example of a report outline

and start grouping the ideas, issues and so on under headings of themes or topics. Refer back to the objective of the report (and to the research objectives and your analysis framework if necessary) – what is the message that you are trying to communicate? Begin to add some structure by ordering and numbering the themes or topics in a way relevant to the aim. The document you have now is your report outline or map. You can now get stuck into the main writing task.

Box 14.5 Establishing the objective of the report: checklist

Think of the reader and ask yourself the following questions:

- Why am I writing it?
- What do I want to achieve?
- Who will read it?
- Why will they want to read it?
- What do they want to know? What do they know already?

THE REPORT LAYOUT

The layout, the visual appearance of what is put down on paper, is a major contributor to the reader's enthusiasm and ability to understand the report. Make good use of white space. Keep print size and style consistent. Use headings to label and identify the structure. Use a simple numbering system to direct the reader. Keep diagrams and tables as close as possible to the relevant text. If you refer to a table or diagram in several places in the text, repeat it so that the reader does not have to refer back to it. Most reports follow a similar structure that consists of an introduction, a methodology chapter, a findings chapter and a summary, conclusions and recommendations chapter. There are variations on this depending on the house style of the organisation or the specific needs or requests of the reader. A more detailed structure or contents list is given in Box 14.6.

Box 14.6 Report headings

- Title
- Abstract or management summary
- Table of contents
- Background and introduction
- Literature review
- Problem identification
- Terms of reference (what the research needs to deliver, research objectives)
- Methodology or approach to the research:
  - research design
  - sample
  - method of data collection
  - questionnaire/discussion guide development
  - limitations of the research
- Analysis or findings
- Discussion and interpretation
- Conclusions
- Recommendations
- Appendices:
  - technical details, e.g. of sample
  - questionnaire/discussion guide in full
  - organisation details
  - CVs of team members

Title

The title of the report is important, particularly if the report is to have a wide circulation or is to be published. It must catch the reader's attention, spark interest in and inform the reader of the main focus or storyline of the report. Coming up with a title that does all this is not as easy as it might seem. It is usually best to use a draft or working title during the preparation of the report and wait until the report is almost complete before deciding on the final title – something in the write-up may suggest something suitable. A brainstorming session or a competition among project team members (with suggestions posted on the website or circulated via email) is a useful way of generating a title. The title can have two parts – a catchy main title that creates interest and a more descriptive sub-title that informs.

Abstract

An abstract is a short, easy to read summary or map of the entire report, typically no more than 500 words long and usually about 150–300. It is common (usually essential) in journal articles or more academic reports but it is good practice to include one in every report you write – it may be the only bit that a busy reader reads. It should inform the reader of the salient facts, allowing them to decide whether to read on; and for those who do read on, it sets the scene. It should include the following:

- the research problem or research questions;
- why this is being researched;
- how the research was conducted, the methods used;
- the main findings; and
- the implications or conclusions.

Although an abstract is best written once the report is finished, you can draft it out as soon as you have done your report outline (see above). This is a useful exercise – it will help you ensure that you are clear about what the message of the report really is. Preparing an accurate, brief but clear abstract is not easy – you may need to prepare several drafts. Instead of an abstract you may need to write a longer summary of the key findings.

Box 14.7 Example of an abstract

Misbehaviour by survey interviewers includes actions forbidden either explicitly or implicitly in codes of ethics, interviewer training or interviewing instructions. As examples of misbehaviour, interviewers can reword questions, answer questions when interviewees refuse to respond or fabricate answers to entire questionnaires. This study investigates the nature and incidence of such interviewer actions in telephone surveys, currently the most popular mode of data collection in marketing research in the United States. It uses both a mail survey and field experiment with samples of survey interviewers to investigate four factors hypothesised to influence misbehaviour by telephone interviewers. Results indicate that misbehaviour by telephone interviewers is ordinary and normal. Recommendations for reducing interviewer actions classified as misbehaviour are provided for research suppliers, marketing managers and marketing academics.

Source: Adapted from Kiecker, P. and Nelson, J. (1996) 'Do interviewers follow telephone survey instructions?', *International Journal of Market Research*, 38, 2, p. 161, www.ijmr.com.

Table of contents

Make sure you have a clear, logical and well-presented table of contents. It will help readers understand the scope and coverage of the report as well as helping them find relevant sections.

Background and introduction

The purpose of this chapter of a report is to set the scene and describe the wider context of the research problem. Include information that will help the reader get to grips with the topic quickly and painlessly. You may have already prepared a similar section for the proposal but things may have changed since then, so write the background and introduction from the point of view of having now done the work.

Box 14.8 Example of an introduction

The objectives of the Healthy Ageing Programme as stated in *Adding Years to Life and Life to Years: A Health Promotion Strategy for Older People* (Brenner and Shelley, 1998) are:

- to improve life expectancy at age 65 and beyond;
- to improve the health status of people aged 65 and beyond;
- to improve the lives and autonomy of older people who are already affected by illness and impairment.

Information on healthy ageing has up to now been fragmented. It is difficult to envisage these objectives being achieved without significantly improved knowledge of existing activities in healthy ageing and some discussion of best practice in this expanding and diverse field. To this end it was necessary to conduct an extensive research and consultation exercise with stakeholders in the field of healthy ageing in Ireland. The aim of this report is to present the key findings from the consultations and from the survey.

Source: Adapted from O'Shea, E. and Connolly, S. (2003) 'Healthy Ageing in Ireland: Policy, Practice and Evaluation', in McGivern, Y. (ed.) *The 2003 Healthy Ageing Conference*, Dublin: National Council on Ageing and Older People. Used with permission.

Literature review

The project may have involved a literature review or a review of previous research on the topic. A literature review chapter should be a synopsis and assessment of that literature or the previous research, with a particular focus on material that has informed the research design, the analysis of the data or the interpretation of the findings. Do not use it merely to show that you know 'the area', and do not write a literature review without some critical thinking. It should achieve the following:

- provide background information on the topic and its wider context;
- provide a brief synopsis and assessment of the findings of previous research and their implications;
- highlight any gaps in knowledge or understanding;
- show why this research is worth doing.

Methodology

This chapter should set out details of how you went about the research, your research design and the methods you used. You should address the following questions:

- What is the structure or design of the research?
- What is the target population and how did you identify it?
- On what basis did you draw your sample and why?
- What are the characteristics of the people you interviewed?
- What data collection methods did you use and why?
- How did you translate the research objectives into a questionnaire or interview guide?
- How did you handle the data?
- How did you approach the analysis of the data?
- What difficulties arose during the research and how were these addressed?
- What are the limitations of the research and the data presented?

Analysis of findings

You can tackle the write-up of your findings in one chapter with sections for each of your main themes or areas, or you can write up each bit in a separate chapter. Whichever way you do it make sure that you plan out the sequence of your sections and chapters in advance of writing anything. Constantly review this report outline to make sure that it addresses the aim of the report, that the sequence is logical, and that the reader can follow the story clearly.

Discussion and interpretation

The purpose of this chapter is to bring together your original research questions, your findings, the previous work discussed in the literature review and the wider context of the research problem as outlined in the introduction. In other words in this chapter you aim to establish the implications of the research findings for the original research problem and the wider business issues. You may also want to make some suggestions about further research that might follow from your findings. In addition you may want to set out here what you would do differently (and why) if you were doing the research over again.

Conclusions and recommendations

You may want to include the conclusions and recommendations in the discussion chapter. Alternatively, you may want to create a separate chapter. The decision will depend on your readership or on house style. Readers are generally busy people with limited time and they may decide to read only the abstract or summary, the introduction and the conclusions and recommendations. The summary, conclusions and recommendations may come at the beginning, even before the introduction, or before the main findings section. Remember – the summary is a short version of the main findings; the conclusion summarises the facts and arguments presented. Do not include any new facts or opinions in the conclusion that have not appeared in the report. Together with the introduction, the conclusion should give the reader the gist of the report. In the recommendations section put your points of action – these must follow directly from the rest of the report. Where the conclusion gives an objective view of the information presented, in the recommendations section you may give your suggestions for action.

Appendices

The purpose of an appendix is to hold all the information that is not directly relevant to the story but may be important to readers who need more detail (to evaluate the quality of the work, or to replicate it, for example). It should contain technical and methodological details, for example the sampling procedure and the sample, how the data were handled, what weighting, if any, was used. It should also contain a full version of the questionnaire or discussion guide; and details of the organisation(s) that carried out the work, perhaps even CVs or résumés of team members. Depending on the type of report the appendix may also contain a full bibliography of references cited and used. Data tables, transcriptions of interviews, field notes or coding schemes may be contained in an appendix but are more usually presented separately, if at all.

Box 14.9 Example of summary, conclusions and recommendations

Summary

The research shows that housing exerts a critical influence on older people's well-being. There are several aspects of housing that we found to be important:

- the dwelling – the quality of the building itself;
- the location;
- the house as an asset or form of wealth;
- as a source of income;
- as a bequest.

Dwellings provide shelter and comfort, but they also locate their occupants in relation to relatives, neighbours and services; they are often valuable assets, they are usually the main form of the older person's wealth, and they can be important in the family dynamics because of their potential as bequests to heirs.

Conclusions

Housing is a critical factor in the quality of life of older people. Many older Irish people are in a paradoxical situation . . .: they are housing poor and housing rich at the same time – many live in houses that are no longer suitable for their needs but which are worth a substantial amount of money . . .

Recommendations

Market solutions might include the following:

- the provision of suitable housing in towns, which allows older people to trade sideways, or down;
- equity release schemes to free capital tied up in the property;
- clawback schemes – where local authorities renovate a property but can reclaim some or all of the cost of doing so if the owner dies within a certain time period and the house is passed on to the next generation.

Source: Adapted from Fahey, T. (2001) 'Housing, social interaction and participation among older Irish people', in McGivern, Y. (ed.), *Towards a Society for All Ages*, Dublin: National Council on Ageing and Older People. © 2001 National Council on Ageing and Older People. Used with permission.

STARTING TO WRITE

It is likely that you will write about three or four draft versions of the report before you are satisfied that it gets your message across. No one gets it right first time. The important thing is not trying to get it right first time but to start writing. Do not be afraid to start. No one may even see the first draft. It is not the final product. In an early draft you are still formulating your ideas and crystallising your thinking. You can start writing before you have the data. Start with the background to the problem or the problem definition. Starting with fairly straightforward sections that you may have covered in the proposal will help you write your way into it. It will also help you establish the aim and focus of the issues and it may make you better and more efficient at interrogating the data when you get them.

Structure

When the data tables and analyses or the tapes and transcripts arrive, work through them systematically. Once you get to grips with the data and understand what they are saying start putting down all your thoughts and ideas – as you work through the research results write down what is interesting, meaningful and relevant, including thoughts and insights that pop into your head. Do not be concerned about how crafted or polished the language is at this stage, or the order of ideas or themes. Once you have dumped down all your ideas you can then start working through them to structure the material and give it a logical order in line with the report's objective. There are lots of ways of organising the flow of a report – there is no one right way. To help you structure it you can write all your major themes down on separate cards, or in boxes on a flow chart, and move them around to see how they best fit together to make the story flow.

Remember, a paragraph is a theme, a group of related sentences, so separate your themes into paragraphs – this will also make the reading easy and clear. Build a map into your report by making the first sentence in a paragraph and the first paragraph in a section a summary of what you are going to say in the subsequent sentences and paragraphs. This makes the report more readable, and enables the reader to get to grips with content relatively easily.

Vary the length of sentences, and in writing and editing them remember that a sentence is a unit of thought and so should contain one idea only. Try to keep your sentences to about 15 to 20 words – it helps with readability.

Language

Once you have the structure more or less sorted out you can tackle the language. Sorting out the structure will have helped you to clarify the ideas and the message; editing the language will help you take this a stage further. Use the language that you use every day and use the active voice rather than the passive. Reports are hard to read when they contain too many sentences in the passive voice, or too many long words, too much jargon, and too many long sentences and long paragraphs. Get rid of redundant words and phrases, including unnecessary adjectives and adverbs. It will have the effect of making your ideas sharper and more focused.

Getting feedback

Is it readable? Is it understandable? Is it accurate? Give a draft to a colleague and ask him or her to read it and give you feedback. The problems feedback might uncover at this stage are that your ideas and your expression of them and the logic are not yet clear. If at this stage someone starts picking on your choice of words or your sentence construction remember it for later, but ignore it for now. Now is the time to get the ideas and the message or argument clear. There should be a thread or storyline that runs through the report which leads the reader to your conclusions and to the overall picture. Read your draft out loud and see what the language sounds like. It should be easy on the ear. If it jars, rewrite it. Rewriting should focus on achieving brevity and adding clarity while at the same time maintaining accuracy. Remember, too, that you have an ethical responsibilty to your client/reader to present a sound and accurate account of the research, and to make clear what is 'fact' and what is your interpretation. Check your draft against the list in Box 14.10. You may also find it useful to read the MRS Code of Conduct rules for the reporting of findings in Box 14.13 below.

Box 14.10 Checking a report draft

- Is the table of contents complete?
- Are all the chapters/sections present?
- Is the structure clear?
- Are the topics within each chapter in a logical order?
- Are there good links between sections?
- Is there anything that would be better off in an appendix?
- How informative and attention getting is the title?
- Is the abstract an accurate summary of the entire report?
- Does the background set the scene in enough detail? Does it contain enough information for a newcomer to the topic to understand the issues and the need for research?
- Have you clearly stated the research objectives?
- Does the literature review present relevant material?
- Have you explained the research design and methods clearly?
- Are the limitations of the research (and the findings) identified?
- Have you distinguished clearly between findings and interpretation, between 'facts' and speculation or opinion?
- Have all (and only) the relevant data been used?
- Are any assumptions made in interpreting the data clearly stated?
- Does the summary cover the key findings?
- Do your conclusions include only material mentioned in the main body of the report?
- Are the recommendations based on a full understanding of the wider context?
- Is the story easy to follow?
- Are there adequate and accurate headings (and labels on charts)?
- Does each chapter or section have an opening and closing summary?
- Is the report easy to read?
- Have you used the active voice rather than the passive?
- Have you removed all unnecessary words and phrases?
- Have you checked that you don't have too many long words?
- Have you removed all unnecessary jargon and technical language?
- Have you varied the length of sentences and paragraphs?
- Are tables and diagrams as close to the relevant text as possible?
- Are pages, chapters, paragraphs, tables and diagrams numbered?
- Have you checked the spelling and grammar?
- Have you used plenty of white space?
- Are all bibliographic references included and presented in the agreed way?
- Does the report conform to the house style or meet the requirements of the client?

Letting go

When it is done, let it go. It is often assumed that taking more time is better than taking less time. That is not always the case, and time spent at the end polishing it is usually better spent up front thinking about the objective of the report, planning it out and devising an effective structure and a logical order.

Presenting data in tables, diagrams and charts

We looked at aspects of data presentation or data display in relation to data processing and analysis in Chapters 11 and 12. The aim of data display is twofold: to reduce the amount of data; and to present data in such a way that it becomes information. We saw the importance (the 'so what') of this above in discussing how to get the message across to the client and the end users of the data – how to help them learn from it and apply it. The ability to reduce the mass of data in your data tables or from tapes and transcripts and display them in summary form (as short written summary statements or in summary tables, charts or diagrams) in a way that tells the story is an important skill.

WRITTEN SUMMARY STATEMENTS

Some types of data are best presented as written statements. Written summary statements are useful for drawing the audience's or the reader's attention to key messages in the presentation or report. If well written they are easy to understand and can be used to convey the meaning of complex data. For a presentation, however, they can lack the impact of a good graphic or visual display. Here are some guidelines that will help you obtain maximum impact from any written chart, even summaries contained in a report:

Text
- the text should be easy to read;
- the typeface should be large enough for most people to read easily;
- the typeface should be easy on the eye (if different typefaces are used on the same chart they should complement each other, otherwise the end result may look untidy);
- the text should be in a colour that does not clash with or fade into the background.

Words and grammar
- use short words;
- avoid too many abbreviations;
- do not reduce sentences so much that the meaning is unclear;
- give each chart a title that clearly explains its content.

Layout
- make use of space – avoid using too much text or text too tightly bunched.

QUALITATIVE DATA TABLES, CHARTS AND DIAGRAMS

Most of the qualitative data you present in a report or in an oral presentation will be in written form – your findings and quotations from respondents. It may also include respondent-produced material, for example from projective and other exercises. The presentation may

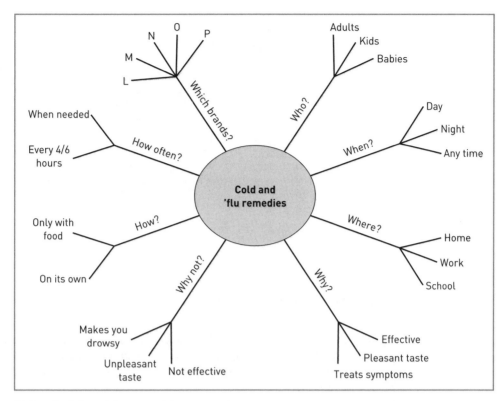

Figure 14.2 Example of a spidergram

also include audio or video clips from interviews or group discussions or film or video of observation (see Case studies 14.1 and 6.2). It is often useful, too, to adapt some of the tables, charts and diagrams you used in analysing the data for inclusion in the report or presentation. For example, a table that shows the relationship between respondent type and a particular buying pattern or a chart or diagram showing the links between key themes or issues in the data or the typical decision-making pathway that you uncovered among the sample might tell the story much more clearly and quickly than a paragraph of text. Figures 14.2 and 14.3 are two examples.

QUANTITATIVE DATA TABLES

The data tables you receive from data processing should not be used in their unadulterated form in a presentation or a report. Invariably they contain too much data, much of which is likely to be irrelevant to the particular point you are trying to make. The data from these tables should be reviewed with the objectives of the report or presentation in mind, and only those data extracted that address these objectives.

Summary tables

The tables used in a presentation or report should be designed so that the reader or viewer does not have to work hard to get the message or see the finding. Each table should have a title that is short but informative. In a report the tables should be numbered. Text describing

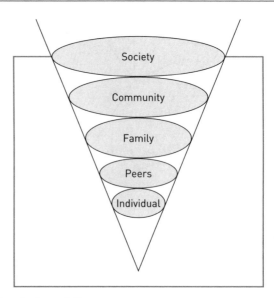

Figure 14.3 Example of a funnel diagram

the content of columns and rows should be clear, and not abbreviated so much that they are hard to understand. The units of measurement of the numbers in the table should be clearly displayed, with base sizes and summary statistics (such as means and standard deviations) included when appropriate.

The layout should make reading the table easy. If numbers are to be compared make sure they are in columns side by side rather than in rows. Avoid cluttering the table with too many lines, or too much text, or using shading or colouring that makes it difficult to read. Make sure the spacing between numbers is consistent and that numbers line up. Keep the numbers in a consistent style; for example, if some numbers have two decimal places and others have one, decide which is more appropriate and use that. Arrange rows and columns in an order that tells a story. For example, a simple rank ordering in terms of content or value often does the trick.

Consider Tables 14.1(a) and 14.1(b), which show fictional data on medication for colds derived from an association grid. With Table 14.1(a) it takes a while to work out what the data are saying. It is not immediately clear which brand is associated with which attributes, or which attributes seem to be more important. In Table 14.1(b) a simple reordering and the addition of another line of data makes the finding more obvious. The two most popular brands, M and N, are considered by most people in the sample to be effective, suitable for use throughout the day, to treat all the symptoms and quick to take effect. More people find N compared to M easy to take and pleasant tasting. Brand P is the third most popular in terms of claimed purchase. It appears to share some characteristics with M and N – effective, treats all the symptoms, quick to take effect; and it is similar to N in that similar proportions say that it is pleasant tasting and easy to take. It differs, however, from both M and N in that a large proportion say that it makes you drowsy and a relatively small proportion, in comparison to M or N, say that it is suitable to use throughout the day. A smaller proportion compared to M, N or P sees Brand O, which shares the 'makes you drowsy' attribute with P and to some extent with L, as effective or as treating all the symptoms of a cold. Relatively few respondents associate Brand L with any of the attributes, with the exception of 'makes you drowsy'.

Table 14.1(a) Data from brand attribute association grid

Attribute	Brand L %	Brand M %	Brand N %	Brand O %	Brand P %
Pleasant tasting	42	67	84	72	78
Makes you drowsy	62	19	25	78	82
Quick to take effect	24	79	76	69	74
Easy to take	38	66	79	79	76
Suitable to use throughout the day	25	83	84	22	29
Treats all the symptoms of a cold	22	82	76	56	79
Effective	27	89	72	62	74
Mean of attribute ratings	32	69	71	63	70

Table 14.1(b) Data from brand attribute association grid – modified version

	Brand M %	Brand N %	Brand P %	Brand O %	Brand L %
Buy now	**82**	**71**	**52**	**38**	**11**
Effective	89	72	74	62	27
Suitable to use throughout the day	83	84	29	22	25
Treats all the symptoms of a cold	82	76	79	56	22
Quick to take effect	79	76	74	69	24
Pleasant tasting	67	84	78	72	42
Easy to take	66	79	76	79	38
Makes you drowsy	19	25	82	78	62
Mean of attribute ratings	69	71	70	63	32

Detailed tables

It is sometimes necessary to provide more detailed tables in a report or in an appendix to a report. In preparing these tables all the above guidelines should be followed. In addition you may want to add in explanatory notes, explaining terms used in the table, the source of the data or a commentary on the findings.

Types of numbers in tables: using indices, ratios and percentage change

If you want to show trends over time it can be useful to transform the data into an index by expressing it as a percentage or proportion of the earliest figure in the time sequence. Table 14.2(a) shows the unit sales for three products from 2002 to 2006, with those for the most recent year, 2006, in the first column.

To get a clearer picture of the relative changes in sales since 2002 we can index the figures to 2002. If we divide the 2002 figure for each product by itself and multiply it by 100 we get 100. To transform each of the figures from 2003 to 2006 we do the same – divide the figure for each year by the 2002 figure for that product and multiply it by 100 to express it in the same units as the 2002 figure. In Table 14.2(b) the data are thus transformed, making the finding clearer. It is now easy to see that, for example, while sales of products Y and Z were the same in 2002, sales of product Z grew faster. Table 14.2(c) is easier to read because the order in which the years appear has been reversed so that the table reads from left to right rather than right to left.

Ratios are a useful way to highlight differences between two or three figures. Here is a fictional example: for every $1 spent on advertising by the anti-drink drive lobby, alcohol manufacturers spend $10 sponsoring motor racing.

Table 14.2(a) Unit sales (millions) 2002–2006

	2006	2005	2004	2003	2002
Product X	376	320	298	246	202
Product Y	499	348	306	298	288
Product Z	636	588	542	322	288

Table 14.2(b) Unit sales (indexed) 2002–2006 (2002 = 100)

	2006	2005	2004	2003	2002
Product X	186	158	148	122	100
Product Y	173	121	106	103	100
Product Z	221	204	188	119	100

Table 14.2(c) Unit sales (indexed) 2002–2006 (2002 = 100) – re-ordered

	2002	2003	2004	2005	2006
Product X	100	122	148	158	186
Product Y	100	103	106	121	173
Product Z	100	119	188	204	221

Table 14.3 First and second quarter sales for four models of luxury car

Model	1st qtr	2nd qtr	Change	% gain/loss
Model R	192	79	−113	−59
Model S	440	460	+20	+5
Model U	204	312	+108	+53
Model W	42	72	+30	+71

It may be useful to show the change – the gain or loss – between two figures as a percentage of the gain. If you do this make sure that the base or sample size on which the percentage change is calculated is large enough, otherwise the results might be misleading, as the example in Table 14.3 shows. The percentage gain/loss figures in the last column of Table 14.3 show that Model W has seen the greatest increase in sales – 71 per cent compared to 53 per cent for Model U. Sales for Model W were relatively low to begin with and the percentage gain is exaggerated – it only looks big because of this small base. When base size or sub-sample sizes are small be wary of using percentages – they are misleading, especially when used in comparison with percentages based on more robust base sizes, and in many cases are meaningless.

QUANTITATIVE DATA IN CHARTS AND DIAGRAMS

A well-designed chart can make the material in reports and presentations more interesting, easier to get through and easier to understand or take in; it can convey quickly and easily a lot of detailed, even complex data. Designing such charts, however, is not easy. The format must be suitable for the material (see Chapter 12 for more detail); and the chart or diagram should convey the message clearly and accurately – the message should jump out at the audience or the reader.

Here are some general guidelines for effective chart design:

■ Avoid anything that makes reading and understanding charts difficult.
■ The title should explain the content clearly and succinctly.

- The text should be large enough to read easily (on a presentation chart about 32-point; in a report, 12-point).
- The text should stand out from the background (the colour should enhance the text, not distract from it or make it look blurred).
- The chart design should be as plain as possible (avoid distracting designs, vertical lines and shading, especially cross-hatching, which can be hard on the eye; in fact, avoid shading at all if possible).
- Label sections or elements of the chart rather than use a legend or key to which the audience or reader have to refer to understand the chart.
- Ensure that scales are labelled with units of measurement and that the scale does not exaggerate relationships or mislead (see Tufte, 2001).
- Do not overcrowd or obscure the chart with labels – it should contain only the text and numbering necessary for interpretation.
- The text included should tell the reader or viewer how to read the chart and should direct attention to the relevant finding.
- Labels and other text should not be abbreviated so much that their meaning is difficult to decipher.

It is important that all aspects of the chart are integrated so that reading it and understanding the message is easy and straightforward – the chart designer has done all the work and the reader is able to see what is going on almost immediately.

Box 14.11 Using a chart format: a quick guide

Pie charts
- useful for categorical data only (nominal or ordinal level variables);
- if you want to show how the whole of something divides up into parts;
- make sure to put segments of the pie chart in a logical order;
- do not use if you have a lot of categories to display.

Bar charts
- useful for categorical data only;
- good for comparing frequencies or percentages of two or more values or variables;
- can use vertical or horizontal bars;
- order bars in a way that is meaningful;
- two or more sets of bars can be displayed on one chart, as in Figure 12.5 (a) and (b);
- can divide the bar into sections with each representing measurements that relate to each other in some way (see Figures 12.6 and 12.7).

Histogram
- useful for displaying continuous data (interval or ratio level of measurement, e.g. age bands, income groups);
- order bars in a way that is meaningful (see Figure 12.8).

Line charts
- useful for displaying continuous data.

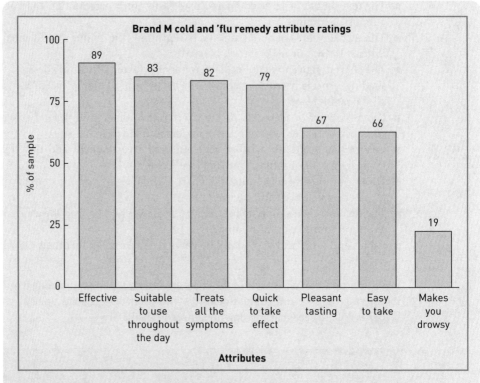

Figure 14.4 Example of a simple bar chart

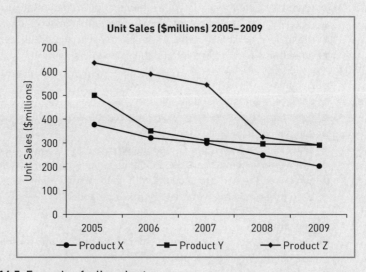

Figure 14.5 Example of a line chart

Figure 14.6 Example of a pictogram

Scatterplots
■ useful for bivariate rather than univariate data, e.g. to show relationship between two variables.

Other types of charts to consider
■ pictograms, geographical maps.

Evaluating the quality of research

Throughout the book we have discussed the things you need to do in order to commission or conduct high-quality research. Imagine now that the research has been completed and the findings delivered. Assuming you were happy with the proposal and the research design proposed in it, you now need to review how the research was executed and how the findings were delivered.

DID YOU GET WHAT YOU ASKED FOR?

First of all consider: did you get what you asked for in the brief or what you were promised in the proposal? If there were problems, what steps were taken to resolve them? Was the problem brought to your attention in a timely manner? For example, if the sample was not achieved, did the researcher explain why? Is the explanation credible? Is it clear what effect this might have on the overall robustness or credibility of the data? Are you satisfied with this explanation? If the recruitment for a group discussion did not match the criteria set down, or the group did not work particularly well, did the researcher continue with the group? Were findings from that group included in the analysis? Did the researcher recruit or offer to recruit a replacement group (Lovett, 2001)? Are you satisfied that the researcher did all that was possible?

Execution of the research

In choosing a research supplier you may have reviewed how well they conducted research for others (via a credentials pitch, an office visit, informal soundings or discussions and so on).

Box 14.12 Added value

You will no doubt have heard or seen reference made to the concept of 'added value', perhaps in the context of what the client gets from the research and from the research provider. But what does 'added value' mean?

There is no one common or agreed definition. In general terms, it is about 'going beyond', delivering a product or a service that is beyond the expectations of the client.

Carrying out the research to a high standard is a given. 'Adding value' could mean thinking about the usefulness of the research findings to the client's problem (seeing things from the client's point of view) and so seeing what the research findings mean to the 'big picture' – that is, understanding and communicating what the findings mean for the decision or course of action the client has to take in relation to the problem, taking into account the wider context of his or her business and the environment it operates in. Smith (2005) says something about this when he says that:

> . . . market research is not just about selling . . .'content' – data or transcripts – but the sum of the experiences that exist within the heads of market researchers about what all this 'content' means . . . [Clients] look to [researchers] to present compelling evidence-based arguments and to reassure them . . . about what constitutes a sensible course of action.

Some may say, however, that this is not added value but merely the sort of thing they expect to get from the researcher!

But how was their research for you? The evidence may be found in the end product; you may also have had a chance to see for yourself during the research process. Think about how you would rate the following:

- the fieldwork briefing or briefing notes;
- the fieldwork and fieldwork supervision;
- quality control and back-checking procedures;
- data entry, verification, editing and coding and data analysis;
- the level of expertise and experience of the providers.

For example: Did the interviewers follow the sampling instructions and/or the questionnaire instructions? Did you get detail in responses to open-ended questions? Were there a lot of 'No responses' or 'Don't knows'? Was the coding frame a good reflection of the verbatim comments? Were the data tables error free? Were there any discrepancies between data in tables and data in the presentation or report?

Project management and the relationship/interface

From a project management point of view there are some tangibles and some intangibles. Ask yourself these questions:

- How satisfied are you with how the project was managed?
- Was the senior researcher who took the brief involved throughout the project?
- How well were you kept informed of progress?
- Were key deadlines met?
- How well did the researchers handle any problems that arose?
- Did the researchers provide added value – anything above and beyond what was expected?
- Were they aware of the issues facing your industry/area?
- Did they show interest in the decisions that you have to make? Were they enthusiastic?
- Was the service provided value for money?

Delivery and interpretation

Review the report (the checklist in Box 14.10 is useful). Review the presentation: how effectively were the findings communicated? In reviewing both presentation and report ask yourself the following:

- Is it clear what action is to be taken, what the next steps are, or are you left saying 'So what?'
- Has the researcher understood the problem and how it relates to the wider context of your business?
- Did you get information or data? Did the researcher relate the findings to the research problem and the wider business problem?
- Is there a clear distinction between facts or other data and opinion and speculation?
- What is the researcher's interpretation of the evidence? Are other possible interpretations given?
- Does the researcher give a clear line of argument? Is that argument solid – is it backed up by evidence?
- Is there evidence against the argument? How has that been handled?
- Is the researcher aware or does he or she state the assumptions and/or limitations in the approach or solution to the problem?
- Do the findings match your own understanding or knowledge of the issues? Is there anything odd or unusual? If so, is there a plausible and credible explanation for it?
- Based on the data you have seen (tables, transcripts or tapes) would you have made the same interpretation and reached the same conclusion based on this evidence and your knowledge of the issues?

Quality, suitability and contribution of the evidence for its end use

Ask the end users of the research:

- Was the research evidence used?
- Was the evidence credible?
- Did it make a contribution to advancing understanding or knowledge?
- Was the research of value in producing evidence for decision making?
- Was the evidence robust enough?
- Was it complete – did it cover the issues?
- What other evidence did you wish you had? (Why was it not there? Was it in the brief and not addressed or was it not included?)

Box 14.13 Professional practice and the MRS Code of Conduct: reporting findings

The following rules cover the researcher's responsibilities in reporting the findings from research. The full Code of Conduct and the ICC/ESOMAR Code are available at www.mrs.org.uk.

B49 Members must ensure that research conclusions disseminated by them are clearly and adequately supported by the data.

B50 Members must comply with reasonable requests to make available to anyone the technical information necessary to assess the validity of any published findings from a research project.

B51 Members must ensure that their names, or those of their employer, are only used in connection with any research project as an assurance that the latter has been carried out in conformity with the Code if they are satisfied on reasonable grounds that the project has in all respects met the Code's requirements.

B52 Members must allow Clients to arrange checks on the quality of fieldwork and data preparation provided that the Client pays any additional costs involved in this.

B53 Members must provide Clients with sufficient technical details to enable Clients to assess the validity of results of research projects carried out on their behalf.

B54 Members must ensure that data tables include sufficient technical information to enable reasonable interpretation of the validity of the results.

B55 Members must ensure that reports include sufficient information to enable reasonable interpretation of the validity of the results.

B56 Members must ensure that reports and presentations clearly distinguish between facts and interpretation.

B57 Members must ensure that when interpreting data they make clear which data they are using to support their interpretation.

B58 Members must ensure that qualitative reports and presentations accurately reflect the findings of the research in addition to the research practitioner's interpretations and conclusions.

B59 Members must take reasonable steps to check and where necessary amend any Client-prepared materials prior to publication to ensure that the published research results will not be incorrectly or misleadingly reported.
    Comment: This means that Members are expected to take reasonable steps to ensure that any press releases include either final report details (including question wording for any questions quoted) or details of where the information can be obtained (e.g. via a website link).

B60 Members must take reasonable steps to ensure that findings from a research project, published by themselves or in their employer's name, are not incorrectly or misleadingly presented.

B61 If Members are aware, or ought reasonably to be aware, that findings from a research project have been incorrectly or misleadingly reported by a Client he/she must at the earliest opportunity: refuse permission for the Client to use their name further in connection with the incorrect or misleading published findings; and publish in an appropriate forum the relevant technical details of the project to correct any incorrect or misleading reporting.

Source: MRS Code of Conduct 2005. Used with permission.

Chapter summary

- Presentations and reports are important as a means of crystallising the thinking about the findings; as a channel for disseminating the findings; as a way of influencing the client in a course of action; and as a way of selling the expertise of the researcher. Presentations give client and researcher an opportunity to discuss the findings and explore their implications; the report brings together in one document the detail of the project and so acts as a record for the work completed. Reports and presentations are useful in evaluating the quality of research and research supplier.

- In both presentation and report the aim is to communicate the findings clearly, accurately and effectively. Be clear about what you are trying to achieve. Think of the audience and tailor the message to them. Edit the content ruthlessly; present only those data or findings that shed light on the issue.

- Prepare thoroughly for a presentation – know the material inside out; practise your delivery. Choose and design your visual aids to enhance the message. Think about the logistics – the equipment, the size of the room, the size of the audience.

- Clarify the aim of the report, prepare an outline of the content and the structure and start writing. Use everyday language. Develop a storyline that runs through the report leading the reader to your conclusions. Review the draft yourself and give it to a colleague to review.

- Design tables, charts and graphs so that they are easy to read and their message is clear.

- Review the research to determine how useful it was in addressing the decision makers' problem. Review the findings – check if you would have reached the same conclusions. Review the process to determine how well managed and how well executed the research was.

Questions and exercises

1 Take a sample of journal articles (from for example the *International Journal of Market Research*) or research reports.
   (a) Examine each one in terms of (i) structure; and (ii) language, style and overall readability.
   (b) Comment on how effectively the abstract or the executive summary of each article summarises the content.

2 A new researcher has recently joined your department. You are responsible for training him to prepare presentations and reports. Draw up a set of guidelines that the researcher would find useful in (a) structuring a presentation or a report; and (b) helping him prepare effective charts and graphs.

3 You have decided to do a quality and usefulness audit of all the research your organisation has undertaken in the last two years. To help you do this efficiently, prepare a checklist of questions you might use in reviewing each piece of research.

References

Biel, A. (1994) 'The utilisation barrier: the need to make research come alive', *Admap*, September.

Brenner, H. and Shelly, E. (1998) *Adding Years to Life and Life to Years: A Health Promotion Strategy for Older People*, Dublin: Department of Health and Children/National Council on Ageing and Older People.

Emerson, E., Malam, S., Joyce, L. and Muir, J. (2003) ' "Nothing about us without us". Meeting the challenges of a national survey amongst people with learning difficulties', *Proceedings of The Market Research Society Conference*, London: MRS.

Fahey, T. (2001) 'Housing, social interaction and participation among older Irish people', in McGivern, Y. (ed.), *Towards a Society for All Ages*, Dublin: National Council on Ageing and Older People.

Flemming from Thygesen and McGowan, P. (2002) 'Inspiring the organisation to act: a business in denial', *Proceedings of the Market Research Society Conference*, London: MRS.

Kiecker, P. and Nelson, J. (1996) 'Do interviewers follow telephone survey instructions?', *Journal of the Market Research Society*, 38, 2, p. 161.

Lovett, P. (2001) 'Ethics shmethics! As long as you get the next job. A moral dilemma', *Proceedings of the Market Research Society Conference*, London: MRS.

Niven, A. and Imms, M. (2006) 'Connecting with clients: Re-thinking the debrief', *Proceedings of the Market Research Society Conference*, London: MRS.

O'Shea, E. and Connolly, S. (2003) 'Healthy ageing in Ireland: policy, practice and evaluation', in McGivern, Y. (ed.) *The 2003 Healthy Ageing Conference*, Dublin: National Council on Ageing and Older People.

Parsons, J. (2004) 'PowerPoint is not written in stone: business communication and the lost art of story-telling', *Proceedings of the Market Research Society Conference*, London: MRS.

Smith, D. (2005) 'It's not how good you are, it's how good you want to be! Are market researchers really up for "reconstruction"?' *Proceedings of the MRS Conference*, London: MRS.

Tufte, E. (2001) *The Visual Display of Quantitative Information*, Cheshire, CT: Graphics Press.

Walter, P. and Donaldson, S. (2001) 'Seeing is believing', *Proceedings of the Market Research Society Conference*, London: MRS.

Wills, S. and Williams, P. (2004) 'Insight as a strategic asset – the opportunity and the stark reality', *International Journal of Market Research*, 46, 4, pp. 393–410.

Recommended reading

Becker, H. (1986) *Writing for Social Scientists*, Chicago, IL: University of Chicago Press.

Buzan, T. and Buzan, B. (2003) *The Mind Map® Book*, London: BBC Worldwide.

Girden, E.R. (2001) *Evaluating Research Articles From Start to Finish*, London: Sage.

Loosveldt, G., Carton, A. and Billiet, J. (2004) 'Assessment of survey data quality: a pragmatic approach focused on interviewer tasks', *International Journal of Market Research*, 46, 1, pp. 65–82.

Truss, L. (2004) *Eats, Shoots and Leaves: The zero tolerance approach to punctuation*, London: Profile Books.

Tufte, E. (2001) *The Visual Display of Quantitative Information*, Cheshire, CT: Graphics Press.

Waterhouse, K. (1994) *English, Our English (and How to Sing It)*, London: Penguin.

BIBLIOGRAPHY

Adriaenssens, C. and Cadman, L. (1999) 'An adaptation of moderated e-mail focus groups to assess the potential for a new online (Internet) financial services offer in the UK', *Journal of the Market Research Society*, 41, 4, pp. 417–24.

Ajzen, I. and Fishbein, M. (1980) *Understanding Attitudes and Predicting Social Behaviour*, Englewood Cliffs, NJ: Prentice-Hall.

Alexander, M. (2000) 'Codes and contexts: practical semiotics for the qualitative researcher', *Proceedings of the Market Research Society Conference*, London: MRS.

ARK. Northern Ireland Life and Times Survey. ARK. www.ark.ac.uk/nilt.

Babbie, E. (1998) *The Practice of Social Research*, London: Wadsworth.

Baez Ortega, D. and Romo Costamaillere, G. (1997) 'Geodemographics and its application to the study of consumers', *ESOMAR Conference Proceedings, The Dynamics of Change in Latin America*, Amsterdam: ESOMAR.

Bairfelt, S. and Spurgeon, F. (1998) *Plenty of Data, but are we doing enough to fill the information gap?*, Proceedings of the ESOMAR Congress, Amsterdam: ESOMAR.

Balabanovic, J., Oxley, M. and Gerritsen, N. (2003) Asynchronous online discussion forums, *Proceedings of the Market Research Society Conference*, London: MRS.

Becker, H. (1986) *Writing for Social Scientists*, Chicago, IL: University of Chicago Press.

Bertaux, D. and Bertaux-Wiame, I. (1981) 'Life stories in the bakers' trade', in Bertaux, D. (ed.) *Biography and Society: The Life History Approach in the Social Sciences*, London: Sage.

Biel, A. (1994) 'The utilisation barrier – the need to make research come alive', *Admap*, September.

Bijapurkar, R. (1995) *Does market research really contribute to decision making?*, Proceedings of the ESOMAR Congress, Amsterdam: ESOMAR.

Bird, M. and Ehrenberg, A. (1970) 'Consumer attitudes and brand usage', *Journal of the Market Research Society*, 12, 3, pp. 233–47.

Birn, R. (ed.) (2000) *The International Handbook of Market Research Techniques*, 2nd edn. London: Kogan Page.

Blaikie, N. (2003) *Analyzing Quantitative Data: From Description to Explanation*, London: Sage.

Blamires, C. (1995) Segmentations techniques in market research: exploding the mystique around cluster analysis', *Journal of Target Marketing, Measurement and Analysis for Marketing*, 4, 2, pp. 62–73.

Blamires, C., Ray, A. and Askew, P. (1997) 'Electronic data capture: taking advantage of a new era', *Proceedings of the Market Research Society Conference*, London: MRS.

Bock T. and Sergeant, J. (2002) 'Small sample market research', *International Journal of Market Research*, 44, 2, pp. 235–44.

Boulton, D. and Hammersley, M. (1996) 'Analysis of unstructured data', in Sapsford, R. and Jupp, V. (eds) *Data Collection and Analysis*, London: Sage.

Bournemouth University Academic Services (2007) *Citing References – A Brief Guide*. Available at http://www.bournemouth.ac.uk/library/citing_references/citing_refs_main.html.

Brace, I. and Nancarrow, C. (2008) 'Let's get ethical: dealing with socially desirable responding online', *Proceedings of the Market Research Society Conference*, London: MRS.

Brennan, M., Hoek, J. and Astridge, C. (1991) 'The effects of monetary incentives on the response rate and cost-effectiveness of a mail survey', *Journal of the Market Research Society*, 33, 3, pp. 229–41.

Brenner, H. and Shelly, E. (1998) *Adding Years to Life and Life to Years: A Health Promotion Strategy for Older People*, Dublin: Department of Health and Children/National Council on Ageing and Older People.

Bristol, T. and Fern, E. (1996) 'Exploring the atmosphere created by focus group interviews: comparing consumers' feelings across qualitative techniques', *Journal of the Market Research Society*, 38, 2, pp. 185–95.

Brook, O. (2004) 'I know what you did last summer: arts audiences in London 1998–2002', *Proceedings of the Market Research Society Conference*, London: MRS.

Brooker, S., Cawson, P., Kelly, G. and Wattam, C. (2001) 'The prevalence of child abuse and neglect: a survey of young people', *Proceedings of the Market Research Society Conference*, London: MRS.

Brooks, V. (2003) 'Exploitation to engagement: the role of market research in getting close to niche markets', *International Journal of Market Research*, 45, 3, pp. 337–54.

Broussard, G. (2000) 'How advertising frequency can work to build online advertising effectiveness', *International Journal of Market Research*, 42, 4, pp. 439–57.

Browne, N. and Keeley, S. (2004) *Asking the Right Questions: A Guide to Critical Thinking*, London: FT/Prentice Hall.

Bryman, A. and Burgess, R. (eds) (1994) *Analyzing Qualitative Data*, London: Routledge.

Bulmer, M. (ed.) (1982) *Social Research Ethics*, London: Macmillan.

Burgess, R. (1984) *In the Field: An introduction to field research*, London: Allen & Unwin.

Butcher, J., Strutt, S. and Bird, C. (2005) 'How research drove the metamorphosis of a public sector organisation', *Proceedings of the Market Research Society Conference*, London: MRS.

Buzan, T. and Buzan, B. (2003) *The Mind Map® Book*, London: BBC Worldwide.

Callingham, M. and Baker, T. (2002) 'We know what they think, but do we know what they do?', *International Journal of Market Research*, 44, 3, pp. 299–335.

Cambiar, L.L.C. (2004) *Study on Changes in Client Demands from Research Agencies*.

Capron, M., Jeeawody F. and Parnell, A. (2002) 'Never work with children and graduates? BMRB's class of 2001 demonstrate insight to action', *Proceedings of the Market Research Society Conference*, London: MRS.

Casey, M. (1998) 'Analysis: honoring the stories', in Krueger, R. (ed.), *Analyzing and Reporting Focus Group Results*, London: Sage.

The Center For Army Leadership (2004) *The US Army Leadership Field Manual*. London: McGraw-Hill.

Chadwick, S. (2005) 'Do we listen to journalists or clients? The real implications of change for the market research industry', *Proceedings of the Market Research Society Conference*, London: MRS.

Childs, R. (1996) 'Buying international research', *Journal of the Market Research Society*, 38, 1, pp. 63–6.

Chisnall, P. (2004) *Marketing Research*, 7th edn. London: McGraw-Hill.

Chrzanowska, J. (2002) *Interviewing Groups and Individuals in Qualitative Market Research*, London: Sage.

Clegg, F. (1991) *Simple Statistics*, Cambridge: Cambridge University Press.

Clough, S. and McGregor, L. (2003) 'Capturing the emerging Zeitgeist: aligning *The Mirror* to the future', *Proceedings of the Market Research Society Conference*, London: MRS.

Codd, E.F., Codd, S.B. and Sally, C.T. (1993) *Providing OLAP (On-line Analytical Processing) to User-Analysts: An IT Mandate*, Toronto, Canada: E.F. Codd and Associates.

Cohen, J. (2005) 'Teenage sex at the margins', *Proceedings of the Market Research Society Conference*, London: MRS.

Collins, L. (1991) 'Everything is true but in a different sense: a new perspective on qualitative research', *Journal of the Market Research Society*, 33, 1, pp. 31–8.

Colwell, J. (1990) 'Qualitative market research: a conceptual analysis and review of practitioner criteria', *Journal of the Market Research Society*, 32, 1, pp. 13–36.

Comley, P. (1999) 'Moderated email groups: computing magazine case study', *Proceedings of the ESOMAR Net Effects Conference*, Amsterdam: ESOMAR.

Comley, P. (2003) 'Innovation in online research – who needs online panels?', *Proceedings of the Market Research Society Conference*, London: MRS.

Converse, J. and Presser, S. (1986) *Survey Questions: Handcrafting the standardized questionnaire*, London: Sage.

Cooper, P. and Branthwaite, A. (1977) 'Qualitative technology: new perspectives on measurement and meaning through qualitative research', *Proceedings of the Market Research Society Conference*, London: MRS.

Cooper, P. and Tower, R. (1992) 'Inside the consumer mind: consumer attitudes to the arts', *Journal of the Market Research Society*, 34, 4, pp. 299–311.

Cowan, D. (1995) 'The importance of good consumer information: information – generals can't do without it. Why do CEOs think they can?', *Admap*, July.

Crouch, S. and Housden, M. (2003) *Marketing Research for Managers*, London: Butterworths.

Cursai, C. (2001) 'A critical evaluation of face-to-face interviewing vs. computer-mediated interviewing', *International Journal of Marketing Research*, 43, 4.

Dale, A., Arber, S. and Procter, M. (1988) *Doing Secondary Analysis*, London: Unwin Hyman.

Davidson, G. and Payne, C. (2008) 'How research saves scapegoat brands©: retaining brand and business perspective in troubled times', *Proceedings of the Market Research Society Conference*, London: MRS.

Denzin, N. and Lincoln, Y. (eds) (1994) *A Handbook of Qualitative Research*, London: Sage.

Desai, P. (2002) *Methods Beyond Interviewing in Qualitative Market Research*, London: Sage.

Desai, P., Roberts, K. and Roberts, C. (2004) 'Dreaming the global future: identity, culture and the media in a multicultural age', *Proceedings of the Market Research Society Conference*, London: MRS.

Desai, P. and Sills, A. (1996) 'Qualitative research among ethnic minority communities', *Journal of the Market Research Society*, 38, 3.

De Vaus, D. (2001) *Research Design in Social Research*, London: Sage.

Devine, P., *User Documentation* (www.ark.ac.uk/nilt).

Dilly, R. (1995) *Data Mining: An Introduction*, www.pcc.qub.ac.uk/tec/courses/datamining/stu_notes/dm_book_1.html.

Duffy, B. (2003) 'Response order effects: how do people read?', *International Journal of Market Research*, 45, 4, pp. 457–66.

Edgar, L. and McErlane, C. (2002) 'Professional development: the future's in diamonds', *Proceedings of the Market Research Society Conference*, London: MRS.

Ehrenberg, A. (1982) *A Primer in Data Reduction*, London: Wiley.

Emerson, E., Malam, S., Joyce, L. and Muir, J. (2003) ' "Nothing about us without us." Meeting the challenges of a national survey amongst people with learning difficulties', *Proceedings of the Market Research Society Conference*, London: MRS.

Engel, J.F., Blackwell, R.D. and Miniard, P.W. (1993) *Consumer Behavior*, 7th edn. Fort Worth, TX: The Dryden Press.

Ereaut, G. (2002) *Analysis and Interpretation in Qualitative Market Research*, London: Sage.

Ereaut, G., Imms, M. and Callingham, M. (eds) (2002) *Qualitative Market Research: Principle and practice*, London: Sage.

ESOMAR (2007) *Global Prices Study*, Amsterdam: ESOMAR.

Fahey, T. (2001) 'Housing, social interaction and participation among older Irish people', in McGivern, Y. (ed.), *Towards a Society for All Ages*, Dublin: National Council on Ageing and Older People.

Fishbein, M. (ed.) (1967) *Readings in Attitude Theory and Measurement*, New York: Wiley.

Fishbein, M. and Ajzen, I. (1975) *Belief, Attitude, Intention and Behaviour*, Reading, MA: Addison-Wesley.

Flemming, from Thygesen and McGowan, P. (2002) 'Inspiring the organisation to act: a business in denial', *Proceedings of the Market Research Society Conference*, London: MRS.

Fleming, P., Ni Ruaidhe, S. and McGarry, K. (2004) ' "I shouldn't be here": the experiences of working adults living at home'. Unpublished qualitative research project, MSc. in Applied Social Research.

Foreman, J. and Collins, M. (1991) 'The viability of random digit dialling in the UK', *Journal of the Market Research Society*, 33, 3, pp. 219–27.

Gabriel, C. (1990) 'The validity of qualitative market research', *Journal of the Market Research Society*, 32, 4, pp. 507–20.

Gale, B.T. (1994) *Managing Customer Value*, New York: Simon & Schuster.

Gibaldi, J. (2003) *MLA Handbook for Writers of Research Papers*, New York: The Modern Language Association of America.

Gibson, S., Teanby, D. and Donaldson, S. (2004) 'Bridging the gap between dreams and reality . . . building holistic insights from an integrated consumer understanding', *Proceedings of the Market Research Society Conference*, London: MRS.

Girden, E.R. (2001) *Evaluating Research Articles From Start to Finish*, London: Sage.

Glaser, B. and Strauss, A. (1967) *The Discovery of Grounded Theory*, Chicago, IL: Aldine.

Gold, R. (1958) 'Roles in sociological field observations', *Social Forces*, 36, 33, pp. 217–23.

Goodyear, M. (1996) 'Divided by a common language: diversity and deception in the world of global marketing', *Journal of the Market Research Society*, 38, 2, pp. 105–22.

Gordon, W. (1999) *Goodthinking: A guide to qualitative research*, Henley-on-Thames: Admap.

Gordon, W. and Robson, S. (1980) 'Respondent through the looking glass: towards a better understanding of the qualitative interviewing process', *Proceedings of the Market Research Society Conference*, London: MRS.

Gosschalk, B. (1999) 'Opinion formers' views on market research', *Admap*, April.

Granville, S., Campbell-Jack, D. and Lamplugh, T. (2005) 'Perception, prevention, policing and the challenges of researching anti-social behaviour', *Proceedings of the Market Research Society Conference*, London: MRS.

Griffiths, J., Salari, S., Rowland, G. and Beasley-Murray, J. (2004) 'The Qual remix', *Proceedings of the Market Research Society Conference*, London: MRS.

Habershon, J. (2005) 'Capturing emotions', *Proceedings of the Market Research Society Conference*, London: MRS.

Hakim, C. (1982) *Secondary Analysis in Social Research*, London: Allen & Unwin.

Hall, K. and Browning, S. (2001) 'Quality time – cohort and observation combined: a charity case', *Proceedings of the Market Research Society Conference*, London: MRS.

Hammersley, M. and Atkinson, P. (1995) *Ethnography: Principles in Practice*, London: Routledge.

Harris, P. (1981) 'Recent developments in the multivariate analysis of market research data', *Proceedings of the Market Research Society Conference*, London: MRS.

Harvey, M. and Evans, M. (2001) 'Decoding competitive propositions: a semiotic alternative to traditional advertising research', *Proceedings of the Market Research Society Conference*, London: MRS.

Hedges, A. (2002) *Commissioning Social Research: A Good Practice Guide*, London: Social Research Association. Also available at www.the-sra.org.uk/commissioning._sr.htm.

Hofstede, G. (1984) *Culture's Consequences*, London: Sage.

Hofstede, G. (1991) *Cultures and Organizations – Software of the Mind*, London: HarperCollins.

Holden, J. and Griffiths, G. (2004) 'The way we live now (Daily Life in the 21st century)', *Proceedings of the Market Research Society Conference*, London: MRS.

Holmes, D. (1998) *Market Research: A Backroom Support Function or Vanguard of Knowledge Management*, Amsterdam: ESOMAR.

Hornsby-Smith, M. (1993) 'Gaining access', in Gilbert, N. (ed.) *Researching Social Life*, London: Sage.

Hurrell, G., Collins, M., Sykes, W. and Williams, V. (1997) 'Solpadol – a successful case of brand positioning', *Journal of the Market Research Society*, 39, 3, pp. 463–80.

Ibeh, K. and Brock, J. (2004) 'Conducting survey research among organisational populations in developing countries: can the drop and collect technique make a difference?', *International Journal of Market Research*, 46, 3, pp. 375–83.

The ICC/ESOMAR International Code of Marketing and Social Research Practice (www.esomar.org).

Inmon, W.H. (1996) *Building the Data Warehouse*, 2nd edn. New York: John Wiley & Sons, Inc.

Johnson, M. (1997) 'The application of geodemographics to retailing: meeting the needs of the catchment', *Journal of the Market Research Society*, 39, 1, pp. 201–24.

Junker, B. (1960) *Fieldwork: An Introduction to the Social Sciences*, Chicago: Chicago University Press.

Katz, J. (1983) 'A theory of qualitative methodology: the social science system of analytic fieldwork', in Emerson, R. (ed.) *Contemporary Field Research*, Boston, MA: Little, Brown.

Kaushik, M. and Sen, A. (1990) 'Semiotics and qualitative research', *Journal of the Market Research Society*, 32, 2, pp. 227–42.

Kenyon, A. (2004) 'Exploring phenomenological research: pre-testing focus group techniques with young people', *International Journal of Market Research*, 46, 4, pp. 427–41.

Kiecker, P. and Nelson, J. (1996) 'Do interviewers follow telephone survey instructions?', *Journal of the Market Research Society*, 38, 2, p. 161.

Kirk, J. and Miller, M. (1986) *Reliability and Validity in Qualitative Research*, Newbury Park, CA: Sage.

Kish, L. (1949) 'A procedure for objective respondent selection within the household', *Journal of the American Statistical Association*, 44, pp. 380–87.

Kish, L. (1965) *Survey Sampling*, New York: Wiley.

Kreinczes, G. (1990) 'Why research is undervalued', *Admap*, March.

Krueger, R. (1998) *Moderating Focus Groups*, London: Sage.

Kumar, V. (2000) *International Marketing Research*, Upper Saddle River, NJ: Prentice-Hall.

Langmaid, R. and Andrews, M. (2003) *Breakthrough Zone*, London: Wiley & Co.

Langmaid, R. (2005) '21st century qualitative research', *Proceedings of the Market Research Society Conference*, London: MRS.

Lawes, R. (2002) 'De-mystifying semiotics: some key questions answered', *Proceedings of the Market Research Society Conference*, London: MRS.

Lee, R. (1992) *Doing Research on Sensitive Topics*, London: Sage.

Leventhal, B. (1997) 'An approach to fusing market research with database marketing', *Journal of the Market Research Society*, 39, 4, pp. 545–58.

Leventhal, B. and Moy, C. (2003) 'Opportunities to leverage the census for research and marketing', *Proceedings of the Market Research Society Conference*, London: MRS.

Lewins, A. and Silver, C. (2006) *Choosing CAQDAS Software*, CAQDAS Networking Project: http://caqdas.soc.surrey.ac.uk.

Lewins, A. and Silver, C. (2007) *Using Software in Qualitative Research: A Step-by-Step Guide*, London: Sage.

Loosveldt, G., Carton, A. and Billiet, J. (2004) 'Assessment of survey data quality: a pragmatic approach focused on interviewer tasks', *International Journal of Market Research*, 46, 1, pp. 65–82.

Lovett, P. (2001) 'Ethics shmethics! As long as you get the next job. A moral dilemma', *Proceedings of the Market Research Society Conference*, London: MRS.

Macfarlane, P. (2003) 'Breaking through the boundaries: MR techniques to understand what individual customers really want, and acting on it', *Proceedings of the Market Research Society Conference*, London: MRS.

McIntosh, A. and Davies, R. (1970 and 1996) 'The sampling of non-domestic populations', *Journal of the Market Research Society*, 12, 4, pp. 217–32 and 38, 4, pp. 429–46.

McPhee, N. (2002) 'Gaining insight on business and organisational behaviour: the qualitative dimension', *International Journal of Market Research*, 44, 1, pp. 53–70.

Madden, M.J., Ellen, P.S. and Ajzen, I. (1992) 'A comparison of the theory of planned behavior and the theory of reasoned action', *Personality and Social Psychology Bulletin*, 18, 1, pp. 3–9.

Mariampolski, H. (1999) 'The power of ethnography', *Journal of the Market Research Society*, 41, 1, pp. 75–87.

The MRS Code of Conduct (2005) (www.mrs.org.uk).

MRS Questionnaire Design Guidelines available from the MRS website at www.mrs.org.uk/standards/quant.htm.

The Market Research Society Guidelines on Qualitative Research available from the MRS and at the MRS website (www.mrs.org.uk).

Marks, L. (ed.) (2000) *Qualitative Research in Context*, Henley-on-Thames: Admap.

Marsden, P. (2002) 'What "Healthy-Living" means to consumers: trialling a new qualitative research technique', *International Journal of Market Research*, 44, 2, pp. 223–34.

Marsh, C. and Scarbrough, E. (1990) 'Testing nine hypotheses about quota sampling', *Journal of the Market Research Society*, 32, 4, pp. 485–506.

Mason, J. (2004) *Qualitative Researching*, London: Sage.

Mattinson, D. (1999) 'People power in politics', *Journal of the Market Research Society*, 41, 1, pp. 87–95.

Maughan, B. (2004) 'Investigator-based interviews', *International Journal of Market Research*, 46, 1, pp. 99–107.

Miles, K., Bright, D. and Kemp, J. (2000) 'Improving the research interview experience', *Proceedings of the Market Research Society Conference*, London: MRS.

Miles, M. and Huberman, A.M. (1994) *Qualitative Data Analysis: An expanded sourcebook*, London: Sage.

Morgan, D., quoted in Krueger, R. (1998) *Analyzing and Reporting Focus Group Results*, London: Sage, Chapter 8, p. 93.

Morris, D. (1994) *Bodytalk: A world guide to gestures*, London: Jonathan Cape.

Morrison, L., Colman, A. and Preston, C. (1997) 'Mystery customer research: cognitive processes affecting accuracy', *Journal of the Market Research Society*, 39, 2, pp. 349–61.

Moser, C.A. and Kalton, G. (1971) *Survey Methods in Social Investigation*, 2nd edn. Aldershot: Dartmouth.

Murcott, A. (1997) 'The Phd: some informal notes' unpublished paper, School of Health and Social Care, South Bank University, London.

Mytton, G. (1996) 'Research in new fields', *Journal of the Market Research Society*, 38, 1, pp. 19–31.

Niven, A. and Imms, M. (2006) 'Connecting with clients: Re-thinking the debrief', *Proceedings of the Market Research Society Conference*, London: MRS.

O'Connor, J. and Seymour, J. (1993) *Introducing NLP*, London: HarperCollins.

Office of National of Statistics (2000) *The UK 2000 Time Use Survey*, www.statistics.gov.uk/TimeUse/default.asp.

Oppenheim, A. (2000) *Questionnaire Design, Interviewing and Attitude Measurement*, London: Continuum.

Orton, S. and Samuels, J. (1988, 1997) 'What we have learned from researching AIDS', *Journal of the Market Research Society*, 39, 1, pp. 175–200.

Osgood, C., Suci, G. and Tannebaum, R. (1957) *The Measurement of Meaning*, Urbana, IL: University of Illinois Press.

O'Shea, E. and Connolly, S. (2003) 'Healthy Ageing in Ireland: Policy, Practice and Evaluation', in McGivern, Y. (ed.) *The 2003 Healthy Ageing Conference*, Dublin: National Council on Ageing and Older People.

Pallant, J. (2004) *SPSS Survival Manual: A Step-by-Step Guide to Data Analysis Using SPSS Version 12*, 2nd edn. London: Open University Press.

Palmer, S. and Kaminow, D. (2005) 'KERPOW!! KERCHING!! Understanding and Positioning the SPIDER-MAN Brand', *Proceedings of the Market Research Society Conference*, London: MRS.

Parsons, J. (2004) 'PowerPoint is not written in stone: business communication and the lost art of storytelling', *Proceedings of the Market Research Society Conference*, London: MRS.

Passingham, P. (1998) 'Grocery retailing and the loyalty card', *Journal of the Market Research Society*, 40, 1, pp. 55–63.

Payne, S. (1951) *The Art of Asking Questions*, Princeton, NJ: Princeton University Press.

Poynter, R. and Ashby, Q. (2005) 'Quick, quick, slow! The case for slow research', *Proceedings of the Market Research Society Conference*, London: MRS.

Punch, K. (2000) *Developing Effective Research Proposals*, London: Sage.

Pyke, A. (2000) 'It's all in the brief', *Proceedings of the Market Research Society Conference*, London: MRS.

Qualitative recruitment: Report of the Industry Working Party (1996) *Journal of the Market Research Society*, 38, pp. 135–43.

Renzetti, C. and Lee, R. (eds) (1993) *Researching Sensitive Topics*, London: Sage.

The Research and Development sub-committee on Qualitative Research (1979) 'Qualitative research: a summary of the concepts involved', *Journal of the Market Research Society*, 21, 2, pp. 107–24.

The *Research Works* series: papers from the AMSO (now BMRA) Research Effectiveness Awards, Henley-on-Thames: NTC.

Rettie, R., Robinson, H., Radke, A. and Ye, X. (2007) 'The use of CAQDAS in the UK Market Research Industry', in *Advances in Qualitative Computing Conference Proceedings*, http://caqdas.soc.surrey.ac.uk/conference/conference07.htm.

Ritchie, J. and Spencer, L. (1994) 'Qualitative data analysis for applied policy research', in Bryman, R. and Burgess, A. (eds) *Analyzing Qualitative Data*, London: Routledge.

Robson, S. (1991) 'Ethics: informed consent or misinformed compliance?', *Journal of the Market Research Society*, 33, 1, pp. 19–28.

Robson, S. and Hedges, A. (1993) 'Analysis and interpretation of qualitative findings: report of the Market Research Society Qualitative Interest Group', *Journal of the Market Research Society*, 35, 1, pp. 23–35.

Rose, J., Sykes, L. and Woodcock, D. (1995) 'Qualitative recruitment: the industry working party report', *Proceedings of the Market Research Society Conference*, London: MRS.

Rowntree, D. (2003) *Statistics Without Tears: A Primer for Non-mathematicians*, London: Allyn and Bacon.

Rubin, H. and Rubin, I. (1995) *Qualitative Interviewing: The art of hearing data*, London: Sage.

Sampson, P. (1967 and 1996) 'Commonsense in qualitative research', *Journal of the Market Research Society*, 9, 1, pp. 30–8 and 38, 4, pp. 331–9.

Sampson, P. (1980) 'The technical revolution of the 1970s: will it happen in the 1980s?', *Journal of the Market Research Society*, 22, 3, pp. 161–78.

Sampson, P. (1985) 'Qualitative research in Europe: the state of the art and the art of the state', ESOMAR Congress, Wiesbaden.

Sampson, P. and Harris, P. (1970) 'A users' guide to Fishbein', *Journal of the Market Research Society*, 12, 3, pp. 145–68.

Schlackman, W. (1984) 'A discussion of the use of sensitivity panels in market research', *Proceedings of the Market Research Society Conference*, London: MRS.

Scottish Executive (2003) Scotland's People: Results from the 2003 Scottish Household Survey.

Shields, G. (2001) 'Meeting the need for actionable consumer insight: the Scottish Courage perspective', *Proceedings of the Market Research Society Conference*, London: MRS.

Shipman, M. (1997) *The Limitations of Social Research*, London: Longman.

Siddall, J., Stride, C. and Sargent, J. (1987) 'Are you homosexual, heterosexual or bisexual? If so, you could develop AIDS', *Proceedings of the Market Research Society Conference*, London: MRS.

Silverman, D. (1999) *Doing Qualitative Research*, London: Sage.

Simmons, S. and Lovejoy, A. (2003) 'Oh no, the consultants are coming!', *Proceedings of the Market Research Society Conference*, London: MRS.

Smith, D. (2005) 'It's not how good you are, it's how good you want to be! Are market researchers really up for "reconstruction"?', *Proceedings of the Market Research Society Conference*, London: MRS.

Smith, D. and Fletcher, J. (2001) *Inside Information: Making sense of marketing data*, London: Wiley.

Smith, D. and Fletcher, J. (2004) *The Art and Science of Interpreting Market Research Evidence*, Chichester: Wiley.

Sorrell, M. (2002) Keynote speech to ARF Annual conference.

Spackman, N. (1993) 'Judging the value of research', *Admap*, January.

Spackman, N., Barker, A. and Nancarrow, C. (2000) 'Happy New Millennium: a research paradigm for the 21st century'. *Proceedings of the Market Research Society Conference*, London: MRS, pp. 45–53.

Sparre, M. and Steen, J. (2000) 'Advantages of conducting employee research on the Internet: a case study', *Proceedings of the ESOMAR Net Effects Conference*, Dublin: ESOMAR.

Stoker, S. (1999a) 'Good data housekeeping', in *DM Direct*, August, www.dmreview.com/dmdirect.

Stoker, S. (1999b) 'Building an information warehouse', in *DM Direct*, December, www.dmreview.com/dmdirect.

Strauss, A. (1987) *Qualitative Analysis for Social Scientists*, Cambridge: Cambridge University Press.

Strauss, A. and Corbin, J. (1998) *Basics of Qualitative Research*, London: Sage.

Sudman, S. and Bradburn, N. (1983) *Asking Questions*, San Francisco, CA: Jossey-Bass.

Sykes, W. (1990) 'Validity and reliability in qualitative market research: a review of the literature', *Journal of the Market Research Society*, 32, 3, pp. 289–328.

Tabachnick, B. and Fidell, L. (2006) *Using Multivariate Statistics*, 5th edn. New York: Allyn & Bacon.

Tanner, V. (2005) 'Using investment-based techniques to prove the "Bottom Line" value of research and give CEOs what they want', *Proceedings of the Market Research Society Conference*, London: MRS.

Taraborelli, P. (1993) 'Becoming a carer', in Gilbert, N. (ed.) *Researching Social Life*, London: Sage.

Truss, L. (2004) *Eats, Shoots and Leaves: The zero tolerance approach to punctuation*, London: Profile Books.

Tuck, M. (1976) *How People Choose*, London: Methuen.

Tuckman, B. (1965) 'Developmental sequence of small groups', *Pyschological Bulletin*, 63, pp. 384–99.

Tuckman, B. and Jenson, M. (1977) 'Stages of small group development re-visited', *Group and Organizational Studies*, 2, pp. 419–27.

Tufte, E. (2001) *The Visual Display of Quantitative Information*, Cheshire, CT: Graphics Press.

Tukey, J. (1977) *Exploratory Data Analysis*, Reading, MA: Addison Wesley.

Valentine, V. (2002) 'Repositioning research: a new MR language model', *International Journal of Market Research*, 44, 2, pp. 163–92.

Walkowski, J. (2001) 'Online qualitative research for Motorola: lessons learned', *Proceedings of the Association for Qualitative Research/Qualitative Research Consultants Association*, Paris: Association for Qualitative Research.

Walter, P. and Donaldson, S. (2001) 'Seeing is believing', *Proceedings of the Market Research Society Conference*, London: MRS.

Warren, M. (1991) 'Another day, another debrief: the use and assessment of qualitative research', *Journal of the Market Research Society*, 33, 1, pp. 13–18.

Waterhouse, K. (1994) *English, Our English (and How to Sing It)*, London: Penguin.

Wells, S. (1991) 'Wet towels and whetted appetites or a wet blanket? The role of analysis in qualitative research', *Journal of the Market Research Society*, 33, 1, pp. 39–44.

Whitehead,, C., Stockdale, J. and Razzu, G. (2003) *The Economic and Social Costs of Anti-Social Behaviour: A Review*. London: London School of Economics and Political Science.

Wills, S. and Webb, S. (2006) 'Measuring the value of insight – it can and must be done', *Proceedings of the Market Research Society Conference*, London: MRS.

Wills, S. and Williams, P. (2004) 'Insight as a strategic asset: the opportunity and the stark reality', *International Journal of Market Research*, 46, 4, pp. 393–410.

Wilsdon, M. (1996) 'Getting it done properly: the role of the co-ordinator in multi-country research', *Journal of the Market Research Society*, 38, 1, pp. 67–71.

Winkler, J.T. (1987) 'The fly on the wall of the inner sanctum: observing company directors at work', in Moyser, G. and Wagstaffe, M. (eds), *Research Methods for Elite Studies*, London: Allen Unwin.

Wissing, A. (2000) 'Using the Internet to measure advertising effectiveness', *Proceedings of the ESOMAR Net Effects Conference*, Dublin: ESOMAR.

Yu, J., Albaum, G. and Swenson, M. (2003) 'Is central tendency error inherent in the use of semantic differential scales in different cultures?', *International Journal of Market Research*, 45, 3, pp. 213–28.

Yu, J. and Cooper, H. (1983) 'A quantitative review of research design effects on response rates to questionnaires', *Journal of the Market Research Society*, 20, 1, pp. 36–44.

INDEX